Web
Intern
Atlas
NEW EDITION

Webster's International Atlas

NEW EDITION

Created in Cooperation with the Editors of
MERRIAM-WEBSTER

A Division of Merriam-Webster, Incorporated
Springfield, Massachusetts

This edition published by
Federal Street Press,
a Division of Merriam-Webster, Incorporated
P.O. Box 281
Springfield, MA 01102

Federal Street Press books are available for bulk purchase for sales promotion and premium use. For details write the manager of special sales, Federal Street Press, P.O. Box 281, Springfield, MA 01102

ISBN 13 978-1-59695-019-1
ISBN 10 1-59695-019-6

Printed in Singapore

07 08 09 10 5 4 3 2 1

Contents

Preface

This atlas provides basic information about each of the 194 countries of the world, the fifty states, the District of Columbia, and the five territories of the United States. It has been completely revised and updated to incorporate the most current information available.

A full page is provided for each country, two for each state, and one for each territory with information including a full-color map showing both populated places and major natural features, a locator map, and a fact box containing important information about the country, state, or territory. There is also a representation of the country, state, or territory flag with a brief flag history.

Additional information appears in tables that show country capitals, membership in international organizations, longest rivers, tallest mountains, and largest lakes. There is also a country by country listing of the largest cities with their geographical coordinates.

This colorful, compact book was created by the editors of Encyclopaedia Britannica in association with the editors of Merriam-Webster. It has been designed as a handy, affordable resource to help readers better understand our changing world.

Map Abbreviations

Ala.	Alabama
Ark.	Arkansas
Arm.	Armenia
ASEAN	Association of Southeast Asian Nations
Azer.	Azerbaijan
Belg.	Belgium
Calif.	California
C.A.R.	Central African Republic
Caricom	Caribbean Community
CFA	Communauté Financière Africaine (African Financial Community)
Conn.	Connecticut
D.C.	District of Columbia
Del.	Delaware
Dem.	Democratic
Den.	Denmark
E	east(ern)
Fla.	Florida
Fr.	France
ft.	foot (feet)
GNP	gross national product
I.	Island
Ill.	Illinois
Ind.	Indiana
Indon.	Indonesia
Is.	Islands
km.	kilometer(s)
La.	Louisiana
Mass.	Massachusetts
Md.	Maryland
mi.	mile(s)
Mich.	Michigan
Minn.	Minnesota
Miss.	Mississippi
Mt.	Mount
Mtn.	Mountain
Mts.	Mountains
N	north(ern)
Nat'l	National
N.C.	North Carolina
NE	northeast(ern)
N.H.	New Hampshire
N.J.	New Jersey
N.P.	National Park
NW	northwest(ern)
N.Y.	New York
N.Z.	New Zealand
Okla.	Oklahoma
Penin.	Peninsula
Penn.	Pennsylvania
Pk.	Peak
Port.	Portugal
Pt.	Point
Rep.	Republic
R.I.	Rhode Island
S	south(ern)
S.C.	South Carolina
SE	southeast(ern)
sq.	square
St.	Saint
SW	southwest(ern)
Switz.	Switzerland
Tenn.	Tennessee
Turkmen.	Turkmenistan
U.A.E.	United Arab Emirates
U.K.	United Kingdom
U.S.	United States
Va.	Virginia
Vt.	Vermont
W	west(ern)
Wash.	Washington
Wis.	Wisconsin
W.Va.	West Virginia

Guide to Map Projections

Technically, the earth is not round but is flattened at the poles and takes a shape most accurately described as an ellipsoid. The deviation from a perfect sphere is relatively minor, and although the distinction is of critical importance in surveying and geodesy, for most purposes it can be assumed that the earth is spherical.

A globe is the only true means of representing the surface of the earth and maintaining accurate relationships of location, direction, and distance, but it is often more desirable to have a flat map for reference. However, in order for a round globe to be portrayed as a flat map, various parts of the globe's surface must stretch or shrink, thereby altering the geometric qualities associated with it. To control this distortion, a systematic transformation of the sphere's surface must be made. The transformation and resultant new surface is usually derived mathematically and is referred to as the map projection.

An infinite number of map projections can be conceived, but the only ones which are effective are those projections which ensure that the spatial relationships between true (known) locations on the three-dimensional sphere are preserved on the two-dimensional flat map.

The four basic spatial properties of location are area, angle, distance, and direction. No map projection can preserve all four of these basic properties simultaneously. In fact, every map will possess some level of distortion in one or more of these dimensions. The map surface can be developed such that individual properties are preserved to a certain extent, or that certain combinations of properties are preserved to some extent, but every projection is, in some way, a compromise and must distort some properties in order to portray others accurately.

Choosing a Map Projection

The question of which map projection is best might be better stated as which map projection is most appropriate for the intended purpose of the map. For example, navigation demands correct direction, while road atlases will be concerned with preserving distance. Another important consideration is the extent and area of the region to be mapped. Some common guidelines include the use of cylindrical projections for low latitudes, conic projections for middle latitudes, and azimuthal projections for polar views. World maps are rather special cases and are commonly shown on a class of projection that may be neither equal-area nor conformal, referred to as compromise projections, typically on an oval grid.

Common Map Projections

Name	Class	Attribute	Common Uses
Mercator	Cylindrical	Conformal	Best suited for navigation uses, but often used inappropriately for world maps.
Sinusoidal	(Pseudo-cylindrical)	Equal-area	Used occasionally for world maps and in combination with Mollweide to derive other projections.
Mollweide	(Pseudo-cylindrical)	Equal-area	Used for world maps, especially for showing thematic content.
Lambert Conformal Conic	Conic	Conformal	Used extensively for mapping areas of extensive east-west extent in the mid-latitudes (such as the U.S.).
Albers Equal-area	Conic	Equal-area	Similar to Lambert Conformal Conic in use.
Polyconic	Polyconic	Neither Equal-area nor Conformal	Used by U.S. Geological Survey in mapping topographic quadrangles and was used for early coastal charts and some military mapping.
Bonne	(Pseudo-conic)	Equal-Area	Frequently used in atlases for showing continents.
Gnomonic	Azimuthal	Equal-Area	Used most frequently in navigation.
Stereographic	Azimuthal	Conformal	Most often used for topographic maps of polar regions and for navigation.
Orthographic	Azimuthal	Neither Equal-area nor Conformal	Most popular use is for pictorial views of earth, especially as seen from space.

Map Legend

Cities and Towns

Ottawa — National Capital

Edinburgh — Second level political capital

São Paulo — City symbol

Other administrative center

Boundaries

International

Disputed

Defacto

Line of control

Political subdivisions

Other Features

SERENGETI NATIONAL PARK — National park

Mount Everest 29,028 ft. — Mountain Peak

Dam

Falls

Rapids

River

Intermittent river

Canal

Aqueduct

Reef

Countries of the World

AFGHANISTAN

Scale 1: 19,568,000
0 80 160 mi
0 120 240 km

Official name: Islamic Republic of Afghanistan
Head of state and government: President
Official languages: Dari (Persian); Pashto
Monetary unit: afghani
Area: 249,347 sq. mi. (645,807 sq. km.)
Population (2005): 23,867,000
GDP per capita (2003): U.S.$340
Principal exports (2003–04): dried fruits 41.0%, skins 20.1%, carpets and handicrafts 14.6% *to:* Pakistan 68.9% India 7.6%; Russia 5.6%

Ethnolinguistic Composition

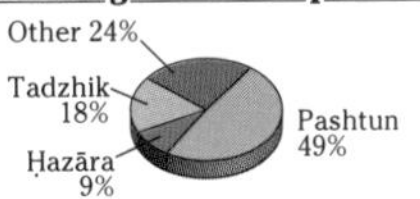

After the fall of the Taliban in January 2002, the new Afghan Interim Authority brought back the 1928 tricolor (black for the past, red for blood shed for independence, and green for hope), adding: the Arabic "Afghanistan" and "There is no deity but God; Muhammad is the messenger of God." It keeps the mosque, two flags, and wheat.

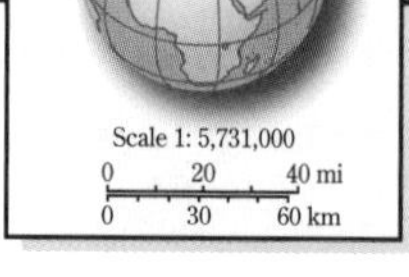

ALBANIA

Scale 1: 5,731,000

0 20 40 mi

0 30 60 km

Official name: Republic of Albania
Head of government: Prime Minister
Official language: Albanian
Monetary unit: lek
Area: 11,082 sq. mi. (28,703 sq. km.)
Population (2005): 3,130,000
GNP per capita (2004): U.S.$2,080
Principal exports (2003): textiles and clothing 34.8%, footwear 29.9%, base and fabricated metals 11.1% *to:* Italy 74.9%; Greece 13.8%; Germany 3.4%; Serbia and Montenegro 2.3%

Religious Affiliation

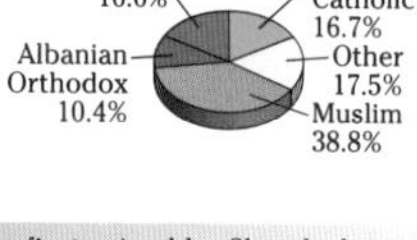

Nonreligious 16.6%
Roman Catholic 16.7%
Albanian Orthodox 10.4%
Other 17.5%
Muslim 38.8%

On Nov. 28, 1443, the flag was first raised by Skanderbeg, the national hero. After independence from Turkish rule was proclaimed on Nov. 28, 1912, the flag was flown by various regimes, each of which identified itself by adding a symbol above the double-headed eagle. The current flag, which features only the eagle, was adopted on May 22, 1993.

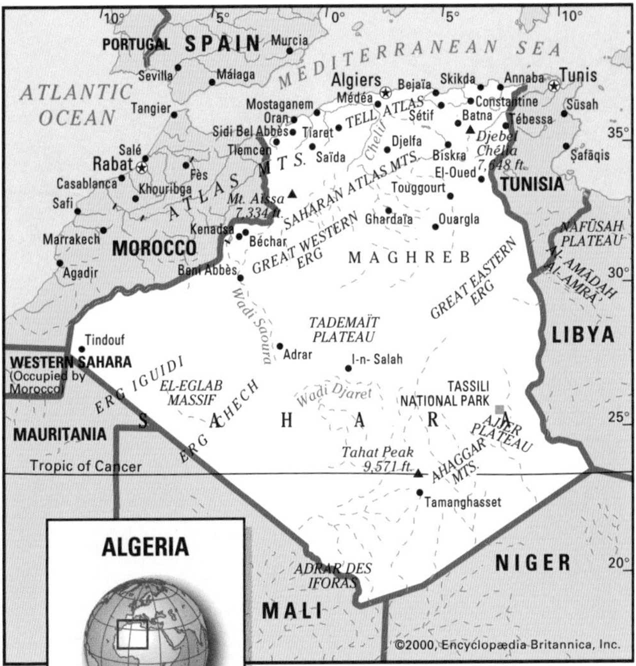

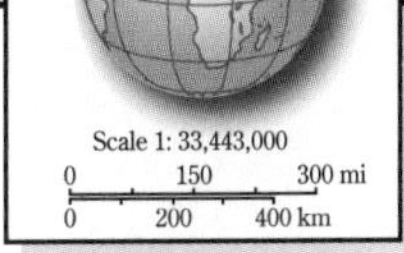

ALGERIA

Scale 1: 33,443,000

0 150 300 mi

0 200 400 km

Ethnic Composition

Other 0.2%

Arab 73.6%

Berber 26.2%

Official name: People's Democratic Republic of Algeria
Head of government: Prime Minister
Official language: Arabic
Monetary unit: Algerian dinar
Area: 919,595 sq. mi. (2,381,741 sq. km.)
Population (2005): 32,854,000
GNP per capita (2004): U.S.$2,280
*Principal exports (*2003): crude petroleum 31.6%; natural gas 30.7%; refined petroleum 12.3% *to:* Italy 20.1%; U.S. 14.2%; France 13.6%; Spain 12.1%; The Netherlands 9.0%; Turkey 5.1%

In the early 19th century, during the French conquest of North Africa, Algerian resistance fighters led by Emir Abdelkader supposedly raised the current flag. Its colors and symbols are associated with Islam and the Arab dynasties of the region. The flag was raised over an independent Algeria on July 2, 1962.

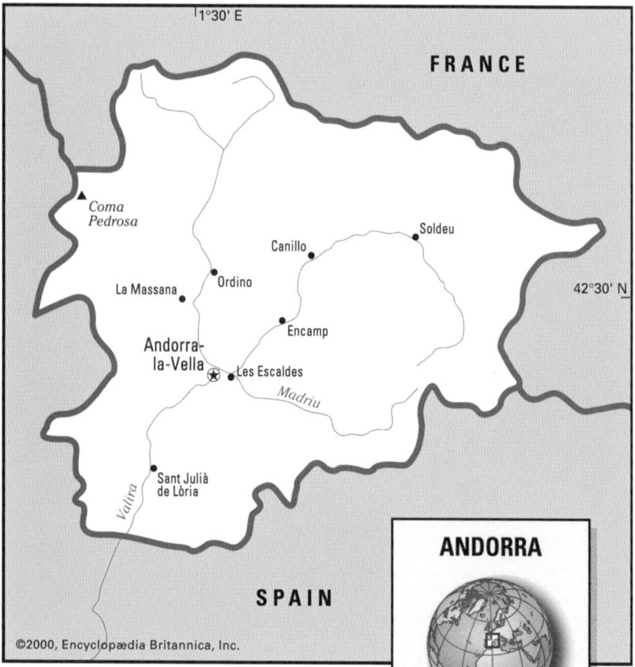
1°30' E
FRANCE
Coma
Pedrosa
Soldeu
Canillo
Ordino
La Massana
42°30' N
Encamp
Andorra-
la-Vella
Les Escaldes
Madriu
Sant Julià
de Lòria
Valira
SPAIN
©2000, Encyclopædia Britannica, Inc.
ANDORRA
Scale 1: 425,000
0 2 4 mi
0 3 6 km

Official name: Principality of Andorra
Head of government: Head of Government
Official language: Catalan
Monetary units: French franc, Spanish peseta
Area: 179 sq. mi. (464 sq. km.)
Population (2005): 74,800
GDP per capita (2001): U.S.$22,120
Principal exports (2003): transport equipment 22.3%; electrical machinery 22.2%; optical and photo equipment 14.1% *to:* Spain 55.7%; France 19.2%; Germany 12.4%

Ethnic Composition

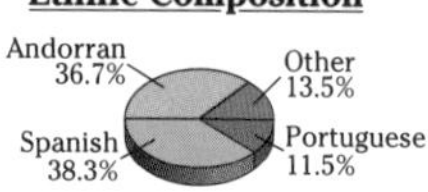
Andorran
36.7%
Other
13.5%
Spanish
38.3%
Portuguese
11.5%

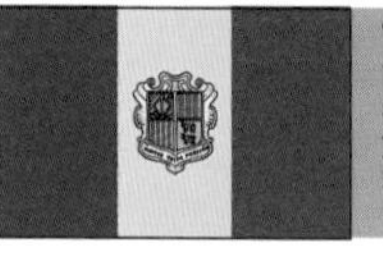

The flag may date to 1866, but the first legal authority for it is unknown. The design was standardized in July 1993. Possible sources for its colors are the flags of neighboring Spain (red-yellow-red) and France (blue-white-red). The coat of arms incorporates both French and Spanish elements dating to the 13th century or earlier.

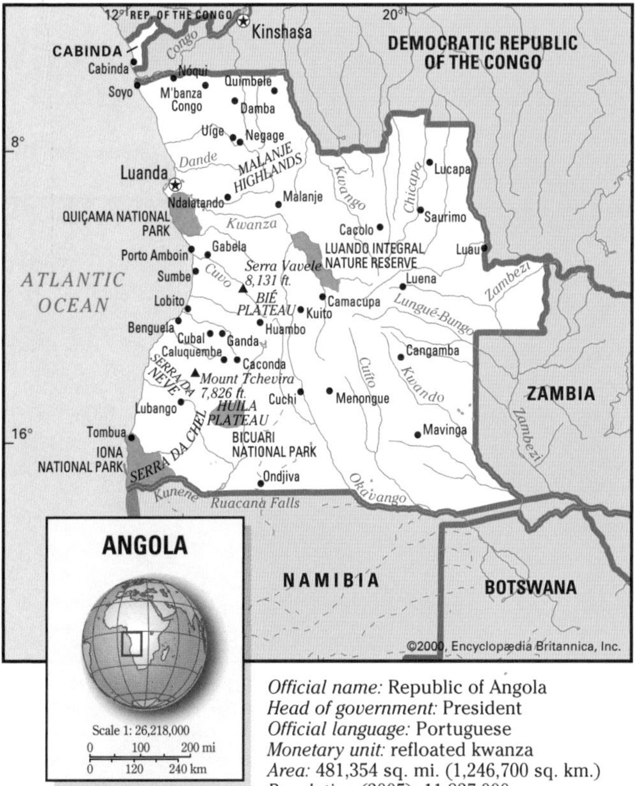

Scale 1: 26,218,000

0 100 200 mi

0 120 240 km

Ethnic Composition

Ovimbundu 25.2%; Kimbunde 23.1%; Kongo 12.6%; Other 39.1%

Official name: Republic of Angola
Head of government: President
Official language: Portuguese
Monetary unit: refloated kwanza
Area: 481,354 sq. mi. (1,246,700 sq. km.)
Population (2005): 11,827,000
GNP per capita (2004): U.S.$1,030
Principal exports (2003): crude petroleum 89.0%; diamonds 8.3%; refined petroleum 1.4% *to:* U.S. 47.1%; China 23.1%; Taiwan 8.7%; France 7.3%

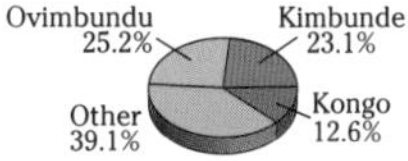

After Portugal withdrew from Angola on Nov. 11, 1975, the flag of the leading rebel group gained recognition. Inspired by designs of the Viet Cong and the former Soviet Union, it includes a star for internationalism and progress, a cogwheel for industrial workers, and a machete for agricultural workers. The black stripe is for the African people.

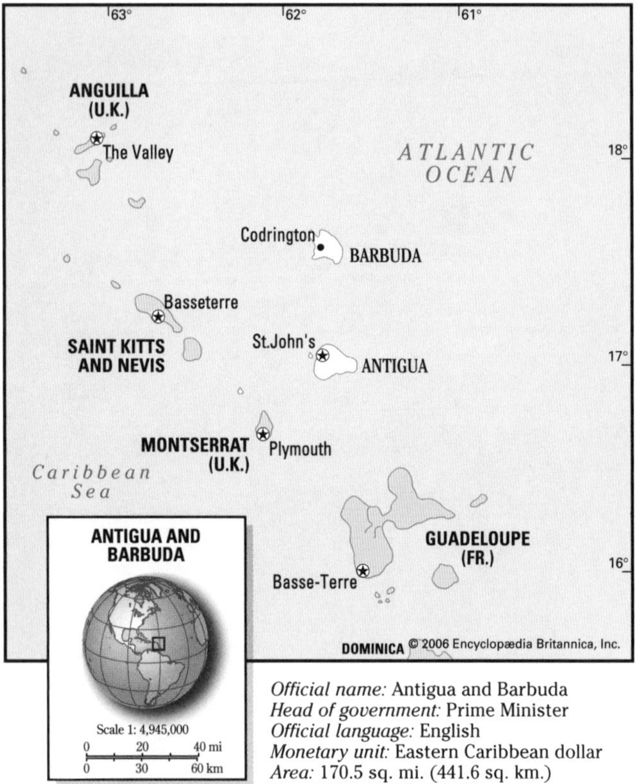

Official name: Antigua and Barbuda
Head of government: Prime Minister
Official language: English
Monetary unit: Eastern Caribbean dollar
Area: 170.5 sq. mi. (441.6 sq. km.)
Population (2005): 77,800
GNP per capita (2004): U.S.$10,000
Principal exports (1999): reexports [significantly, petroleum products reexported to neighboring islands] 60.3%; domestic exports 39.7%
to (1998): Barbados 9.5%; Trinidad and Tobago 7.3%; Saint Lucia 7.3%

Religious Affiliation

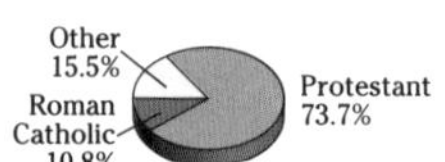

When "associated statehood" was granted by Britain on Feb. 27, 1967, the flag was introduced, and it remained after independence (Nov. 1, 1981). Red is for the dynamism of the people, the V-shape is for victory, and the sun is for the climate. Black is for the majority population and the soil, blue is for the sea, and white is for the beaches.

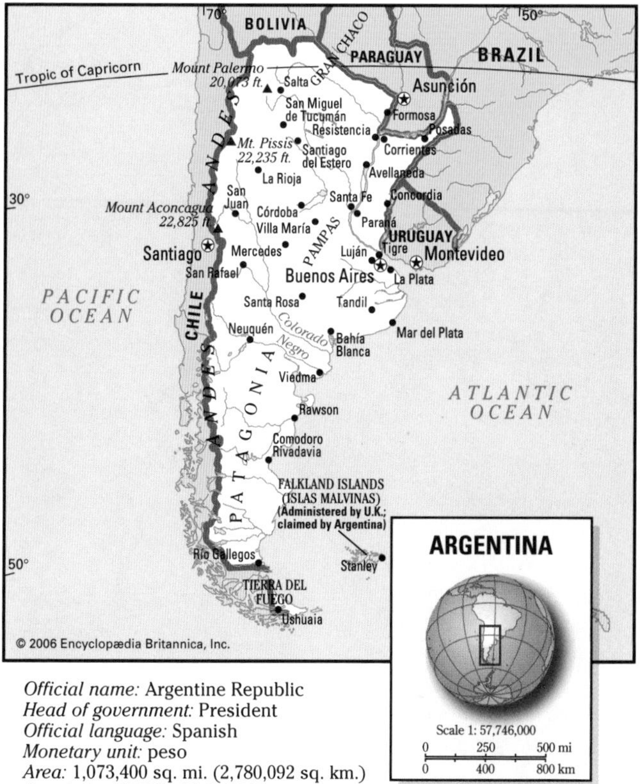

ARGENTINA

Scale 1: 57,746,000

0 250 500 mi

0 400 800 km

Official name: Argentine Republic
Head of government: President
Official language: Spanish
Monetary unit: peso
Area: 1,073,400 sq. mi. (2,780,092 sq. km.)
Population (2005): 38,592,000
GNP per capita (2004): U.S.$3,270
Principal exports (2001): food products and live animals 31.6%; crude petroleum 9.0%; road vehicles 7.4% *to:* Brazil 23.3%; U.S. 10.9%; Chile 10.7%; China 4.2%

Ethnic Composition

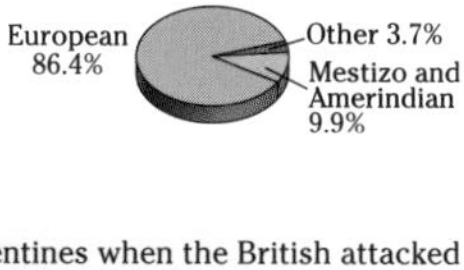

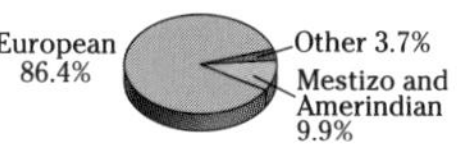

The uniforms worn by Argentines when the British attacked Buenos Aires (1806) and the blue ribbons worn by patriots in 1810 may have been the origin of the celeste-white-celeste flag hoisted on Feb. 12,1812. The flag's golden "sun of May" was added on Feb. 25,1818, to commemorate the yielding of the Spanish viceroy in 1810.

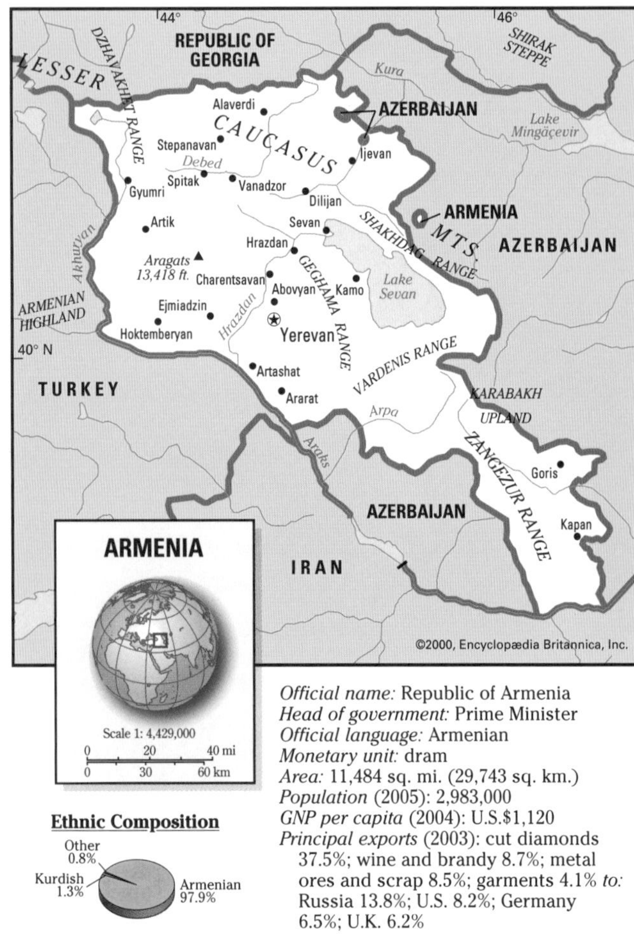

Official name: Republic of Armenia
Head of government: Prime Minister
Official language: Armenian
Monetary unit: dram
Area: 11,484 sq. mi. (29,743 sq. km.)
Population (2005): 2,983,000
GNP per capita (2004): U.S.$1,120
Principal exports (2003): cut diamonds 37.5%; wine and brandy 8.7%; metal ores and scrap 8.5%; garments 4.1% *to:* Russia 13.8%; U.S. 8.2%; Germany 6.5%; U.K. 6.2%

In 1885 an Armenian priest proposed adopting the "rainbow flag given to the Armenians when Noah's Ark came to rest on Mt. Ararat." On Aug. 1, 1918, a flag was sanctioned with stripes of red (possibly symbolizing blood), blue (for homeland), and orange (for courage and work). Replaced during Soviet rule, it was readopted on Aug. 24, 1990.

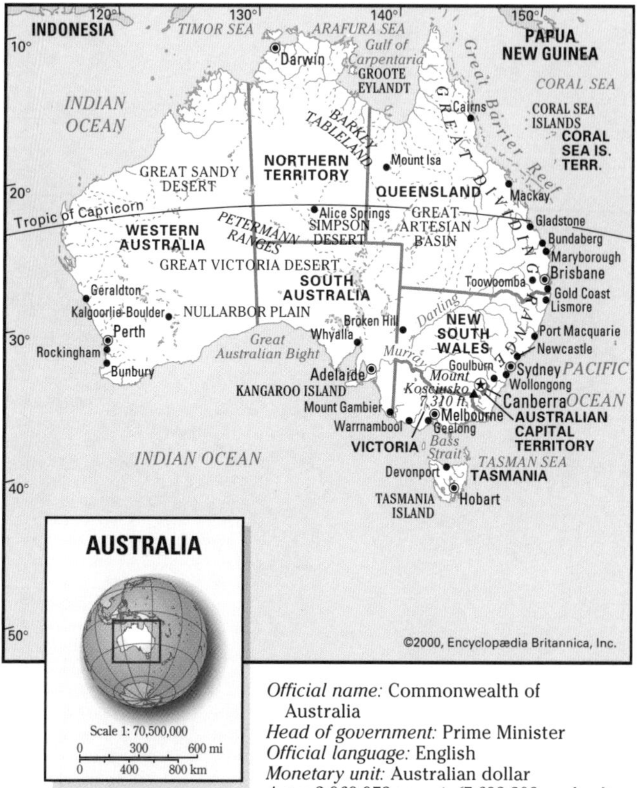

AUSTRALIA

Scale 1: 70,500,000

0 300 600 mi

0 400 800 km

Official name: Commonwealth of Australia
Head of government: Prime Minister
Official language: English
Monetary unit: Australian dollar
Area: 2,969,978 sq. mi. (7,692,208 sq. km.)
Population (2005): 20,345,000
GNP per capita (2004): U.S.$26,900
Principal exports (2002–03): mineral fuels 20.6%, crude materials excluding fuels 18.6%, food 15.9%, machinery and transport equipment 11.7% *to:* Japan 18.8%; U.S. 9.0%; South Korea 7.9; Singapore 4.0%

Age Breakdown

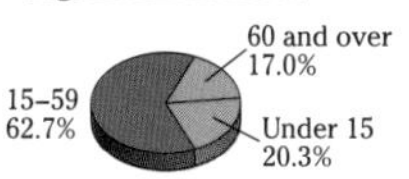

After Australian confederation was achieved on Jan. 1, 1901, the flag was chosen in a competition. Like the blue flags of British colonies, it displays the Union Jack in the canton. Also shown are the Southern Cross and a "Commonwealth Star." The design became official on May 22, 1909, and it was recognized as the national flag on Feb. 14, 1954.

AUSTRIA

Scale 1: 8,842,000

0 40 80 mi

0 40 80 120 km

Official name: Republic of Austria
Head of government: Chancellor
Official language: German
Monetary unit: euro
Area: 32,383 sq. mi. (83,871 sq. km.)
Population (2005): 8,168,000
GNP per capita (2004): U.S.$32,300
Principal exports (2002): machinery and transport equipment 32.9%, chemical products 10.2%, vehicles 9.8%, paper and paper products 4.6% *to:* Germany 32.1%; Italy 8.6%; United States 6.0%; Switzerland 4.5%

Religious Affiliation

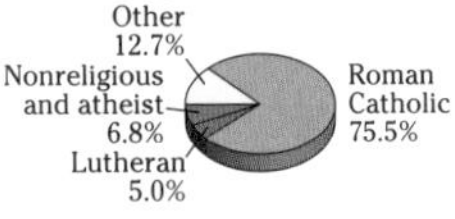

Roman Catholic 75.5%
Other 12.7%
Nonreligious and atheist 6.8%
Lutheran 5.0%

The colors of the Austrian coat of arms date from the seal of Duke Frederick II in 1230. With the fall of the Austro-Hungarian Empire in 1918, the new Austrian republic adopted the red-white-red flag. The white is sometimes said to represent the Danube River. The imperial eagle, with one or two heads, has been an Austrian symbol for centuries.

AZERBAIJAN

Scale 1: 8,146,000

Official name: Republic of Azerbaijan
Head of government: President
Official language: Azerbaijani
Monetary unit: manat
Area: 33,400 sq. mi. (86,600 sq. km.)
Population (2005): 8,381,000
GNP per capita (2004): U.S.$950
Principal exports (2004): crude petroleum 68.1%, refined petroleum 19.6% *to:* Italy 44.7%; Israel 9.0%; Russia 5.8%; Georgia 5.2%

Ethnic Composition

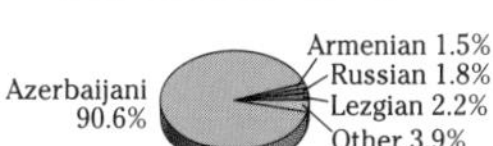

In the early 20th century anti-Russian nationalists exhorted the Azerbaijanis to "Turkify, Islamicize, and Europeanize," and the 1917 flag was associated with Turkey and Islam. In 1918 the crescent and star (also symbols of Turkic peoples) were introduced. Suppressed under Soviet rule, the flag was re-adopted on Feb. 5, 1991.

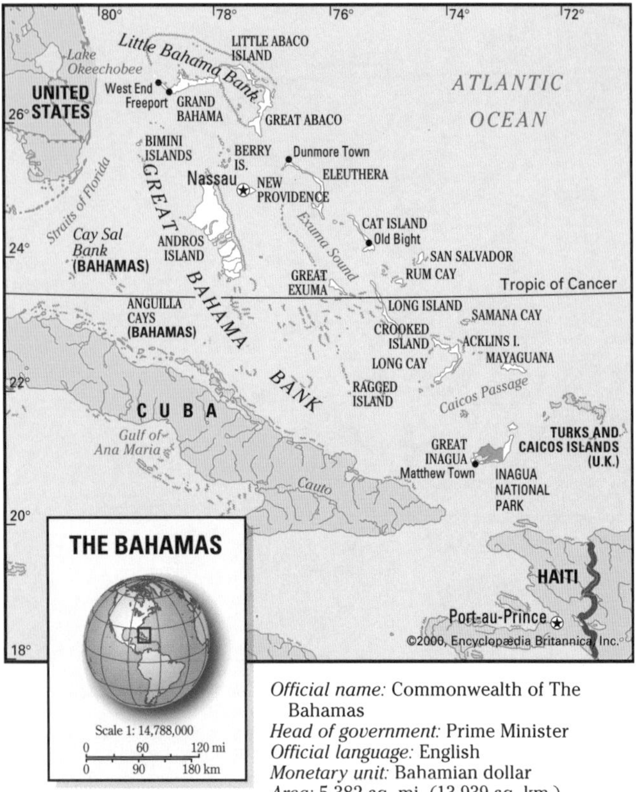

THE BAHAMAS

Scale 1: 14,788,000

©2000, Encyclopædia Britannica, Inc.

Ethnic Composition

Black 70.3%
Other 1.1%
Mulatto 14.2%
White 14.4%

Official name: Commonwealth of The Bahamas
Head of government: Prime Minister
Official language: English
Monetary unit: Bahamian dollar
Area: 5,382 sq. mi. (13,939 sq. km.)
Population (2005): 323,000
GNP per capita (2003): U.S.$10,450
Principal exports (2003): crayfish 19.1%, polystyrene 19.1%, refined petroleum 18.3%, rum 10.2% *to:* U.S. 35.2%; Peru 10.0%; Germany 9.7%; Spain 9.7%; France 7.7%

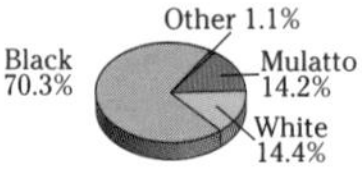

The flag of The Bahamas was adopted on July 10, 1973, the date of independence from Britain. Several entries from a competition were combined to create the design. The two aquamarine stripes are for the surrounding waters, the gold stripe is for the sand and other rich land resources, and the black triangle is for the people and their strength.

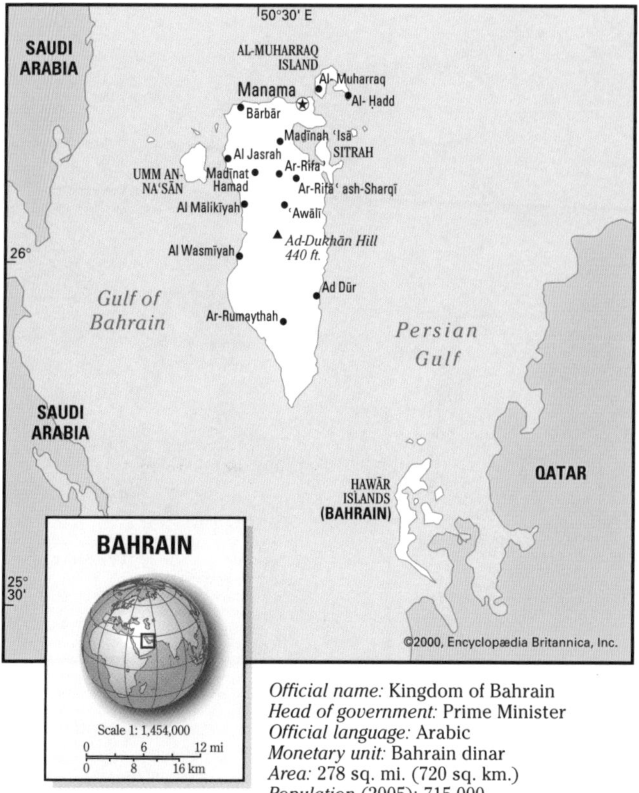

50°30' E
SAUDI ARABIA
AL-MUHARRAQ ISLAND
Manama
Al-Muharraq
Al-Ḥadd
Bārbār
Madīnah 'Isā
Al Jasrah
SITRAH
Ar-Rifā'
UMM AN-NA'SĀN
Madīnat Ḥamad
Ar-Rifā' ash-Sharqī
Al Mālikīyah
'Awālī
Ad-Dukhān Hill 440 ft.
26°
Al Wasmīyah
Ad Dūr
Gulf of Bahrain
Ar-Rumaythah
Persian Gulf
SAUDI ARABIA
QATAR
HAWĀR ISLANDS (BAHRAIN)
BAHRAIN
25° 30'
©2000, Encyclopædia Britannica, Inc.
Scale 1: 1,454,000
0 6 12 mi
0 8 16 km

Official name: Kingdom of Bahrain
Head of government: Prime Minister
Official language: Arabic
Monetary unit: Bahrain dinar
Area: 278 sq. mi. (720 sq. km.)
Population (2005): 715,000
GNP per capita (2003): U.S.$11,880
Principal exports (2003): petroleum products 70.9%, base metals including aluminum 13.8%, textiles and clothing 4.3% *to:* Saudi Arabia 24.0%; United States 14.6%; Taiwan 10.2%; India 5.8%; U.A.E. 5.7%

Religious Affiliation

Other 7.1%
Christian 10.5%
Sunni Muslim 24.4%
Shi'i Muslim 58.0%

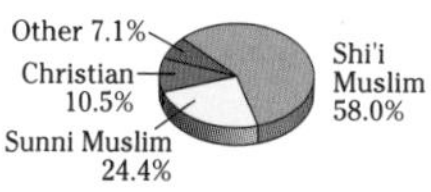

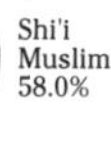

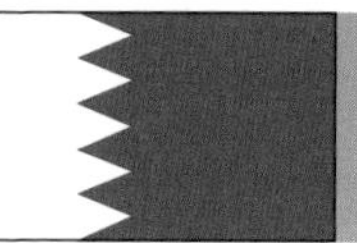

Red in this flag represents the Kharijite sect of Islam, dominant about 1820, and white stands for amity with the British, who brought peace to the strife-torn Persian Gulf then. After many versions of the design had been used by Bahrain, on February 14, 2002 it adopted the current flag, specifying that the dividing line must be serrated into five white triangles.

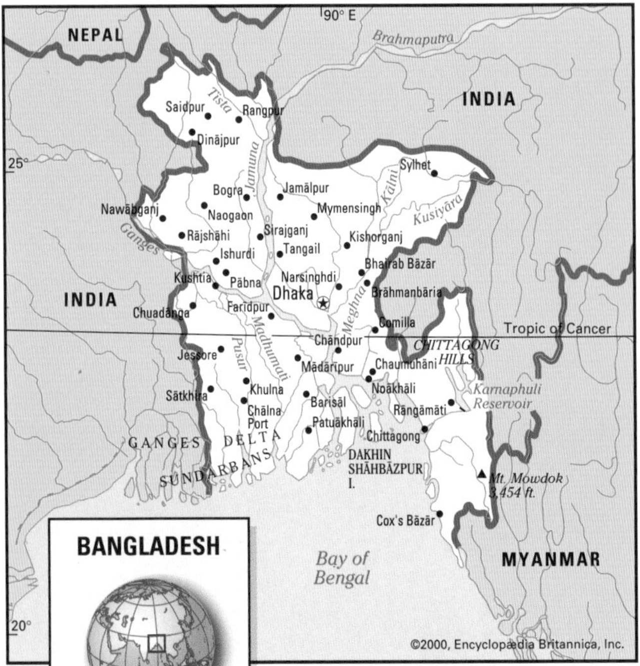

BANGLADESH

Scale 1: 11,181,000

0 50 100 mi

0 80 160 km

Religious Affiliation

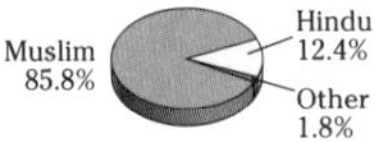

Muslim 85.8%

Hindu 12.4%

Other 1.8%

Official name: People's Republic of Bangladesh
Head of government: Prime Minister
Official language: Bengali
Monetary unit: Bangladesh taka
Area: 56,977 sq. mi. (147,570 sq. km.)
Population (2005): 137,636,000
GNP per capita (2004): U.S.$440
Principal exports (2003–04): garments 46.5%, hoisery and knitwear 28.3%, frozen fish and shrimp 5.1% *to:* U.S. 24.6%; Germany 13.3%; U.K. 10.9%; France 5.6%

The flag is dark green to symbolize Islam, plant life, and the hope placed in Bengali youth. Its original design included a red disk and a silhouette of the country. On Jan. 13, 1972, the silhouette was removed and the disk shifted off-center. The disk is the "rising sun of a new country" colored by the blood of those who fought for independence.

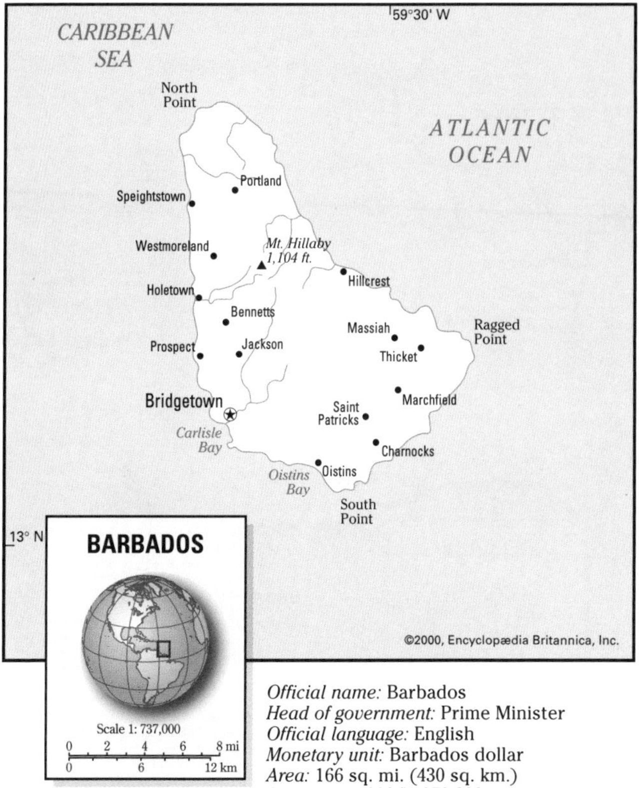
59°30' W
CARIBBEAN SEA
ATLANTIC OCEAN
North Point
Portland
Speightstown
Westmoreland
Mt. Hillaby 1,104 ft.
Hillcrest
Holetown
Bennetts
Massiah
Ragged Point
Prospect
Jackson
Thicket
Marchfield
Bridgetown
Saint Patricks
Carlisle Bay
Charnocks
Oistins
Oistins Bay
South Point
13° N
BARBADOS
Scale 1: 737,000
0 2 4 6 8 mi
0 6 12 km
©2000, Encyclopædia Britannica, Inc.

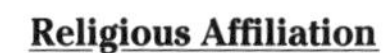

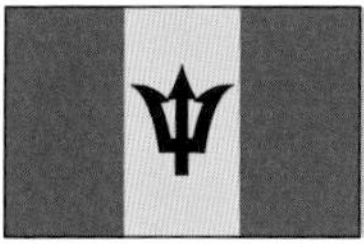

Official name: Barbados
Head of government: Prime Minister
Official language: English
Monetary unit: Barbados dollar
Area: 166 sq. mi. (430 sq. km.)
Population (2005): 270,000
GNP per capita (2003): U.S.$9,270
Principal exports (2003): food and beverages 25.3%, rum 7.0%, chemicals 8.3%, other manufactures 17.5% *to:* (2002): United States 16.5%; United Kingdom 11.9%; Trinidad and Tobago 11.0%; Jamaica 7.0

Religious Affiliation

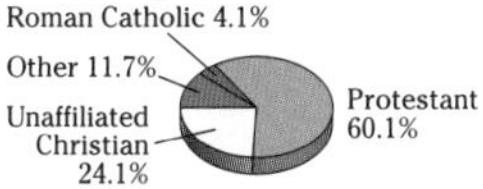
Roman Catholic 4.1%
Other 11.7%
Unaffiliated Christian 24.1%
Protestant 60.1%

The flag was designed by Grantley Prescod, a Barbadian art teacher. Its stripes of blue-yellow-blue are for sea, sand, and sky. The black trident head was inspired by the colonial flag of Barbados, which featured a trident-wielding Poseidon, or Neptune, figure. The flag was first hoisted on Nov. 30, 1966, the date of independence from Britain.

Official name: Republic of Belarus
Head of government: President
Official languages: Belarusian; Russian
Monetary unit: ruble
Area: 80,200 sq. mi. (207,600 sq. km.)
Population (2005): 9,776,000
GNP per capita (2004): U.S.$2,120
Principal exports (2002): refined petroleum 18.3%, road vehicles 8.9%, nonelectrical machinery 8.3%, food 6.7% *to:* Russia 47.0%; United Kingdom 8.3%; The Netherlands 6.7%; Poland 5.3%

Ethnic Composition

Ukrainian 2.4%
Other 5.0%
Russian 11.4%
Belarusian 81.2%

In 1951 the former Soviet republic created a striped flag in red (for communism) and green (for fields and forests), with the hammer, sickle, and star of communism. In 1991–95 an older design was used, but the Soviet-era flag was then altered and readopted without communist symbols. The vertical stripe is typical of embroidery on peasant clothing.

Official name: Kingdom of Belgium
Head of government: Prime Minister
Official languages: Dutch; French; German
Monetary unit: euro
Area: 11,787 sq. mi. (30,528 sq. km.)
Population (2005): 10,432,000
GNP per capita (2004): U.S.$34,370
Principal exports (2002): machinery and transport equipment 27.8%, pharmaceuticals 10.1%, food and live animals 7.6%, organic chemicals 5.9% *to:* Germany 17.4%; France 17.1%; The Netherlands 13.0%

A gold shield and a black lion appeared in the seal of Count Philip of Flanders as early as 1162, and in 1787 cockades of black-yellow-red were used in a Brussels revolt against Austria. After a war for independence, the flag was recognized on Jan. 23, 1831. By 1838 the design, which was influenced by the French tricolor, became standard.

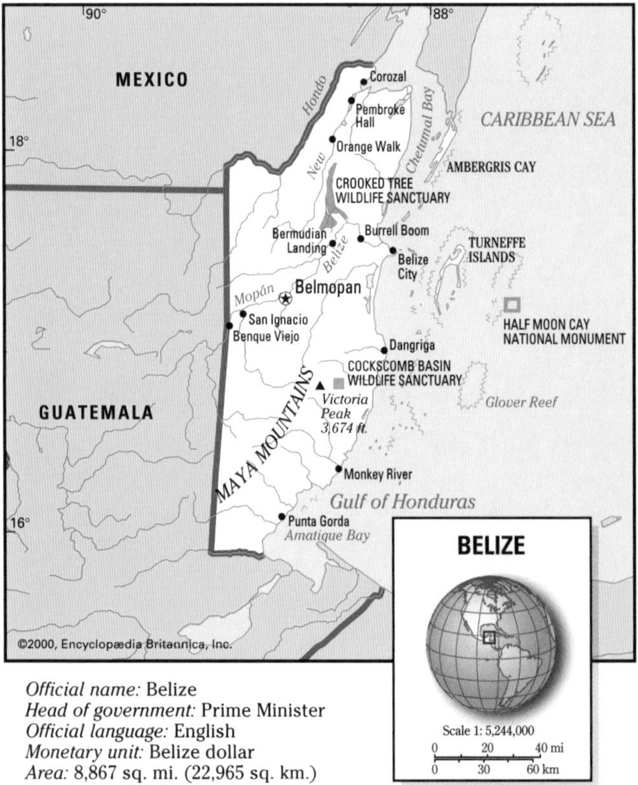
90°
88°
18°
16°
MEXICO
Corozal
Hondo
Pembroke Hall
Orange Walk
New
Chetumal Bay
CARIBBEAN SEA
AMBERGRIS CAY
CROOKED TREE WILDLIFE SANCTUARY
Bermudian Landing
Burrell Boom
Belize
Belize City
TURNEFFE ISLANDS
Mopán
Belmopan
San Ignacio
Benque Viejo
HALF MOON CAY NATIONAL MONUMENT
Dangriga
COCKSCOMB BASIN WILDLIFE SANCTUARY
MAYA MOUNTAINS
Victoria Peak 3,674 ft.
Glover Reef
GUATEMALA
Monkey River
Gulf of Honduras
Punta Gorda
Amatique Bay
©2000, Encyclopædia Britannica, Inc.
BELIZE
Scale 1: 5,244,000
0 20 40 mi
0 30 60 km

Official name: Belize
Head of government: Prime Minister
Official language: English
Monetary unit: Belize dollar
Area: 8,867 sq. mi. (22,965 sq. km.)
Population (2005): 291,000
GNP per capita (2004): U.S.$3,100
Principal exports (2003): domestic exports 60.4%, of which seafood products 17.4%, citrus concentrate 12.4%, raw sugar 11.2%, bananas 8.3%, garments 5.0%; reexports 39.6% *to:* United States 55.6%; United Kingdom 24.0%

Ethnic Composition

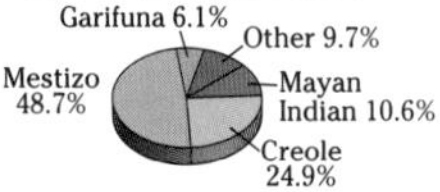
Garifuna 6.1%
Other 9.7%
Mayan Indian 10.6%
Creole 24.9%
Mestizo 48.7%

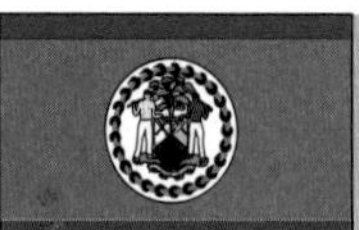

The flag of Belize (former British Honduras) was based on the flag of the nationalist People's United Party. Its coat of arms shows a mahogany tree, a shield, and a Creole and a Mestizo. The red stripes, symbolic of the United Democratic Party, were added on independence day (Sept. 21, 1981), when the flag was first officially hoisted.

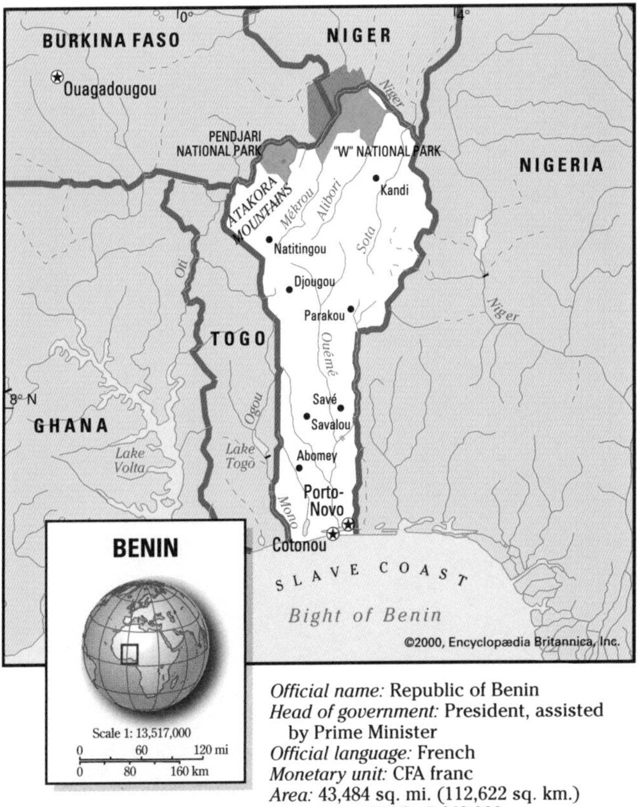

BENIN

Scale 1: 13,517,000

0 60 120 mi

0 80 160 km

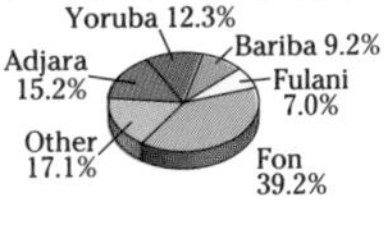

Official name: Republic of Benin
Head of government: President, assisted by Prime Minister
Official language: French
Monetary unit: CFA franc
Area: 43,484 sq. mi. (112,622 sq. km.)
Population (2005): 7,649,000
GNP per capita (2004): U.S.$530
Principal exports (2003): domestic exports 66.2%, of which cotton yarn 28.9%; reexport 33.8% *to* (2001): India 31.0%; Brazil 6.0%; Indonesia 6.0%; Ghana 6.0%

Ethnic Composition

Yoruba 12.3%
Bariba 9.2%
Adjara 15.2%
Fulani 7.0%
Other 17.1%
Fon 39.2%

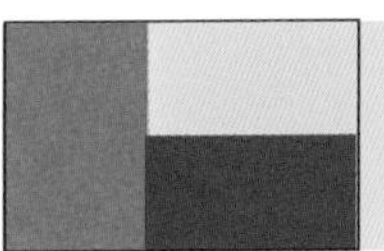

Adopted on Nov. 16, 1959, the flag of the former French colony used the Pan-African colors. Yellow was for the savannas in the north and green was for the palm groves in the south. Red stood for the blood of patriots. In 1975 a Marxist-oriented government replaced the flag, but after the demise of Communism it was restored on Aug. 1, 1990.

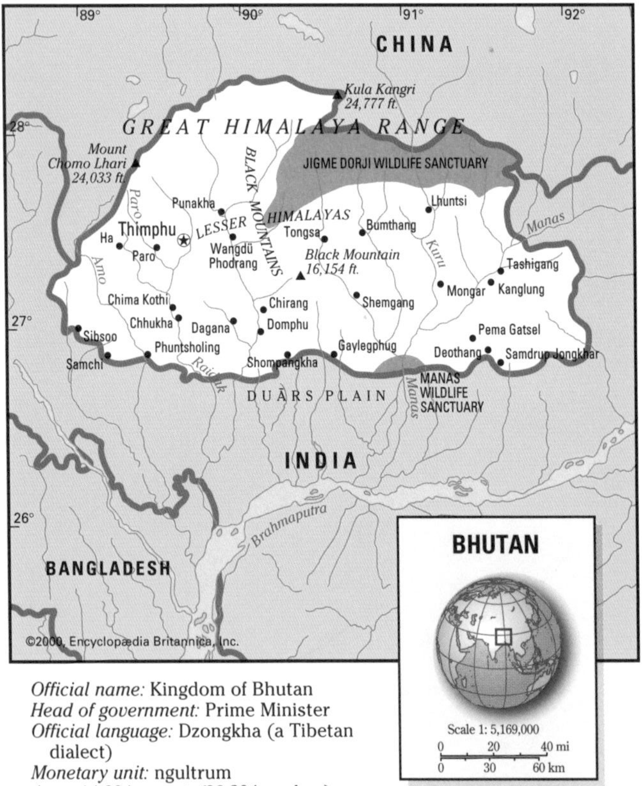

Official name: Kingdom of Bhutan
Head of government: Prime Minister
Official language: Dzongkha (a Tibetan dialect)
Monetary unit: ngultrum
Area: 14,824 sq. mi. (38,394 sq. km.)
Population (2005): 776,000
GNP per capita (2004): U.S.$760
Principal exports (2001): electricity 48.1%, calcium carbide 13.3%, ferrosilicon 12.6%, cement 9.6% *to:* India 94.1%; Bangladesh 4.5%

Ethnic Composition

The flag of Bhutan ("Land of the Dragon") features a dragon grasping jewels; this represents natural wealth and perfection. The white color is for purity and loyalty, the gold is for regal power, and the orange-red is for Buddhist sects and religious commitment. The flag may have been introduced as recently as 1971.

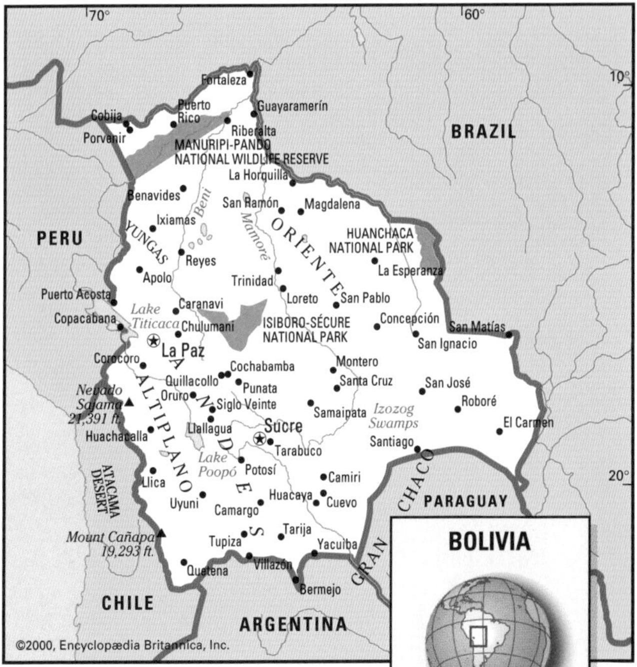

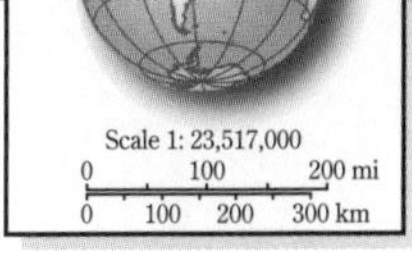

Official name: Republic of Bolivia
Head of government: President
Official languages: Spanish; Aymara; Quechua
Monetary unit: boliviano
Area: 424,164 sq. mi. (1,098,581 sq. km.)
Population (2005): 8,858,000
GNP per capita (2004): U.S.$960
Principal exports (2003): natural gas 23.0%, food products 18.3%, zinc ores 7.4%, petroleum 5.8% *to:* Brazil 29.9%; U.S. 14.2%; Colombia 10.3%; Switzerland 10.0%

Ethnic Composition

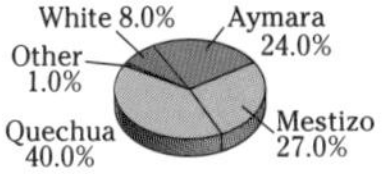

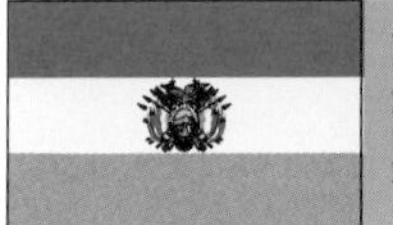

A version of the flag was first adopted on July 25, 1826, but on Nov. 5, 1851, the order of the stripes was changed to red-yellow-green. The colors were often used by the Aymara and Quechua peoples; in addition, red is for the valor of the army, yellow for mineral resources, and green for the land. The current flag law dates from July 14, 1888.

BOSNIA AND HERZEGOVINA

Ethnic Composition

Official name: Bosnia and Herzegovina
Head of government: Prime Minister
Official language: Bosnian
Monetary unit: marka
Area: 19,772 sq. mi. (51,209 sq. km.)
Population (2005): 3,853,000
GNP per capita (2003): U.S.$1,540
Principal exports (2003): *to:* Croatia 17.9%; Germany 15.4%; Serbia and Montenegro 15.3%; Italy 13.4%; Slovenia 9.7%

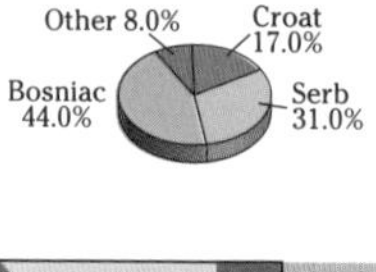

Under communist Yugoslavia (1946 to 1992), the Socialist Republic of Bosnia and Herzegovina flew a red banner with a small Yugoslav national flag in the canton. At independence, March 3, 1992, there was no flag acceptable to Bosnians, Serbs, and Croats. So, the UN established a flag (February 4, 1998) not symbolic of any ethnic, religious, or political group.

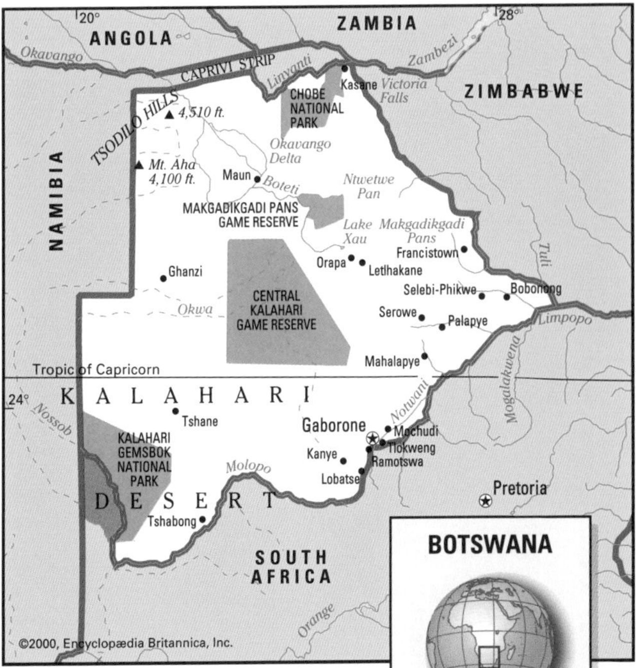

BOTSWANA

Scale 1: 17,673,000

0 80 160 mi

0 120 240 km

Official name: Republic of Botswana
Head of government: President
Official language: English
Monetary unit: pula
Area: 224,848 sq. mi. (582,356 sq. km.)
Population (2005): 1,765,000
GNP per capita (2004): U.S.$4,340
Principal exports (2002): diamonds 83.3%, copper-nickel matte 3.2%, textiles 2.0%, *to:* U.K. 85.7%; Customs Union of Southern Africa 6.5%; Zimbabwe 2.6%

Ethnic Composition

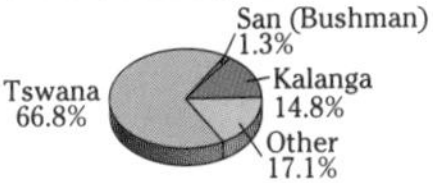

Tswana 66.8%
San (Bushman) 1.3%
Kalanga 14.8%
Other 17.1%

Adopted in 1966, the flag was designed to contrast symbolically with that of neighboring South Africa, where apartheid was then in effect. The black and white stripes in Botswana's flag are for racial cooperation and equality. The background symbolizes water, a scarce resource in the expansive Kalahari Desert.

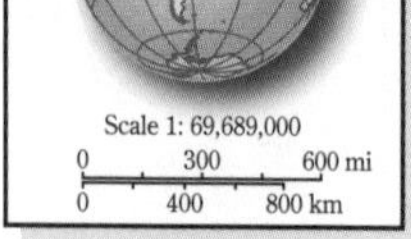

BRAZIL

Scale 1: 69,689,000

0 300 600 mi

0 400 800 km

Official name: Federative Republic of Brazil
Head of government: President
Official language: Portuguese
Monetary unit: real
Area: 3,287,612 sq. mi. (8,514,877 sq. km.)
Population (2005): 184,016,000
GNP per capita (2004): U.S.$3,090
Principal exports (2001): food products 20.0%, transport equipment 13.6%, machinery and apparatus 13.1%, iron and steel 5.5% *to* (2002): U.S. 25.4%; The Netherlands 5.3%; Germany 4.2%; China 4.2%

Ethnic Composition

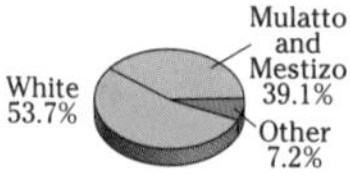

White 53.7%
Mulatto and Mestizo 39.1%
Other 7.2%

The original flag was introduced on Sept. 7, 1822, when Dom Pedro declared independence from Portugal. In 1889 the blue disk and the motto Ordem e Progresso ("Order and Progress") were added. The Brazilian states and territories are symbolized by the constellations of stars. Green is for the land, while yellow is for gold and other mineral wealth.

BRUNEI

Scale 1: 2,249,000

Official name: State of Brunei, Abode of Peace
Head of government: Sultan
Official language: Malay
Monetary unit: Brunei dollar
Area: 2,226 sq. mi. (5,765 sq. km.)
Population (2005): 364,000
GNP per capita (2003): U.S.$20,360
Principal exports (2004): crude petroleum 57.4%, natural gas 34.0%, garments 3.6% *to:* Japan 41.0%; ASEAN 20.2%; South Korea 11.2%; Australia 8.4%; China 6.7%

Ethnic Composition

Other indigenous 3.6%
Chinese 10.9%
Indian and other 19.3%
Malay 66.2%

On becoming independent from Britain, January 1, 1984, Brunei adopted this flag. The colors stand for the sultan (yellow) and his two ministers (white and black), while red is for the national coat of arms in the center. Its crescent is for Islam, the state religion, and reads, "Always render service by the guidance of God." The ribbon below says, "Brunei, abode of peace."

Official name: Republic of Bulgaria
Head of government: Prime Minister
Official language: Bulgarian
Monetary unit: lev
Area: 42,858 sq. mi. (111,002 sq. km.)
Population (2005): 7,740,000
GNP per capita (2004): U.S.$2,740
Principal exports (2004): clothing and footware 19.4%, iron and steel 10.1%, machinery and transport equipment 9.7%, petroleum products 7.8% *to:* Italy 13.1%; Germany 10.2%; Turkey 10.0%; Belgium 6.0%

Ethnic Composition

The flag was based on the Russian flag of 1699, but with green substituted for blue. Under communist rule, a red star and other symbols were added, but the old tricolor was reestablished on Nov. 27, 1990. The white is for peace, love, and freedom; green is for agriculture; and red is for the independence struggle and military courage.

BURKINA FASO

Scale 1: 14,037,000

0 60 120 mi

0 90 180 km

Official name: Burkina Faso
Head of government: Prime Minister
Official language: French
Monetary unit: CFA franc
Area: 103,456 sq. mi. (267,950 sq. km.)
Population (2005): 13,492,000
GNP per capita (2004): U.S.$360
Principal exports (2002): raw cotton 54.1%, hides and skins 11.0%, live animals 8.8% *to:* France 45.3%; Côte d'Ivoire 9.2%; Singapore 5.1%; Mali 4.0%; Japan 3.0%

Ethnic Composition

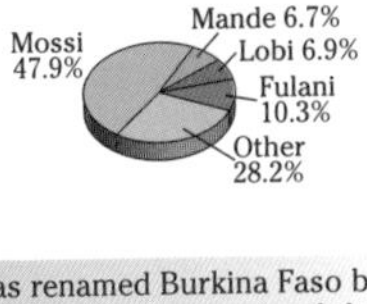

Mossi 47.9%
Mande 6.7%
Lobi 6.9%
Fulani 10.3%
Other 28.2%

On Aug. 4, 1984, Upper Volta was renamed Burkina Faso by the revolutionary government of Thomas Sankara, and the current flag was adopted with Pan-African colors. The yellow star symbolizes leadership and revolutionary principles. The red stripe is said to stand for the revolutionary struggle, while the green stripe represents hope and abundance.

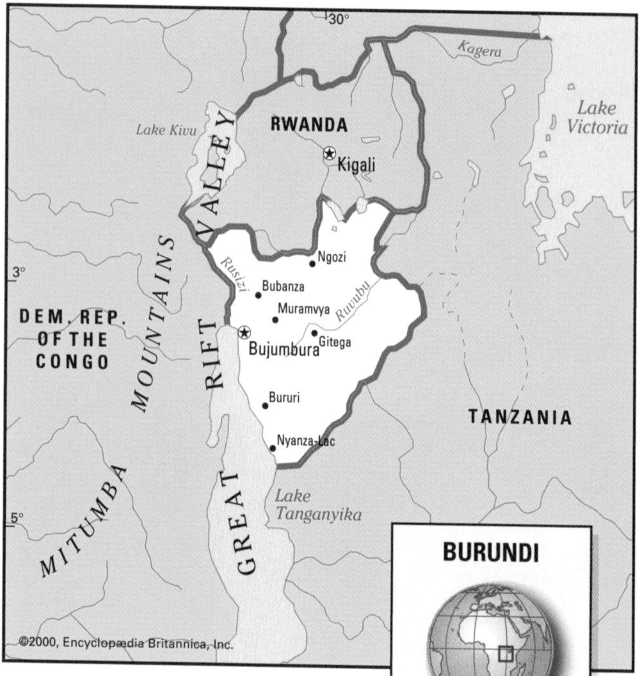

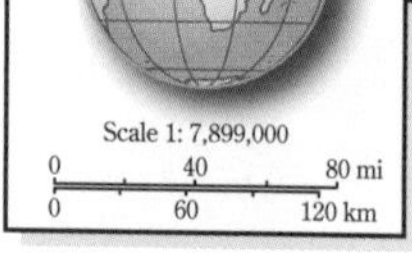

BURUNDI

Scale 1: 7,899,000

0 40 80 mi

0 60 120 km

Official name: Republic of Burundi
Head of government: President, assisted by Vice President
Official languages: Rundi; French
Monetary unit: Burundi franc
Area: 10,740 sq. mi. (27,816 sq. km.)
Population (2005): 7,795,000
GNP per capita (2004): U.S.$100
Principal exports (2003): coffee 61.4%, tea 21.3%, refined sugar 6.2% *to:* (2003): Switzerland 32.0%; United Kingdom 16.4%; Belgium-Luxembourg 5.7%; Rwanda 5.7%

Ethnic Composition

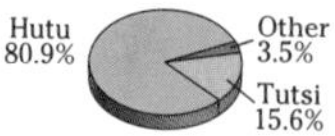

Hutu 80.9%
Other 3.5%
Tutsi 15.6%

The flag became official on June 28, 1967. Its white saltire (diagonal cross) and central disk symbolize peace. The red color is for the independence struggle, and green is for hope. The stars correspond to the national motto, "Unity, Work, Progress." They also recall the Tutsi, Hutu, and Twa peoples and the pledge to God, king, and country.

Official name: Kingdom of Cambodia
Head of government: First Prime Minister
Official language: Khmer
Monetary unit: riel
Area: 69,898 sq. mi. (181,035 sq. km.)
Population (2005): 13,327,000
GDP per capita (2004): U.S.$320
Principal exports (2001): domestic exports 94.4%, of which garments 80.0%, rubber 4.7%, rice 4.3%, fish 1.8%, sawn timber and logs 1.2%; reexports 5.6% *to:* U.S. 59.8%; Germany 10.4%; U.K. 7.4%

Ethnic Composition

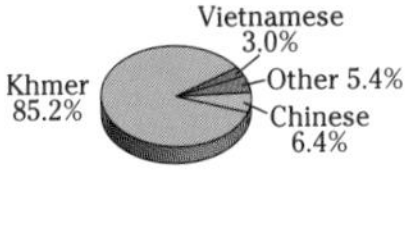

Artistic representations of the central ruined temple of Angkor Wat, a 12th-century temple complex, have appeared on Khmer flags since the 19th century. The current flag design dates to 1948. It was replaced in 1970 under the Khmer Republic and in 1976 under communist leadership, but it was again hoisted on June 29, 1993.

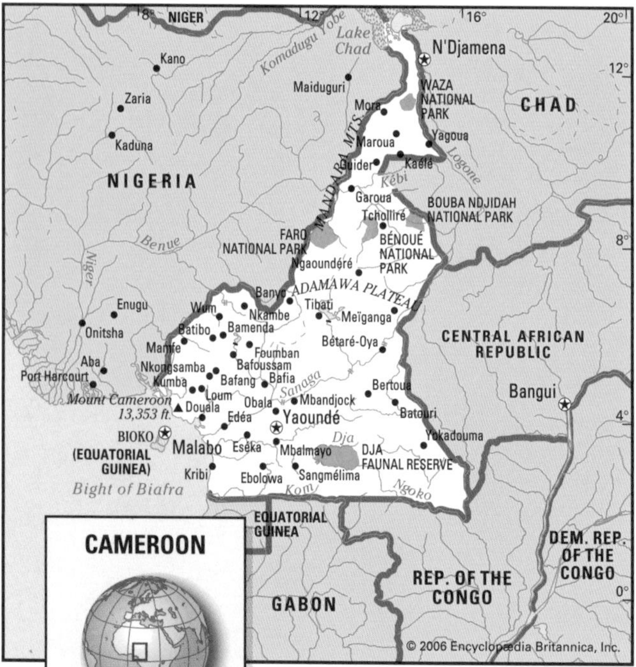

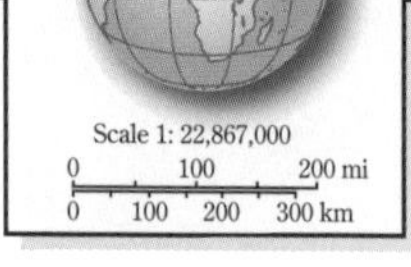

CAMEROON

Scale 1: 22,867,000

0 100 200 mi

0 100 200 300 km

Official name: Republic of Cameroon
Head of government: Prime Minister
Official languages: French; English
Monetary unit: CFA franc
Area: 183,569 sq. mi. (475,442 sq. km.)
Population (2005): 16,988,000
GNP per capita (2004): U.S.$800
Principal exports (2004): crude petroleum 49.9%, aluminum 7.3%, cocoa beans 7.0%, cotton 6.6%, lumber 6.5% *to* (2003): Spain 20.3%; Italy 15.0%; The Netherlands 11.9%; France 10.6%; U.S. 8.4%

Ethnic Composition

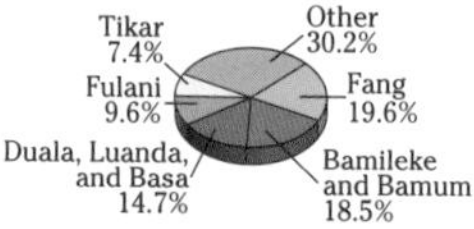

Tikar 7.4%
Fulani 9.6%
Duala, Luanda, and Basa 14.7%
Other 30.2%
Fang 19.6%
Bamileke and Bamum 18.5%

The flag was officially hoisted on Oct. 29, 1957, prior to independence (Jan. 1, 1960). Green is for the vegetation of the south, yellow for the savannas of the north, and red for union and sovereignty. Two yellow stars were added (for the British Cameroons) in 1961, but these were replaced in 1975 by a single star symbolizing national unity.

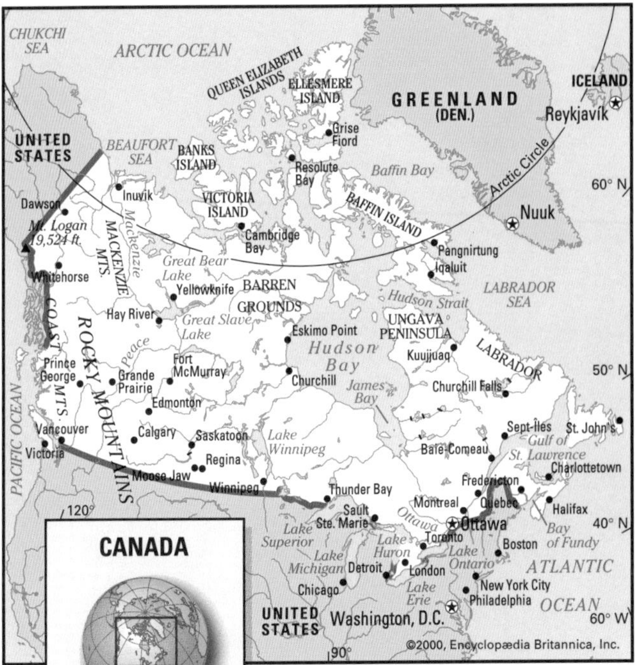

CANADA

Scale 1: 75,618,000
0 300 600 mi
0 300 600 900 km

©2000, Encyclopædia Britannica, Inc.

Official name: Canada
Head of government: Prime Minister
Official languages: English; French
Monetary unit: Canadian dollar
Area: 3,855,103 sq. mi. (9,984,670 sq. km.)
Population (2005): 32,227,000
GNP per capita (2004): U.S.$28,390
Principal exports (2004): transport equipment 25.6%, machinery and apparatus 16.7%, base metals 7.5%, food products 7.1%, natural gas 6.5%, crude petroleum 6.1% *to:* U.S. 87.2%; Japan 2.1%; U.K. 1.1%; China 1.0%; Germany 0.7%

Ethnic Origin

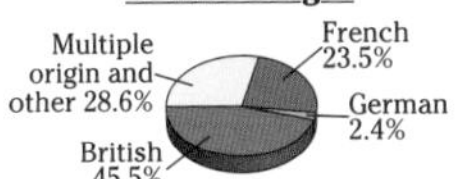

During Canada's first century of independence the Union Jack was still flown, but with a Canadian coat of arms. The maple leaf design, with the national colors, became official on Feb. 15, 1965. Since 1868 the maple leaf has been a national symbol, and in 1921 a red leaf in the coat of arms stood for Canadian sacrifice during World War I.

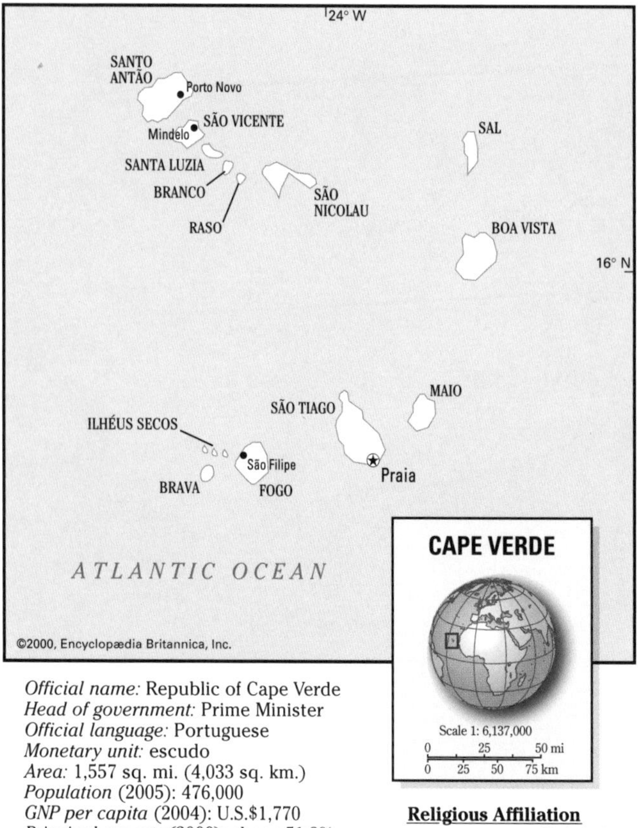

24° W
SANTO ANTÃO
Porto Novo
SÃO VICENTE
Mindelo
SAL
SANTA LUZIA
BRANCO
SÃO NICOLAU
RASO
BOA VISTA
16° N
MAIO
SÃO TIAGO
ILHÉUS SECOS
São Filipe
Praia
BRAVA
FOGO
CAPE VERDE
ATLANTIC OCEAN
©2000, Encyclopædia Britannica, Inc.
Scale 1: 6,137,000
0 25 50 mi
0 25 50 75 km

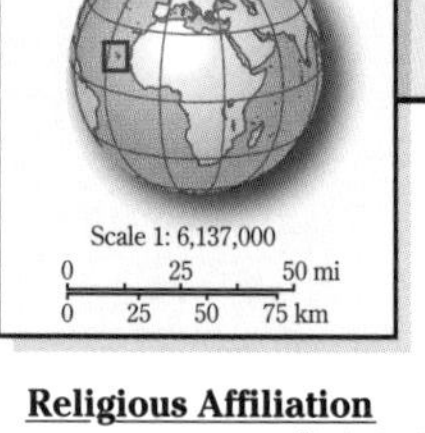

Official name: Republic of Cape Verde
Head of government: Prime Minister
Official language: Portuguese
Monetary unit: escudo
Area: 1,557 sq. mi. (4,033 sq. km.)
Population (2005): 476,000
GNP per capita (2004): U.S.$1,770
Principal exports (2000): shoes 51.8%, clothing 35.1%, fish 4.8% *to* (2003): Portugal 70.8%; U.S. 22.5%; Germany 1.1%

Religious Affiliation

Roman Catholic 91.4%
Protestant and other 5.8%
Muslim 2.8%

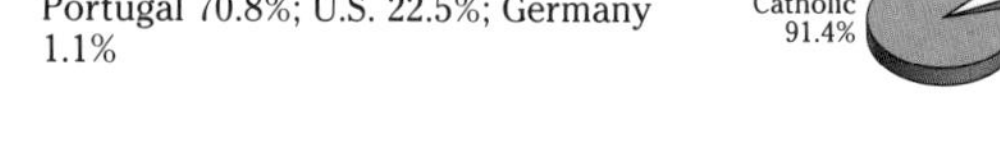

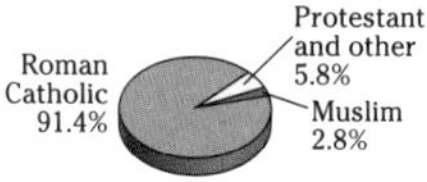

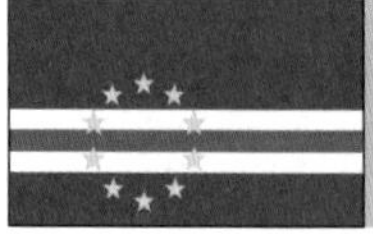

After the elections of 1991, the flag was established with a blue field bearing a ring of 10 yellow stars to symbolize the 10 main islands of Cape Verde. The stripes of white-red-white suggest peace and national resolve. Red, white, and blue also are a symbolic link to Portugal and the United States. The new flag became official on Sept. 25, 1992.

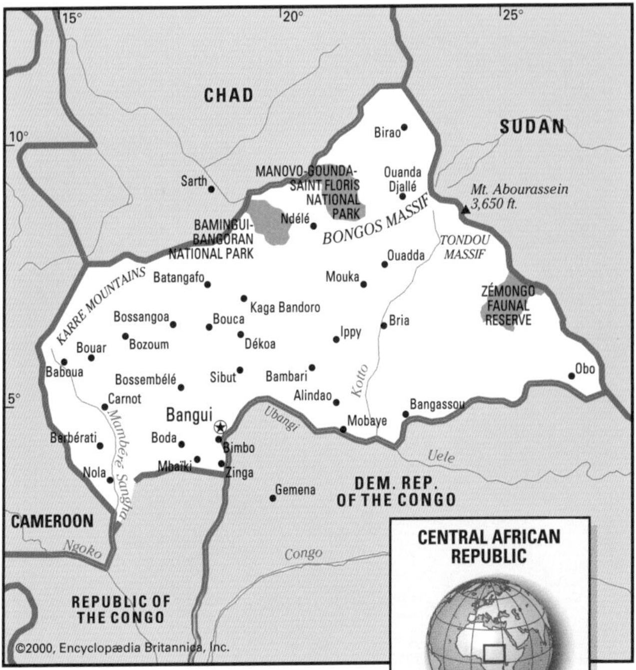

Official name: Central African Republic
Head of government: President assisted by Prime Minister
Official languages: French; Sango
Monetary unit: CFA franc
Area: 240,324 sq. mi. (622,436 sq. km.)
Population (2005): 4,038,000
GNP per capita (2004): U.S.$310
Principal exports (2002): wood 49.0%, diamonds 35.8%, cotton 6.3%, coffee 1.0% *to:* Belgium-Luxembourg 71.0%; Spain 7.0%; Italy 6.4%; France 3.0%

Religious Affiliation

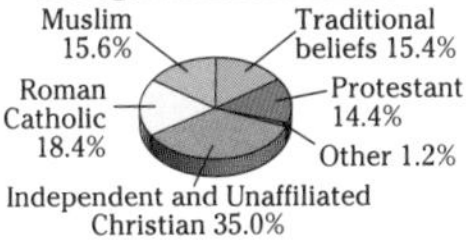

Muslim 15.6%
Traditional beliefs 15.4%
Roman Catholic 18.4%
Protestant 14.4%
Other 1.2%
Independent and Unaffiliated Christian 35.0%

Barthélemy Boganda designed the flag in 1958. It combines French and Pan-African colors. The star is a guide for progress and an emblem of unity. The blue stripe is for liberty, grandeur, and the sky; the white is for purity, equality, and candor; the green and yellow are for forests and savannas; and the red is for the blood of humankind.

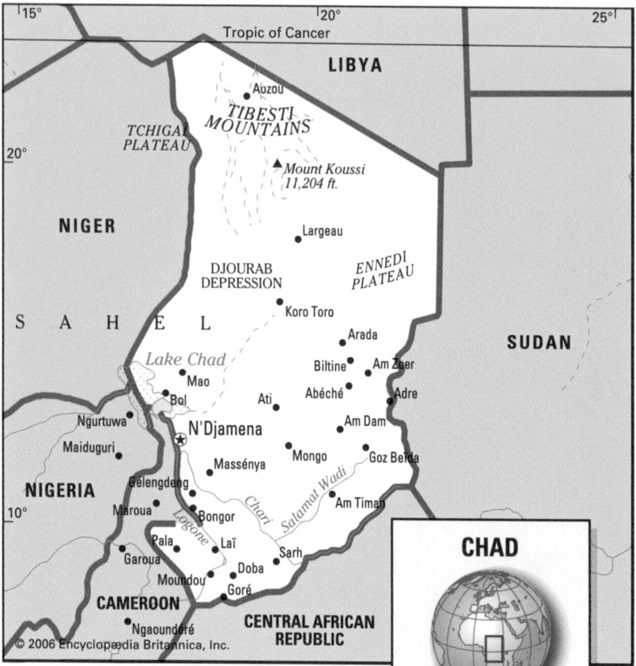
15°
20°
25°
Tropic of Cancer
LIBYA
Aozou
TIBESTI MOUNTAINS
TCHIGAI PLATEAU
20°
Mount Koussi 11,204 ft.
NIGER
Largeau
DJOURAB DEPRESSION
ENNEDI PLATEAU
Koro Toro
S A H E L
Arada
SUDAN
Lake Chad
Biltine
Am Zoer
Mao
Abéché
Adre
Bol
Ati
Ngurtuwa
Am Dam
N'Djamena
Maiduguri
Mongo
Goz Beïda
Massénya
Gélengdeng
NIGERIA
Salamat Wadi
Am Timan
10°
Maroua
Chari
Bongor
Logone
Pala
Laï
Sarh
Garoua
Doba
Moundou
Goré
CAMEROON
Ngaoundéré
CENTRAL AFRICAN REPUBLIC
© 2006 Encyclopædia Britannica, Inc.
CHAD
Scale 1: 30,270,000
0
150
300 mi
0
200
400 km

Official name: Republic of Chad
Head of government: Prime Minister
Official languages: Arabic; French
Monetary unit: CFA franc
Area: 495,755 sq. mi. (1,284,000 sq. km.)
Population (2005): 9,657,000
GNP per capita (2004): U.S.$260
Principal exports (2003): petroleum products 49.3%, live cattle 21.0%, cotton fiber 15.8% *to:* U.S. 25.0%; Germany 17.0%; Portugal 16.0%; France 7.0%

Religious Affiliation

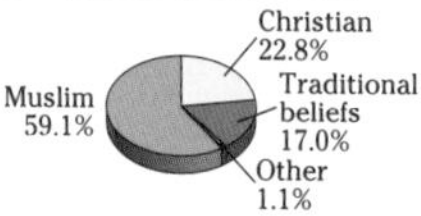
Christian 22.8%
Traditional beliefs 17.0%
Muslim 59.1%
Other 1.1%

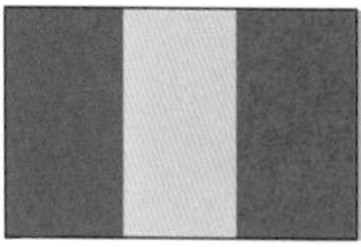

In 1958 a tricolor of green-yellow-red (the Pan-African colors) was proposed, but that design was already used by the Mali-Senegal federation, another former French colony. Approved on Nov. 6, 1959, the current flag substitutes blue for the original green stripe. Blue is for hope and sky, yellow for the sun, and red for the unity of the nation.

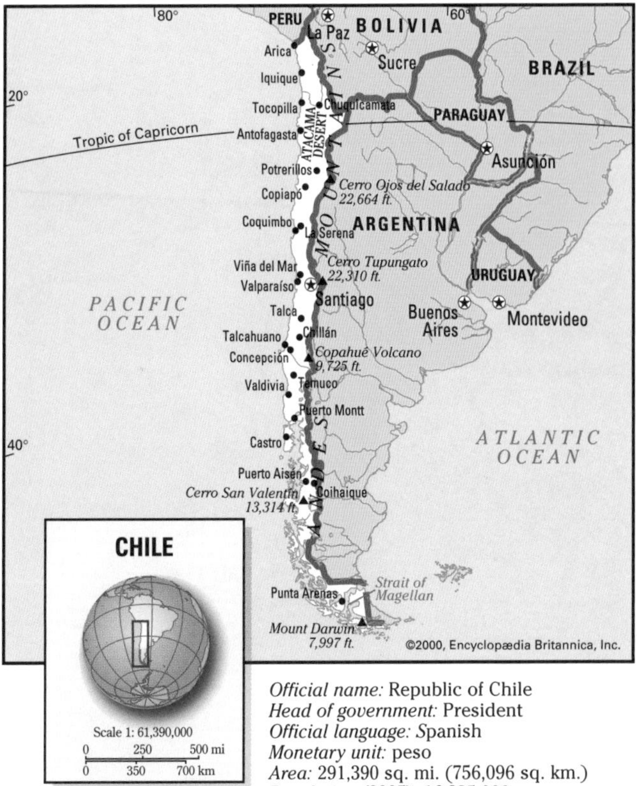
80°
60°
20°
40°
PERU
La Paz
BOLIVIA
Sucre
BRAZIL
Arica
Iquique
Tocopilla
Chuquicamata
PARAGUAY
Tropic of Capricorn
Antofagasta
ATACAMA DESERT
Asunción
Potrerillos
Cerro Ojos del Salado
22,664 ft.
Copiapó
Coquimbo
La Serena
ARGENTINA
ANDES MOUNTAINS
Viña del Mar
Cerro Tupungato
22,310 ft.
URUGUAY
Valparaíso
Santiago
PACIFIC OCEAN
Talca
Buenos Aires
Montevideo
Chillán
Talcahuano
Concepción
Copahuê Volcano
9,725 ft.
Valdivia
Temuco
Puerto Montt
ATLANTIC OCEAN
Castro
Puerto Aisén
Cerro San Valentín
13,314 ft.
Coihaique
Strait of Magellan
Punta Arenas
Mount Darwin
7,997 ft.
©2000, Encyclopædia Britannica, Inc.
CHILE
Scale 1: 61,390,000
0 250 500 mi
0 350 700 km

Official name: Republic of Chile
Head of government: President
Official language: Spanish
Monetary unit: peso
Area: 291,390 sq. mi. (756,096 sq. km.)
Population (2005): 16,295,000.
GNP per capita (2004): U.S.$4,910.
Principal exports (2003): copper 36.3%, food 16.0%, chemicals 8.4%, fruit 8.1% *to:* U.S. 16.2%; Japan 10.5%; China 8.6%; South Korea 4.7%; Mexico 4.3%

Religious Affiliation

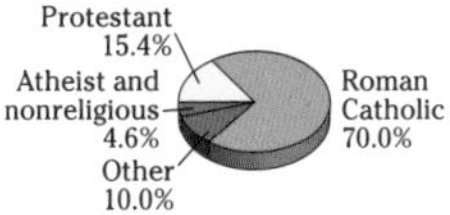
Protestant
15.4%
Atheist and
nonreligious
4.6%
Other
10.0%
Roman
Catholic
70.0%

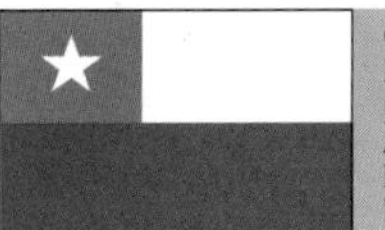

On Oct. 18, 1817, the flag was established for the new republic. The blue is for the sky, and the star is "a guide on the path of progress and honor." The white is for the snow of the Andes Mountains while the red recalls the blood of patriots. In the 15th century the Araucanian Indians gave red-white-blue sashes to their warriors.

Ⓐ Administered by Pakistan; claimed by India
Ⓑ Administered by India
Ⓒ Administered by China; claimed by India
Ⓓ Administered by India; claimed by China

RUSSIA
KAZAKHSTAN
MONGOLIA
ALTAI MTS.
JUNGGAR BASIN
Ürümqi
Tashkent
Bishkek
UZBEKISTAN
KYRGYZSTAN
TIEN SHAN
Victory Peak 24,400 ft.
Dushanbe
TAJIKISTAN
PAMIRS
Tarim
TAKLA MAKAN DESERT
Lop Nur
GOBI
AFGHANISTAN
Kabul
QAIDAM BASIN
KUNLUN MTS.
Koko Nor
Xining
Lanzhou
Islamabad
PLATEAU OF TIBET
HIMALAYAS
Tongtian
PAKISTAN
WENCHUAN WOLONG NATURE RESERVE
SICHUAN BASIN
New Delhi
Mount Everest 29,035 ft.
Lhasa
NEPAL
Nu
Kathmandu
HIMALAYAS
BHUTAN
Thimphu
INDIA
INDIA
Mount Yulongxue 18,355 ft.
Kunming
Red
BANGLADESH
Dhaka
MYANMAR
LAOS
THAILAND
Bay of Bengal

CHINA

Scale 1: 49,053,000

0 200 400 mi

0 300 600 km

Age Breakdown

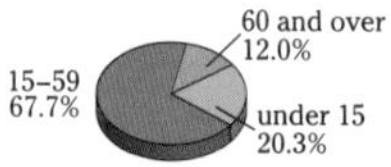

60 and over 12.0%

15–59 67.7%

under 15 20.3%

The flag was hoisted on Oct. 1, 1949. The red is for communism and the Han Chinese. The large star was originally for the Communist Party, and the smaller stars were for the proletariat, the peasants, the petty bourgeoisie, and the "patriotic capitalists." The large star was later said to stand for China, the smaller stars for minorities.

Official name: People's Republic of China
Head of government: Premier
Official language: Mandarin Chinese
Monetary unit: Renminbi (yuan)
Area: 3,696,100 sq. mi. (9,572,900 sq. km.)
Population (2005): 1,304,369,000
GNP per capita (2003): U.S.$2,100
Principal exports (2002): machinery and apparatus 39.0%, of which computers 11.1%; garments 12.7%; textile yarn and fabrics 6.4%; toys and games 3.9% *to* (2004): U.S. 21.1%; Hong Kong 17.0; Japan 12.4%; South Korea 4.7%; Germany 4.0%

COLOMBIA

Scale 1: 26,728,000

0 100 200 mi

0 100 200 300 km

Official name: Republic of Colombia
Head of government: President
Official language: Spanish
Monetary unit: peso
Area: 440,762 sq. mi. (1,141,568 sq. km.)
Population (2005): 42,954,000
GNP per capita (2004): U.S.$2,000
Principal exports (2004): crude and refined petroleum 25.3%, coal 11.1%, chemicals 10.4%, textiles and clothing 8.2%, machinery and equipment 7.4%, food 7.3% *to:* U.S. 39.4%; EU 14.0%; Venezuela 9.7%; Mexico 3.1%

Ethnic Composition

Mestizo 47.3%
Mulatto 23.0%
White 20.0%
Other 9.7%

In the early 19th century "the Liberator" Simon Bolivar created a yellow-blue-red flag for New Granada (which included Colombia, Venezuela, Panama, and Ecuador). The flag symbolized the yellow gold of the New World separated by the blue ocean from the red of "bloody Spain." The present Colombian flag was established on Nov. 26, 1861.

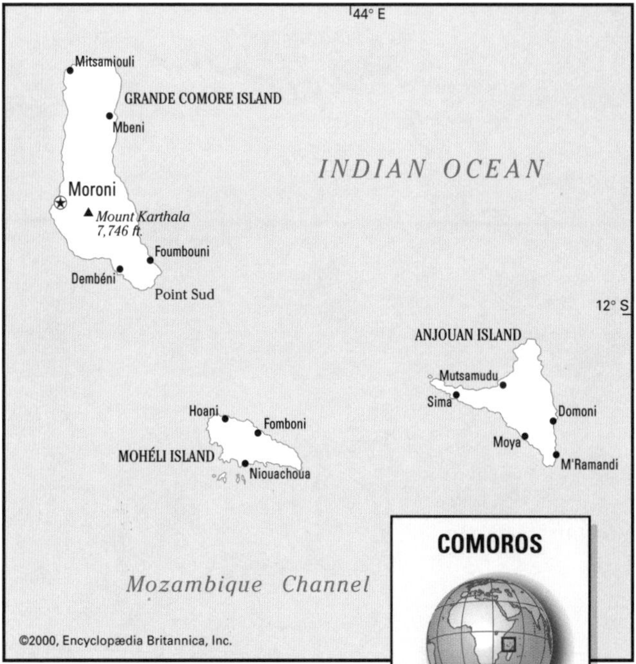
44° E
Mitsamiouli
GRANDE COMORE ISLAND
Mbeni
INDIAN OCEAN
Moroni
Mount Karthala
7,746 ft.
Foumbouni
Dembéni
Point Sud
12° S
ANJOUAN ISLAND
Mutsamudu
Sima
Domoni
Moya
M'Ramandi
Hoani
Fomboni
MOHÉLI ISLAND
Niouachoua
Mozambique Channel
©2000, Encyclopædia Britannica, Inc.

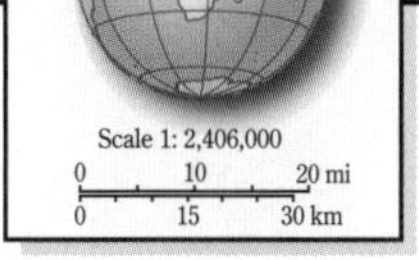
COMOROS
Scale 1: 2,406,000
0 10 20 mi
0 15 30 km

Official name: Union of the Comoros
Head of government: President assisted by Vice Presidents
Official languages: Comorian; Arabic; French
Monetary unit: Comorian franc
Area: 719 sq. mi. (1,862 sq. km.)
Population (2005): 614,000
GNP per capita (2004): U.S.$530
Principal exports (2002): vanilla 61.6%, cloves 24.1%, ylang-ylang 11.6% *to:* France 46.1%; Germany 18.8%; U.S. 11.4%; Madagascar 5.8%

Age Breakdown

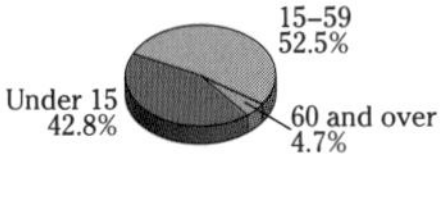
15–59
52.5%
Under 15
42.8%
60 and over
4.7%

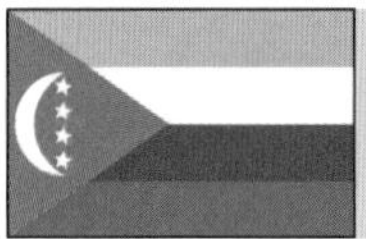

After more than 76 years of independence from France, and many different flags, on December 23, 2001, Comoros raised the current flag, in conjunction with a new constitution meant to ensure national unity. A variation of a design from 1963, its green background and its crescent reflect Islam, and its four white stars represent the islands in the Comoros archipelago.

DEMOCRATIC REPUBLIC OF THE CONGO

Scale 1: 31,104,000

0 150 300 mi

0 150 300 450 km

©2000, Encyclopædia Britannica, Inc.

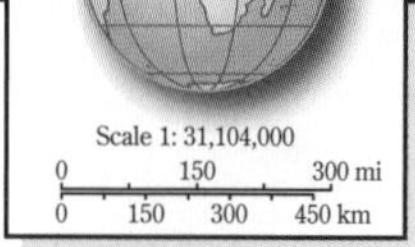

Ethnic Composition

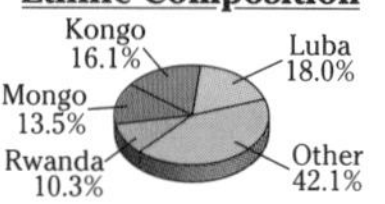

Official name: Democratic Republic of the Congo
Head of government: President assisted by Vice Presidents
Official languages: French; English
Monetary unit: Congo franc
Area: 905,354 sq. mi. (2,344,858 sq. km.)
Population (2005): 57,549,000
GNP per capita (2004): U.S.$120
Principal exports (2001): diamonds 52.5%, crude petroleum 22.8%, cobalt 8.0%, copper 4.8%, gold 2.4% *to:* Belgium-Luxembourg 42.5%; Finland 17.8%; Zimbabwe 12.2%; U.S. 9.2%; China 6.5%

Also called the flag of Congo-Kinshasa, the 1877 blue flag, with a star for light in the "Dark Continent," was returned February 18, 2006. Independent from Belgium in 1960, in 1971 Congo's name changed to Zaire, and there was a new flag. The revolution under the leadership of Laurent Kabila brought back the name of Congo in 1997.

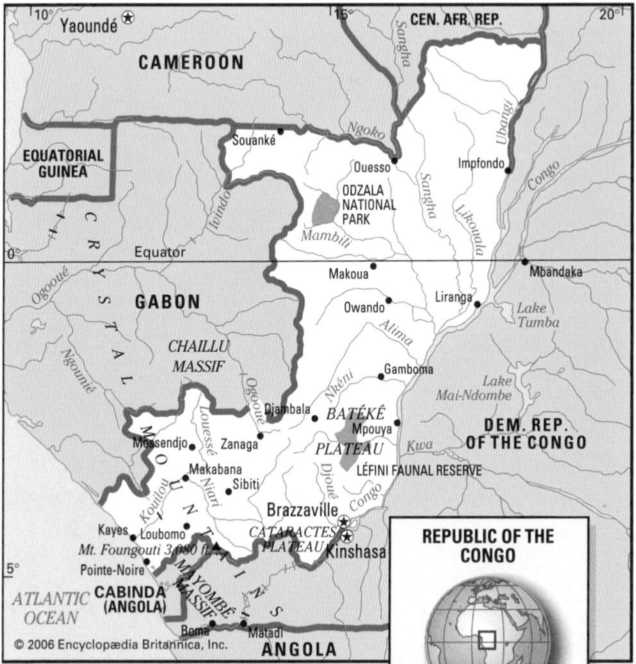

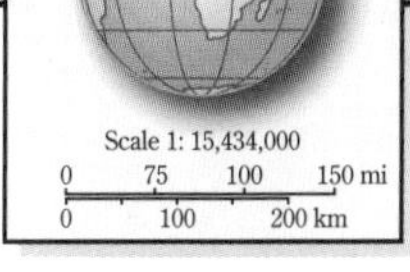

REPUBLIC OF THE CONGO

Scale 1: 15,434,000

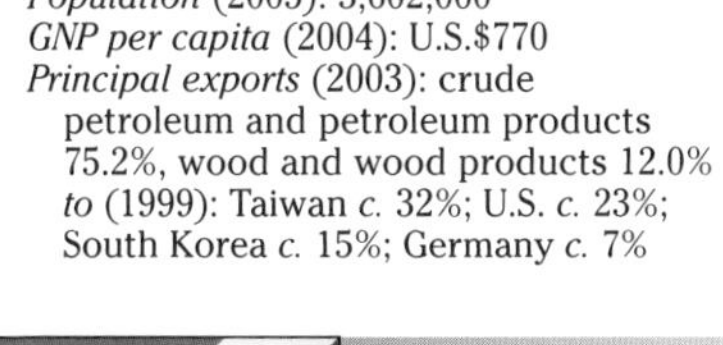

Official name: Republic of the Congo
Head of government: President
Official language: French
Monetary unit: CFA franc
Area: 132,047 sq. mi. (342,000 sq. km.)
Population (2005): 3,602,000
GNP per capita (2004): U.S.$770
Principal exports (2003): crude petroleum and petroleum products 75.2%, wood and wood products 12.0% *to* (1999): Taiwan *c.* 32%; U.S. *c.* 23%; South Korea *c.* 15%; Germany *c.* 7%

Ethnic Composition

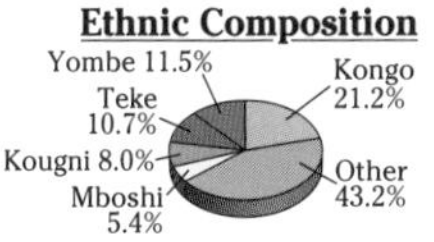

First adopted on Sept. 15, 1959, the flag uses the Pan-African colors. Green was originally said to stand for Congo's agriculture and forests, and yellow for friendship and the nobility of the people, but the red was unexplained. Altered in 1969 by a Marxist government, the flag was restored to its initial form on June 10, 1991.

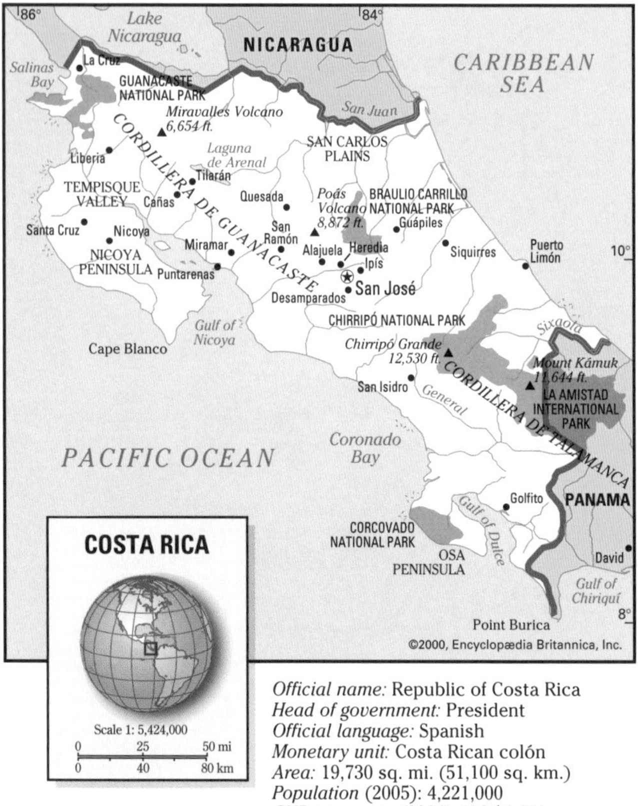

86°
84°
Lake Nicaragua
NICARAGUA
CARIBBEAN SEA
Salinas Bay
La Cruz
GUANACASTE NATIONAL PARK
Miravalles Volcano 6,654 ft.
San Juan
CORDILLERA DE GUANACASTE
Liberia
Laguna de Arenal
SAN CARLOS PLAINS
Tilarán
TEMPISQUE VALLEY
Cañas
Quesada
Poás Volcano 8,872 ft.
BRAULIO CARRILLO NATIONAL PARK
Guápiles
Santa Cruz
Nicoya
San Ramón
NICOYA PENINSULA
Miramar
Alajuela
Heredia
Siquirres
Puerto Limón
10°
Ipís
Puntarenas
San José
Desamparados
CHIRRIPÓ NATIONAL PARK
Gulf of Nicoya
Sixaola
Cape Blanco
Chirripó Grande 12,530 ft.
Mount Kámuk 11,644 ft.
CORDILLERA DE TALAMANCA
San Isidro
General
LA AMISTAD INTERNATIONAL PARK
PACIFIC OCEAN
Coronado Bay
Golfito
PANAMA
Gulf of Dulce
CORCOVADO NATIONAL PARK
OSA PENINSULA
David
Gulf of Chiriquí
8°
Point Burica
©2000, Encyclopædia Britannica, Inc.
COSTA RICA
Scale 1: 5,424,000
0 25 50 mi
0 40 80 km

Official name: Republic of Costa Rica
Head of government: President
Official language: Spanish
Monetary unit: Costa Rican colón
Area: 19,730 sq. mi. (51,100 sq. km.)
Population (2005): 4,221,000
GNP per capita (2004): U.S.$4,670
Principal exports (2002): food 30.2%, of which bananas 9.7%; office machines and computer parts 18.1%; apparel 8.0% *to:* United States 25.1%; The Netherlands 6.9%; U.K. 5.0%; Mexico 4.1%; China 3.9%

Ethnic Composition

White 77.0%
Mestizo 17.0%
Other 6%

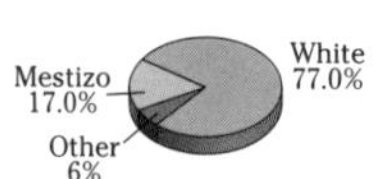

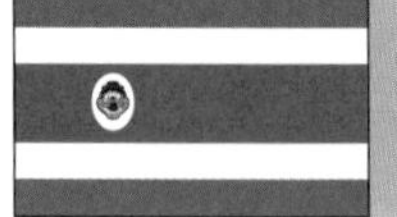

The blue and white stripes originated in the flag colors of the United Provinces of Central America (1823–40). On Sept. 29, 1848, the red stripe was added to symbolize sunlight, civilization, and "true independence." The current design of the coat of arms, which is included on government flags, was established in 1964.

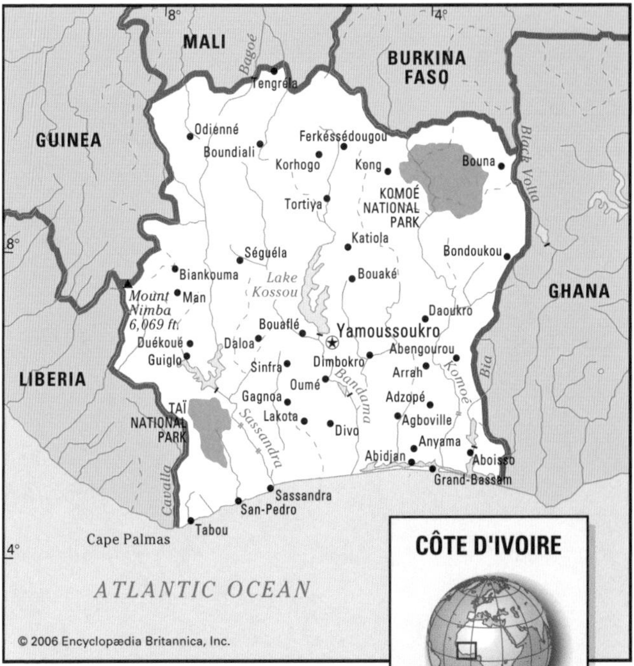

CÔTE D'IVOIRE

Scale 1: 12,565,000

0 60 120 mi

0 80 160 km

Official name: Republic of Côte d'Ivoire [Ivory Coast]
Head of government: Prime Minister
Official language: French
Monetary unit: CFA franc
Area: 123,863 sq. mi. (320,803 sq. km.)
Population (2005): 17,298,000
GNP per capita (2004): U.S.$770
Principal exports (2002): cocoa beans 44.3%, crude petroleum and petroleum products 11.3%, machinery and transport equipment 8.9%, wood 5.1%, coffee 2.4% *to:* France 17.9%; The Netherlands 16.7%; U.S. 6.7%; Spain 5.3%

Religious Affiliation

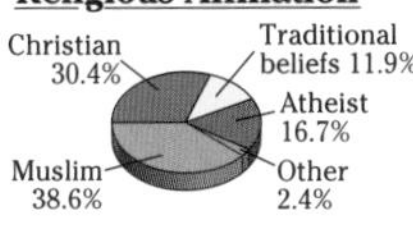

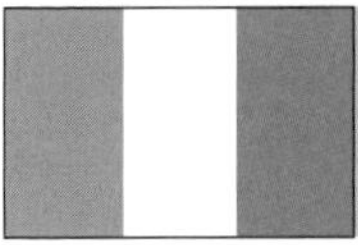

Adopted on Aug. 7, 1959, the flag of the former French colony has three stripes corresponding to the national motto (Unity, Discipline, Labor). The orange is for growth, the white is for peace emerging from purity and unity, and the green is for hope and the future. Unofficially the green is for forests and the orange is for savannas.

CROATIA

Scale 1: 7,071,000

0 30 60 mi

0 30 60 90 km

Official name: Republic of Croatia
Head of government: Prime Minister
Official language: Croatian
Monetary unit: kuna
Area: 21,851 sq. mi. (56,594 sq. km.)
Population (2005): 4,440,000
GNP per capita (2004): U.S.$6,590
Principal exports (2001): machinery and transport equipment 29.4%, chemical products 10.6%, clothing 10.5%, crude petroleum and petroleum products 7.4%, food 6.9% *to:* Italy 26.4%; Bosnia and Herzegovina 14.5%; Germany 11.9%; Slovenia 8.3%; Austria 7.8%

Ethnic Composition

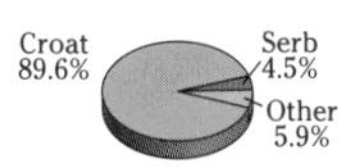

During the European uprisings of 1848, Croatians designed a flag based on that of Russia. In April 1941 the fascistic Ustasa used this flag, adding the checkered shield of Croatia. A communist star soon replaced the shield, but the current flag was adopted on Dec. 22, 1990. Atop the shield is a "crown" inlaid with historic coats of arms.

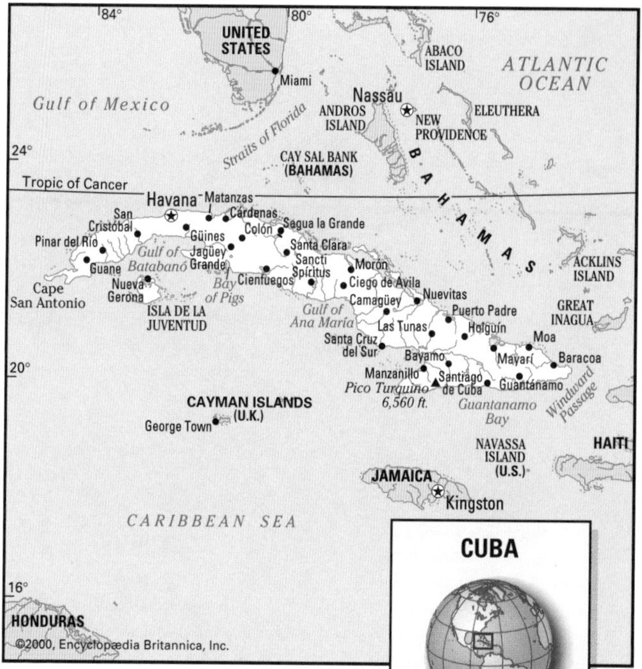

CUBA

Scale 1: 18,754,000

0 70 140 mi

0 100 200 km

Official name: Republic of Cuba
Head of government: President
Official language: Spanish
Monetary unit: Cuban peso
Area: 42,804 sq. mi. (110,861 sq. km.)
Population (2005): 11,269,000
GDP per capita (2003): U.S.$2,880
Principal exports (2004): raw sugar 32.6%, nickel 27.8%, tobacco and tobacco products 15.8%, fish 4.6% *to:* The Netherlands 23.5%; Canada 21.9%; China 8.3%; Russia 7.8%; Spain 6.6%

Religious Affiliation

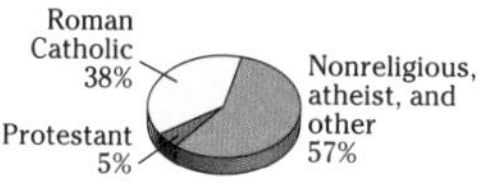

Roman Catholic 38%
Protestant 5%
Nonreligious, atheist, and other 57%

In the mid-19th century Cuban exiles designed the flag, which was later carried into battle against Spanish forces. It was adopted on May 20, 1902. The stripes were for the three military districts of Cuba and the purity of the patriotic cause. The red triangle was for strength, constancy, and equality, and the white star symbolized independence.

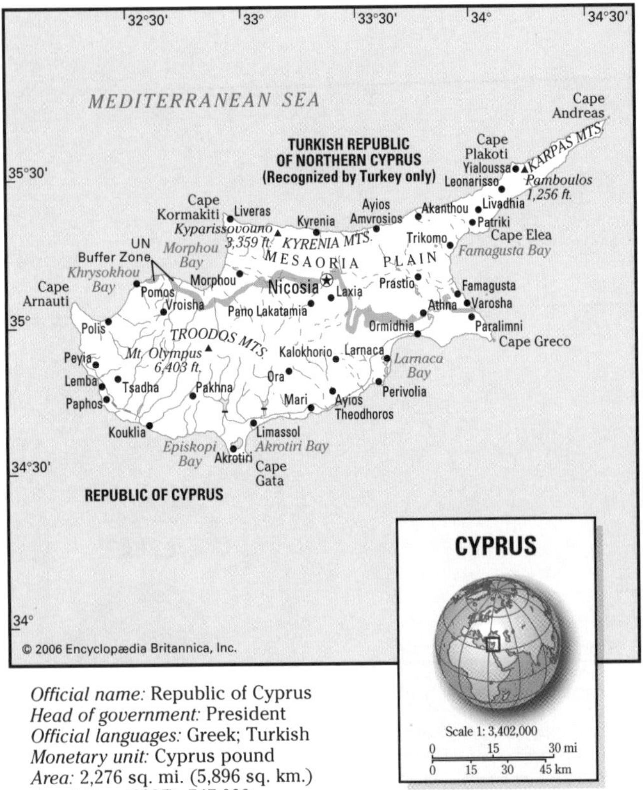

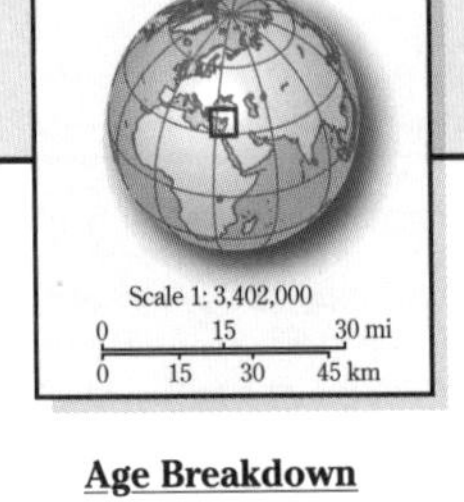

Official name: Republic of Cyprus
Head of government: President
Official languages: Greek; Turkish
Monetary unit: Cyprus pound
Area: 2,276 sq. mi. (5,896 sq. km.)
Population (2005): 747,000
GNP per capita (2004): U.S.$17,580
Principal exports (2003): domestic exports 52.9%, of which ships' stores 9.7%, pharmaceuticals 8.1%, citrus fruit 4.0%; reexport 47.1% *to:* U.K. 24.4%; France 11.0%; Germany 7.2%; Greece 6.4%

Age Breakdown

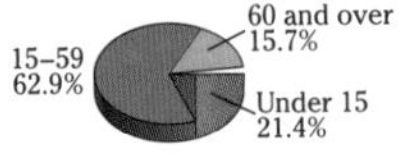

On Aug. 7, 1960, the Republic of Cyprus was proclaimed with a national flag of a neutral design. It bears the island in silhouette and a green olive wreath, for peace. In 1974 there was a Turkish invasion of the island. A puppet government, which adopted a flag based on the Turkish model, was set up on the northern third of Cyprus.

CZECH REPUBLIC

Scale 1: 6,810,000

0 20 40 mi

0 40 60 km

Official name: Czech Republic
Head of government: Prime Minister
Official language: Czech
Monetary unit: koruna
Area: 30,450 sq. mi. (78,866 sq. km.)
Population (2005): 10,235,000
GNP per capita (2004): U.S.$9,150
Principal exports (2003): machinery and apparatus 27.7%, motor vehicles 16.2%, fabricated metals 6.7%, base metals 5.6%, chemicals 5.4% *to:* Germany 37.1%; Slovakia 8.0%; Austria 6.3%; U.K. 5.4%; Poland 4.8%

Ethnic Composition

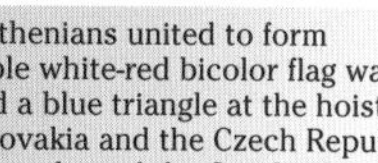

Czech 90.4%
Other 5.9%
Moravian 3.7%

When Czechs, Slovaks, and Ruthenians united to form Czechoslovakia in 1918, a simple white-red bicolor flag was chosen; in 1920 it incorporated a blue triangle at the hoist. Czechoslovakia divided into Slovakia and the Czech Republic in 1993, but the latter country readopted the Czechoslovak flag as its own.

DENMARK

Scale 1: 6,930,000
0 20 40 mi
0 30 60 km

Official name: Kingdom of Denmark
Head of government: Prime Minister
Official language: Danish
Monetary unit: Danish krone
Area: 16,640 sq. mi. (43,098 sq. km.)
Population (2005): 5,416,000
GNP per capita (2004): U.S.$40,650
Principal exports (2004): machinery and apparatus 23.2%, food and beverages 21.8%, pharmaceuticals 7.5%, petroleum products 7.2%, furniture 3.6% *to:* Germany 17.9%; Sweden 12.9%; United Kingdom 12.7%; Norway 5.4%

Age Breakdown

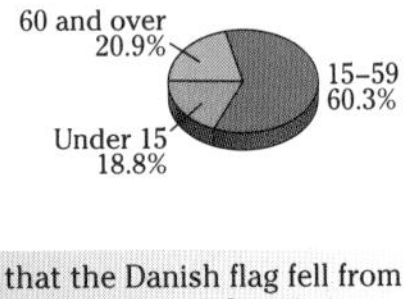

60 and over 20.9%
15–59 60.3%
Under 15 18.8%

A traditional story claims that the Danish flag fell from heaven on June 15, 1219, but the previously existing war flag of the Holy Roman Empire was of a similar design, with its red field symbolizing battle and its white cross suggesting divine favor. In 1849 the state and military flag was altered and adopted as a symbol of the Danish people.

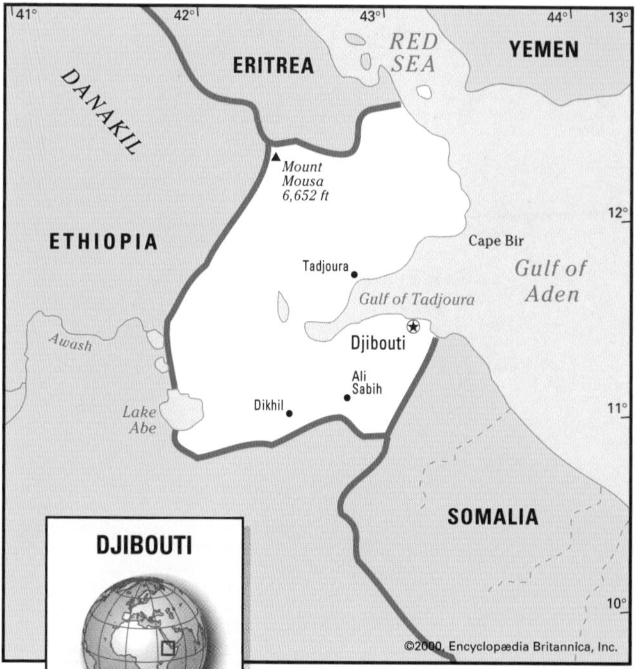
41°
42°
43°
44°
13°
12°
11°
10°
RED SEA
YEMEN
ERITREA
DANAKIL
Mount Mousa 6,652 ft
ETHIOPIA
Cape Bir
Tadjoura
Gulf of Aden
Gulf of Tadjoura
Awash
Djibouti
Ali Sabih
Dikhil
Lake Abe
SOMALIA
©2000, Encyclopædia Britannica, Inc.
DJIBOUTI
Scale 1: 5,534,000
0 25 50 mi
0 25 50 75 km

Official name: Republic of Djibouti
Head of government: President
Official languages: Arabic; French
Monetary unit: Djibouti franc
Area: 8,950 sq. mi. (23,200 sq. km.)
Population (2005): 477,000
GNP per capita (2004): U.S.$1,030
Principal exports (2001): aircraft parts 24.5%, hides and skins 20.6%, leather 7.8%, live animals 6.9% *to:* Somalia 61.4%; Yemen 21.7%; Pakistan 6.0%; Ethiopia 4.8%

Ethnic Composition

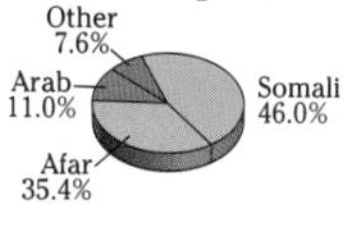
Other 7.6%
Arab 11.0%
Somali 46.0%
Afar 35.4%

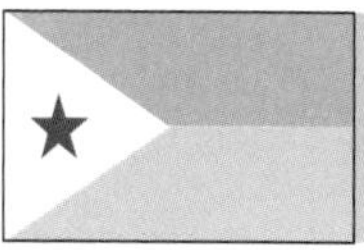

First raised by anti-French separatists, the flag was officially hoisted on June 27, 1977. The color of the Afar people, green, stands for prosperity. The color of the Issa people, light blue, symbolizes sea and sky, and recalls the flag of Somalia. The white triangle is for equality and peace; the red star is for unity and independence.

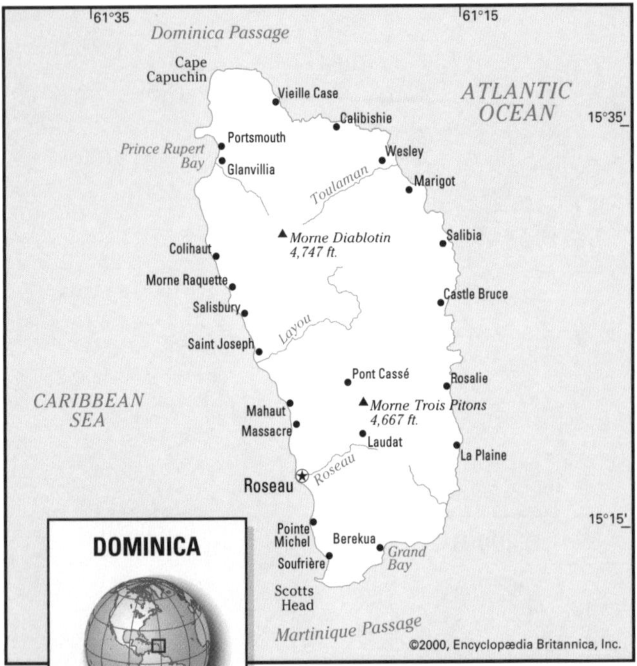

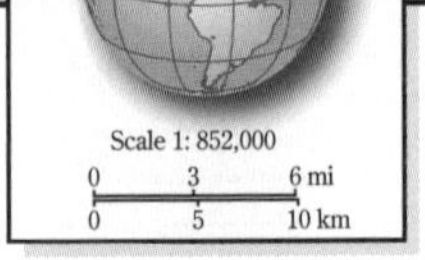

61°35
61°15
Dominica Passage
Cape Capuchin
Vieille Case
Calibishie
ATLANTIC OCEAN
15°35'
Portsmouth
Prince Rupert Bay
Glanvillia
Wesley
Toulaman
Marigot
Morne Diablotin 4,747 ft.
Salibia
Colihaut
Morne Raquette
Castle Bruce
Salisbury
Layou
Saint Joseph
Pont Cassé
Rosalie
CARIBBEAN SEA
Mahaut
Morne Trois Pitons 4,667 ft.
Massacre
Laudat
La Plaine
Roseau
Roseau
15°15'
Pointe Michel
Berekua
Grand Bay
Soufrière
Scotts Head
Martinique Passage
©2000, Encyclopædia Britannica, Inc.

DOMINICA
Scale 1: 852,000
0 3 6 mi
0 5 10 km

Official name: Commonwealth of Dominica
Head of government: Prime Minister
Official language: English
Monetary unit: East Caribbean dollar
Area: 285.3 sq. mi. (739.0 sq. km.)
Population (2005): 69,000
GNP per capita (2004): U.S.$3,650
Principal exports (2000): agricultural exports 37.5%, of which bananas 25.9%; coconut-based laundry and toilet soaps 25.0%, cosmetics 13.7% *to* (2003): Japan 27.1%; U.K. 16.4%; Jamaica 15.1%; U.S. 6.6%

Religious Affiliation

Other 12.7%
Roman Catholic 70.1%
Protestant 17.2%

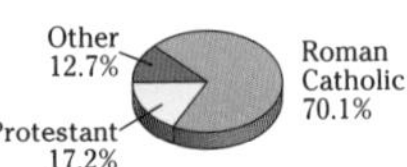

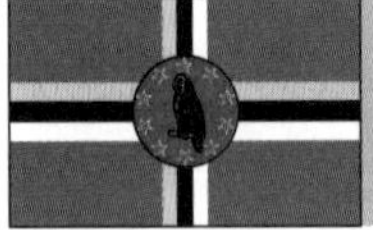

The flag was hoisted on Nov. 3, 1978, at independence from Britain. Its background symbolizes forests; its central disk is red for socialism and bears a sisserou (a rare local bird). The stars are for the parishes of the island. The cross of yellow, white, and black is for the Carib, Caucasian, and African peoples and for fruit, water, and soil.

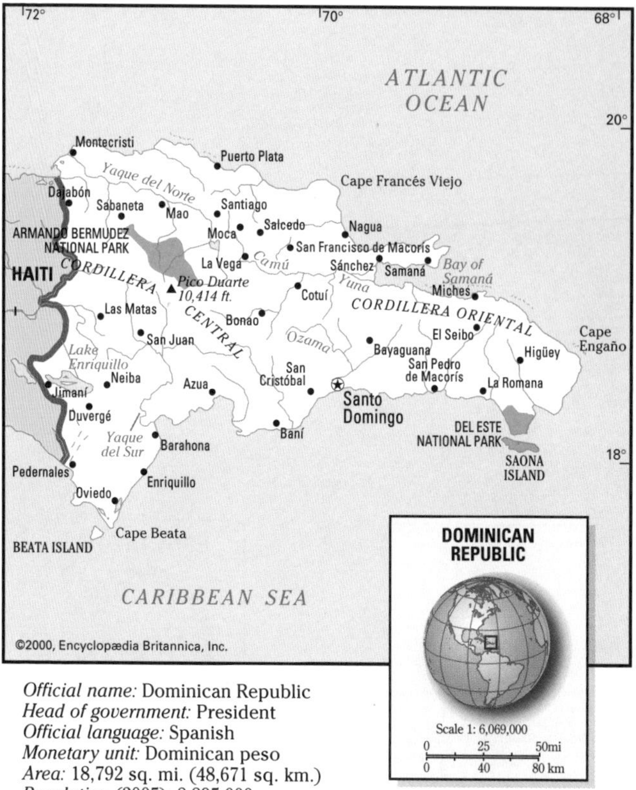

DOMINICAN REPUBLIC

Scale 1: 6,069,000

0 25 50mi

0 40 80 km

Official name: Dominican Republic
Head of government: President
Official language: Spanish
Monetary unit: Dominican peso
Area: 18,792 sq. mi. (48,671 sq. km.)
Population (2005): 8,895,000
GNP per capita (2004): U.S.$2,080
Principal exports (2004): reexport of free zones 76.8%; ferronickel 6.8%; ships' stores 4.1% *to* (2003): U.S. 83.8%; U.K. 1.5%; Haiti 1.5%

Ethnic Composition

On Feb. 28, 1844, Spanish-speaking Dominican revolutionaries added a white cross to the simple blue-red flag of eastern Hispaniola, in order to emphasize their Christian heritage. On November 6 of that same year the new constitution established the flag, but with the colors at the fly end reversed so that the blue and red would alternate.

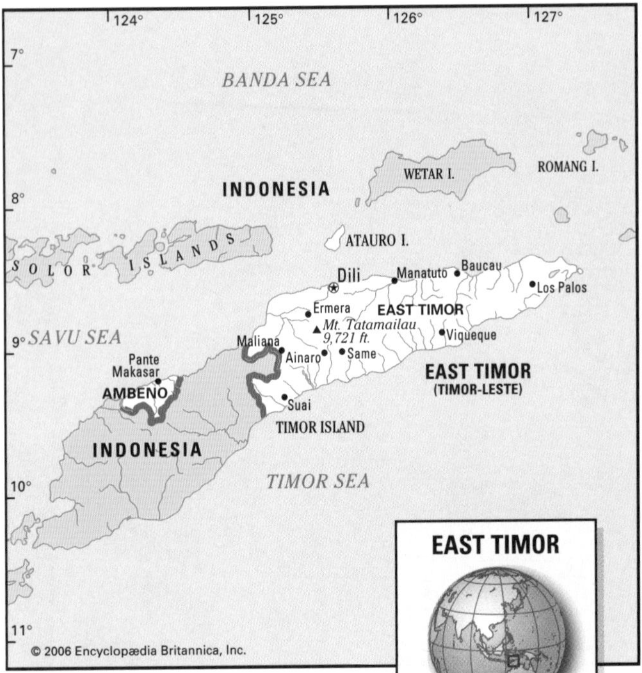

EAST TIMOR

Scale 1: 6,801,000

Official name: Democratic Republic of Timor-Leste
Head of government: Prime Minister
Official languages: Tetum; Portuguese
Monetary unit: U.S. dollar
Area: 5,639 sq. mi. (14,604 sq. km.)
Population (2005): 975,000
GNP per capita (2004): U.S.$550
Principal exports (2004): coffee 86.1% *to:* Australia 41.7%; Japan 22.8%; Portugal 13.0%; U.S. 4.1%

Ethnic Composition

East Timorese 80.0%
West Timorese 20.0%

After Indonesia's withdrawal in 1999, East Timor came under the UN flag. The new national flag was adopted on May 20, 2002, when East Timor gained full sovereignty. The black is for more than four centuries of colonial repression, the yellow the struggle for independence, and the red the suffering of the East Timorese. The white star symbolizes hope.

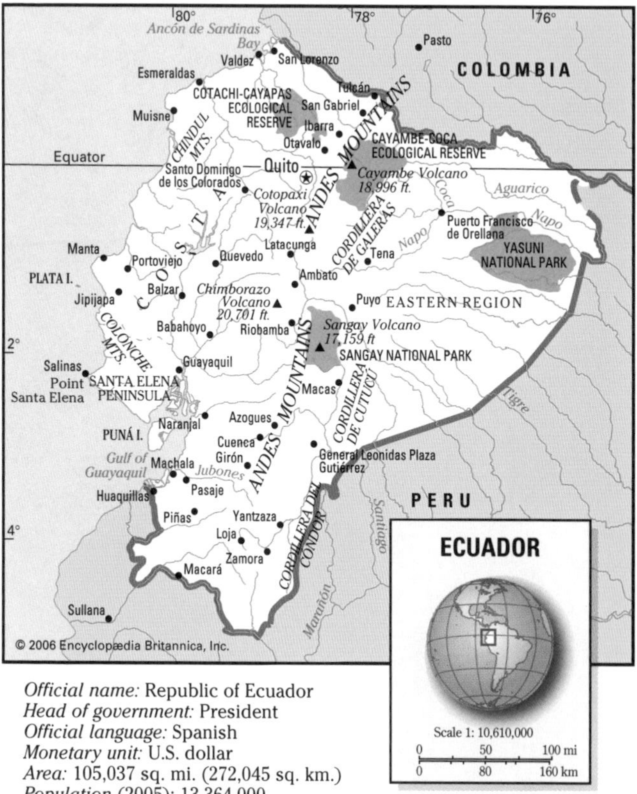

80°
78°
76°
Ancón de Sardinas Bay
Pasto
COLOMBIA
Valdez
San Lorenzo
Esmeraldas
COTACHI-CAYAPAS ECOLOGICAL RESERVE
Tulcán
San Gabriel
Muisne
Ibarra
CHINDUL MTS.
ANDES MOUNTAINS
Otavalo
CAYAMBE-COCA ECOLOGICAL RESERVE
Equator
Santo Domingo de los Colorados
Quito
Cayambe Volcano 18,996 ft.
Coca
Aguarico
Cotopaxi Volcano 19,347 ft.
CORDILLERA DE GALERAS
Puerto Francisco de Orellana
Napo
Manta
Latacunga
YASUNI NATIONAL PARK
Portoviejo
Quevedo
Tena
COSTA
PLATA I.
Ambato
Jipijapa
Balzar
Chimborazo Volcano 20,701 ft.
Puyo
EASTERN REGION
Babahoyo
Riobamba
Sangay Volcano 17,159 ft
COLONCHE MTS.
2°
SANGAY NATIONAL PARK
Salinas
Guayaquil
Point Santa Elena
SANTA ELENA PENINSULA
Macas
Tigre
Naranjal
Azogues
CORDILLERA DE CUTUCÚ
PUNÁ I.
Cuenca
Gulf of Guayaquil
Machala
Girón
Jubones
General Leonidas Plaza Gutiérrez
Huaquillas
Pasaje
PERU
Santiago
Piñas
Yantzaza
4°
Loja
Zamora
CORDILLERA DEL CONDOR
Macará
Marañón
Sullana
© 2006 Encyclopædia Britannica, Inc.
ECUADOR
Scale 1: 10,610,000
0 50 100 mi
0 80 160 km

Official name: Republic of Ecuador
Head of government: President
Official language: Spanish
Monetary unit: U.S. dollar
Area: 105,037 sq. mi. (272,045 sq. km.)
Population (2005): 13,364,000
GNP per capita (2004): U.S.$2,178
Principal exports (2004): crude petroleum 50.9%, bananas and plantains 13.4%, shrimp 10.1%, cut flowers 4.5% *to:* U.S. 42.9%; Peru 7.9%; Italy 4.6%; Colombia 3.9%; Germany 2.5%

Ethnic Composition

Amerindian 40.8%
White 10.6%
Black 5.0%
Other 1.6%
Mestizo 42.0%

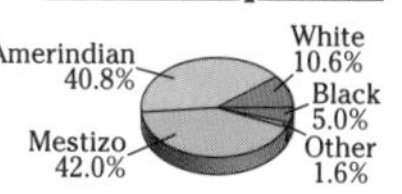

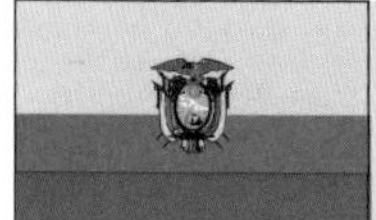

Victorious against the Spanish on May 24, 1822, Antonio José de Sucre hoisted a yellow-blue-red flag. Other flags were later used, but on Sept. 26, 1860, the current flag design was adopted. The coat of arms is displayed on the flag when it is used abroad or for official purposes, to distinguish it from the flag of Colombia.

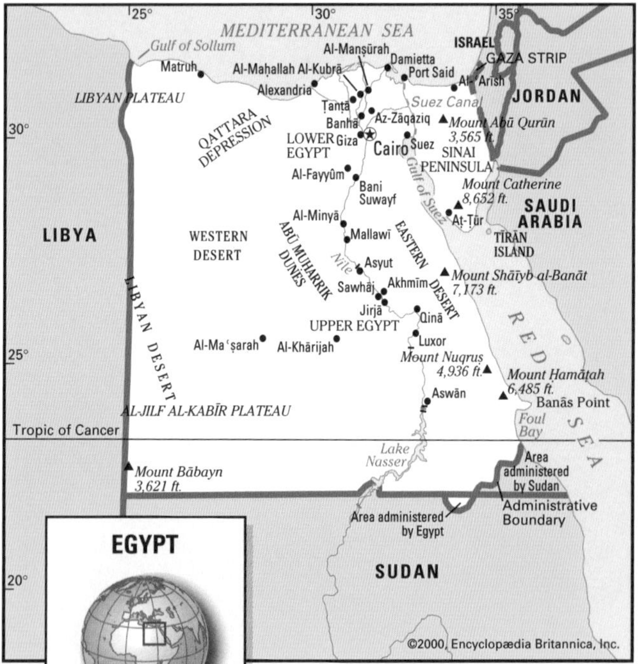

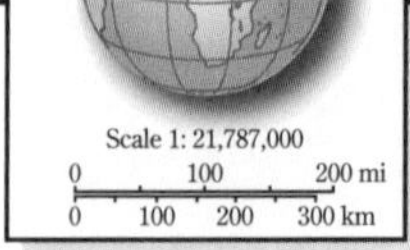

Official name: Arab Republic of Egypt
Head of government: Prime Minister
Official language: Arabic
Monetary unit: Egyptian pound
Area: 385,229 sq. mi. (997,739 sq. km.)
Population (2005): 70,457,000
GNP per capita (2004): U.S.$1,310
Principal exports (2004): petroleum and petroleum products 40.0%, finished goods 27.2%, semi-manufactured goods 14.1%, raw cotton 6.3% *to:* U.S. 13.6%; Italy 12.5%; U.K. 8.1%; France 4.8%; Germany 4.8%

Religious Affiliation

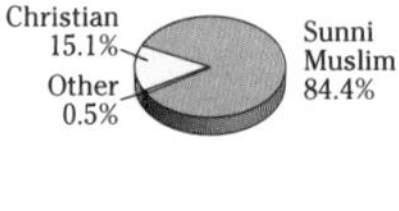

Christian 15.1%
Other 0.5%
Sunni Muslim 84.4%

The 1952 revolt against British rule established the red-white-black flag with a central gold eagle. Two stars replaced the eagle in 1958, and in 1972 a federation with Syria and Libya was formed, adding instead the hawk of Quraysh (the tribe of Muhammad). On Oct. 9, 1984, the eagle of Saladin (a major 12th-century ruler) was substituted.

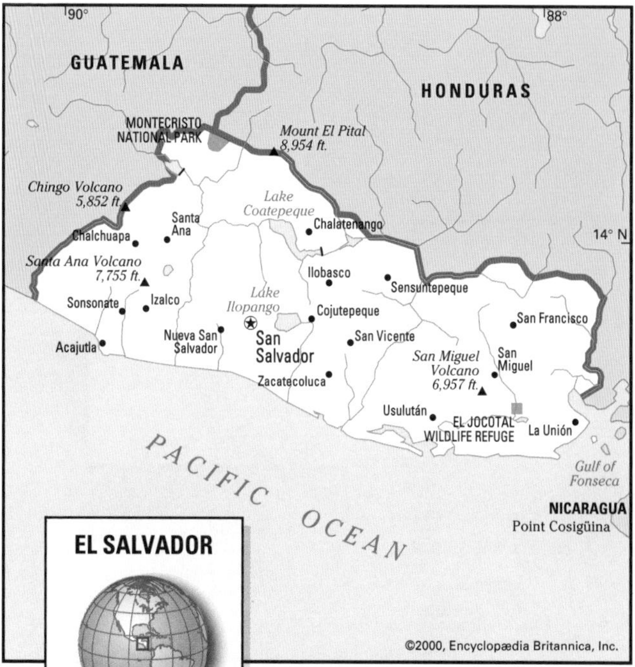

EL SALVADOR

Scale 1: 3,810,000
0 25 mi
0 20 40 km

Official name: Republic of El Salvador
Head of government: President
Official language: Spanish
Monetary unit: U.S. dollar
Area: 8,124 sq. mi. (21,041 sq. km.)
Population (2005): 6,881,000
GNP per capita (2004): U.S.$2,350
Principal exports (2004): reexports 55.2%, domestic export 44.8%, of which yarn and fabrics 6.8%, chemicals 4.8%, coffee 3.8% *to:* United States 65.4%; Guatemala 11.7%; Honduras 6.3%; Nicaragua 3.9%; Costa Rica 3.0%

Age Breakdown

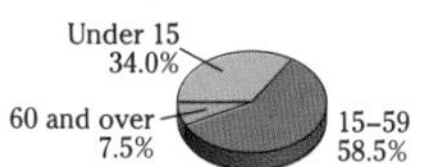

In the early 19th century a blue-white-blue flag was designed for the short-lived United Provinces of Central America, in which El Salvador was a member. On Sept. 15, 1912, the flag was reintroduced in El Salvador. The coat of arms in the center resembles that used by the former federation and includes the national motto, "God, Union, Liberty."

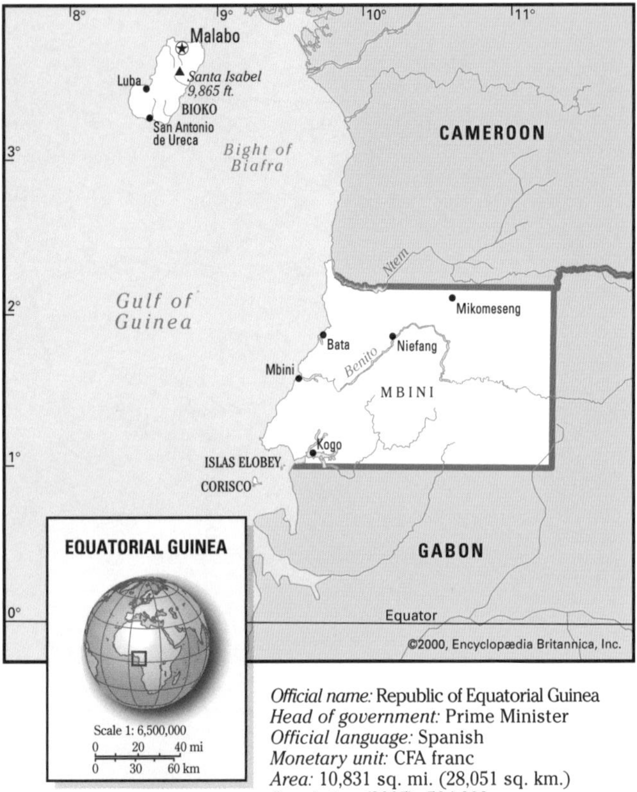
8°
9°
10°
11°
3°
2°
1°
0°
Malabo
Luba
Santa Isabel
9,865 ft.
BIOKO
San Antonio
de Ureca
Bight of
Biafra
CAMEROON
Ntem
Gulf of
Guinea
Mikomeseng
Bata
Niefang
Benito
Mbini
MBINI
Kogo
ISLAS ELOBEY
CORISCO
GABON
Equator
©2000, Encyclopædia Britannica, Inc.
EQUATORIAL GUINEA
Scale 1: 6,500,000
0 20 40 mi
0 30 60 km

Ethnic Composition

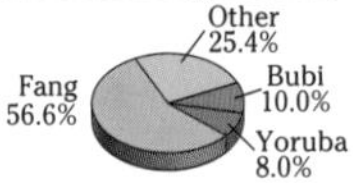
Other
25.4%
Bubi
10.0%
Fang
56.6%
Yoruba
8.0%

Official name: Republic of Equatorial Guinea
Head of government: Prime Minister
Official language: Spanish
Monetary unit: CFA franc
Area: 10,831 sq. mi. (28,051 sq. km.)
Population (2005): 504,000
GDP per capita (2004): U.S.$9,110
Principal exports (2004): petroleum products and natural gas 98.4%, timber 1.0% *to:* U.S. 33.2%; Spain 25.4%; China 14.2%; Canada 12.7%; Italy 6.3%; France 3.6%

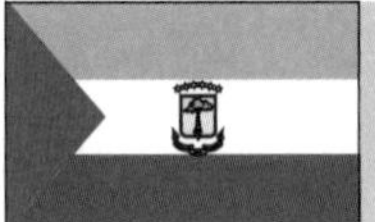

The flag was first hoisted at independence (Oct. 12, 1968). Its coat of arms shows the silk-cotton tree, or god tree, which recalls early Spanish influence in the area. The sea, which links parts of the country, is reflected in the blue triangle. The green is for vegetation, white is for peace, and red is for the blood of martyrs in the liberation struggle.

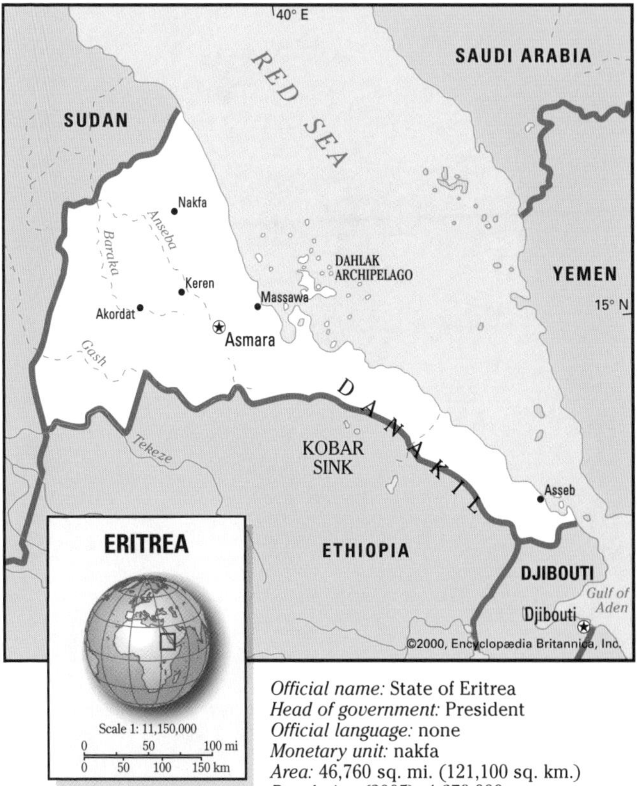

ERITREA

Scale 1: 11,150,000

0 50 100 mi

0 50 100 150 km

©2000, Encyclopædia Britannica, Inc.

Ethnolinguistic Composition

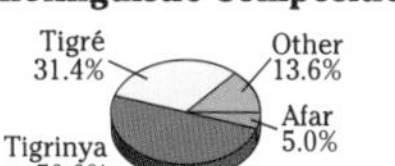

Official name: State of Eritrea
Head of government: President
Official language: none
Monetary unit: nakfa
Area: 46,760 sq. mi. (121,100 sq. km.)
Population (2005): 4,670,000
GNP per capita (2004): U.S.$180
Principal exports (2002): raw sugar 60.8%, synthetic woven fabrics 4.4%, vegetables and fruits 3.3%, fish 2.9% *to:* The Sudan 82.7%; Italy 4.9%; Djibouti 2.1%

Officially hoisted at the proclamation of independence on May 24, 1993, the national flag was based on that of the Eritrean People's Liberation Front. The red triangle is for the blood of patriots, the green is for agriculture, and the blue is for maritime resources. Around a central branch is a circle of olive branches with 30 leaves.

ESTONIA

Scale 1: 4,840,000

0 20 40 mi

0 30 60 km

Ethnic Composition

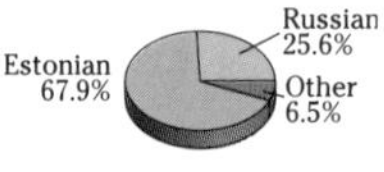

Estonian 67.9%

Russian 25.6%

Other 6.5%

Official name: Republic of Estonia
Head of government: Prime Minister
Official language: Estonian
Monetary unit: kroon
Area: 16,769 sq. mi. (43,431 sq. km.)
Population (2005): 1,345,000
GNP per capita (2004): U.S.$7,010
Principal exports (2004): machinery 27.2%, wood and paper products 15.7%, textile and apparel 9.0%, household furnishings 8.5% *to:* Finland 21.3%; Sweden 15.3%; Germany 8.4%; Latvia 7.9%; Russia 5.6%; Lithuania 4.4%

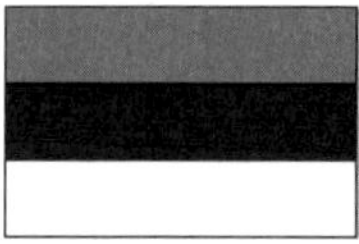

In the late 19th century an Estonian students' association adopted the blue-black-white flag. Blue was said to stand for the sky, black for the soil, and white for aspirations to freedom and homeland. The flag was officially recognized on July 4, 1920. It was replaced under Soviet rule, and readopted on Oct. 20, 1988.

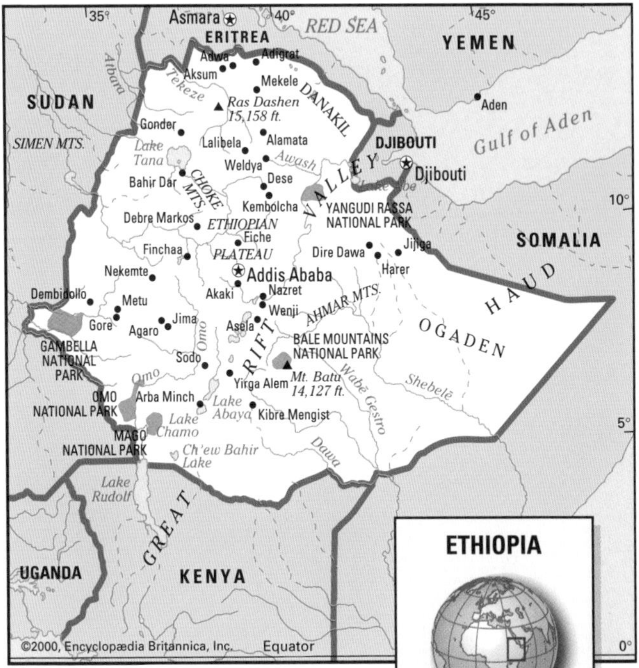

ETHIOPIA

Scale 1: 25,422,000
0 100 200 mi
0 200 400 km

Official name: Federal Democratic Republic of Ethiopia
Head of government: Prime Minister
Official language: none
Monetary unit: birr
Area: 435,186 sq. mi. (1,127,127 sq. km.)
Population (2005): 73,053,000
GNP per capita (2004): U.S.$110
Principal exports (2003–04): coffee 37.2%, khat 14.7%, sesame seed 13.8%, gold 8.1%, leather 7.5% *to:* Djibouti 13.4%; Germany 11.4%; Saudi Arabia 7.0%; Japan 6.8%; Italy 6.5%

Ethnolinguistic Composition

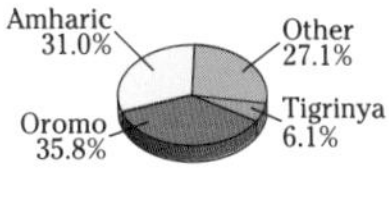

Amharic 31.0%
Other 27.1%
Tigrinya 6.1%
Oromo 35.8%

The flag is red (for sacrifice), green (for labor, development, and fertility), and yellow (for hope, justice, and equality). Tricolor pennants were used prior to the official flag of Oct. 6, 1897, and a tricolor was flown by antigovernment forces in 1991. On Feb. 6, 1996, the disk (for peace) and star (for unity and the future) were added.

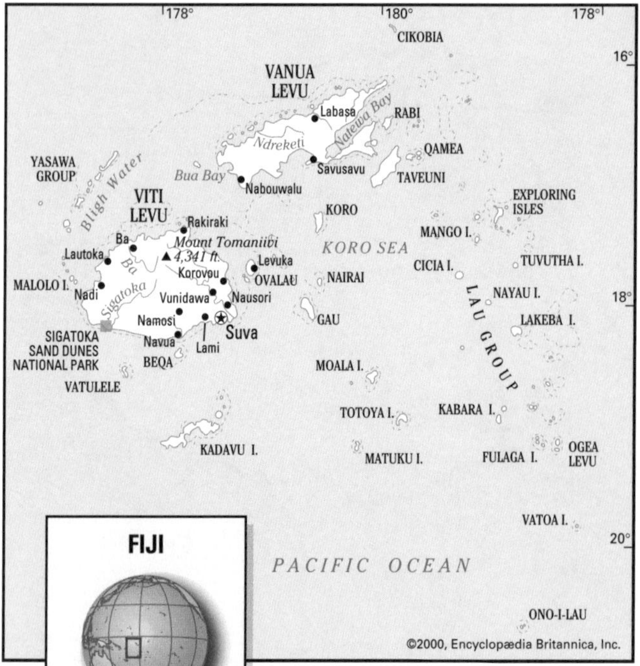

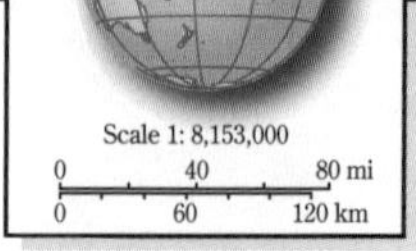

FIJI

Scale 1: 8,153,000

0 40 80 mi

0 60 120 km

Official name: Republic of the Fiji Islands
Head of government: Prime Minister
Official languages: English, Fijian, and Hindustani have equal status
Monetary unit: Fiji dollar
Area: 7,055 sq. mi. (18,272 sq. km.)
Population (2005): 846,000
GNP per capita (2004): U.S.$2,690
Principal exports (2004): clothing 21.8%, reexports 18.5%, sugar 15.2%, gold 7.5%, fish 7.2% *to:* Australia 22.5%; United Kingdom 13.0%; Singapore 8.4%; New Zealand 5.1%

Ethnic Composition

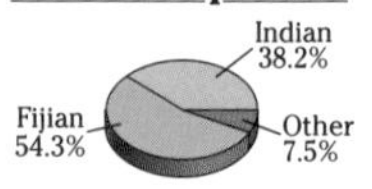

The national flag, introduced on Oct. 10, 1970, is a modified version of Fiji's colonial flag. It includes the Union Jack on a light blue field. The shield has the red cross of St. George on a white background, below a yellow lion, which holds a cocoa pod. Local symbols (sugar cane, coconuts, bananas, and the Fiji dove) are also shown.

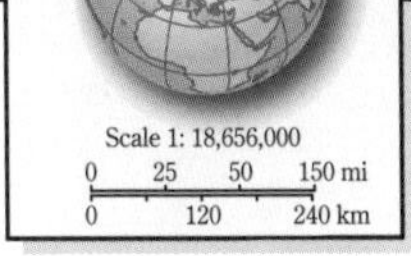

Official name: Republic of Finland
Head of government: Prime Minister
National languages: Finnish; Swedish
Monetary unit: euro
Area: 130,559 sq. mi. (338,145 sq. km.)
Population (2005): 5,244,000
GNP per capita (2004): U.S.$32,790
Principal exports (2003): electrical machinery 23.3%, paper, paper products, and publishing 17.3%, nonelectrical machinery 11.1%, wood and wood products 5.4% *to:* Sweden 11.0%; Germany 10.7%; Russia 8.9%; U.K. 7.1%; U.S. 6.4%

Religious Affiliation

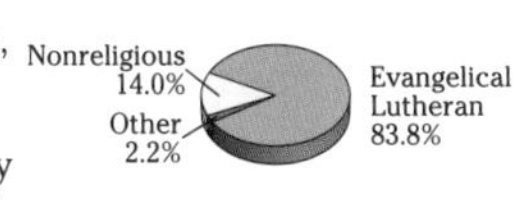

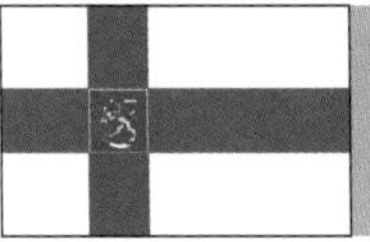

In 1862, while Finland was under Russian control, a flag was proposed that would have a white background for the snows of Finland and blue for its lakes. The blue was in the form of a "Nordic cross" similar to those used by other Scandinavian countries. The flag was officially adopted by the newly independent country on May 29, 1918.

FRANCE

Scale 1: 18,620,000

0 80 160 mi

0 80 160 240 km

Religious Affiliation

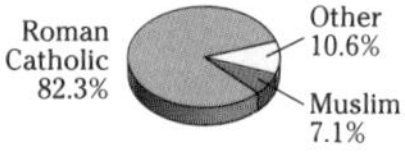

Roman Catholic 82.3%
Other 10.6%
Muslim 7.1%

Official name: French Republic
Head of government: Prime Minister
Official language: French
Monetary unit: euro
Area: 210,026 sq. mi. (543,965 sq. km.)
Population (2005): 60,733,000
GNP per capita (2004): U.S.$30,090
Principal exports (2002): machinery and transport equipment 43.7%, chemical products 14.9%, food 7.9%, iron and steel 3.2%, perfume and cosmetics 2.9% *to:* Germany 14.5%; U.K. 10.3%; Spain 9.7%; Italy 9.1%; U.S. 8.1%; Belgium 7.2%

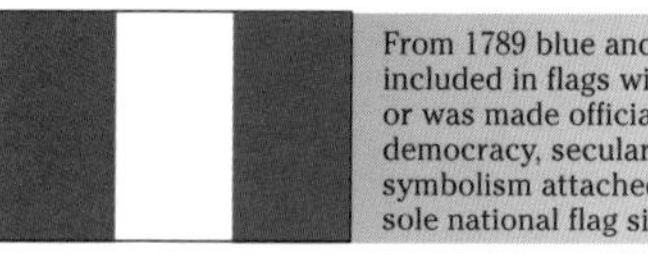

From 1789 blue and red, the traditional colors of Paris, were included in flags with Bourbon royal white. In 1794 the tricolor was made official. It embodied liberty, equality, fraternity, democracy, secularism, and modernization, but there is no symbolism attached to the individual colors. It has been the sole national flag since March 5, 1848.

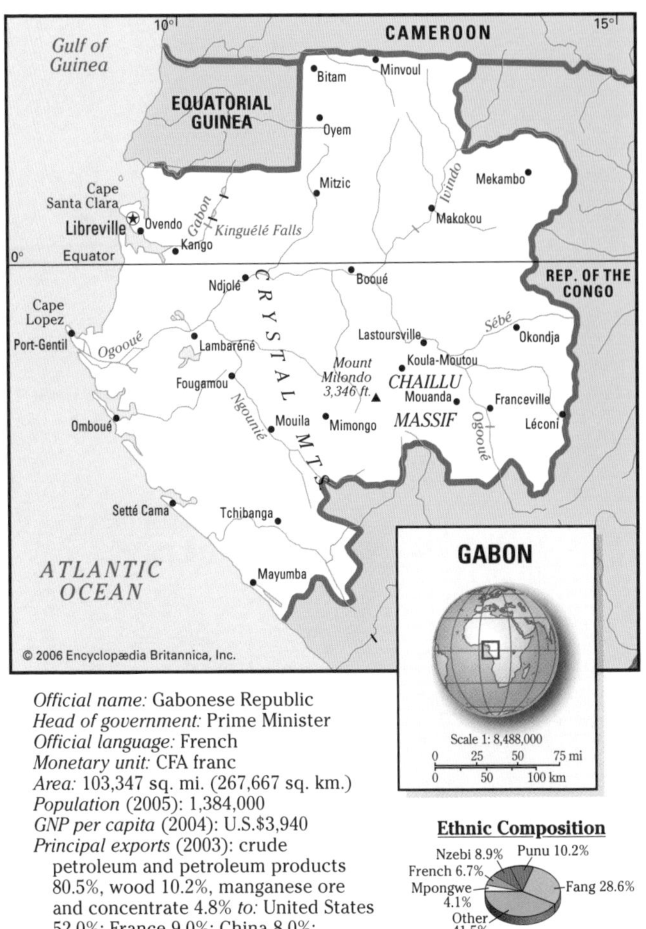

Official name: Gabonese Republic
Head of government: Prime Minister
Official language: French
Monetary unit: CFA franc
Area: 103,347 sq. mi. (267,667 sq. km.)
Population (2005): 1,384,000
GNP per capita (2004): U.S.$3,940
Principal exports (2003): crude petroleum and petroleum products 80.5%, wood 10.2%, manganese ore and concentrate 4.8% *to:* United States 52.0%; France 9.0%; China 8.0%; Trinidad and Tobago 3.0%

Ethnic Composition

Nzebi 8.9%
Punu 10.2%
French 6.7%
Mpongwe 4.1%
Fang 28.6%
Other 41.5%

After proclaiming independence from France, Gabon adopted its national flag on Aug. 9, 1960. The central yellow stripe is for the Equator, which runs through the country. Green stands for the tropical forests that are one of Gabon's most important resources. Blue represents its extensive coast along the South Atlantic Ocean.

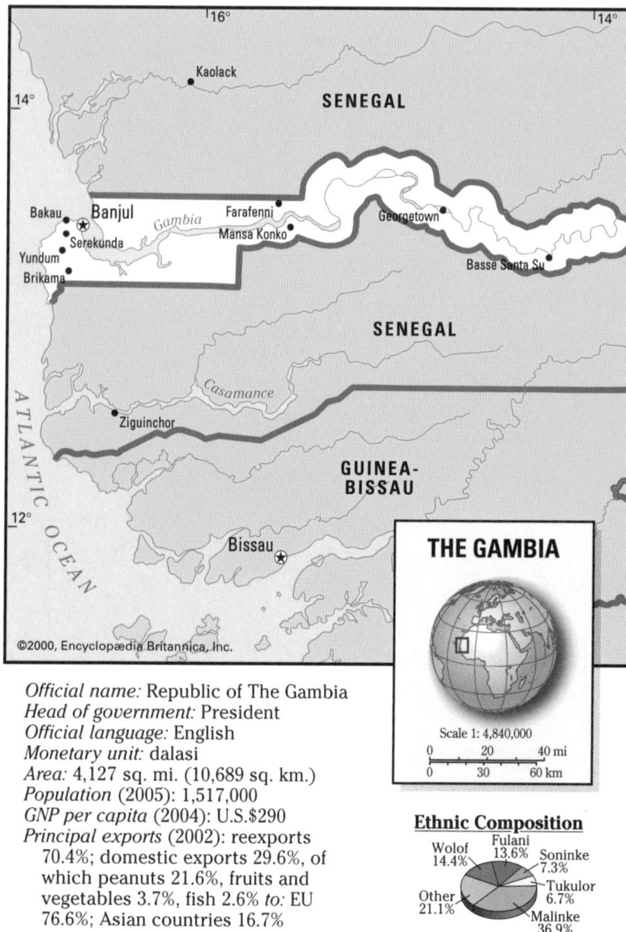

Official name: Republic of The Gambia
Head of government: President
Official language: English
Monetary unit: dalasi
Area: 4,127 sq. mi. (10,689 sq. km.)
Population (2005): 1,517,000
GNP per capita (2004): U.S.$290
Principal exports (2002): reexports 70.4%; domestic exports 29.6%, of which peanuts 21.6%, fruits and vegetables 3.7%, fish 2.6% *to:* EU 76.6%; Asian countries 16.7%

The Gambia achieved independence from Britain on Feb. 18, 1965, under the current flag. The center stripe is blue to symbolize the Gambia River. The red stripe is for the sun and the equator. The green stripe is for agricultural produce (peanuts, grains, and citrus fruits), while the white stripes are said to stand for peace and unity.

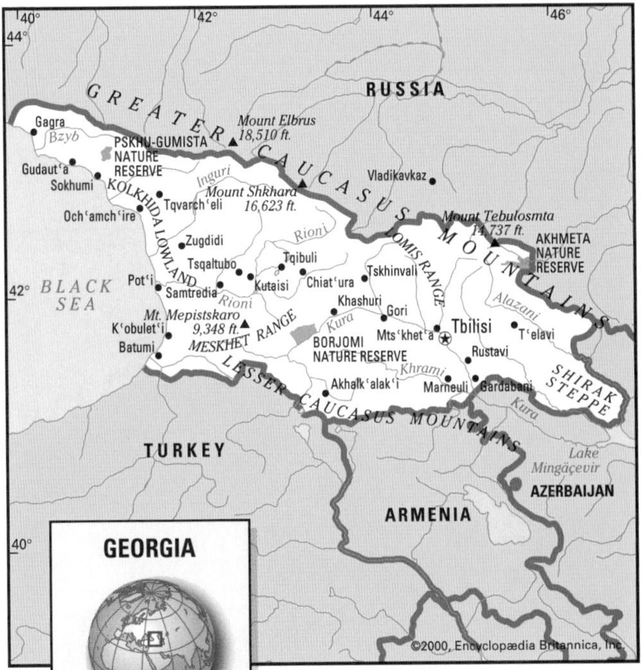

GEORGIA

Scale 1: 7,957,000

0 25 50 75 mi

0 60 120 km

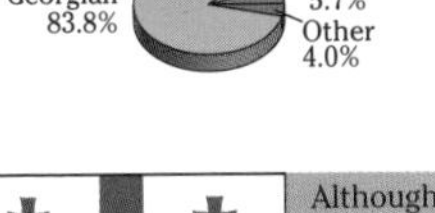

Ethnic Composition

Georgian 83.8%

Azerbaijani 6.5%

Armenian 5.7%

Other 4.0%

Official name: Georgia
Head of government: President assisted by Prime Minister
Official language: Georgian
Monetary unit: lari
Area: 27,086 sq. mi. (70,152 sq. km.)
Population (2005): 4,496,000
GNP per capita (2004): U.S.$1,040
Principal exports (2003): food and beverages 35.4%, iron and steel 24.5%, mineral fuels 12.0% *to:* Russia 18.0%; Turkey 17.7%; Turkmenistan 12.6%; Switzerland 7.1%; Armenia 6.6%

Although independent from Russia in 1991, Georgia adopted this flag only on January 14, 2004, after the next government change. The Cross of St. George and four smaller ones on this flag probably first were used in the 14th century, but Russia suppressed all such designs when annexing Georgia in 1801. Cherry red is the national color, and white stands for hope.

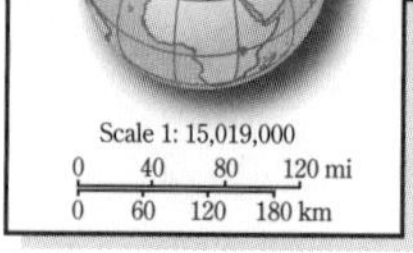

GERMANY

Scale 1: 15,019,000

Official name: Federal Republic of Germany
Head of government: Chancellor
Official language: German
Monetary unit: euro
Area: 137,847 sq. mi. (357,023 sq. km.)
Population (2005): 82,467,000
GNP per capita (2004): U.S.$30,120
Principal exports (1995): machinery 26.3%, transport equipment 23.4%, chemicals and chemical products 11.8%, base metals 4.5% *to:* France 10.3%; U.S. 8.8%; U.K. 8.3%; Italy 7.1%; The Netherlands 6.2%; Belgium 5.6%

Age Breakdown

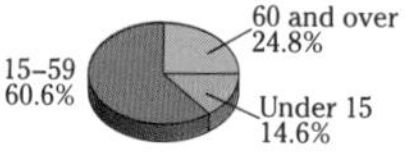

60 and over 24.8%
15–59 60.6%
Under 15 14.6%

In the early 19th century German nationalists displayed black, gold, and red on their uniforms and tricolor flags. The current flag was used officially from 1848 to 1852 and re-adopted by West Germany on May 9, 1949. East Germany flew a similar flag but only the flag of West Germany was maintained upon reunification in 1990.

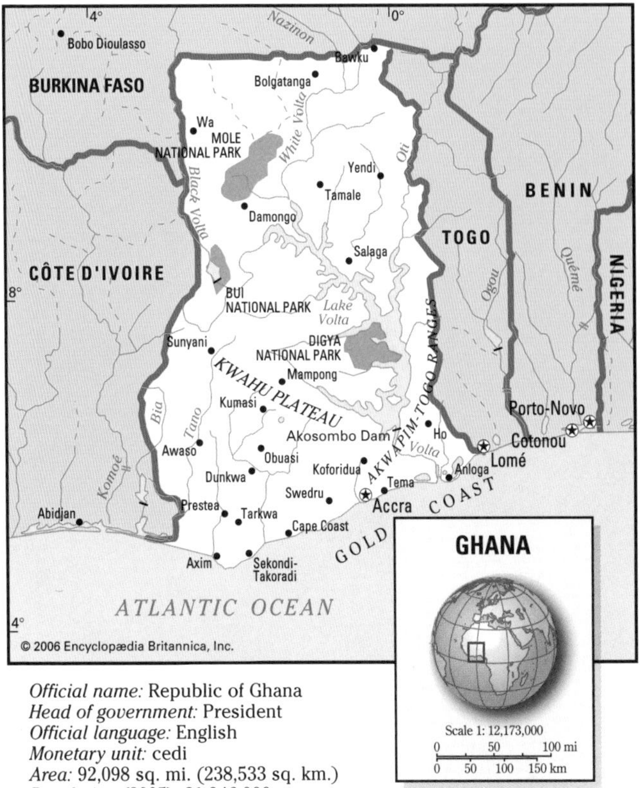

GHANA

Scale 1: 12,173,000

0 50 100 mi

0 50 100 150 km

Official name: Republic of Ghana
Head of government: President
Official language: English
Monetary unit: cedi
Area: 92,098 sq. mi. (238,533 sq. km.)
Population (2005): 21,946,000
GNP per capita (2004): U.S.$380
Principal exports (2004): cocoa beans and products 38.5%, gold 30.2%, sawn wood 7.6% *to:* United Kingdom 10.9%; The Netherlands 11.1%; France 6.9%; U.S. 6.0%; Belgium 4.8%

Ethnic Composition

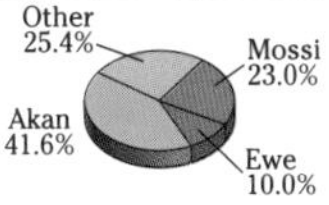

Other 25.4%
Mossi 23.0%
Akan 41.6%
Ewe 10.0%

On March 6, 1957, independence from Britain was granted and a flag, based on the red-white-green tricolor of a nationalist organization, was hoisted. A black "lodestar of African freedom" was added and the white stripe was changed to yellow, symbolizing wealth. Green is for forests and farms, red for the independence struggle.

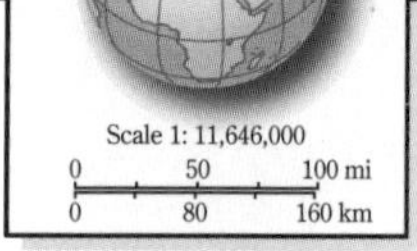

GREECE

Scale 1: 11,646,000

0 50 100 mi

0 80 160 km

Official name: Hellenic Republic
Head of government: Prime Minister
Official language: Greek
Monetary unit: euro
Area: 50,949 sq. mi. (131,957 sq. km.)
Population (2005): 11,088,000
GNP per capita (2004): U.S.$16,610
Principal exports (2000): food 14.6%, of which fruits and nuts 6.0%, clothing and apparel 12.8%; refined petroleum 12.5%; machinery 9.8%; aluminum 4.2% *to* (2003): Germany 12.6%; Italy 10.5%; U.K. 7.1%; U.S. 6.5%

Age Breakdown

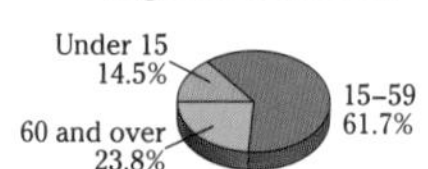

In March 1822, during the revolt against Ottoman rule, the first Greek national flags were adopted; the most recent revision to the flag was made on Dec. 22, 1978. The colors symbolize Greek Orthodoxy while the cross stands for "the wisdom of God, freedom and country." The stripes are for the battle cry for independence: "Freedom or Death."

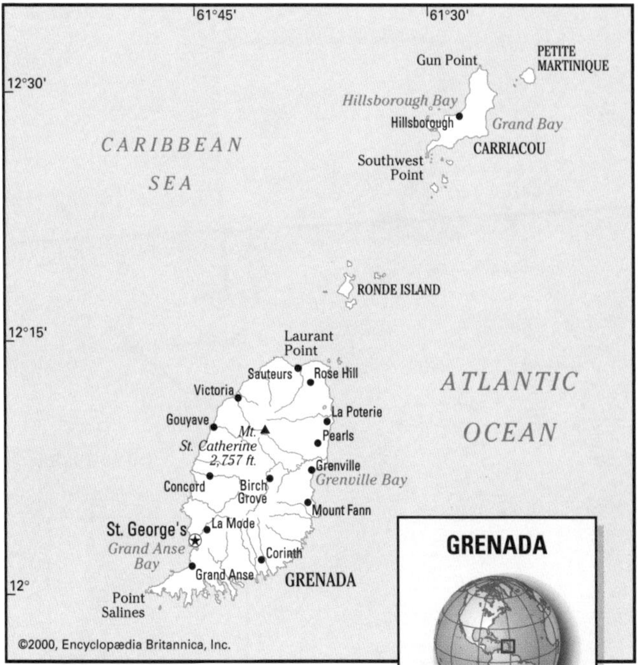

Official name: Grenada
Head of government: Prime Minister
Official language: English
Monetary unit: East Caribbean dollar
Area: 133 sq. mi. (344 sq. km.)
Population (2005): 103,000
GNP per capita (2004): U.S.$3,760
Principal exports (2004): domestic exports 78.7%, of which nutmeg 31.6%, fish 9.7%, flour 8.7%, cocoa beans 6.5%; reexports 21.3% *to:* Saint Lucia 11.8%; U.S. 11.6%; The Netherlands 8.1%; Antigua and Barbuda 8.0%

Religious Affiliation

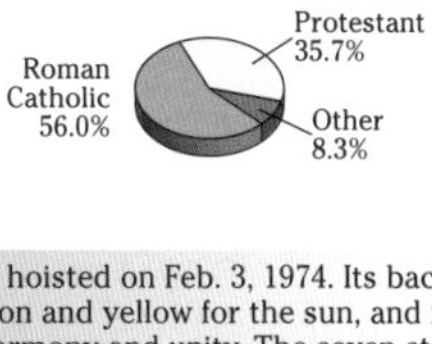

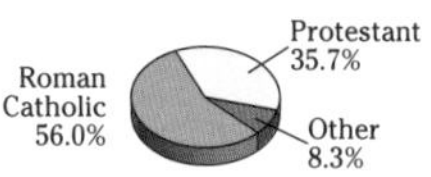

Grenada's flag was officially hoisted on Feb. 3, 1974. Its background is green for vegetation and yellow for the sun, and its red border is symbolic of harmony and unity. The seven stars are for the original administrative subdivisions of Grenada. Nutmeg, a crop for which the "Isle of Spice" is internationally known, is represented as well.

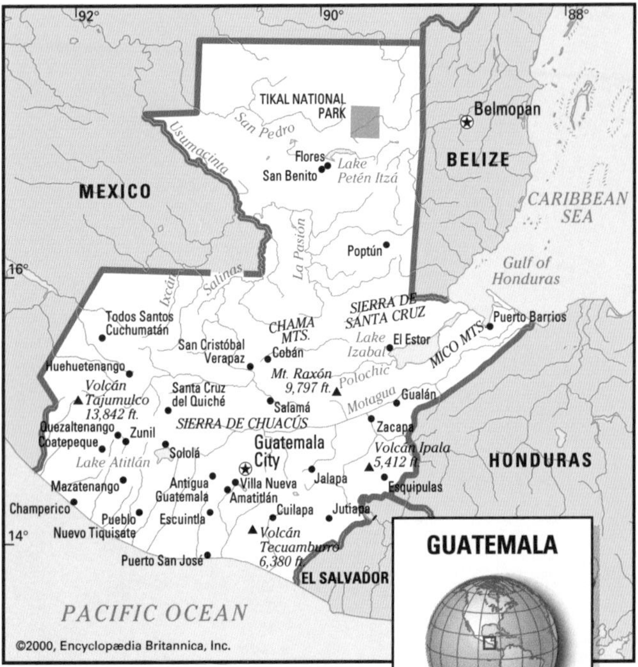

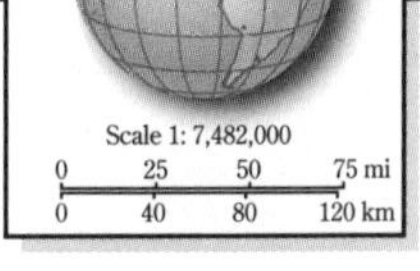

GUATEMALA

Scale 1: 7,482,000

Official name: Republic of Guatemala
Head of government: President
Official language: Spanish
Monetary unit: quetzal
Area: 42,130 sq. mi. (109,117 sq. km.)
Population (2005): 12,599,000
GNP per capita (2004): U.S.$2,130
Principal exports (2004): chemical 17.7%, coffee 11.2%, bananas 7.8%, crude petroleum 6.1% *to:* United States 29.3%; El Salvador 18.6%; Honduras 11.6%; Costa Rica 6.2%; Nicaragua 6.0%

Ethnic Composition

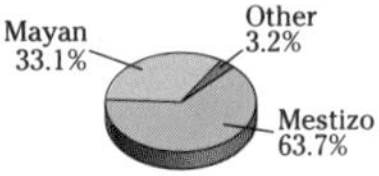

Mayan 33.1%
Other 3.2%
Mestizo 63.7%

The flag was introduced in 1871. It has blue and white stripes (colors of the former United Provinces of Central America) and a coat of arms with the quetzal (the national bird), a scroll, a wreath, and crossed rifles and sabres. Different artistic variations have been used but on Sept. 12, 1968, the present pattern was established.

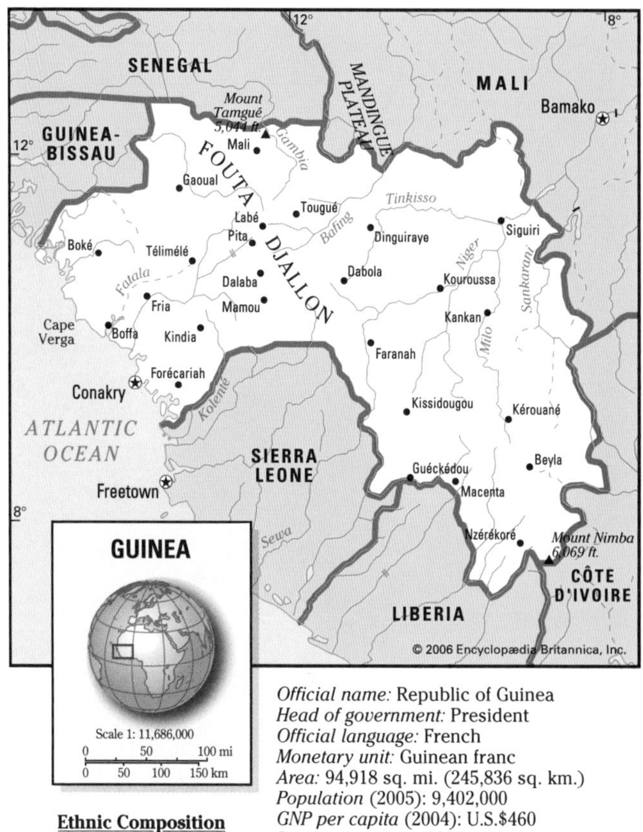

Ethnic Composition

Other 27.2%
Malinke 23.2%
Fulani 38.6%
Susu 11%

Official name: Republic of Guinea
Head of government: President
Official language: French
Monetary unit: Guinean franc
Area: 94,918 sq. mi. (245,836 sq. km.)
Population (2005): 9,402,000
GNP per capita (2004): U.S.$460
Principal exports (2004): bauxite 39.0%, alumina 20.3%, gold 18.9%, diamonds 6.5%, cotton 5.6%, coffee 3.1% *to:* South Korea 15.6%; Russia 13.1%; Spain 12.3; Ireland 9.1%; U.S. 7.5%; Germany 6.2%

The flag was adopted on Nov. 12, 1958, one month after independence from France. Its simple design was influenced by the French tricolor. The red is said to be a symbol of sacrifice and labor, while the yellow is for mineral wealth, the tropical sun, and justice. Green symbolizes agricultural wealth and the solidarity of the people.

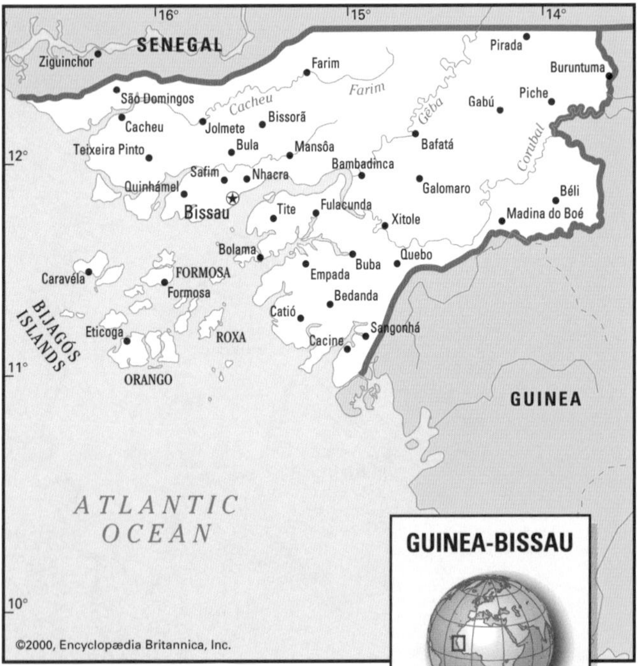

GUINEA-BISSAU

Scale 1: 4,928,000

0 15 35 45 mi

0 30 60 km

Official name: Republic of Guinea-Bissau
Head of government: Prime Minister
Official language: Portuguese
Monetary unit: CFA franc
Area: 13,948 sq. mi. (36,125 sq. km.)
Population (2005): 1,413,000
GNP per capita (2004): U.S.$160
Principal exports (2003): cashews 89.5%, cotton 1.9%, wood products 1.4% *to:* India 62.0%; Thailand 23.5%; Portugal 2.9%

Ethnic Composition

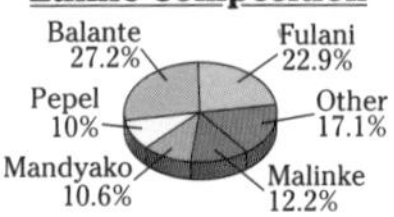

Balante 27.2%
Fulani 22.9%
Pepel 10%
Other 17.1%
Mandyako 10.6%
Malinke 12.2%

The flag has been used since the declaration of independence from Portugal on Sept. 24, 1973. The black star on the red stripe was for African Party leadership, the people, and their will to live in dignity, freedom, and peace. Yellow was for the harvest and other rewards of work, and green was for the nation's vast jungles and agricultural lands.

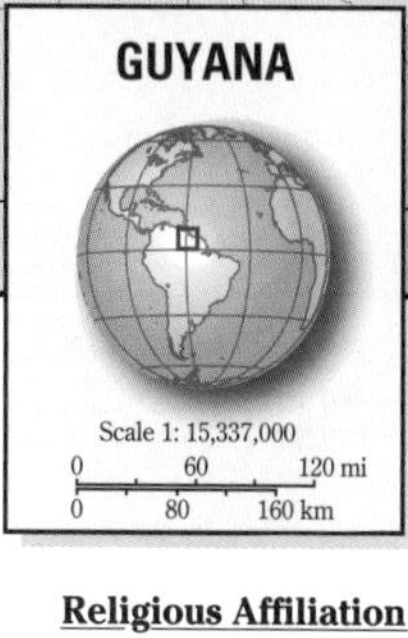

GUYANA

Scale 1: 15,337,000

0 60 120 mi

0 80 160 km

Official name: Co-operative Republic of Guyana
Head of government: President
Official language: English
Monetary unit: Guyana dollar
Area: 83,044 sq. mi. (215,083 sq. km.)
Population (2005): 751,000
GNP per capita (2004): U.S.$990
Principal exports (2004): gold 25.1%, sugar 23.6%, shrimp 10.1%, rice 9.5%, timber 7.8% *to* (2001): United States 22.0%; Canada 20.0%; United Kingdom 12.0%; Netherlands Antilles 12.0%

Religious Affiliation

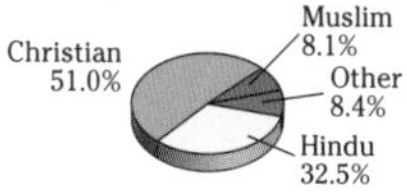

Christian 51.0%
Muslim 8.1%
Other 8.4%
Hindu 32.5%

Upon independence from Britain on May 26, 1966, the flag was first hoisted. The green stands for jungles and fields, white suggests the rivers which are the basis for the Indian word guiana ("land of waters"), red is for zeal and sacrifice in nation-building, and black is for perseverance. The flag is nicknamed "The Golden Arrowhead."

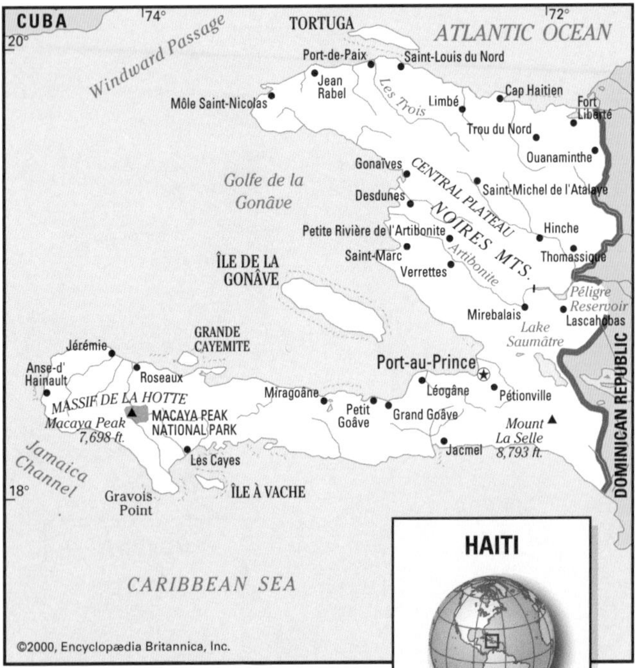

CUBA
74°
72°
20°
18°
TORTUGA
ATLANTIC OCEAN
Windward Passage
Port-de-Paix
Saint-Louis du Nord
Jean Rabel
Môle Saint-Nicolas
Les Trois
Limbé
Cap Haitien
Fort Liberté
Trou du Nord
Ouanaminthe
Gonaïves
CENTRAL PLATEAU
Saint-Michel de l'Atalaye
Golfe de la Gonâve
Desdunes
NOIRES MTS.
Petite Rivière de l'Artibonite
Hinche
Saint-Marc
Artibonite
Thomassique
ÎLE DE LA GONÂVE
Verrettes
Péligre Reservoir
Mirebalais
Lascahobas
Lake Saumâtre
GRANDE CAYEMITE
Jérémie
Port-au-Prince
Anse-d'Hainault
Roseaux
Léogâne
Pétionville
MASSIF DE LA HOTTE
Miragoâne
Petit Goâve
Grand Goâve
MACAYA PEAK NATIONAL PARK
Macaya Peak 7,698 ft.
Mount La Selle 8,793 ft.
Jacmel
Les Cayes
Jamaica Channel
Gravois Point
ÎLE À VACHE
DOMINICAN REPUBLIC
CARIBBEAN SEA

HAITI

Scale 1: 4,550,000
0 20 40 mi
0 30 60 km

Official name: Republic of Haiti
Head of government: Prime Minister
Official languages: Haitian Creole; French
Monetary unit: gourde
Area: 10,695 sq. mi. (27,700 sq. km.)
Population (2005): 8,528,000
GNP per capita (2004): U.S.$390
Principal exports (2003): reexports 83.5%, of which clothing and apparel 82.1%; cacao 1.8%; mango 1.4%, coffee 1.1% *to:* United States 81.8%; Dominican Republic 7.2%; Canada 4.2%

Religious Affiliation

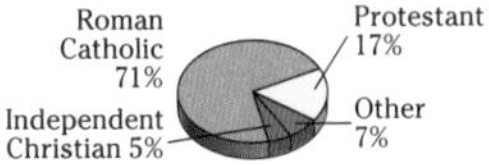

Roman Catholic 71%
Protestant 17%
Other 7%
Independent Christian 5%

After the French Revolution of 1789 Haiti underwent a slave revolt, but the French tricolor continued in use until 1803. The new blue-red flag represented the black and mulatto populations only. A black-red flag was used by various dictators, including François "Papa Doc" Duvalier and his son, but on Feb. 25, 1986, the old flag was reestablished.

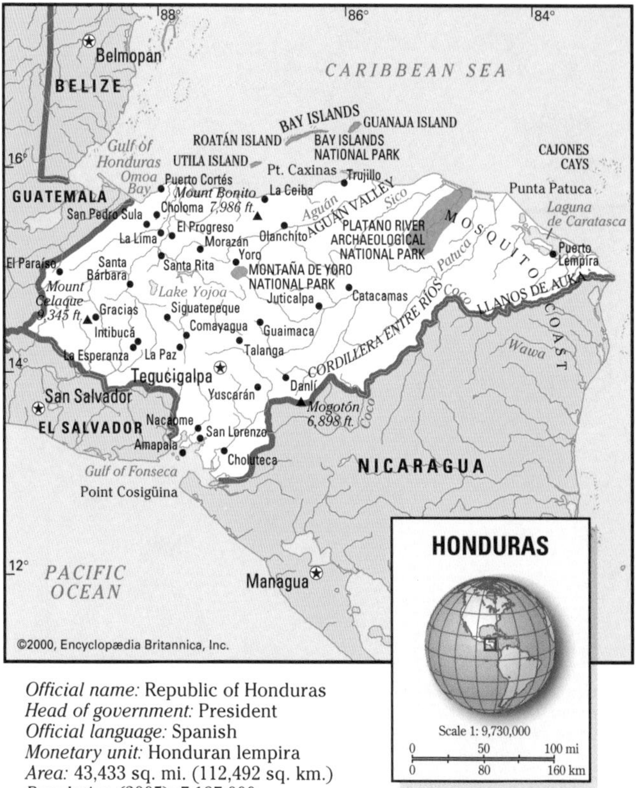

HONDURAS

Scale 1: 9,730,000

0 50 100 mi

0 80 160 km

Official name: Republic of Honduras
Head of government: President
Official language: Spanish
Monetary unit: Honduran lempira
Area: 43,433 sq. mi. (112,492 sq. km.)
Population (2005): 7,187,000
GNP per capita (2004): U.S.$1,030
Principal exports (2004): coffee 16.4%, bananas 13.6%, shrimp and lobsters 10.5%, gold 4.8%, palm oil 3.5% *to:* United States 41.5%; El Salvador 10.9%; Guatemala 7.3%; Germany 5.9%; Belgium 4.2%

Ethnic Composition

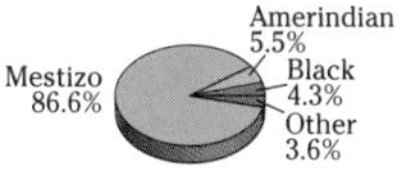

Mestizo 86.6%
Amerindian 5.5%
Black 4.3%
Other 3.6%

Since Feb. 16, 1866, the Honduran flag has retained the blue-white-blue design of the flag of the former United Provinces of Central America, but with five central stars symbolizing the states of Honduras, El Salvador, Nicaragua, Costa Rica, and Guatemala. The flag design has often been associated with Central American reunification attempts.

Official name: Republic of Hungary
Head of government: Prime Minister
Official language: Hungarian
Monetary unit: forint
Area: 35,919 sq. mi. (93,030 sq. km.)
Population (2005): 10,078,000
GNP per capita (2004): U.S.$8,270
Principal exports (2002):
telecommunication equipment 15.5%, electrical machinery 11.2%, power-generating machinery 10.9%, road vehicles 8.7% *to:* Germany 31.0%; Austria 6.7%; France 5.6%; Italy 5.6%

Religious Affiliation

The colors of the Hungarian flag were mentioned in a 1608 coronation ceremony, but they may have been used since the 13th century. The tricolor was adopted on Oct. 12, 1957, after the abortive revolution of 1956. The white is said to symbolize Hungary's rivers, the green its mountains, and the red the blood shed in its many battles.

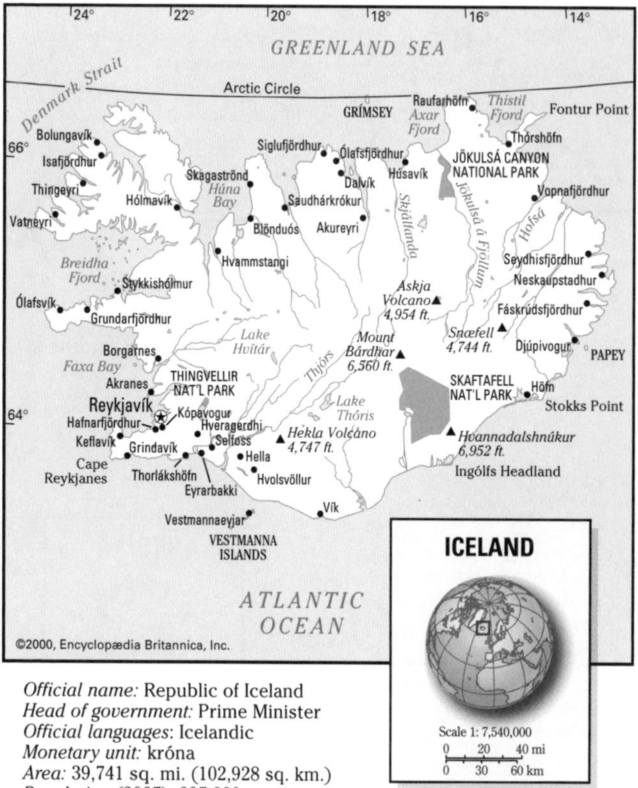

24° 22° 20° 18° 16° 14°
GREENLAND SEA
Denmark Strait
Arctic Circle
GRÍMSEY
Raufarhöfn
Thistil Fjord
Axar Fjord
Fontur Point
Thórshöfn
Bolungavík
66°
Isafjördhur
Siglufjördhur
Ólafsfjördhur
Húsavík
JÖKULSÁ CANYON NATIONAL PARK
Dalvík
Skagaströnd
Thingeyri
Húna Bay
Vopnafjördhur
Hólmavík
Saudhárkrókur
Vatneyri
Blönduós
Akureyri
Skjálfanda
Jökulsá á Fjöllum
Hofsá
Hvammstangi
Seydhisfjördhur
Breidha Fjord
Stykkishólmur
Askja Volcano 4,954 ft.
Neskaupstadhur
Ólafsvík
Grundarfjördhur
Fáskrúdsfjördhur
Lake Hvítár
Mount Bárdhar 6,560 ft.
Snæfell 4,744 ft.
Djúpivogur
PAPEY
Borgarnes
Faxa Bay
Thjórs
Akranes
THINGVELLIR NAT'L PARK
SKAFTAFELL NAT'L PARK
Höfn
Reykjavík
Stokks Point
64°
Kópavogur
Lake Thóris
Hafnarfjördhur
Hveragerdhi
Hekla Volcano 4,747 ft.
Hvannadalshnúkur 6,952 ft.
Keflavík
Selfoss
Grindavík
Hella
Cape Reykjanes
Thorlákshöfn
Hvolsvöllur
Ingólfs Headland
Eyrarbakki
Vík
Vestmannaeyjar
VESTMANNA ISLANDS
ATLANTIC OCEAN

ICELAND

Scale 1: 7,540,000
0 20 40 mi
0 30 60 km

Official name: Republic of Iceland
Head of government: Prime Minister
Official languages: Icelandic
Monetary unit: króna
Area: 39,741 sq. mi. (102,928 sq. km.)
Population (2005): 295,000
GNP per capita (2004): U.S.$38,620
Principal exports (2004): marine products 60.2%, of which cod 23.7%; aluminum 18.0% *to:* United Kingdom 19%; Germany 17.7%; The Netherlands 10.7%; U.S. 9.3%; Spain 6.9%

Age Breakdown

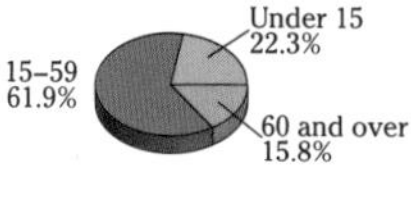

Under 15 22.3%
15–59 61.9%
60 and over 15.8%

Approval for an Icelandic flag was given by the king of Denmark on June 19, 1915; it became a national flag on Dec. 1, 1918, when the separate kingdom of Iceland was proclaimed. The flag was retained upon the creation of a republic on June 17, 1944. The design has a typical "Scandinavian cross."

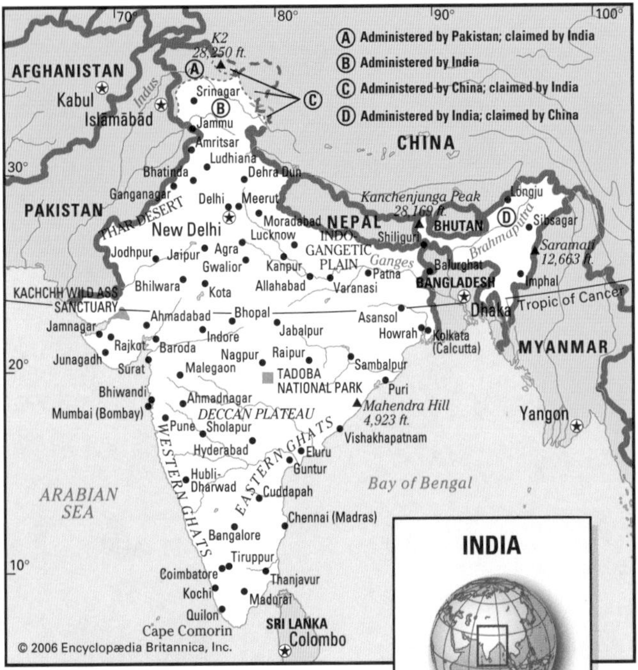

Official name: Republic of India
Head of government: Prime Minister
Official languages: Hindi; English
Monetary unit: Indian rupee
Area: 1,222,559 sq. mi. (3,166,414 sq. km.)
Population (2005): 1,103,371,000
GNP per capita (2004): U.S.$620
Principal exports (2004): engineering goods 20.7%, cut and polished diamonds and jewelry 17.3%, chemicals 15.0%, food 10.1%, petroleum products 8.1%, garments 7.6% *to:* U.S. 16.7%; U.A.E. 9.0%; China 5.8%; Singapore 4.8%; Hong Kong 4.6%; U.K. 4.5%

Linguistic Composition

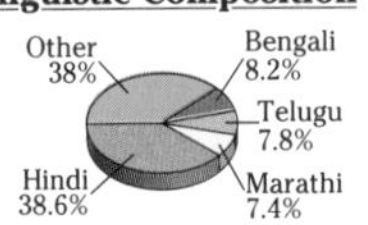

Earlier versions of the flag were used from the 1920s, but the current flag was hoisted officially on July 22, 1947. The orange was said to stand for courage and sacrifice, white for peace and truth, and green for faith and chivalry. The blue wheel is a chakra, associated with Emperor Asoka's attempts to unite India in the 3rd century BC.

Official name: Republic of Indonesia
Head of government: President
Official language: Indonesian
Monetary unit: Indonesian rupiah
Area: 730,024 sq. mi. (1,890,754 sq. km.)
Population (2005): 222,781,000
GNP per capita (2004): U.S.$1,140
Principal exports (2004–05): petroleum products and natural gas 21.9%, machinery and apparatus 13.9%, textiles 10.3%, base metals 6.5%, rubber products 5.6% *to:* Japan 21.8%; U.S. 13.5%; Singapore 7.4%; China 7.5%

Indonesia's red and white flag was associated with the Majapahit empire which existed from the 13th to the 16th century. It was adopted on Aug. 17, 1945, and it remained after Indonesia won its independence from The Netherlands in 1949. Red is for courage and white for honesty. The flag is identical, except in dimensions, to the flag of Monaco.

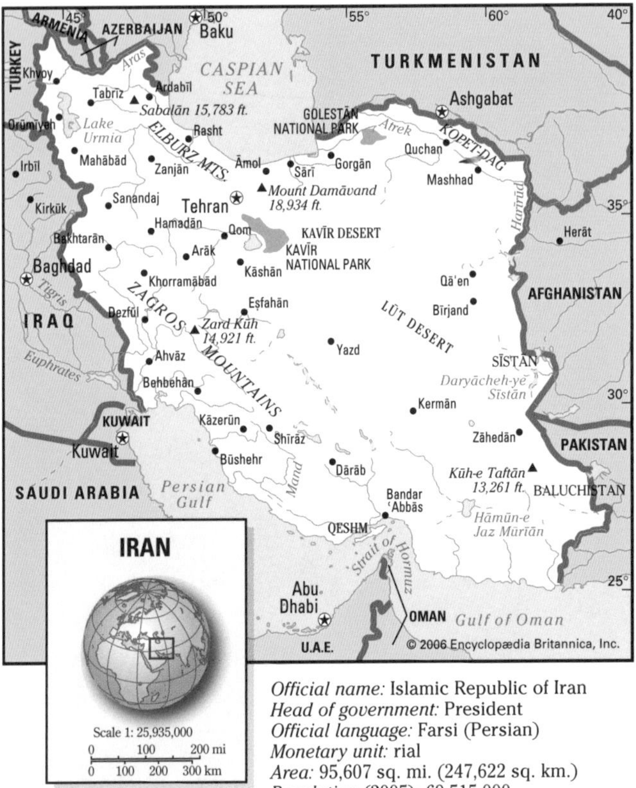

IRAN

Scale 1: 25,935,000

0 100 200 mi

0 100 200 300 km

Ethnic Composition

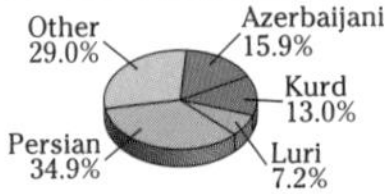

Other 29.0%
Azerbaijani 15.9%
Kurd 13.0%
Luri 7.2%
Persian 34.9%

Official name: Islamic Republic of Iran
Head of government: President
Official language: Farsi (Persian)
Monetary unit: rial
Area: 95,607 sq. mi. (247,622 sq. km.)
Population (2005): 69,515,000
GNP per capita (2004): U.S.$2,300
Principal exports (2002): crude and refined petroleum 85.4%, carpets 1.9%, nuts 1.7% *to:* Japan 23.0%; China 10.2%; Italy 6.6%; Taiwan 6.4%; South Korea 5.0%

The tricolor flag was recognized in 1906 but altered after the revolution of 1979. Along the central stripe are the Arabic words Allahu akbar ("God is great"), repeated 22 times. The coat of arms can be read as a rendition of the word Allah, as a globe, or as two crescents. The green is for Islam, white is for peace, and red is for valor.

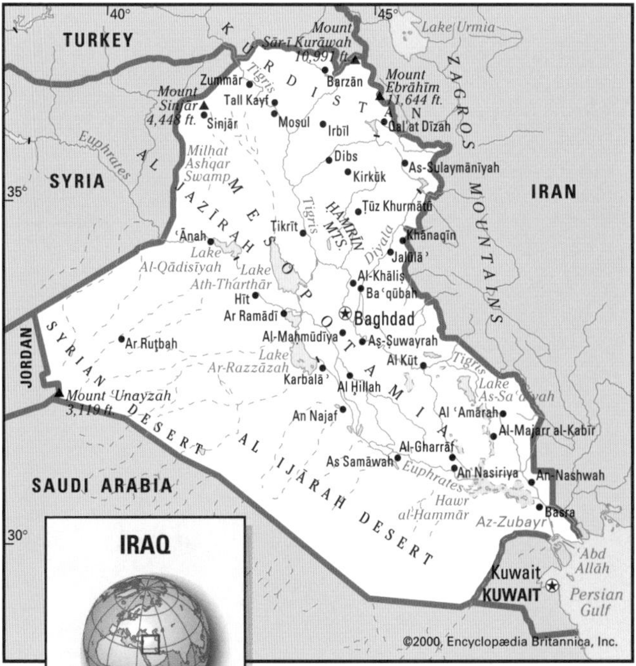

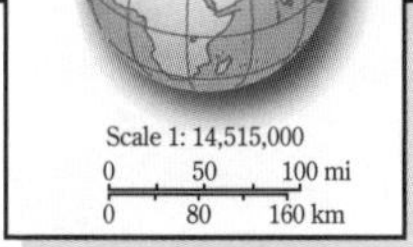

IRAQ

Scale 1: 14,515,000
0 50 100 mi
0 80 160 km

Ethnic Composition

Arab 64.7%
Kurd 23.0%
Other 12.3%

Official name: Republic of Iraq
Head of government: President assisted by Prime Minister
Official languages: Arabic; Kurdish
Monetary unit: Iraqi dinar
Area: 167,618 sq. mi. (434,128 sq. km.)
Population (2005): 27,818,000
GNP per capita (2003): U.S.$540
Principal exports (2003): crude petroleum 82.8%, food 5.0% *to:* U.S. 55.8%; Spain 8.0%; Japan 7.3%; Italy 6.5%; Canada 5.8%

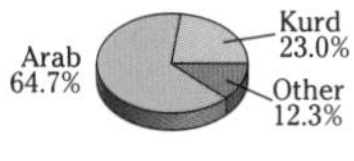

The new Iraqi interim government raised this flag on June 28, 2004, about a year after the fall of dictator Saddam Hussein. Its three green stars expressed Iraq's 1963 desire to unite with Egypt and Syria. The colors honor a 13th-century poem by Safi al-Din al-Hilli (see Kuwait, p. 91). The Kufic script says, "God is great."

Official name: Ireland
Head of government: Prime Minister
Official languages: Irish; English
Monetary unit: euro
Area: 27,133 sq. mi. (70,273 sq. km.)
Population (2005): 4,152,000
GNP per capita (2004): U.S.$34,280
Principal exports (2002): organic chemicals 18.8%, office machines 18.5%, pharmaceuticals 16.7%, electronic microcircuits 8.6% *to:* U.K. 24.0%; U.S. 17.6%; Belgium 14.4%; Germany 7.2%; France 5.0%

In the 19th century various tricolor flags and ribbons became symbolic of Irish opposition to British rule. Many of them included the colors green (for the Catholics), orange (for the Protestants), and white (for the peace between the two groups). The tricolor in its modern form was recognized by the constitution on Dec. 29, 1937.

LEBANON
Mount Meron 3,692 ft.
UN Forces deployment area
Qiryat Shemona
GOLAN HEIGHTS (Israeli occupied)
SYRIA
Karmi'el
Rama
Haifa
Qiryat Ata
Lake Tiberias
Mount Carmel 1,789 ft.
Nazareth
Bet She'an
MEDITERRANEAN SEA
Hadera
Janin
Netanya
WEST BANK
Jordan
Herzliyya
Tel Aviv-Yafo
Petah Tiqwa
Bat Yam
Holon
Ram Allah
Amman
Rehovot
Ashdod
Ashqelon
Jerusalem
Bet Shemesh
Bethlehem
Dead Sea -1,312 ft.
Note:
Final Status of Gaza Strip and West Bank to be determined.
GAZA STRIP
Gaza
Hebron
En-gedi
JUDAEA
Beersheba
Nir Yizhaq
'Arad
Dimona
JORDAN
Hazeva
NEGEV
'En Yahav
HA-'ARAVA VALLEY
EGYPT
Mount Ramon 3,395 ft.
SINAI PENINSULA
Elat
34°
36°
32°
30°

ISRAEL

Scale 1: 6,360,000
0 25 50 mi
0 40 80 km

Official name: State of Israel
Head of government: Prime Minister
Official languages: Hebrew; Arabic
Monetary unit: New (Israeli) sheqel
Area: 8,367 sq. mi. (21,671 sq. km.)
Population (2005): 6,677,000
GNP per capita (2004): U.S.$17,380
Principal exports (2002): cut diamonds 28.2%, telecommunication equipment 9.2%, rough diamonds 6.5%, organic chemicals 3.9%, aircraft parts 3.6% *to:* U.S. 40.2%; Belgium 6.3%; Hong Kong 4.7%; U.K. 3.9%; Germany 3.5%

Religious Affiliation

Jewish 76.2%
Muslim 15.7%
Other 8.1%

Symbolic of the traditional *tallit,* or Jewish prayer shawl, and including the Star of David, the flag was used from the late 19th century. It was raised when Israel proclaimed independence on May 14, 1948, and the banner was legally recognized on Nov. 12, 1948. A dark blue was also substituted for the traditional lighter shade of blue.

ITALY

Scale 1: 18,825,000

Official name: Italian Republic
Head of government: Prime Minister
Official language: Italian
Monetary unit: euro
Area: 116,324 sq. mi. (301,277 sq. km.)
Population (2005): 57,989,000
GNP per capita (2004): U.S.$26,120
Principal exports (2004): machinery and transport equipment 31.6%, chemicals 9.7%, fabricated metals 9.6%, textiles and wearing apparel 9.2%, electrical equipment 9.1% *to:* Germany 13.7%; France 12.1%; U.S. 8.0%; Spain 7.3%; U.K. 6.9%; Switzerland 4.1%

Age Breakdown

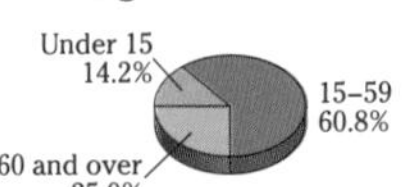

The first Italian national flag was adopted on Feb. 25, 1797, by the Cispadane Republic. Its stripes were vertically positioned on May 11, 1798, and thereafter it was honored by all Italian nationalists. The design was guaranteed by a decree (March 23, 1848) of King Charles Albert of Sardinia, ordering troops to carry the flag into battle.

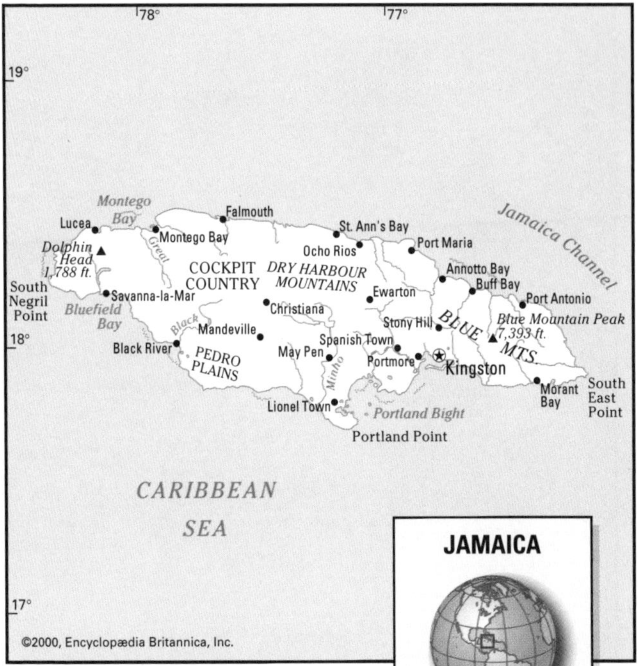

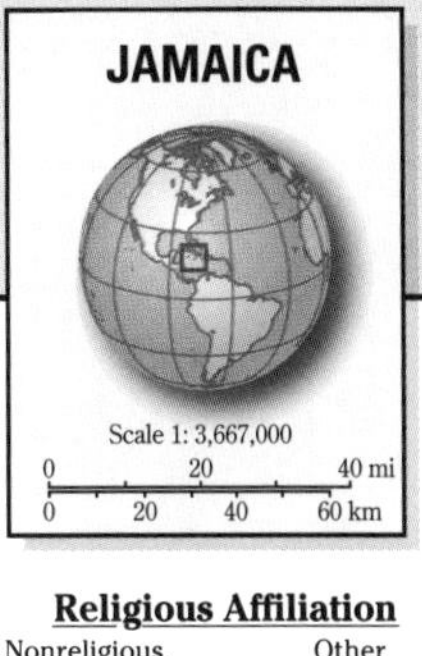

78°
77°
19°
18°
17°
Montego Bay
Lucea
Falmouth
Montego Bay
St. Ann's Bay
Ocho Rios
Port Maria
Jamaica Channel
Dolphin Head 1,788 ft.
Great
COCKPIT COUNTRY
DRY HARBOUR MOUNTAINS
Annotto Bay
Buff Bay
South Negril Point
Savanna-la-Mar
Ewarton
Port Antonio
Bluefield Bay
Christiana
Stony Hill
BLUE MTS.
Blue Mountain Peak 7,393 ft.
Black
Mandeville
Spanish Town
Black River
PEDRO PLAINS
May Pen
Portmore
Kingston
Minho
Morant Bay
South East Point
Lionel Town
Portland Bight
Portland Point
CARIBBEAN SEA
©2000, Encyclopædia Britannica, Inc.

JAMAICA
Scale 1: 3,667,000
0
20
40 mi
0
20
40
60 km

Official name: Jamaica
Head of government: Prime Minister
Official language: English
Monetary unit: Jamaica dollar
Area: 4,244 sq. mi. (10,991 sq. km.)
Population (2005): 2,736,000
GNP per capita (2004): U.S.$2,900
Principal exports (2004): alumina 51.9%, chemical products and mineral fuels 17.9%, wearing apparel 8.0%, refined sugar 6.2%, bauxite 5.0% *to* (2003): United States 28.8%, Canada 16.1%; U.K. 12.8%

Religious Affiliation

Nonreligious 20.9%
Other 14.4%
Roman Catholic 2.6%
Protestant 61.2%
Rastafarian 0.9%

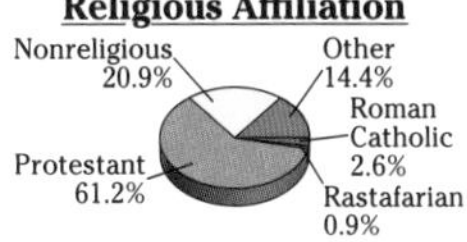

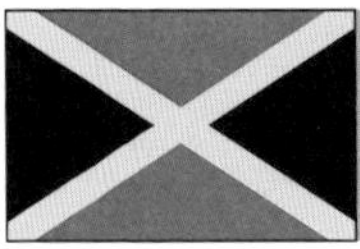

The flag was designed prior to independence from Britain (Aug. 6, 1962). The black color stood for hardships faced by the nation, green for agriculture and hope, and yellow for the natural wealth of Jamaica. This was summed up in the phrase, "Hardships there are, but the land is green and the sun shineth."

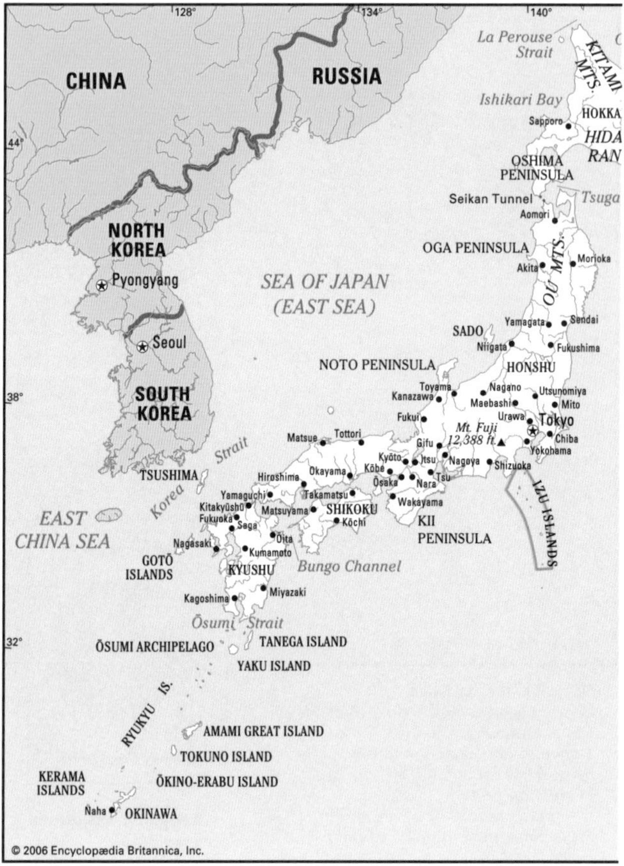

128°
134°
140°
44°
38°
32°
CHINA
RUSSIA
La Perouse Strait
Ishikari Bay
Sapporo
OSHIMA PENINSULA
Seikan Tunnel
Aomori
NORTH KOREA
Pyongyang
OGA PENINSULA
Akita
Morioka
OU MTS.
SEA OF JAPAN (EAST SEA)
Seoul
SADO
Yamagata
Sendai
Niigata
Fukushima
HONSHU
NOTO PENINSULA
SOUTH KOREA
Toyama
Kanazawa
Nagano
Maebashi
Utsunomiya
Mito
Fukui
Urawa
Tokyo
Mt. Fuji 12,388 ft.
Chiba
Yokohama
Matsue
Tottori
Gifu
Kyōto
Nagoya
Shizuoka
Kōbe
Ōsaka
Nara
Tsu
Okayama
Hiroshima
TSUSHIMA
Korea Strait
Yamaguchi
Takamatsu
Wakayama
Kitakyūshū
Matsuyama
SHIKOKU
Kōchi
KII PENINSULA
IZU ISLANDS
EAST CHINA SEA
Fukuoka
Saga
Ōita
Nagasaki
Kumamoto
GOTŌ ISLANDS
KYUSHU
Bungo Channel
Miyazaki
Kagoshima
Ōsumi Strait
ŌSUMI ARCHIPELAGO
TANEGA ISLAND
YAKU ISLAND
RYUKYU IS.
AMAMI GREAT ISLAND
TOKUNO ISLAND
KERAMA ISLANDS
ŌKINO-ERABU ISLAND
Naha
OKINAWA
© 2006 Encyclopædia Britannica, Inc.

The flag features a red sun on a cool white background. Traditionally, the sun goddess founded Japan in the 7th century BC and gave birth to its first emperor, Jimmu. Even today the emperor is known as the "Son of the Sun" and the popular name for the country is "Land of the Rising Sun." The current flag design was adopted on Aug. 5, 1854.

Official name: Japan
Head of government: Prime Minister
Official language: Japanese
Monetary unit: yen
Area: 145,898 sq. mi. (377,873 sq. km.)
Population (2005): 128,085,000
GNP per capita (2004): U.S.$37,180
Principal exports (2001): machinery and apparatus 44.4%, road vehicles and parts 18.6%, base and fabricated metals 5.9% *to:* United States 30.0%; China 7.7%; South Korea 6.3%; Taiwan 6.0%; Hong Kong 5.8%

Age Breakdown

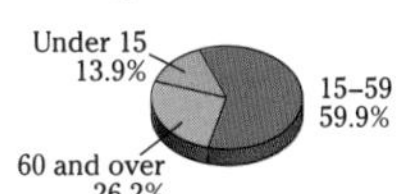

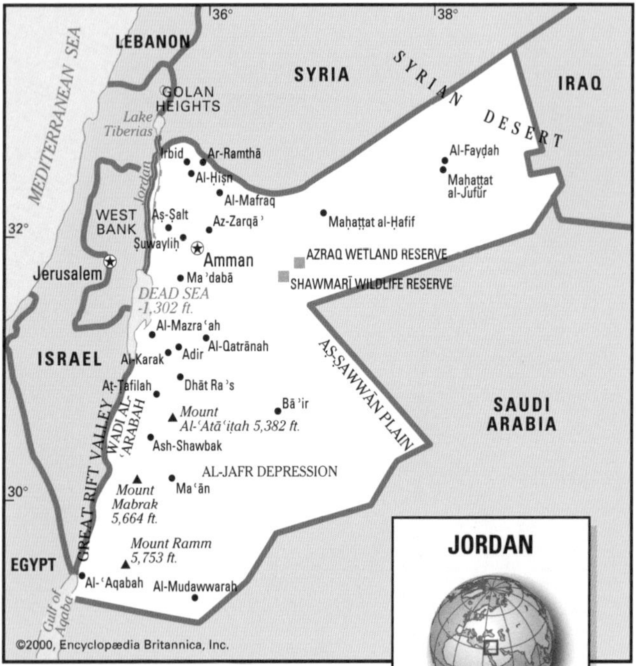

Official name: Hashemite Kingdom of Jordan
Head of government: King assisted by Prime Minister
Official language: Arabic
Monetary unit: Jordan dinar
Area: 34,495 sq. mi. (89,342 sq. km.)
Population (2005): 5,182,000
GNP per capita (2004): U.S.$2,140
Principal exports (2004): domestic exports 76.7%, of which clothing 20.5%, chemicals 17.8%, potash 6.6%; reexports 23.3% *to:* United States 29.0%; Iraq 13.4; India; 8.4%; Saudi Arabia 6.5%; Israel 4.1%

Religious Affiliation

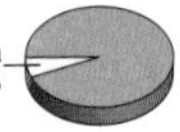

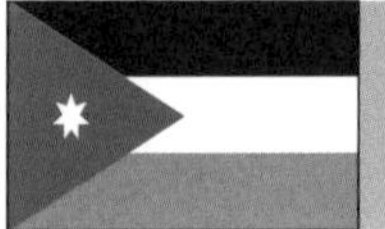

In 1917 Husayn ibn Ali raised the Arab Revolt flag. With the addition of a white seven-pointed star, this flag was adopted by Transjordan on April 16, 1928, and retained upon the independence of Jordan on March 22, 1946. White is for purity, black for struggle and suffering, red for bloodshed, and green for Arab lands.

Official name: Republic of Kazakhstan
Head of government: President assisted by Prime Minister
Official language: Kazakh
Monetary unit: tenge
Area: 1,052,100 sq. mi. (2,724,900 sq. km.)
Population (2005): 15,186,000
GNP per capita (2004): U.S.$2,260
Principal exports (2003): mineral fuels 64.3%, base metals 20.4%, food 5.1% *to:* Bermuda 17.0%; Russia 15.2%; Switzerland 13.0%; China 12.8%; Italy 7.8%

Ethnic Composition

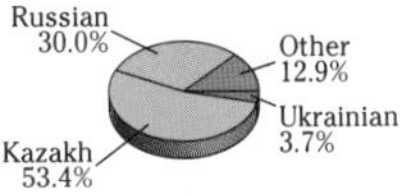

Russian 30.0%
Other 12.9%
Ukrainian 3.7%
Kazakh 53.4%

The flag was adopted in June 1992. Light blue is a traditional color of the nomads of Central Asia; it symbolizes peace and well-being. The golden sun and eagle represent freedom and the high ideals of the Kazakhs. Along the edge is a band of traditional Kazakh ornamentation; the band was originally in red but is now in golden yellow.

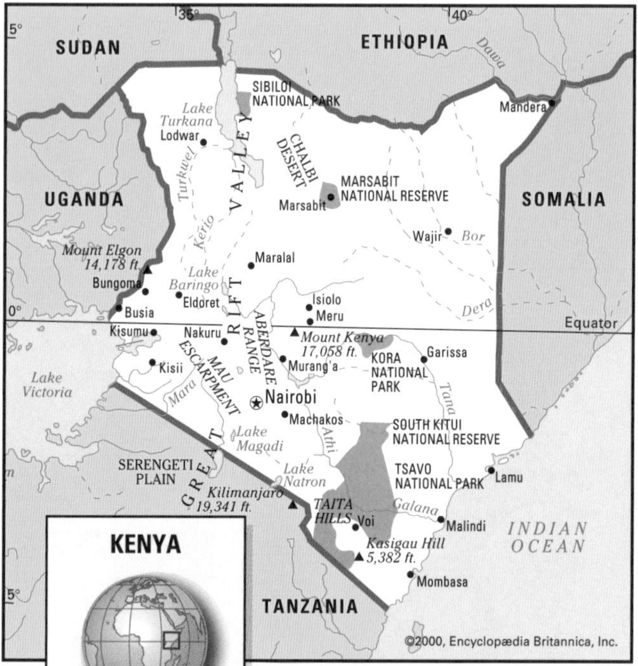

KENYA

Scale 1: 17,833,000

0 50 100 150 mi

0 100 200 km

Official name: Republic of Kenya
Head of government: President
Official languages: Swahili; English
Monetary unit: Kenya shilling
Area: 224,961 sq. mi. (582,646 sq. km.)
Population (2005): 33,830,000
GNP per capita (2004): U.S.$400
Principal exports (2002): tea 21.4%, cut flowers 13.8%, petroleum products 7.6%, coffee 4.1% *to* (2001): Uganda 17.4%; United Kingdom 12.5%; The Netherlands 6.5%; Pakistan 6.1%; U.S. 5.6%

Ethnic Composition

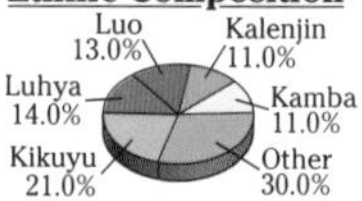

Luo 13.0%
Kalenjin 11.0%
Luhya 14.0%
Kamba 11.0%
Kikuyu 21.0%
Other 30.0%

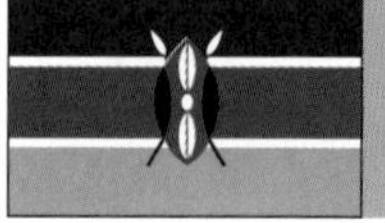

Upon independence from Britain (Dec. 12, 1963), the Kenyan flag became official. It was based on the flag of the Kenya African National Union. Black is for the people, red for humanity and the struggle for freedom, green for the fertile land, and white for unity and peace. The shield and spears are traditional weapons of the Masai people.

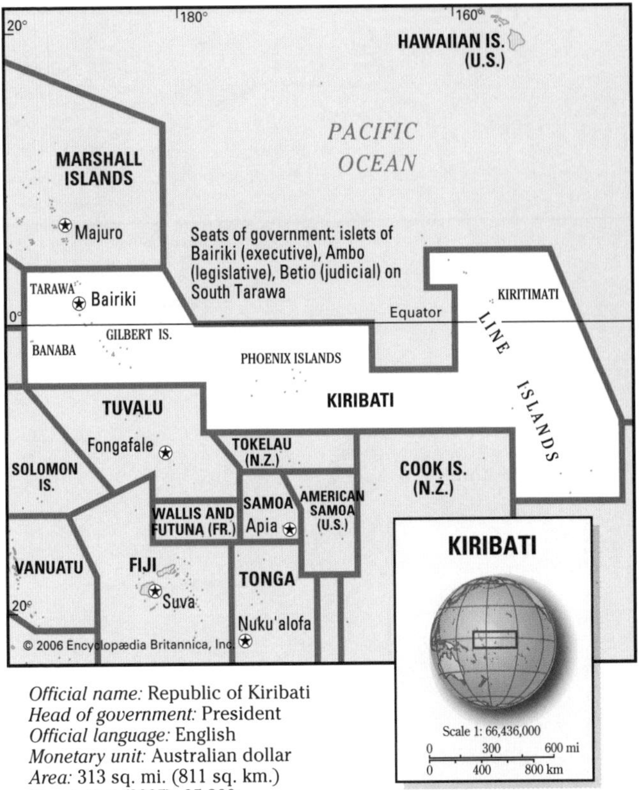

Official name: Republic of Kiribati
Head of government: President
Official language: English
Monetary unit: Australian dollar
Area: 313 sq. mi. (811 sq. km.)
Population (2005): 95,300
GNP per capita (2004): U.S.$970
Principal exports (2001): domestic exports 82.4%, of which copra 22.8%, aquarium fish 17.1%, seaweed 4.8%; reexports 17.6% *to:* Japan 45.8%; Thailand 24.8%; South Korea 10.7%; Bangladesh 5.5%

Age Breakdown

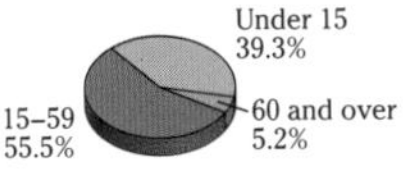

Under 15 39.3%
15–59 55.5%
60 and over 5.2%

Great Britain acquired the Gilbert and Ellice Islands in the 19th century. In 1975 the Gilbert Islands separated from the Ellice Islands to form Kiribati, and a new flag was adopted based on the coat of arms granted to the islands in 1937. It has waves of white and blue, for the Pacific Ocean, as well as a yellow sun and a local frigate bird.

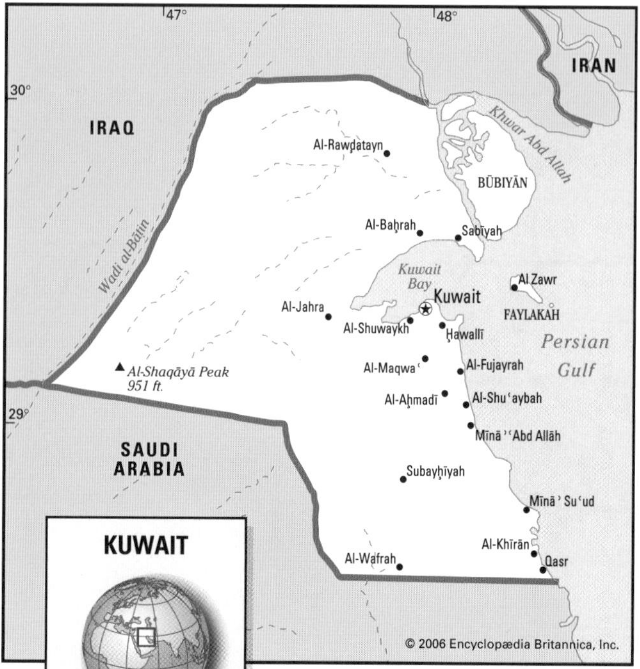
47°
48°
30°
29°
IRAQ
IRAN
SAUDI ARABIA
Wadi al-Bāṭin
Al-Rawḍatayn
Khwar Abd Allah
BŪBIYĀN
Al-Baḥrah
Sabīyah
Kuwait Bay
Kuwait
Al Zawr
FAYLAKAH
Al-Jahra
Al-Shuwaykh
Ḥawallī
Persian Gulf
Al-Maqwaʿ
Al-Fujayrah
Al-Shaqāyā Peak 951 ft.
Al-Aḥmadī
Al-Shuʿaybah
Mīnāʾ ʿAbd Allāh
Subayḥīyah
Mīnāʾ Suʿud
Al-Khīrān
Al-Wafrah
Qasr
© 2006 Encyclopædia Britannica, Inc.

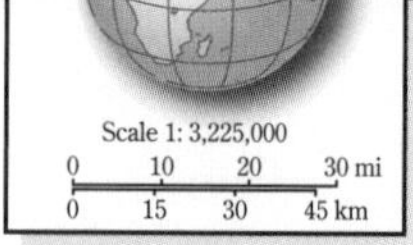
KUWAIT
Scale 1: 3,225,000
0 10 20 30 mi
0 15 30 45 km

Official name: State of Kuwait
Head of government: Emir assisted by Prime Minister
Official language: Arabic
Monetary unit: Kuwaiti dinar
Area: 6,880 sq. mi. (17,818 sq. km.)
Population (2005): 2,847,000
GNP per capita (2004): U.S.$17,970
Principal exports (2003): crude petroleum and petroleum products 91.9%, ethylene products 3.0% *to:* Japan 22.1%; South Korea 13.1%; U.S. 12.0%; Taiwan 10.7%; Singapore 10.2%

Religious Affiliation

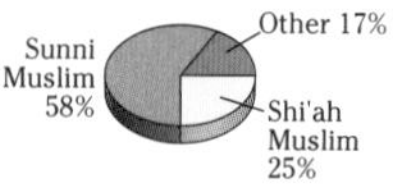
Other 17%
Sunni Muslim 58%
Shi'ah Muslim 25%

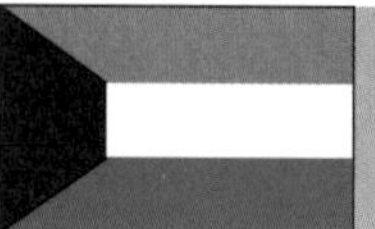

The red flag of Kuwait, in use since World War I, was replaced by the current flag on Oct. 24, 1961, shortly after independence from Britain. The symbolism is from a poem written over six centuries ago. The green stands for Arab lands, black is for battles, white is for the purity of the fighters, and red is for the blood on their swords.

KYRGYZSTAN

Scale 1: 13,484,000

Official name: Kyrgyz Republic
Head of government: President assisted by Prime Minister
Official languages: Kyrgyz; Russian
Monetary unit: som
Area: 77,199 sq. mi. (199,945 sq. km.)
Population (2005): 5,146,000
GNP per capita (2004): U.S.$400
Principal exports (2001): nonferrous metals 51.7%, machinery and apparatus 12.0%, electricity 9.8%, agricultural products 9.5% *to:* Switzerland 26.1%; Germany 19.8%; Russia 13.5%; Uzbekistan 10.1%

Ethnic Composition

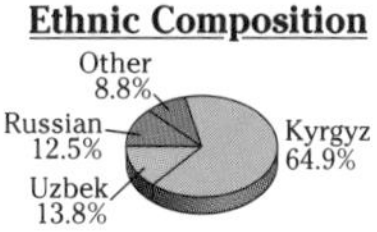

Kyrgyz 64.9%
Uzbek 13.8%
Russian 12.5%
Other 8.8%

The Kyrgyz flag replaced a Soviet-era design on March 3, 1992. The red recalls the flag of the national hero Mansas the Noble. The central yellow sun has 40 rays, corresponding to the followers of Mansas and the tribes he united. On the sun is the stylized view of the roof of a yurt, a traditional nomadic home that is now seldom used.

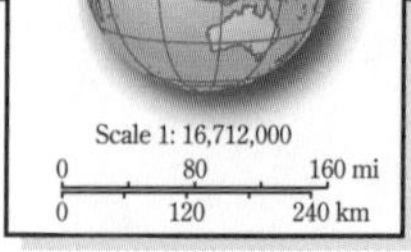

LAOS

Scale 1: 16,712,000

0 80 160 mi

0 120 240 km

Ethnic Composition

Lao-Lum 53.0%
Lao-Theung 23.0%
Lao-Tai 13.0%
Other 11.0%

Official name: Lao People's Democratic Republic
Head of government: Prime Minister
Official language: Lao
Monetary unit: kip
Area: 91,429 sq. mi. (236,800 sq. km.)
Population (2005): 5,924,000
GNP per capita (2004): U.S.$390
Principal exports (2002): garments 30.8%, electricity 30.4%, wood products 27.5%, coffee 5.0% *to* (2001): Vietnam 41.5%; Thailand 14.8%; France 6.1%; Germany 4.6%; Belgium 2.2%

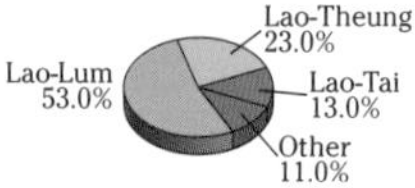

The Lao flag was first used by anticolonialist forces from the mid-20th century. The white disk honored the Japanese who had supported the Lao independence movement, but it also symbolized a bright future. Red was said to stand for the blood of patriots and blue was for the promise of future prosperity. The flag was adopted on Dec. 2, 1975.

Official name: Republic of Latvia
Head of government: Prime Minister
Official language: Latvian
Monetary unit: lats
Area: 24,938 sq. mi. (64,589 sq. km.)
Population (2005): 2,299,000
GNP per capita (2004): U.S.$5,460
Principal exports (2002): wood and wood products 33.6%, base and fabricated metals 13.2%, textiles and clothing 12.8% *to:* Germany 15.5%; U.K. 14.6%; Sweden 10.5%; Lithuania 8.4%

The basic flag design was used by a militia unit in 1279, according to a 14th century source. Popularized in the 19th century among anti-Russian nationalists, the flag flew in 1918 and was legally adopted on Jan. 20, 1923. Under Soviet control the flag was suppressed, but it was again legalized in 1988 and flown officially from Feb. 27, 1990.

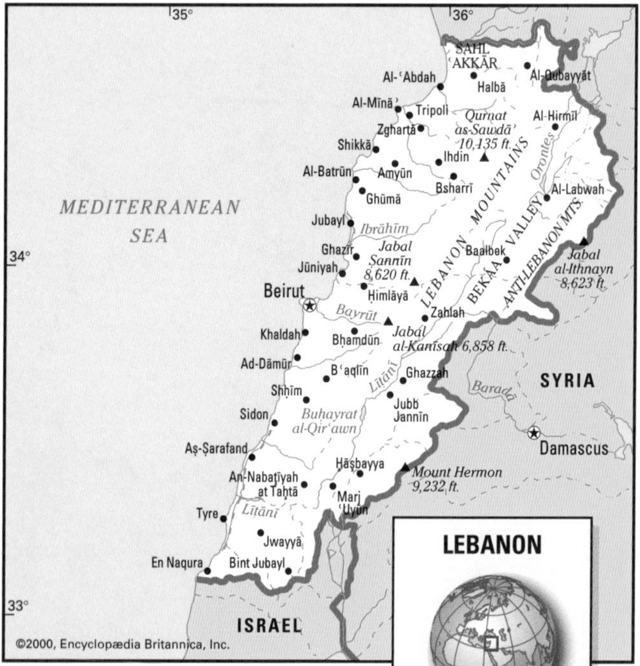

LEBANON

Scale 1: 2,833,000

0 10 20 30 mi

0 20 40 km

Official name: Lebanese Republic
Head of government: Prime Minister
Official language: Arabic
Monetary unit: Lebanese pound
Area: 4,016 sq. mi. (10,400 sq. km.)
Population (2005): 3,577,000
GNP per capita (2004): U.S.$4,980
Principal exports (2004): precious metals 16.4%, electrical equipment 15.7%, base metals 13.0%, chemicals 8.5%, food 8.5% *to:* Iraq 14.6%; Switzerland 10.7%; Syria 8.3%; U.A.E. 7.7%

Ethnic Composition

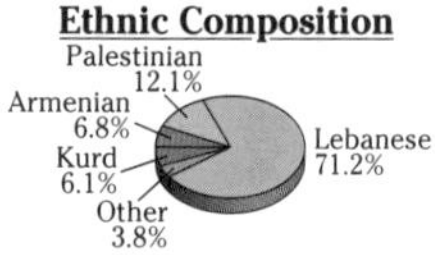

Palestinian 12.1%
Armenian 6.8%
Kurd 6.1%
Other 3.8%
Lebanese 71.2%

On Sept. 1, 1920, French-administered Lebanon adopted a flag based on the French tricolor. The current red-white flag was established by the constitution of 1943, which divided power among the Muslim and Christian sects. On the central stripe is a cedar tree, which is a biblical symbol for holiness, peace, and eternity.

LESOTHO

Scale 1: 3,679,000
0 10 20 30 mi
0 20 40 km

Official name: Kingdom of Lesotho
Head of government: Prime Minister
Official languages: Sotho; English
Monetary unit: loti
Area: 11,720 sq. mi. (30,355 sq. km.)
Population (2005): 2,031,000
GNP per capita (2004): U.S.$740
Principal exports (2001): manufactured goods (mostly clothing) 74.7%, machinery 10.5%, beverages 3.6%, wool 2.5% *to:* North America (mostly the United States) 62.8%; Customs Union of Southern Africa 37.0%

Ethnic Composition

Sotho 80.3%
Zulu 14.4%
Other 5.3%

The flag was hoisted on Jan. 20, 1987, after the military overthrew the government of prime minister Leabua Jonathan. It contains a white triangle (for peace) on which are an animal-skin shield and traditional weapons used in battles to preserve Sotho independence. The green triangle is for prosperity, and the blue stripe is for rain.

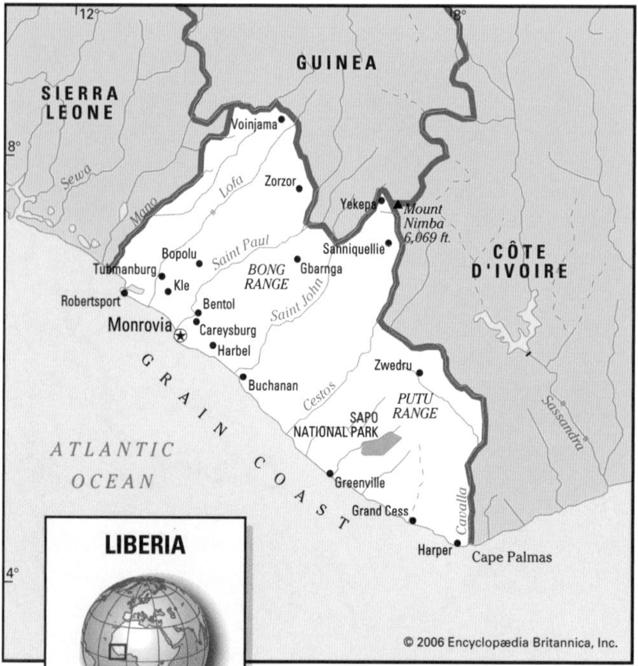

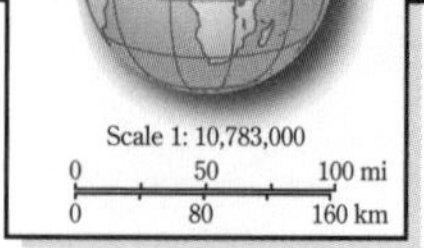

LIBERIA

Scale 1: 10,783,000
0 50 100 mi
0 80 160 km

Official name: Republic of Liberia
Head of government: Chairman
Official language: English
Monetary unit: Liberian dollar
Area: 38,250 sq. mi. (99,067 sq. km.)
Population (2005): 2,900,000
GNP per capita (2004): U.S.$110
Principal exports (2004): rubber 90.0%, cocoa beans 3.4% *to:* U.S. 61.4%; Belgium 29.5%; China 5.3%; France 1.6%

Religious Affiliation

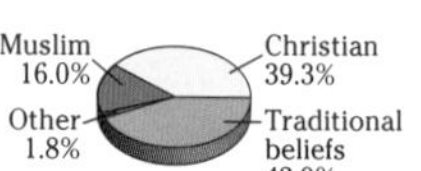

In the 19th century land was purchased on the African coast by the American Colonization Society, in order to return freed slaves to Africa. On April 9, 1827, a flag based on that of the United States was adopted, featuring a white cross. On Aug. 24, 1847, after independence, the cross was replaced by a star and the number of stripes was reduced.

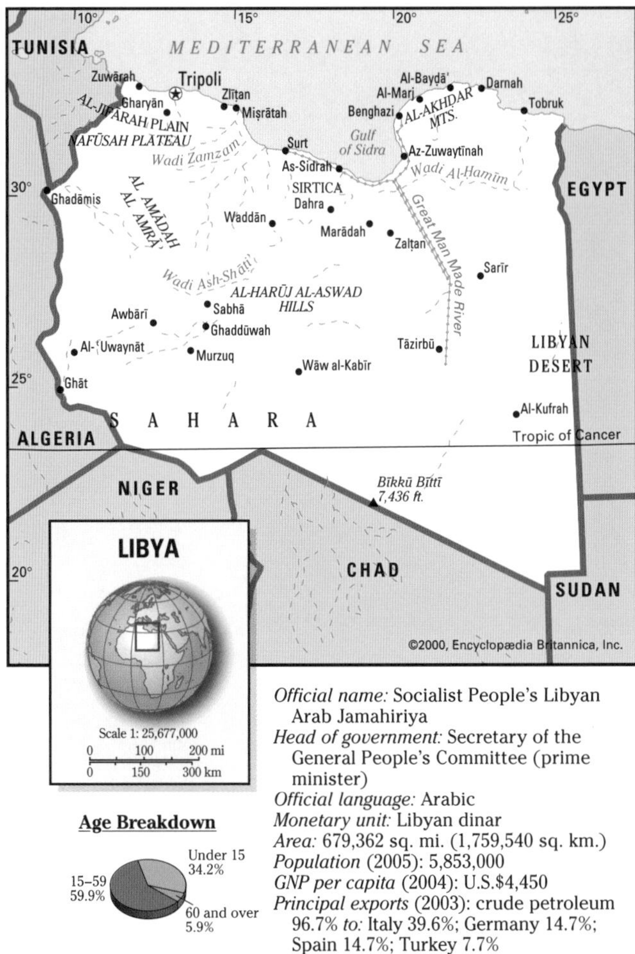

Official name: Socialist People's Libyan Arab Jamahiriya
Head of government: Secretary of the General People's Committee (prime minister)
Official language: Arabic
Monetary unit: Libyan dinar
Area: 679,362 sq. mi. (1,759,540 sq. km.)
Population (2005): 5,853,000
GNP per capita (2004): U.S.$4,450
Principal exports (2003): crude petroleum 96.7% *to:* Italy 39.6%; Germany 14.7%; Spain 14.7%; Turkey 7.7%

After the coup d'état of 1969, Muammar al-Qaddafi adopted a flag based on the Egyptian flag. When the Egyptian president Anwar el-Sadat made peace with Israel, however, Qaddafi broke diplomatic relations and replaced the flag. In November 1977 he established a plain green banner, symbolizing promises of agricultural wealth.

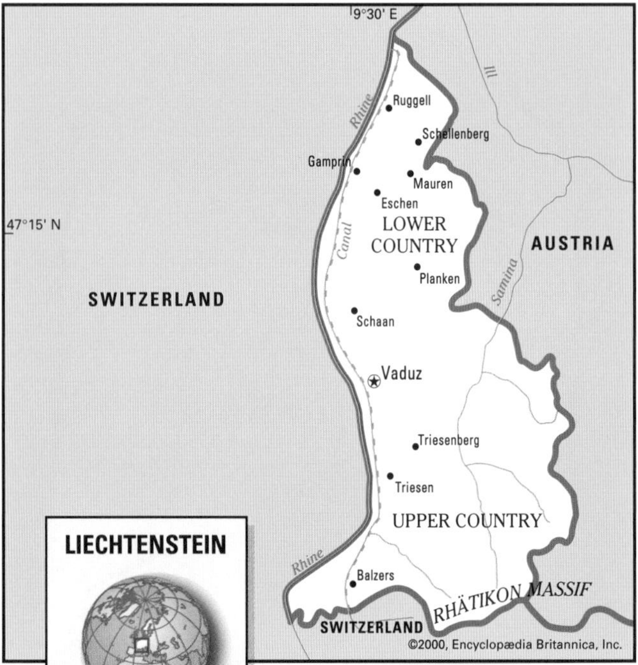
9°30' E
47°15' N
Rhine
Ill
Ruggell
Schellenberg
Gamprin
Mauren
Eschen
LOWER
COUNTRY
AUSTRIA
Canal
Samina
Planken
SWITZERLAND
Schaan
Vaduz
Triesenberg
Triesen
UPPER COUNTRY
Rhine
Balzers
RHÄTIKON MASSIF
SWITZERLAND
©2000, Encyclopædia Britannica, Inc.

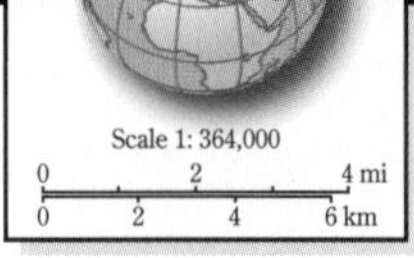
LIECHTENSTEIN
Scale 1: 364,000
0 2 4 mi
0 2 4 6 km

Religious Affiliation

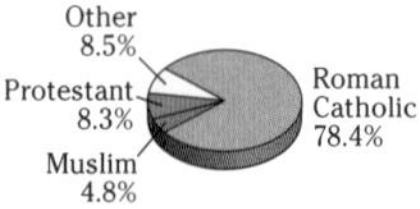
Other
8.5%
Protestant
8.3%
Muslim
4.8%
Roman
Catholic
78.4%

Official name: Principality of Liechtenstein
Head of government: Head of Government
Official language: German
Monetary unit: Swiss franc
Area: 61.8 sq. mi. (160.0 sq. km.)
Population (2005): 34,800
GNP per capita (2001): U.S.$67,510
Principal exports (2003): machinery and apparatus 33.9%, fabricated metals 14.8%, glass and ceramics 9.1%, chemicals 4.5% *to:* Germany 21.7%; U.S. 17.3%; France 11.6%; Austria 9.8%; Italy 7.6%

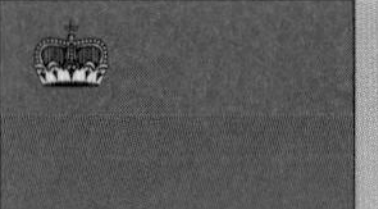

The blue-red flag was given official status in October 1921. At the 1936 Olympics it was learned that this same flag was used by Haiti; thus, in 1937 a yellow crown was added, which symbolizes the unity of the people and their prince. Blue stands for the sky, red for the evening fires in homes. The flag was last modified on Sept. 18, 1982.

Official name: Republic of Lithuania
Head of government: Prime Minister
Official language: Lithuanian
Monetary unit: litas
Area: 25,212 sq. mi. (65,300 sq. km.)
Population (2005): 3,413,000
GNP per capita (2004): U.S.$5,740
Principal exports (2002): mineral fuels 19.0%, transport equipment 15.9%, textiles and clothing 15.0%, food 10.8%, machinery 9.9% *to:* U.K. 13.5%; Russia 12.1%; Germany 10.3%; Latvia 9.6%; Denmark 5.0%

Ethnic Composition

Lithuanian 83.5%
Polish 6.7%
Russian 6.3%
Other 3.5%

The tricolor flag of Lithuania was adopted on Aug. 1, 1922. It was long suppressed under Soviet rule until its reestablishment on March 20, 1989. The yellow color suggests ripening wheat and freedom from want. Green is for hope and the forests of the nation, while red stands for love of country, sovereignty, and valor in defense of liberty.

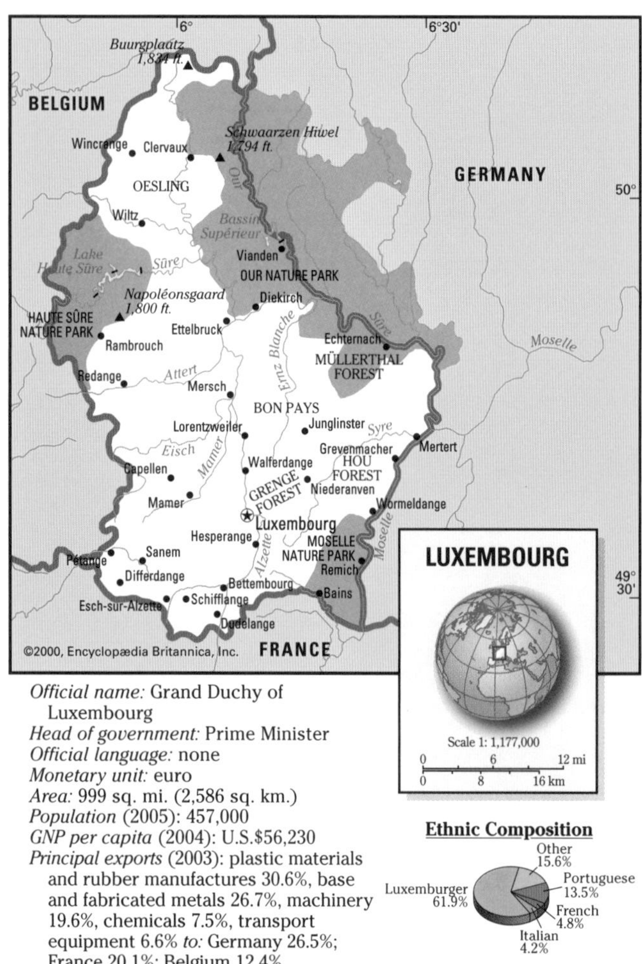

Official name: Grand Duchy of Luxembourg
Head of government: Prime Minister
Official language: none
Monetary unit: euro
Area: 999 sq. mi. (2,586 sq. km.)
Population (2005): 457,000
GNP per capita (2004): U.S.$56,230
Principal exports (2003): plastic materials and rubber manufactures 30.6%, base and fabricated metals 26.7%, machinery 19.6%, chemicals 7.5%, transport equipment 6.6% *to:* Germany 26.5%; France 20.1%; Belgium 12.4%

In the 19th century the national colors, from the coat of arms of the dukes of Luxembourg, came to be used in a tricolor of red-white-blue, coincidentally the same as the flag of The Netherlands. To distinguish it from the Dutch flag, the proportions were altered and the shade of blue was made lighter. It was recognized by law on Aug. 16, 1972.

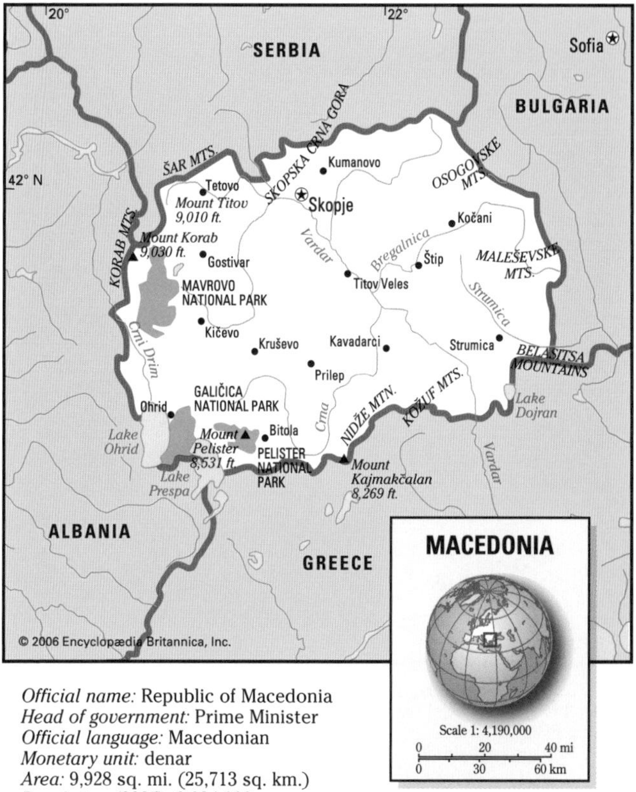
20°
22°
SERBIA
Sofia
BULGARIA
42° N
ŠAR MTS.
SKOPSKA CRNA GORA
Kumanovo
OSOGOVSKE MTS.
Tetovo
Mount Titov
9,010 ft.
Skopje
Kočani
KORAB MTS.
Mount Korab
9,030 ft.
Gostivar
Vardar
Bregalnica
Štip
MALEŠEVSKE MTS.
MAVROVO NATIONAL PARK
Titov Veles
Strumica
Crni Drim
Kičevo
Kruševo
Kavadarci
Strumica
BELASITSA MOUNTAINS
Prilep
KOŽUF MTS.
GALIČICA NATIONAL PARK
NIDŽE MTN.
Crna
Ohrid
Lake Dojran
Lake Ohrid
Mount Pelister
8,531 ft.
Bitola
PELISTER NATIONAL PARK
Mount Kajmakčalan
8,269 ft.
Lake Prespa
Vardar
ALBANIA
GREECE
© 2006 Encyclopædia Britannica, Inc.
MACEDONIA
Scale 1: 4,190,000
0
20
40 mi
0
30
60 km

Official name: Republic of Macedonia
Head of government: Prime Minister
Official language: Macedonian
Monetary unit: denar
Area: 9,928 sq. mi. (25,713 sq. km.)
Population (2005): 2,034,000
GNP per capita (2004): U.S.$2,350
Principal exports (2002): clothing 30.0%, iron and steel 14.0%, tobacco 6.8%, food and live animals 6.7%, chemicals 6.2% *to:* Serbia and Montenegro 20.8%; Germany 18.9%; Greece 13.7%; Italy 8.0%; Croatia 4.8%

Ethnic Composition

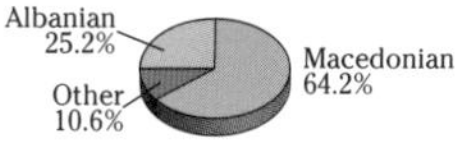
Albanian
25.2%
Macedonian
64.2%
Other
10.6%

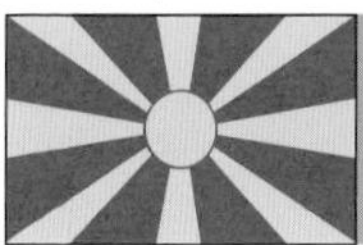

A "starburst" flag replaced the communist banner on Aug. 11, 1992. The starburst was a symbol of Alexander the Great and his father, Philip of Macedon, but its use by Macedonia was opposed by Greece. Thus on Oct. 6, 1995, the similar "golden sun" flag was chosen instead. The gold and red colors originated in an early Macedonian coat of arms.

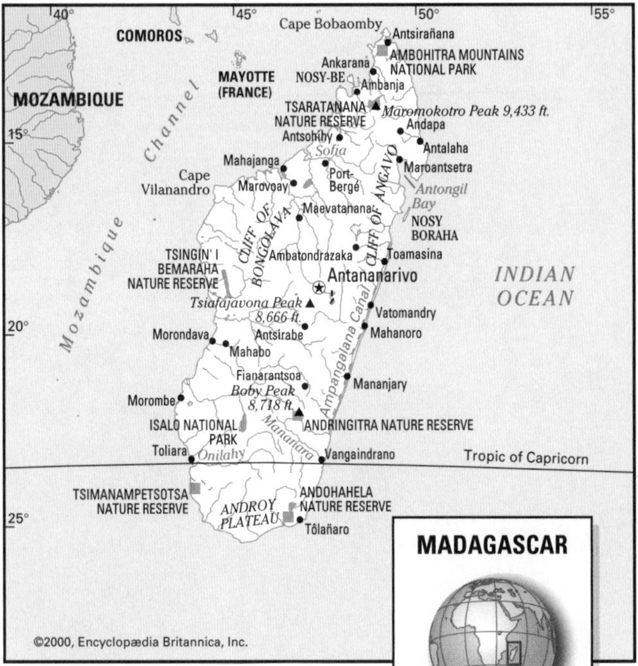

MADAGASCAR

Scale 1: 25,920,000

0 100 200 mi

0 150 300 km

Official name: Republic of Madagascar
Head of government: President assisted by Prime Minister
Official language: none
Monetary unit: ariary (MGA)
Area: 226,662 sq. mi. (587,051 sq. km.)
Population (2005): 18,606,000
GNP per capita (2004): U.S.$300
Principal exports (2004): textiles and clothing 52.0%, vanilla 13.0%, shellfish 5.2%, cloves 3.0% *to:* U.S. 35.5%; France 30.5%; Germany 7.0%; Mauritius 4.6%; Italy 3.4%

Religious Affiliation

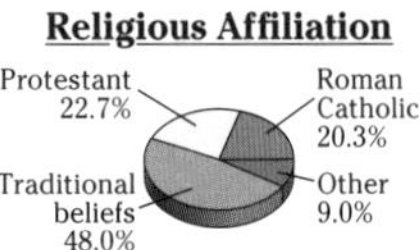

The Madagascar flag was adopted on Oct. 16, 1958, by the newly proclaimed Malagasy Republic, formerly a French colony. The flag combines the traditional Malagasy colors of white and red with a stripe of green. The white and red are said to stand for purity and sovereignty, while the green represents the coastal regions and symbolizes hope.

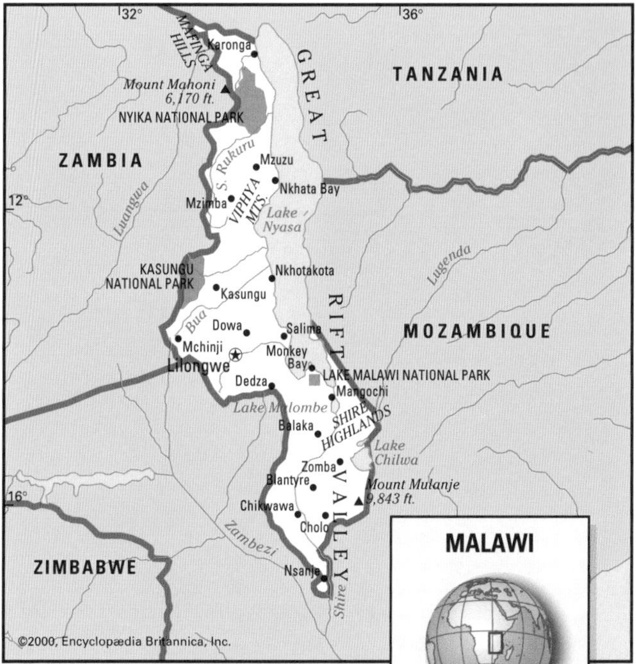

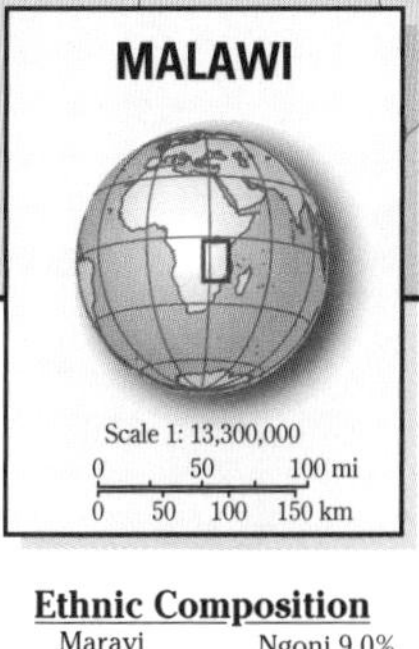

MALAWI

Scale 1: 13,300,000

0 50 100 mi

0 50 100 150 km

Official name: Republic of Malawi
Head of government: President
Official language: none
Monetary unit: Malawi kwacha
Area: 45,747 sq. mi. (118,484 sq. km.)
Population (2005): 12,707,000
GNP per capita (2004): U.S.$170
Principal exports (2003): tobacco 52.0%, sugar 14.9%, tea 7.4%; reexports 2.0% *to* (2004): South Africa 13.4%; U.S. 12.2%; Germany 11.9%; Egypt 8.6%; U.K. 6.8%

Ethnic Composition

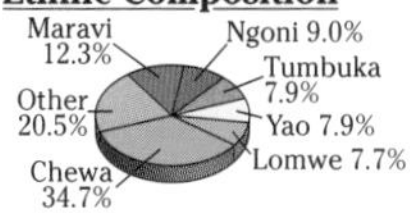

Maravi 12.3%
Ngoni 9.0%
Tumbuka 7.9%
Other 20.5%
Yao 7.9%
Lomwe 7.7%
Chewa 34.7%

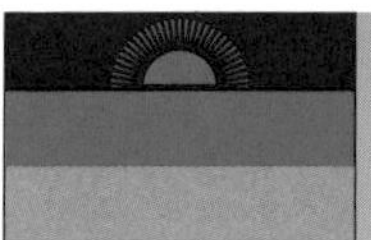

The flag of the Malawi Congress Party was striped black for the African people, red for the blood of martyrs, and green for the vegetation and climate. The country's name means "flaming waters," referring to the setting sun on Lake Malawi. With independence on July 6, 1964, a new flag was created by adding the sun symbol to the party flag.

Official name: Malaysia
Head of government: Prime Minister
Official language: Malay
Monetary unit: ringgit, or Malaysian dollar
Area: 127,355 sq. mi. (329,847 sq. km.)
Population (2005): 26,130,000
GNP per capita (2004): U.S.$4,650
Principal exports (2002): microcircuits, transistors, and valves 20.5%, computers/office machines 18.4%, telecommunication equipment 5.4%, crude petroleum 3.3% *to:* U.S. 20.2%; Singapore 17.1%; Japan 11.2%

Ethnic Composition

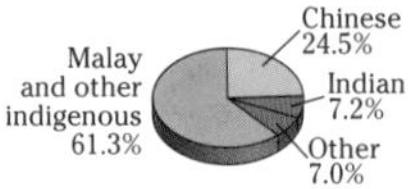

Malay and other indigenous 61.3%
Chinese 24.5%
Indian 7.2%
Other 7.0%

The flag hoisted on May 26, 1950, had 11 stripes, a crescent, and an 11-pointed star. The number of stripes and star points was increased to 14 on Sept. 16, 1963. Yellow is a royal color in Malaysia while red, white, and blue indicate connections with the Commonwealth. The crescent is a reminder that the population is mainly Muslim.

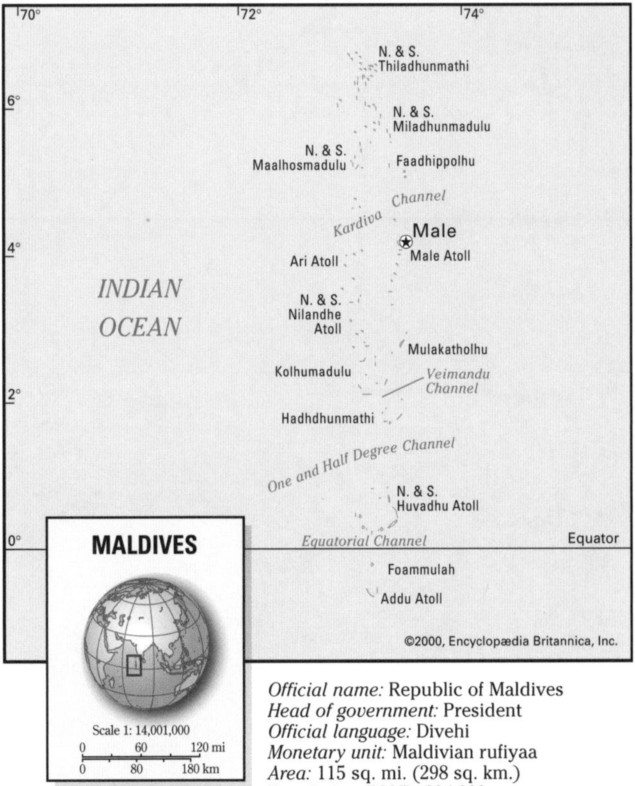
70°
72°
74°
6°
4°
2°
0°
N. & S.
Thiladhunmathi
N. & S.
Miladhunmadulu
N. & S.
Maalhosmadulu
Faadhippolhu
Kardiva Channel
Male
Male Atoll
Ari Atoll
INDIAN
OCEAN
N. & S.
Nilandhe
Atoll
Mulakatholhu
Kolhumadulu
Veimandu
Channel
Hadhdhunmathi
One and Half Degree Channel
N. & S.
Huvadhu Atoll
Equatorial Channel
Equator
Foammulah
Addu Atoll
©2000, Encyclopædia Britannica, Inc.
MALDIVES
Scale 1: 14,001,000
0 60 120 mi
0 80 180 km

Official name: Republic of Maldives
Head of government: President
Official language: Divehi
Monetary unit: Maldivian rufiyaa
Area: 115 sq. mi. (298 sq. km.)
Population (2005): 294,000
GNP per capita (2004): U.S.$2,510
Principal exports (2004): domestic export 70.9%, of which fish 50.6%; garments 18.4%; reexports 29.1% *to:* United States 26.5%; Thailand 23.5%; Sri Lanka 12.3%; Japan 11.7%; U.K. 9.8%

Age Breakdown

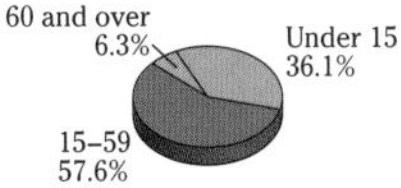
60 and over
6.3%
Under 15
36.1%
15–59
57.6%

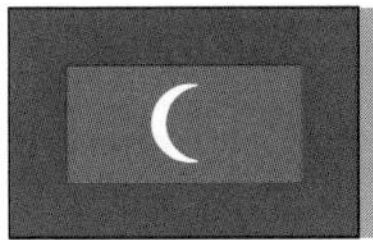

Maldivian ships long used a plain red ensign like those flown by Arabian and African nations. While a British protectorate in the early 20th century, the Maldives adopted a flag which was only slightly altered upon independence (July 26, 1965). The green panel and white crescent are symbolic of Islam, progress, prosperity, and peace.

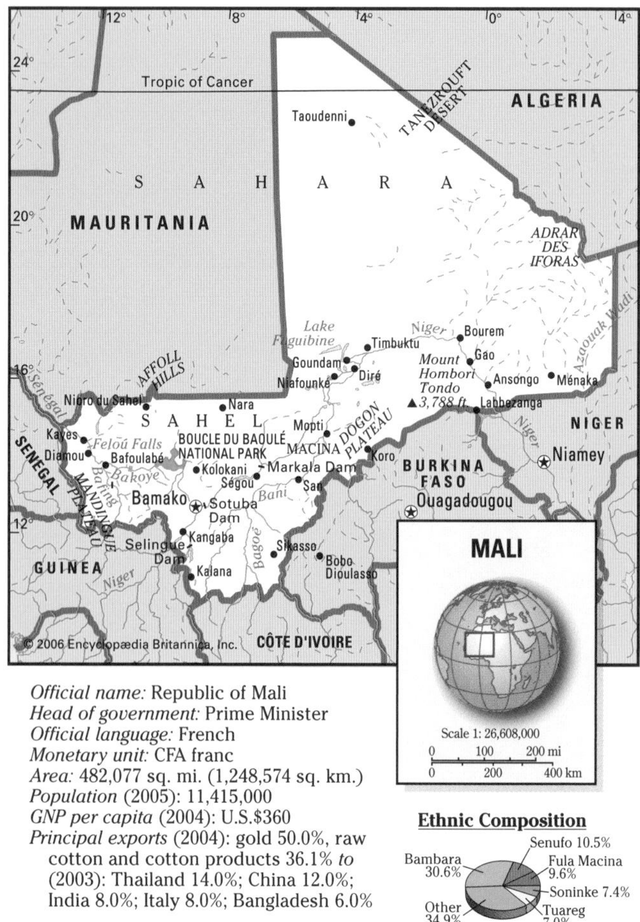

Official name: Republic of Mali
Head of government: Prime Minister
Official language: French
Monetary unit: CFA franc
Area: 482,077 sq. mi. (1,248,574 sq. km.)
Population (2005): 11,415,000
GNP per capita (2004): U.S.$360
Principal exports (2004): gold 50.0%, raw cotton and cotton products 36.1% *to* (2003): Thailand 14.0%; China 12.0%; India 8.0%; Italy 8.0%; Bangladesh 6.0%

Ethnic Composition

Bambara 30.6%
Senufo 10.5%
Fula Macina 9.6%
Soninke 7.4%
Tuareg 7.0%
Other 34.9%

Designed for the Mali-Senegal union of 1959, the flag originally included a human figure, the Kanaga, in its center. In 1960 Senegal and Mali divided. Muslims in Mali objected to the Kanaga, and on March 1, 1961, the figure was dropped. Green, yellow, and red are the Pan-African colors and are used by many former French territories.

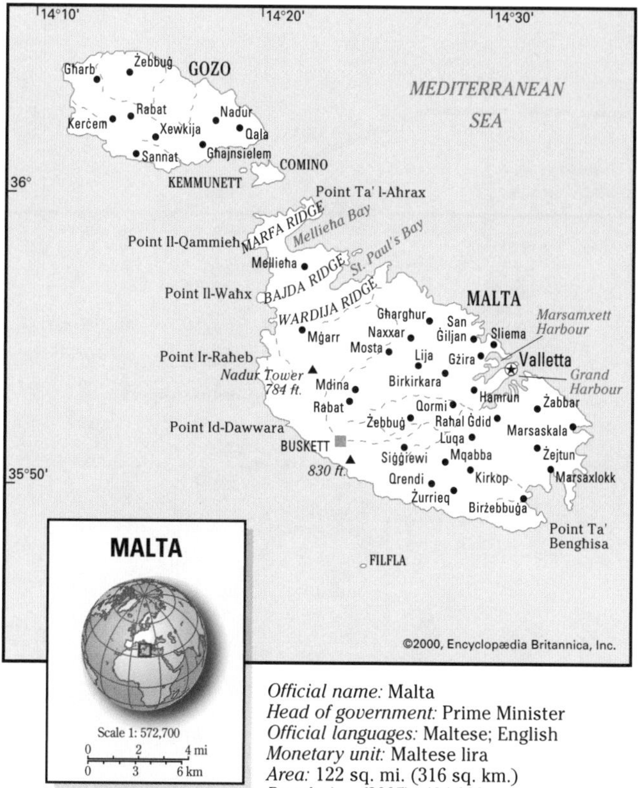

14°10' 14°20' 14°30'

GOZO
Għarb
Żebbuġ
Rabat
Nadur
Kerċem
Xewkija
Qala
Sannat
Għajnsielem
COMINO
KEMMUNETT
36°
MEDITERRANEAN SEA
Point Ta' l-Aħrax
MARFA RIDGE
Mellieħa Bay
St. Paul's Bay
Point Il-Qammieħ
Mellieħa
BAJDA RIDGE
Point Il-Waħx
WARDIJA RIDGE
MALTA
Għargħur
San Ġiljan
Sliema
Marsamxett Harbour
Mġarr
Naxxar
Mosta
Lija
Gżira
Valletta
Point Ir-Raħeb
Nadur Tower 784 ft.
Mdina
Birkirkara
Grand Harbour
Rabat
Qormi
Ħamrun
Żabbar
Żebbuġ
Raħal Ġdid
Point Id-Dawwara
Marsaskala
BUSKETT
Luqa
Siġġiewi
Mqabba
Żejtun
830 ft.
Kirkop
Marsaxlokk
35°50'
Qrendi
Żurrieq
Birżebbuġa
Point Ta' Benghisa
FILFLA

MALTA

Scale 1: 572,700
0 2 4 mi
0 3 6 km

Official name: Malta
Head of government: Prime Minister
Official languages: Maltese; English
Monetary unit: Maltese lira
Area: 122 sq. mi. (316 sq. km.)
Population (2005): 404,000
GNP per capita (2004): U.S.$12,250
Principal exports (2004): machinery and transport equipment 63.9%, basic manufactures 18.8%, crude petroleum 4.4% *to:* Singapore 15.2%; U.S. 11.6%; France 10.9%; U.K. 10.0%; Germany 8.9%

Age Breakdown

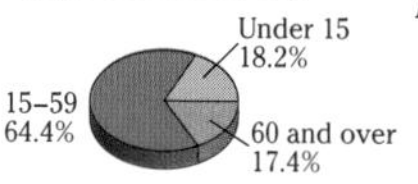

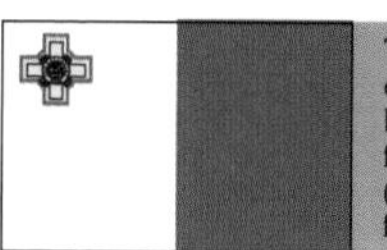

The Maltese flag was supposedly based on an 11th-century coat of arms, and a red flag with a white cross was used by the Knights of Malta from the Middle Ages. The current flag dates from independence within the Commonwealth (Sept. 21, 1964). The George Cross was granted by the British for the heroic defense of the island in World War II.

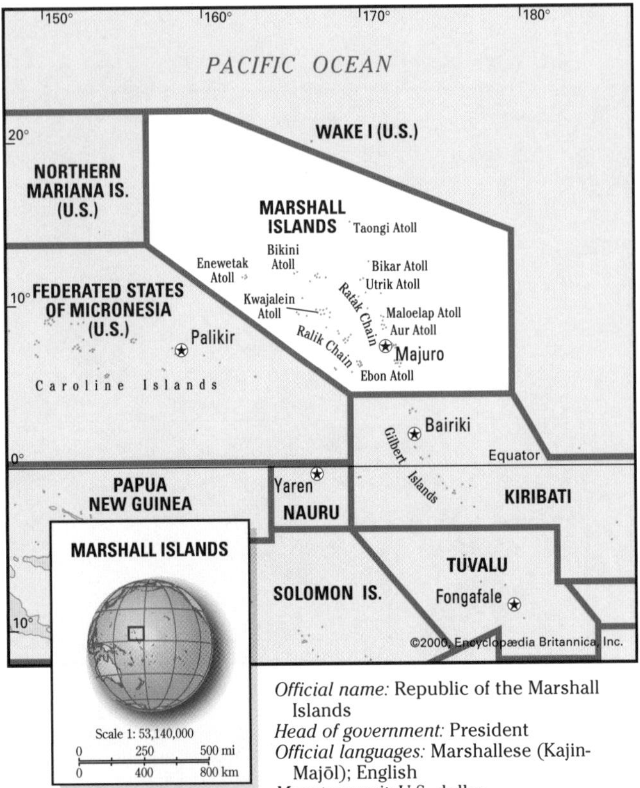
150°
160°
170°
180°
PACIFIC OCEAN
20°
WAKE I (U.S.)
NORTHERN MARIANA IS. (U.S.)
MARSHALL ISLANDS
Taongi Atoll
Bikini Atoll
Enewetak Atoll
Bikar Atoll
Utrik Atoll
Ratak Chain
Kwajalein Atoll
Maloelap Atoll
Aur Atoll
Ralik Chain
Majuro
Ebon Atoll
10°
FEDERATED STATES OF MICRONESIA (U.S.)
Palikir
Caroline Islands
Bairiki
Gilbert Islands
Equator
0°
PAPUA NEW GUINEA
Yaren
NAURU
KIRIBATI
TUVALU
SOLOMON IS.
Fongafale
10°
©2000, Encyclopædia Britannica, Inc.
MARSHALL ISLANDS
Scale 1: 53,140,000
0 250 500 mi
0 400 800 km

Official name: Republic of the Marshall Islands
Head of government: President
Official languages: Marshallese (Kajin-Majōl); English
Monetary unit: U.S. dollar
Area: 70.05 sq. mi. (181.43 sq. km.)
Population (2005): 56,300
GNP per capita (2004): U.S.$2,710
Principal exports (2000): chilled fish n.a.; crude coconut oil 14.7%, aquarium fish 6.2% *to:* U.S. *c.* 71%; other *c.* 29%

Religious Affiliation

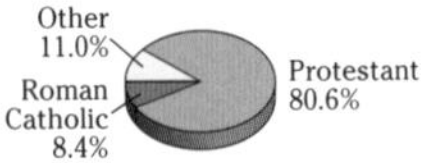
Other 11.0%
Roman Catholic 8.4%
Protestant 80.6%

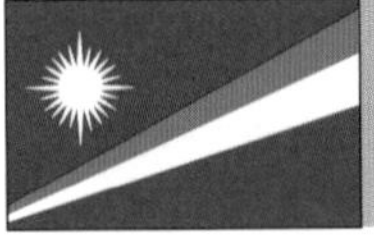

The island nation hoisted its flag on May 1, 1979. The blue stands for the ocean. The white is for brightness while the orange is for bravery and wealth. The two stripes joined symbolize the Equator, and they increase in width to show growth and vitality. The rays of the star are for the municipalities; its four long rays recall a Christian cross.

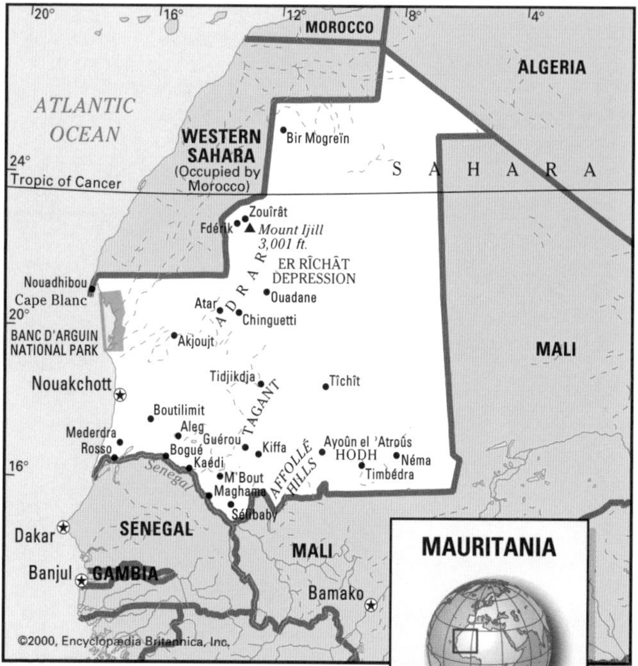

MAURITANIA

Scale 1: 26,914,000
0 100 200 mi
0 200 400 km

Official name: Islamic Republic of Mauritania
Head of government: Chairman of the Military Council for Justice and Democracy
Official language: Arabic
Monetary unit: ouguiya
Area: 398,000 sq. mi. (1,030,700 sq. km.)
Population (2005): 3,069,000
GNP per capita (2004): U.S.$420
Principal exports (2002): iron ore 55.6%, fish 43.4% *to:* Italy 14.8%; France 14.4%; Spain 12.1%; Germany 10.8%

Age Breakdown

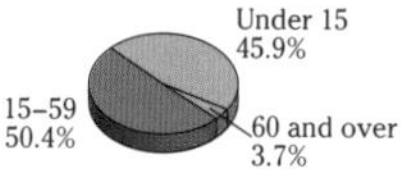

Under 15 45.9%
15–59 50.4%
60 and over 3.7%

In 1958 Mauritania was granted autonomous status within the French Community. The current flag replaced the French tricolor on April 1, 1959, and no changes were made to the design at independence (Nov. 28, 1960). The green background of the flag and its star and crescent are traditional Muslim symbols that have been in use for centuries.

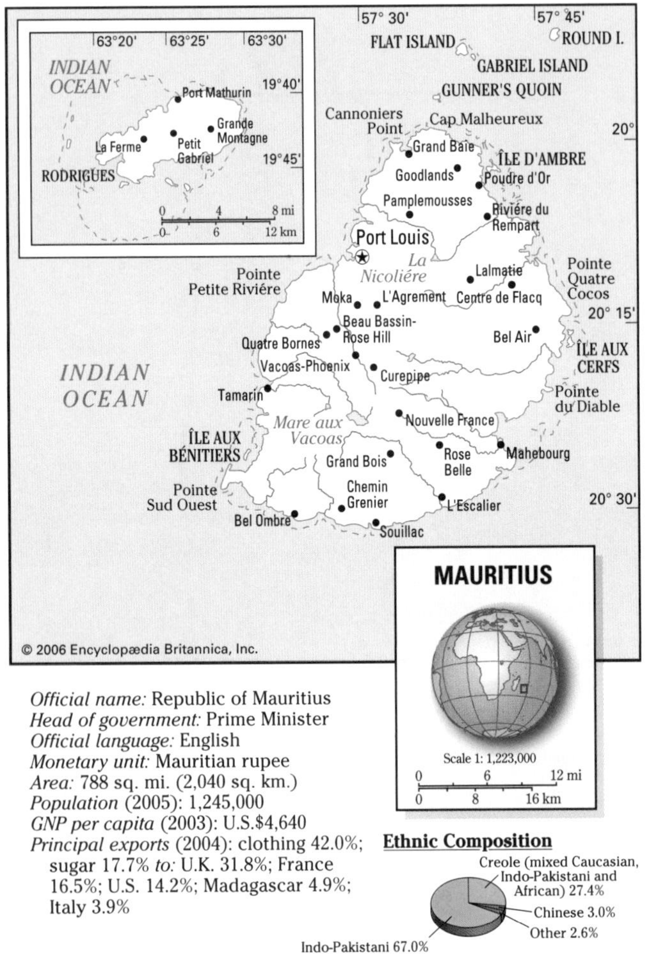

Official name: Republic of Mauritius
Head of government: Prime Minister
Official language: English
Monetary unit: Mauritian rupee
Area: 788 sq. mi. (2,040 sq. km.)
Population (2005): 1,245,000
GNP per capita (2003): U.S.$4,640
Principal exports (2004): clothing 42.0%; sugar 17.7% *to:* U.K. 31.8%; France 16.5%; U.S. 14.2%; Madagascar 4.9%; Italy 3.9%

In 1968 this flag was first flown on March 12, at the time of Mauritius's independence from the United Kingdom. The flag's red stands for the struggle for freedom, while the blue represents the Indian Ocean. The light of independence is shown by yellow. Green is for agriculture and the year-round flourishing of the island's plant life.

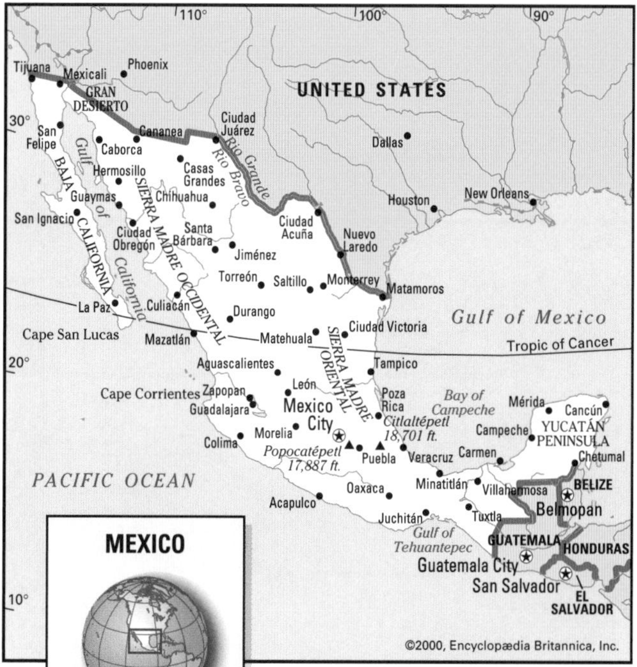

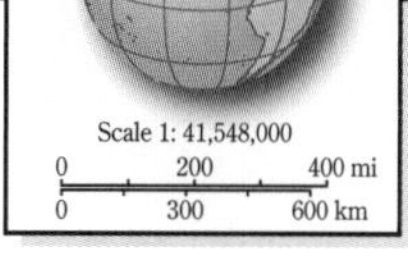

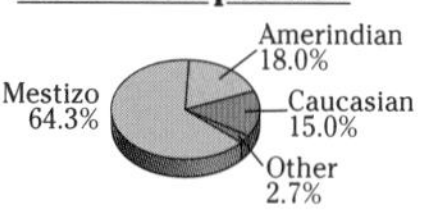

Official name: United Mexican States
Head of government: President
Official language: Spanish
Monetary unit: Mexican peso
Area: 758,449 sq. mi. (1,964,375 sq. km.)
Population (2005): 107,029,000
GNP per capita (2004): U.S.$6,770
Principal exports (2004): non-maquiladora sector 53.6%, of which road vehicles and parts 13.5%, crude petroleum 11.3%, machinery 8.6%; maquiladora sector 46.4%, of which electronics 21.7%, nonelectrical machinery 11.3% *to:* U.S. 87.6%; Canada 1.7%; Germany 0.9%

Ethnic Composition

Mestizo 64.3%
Amerindian 18.0%
Caucasian 15.0%
Other 2.7%

The green-white-red tricolor was officially established in 1821. Green is for independence, white for Roman Catholicism, and red for union. The emblem depicts the scene supposedly witnessed by the Aztecs in 1325: an eagle with a snake in its beak standing upon a cactus growing out of rocks in the water. The flag was modified on Sept. 17, 1968.

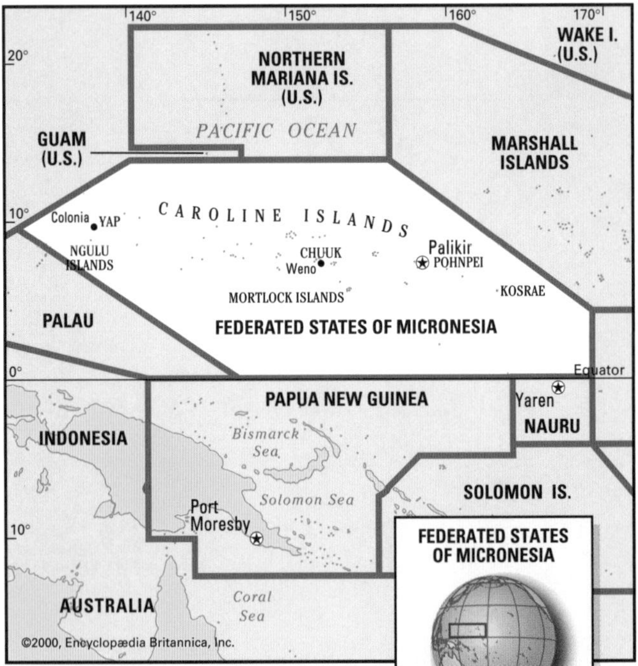
140°
150°
160°
170°
20°
10°
0°
10°
WAKE I. (U.S.)
NORTHERN MARIANA IS. (U.S.)
PACIFIC OCEAN
GUAM (U.S.)
MARSHALL ISLANDS
CAROLINE ISLANDS
Colonia
YAP
NGULU ISLANDS
CHUUK
Weno
Palikir
POHNPEI
KOSRAE
MORTLOCK ISLANDS
PALAU
FEDERATED STATES OF MICRONESIA
Equator
PAPUA NEW GUINEA
Yaren
NAURU
INDONESIA
Bismarck Sea
Solomon Sea
SOLOMON IS.
Port Moresby
AUSTRALIA
Coral Sea
©2000, Encyclopædia Britannica, Inc.

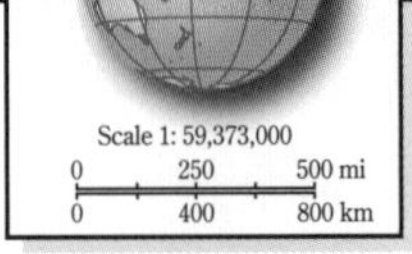
FEDERATED STATES OF MICRONESIA
Scale 1: 59,373,000
0
250
500 mi
0
400
800 km

Official name: Federated States of Micronesia
Head of government: President
Official language: none
Monetary unit: U.S. dollar
Area: 270.8 sq. mi. (701.4 sq. km.)
Population (2005): 113,000
GNP per capita (2004): U.S.$1,990
Principal exports (2002): marine products 63.3%, clothing and textiles 24.9%, betel nuts 6.1% *to:* United States 25.5%; Guam 7.9%; Northern Marianas 3.4%; unspecified 44.0%

Ethnic Composition

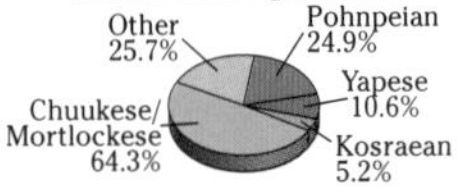
Other 25.7%
Pohnpeian 24.9%
Yapese 10.6%
Chuukese/ Mortlockese 64.3%
Kosraean 5.2%

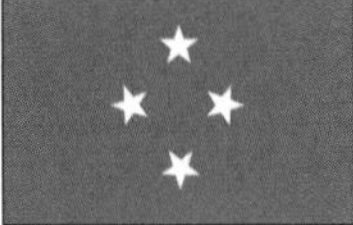

On Nov. 30, 1978, the flag of the former United States trust territory was approved by an interim congress. Based on the symbolism of the territory, the flag has stars for the four states of Micronesia. After sovereignty was granted in 1986, a dark blue background (for the Pacific Ocean) was substituted for the original "United Nations blue."

MOLDOVA

Scale 1: 5,251,000

0 20 40 mi

0 30 60 km

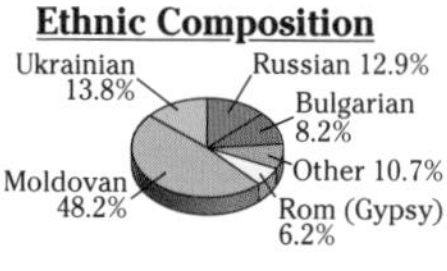

©2000, Encyclopædia Britannica, Inc.

Official name: Republic of Moldova
Head of government: Prime Minister
Official language: Romanian
Monetary unit: Moldovan leu
Area: 13,068 sq. mi. (33,845 sq. km.)
Population (2005): 4,206,000
GNP per capita (2004): U.S.$710
Principal exports (2004): food, beverages, and tobacco 35.1%; textiles and apparel 17.3% *to:* Russia 55.8%; Italy 13.9%; Romania 10.0%; Germany 7.3%; Ukraine 6.6%

Ethnic Composition

Moldovan 48.2%
Ukrainian 13.8%
Russian 12.9%
Bulgarian 8.2%
Other 10.7%
Rom (Gypsy) 6.2%

By 1989, Moldovans protested against communist rule, and the traditional tricolor of blue-yellow-red, which had flown briefly in 1917–18, became a popular symbol. It replaced the communist flag in May 1990 and remained after independence in 1991. The shield has an eagle on whose breast are an aurochs head, a crescent, a star, and a flower.

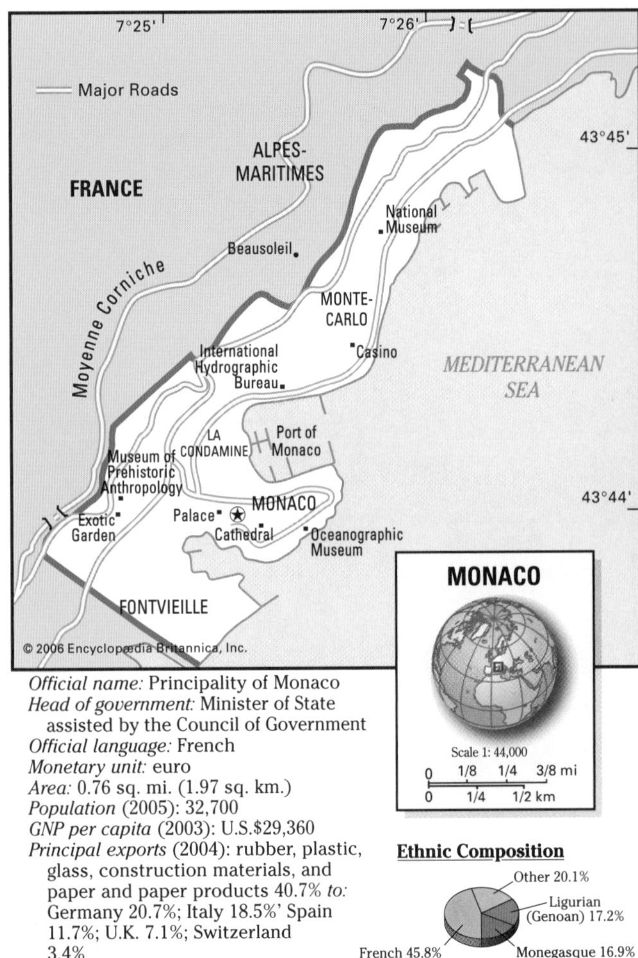

Official name: Principality of Monaco
Head of government: Minister of State assisted by the Council of Government
Official language: French
Monetary unit: euro
Area: 0.76 sq. mi. (1.97 sq. km.)
Population (2005): 32,700
GNP per capita (2003): U.S.$29,360
Principal exports (2004): rubber, plastic, glass, construction materials, and paper and paper products 40.7% *to:* Germany 20.7%; Italy 18.5%' Spain 11.7%; U.K. 7.1%; Switzerland 3.4%

Ethnic Composition

Other 20.1%
Ligurian (Genoan) 17.2%
Monegasque 16.9%
French 45.8%

Used at the United Nations and by private citizens, Monaco's national flag's plain red and white are from the ruling Grimaldi family's coat of arms. The coat of arms shows a red and white shield flanked by Franciscan monks. Francois Grimaldi disguised himself as such a monk in capturing the fortress of Monaco in 1297.

MONGOLIA

Scale 1: 36,059,000

0 150 300 mi

0 200 400 km

Official name: Mongolia
Head of government: Prime Minister
Official language: Khalkha Mongolian
Monetary unit: tugrik
Area: 603,930 sq. mi. (1,564,160 sq. km.)
Population (2005): 2,550,000
GNP per capita (2004): U.S.$590
Principal exports (2001): copper concentrate 28.1%, gold 14.3%, cashmere products 13.4%, fluorspar 3.8% *to* (2004): China 50.7%; U.S. 26.3%; Canada 5.3%; U.K. 4.3%

Ethnic Composition

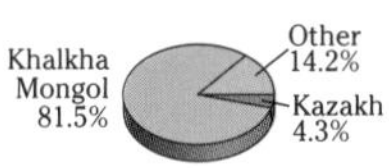

In 1945, the flag symbolizing communism (red) and Mongol nationalism (blue) was established. Near the hoist is a *soyonba*, a grouping of philosophical symbols (flame, sun, moon, yin-yang, triangles, and bars). Yellow traditionally stood for Lamaist Buddhism. On Jan. 12, 1992, a five-pointed star (for Communism) was removed from the flag.

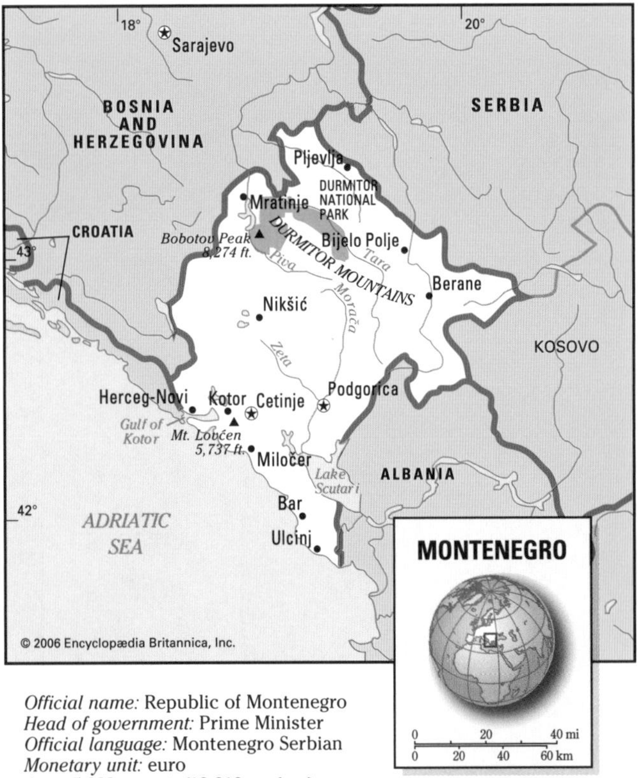
18°
Sarajevo
20°
BOSNIA AND HERZEGOVINA
SERBIA
Pljevlja
DURMITOR NATIONAL PARK
Mratinje
CROATIA
Bobotov Peak 8,274 ft.
DURMITOR MOUNTAINS
Bijelo Polje
Tara
Piva
43°
Berane
Nikšić
Morača
KOSOVO
Zeta
Herceg-Novi
Kotor
Cetinje
Podgorica
Gulf of Kotor
Mt. Lovćen 5,737 ft.
Miločer
Lake Scutari
ALBANIA
42°
Bar
ADRIATIC SEA
Ulcinj
MONTENEGRO
0 20 40 mi
0 20 40 60 km
© 2006 Encyclopædia Britannica, Inc.

Official name: Republic of Montenegro
Head of government: Prime Minister
Official language: Montenegro Serbian
Monetary unit: euro
Area: 5,333 sq. mi. (13,812 sq. km.)
Population (2005): 618,000
GDP per capita (2004): U.S.$3,080
Principal exports (2003): products of aluminum industry 87.4%; tobacco products 3.6% *to:* Switzerland 84.0%; Italy 6.1%; U.S. Virgin Islands 2.7%

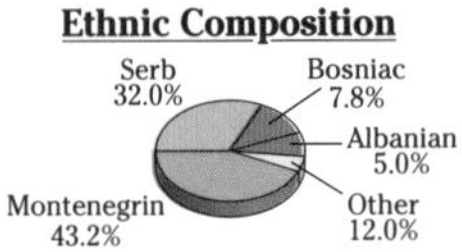
Ethnic Composition
Serb 32.0%
Bosniac 7.8%
Albanian 5.0%
Other 12.0%
Montenegrin 43.2%

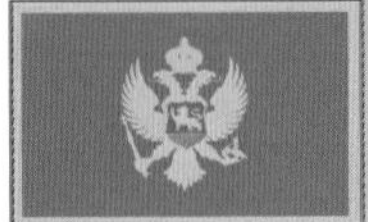

Independent in 1878, Montenegro flew the Russian-inspired red-blue-white flag. After World War I, it became part of Yugoslavia, without its own flag. Serbia-Montenegro stayed in Yugoslavia after the other republics seceded in the 1990s. In 2004, Montenegro adopted this new flag, showing the arms of the ancient Njegoš dynasty, and became independent in 2006.

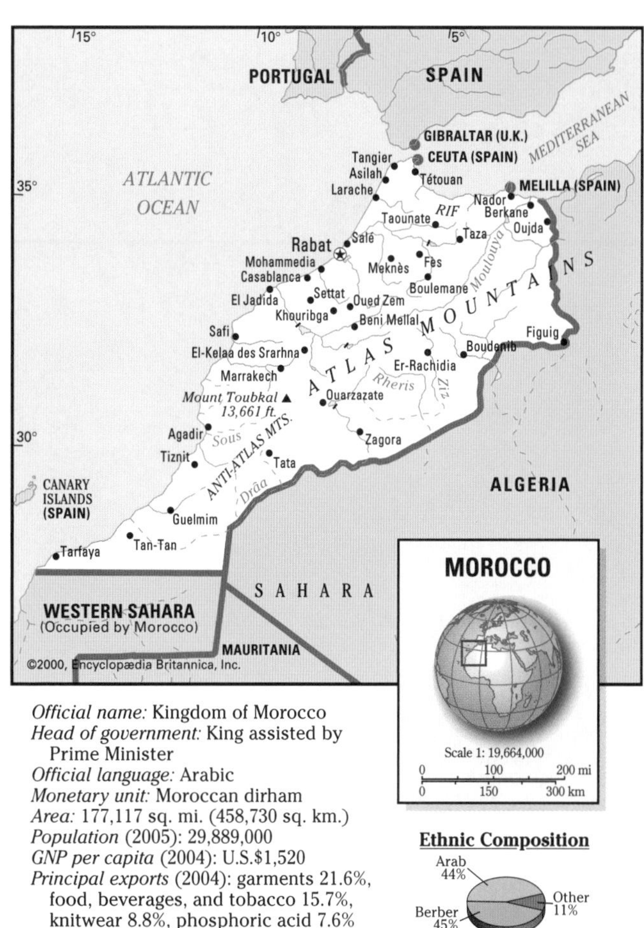

Official name: Kingdom of Morocco
Head of government: King assisted by Prime Minister
Official language: Arabic
Monetary unit: Moroccan dirham
Area: 177,117 sq. mi. (458,730 sq. km.)
Population (2005): 29,889,000
GNP per capita (2004): U.S.$1,520
Principal exports (2004): garments 21.6%, food, beverages, and tobacco 15.7%, knitwear 8.8%, phosphoric acid 7.6% *to:* France 33.1%; Spain 17.4%; U.K. 7.7%; U.S. 4.1%

Ethnic Composition

Arab 44%
Other 11%
Berber 45%

After Morocco was subjected to the rule of France and Spain in the 20th century, the plain red flag, which had been displayed on its ships, was modified on Nov. 17, 1915. To its center was added the ancient pentagram known as the "Seal of Solomon." The flag continued in use even after the French granted independence in 1956.

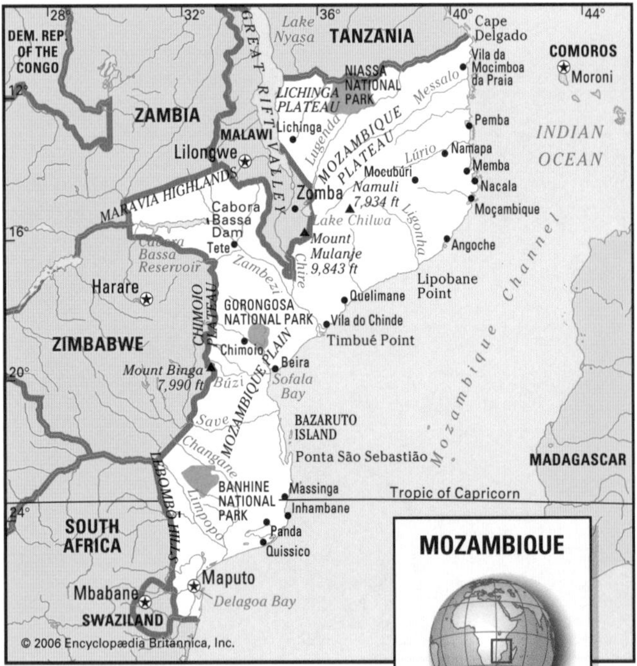

MOZAMBIQUE

Scale 1: 26,326,000

0 75 150 225 mi

0 100 200 300 km

Official name: Republic of Mozambique
Head of government: President
Official language: Portuguese
Monetary unit: metical
Area: 313,661 sq. mi. (812,379 sq. km.)
Population (2005): 19,407,000
GNP per capita (2004): U.S.$250
Principal exports (2003): aluminum 54.4%, electricity 10.9%, prawns 7.3%, cotton 3.1% *to:* Belgium 43.5%; South Africa 16.2%; Spain 6.7%

Ethnic Composition

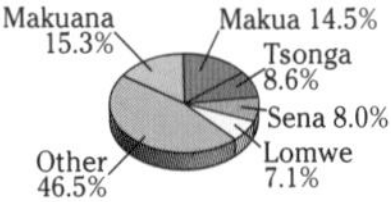

Makuana 15.3%
Makua 14.5%
Tsonga 8.6%
Sena 8.0%
Lomwe 7.1%
Other 46.5%

In the early 1960s, anti-Portuguese groups adopted flags of green (for forests), black (for the majority population), white (for rivers and the ocean), gold (for peace and mineral wealth), and red (for the blood of liberation). The current flag was readopted in 1983; on its star are a book, a hoe, and an assault rifle.

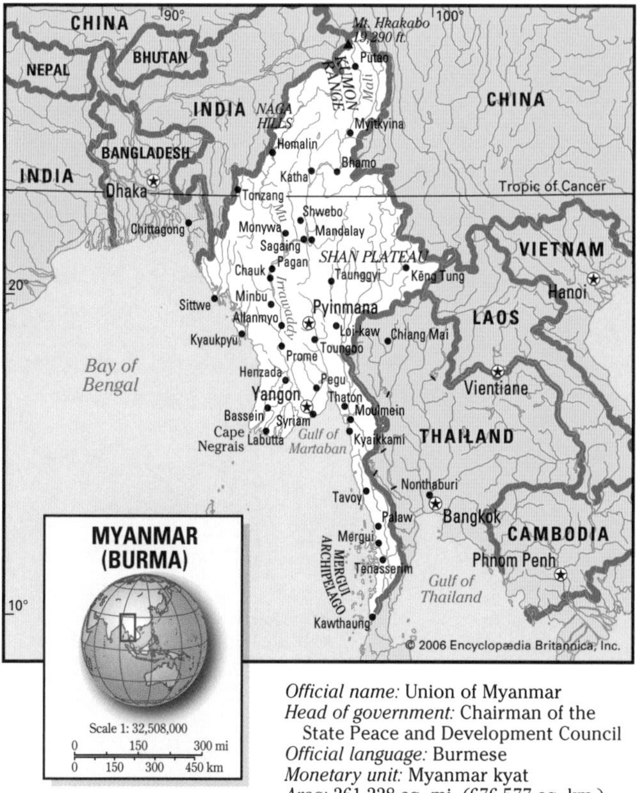

MYANMAR (BURMA)

Scale 1: 32,508,000
0 150 300 mi
0 150 300 450 km

Ethnic Composition

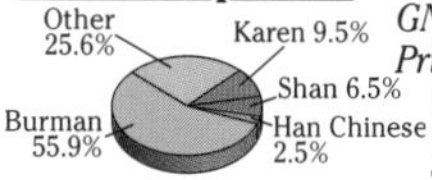

Burman 55.9%
Other 25.6%
Karen 9.5%
Shan 6.5%
Han Chinese 2.5%

Official name: Union of Myanmar
Head of government: Chairman of the State Peace and Development Council
Official language: Burmese
Monetary unit: Myanmar kyat
Area: 261,228 sq. mi. (676,577 sq. km.)
Population (2005): 46,997,000
GNP per capita (2004): U.S.$1,070
Principal exports (2002-03): mineral fuels 29.6%, food, beverages, and tobacco 19.0%, garments 14.0%, wood 9.4% *to:* Thailand 37.0%; India 14.0%; China 6.2%; Japan 5.1%; U.K. 4.0%

The current flag design dates to Jan. 4, 1974. Its 14 stars, for the states and divisions of Myanmar, form a circle around a cogwheel, for industrial workers, and ears and leaves of rice, symbolizing the peasantry. Blue is for truthfulness and strength; red for bravery, unity, and determination; and white for truth, purity, and steadfastness.

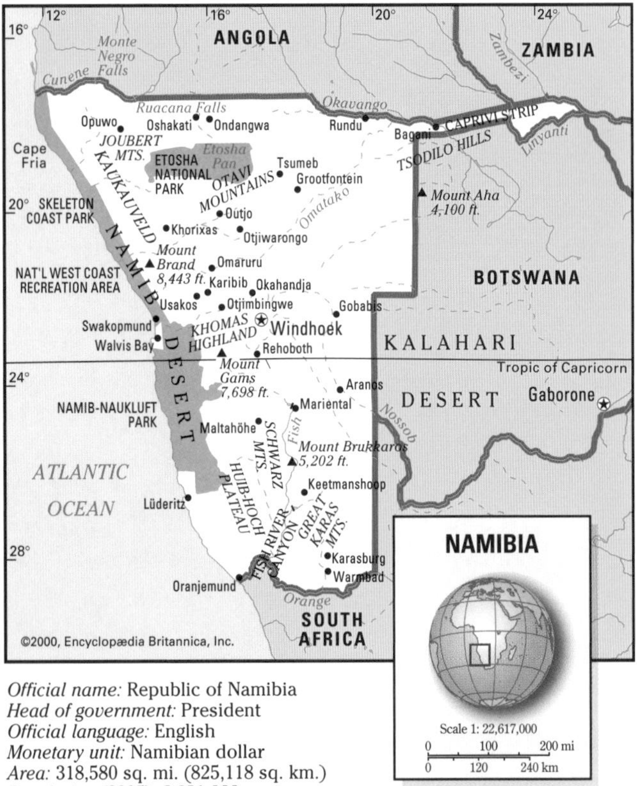

NAMIBIA

Scale 1: 22,617,000

Official name: Republic of Namibia
Head of government: President
Official language: English
Monetary unit: Namibian dollar
Area: 318,580 sq. mi. (825,118 sq. km.)
Population (2005): 2,031,000
GNP per capita (2004): U.S.$2,370
Principal exports (2003): diamonds 40.9%, other minerals 14.6%, meat preparations 6.3% *to:* South Africa 31.5%; Angola 24.9%; Spain 12.8%; U.K. 10.4%; U.S. 2.7%

Ethnic Composition

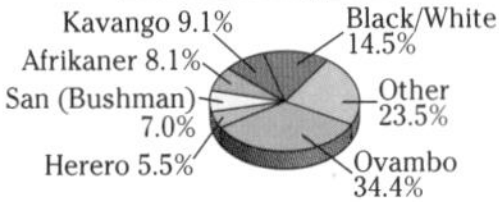

Kavango 9.1%
Afrikaner 8.1%
San (Bushman) 7.0%
Herero 5.5%
Black/White 14.5%
Other 23.5%
Ovambo 34.4%

The flag was adopted on Feb. 2, 1990, and hoisted on independence from South Africa, March 21, 1990. Its colors are those of the South West Africa People's Organization: blue (for sky and ocean), red (for heroism and determination), and green (for agriculture). The gold sun represents life and energy while the white stripes are for water resources.

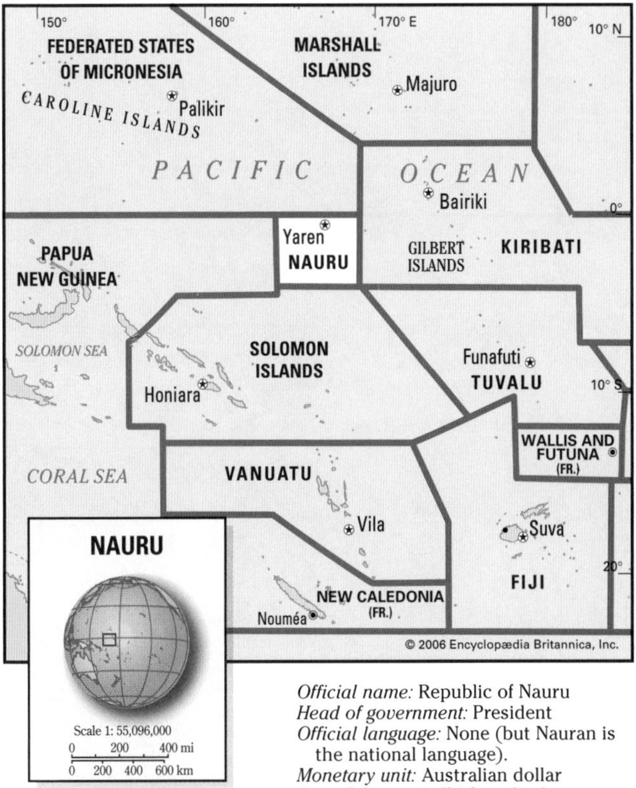
150°
160°
170° E
180°
10° N
FEDERATED STATES OF MICRONESIA
MARSHALL ISLANDS
Majuro
CAROLINE ISLANDS
Palikir
PACIFIC OCEAN
Bairiki
0°
Yaren
NAURU
GILBERT ISLANDS
KIRIBATI
PAPUA NEW GUINEA
SOLOMON SEA
SOLOMON ISLANDS
Honiara
Funafuti
TUVALU
10° S
WALLIS AND FUTUNA (FR.)
CORAL SEA
VANUATU
Vila
Suva
FIJI
20°
NEW CALEDONIA (FR.)
Nouméa
NAURU
Scale 1: 55,096,000
0 200 400 mi
0 200 400 600 km
© 2006 Encyclopædia Britannica, Inc.

Official name: Republic of Nauru
Head of government: President
Official language: None (but Nauran is the national language).
Monetary unit: Australian dollar
Area: 8.2 sq. mi. (21.2 sq. km.)
Population (2005): 10,200
GNP per capita (2003): U.S.$3,740
Principal exports (1999): phosphate, virtually 100% *to* (2002): India 46.3%; South Korea 18.4%; Austrailia 10.6%; New Zealand 7.8%; U.S. 2.8%

Ethnic Composition

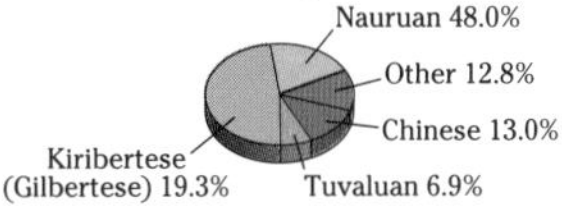
Nauruan 48.0%
Other 12.8%
Chinese 13.0%
Kiribertese (Gilbertese) 19.3%
Tuvaluan 6.9%

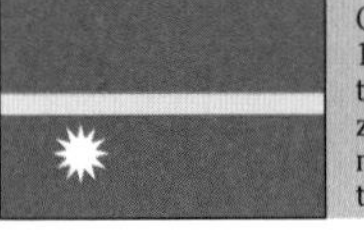

Celebrating its independence from Australia on January 31, 1968, Nauru showed this flag chosen from a local competition. The blue field is for the Pacific Ocean. Its yellow horizontal stripe stands for the equator, which lies about 40 miles north of the island republic. Representing the original 12 tribes of Nauru is the 12-pointed white star beneath.

NEPAL

Scale 1: 12,731,000

0 60 120 mi

0 90 180 km

Official name: Kingdom of Nepal
Head of government: King
Official language: Nepali
Monetary unit: Nepalese rupee
Area: 56,827 sq. mi. (147,181 sq. km.)
Population (2005): 27,133,000
GNP per capita (2004): U.S.$260
Principal exports (2000-01): garments 23.6%, carpets 15.4%, pashminas 12.4%, vegetable ghee 6.4% *to:* India 48.8%; U.S. 22.5%; Germany 8.5%; U.K. 2.8%; France 2.2%

Religious Affiliation

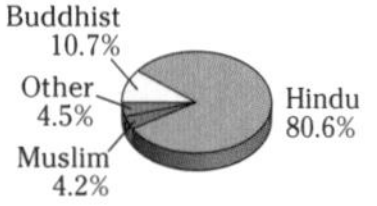

Buddhist 10.7%
Other 4.5%
Muslim 4.2%
Hindu 80.6%

Established on Dec. 16, 1962, Nepal's flag consists of two united pennant shapes; it is the only non-rectangular national flag in the world. In the upper segment is a moon with a crescent attached below; in the bottom segment appears a stylized sun. The symbols are for different dynasties and express a hope for the immortality of the nation. The crimson and blue colors are common in Nepali art.

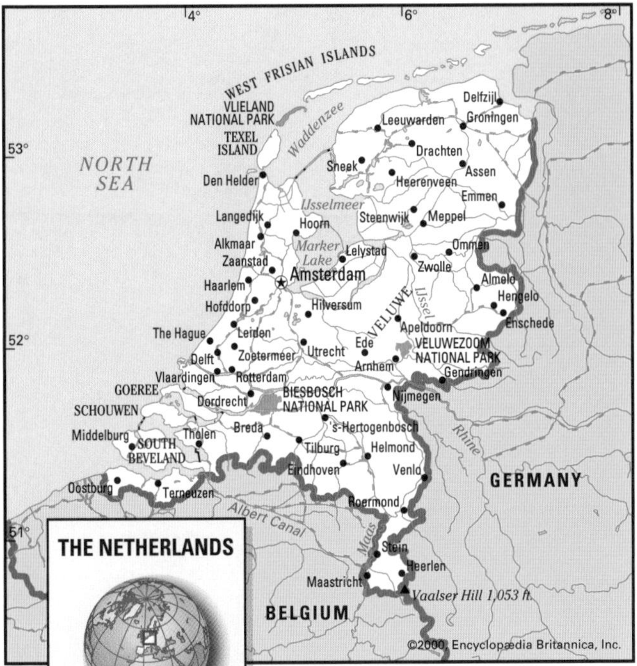

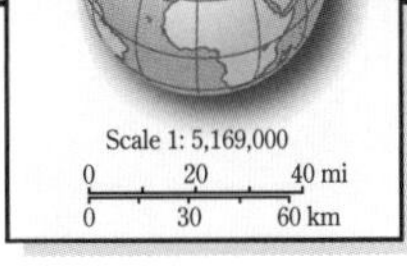

THE NETHERLANDS

Scale 1: 5,169,000

0 20 40 mi
0 30 60 km

Official name: Kingdom of The Netherlands
Head of government: Prime Minister
Official language: Dutch
Monetary unit: euro
Area: 16,033 sq. mi. (41,526 sq. km.)
Population (2005): 16,306,000
GNP per capita (2003): U.S.$26,310
Principal exports (2003): chemicals 16.7%, food 12.6%, computers and parts 10.5%, mineral fuels 8.3% *to:* Germany 24.4%; Belgium-Luxembourg 11.9%; U.K. 10.3%; France 10.0%

Religious Affiliation

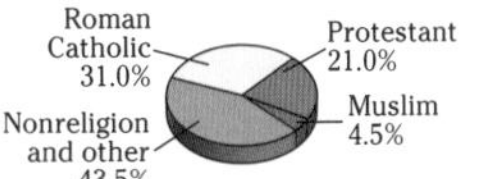

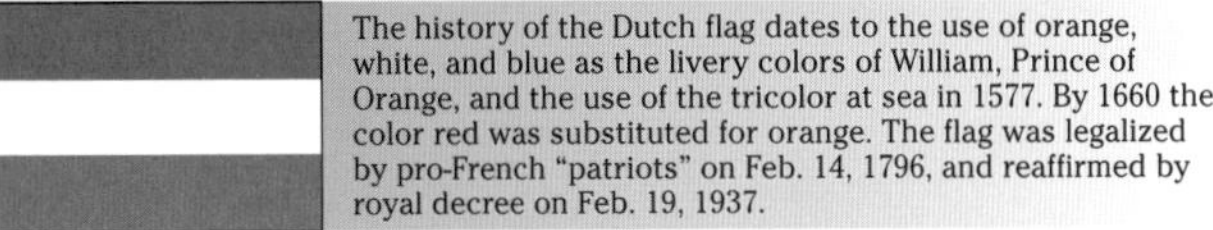

The history of the Dutch flag dates to the use of orange, white, and blue as the livery colors of William, Prince of Orange, and the use of the tricolor at sea in 1577. By 1660 the color red was substituted for orange. The flag was legalized by pro-French "patriots" on Feb. 14, 1796, and reaffirmed by royal decree on Feb. 19, 1937.

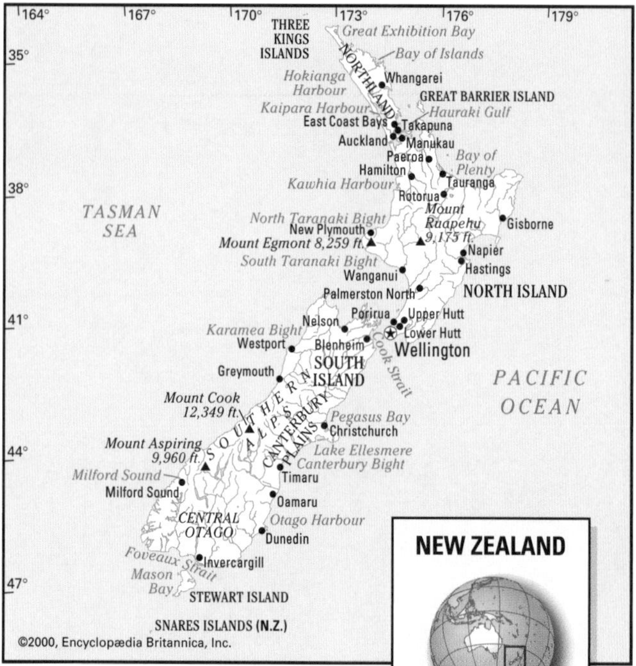

164°
167°
170°
173°
176°
179°
35°
38°
41°
44°
47°
THREE KINGS ISLANDS
Great Exhibition Bay
NORTHLAND
Bay of Islands
Hokianga Harbour
Whangarei
GREAT BARRIER ISLAND
Kaipara Harbour
Hauraki Gulf
East Coast Bays
Takapuna
Auckland
Manukau
Paeroa
Bay of Plenty
Hamilton
Kawhia Harbour
Tauranga
Rotorua
TASMAN SEA
Mount Ruapehu 9,175 ft.
North Taranaki Bight
New Plymouth
Gisborne
Mount Egmont 8,259 ft.
Napier
South Taranaki Bight
Hastings
Wanganui
Palmerston North
NORTH ISLAND
Porirua
Upper Hutt
Nelson
Karamea Bight
Lower Hutt
Westport
Blenheim
Wellington
Cook Strait
SOUTH ISLAND
Greymouth
PACIFIC OCEAN
SOUTHERN ALPS
Mount Cook 12,349 ft.
CANTERBURY PLAINS
Pegasus Bay
Christchurch
Mount Aspiring 9,960 ft.
Lake Ellesmere
Canterbury Bight
Milford Sound
Timaru
Milford Sound
Oamaru
CENTRAL OTAGO
Otago Harbour
Dunedin
Foveaux Strait
Invercargill
Mason Bay
STEWART ISLAND
SNARES ISLANDS (N.Z.)
©2000, Encyclopædia Britannica, Inc.
NEW ZEALAND
Scale 1: 23,005,000
0
100
200 mi
0
150
300 km

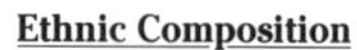

Official name: New Zealand
Head of government: Prime Minister
Official languages: English; Maori
Monetary unit: New Zealand dollar
Area: 104,454 sq. mi. (270,534 sq. km.)
Population (2005): 4,096,000
GNP per capita (2004): U.S.$20,310
Principal exports (2003): dairy products 16.1%, beef and sheep meat 13.1% wood and paper products 8.1%, machinery 4.6%, fish 4.1% *to:* Australia 20.9%; U.S. 14.9%; Japan 11.5%; China 5.0%; U.K. 4.6%

Ethnic Composition

Maori 13.5%
Asian 6.1%
European 73.8%
Other Polynesian 6.0%
Other 0.6%

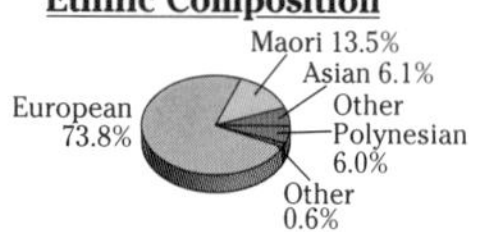

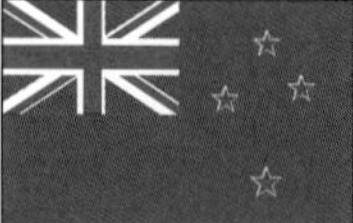

The Maori of New Zealand accepted British control in 1840, and a colonial flag was adopted on Jan. 15, 1867. It included the Union Jack in the canton and the letters "NZ" at the fly end. Later versions used the Southern Cross. Dominion status was granted on Sept. 26, 1907, and independence on Nov. 25, 1947, but the flag was unchanged.

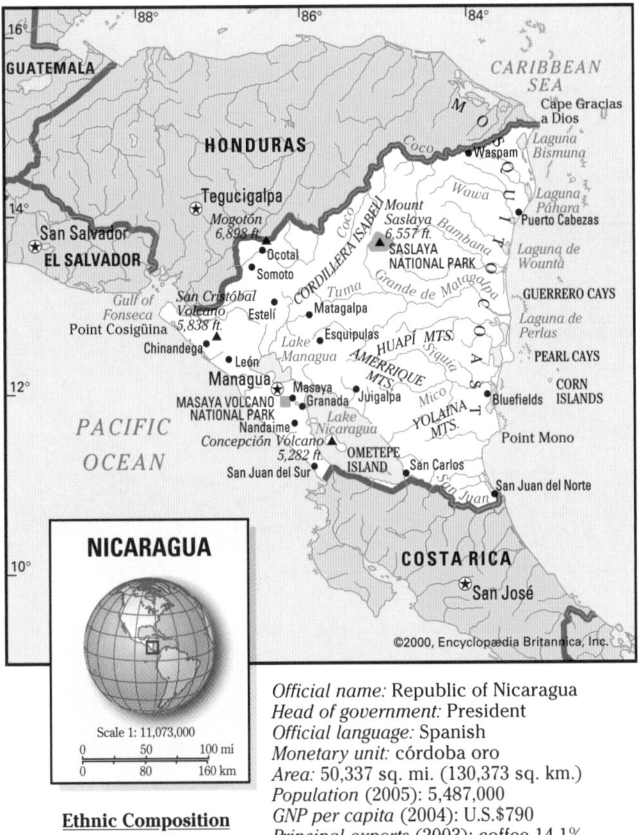

NICARAGUA

Scale 1: 11,073,000

0 50 100 mi

0 80 160 km

Official name: Republic of Nicaragua
Head of government: President
Official language: Spanish
Monetary unit: córdoba oro
Area: 50,337 sq. mi. (130,373 sq. km.)
Population (2005): 5,487,000
GNP per capita (2004): U.S.$790
Principal exports (2003): coffee 14.1%, beef 13.5%, lobster 6.0%, gold 5.8%, shrimp 5.5% *to:* United States 33.4%; El Salvador 17.3%; Costa Rica 8.1%; Honduras 7.2%; Mexico 4.6%

Ethnic Composition

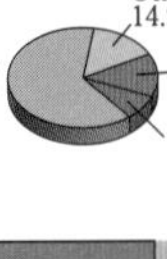

Mestizo 63.1%
Other 14.9%
White 14%
Black 8.0%

On Aug. 21, 1823, a blue-white-blue flag was adopted by the five member states of the United Provinces of Central America, which included Nicaragua. From the mid-19th century various flag designs were used in Nicaragua, but the old flag was readopted in 1908, with a modified coat of arms, and reaffirmed by law on Aug. 27, 1971.

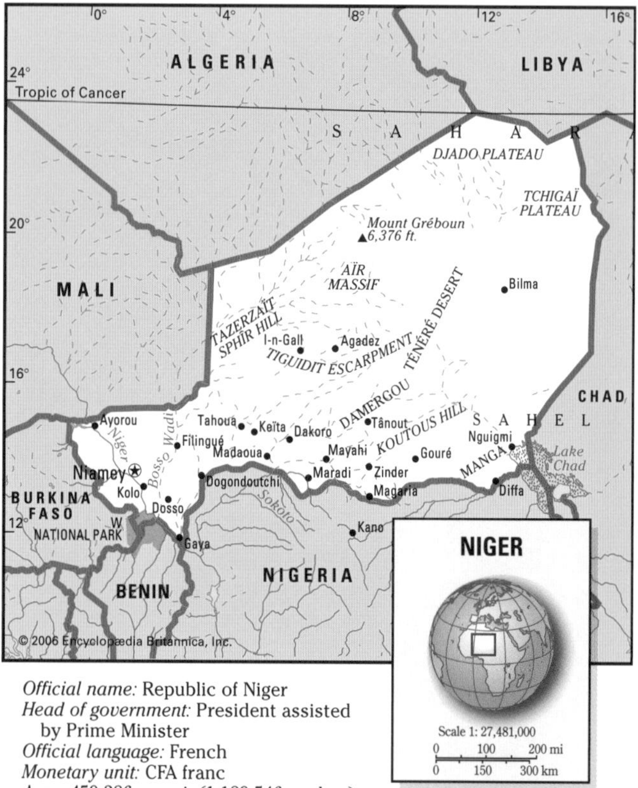

NIGER

Scale 1: 27,481,000
0 100 200 mi
0 150 300 km

Official name: Republic of Niger
Head of government: President assisted by Prime Minister
Official language: French
Monetary unit: CFA franc
Area: 459,286 sq. mi. (1,189,546 sq. km.)
Population (2005): 12,163,000
GNP per capita (2004): U.S.$230
Principal exports (2003): uranium 32.2%, reexports 17.9%, live cattle 17.5%, onions 7.7% *to:* France 37.1%; Nigeria 33.6%; Japan 17.2%; Spain 3.8%

Ethnolinguistic Composition

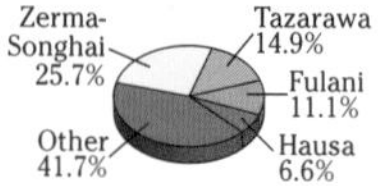

Zerma-Songhai 25.7%
Tazarawa 14.9%
Fulani 11.1%
Hausa 6.6%
Other 41.7%

The flag of Niger was chosen on Nov. 23, 1959. The white color is for purity, innocence, and civic spirit. The orange is for the Sahara Desert and the heroic efforts of citizens to live within it, while the orange central disk represents the sun. The green color stands for agriculture and hope; it is suggestive of the Niger River valley.

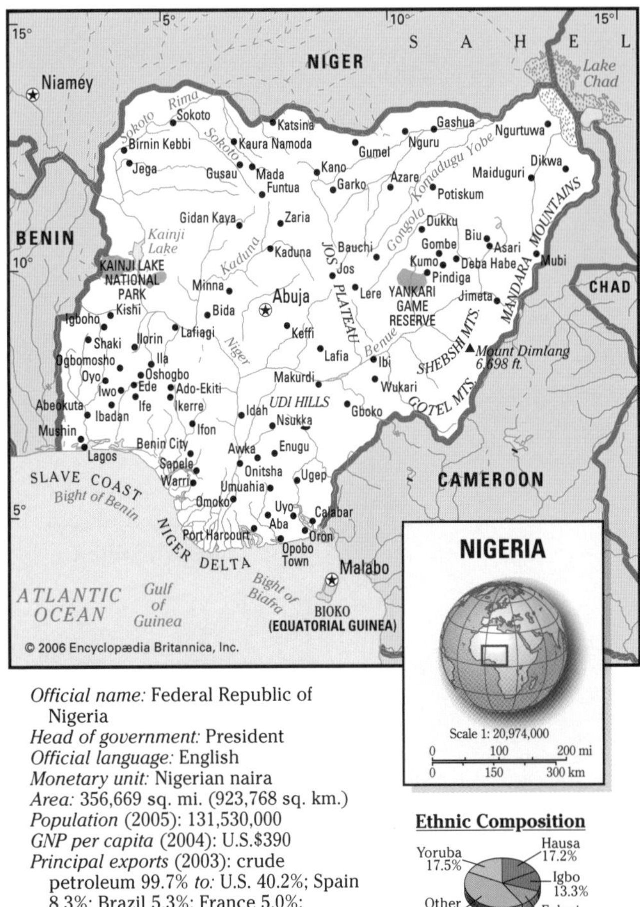

Official name: Federal Republic of Nigeria
Head of government: President
Official language: English
Monetary unit: Nigerian naira
Area: 356,669 sq. mi. (923,768 sq. km.)
Population (2005): 131,530,000
GNP per capita (2004): U.S.$390
Principal exports (2003): crude petroleum 99.7% *to:* U.S. 40.2%; Spain 8.3%; Brazil 5.3%; France 5.0%; Indonesia 4.6%; Japan 4.1%; India 4.0%

Ethnic Composition

Yoruba 17.5%
Hausa 17.2%
Igbo 13.3%
Fulani 10.7%
Other 41.3%

The Nigerian flag became official upon independence from Britain on Oct. 1, 1960. The flag design is purposefully simple in order not to favor the symbolism of any particular ethnic or religious group. Agriculture is represented by the green stripes while unity and peace are symbolized by the white stripe.

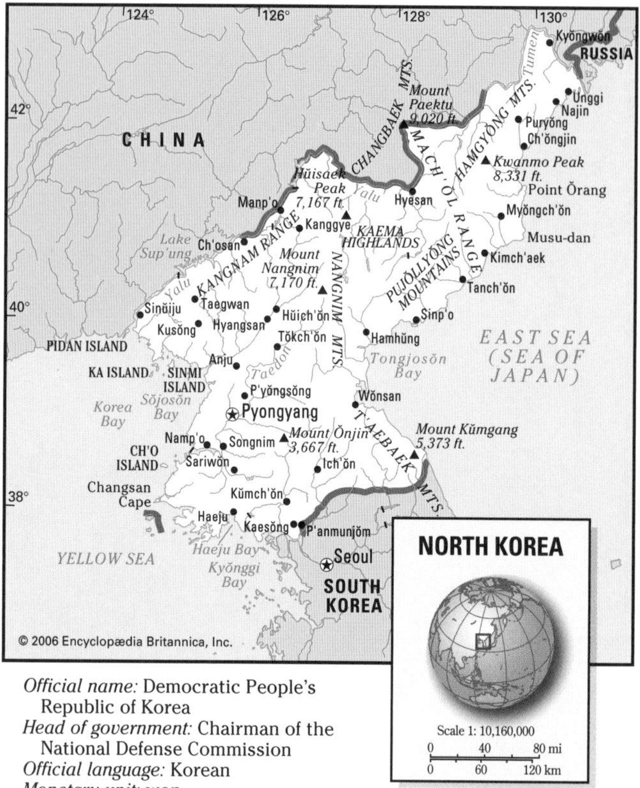

NORTH KOREA

Scale 1: 10,160,000
0 40 80 mi
0 60 120 km

Official name: Democratic People's Republic of Korea
Head of government: Chairman of the National Defense Commission
Official language: Korean
Monetary unit: won
Area: 47,399 sq. mi. (122,762 sq. km.)
Population (2005): 22,488,000
GNP per capita (2004): U.S.$930
Principal exports (2002): agricultural products 39.3%, textiles 16.7%, machinery and apparatus 11.6%, mineral fuels 9.5% *to:* South Korea 27.0%; China 26.9%; Japan 23.3%

Age Breakdown

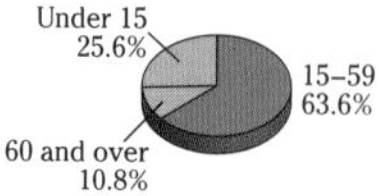

Under 15 25.6%
15–59 63.6%
60 and over 10.8%

The traditional Korean Taeguk flag (still used by South Korea) was official in North Korea until July 10, 1948, when the current flag was introduced. Its red stripe and star are for the country's commitment to communism, while blue is said to stand for a commitment to peace. The white stripes stand for purity, strength, and dignity.

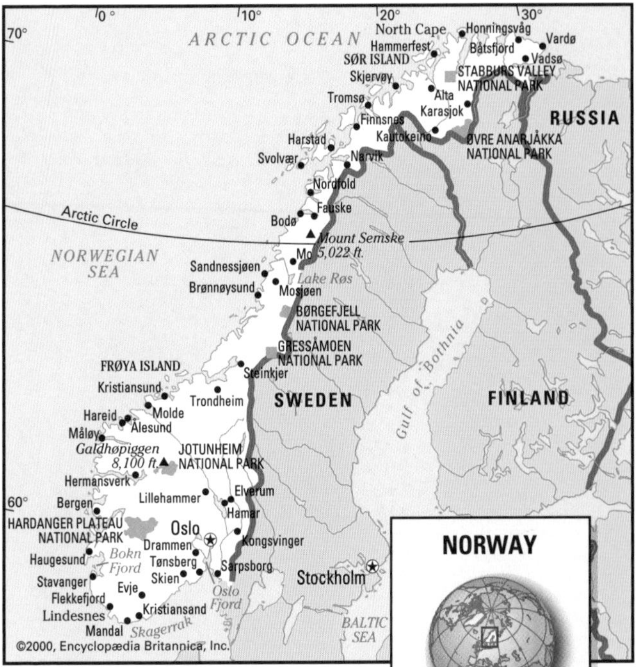

Official name: Kingdom of Norway
Head of government: Prime Minister
Official language: Norwegian
Monetary unit: Norwegian krone
Area: 148,726 sq. mi. (385,199 sq. km.)
Population (2005): 4,617,000
GNP per capita (2004): U.S.$52,030
Principal exports (2003): crude petroleum 42.7%, natural gas 12.9%, machinery and transport equipment 11.3%, metals and metal products 8.4%, fish 5.2% *to:* U.K. 21.3%; Germany 13.0%; The Netherlands 9.6%; France 8.2%; Sweden 7.4%

Age Breakdown

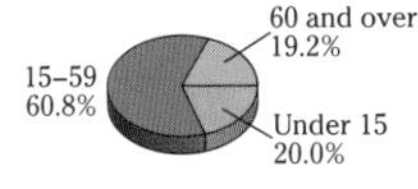

The first distinctive Norwegian flag was created in 1814 while the country was under Swedish rule. It was based on the red Danish flag with its white cross. In 1821 the Norwegian parliament developed the current flag design. From 1844 to 1899, six years before independence, the official flag included a symbol of Swedish-Norwegian union.

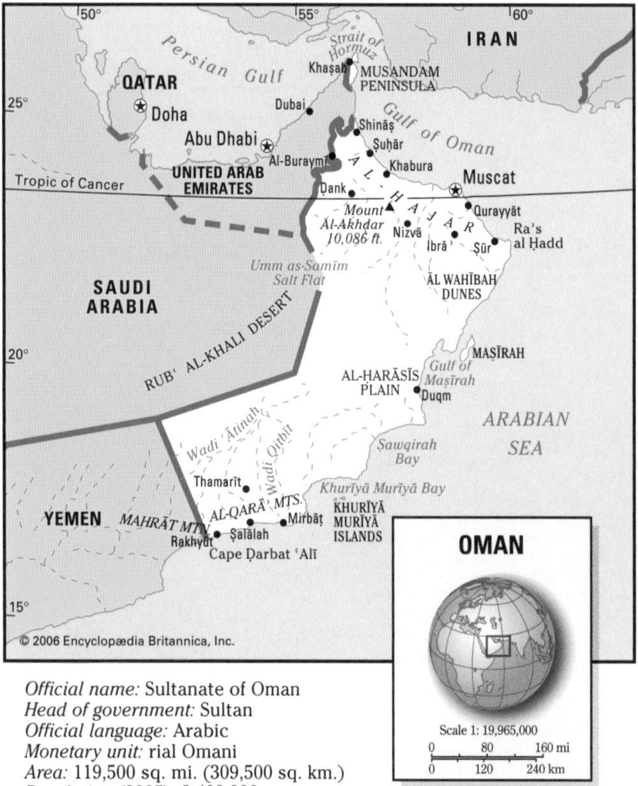

OMAN

Scale 1: 19,965,000

0 80 160 mi

0 120 240 km

Official name: Sultanate of Oman
Head of government: Sultan
Official language: Arabic
Monetary unit: rial Omani
Area: 119,500 sq. mi. (309,500 sq. km.)
Population (2005): 2,409,000
GNP per capita (2003): U.S.$7,830
Principal exports (2003): petroleum 66.5%, natural gas 13.3%, live animals 1.4%; reexports 13.4%, of which motor vehicles and parts 7.5% *to:* United Arab Emirates 32.7%; Iran 18.3%; Saudi Arabia 8.4%; U.S. 3.6%; Yemen 2.6%

Religious Affiliation

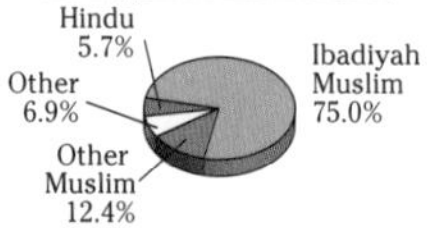

Ibadiyah Muslim 75.0%
Other Muslim 12.4%
Other 6.9%
Hindu 5.7%

The flag dates to Dec. 17, 1970, and it was altered on Nov. 18, 1995. The white is for peace and prosperity, red is for battles, and green is for the fertility of the land. Unofficially, white recalls the imamate, red the sultanate, and green Al-Jabal Al-Akhdar ("The Green Mountain"). The coat of arms has two swords, a dagger, and a belt.

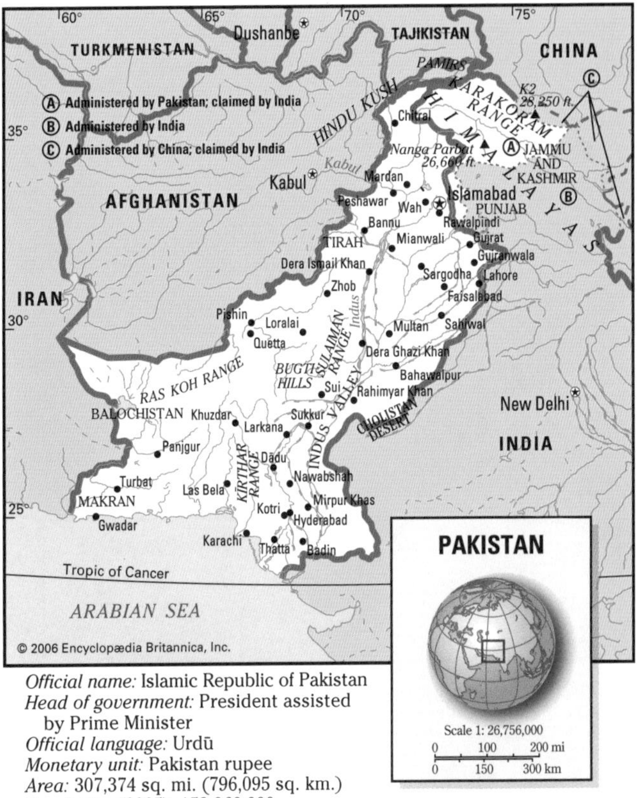

PAKISTAN

Scale 1: 26,756,000
0 100 200 mi
0 150 300 km

Official name: Islamic Republic of Pakistan
Head of government: President assisted by Prime Minister
Official language: Urdū
Monetary unit: Pakistan rupee
Area: 307,374 sq. mi. (796,095 sq. km.)
Population (2005): 153,960,000
GNP per capita (2004): U.S.$600
Principal exports (2004): textile fabrics 58.8%, knitwear 11.3%, bedding 10.1%, ready-made garments 7.5%; leather and leather goods 3.7%; petroleum products 3.4% *to:* U.S. 20.7%; U.A.E. 10.8%; U.K. 6.9%; Germany 5.0%; Saudi Arabia 4.5%

Ethnic Composition

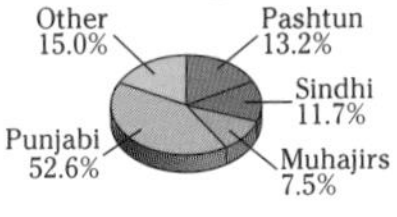

Other 15.0%
Pashtun 13.2%
Sindhi 11.7%
Muhajirs 7.5%
Punjabi 52.6%

On Dec. 30, 1906, the All India Muslim League approved this typically Muslim flag, with its star and crescent. At independence (Aug. 14, 1947) a white stripe was added for minority religious groups. Also symbolized are prosperity and peace by the green and white colors, progress by the crescent, and knowledge and light by the star.

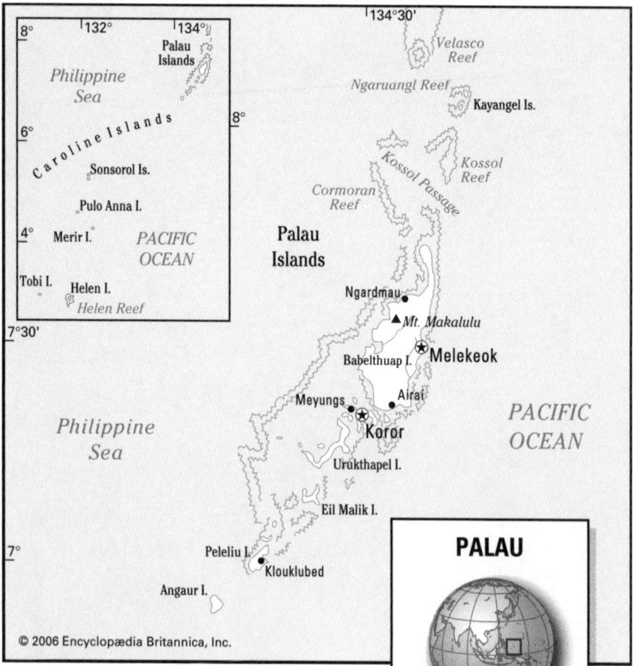

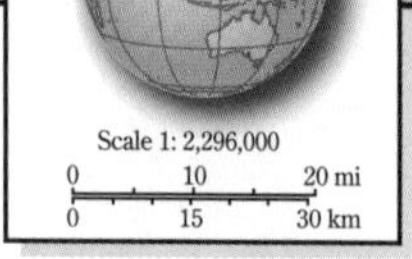

PALAU

Scale 1: 2,296,000

0 10 20 mi

0 15 30 km

Official name: Republic of Palau
Head of government: President
Official languages: Palauan; English
Monetary unit: U.S. dollar
Area: 188 sq. mi. (488 sq. km.)
Population (2005): 21,100
GNP per capita (2004): U.S.$6,870
Principal exports (2001): mostly high-grade tuna and garments *to* (2003): Japan 86.7%; Vietnam 5.9%; Zambia 4.6%

Religious Affiliation

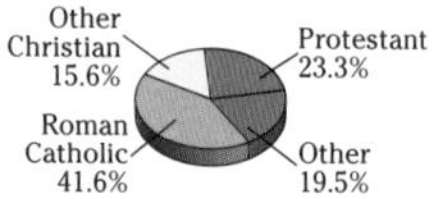

Other Christian 15.6%
Protestant 23.3%
Roman Catholic 41.6%
Other 19.5%

Approved on Oct. 22, 1980, and hoisted on Jan. 1, 1981, the Palauan flag was left unaltered at independence in 1994. The golden disk represents the full moon, which is said on Palau to be propitious for fishing, planting, and other activities and gives the people "a feeling of warmth, tranquillity, peace, love, and domestic unity."

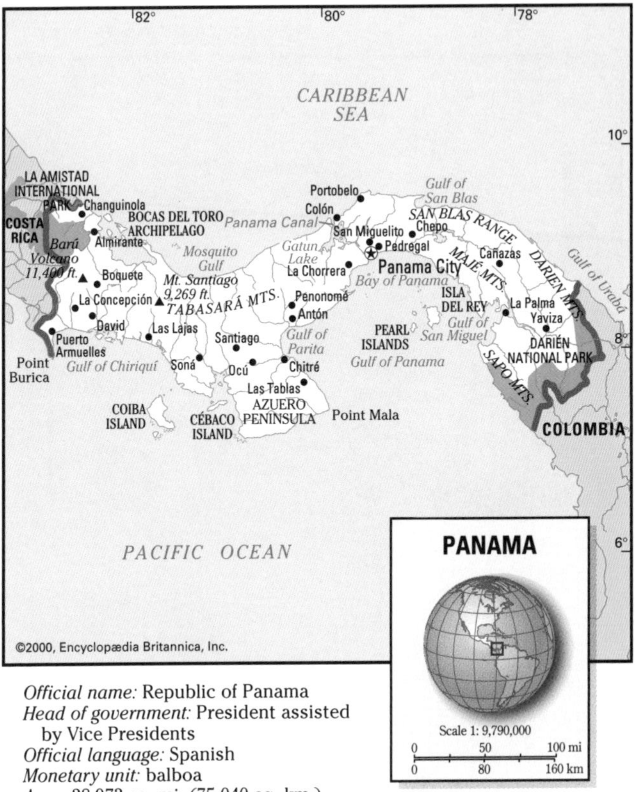

PANAMA

Scale 1: 9,790,000

0 50 100 mi

0 80 160 km

Official name: Republic of Panama
Head of government: President assisted by Vice Presidents
Official language: Spanish
Monetary unit: balboa
Area: 28,973 sq. mi. (75,040 sq. km.)
Population (2005): 3,140,000
GNP per capita (2004): U.S.$4,450
Principal exports (2003): fish 32.6%, shrimp 7.2%, melons 3.3%, unspecified 56.9% *to:* U.S. 50.4%; Sweden 6.0%; Spain 5.7%; Costa Rica 4.2%; Portugal 3.4%

Ethnic Composition

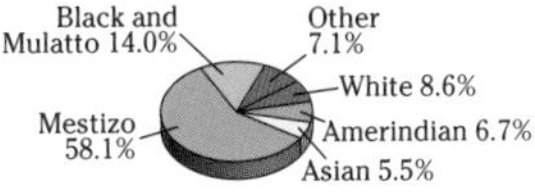

Mestizo	58.1%
Black and Mulatto	14.0%
Other	7.1%
White	8.6%
Amerindian	6.7%
Asian	5.5%

The Panamanian flag became official on July 4, 1904, after independence from Colombia was won through the intervention of the United States, which was determined to construct the Panama Canal. The flag was influenced by the United States, and its quartered design was said to symbolize the power sharing of Panama's two main political parties.

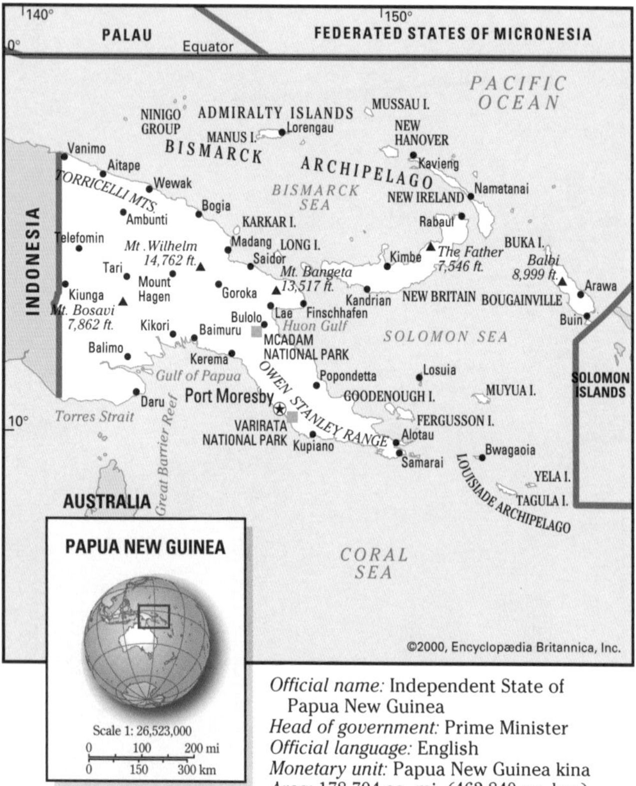

PAPUA NEW GUINEA

Scale 1: 26,523,000

0 100 200 mi

0 150 300 km

Religious Affiliation

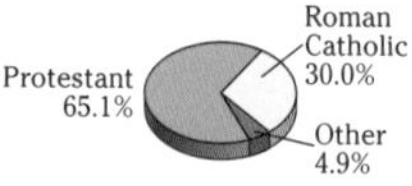

Protestant 65.1%

Roman Catholic 30.0%

Other 4.9%

Official name: Independent State of Papua New Guinea
Head of government: Prime Minister
Official language: English
Monetary unit: Papua New Guinea kina
Area: 178,704 sq. mi. (462,840 sq. km.)
Population (2005): 5,887,000
GNP per capita (2004): U.S.$580
Principal exports (2004): gold 33.8%, crude oil 20.1%, copper ore 18.8%, palm oil 5.3%, logs 4.3% *to:* Australia 45.6%; Japan 10.8%; Germany 7.1%; South Korea 6.1%; China 4.9%

The formerly German-, British-, and Australian-controlled territory officially recognized its flag on March 11, 1971, and flag usage was extended to ships at independence (Sept. 16, 1975). The colors red and black are shown extensively in local art and clothing. Featured emblems are a bird of paradise and the Southern Cross constellation.

Ethnic Composition

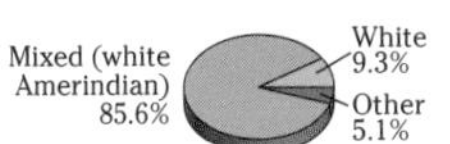

Official name: Republic of Paraguay
Head of government: President
Official languages: Spanish; Guaraní
Monetary unit: Paraguayan Guaraní
Area: 157,048 sq. mi. (406,752 sq. km.)
Population (2005): 5,905,000
GNP per capita (2004): U.S.$1,170
Principal exports (2002): soybean 35.8%, processed meats 7.6%, soybean oil 7.5%, leather goods 6.1%, wood products 5.9% *to:* Brazil 37.1%; Uruguay 17.4%; Cayman Islands 8.2%; Chile 5.2%; U.S. 3.9%

Under the dictator José Gaspar Rodríguez de Francia (1814–40) the French colors were adopted for the flag. The coat of arms (a golden star surrounded by a wreath) is on the obverse side, but the seal of the treasury (a lion, staff, and liberty cap, with the motto "Peace and Justice") is on the reverse; the flag is unique in this respect.

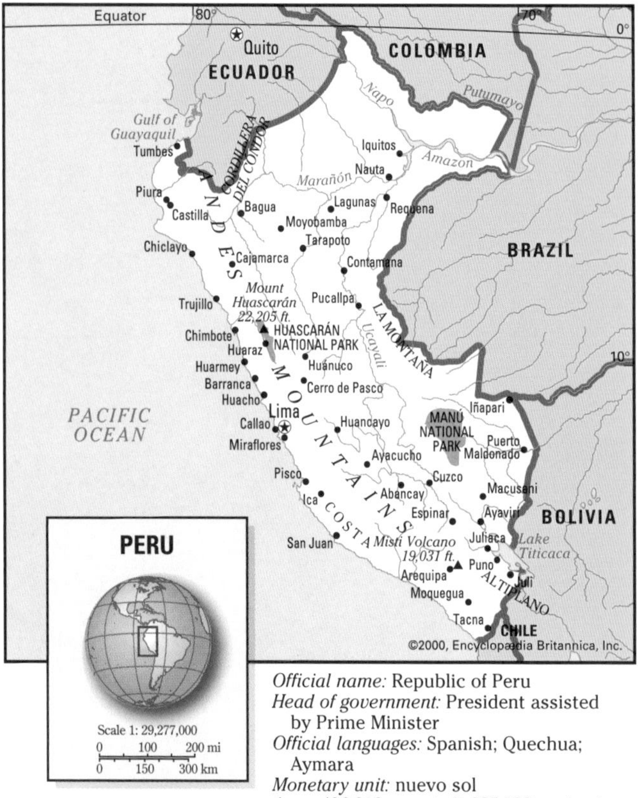

PERU

Scale 1: 29,277,000

0 100 200 mi

0 150 300 km

Ethnic Composition

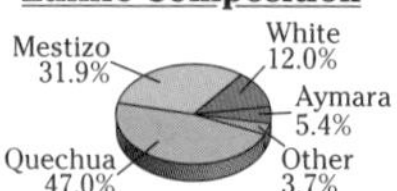

Official name: Republic of Peru
Head of government: President assisted by Prime Minister
Official languages: Spanish; Quechua; Aymara
Monetary unit: nuevo sol
Area: 496,218 sq. mi. (1,285,198 sq. km.)
Population (2005): 27,968,000
GNP per capita (2004): U.S.$2,360
Principal exports (1994): copper 19.4%, gold 18.8%, textiles and clothing 8.7%, fishmeal 7.6%, petroleum 5.1%, zinc 4.6% *to:* U.S. 29.1%; China 9.9%; U.K. 9.2%; Chile 5.1%; Japan 4.4%

Partisans in the early 19th century adopted a red-white-red flag resembling that of Spain, but they soon made its stripes vertical. In 1825 the current design was established. The shield includes figures symbolic of national wealth—the vicuna (a relative of the alpaca), a cinchona tree, and a cornucopia with gold and silver coins.

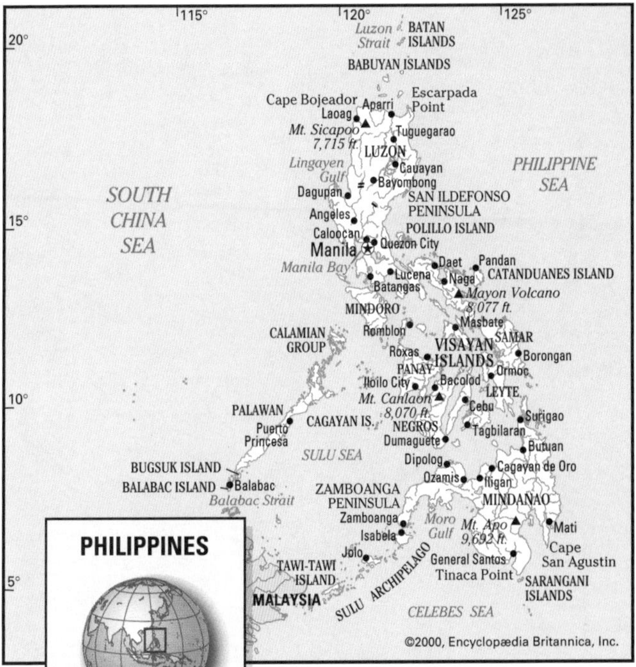

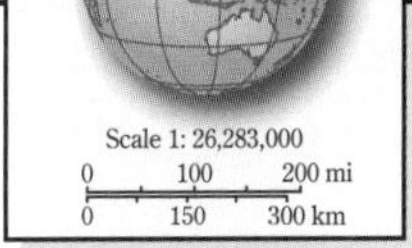

PHILIPPINES

Scale 1: 26,283,000

0 100 200 mi

0 150 300 km

Official name: Republic of the Philippines
Head of government: President
Official languages: Pilipino; English
Monetary unit: Philippine peso
Area: 122,121 sq. mi. (316,294 sq. km.)
Population (2005): 89,191,000
GNP per capita (2004): U.S.$1,090
Principal exports (2004): microcircuits, office machines, and parts 57.1%; garments 4.6%; coconut oil 1.2% *to:* United States 17.4%; Japan 15.8%; Hong Kong 8.3%; Singapore 7.7%

Ethnic Composition

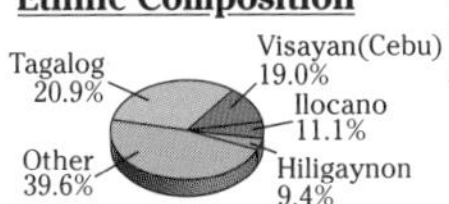

In 1898, during the Spanish-American War, Filipinos established the basic flag in use today; it was officially adopted in 1936. The white triangle is for liberty. The golden sun and stars are for the three main areas of the Philippines: Luzon, the Visayan Islands, and Mindanao. The red color is for courage and the blue color is for sacrifice.

Official name: Republic of Poland
Head of government: Prime Minister
Official language: Polish
Monetary unit: zloty
Area: 120,728 sq. mi. (312,685 sq. km.)
Population (2005): 38,164,000
GNP per capita (2004): U.S.$6,090
Principal exports (2001): machinery and transport equipment 29.3%, furniture 6.9%, food 5.9%, clothing 5.4%, ships and boats 5.2% *to:* Germany 30.0%; Italy 6.1%; France 6.0%; U.K. 5.4%

Age Breakdown

Under 15 18.3%
15–59 65.7%
60 and over 16.0%

The colors of the Polish flag originated in its coat of arms, a white eagle on a red shield, dating from 1295. The precise symbolism of the colors is not known, however. Poland's simple flag of white-red horizontal stripes was adopted on Aug. 1, 1919. The flag was left unaltered under the Soviet-allied communist regime (1944 to 1990).

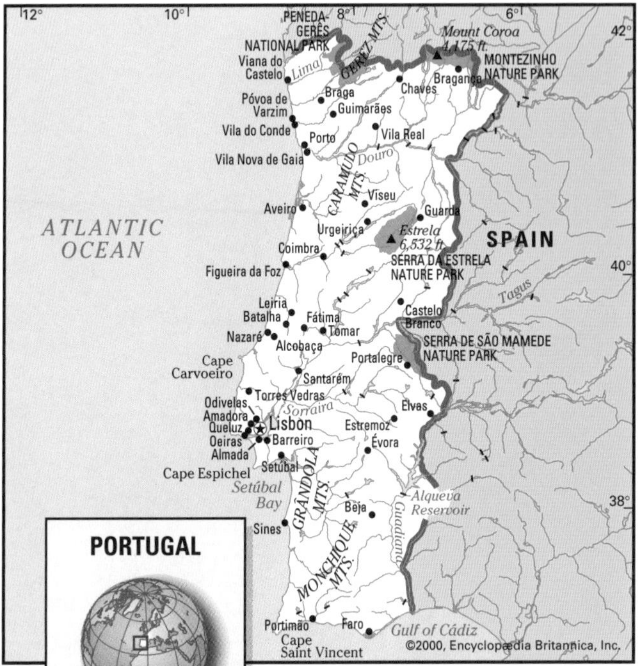

PORTUGAL

Scale 1: 8,756,000

©2000, Encyclopædia Britannica, Inc.

Age Breakdown

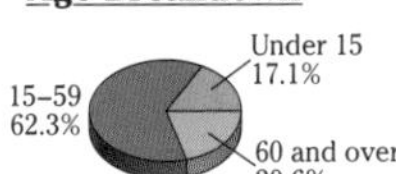

Official name: Portuguese Republic
Head of government: Prime Minister
Official language: Portuguese
Monetary unit: euro
Area: 35,580 sq. mi. (92,152 sq. km.)
Population (2005): 10,513,000
GNP per capita (2004): U.S.$14,350
Principal exports (2002): machinery 19.0%, transport equipment 16.1%, clothing 10.6%, chemicals 5.5%, footwear 5.4% *to:* Spain 20.5%; Germany 18.1%; France 13.3%; United Kingdom 10.5%; U.S. 5.6%

The central shield includes five smaller shields for a victory over the Moors in 1139, and a red border with gold castles. Behind the shield is an armillary sphere (an astronomical device) recalling world explorations and the kingdom of Brazil. Red and green were used in many early Portuguese flags. The current flag dates to June 30, 1911.

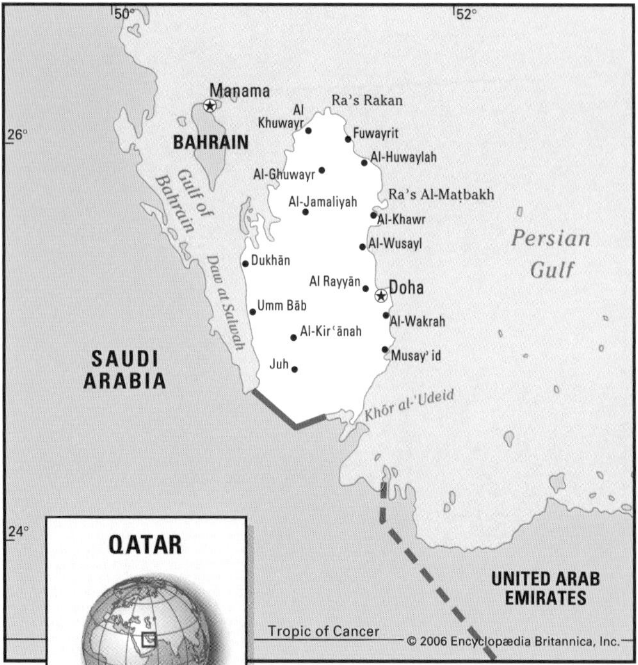
50°
52°
26°
24°
Manama
BAHRAIN
Gulf of Bahrain
Al Khuwayr
Ra's Rakan
Fuwayrit
Al-Huwaylah
Al-Ghuwayr
Al-Jamaliyah
Ra's Al-Maṭbakh
Al-Khawr
Al-Wusayl
Persian Gulf
Dukhān
Dawḥat Salwah
Al Rayyān
Doha
Umm Bāb
Al-Wakrah
Al-Kir'ānah
Musay' id
Juh
SAUDI ARABIA
Khōr al-'Udeid
UNITED ARAB EMIRATES
Tropic of Cancer
© 2006 Encyclopædia Britannica, Inc.
QATAR
Scale 1: 5,305,000
0 20 40 mi
0 30 60 km

Official name: State of Qatar
Head of government: Emir assisted by Prime Minister
Official language: Arabic
Monetary unit: riyal
Area: 4,412 sq. mi. (11,427 sq. km.)
Population (2005): 773,000
GNP per capita (2004): U.S.$37,690
Principal exports (2003): liquefied natural gas 42.6%, crude petroleum 35.0%, refined petroleum 6.7% *to* (2004): Japan 42.2%; South Korea 15.9%; Singapore 9.2%; India 5.4%; U.A.E. 2.9%

Ethnic Composition

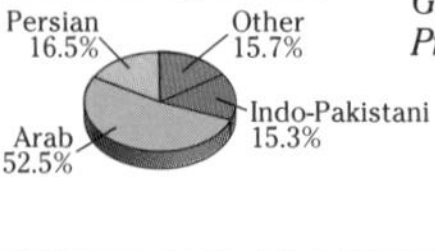
Persian 16.5%
Other 15.7%
Indo-Pakistani 15.3%
Arab 52.5%

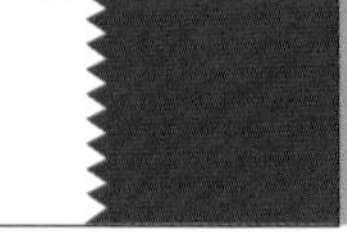

The 1868 treaty between Great Britain and Qatar may have inspired the creation of the flag. Qataris chose mauve or maroon instead of red (a more typical color among Arab countries) perhaps to distinguish it from the flag used in Bahrain. Passages from the Quran, in Arabic script, have sometimes been added to the flag.

ROMANIA

Scale 1: 10,966,000

0 50 100 mi

0 80 160 km

Official name: Romania
Head of government: Prime Minister
Official language: Romanian
Monetary unit: (new) leu
Area: 92,043 sq. mi. (238,391 sq. km.)
Population (2005): 21,602,000
GNP per capita (2004): U.S.$2,920
Principal exports (2002): textiles and clothing 25.3%, electrical and telecommunication equipment 10.3%, footwear 8.4%, nonelectrical machinery 5.3% *to:* Italy 25.0%; Germany 15.6%; France 7.6%; Turkey 4.2%

Ethnic Composition

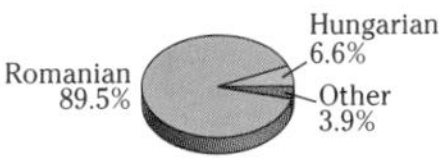

Romanian 89.5%
Hungarian 6.6%
Other 3.9%

In 1834 Walachia, an ancient region of Romania, chose a naval ensign with stripes of red, blue, and yellow. The modern Romanian tricolor was created in 1848 and flown for a brief time. In 1867 Romania reestablished the vertical tricolor, and with the fall of the 20th-century communist regime, it was defined on Dec. 27, 1989.

Tsar Peter the Great visited the Netherlands in order to modernize the Russian navy, and in 1699 he chose a Dutch-influenced flag for Russian ships. The flag soon became popular on land as well. After the Russian Revolution it was replaced by the communist red banner, but the tricolor again became official on Aug. 21, 1991.

Official name: Russian Federation
Head of government: President
Official language: Russian
Monetary unit: ruble
Area: 6,592,800 sq. mi. (17,075,400 sq. km.)
Population (2005): 143,420,000
GNP per capita (2004): U.S.$3,410
Principal exports (2004): fuels and lubricants 58.2%, of which crude petroleum 32.3%, natural gas 12.3%; ferrous and nonferrous metals 16.8%; machinery 7.2%; chemicals 6.4% *to:* The Netherlands 8.4%; Germany 7.3%; Italy 6.7%; China 5.6%

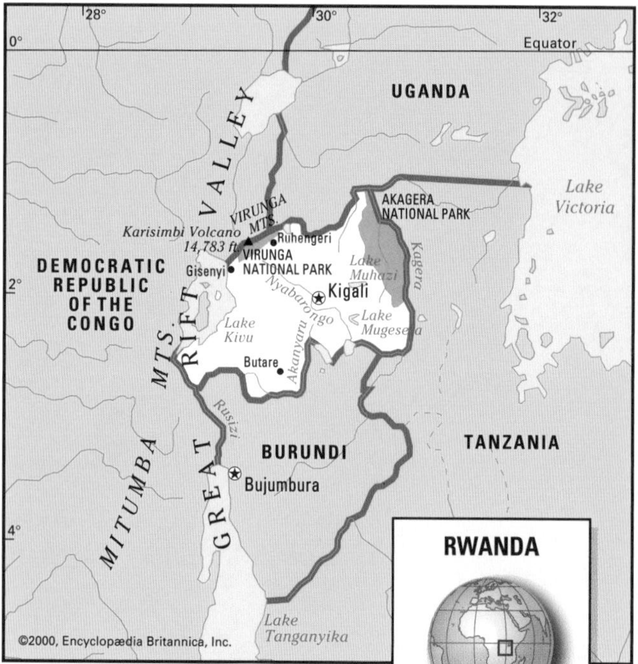

RWANDA

Scale 1: 8,930,000

0 40 80 mi

0 60 120 km

Official name: Republic of Rwanda
Head of government: President assisted by Prime Minister
Official languages: Rwanda; French; English
Monetary unit: Rwanda franc
Area: 10,169 sq. mi. (26,338 sq. km.)
Population (2005): 8,574,000
GNP per capita (2004): U.S.$220
Principal exports (2003): tea 35.7%, coffee 23.8%, cassiterite 7.1% *to* (2002): Indonesia 30.8%; Germany 14.6%; Hong Kong 8.9%; South Africa 5.5%

Age Breakdown

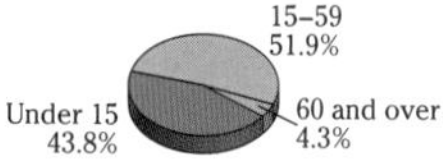

15–59 51.9%
Under 15 43.8%
60 and over 4.3%

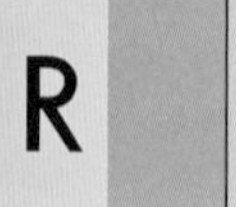

December 31, 2001 Rwanda raised this flag to promote unity, work ethic, heroism, and self-assurance. Under Belgium, minority Tutsi ruled feudally until 1959, when the Hutu majority revolted and took power. Rwanda won independence from Belgium in 1962. In 1994 Tutsis were back, after suffering hundreds of thousands of killings by Hutu.

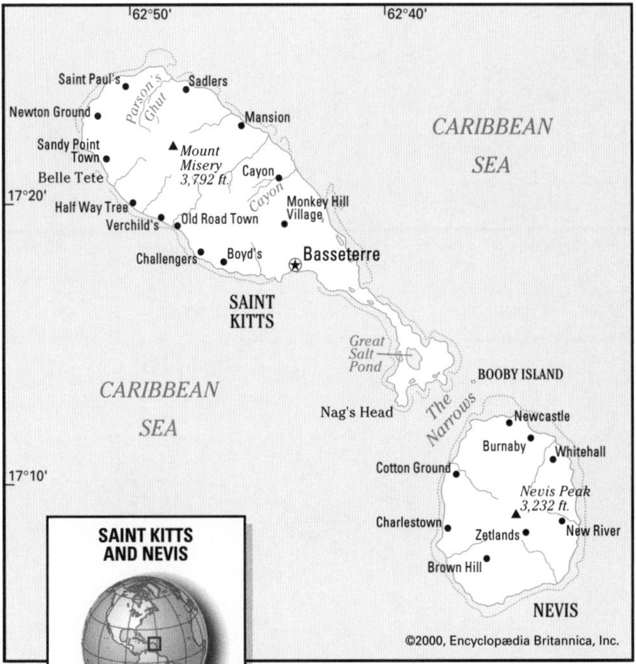

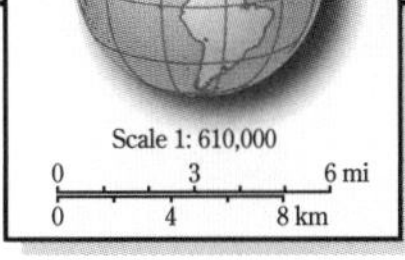

62°50'
62°40'
17°20'
17°10'
Saint Paul's
Sadlers
Parson's Ghut
Newton Ground
Mansion
Sandy Point Town
Mount Misery 3,792 ft.
Belle Tete
Cayon
Cayon
Half Way Tree
Verchild's
Old Road Town
Monkey Hill Village
Challengers
Boyd's
Basseterre
SAINT KITTS
CARIBBEAN SEA
Great Salt Pond
BOOBY ISLAND
CARIBBEAN SEA
Nag's Head
The Narrows
Newcastle
Burnaby
Whitehall
Cotton Ground
Nevis Peak 3,232 ft.
Charlestown
Zetlands
New River
Brown Hill
NEVIS
©2000, Encyclopædia Britannica, Inc.

SAINT KITTS AND NEVIS
Scale 1: 610,000
0 3 6 mi
0 4 8 km

Official name: Federation of Saint Kitts and Nevis
Head of government: Prime Minister
Official language: English
Monetary unit: Eastern Caribbean dollar
Area: 104.0 sq. mi. (269.4 sq. km.)
Population (2005): 46,600
GNP per capita (2004): U.S.$7,600
Principal exports (2000): electronic and electrical goods 56.1%, raw sugar 21.0%, telecommunication equipment 3.2% *to:* United States 66.6%; U.K. 7.6%; Canada 6.8%; Portugal 6.0%; Germany 2.9%

Religious Affiliation

Protestant 84.6%
Other 8.7%
Roman Catholic 6.7%

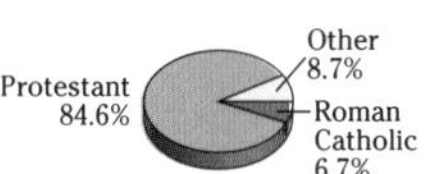

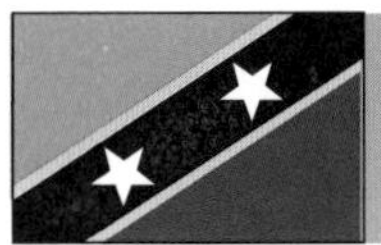

On Sept. 18, 1983, at the time of its independence from Britain, St. Kitts and Nevis hoisted the current flag. It has green (for fertility), red (for the struggle against slavery and colonialism), and black (for African heritage). The yellow flanking stripes are for sunshine, and the two stars, one for each island, are for hope and liberty.

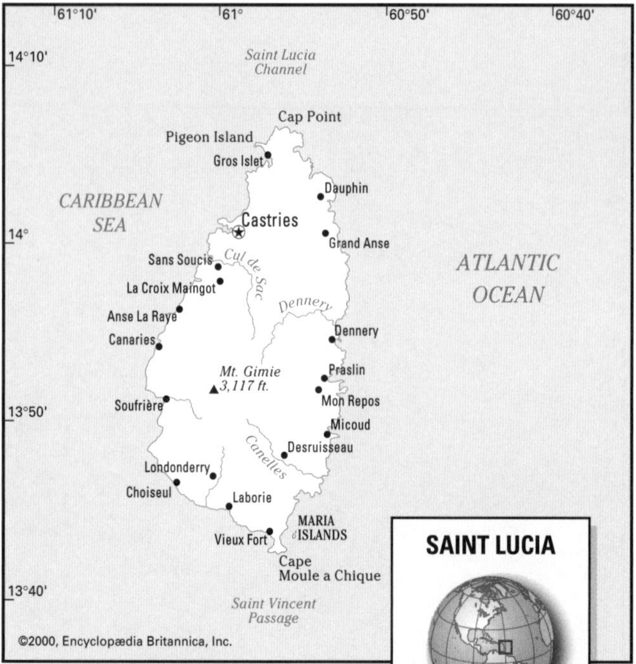
61°10'
61°
60°50'
60°40'
14°10'
14°
13°50'
13°40'
Saint Lucia Channel
Cap Point
Pigeon Island
Gros Islet
Dauphin
CARIBBEAN SEA
Castries
Grand Anse
Sans Soucis
Cul de Sac
La Croix Maingot
Anse La Raye
Dennery
Canaries
Dennery
ATLANTIC OCEAN
Mt. Gimie
3,117 ft.
Praslin
Soufrière
Mon Repos
Micoud
Canelles
Desruisseau
Londonderry
Choiseul
Laborie
MARIA ISLANDS
Vieux Fort
Cape
Moule a Chique
Saint Vincent Passage
©2000, Encyclopædia Britannica, Inc.
SAINT LUCIA
Scale 1: 945,000
0 4 8 mi
0 6 12 km

Official name: Saint Lucia
Head of government: Prime Minister
Official language: English
Monetary unit: Eastern Caribbean dollar
Area: 238 sq. mi. (617 sq. km.)
Population (2005): 161,000
GNP per capita (2004): U.S.$4,310
Principal exports (2002): bananas 49.9%; beer and ale 15.9%; clothing 3.2%; electronic equipment 3.2% *to:* United Kingdom 37.6%; United States 20.3%; Trinidad and Tobago 11.8%; Barbados 9.7%; Dominica 5.3%

Ethnic Composition

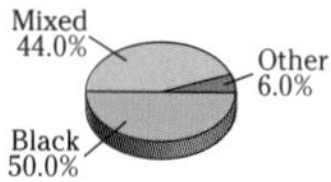
Mixed
44.0%
Other
6.0%
Black
50.0%

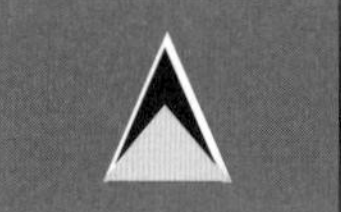

Upon independence from Britain, February 22, 1979, Saint Lucia raised this flag. The blue reflects the surrounding Atlantic Ocean and the Caribbena Sea. Its yellow triangle prepresents its tropical sunshine that tourists love, and its black triangle symbolizes the Pitons, ancient volcanic cones found in the southwest, while the adjoining white indicates racial harmony.

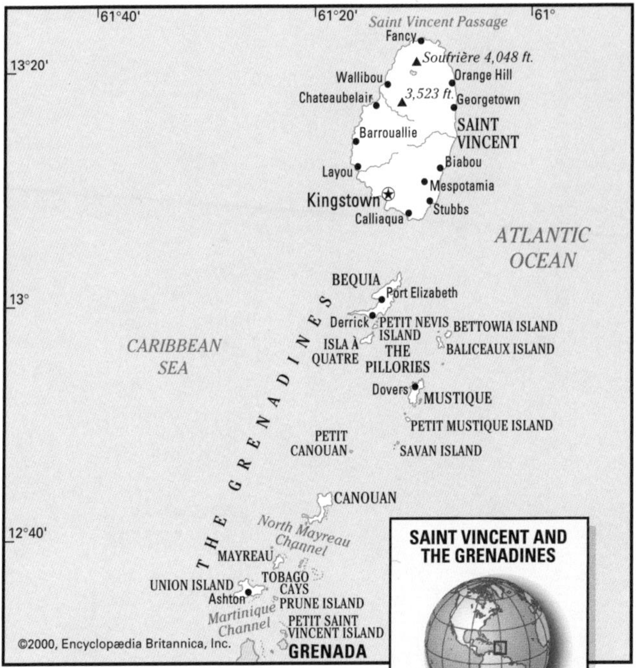

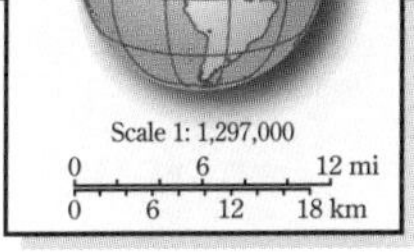

Official name: Saint Vincent and the Grenadines
Head of government: Prime Minister
Official language: English
Monetary unit: Eastern Caribbean dollar
Area: 150.3 sq. mi. (389.3 sq. km.)
Population (2005): 119,000
GNP per capita (2004): U.S.$3,650
Principal exports (1993): domestic exports 92.2%, of which bananas 40.4%, flour 11.5%, rice 10.7%; reexports 7.8% *to:* United Kingdom 38.8%; Barbados 10.6%; Trinidad and Tobago 9.0%; St. Lucia 8.3%

Ethnic Composition

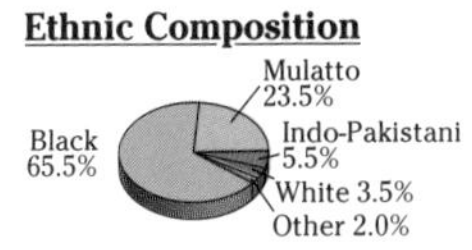

At independence from Britain in 1979 a national flag was designed, but it was replaced by the current flag on Oct. 22, 1985. The three green diamonds are arranged in the form of a V. Green is for the rich vegetation and the vitality of the people, yellow is for sand and personal warmth, and blue is for sea and sky.

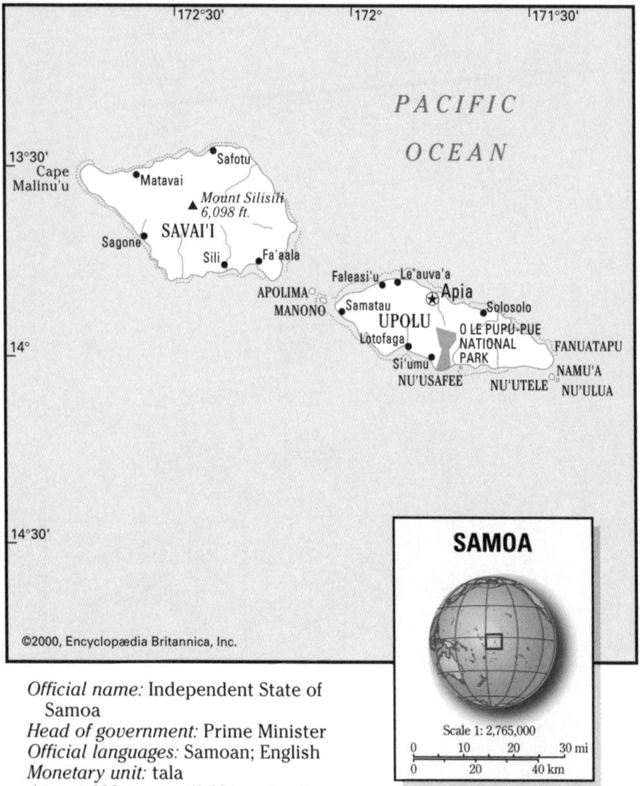

Official name: Independent State of Samoa
Head of government: Prime Minister
Official languages: Samoan; English
Monetary unit: tala
Area: 1,093 sq. mi. (2,831 sq. km.)
Population (2005): 185,000
GNP per capita (2004): U.S.$1,860
Principal exports (2001-02): fresh fish 66.9%, garments 11.5%, beer 6.7%, coconut cream 6.6% *to:* American Samoa 52.3%; United States 32.2%; New Zealand 6.8%; Germany 3.4%

Religious Affiliation

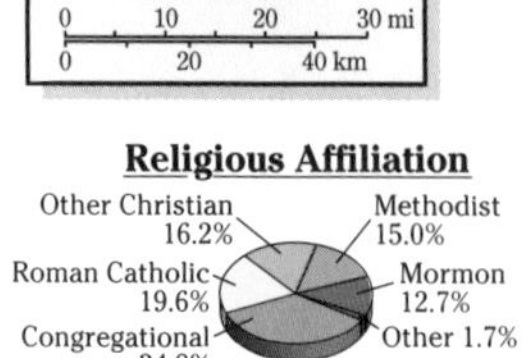

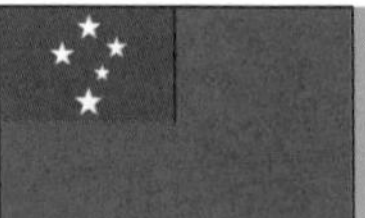

The first national flag of Samoa may date to 1873. Under British administration, a version of the current flag was introduced on May 26, 1948. On Feb. 2, 1949, a fifth star was added to the Southern Cross. White in the flag is said to stand for purity, blue for freedom, and red for courage. The flag was left unaltered upon independence in 1962.

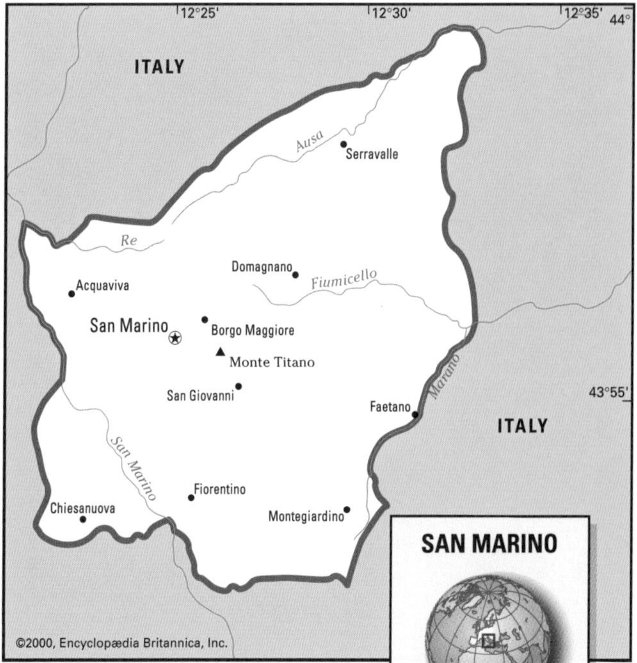
12°25'
12°30'
12°35'
44°
ITALY
Ausa
Serravalle
Re
Domagnano
Fiumicello
Acquaviva
San Marino
Borgo Maggiore
Monte Titano
San Giovanni
Faetano
Marano
43°55'
ITALY
San Marino
Fiorentino
Chiesanuova
Montegiardino
©2000, Encyclopædia Britannica, Inc.
SAN MARINO
Scale 1: 175,500
0 1 2 mi
0 1 2 3 km

Official name: Most Serene Republic of San Marino
Head of government: Captains-Regent (2)
Official language: Italian
Monetary unit: euro
Area: 23.63 sq. mi. (61.19 sq. km.)
Population (2005): 30,100
GNP per capita (2004): U.S.$39,830
Principal exports (2002): wine, wheat, woolen goods, furniture, wood, ceramics, building stone, dairy products, meat, and postage stamps
to: Italy

Ethnic Composition

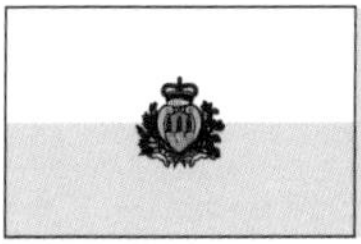

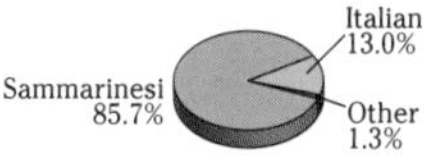
Italian 13.0%
Sammarinesi 85.7%
Other 1.3%

The colors of the flag, blue and white, were first used in the national cockade in 1797. The coat of arms in its present form was adopted on April 6, 1862, when the crown was added as a symbol of national sovereignty. Also in the coat of arms are three towers (Guaita, Cesta, and Montale) from the fortifications on Mount Titano.

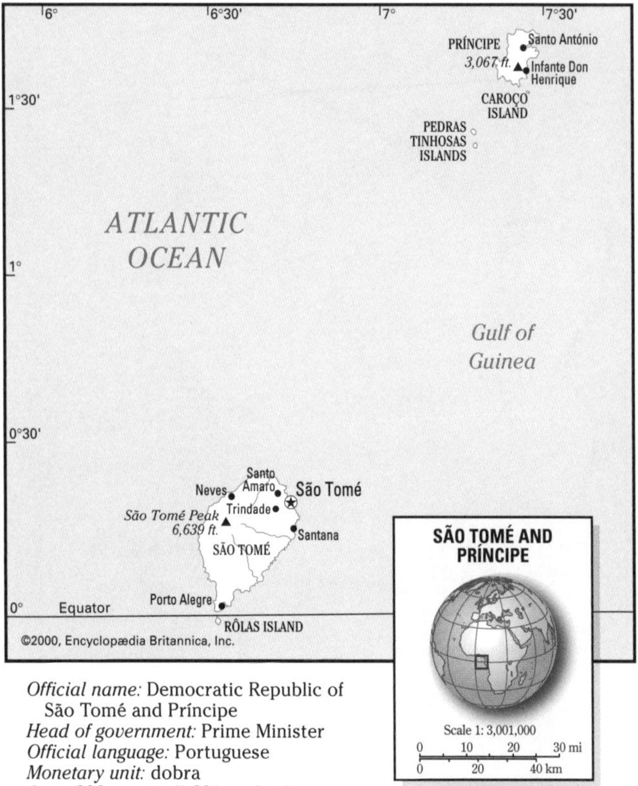
6°
6°30'
7°
7°30'
1°30'
1°
0°30'
0°
Equator
PRÍNCIPE
Santo António
3,067 ft.
Infante Don Henrique
CAROÇO ISLAND
PEDRAS TINHOSAS ISLANDS
ATLANTIC OCEAN
Gulf of Guinea
Santo Amaro
Neves
São Tomé
Trindade
São Tomé Peak 6,639 ft.
Santana
SÃO TOMÉ
Porto Alegre
RÔLAS ISLAND
©2000, Encyclopædia Britannica, Inc.
SÃO TOMÉ AND PRÍNCIPE
Scale 1: 3,001,000
0 10 20 30 mi
0 20 40 km

Official name: Democratic Republic of São Tomé and Príncipe
Head of government: Prime Minister
Official language: Portuguese
Monetary unit: dobra
Area: 386 sq. mi. (1,001 sq. km.)
Population (2005): 157,000
GNP per capita (2004): U.S.$370
Principal exports (2003): cocoa 86.0%
to: The Netherlands *c.* 42%; Portugal *c.* 19%; Angola *c.* 3%

Age Breakdown

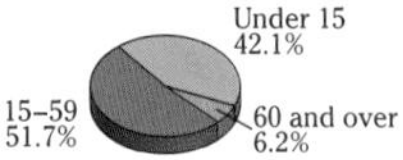
Under 15
42.1%
15–59
51.7%
60 and over
6.2%

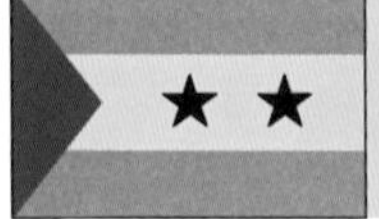

The national flag was adopted upon independence from Portugal on July 12, 1975. Its colors are associated with Pan-African independence. The red triangle stands for equality and the nationalist movement. The stars are for the African population living on the nation's two main islands. Green is for vegetation and yellow is for the tropical sun.

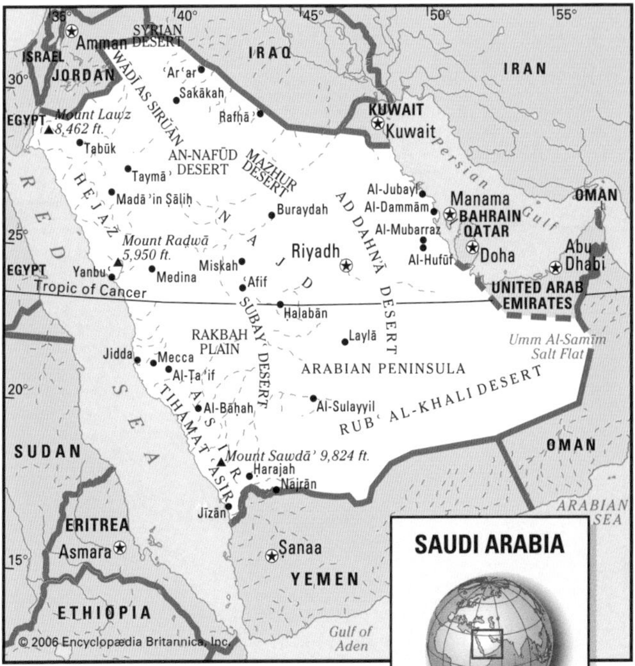

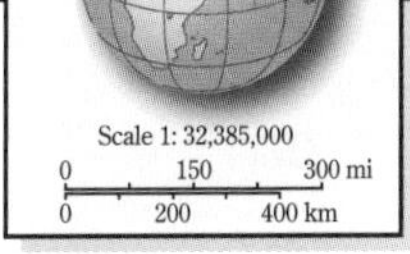

SAUDI ARABIA

Scale 1: 32,385,000

0 150 300 mi

0 200 400 km

Official name: Kingdom of Saudi Arabia
Head of government: King
Official language: Arabic
Monetary unit: Saudi riyal
Area: 830,000 sq. mi. (2,149,690 sq. km.)
Population (2005): 23,230,000
GNP per capita (2004): U.S.$10,430
Principal exports (1993): petroleum 88.8%, other 11.2% *to:* U.S. 18.5%; Japan 15.2%; S. Korea 10.1%; China 5.7%; Singapore 4.1%

Ethnic Composition

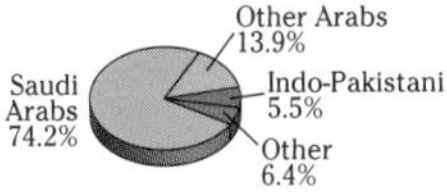

Saudi Arabs 74.2%
Other Arabs 13.9%
Indo-Pakistani 5.5%
Other 6.4%

The Saudi flag, made official in 1932 but altered in 1968, originated in the military campaigns of Muhammad. The color green is associated with Fatima, the Prophet's daughter, and the Arabic inscription is translated as "There is no God but Allah and Muhammad is the Prophet of Allah." The saber symbolizes the militancy of the faith.

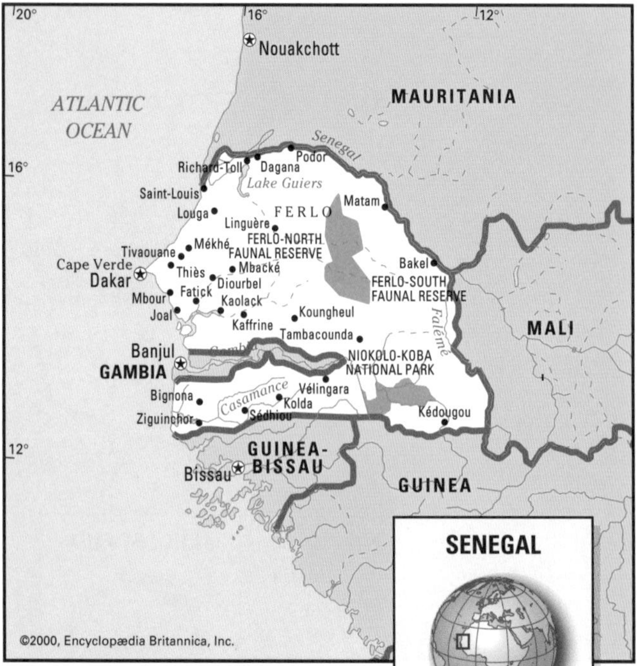

SENEGAL

Scale 1: 14,627,000

0 60 120 mi

0 80 160 km

Official name: Republic of Senegal
Head of government: Prime Minister
Official language: French
Monetary unit: CFA franc
Area: 75,955 sq. mi. (196,722 sq. km.)
Population (2005): 11,706,000
GNP per capita (2004): U.S.$670
Principal exports (2001): fish and crustaceans 28.1%, bunkers and ships' stores 12.0%, phosphorous pentoxide and phosphoric acids 9.5%, peanut oil 9.1% *to* (2003): African countries 37.5%, of which Mali 9.5%; France 12.2%; Italy 8.5%

Ethnic Composition

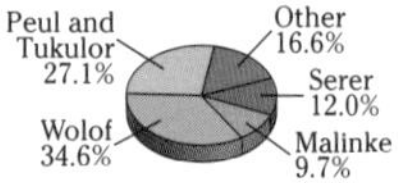

Peul and Tukulor 27.1%
Other 16.6%
Serer 12.0%
Malinke 9.7%
Wolof 34.6%

In a federation with French Sudan (now Mali) on April 4, 1959, Senegal used a flag with a human figure in the center. After the federation broke up in August 1960, Senegal substituted a green star for the central figure. Green is for hope and religion, yellow is for natural riches and labor, and red is for independence, life, and socialism.

SERBIA

Scale 1: 8,452,000

0 40 80 mi

0 60 120 km

Official name: Republic of Serbia
Head of government: Prime Minister
Official language: Serbo-Croatian
Monetary unit: Serbian dinar
Area:[1] 34,116 sq. mi. (88,361 sq. km.)
Population (2005):[1] 9,342,000
GDP per capita (2004):[2] U.S.$3,030
Principal exports (2003):[2] food/beverages 18.0%; basic metals 17.3%; *to:* Bosnia and Herzegovina 15.0%; Italy 13.5%; Germany 10.9%

Age Breakdown

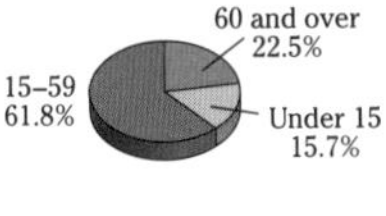

60 and over 22.5%
15–59 61.8%
Under 15 15.7%

[1]Includes Kosovo. [2]Excludes Kosovo

Serbia first became independent in 1878. After World War I, Serbia (with Montenegro), as part of Yugoslavia, had no flag of its own. Again independent in 2006 (from both Montenegro and Yugoslavia), Serbia now flies this flag, adopted in 2004. The four Cyrillic *C*s in the coat of arms are thought to mean, “Only unity will save the Serbs.”

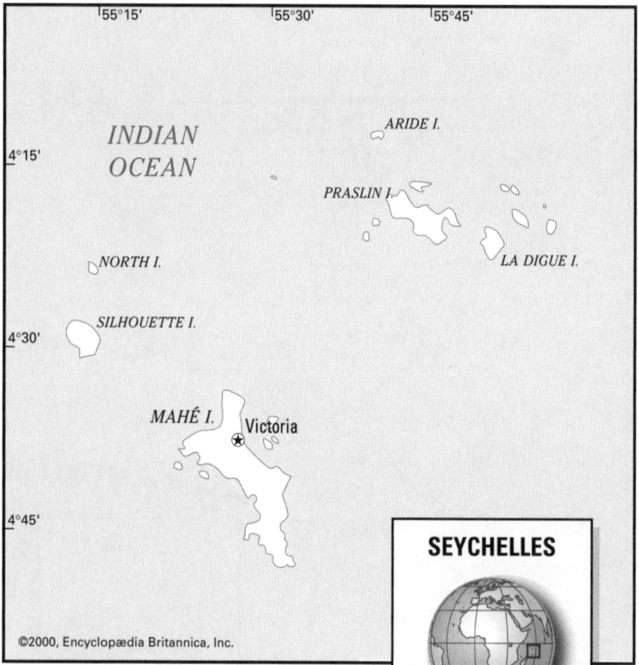

55°15'
55°30'
55°45'
4°15'
4°30'
4°45'
INDIAN OCEAN
ARIDE I.
PRASLIN I.
LA DIGUE I.
NORTH I.
SILHOUETTE I.
MAHÉ I.
Victoria
©2000, Encyclopædia Britannica, Inc.
SEYCHELLES
Scale 1: 1,380,000
0
5
10
15 mi
0
10
20 km

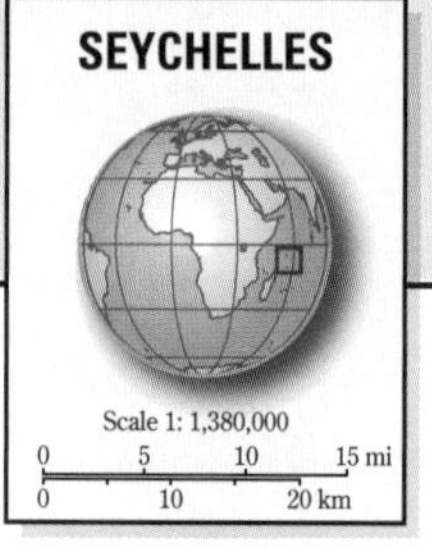

Official name: Republic of Seychelles
Head of government: President
Official language: none
Monetary unit: Seychelles rupee
Area: 176 sq. mi. (455 sq. km.)
Population (2005): 82,800
GNP per capita (2004): U.S.$8,090
Principal exports (2003): canned tuna 69.0%, other fish 3.7%; reexports 23.1%, of which petroleum products 19.8% *to:* United Kingdom 39.2%; France 32.0%; Italy 14.5%; Germany 7.5%

Age Breakdown

Under 15
25.5%
15–59
64.1%
60 and over
10.4%

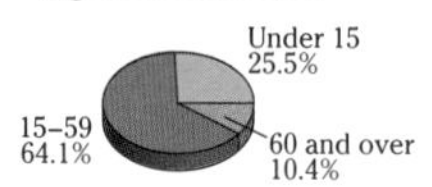

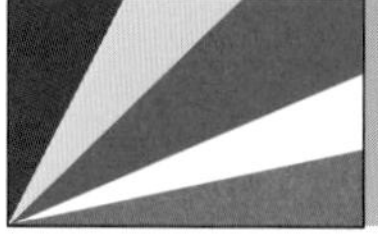

The former British colony underwent a revolution in 1977. The government was democratized in 1993, and on Jan. 8, 1996, a new flag was designed. The blue color is for sky and sea, yellow is for the sun, red is for the people and their work for unity and love, white is for social justice and harmony, and green is for the land and natural environment.

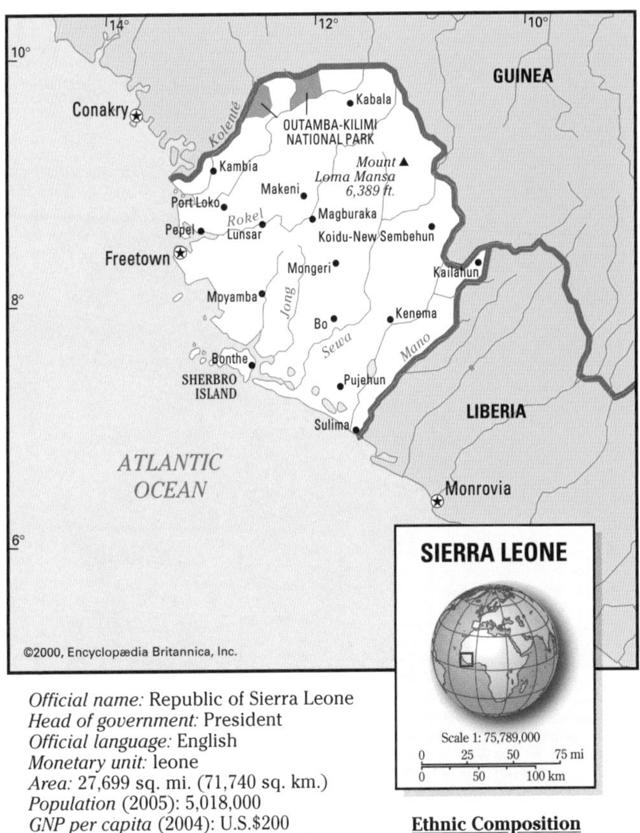

Official name: Republic of Sierra Leone
Head of government: President
Official language: English
Monetary unit: leone
Area: 27,699 sq. mi. (71,740 sq. km.)
Population (2005): 5,018,000
GNP per capita (2004): U.S.$200
Principal exports (2002): diamonds 85.7%, cocoa 2.5% *to:* Belgium 40.6%; U.S. 9.1%; U.K. 8.5%; Germany 7.8%; Japan 5.6%

Ethnic Composition

Mende 26.0%
Temne 24.6%
Limba 7.1%
Kuranko 5.5%
Kono 4.2%
Other 32.6%

Under British colonial control Sierre Leone was founded as a home for freed slaves. With independence on April 27, 1961, the flag was hoisted. Its stripes stand for agriculture and the mountains (green); unity and justice (white); and the aspiration to contribute to world peace, especially through the use of the natural harbor at Freetown (blue).

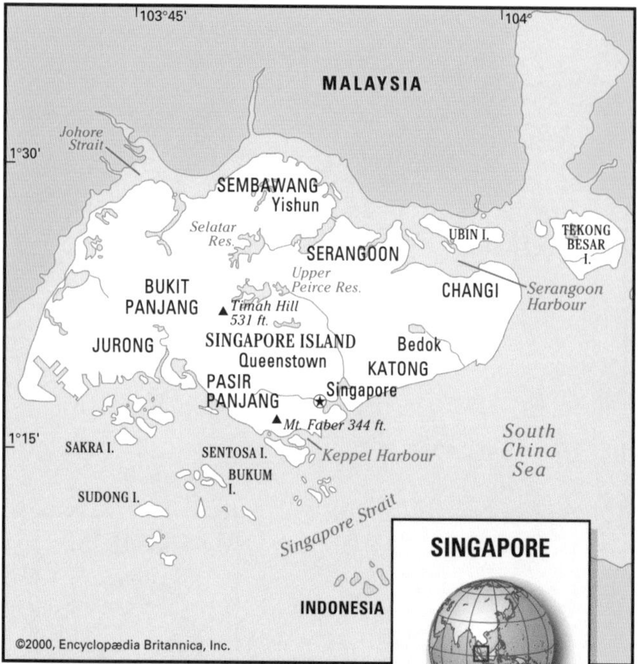

SINGAPORE

Scale 1: 740,000

0 4 8 mi
0 6 12 km

Official name: Republic of Singapore
Head of government: Prime Minister
Official languages: Chinese; Malay; Tamil; English
Monetary unit: Singapore dollar
Area: 269.9 sq. mi. (699.0 sq. km.)
Population (2005): 4,291,000
GNP per capita (2004): U.S.$24,220
Principal exports (2003): electronic valves 20.9%, computers and parts 17.9%, chemicals 11.8%, crude and refined petroleum 10.9%, telecommunications apparatus 4.6% *to:* Malaysia 15.8%; U.S. 13.3%; Hong Kong 10.0%; China 7.0%; Japan 6.7%; Taiwan 4.8%

Ethnic Composition

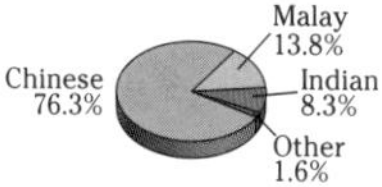

Chinese 76.3%
Malay 13.8%
Indian 8.3%
Other 1.6%

On Dec. 3, 1959, the flag was acquired, and it was retained after separation from Malaysia on Aug. 9, 1965. The red and white stripes stand for universal brotherhood, equality, purity, and virtue. The crescent symbolizes the growth of a young country, while the five stars are for democracy, peace, progress, justice, and equality.

SLOVAKIA

Scale 1: 6,249,000

0 30 60 mi

0 40 80 km

Official name: Slovak Republic
Head of government: Prime Minister
Official language: Slovak
Monetary unit: Slovak koruna
Area: 18,933 sq. mi. (49,035 sq. km.)
Population (2005): 5,384,000
GNP per capita (2004): U.S.$6,480
Principal exports (2002): transport equipment 21.2%, machinery 18.8%, base and fabricated metals 14.3%, mineral fuels 7.2% *to:* Germany 26.0%; Czech Republic 15.2%; Italy 10.7%; Austria 7.7%; Hungary 5.5%

Ethnic Composition

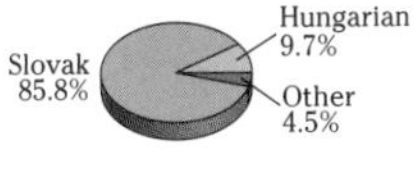

Slovak 85.8%
Hungarian 9.7%
Other 4.5%

In 1189 the kingdom of Hungary (including Slovakia) introduced a double-barred cross in its coat of arms; this symbol was altered in 1848-49 by Slovak nationalists. After a period of communist rule, the tricolor was made official in 1989. On Sept. 3, 1992, the shield was added to the white-blue-red flag to differentiate it from the flag of Russia.

SLOVENIA

Scale 1: 4,314,000

0 20 40 mi
0 30 60 km

Official name: Republic of Slovenia
Head of government: Prime Minister
Official language: Slovene
Monetary unit: Slovene tolar
Area: 7,827 sq. mi. (20,273 sq. km.)
Population (2005): 1,999,000
GNP per capita (2004): U.S.$11,250
Principal exports (2003): machinery and transport equipment 36.5%, of which road vehicles 11.4%; chemicals 13.8%; furniture 6.9% *to:* Germany 23.1%; Italy 13.1%; Croatia 8.9%; Austria 7.3%; France 5.7%

Age Breakdown

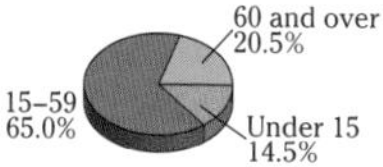

60 and over 20.5%
15–59 65.0%
Under 15 14.5%

Under the current flag Slovenia proclaimed independence on June 25, 1991, but it was opposed for a time by the Yugoslav army. The flag is the same as that of Russia and Slovakia except for the coat of arms. It depicts the peaks of Triglav (the nation's highest mountain), the waves of the Adriatic coast, and three stars on a blue background.

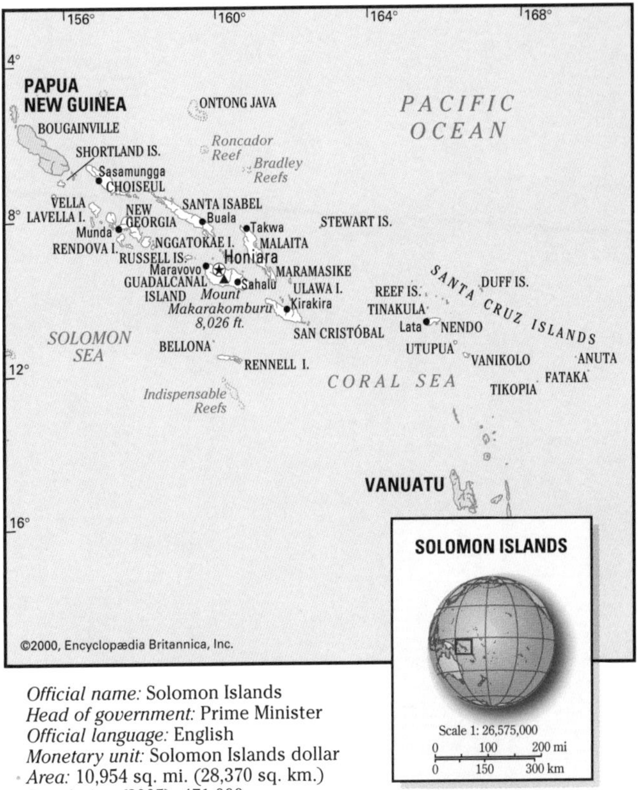
156°
160°
164°
168°
4°
8°
12°
16°
PAPUA
NEW GUINEA
BOUGAINVILLE
SHORTLAND IS.
ONTONG JAVA
Roncador
Reef
Bradley
Reefs
PACIFIC
OCEAN
Sasamungga
CHOISEUL
VELLA
LAVELLA I.
NEW
GEORGIA
Munda
RENDOVA I.
SANTA ISABEL
Buala
Takwa
STEWART IS.
NGGATOKAE I.
MALAITA
RUSSELL IS.
Honiara
Maravovo
MARAMASIKE
GUADALCANAL
ISLAND
Sahalu
Mount
Makarakomburu
8,026 ft.
ULAWA I.
Kirakira
REEF IS.
TINAKULA
SANTA CRUZ ISLANDS
DUFF IS.
Lata
NENDO
SAN CRISTÓBAL
SOLOMON
SEA
BELLONA
RENNELL I.
UTUPUA
VANIKOLO
ANUTA
FATAKA
TIKOPIA
CORAL SEA
Indispensable
Reefs
VANUATU
©2000, Encyclopædia Britannica, Inc.
SOLOMON ISLANDS
Scale 1: 26,575,000
0
100
200 mi
0
150
300 km

Official name: Solomon Islands
Head of government: Prime Minister
Official language: English
Monetary unit: Solomon Islands dollar
Area: 10,954 sq. mi. (28,370 sq. km.)
Population (2005): 471,000
GNP per capita (2004): U.S.$550
Principal exports (2003): timber 66.6%, fish products 16.7%, cacao beans 9.6% *to:* China 25.8%; Japan 17.9%; South Korea 15.2%; Philippines 9.9%; Thailand 6.2%; Singapore 5.6%

Age Breakdown

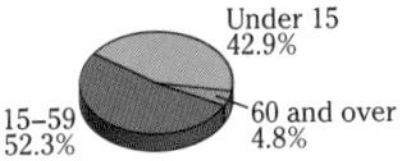
Under 15
42.9%
15–59
52.3%
60 and over
4.8%

The flag was introduced on Nov. 18, 1977, eight months before independence from Britain. The yellow stripe stands for the sun. The green triangle is for the trees and crops of the fertile land, while the blue triangle symbolizes rivers, rain, and the ocean. The five stars represented the original five districts of the island.

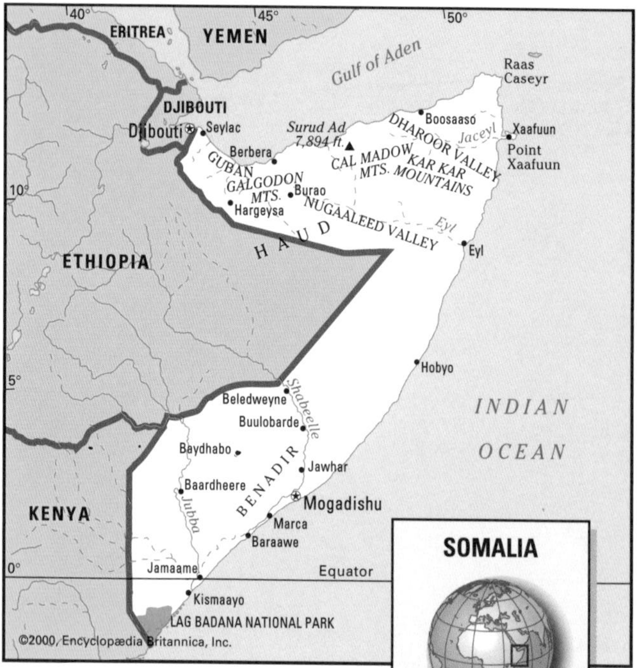

Official name: Somalia
Head of government: President assisted by Prime Minister
Official languages: Somali; Arabic
Monetary unit: Somali shilling
Area: 246,000 sq. mi. (637,000 sq. km.)
Population (2005): 8,228,000
GNP per capita (2004): U.S.$240
Principal exports (2003): agricultural products 45.1%, of which live sheep and goats 25.6% *to* (2004): Thailand 29.0%; U.A.E. 24.0%; Yemen 15.0%; India 8.0%; Oman 6.0%

Age Breakdown

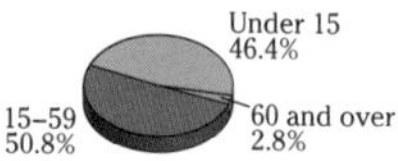

Under 15 46.4%
15–59 50.8%
60 and over 2.8%

From the mid-19th century, areas in the Horn of Africa with Somali populations were divided between Ethiopia, France, Britain, and Italy. On Oct. 12, 1954, with the partial unification of these areas, the flag was adopted with a white star, each point referring to a Somali homeland. The colors were influenced by the colors of the United Nations.

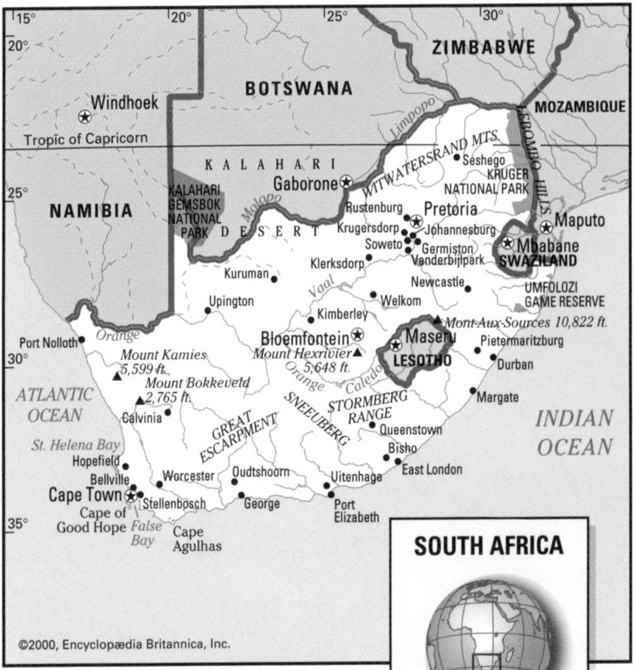

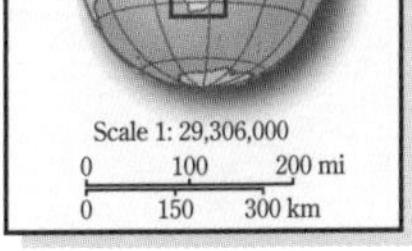

SOUTH AFRICA

Scale 1: 29,306,000
0 100 200 mi
0 150 300 km

Official name: Republic of South Africa
Head of government: President
Official languages: Afrikaans; English; Ndebele; Pedi; Sotho; Swazi; Tsonga; Tswana; Venda; Xhosa; Zulu
Monetary unit: rand
Area: 470,693 sq. mi. (1,219,090 sq. km.)
Population (2005): 46,888,000
GNP per capita (2004): U.S.$3,630
Principal exports (2002): gold *c.* 13%; platinum *c.* 11%; iron and steel 10.5%; road vehicles 10.4%; food 8.2%; diamonds 6.7% *to:* U.K. 10.9%; U.S. 10.1%; Germany 8.2%; Japan 5.6%

Ethnic Composition

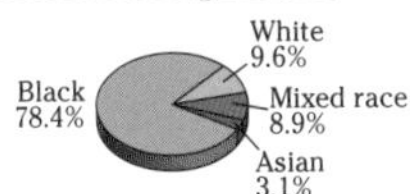

With the decline of apartheid, the flag was hoisted on April 27, 1994, and confirmed in 1996. Its six colors collectively represent Zulus, English or Afrikaners, Muslims, supporters of the African National Congress, and other groups. The Y-symbol stands for "merging history and present political realities" into a united and prosperous future.

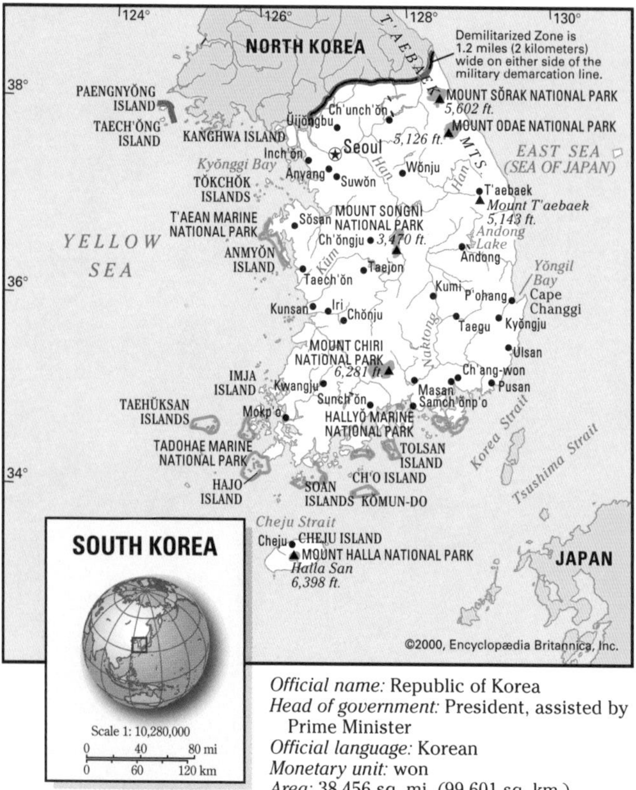

SOUTH KOREA

Scale 1: 10,280,000
0 40 80 mi
0 60 120 km

Official name: Republic of Korea
Head of government: President, assisted by Prime Minister
Official language: Korean
Monetary unit: won
Area: 38,456 sq. mi. (99,601 sq. km.)
Population (2005): 48,294,000
GNP per capita (2004): U.S.$13,980
Principal exports (2003): machinery and apparatus 44.7%, transport equipment 17.8%, chemicals 9.2%, textiles 5.6% *to:* China 18.6%; United States 17.7%; Japan 8.9%; Hong Kong 7.6%; Taiwan 3.6%

Age Breakdown

Under 15 19.6%
15–59 69.7%
60 and over 10.7%

The flag was adopted in August 1882. Its white background is for peace, while the central emblem represents yin-yang (Korean: *um-yang*), the duality of the universe. The black bars recall sun, moon, earth, heaven and other Confucian principles. Outlawed under Japanese rule, the flag was revived in 1945 and slightly modified in 1950 and 1984.

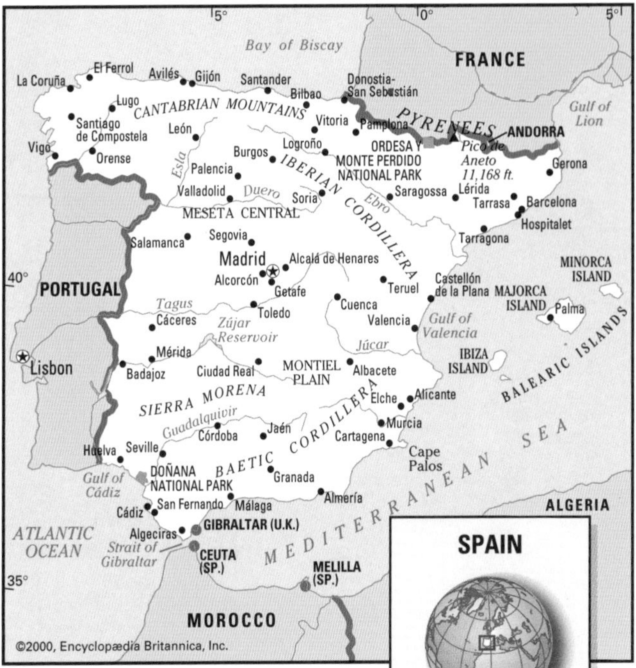

SPAIN

Scale 1: 16,741,000

0 75 150 mi
0 100 200 km

Official name: Kingdom of Spain
Head of government: Prime Minister
Official language: Castilian Spanish
Monetary unit: euro
Area: 195,363 sq. mi. (505,988 sq. km.)
Population (2005): 44,079,000
GNP per capita (2004): U.S.$21,210
Principal exports (2002): transport equipment 22.7%, agricultural products 15.4%, machinery 15.1%, chemicals 8.7% *to:* France 19.0%; Germany 11.5%; Portugal 10.2%; U.K. 9.6%; Italy 9.4%

Ethnic Composition

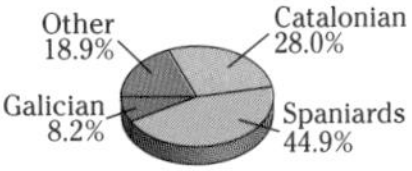

- Catalonian 28.0%
- Spaniards 44.9%
- Galician 8.2%
- Other 18.9%

The colors of the flag have no official symbolic meaning. Introduced in 1785 by King Charles III, the flag was changed only under the Spanish Republic (1931–39). Under different regimes, however, the coat of arms has been altered. The current design dates from Dec. 18, 1981, with the death of Francisco Franco and the resurgence of democracy.

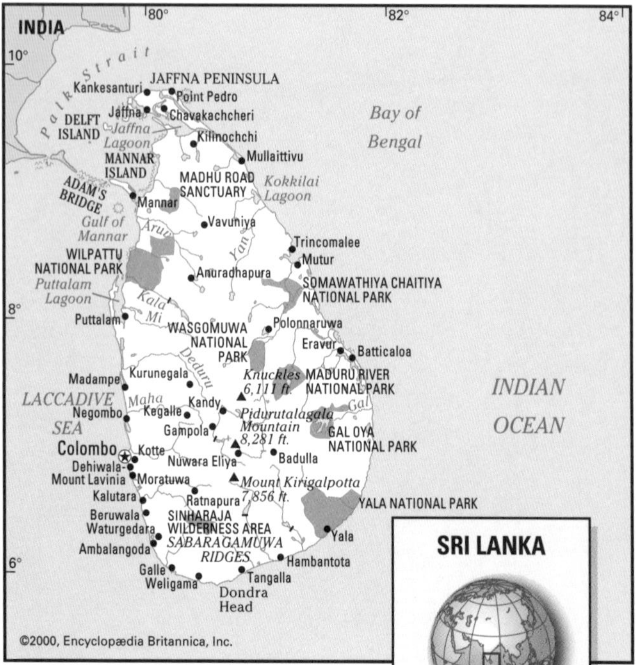

INDIA
Palk Strait
JAFFNA PENINSULA
Kankesanturai
Point Pedro
Jaffna
Chavakachcheri
DELFT ISLAND
Jaffna Lagoon
Kilinochchi
MANNAR ISLAND
Mullaittivu
ADAM'S BRIDGE
Mannar
MADHU ROAD SANCTUARY
Kokkilai Lagoon
Gulf of Mannar
Vavuniya
Aruvi
Yan
Trincomalee
Mutur
WILPATTU NATIONAL PARK
Anuradhapura
Puttalam Lagoon
SOMAWATHIYA CHAITIYA NATIONAL PARK
Kala
Mi
Puttalam
WASGOMUWA NATIONAL PARK
Polonnaruwa
Eravur
Batticaloa
Deduru
Kurunegala
Madampe
Knuckles 6,111 ft.
MADURU RIVER NATIONAL PARK
LACCADIVE SEA
Maha
Kandy
Gal
Negombo
Kegalle
Pidurutalagala Mountain 8,281 ft.
Gampola
GAL OYA NATIONAL PARK
INDIAN OCEAN
Bay of Bengal
Colombo
Kotte
Badulla
Nuwara Eliya
Dehiwala-Mount Lavinia
Moratuwa
Mount Kirigalpotta 7,856 ft.
Kalutara
Ratnapura
YALA NATIONAL PARK
Beruwala
SINHARAJA WILDERNESS AREA
Waturgedara
Yala
SABARAGAMUWA RIDGES
Ambalangoda
Hambantota
Galle
Tangalla
Weligama
Dondra Head
10°
8°
6°
80°
82°
84°

SRI LANKA

Scale 1: 7,798,000
0 30 60 mi
0 50 100 km

Official name: Democratic Socialist Republic of Sri Lanka
Head of government: President
Official languages: Sinhala; Tamil
Monetary unit: Sri Lanka rupee
Area: 25,332 sq. mi. (65,610 sq. km.)
Population (2005): 20,743,000
GNP per capita (2004): U.S.$1,010
Principal exports (2004): clothing and accessories 48.8%, tea 12.8%, precious and semiprecious stones 6.1%, rubber products 4.9% *to:* U.S. 32.4%; U.K. 13.5%; India 6.8%; Belgium 5.1%; Germany 4.7%

Ethnic Composition

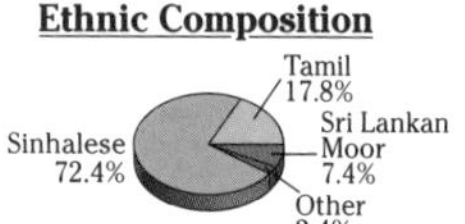

From the 5th century BCE the Lion flag was a symbol of the Sinhalese people. The flag was replaced by the Union Jack in 1815 but readopted upon independence in 1948. The stripes of green (for Muslims) and orange (for Hindus) were added in 1951. In 1972 four leaves of the Bo tree were added as a symbol of Buddhism; the leaves were altered in 1978.

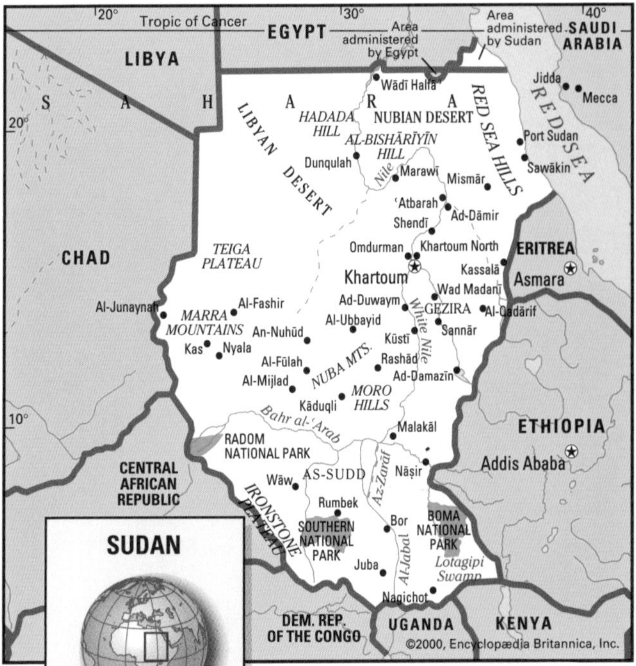

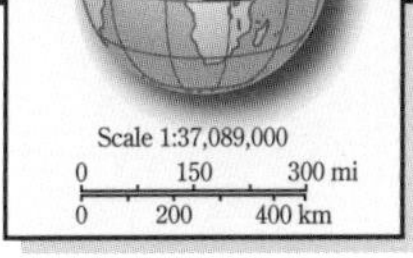

SUDAN

Scale 1:37,089,000

0 150 300 mi

0 200 400 km

Official name: Republic of the Sudan
Head of government: President
Official language: Arabic
Monetary unit: Sudanese dinar
Area: 966,757 sq. mi. (2,503,890 sq. km.)
Population (2005): 36,233,000
GNP per capita (2004): U.S.$530
Principal exports (2004): crude petroleum 78.3%, sesame seeds 4.7%, refined petroleum 3.8%, sheep and goats 3.7%, cotton 2.5% *to:* China 66.9%; Japan 10.6%; Saudi Arabia 4.3%

Ethnic Composition

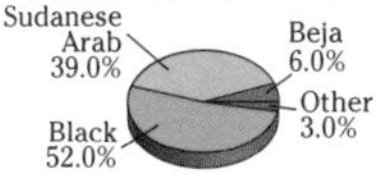

Sudanese Arab 39.0%
Beja 6.0%
Other 3.0%
Black 52.0%

The flag was first hoisted on May 20, 1970. It uses Pan-Arab colors. Black is for al-Mahdi (a leader in the 1800s) and the name of the country (sudan in Arabic means black); white recalls the revolutionary flag of 1924 and suggests peace and optimism; red is for patriotic martyrs, socialism, and progress; and green is for prosperity and Islam.

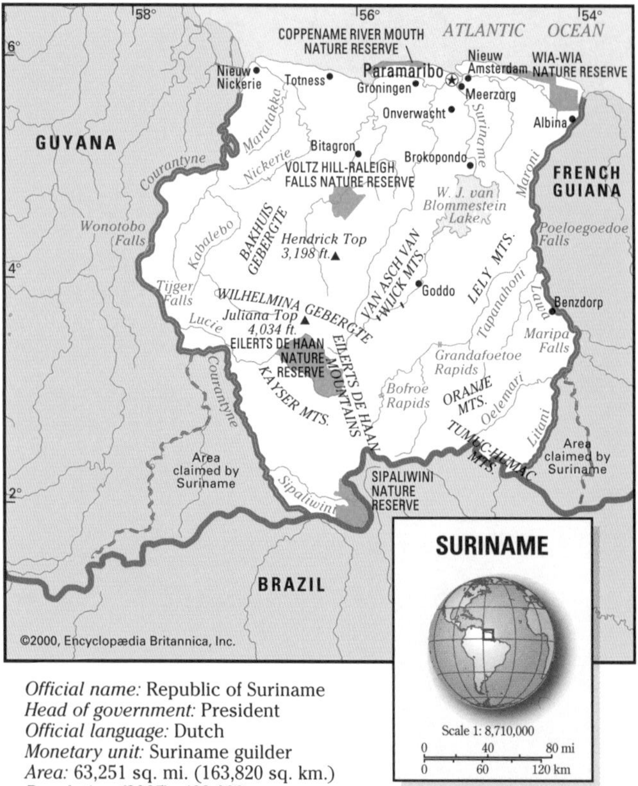

Official name: Republic of Suriname
Head of government: President
Official language: Dutch
Monetary unit: Suriname guilder
Area: 63,251 sq. mi. (163,820 sq. km.)
Population (2005): 493,000
GNP per capita (2004): U.S.$2,250
Principal exports (2003): alumina 52.6%, shrimp and fish 5.8%, crude petroleum 5.4%, rice 2.2% *to:* U.S. 21.0%; Norway 16.5%; France 9.1%; Trinidad and Tobago 6.4%

Ethnic Composition

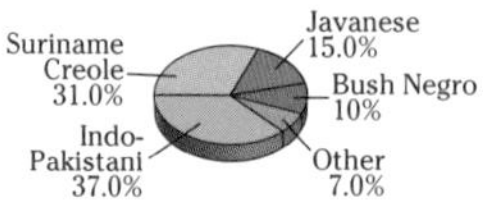

Suriname Creole 31.0%
Javanese 15.0%
Bush Negro 10%
Other 7.0%
Indo-Pakistani 37.0%

Adopted on Nov. 21, 1975, four days before independence from the Dutch, the flag of Suriname features green stripes for jungles and agriculture, white for justice and freedom, and red for the progressive spirit of a young nation. The yellow star is symbolic of the unity of the country, its golden future, and the people's spirit of sacrifice.

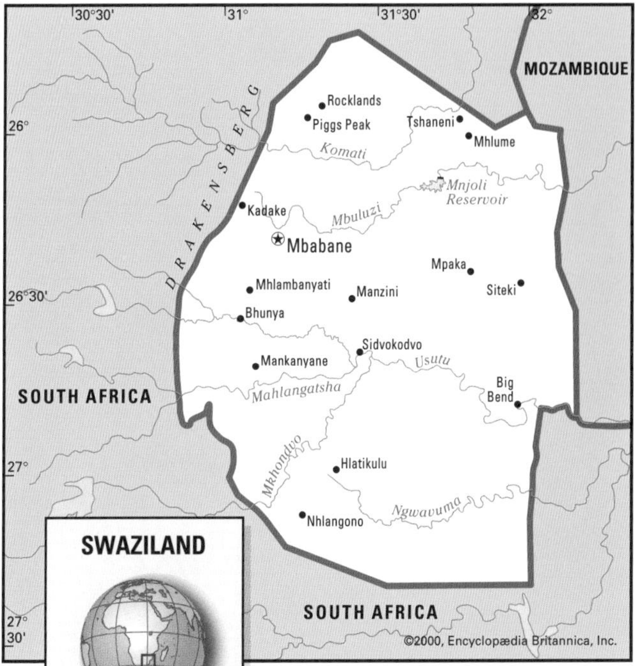

SWAZILAND

Scale 1: 2,956,000
0 10 20 30 mi
0 20 40 km

Ethnic Composition

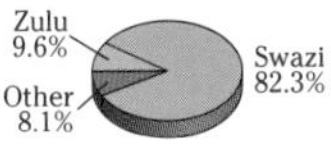

Zulu 9.6%
Other 8.1%
Swazi 82.3%

Official name: Kingdom of Swaziland
Head of government: King, assisted by Prime Minister
Official languages: Swazi; English
Monetary unit: lilangeni
Area: 6,704 sq. mi. (17,364 sq. km.)
Population (2005): 1,032,000
GNP per capita (2004): U.S.$1,660
Principal exports (2004): soft drinks and juices 38.0%, sugar 14.0%, clothing 12.0%, wood and wood products 9.0% *to:* South Africa 78.0%; Mozambique 4.6%; United States 4.0%

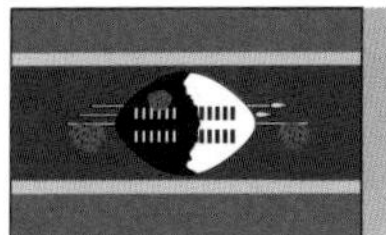

The flag dates to the creation of a military banner in 1941, when Swazi troops were preparing for the Allied invasion of Italy. On April 25, 1967, it was hoisted as the national flag. The crimson stripe stands for past battles, yellow for mineral wealth, and blue for peace. Featured are a Swazi war shield, two spears, and a "fighting stick."

Official name: Kingdom of Sweden
Head of government: Prime Minister
Official language: Swedish
Monetary unit: Swedish krona
Area: 173,860 sq. mi. (450,295 sq. km.)
Population (2005): 9,024,000
GNP per capita (2004): U.S.$35,770
Principal exports (2004): machinery and transport equipment 29.4%, telecommunications equipment and electronics 13.6%; paper products 8.1%, pharmaceuticals 6.5% *to:* U.S. 14.5%; Germany 10.0%; Norway 8.4%; U.K. 7.8%

Age Breakdown

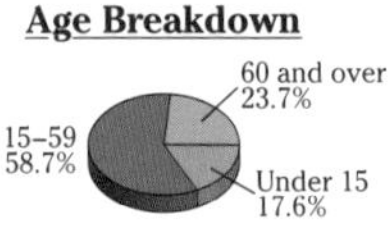

60 and over 23.7%
15–59 58.7%
Under 15 17.6%

From the 14th century the coat of arms of Sweden had a blue field with three golden crowns, and the earlier Folkung dynasty used a shield of blue and white wavy stripes with a gold lion. The off-center "Scandinavian cross" was influenced by the flag of the rival kingdom of Denmark. The current flag law was adopted on July 1, 1906.

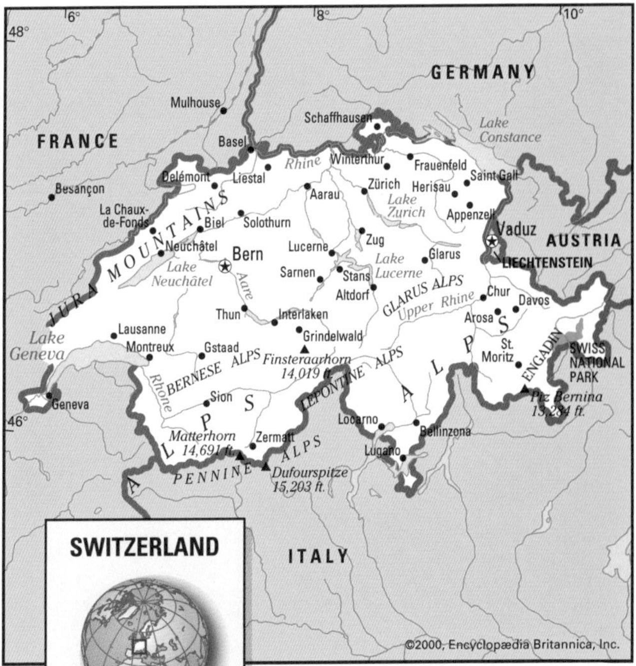

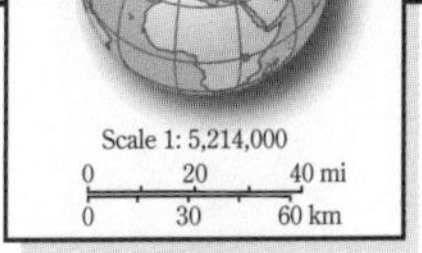

SWITZERLAND

Scale 1: 5,214,000

0 20 40 mi

0 30 60 km

Official name: Swiss Confederation
Head of government: President of the Federal Council
Official languages: French; German; Italian
Monetary unit: Swiss franc
Area: 15,940 sq. mi. (41,284 sq. km.)
Population (2005): 7,519,000
GNP per capita (2004): U.S.$48,230
Principal exports (2002): chemicals 33.4%, machinery and electronics 24.3%, precision instruments, watches, and jewelry 17.3% *to* (2003): Germany 21.2%; France 8.8%; Italy 8.4%; U.K. 4.8%; Japan 3.9%

National Composition

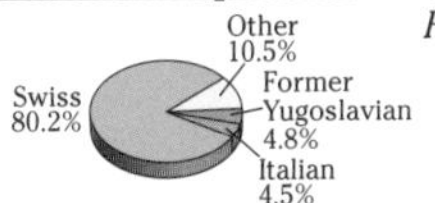

The Swiss flag is ultimately based on the war flag of the Holy Roman Empire. Schwyz, one of the original three cantons of the Swiss Confederation, placed a narrow white cross in the corner of its flag in 1240. This was also used in 1339 at the Battle of Laupen. Following the 1848 constitution, the flag was recognized by the army, and it was established as the national flag on land on Dec. 12, 1889.

SYRIA

Scale 1: 10,048,000

0 50 100 mi

0 80 160 km

Official name: Syrian Arab Republic
Head of government: President
Official language: Arabic
Monetary unit: Syrian pound
Area: 71,498 sq. mi. (185,180 sq. km.)
Population (2005): 17,794,000
GNP per capita (2004): U.S.$1,190
Principal exports (2003): crude petroleum and petroleum products 76.3%, textiles 4.2%, live animals and meat 4.2% *to* (2002): Italy 33.0%; France 14.0%; Turkey 8.0%; Saudi Arabia 8.0%

Ethnic Composition

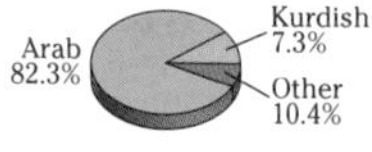

Arab 82.3%
Kurdish 7.3%
Other 10.4%

In 1918 the Arab Revolt flag flew over Syria, which joined Egypt in the United Arab Republic in 1958 and based its new flag on that of the Egyptian revolution of 1952; its stripes were red-white-black, with two green stars for the constituent states. In 1961 Syria broke from the union, but it readopted the flag on March 29, 1980.

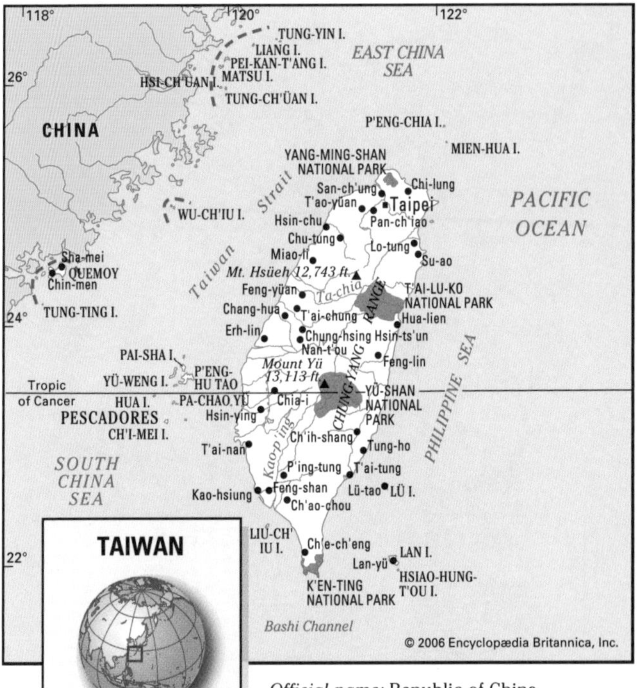

TAIWAN

Scale 1: 8,448,000

Official name: Republic of China
Head of government: Premier
Official language: Mandarin Chinese
Monetary unit: New Taiwan dollar
Area: 13,972 sq. mi. (36,188 sq. km.)
Population (2005): 22,726,000
GNP per capita (2004): U.S.$13,160
Principal exports (2004): nonelectrical machinery, electrical machinery and electronics 50.5%, metal products 10.0%, plastic articles 7.2%, textiles 7.2% *to:* China 19.5%; Hong Kong 17.1%; U.S. 16.2%; Japan 7.6%; Singapore 3.6%

Religious Affiliation

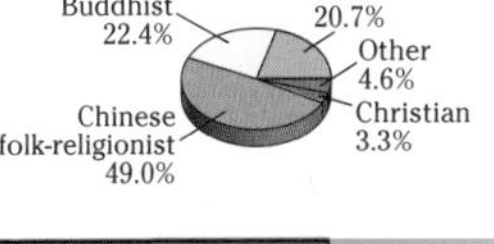

Under Chiang Kai-shek, a new Chinese national flag was adopted on Oct. 28, 1928, and it was carried to Taiwan in 1949–50 when the Nationalists fled the mainland. The three colors stand for the "Three Principles of the People" of the Nationalist (Kuomintang) Party—nationalism, democracy, and socialism.

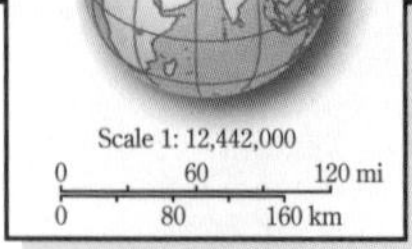

TAJIKISTAN

Scale 1: 12,442,000

0 60 120 mi

0 80 160 km

Ethnic Composition

Tajik 80.0%
Uzbek 15.3%
Other 3.6%
Russian 1.1%

Official name: Republic of Tajikistan
Head of government: Prime Minister
Official language: Tajik (Tojik)
Monetary unit: somoni
Area: 55,300 sq. mi. (143,100 sq. km.)
Population (2005): 6,849,000
GNP per capita (2004): U.S.$280
Principal exports (2004): aluminum 62.6%, cotton fiber 17.7%, electricity 6.6% *to:* The Netherlands 25.4%; Turkey 24.4%; Latvia 9.9%; Switzerland 9.7%; Uzbekistan 9.5%

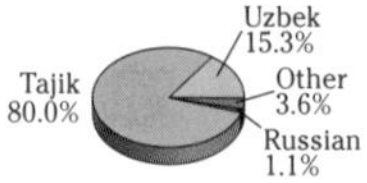

Following independence from the Soviet Union in 1991, Tajikistan developed a new flag on Nov. 24, 1992. The green stripe is for agriculture, while red is for sovereignty. White is for the main crop—cotton. The central crown contains seven stars representing unity among workers, peasants, intellectuals, and other social classes.

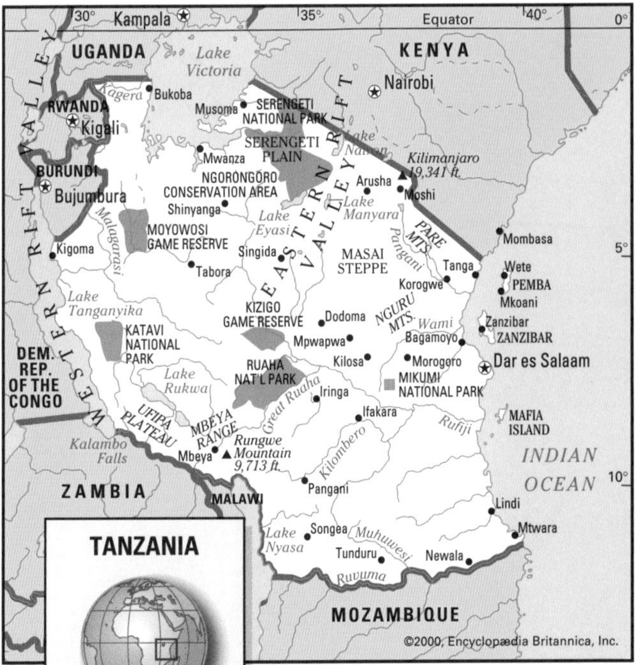

TANZANIA

Scale 1: 21,031,000
0 100 200 mi
0 150 300 km

Religious Affiliation

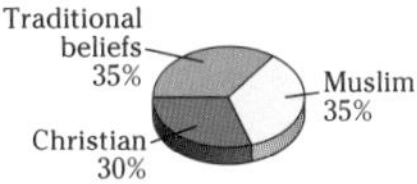

Traditional beliefs 35%
Muslim 35%
Christian 30%

Official name: United Republic of Tanzania
Head of government: President
Official languages: Swahili; English
Monetary unit: Tanzania shilling
Area: 364,017 sq. mi. (942,799 sq. km.)
Population (2005): 36,766,000
GNP per capita (2004): U.S.$330
Principal exports (2002): gold, diamonds and other gemstones 42.4%, cashew nuts 5.8%, tobacco 5.6%, coffee 4.0% *to:* U.K. 18.5%; France 17.4%; Japan 11.0%; India 7.3%

In April 1964 Tanganyika and Zanzibar united, and in July their flag traditions melded to create the current design. The black stripe is for the majority population, while green is for the rich agricultural resources of the land. Mineral wealth is reflected in the yellow fimbriations (narrow borders), while the Indian Ocean is symbolized by blue.

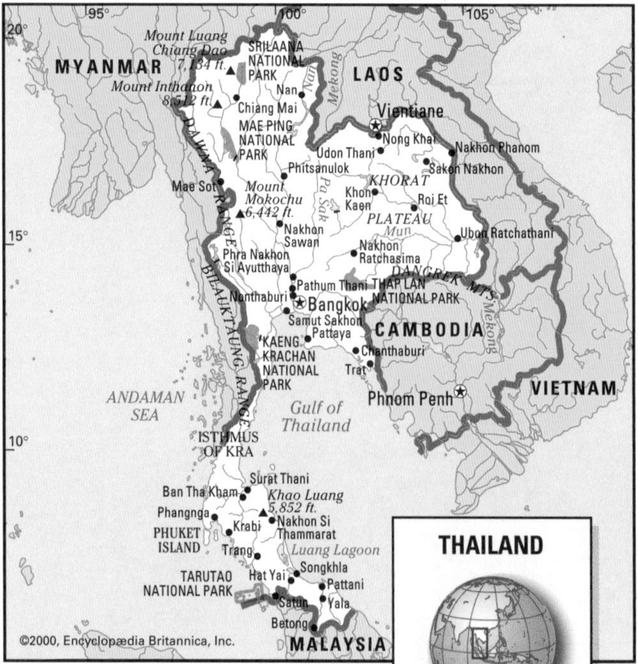

THAILAND

Scale 1: 24,526,000
0 100 200 mi
0 150 300 km

Official name: Kingdom of Thailand
Head of government: Prime Minister
Official language: Thai
Monetary unit: Thai baht
Area: 198,117 sq. mi. (513,120 sq. km.)
Population (2005): 64,186,000
GNP per capita (2004): U.S.$2,540
Principal exports (2001): computers and parts 12.3%, other electronics 7.2%, chemicals 5.7%, garments 5.6% *to:* U.S. 15.9%; Japan 13.9%; China 7.3%; Singapore 7.2%

Ethnic Composition

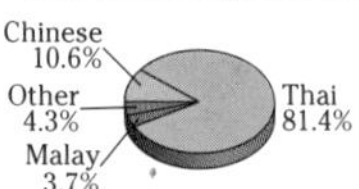

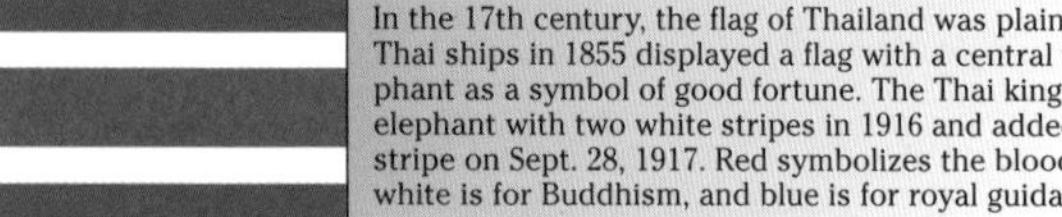

In the 17th century, the flag of Thailand was plain red, and Thai ships in 1855 displayed a flag with a central white elephant as a symbol of good fortune. The Thai king replaced the elephant with two white stripes in 1916 and added the blue stripe on Sept. 28, 1917. Red symbolizes the blood of patriots, white is for Buddhism, and blue is for royal guidance.

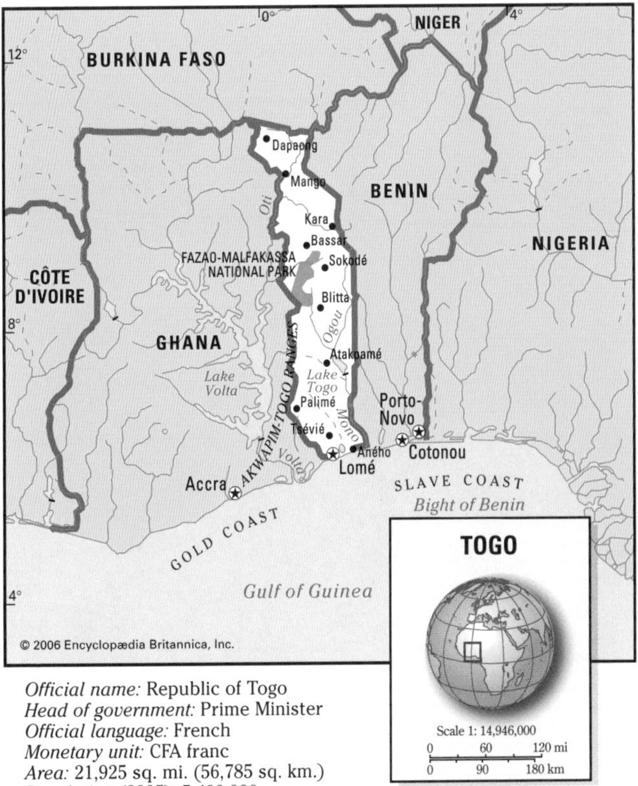

TOGO

Scale 1: 14,946,000

Official name: Republic of Togo
Head of government: Prime Minister
Official language: French
Monetary unit: CFA franc
Area: 21,925 sq. mi. (56,785 sq. km.)
Population (2005): 5,400,000
GNP per capita (2004): U.S.$380
Principal exports (2002): cement 26.5%, phosphates 16.6%, food 16.6%, cotton 15.9%, iron and steel 7.4% *to:* Ghana 21.5%; Benin 13.2%; Burkina Faso 13.0%; Niger 4.6%

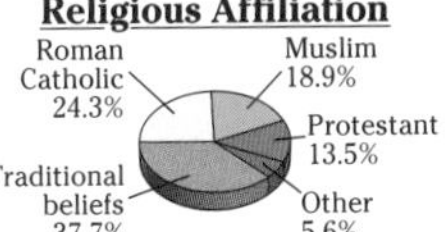

On April 27, 1960, Togo became independent from France under the current flag. Its stripes correspond to the administrative regions and symbolize that the population depends on the land for its sustenance (green) and its own labor for development (yellow). The red is for love, fidelity, and charity, while the white star is for purity and unity.

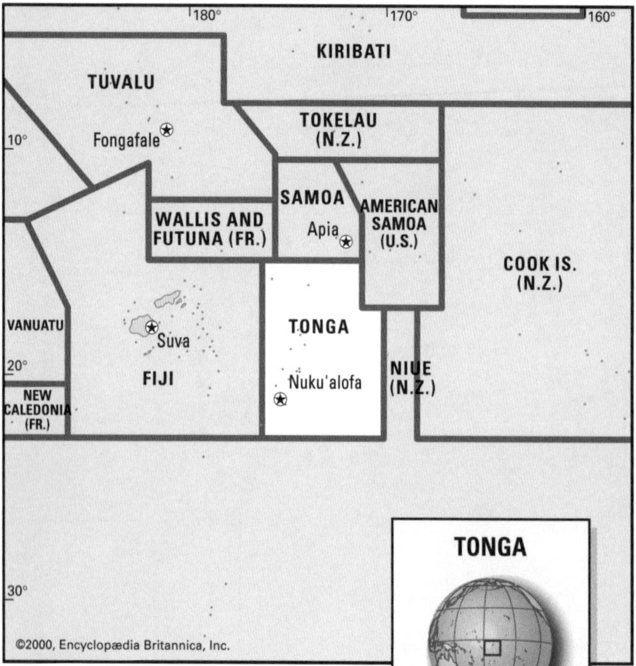

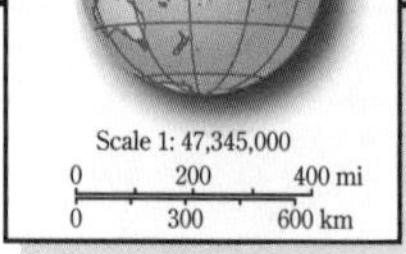

180°
170°
160°
KIRIBATI
TUVALU
Fongafale
10°
TOKELAU
(N.Z.)
SAMOA
Apia
AMERICAN
SAMOA
(U.S.)
WALLIS AND
FUTUNA (FR.)
COOK IS.
(N.Z.)
VANUATU
Suva
TONGA
FIJI
20°
Nuku'alofa
NIUE
(N.Z.)
NEW
CALEDONIA
(FR.)
30°
©2000, Encyclopædia Britannica, Inc.

TONGA
Scale 1: 47,345,000
0 200 400 mi
0 300 600 km

Official name: Kingdom of Tonga
Head of government: King assisted by Privy Council
Official languages: Tongan; English
Monetary unit: pa'anga
Area: 289.5 sq. mi. (749.9 sq. km.)
Population (2005): 98,600
GNP per capita (2004): U.S.$1,830
Principal exports (2003-04): squash 36.6%, fish 32.5%, vanilla beans 14.0% *to:* Japan 39.8%; U.S. 26.6%; New Zealand 6.5%

Religious Affiliation

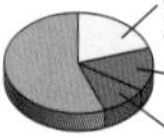

Independent
Christian
20.0%
Protestant
56.0%
Mormon
14.0%
Other
10.0%

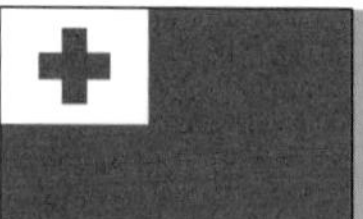

The colors red and white were popular in the Pacific long before the arrival of Europeans. The Tonga constitution (Nov. 4, 1875) established the flag, which was created by King George Tupou I with the advice of a missionary. The cross was chosen as a symbol of the widespread Christian religion, and the color red was related to the blood of Jesus.

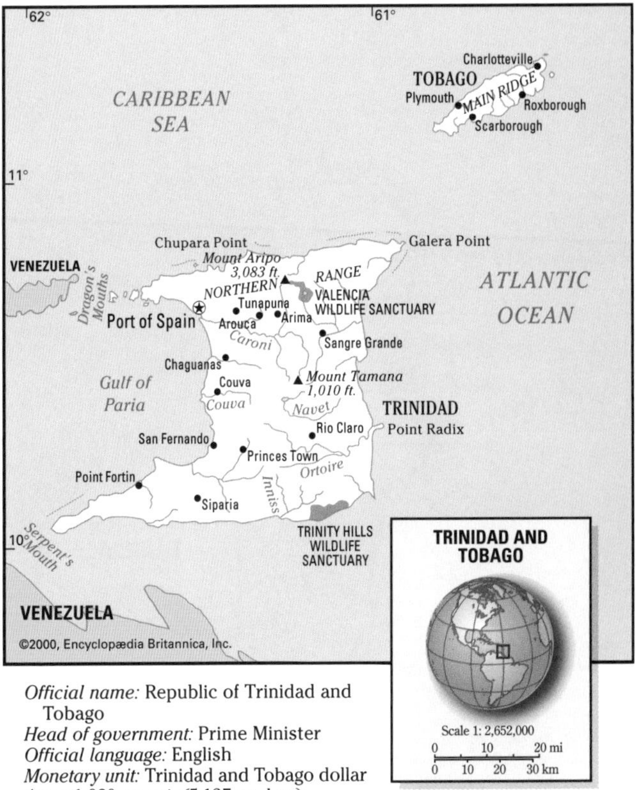

62° 61° 11° 10°

CARIBBEAN SEA

TOBAGO
Charlotteville
Plymouth
MAIN RIDGE
Roxborough
Scarborough

Chupara Point
Galera Point
Mount Aripo 3,083 ft.
NORTHERN RANGE
VALENCIA WILDLIFE SANCTUARY
ATLANTIC OCEAN
VENEZUELA
Dragon's Mouths
Port of Spain
Tunapuna
Arouca
Arima
Caroni
Sangre Grande
Chaguanas
Gulf of Paria
Couva
Couva
Mount Tamana 1,010 ft.
Navet
TRINIDAD
Rio Claro
Point Radix
San Fernando
Princes Town
Ortoire
Point Fortin
Siparia
Inniss
TRINITY HILLS WILDLIFE SANCTUARY
Serpent's Mouth
VENEZUELA

TRINIDAD AND TOBAGO

Scale 1: 2,652,000
0 10 20 mi
0 10 20 30 km

Official name: Republic of Trinidad and Tobago
Head of government: Prime Minister
Official language: English
Monetary unit: Trinidad and Tobago dollar
Area: 1,980 sq. mi. (5,127 sq. km.)
Population (2005): 1,298,000
GNP per capita (2004): U.S.$8,580
Principal exports (2001): refined petroleum 29.4%, floating docks 12.6%, crude petroleum 9.3%, ammonia 8.5% *to:* United States 42.3%; Mexico 7.4%; Jamaica 7.0%

Religious Affiliation

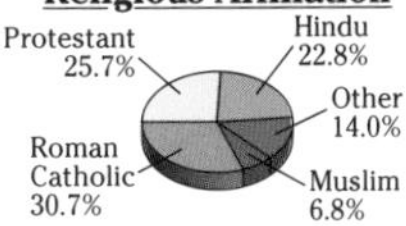

Protestant 25.7%
Hindu 22.8%
Other 14.0%
Roman Catholic 30.7%
Muslim 6.8%

Hoisted on independence day, Aug. 31, 1962, the flag symbolizes earth, water, and fire as well as past, present, and future. Black also is a symbol of unity, strength, and purpose. White recalls the equality and purity of the people and the sea that unites them. Red is for the sun, the vitality of the people and nation, friendliness, and courage.

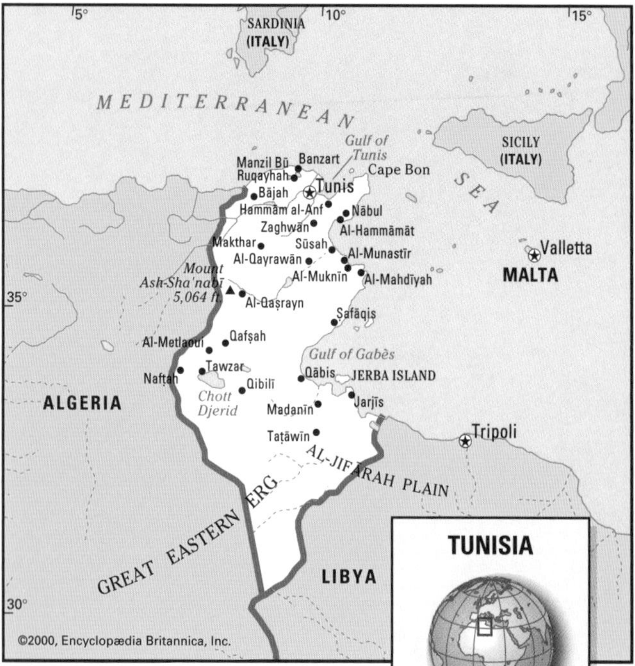

TUNISIA

Scale 1: 15,497,000

Official name: Republic of Tunisia
Head of government: Prime Minister
Official language: Arabic
Monetary unit: dinar
Area: 63,170 sq. mi. (163,610 sq. km.)
Population (2005): 10,038,000
GNP per capita (2004): U.S.$2,630
Principal exports (2004): textiles 37.2%, electrical machinery 11.9%, petroleum 9.6%, motor vehicles 7.3%, iron and steel 6.0% *to:* France 33.1%; Italy 25.3%; Germany 9.2%; Spain 6.1%

Age Breakdown

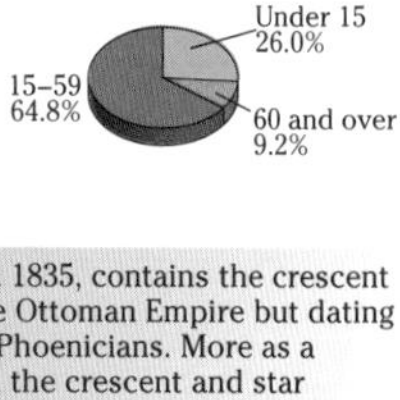

Under 15 26.0%
15–59 64.8%
60 and over 9.2%

The Tunisian flag, established in 1835, contains the crescent and moon, a symbol used by the Ottoman Empire but dating from the ancient Egyptians and Phoenicians. More as a cultural than a religious symbol, the crescent and star came to be associated with Islam because of its widespread adoption in Muslim nations.

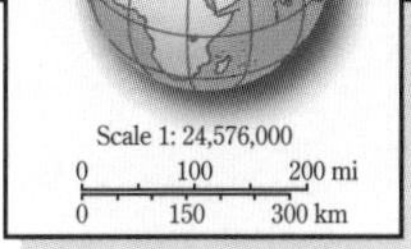

Official name: Republic of Turkey
Head of government: Prime Minister
Official language: Turkish
Monetary unit: Turkish lira
Area: 302,535 sq. mi. (783,562 sq. km.)
Population (2005): 72,083,000
GNP per capita (2004): U.S.$3,750
Principal exports (2003): textiles and clothing 20.3%, vehicles 11.3%, electrical and electronic machinery 7.4%, nonelectrical machinery 6.3%, iron and steel 6.2% *to:* Germany 15.9%; United States 8.0%; U.K. 7.8%; Italy 6.8%; France 6.8%

Religious Affiliation

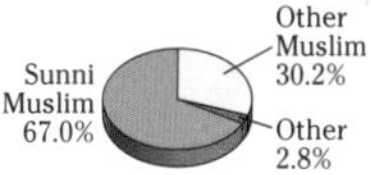

Sunni Muslim 67.0%
Other Muslim 30.2%
Other 2.8%

In June 1793 the flag was established for the navy, although its star had eight points instead of the current five (since about 1844). This design was reconfirmed in 1936 following the revolution led by Ataturk. Various myths are associated with the symbolism of the red color and the star and crescent, but none really explains their origins.

TURKMENISTAN

Scale 1: 19,553,000

Official name: Republic of Turkmenistan
Head of government: President, assisted by a People's Council
Official language: Turkmen
Monetary unit: manat
Area: 188,500 sq. mi. (488,100 sq. km.)
Population (2005): 4,833,000
GNP per capita (2004): U.S.$1,340
Principal exports (2003): natural gas 49.7%, petrochemicals 18.3%, crude petroleum 8.9%, cotton fiber and yarn 5.4% *to* (2004): Ukraine 50.0%; Iran 17.0%; Italy 5.0%; Turkey 5.0%

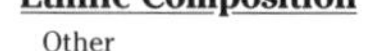

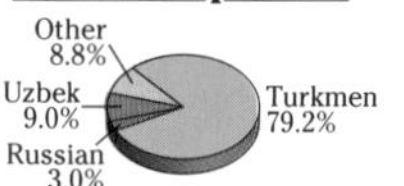

Raised on February 19, 1992, following Turkmenistan's independence from Russia, the flag's stripe holds a design of five carpet motifs associated with local tribes. Green is a symbol of Islam, the white crescent stands for hope, and the stars are for the five senses. In 1997, as a symbol of neutrality, an olive wreath was put on the vertical stripe.

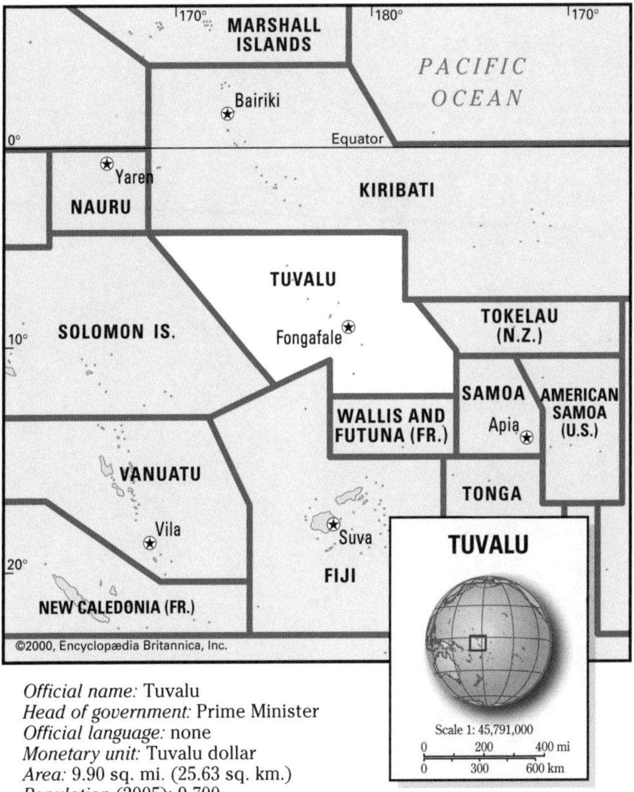

Official name: Tuvalu
Head of government: Prime Minister
Official language: none
Monetary unit: Tuvalu dollar
Area: 9.90 sq. mi. (25.63 sq. km.)
Population (2005): 9,700
GNP per capita (2004): U.S.$2,100
Principal exports (2003): primarily copra, stamps, and handicrafts *to* (2002): Fiji 58.9%; Australia 22.3%; New Zealand 11.4%; Japan 5.7%

Ethnic Composition

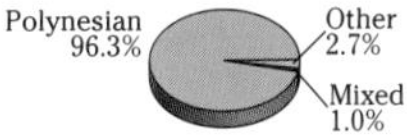

Polynesian 96.3%
Other 2.7%
Mixed 1.0%

On Oct. 1, 1978, three years after separating from the Gilbert Islands, Tuvalu became independent under the current flag. The stars represent the atolls and islands of the country. The Union Jack recalls links with Britain and the Commonwealth. Replaced by supporters of republicanism on Oct. 1, 1995, the flag was reinstated on April 11, 1997.

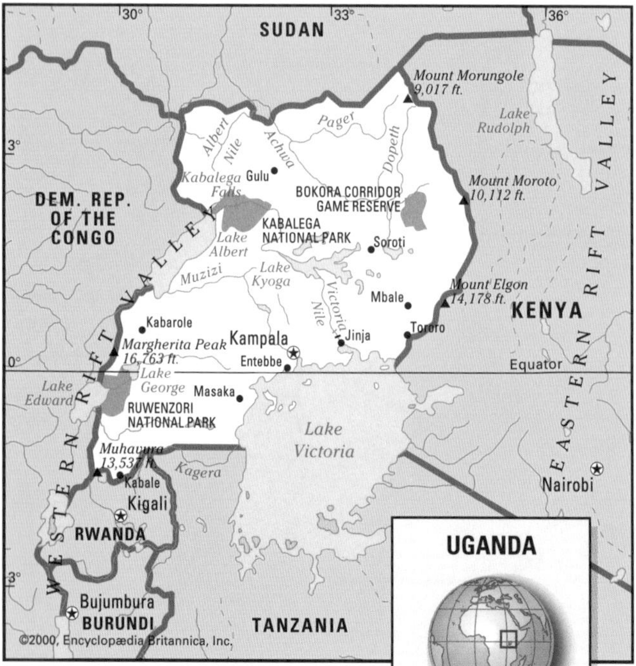

UGANDA

Scale 1: 13,986,000

0 60 120 mi

0 80 160 km

Official name: Republic of Uganda
Head of government: President
Official language: English
Monetary unit: Uganda shilling
Area: 93,065 sq. mi. (241,038 sq. km.)
Population (2005): 87,269,000
GNP per capita (2004): U.S.$270
Principal exports (2004): coffee 18.8%, fish and fish products 15.6%, gold 11.2%, tobacco 6.1%, cotton 6.0%, tea 5.4% *to:* EU countries 36.9%; African countries 34.4%; Switzerland 9.0%; U.A.E. 4.1%

Religious Affiliation

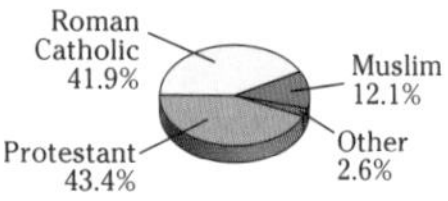

Roman Catholic 41.9%
Muslim 12.1%
Other 2.6%
Protestant 43.4%

The crested crane symbol was selected by the British for Uganda. The flag, established for independence on Oct. 9, 1962, was based on the flag of the ruling Uganda People's Congress (which has three black-yellow-red stripes), with the addition of the crane in the center. Black stands for the people, yellow for sunshine, and red for brotherhood.

Official name: Ukraine
Head of government: Prime Minister
Official language: Ukrainian
Monetary unit: hryvnia
Area: 233,062 sq. mi. (603,628 sq. km.)
Population (2005): 47,075,000
GNP per capita (2004): U.S.$1,260
Principal exports (2004): ferrous metals 39.9%, food 10.6%, chemicals 9.9%, machinery 9.3%, transport equipment 5.2% *to:* Russia 18.0%; Germany 5.8%; Turkey 5.7%; Italy 5.0%; U.S. 4.6%

The first national flag of Ukraine, adopted in 1848, had equal stripes of yellow over blue and was based on the coat of arms of the city of Lviv. In 1918 the stripes were reversed to reflect the symbolism of blue skies over golden wheat fields. A red Soviet banner flew from 1949, but it was replaced by the blue-yellow bicolor on Jan. 28, 1992.

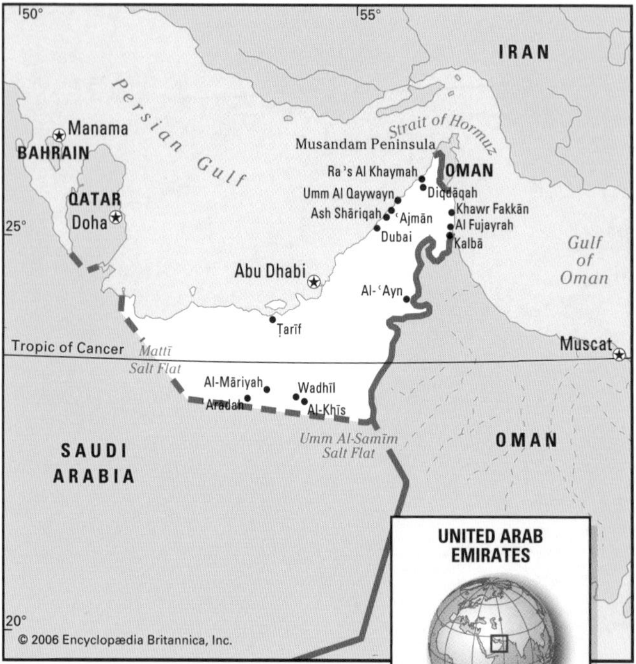

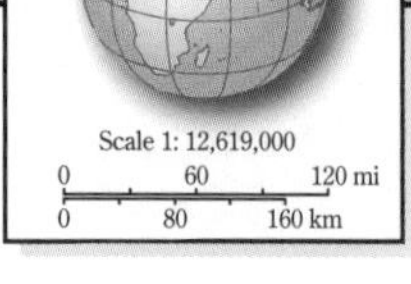

UNITED ARAB EMIRATES

Scale 1: 12,619,000

0 60 120 mi

0 80 160 km

Official name: United Arab Emirates
Head of government: Prime Minister
Official language: Arabic
Monetary unit: UAE dirham
Area: 32,280 sq. mi. (83,600 sq. km.)
Population (2005): 4,690,000
GNP per capita (2004): U.S.$20,000
Principal exports (2001): crude petroleum and refined petroleum 41.3%, natural gas 7.1%, gold 4.4%; reexports 28.9% *to:* Japan 26.1%; South Korea 10.5%; Iran 4.4%; Thailand 3.7%; Singapore 3.4%

Ethnic Composition

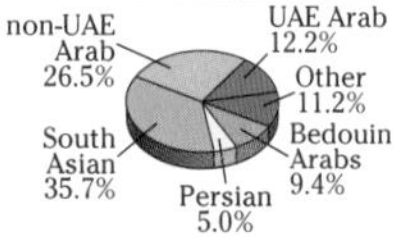

non-UAE Arab 26.5%
UAE Arab 12.2%
Other 11.2%
Bedouin Arabs 9.4%
Persian 5.0%
South Asian 35.7%

On Dec. 2, 1971, six small Arab states formed the United Arab Emirates, and a seventh state joined on Feb. 11, 1972. The flag took its colors from the Arab Revolt flag of 1917. The colors are included in a 13th-century poem which speaks of green Arab lands defended in black battles by blood-red swords of Arabs whose deeds are pure white.

UNITED KINGDOM

Scale 1: 17,114,000

0 50 100 150 mi

0 80 160 240 km

Official name: United Kingdom of Great Britain and Northern Ireland
Head of government: Prime Minister
Official language: English
Monetary unit: pound sterling
Area: 93,635 sq. mi. (242,514 sq. km.)
Population (2005): 60,020,000
GNP per capita (2004): U.S.$33,940
Principal exports (2003): machinery and transport equipment 42.3%, chemicals and chemical products 16.6%, petroleum products 7.8%, food 5.8% *to* (2004): U.S. 15.1%; Germany 11.3%; France 9.7%; Ireland 7.3%

Age Breakdown

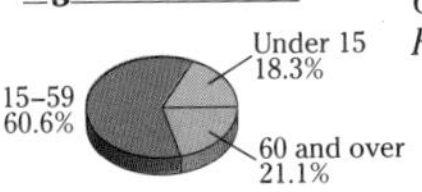

Within the Union Jack are combined the crosses of St. George (a symbol of England), St. Andrew (Scotland), and St. Patrick (Ireland). Its earliest form, called the "Union Flag," or "Great Union," was designed in 1606. The current flag design has been in use since Jan. 1, 1801, when Great Britain and Ireland were joined.

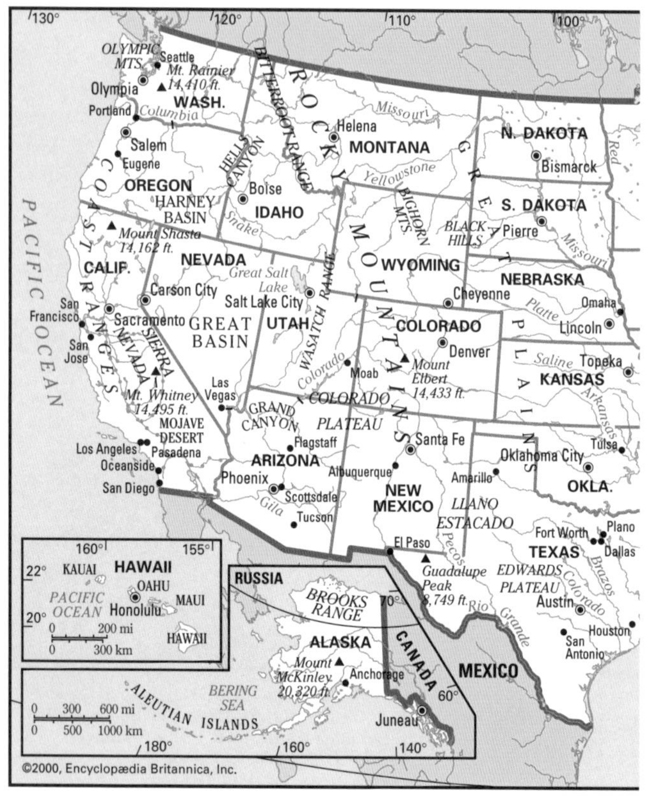

Official name: United States of America
Head of government: President
Official language: none
Monetary unit: dollar
Area: 3,676,487 sq. mi. (9,522,057 sq. km.)
Population (2005): 296,748,000
GNP per capita (2004): U.S.$37,898
Principal exports (2004): chemicals 14.7%, nonelectrical machinery 8.6%, motor vehicles and parts 8.5%, electrical machinery 6.4%, food 6.0% *to:* Canada 23.2%; Mexico 13.5%; Japan 6.6%; United Kingdom 4.4%; China 4.2%; South Korea 3.2%

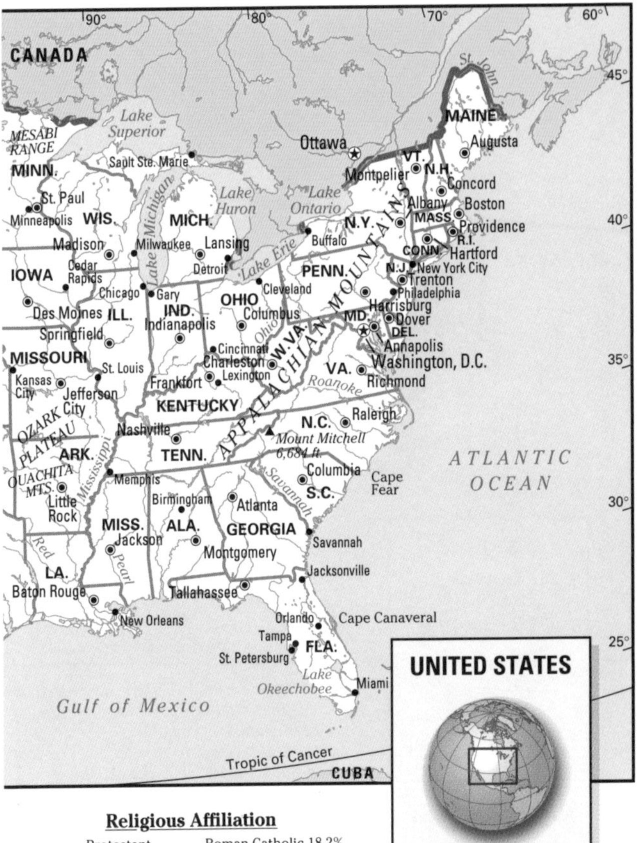

UNITED STATES

Scale 1: 36,770,000

0 150 300 mi

0 200 400 km

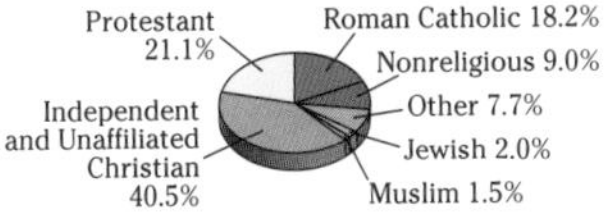

Religious Affiliation

Independent and Unaffiliated Christian	40.5%
Protestant	21.1%
Roman Catholic	18.2%
Nonreligious	9.0%
Other	7.7%
Jewish	2.0%
Muslim	1.5%

The Stars and Stripes has white stars corresponding to the states of the union (50 since July 4, 1960), as well as stripes for the 13 original states. The first unofficial national flag, hoisted on Jan. 1, 1776, had the British Union flag in the canton. The official flag dates to June 14, 1777; its design was standardized in 1912 and 1934.

URUGUAY

Scale 1: 10,810,000

0 50 100 mi

0 80 160 km

Official name: Oriental Republic of Uruguay
Head of government: President
Official language: Spanish
Monetary unit: peso uruguayo
Area: 68,037 sq. mi. (176,215 sq. km.)
Population (2005): 3,256,000
GNP per capita (2004): U.S.$3,950
Principal exports (2004): beef 20.6%, hides and leather goods 9.5%, textiles and textile products 8.1%, dairy products 7.0%, rice 6.2% *to:* U.S. 19.8%; Brazil 16.5%; Argentina 7.6%; Germany 5.2%; Mexico 4.0%

Ethnic Composition

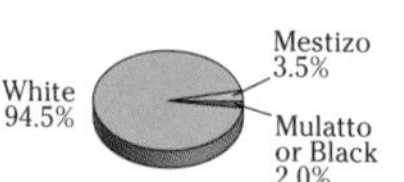

The flag adopted on Dec. 16, 1828, combined symbols of Argentina with the flag pattern of the United States. It was last altered on July 11, 1830. On the canton is the golden "Sun of May," which was seen on May 25, 1810, as a favorable omen for anti-Spanish forces in Buenos Aires, Arg. The stripes are for the original Uruguayan departments.

Official name: Republic of Uzbekistan
Head of government: Prime Minister
Official language: Uzbek
Monetary unit: sum
Area: 172,700 sq. mi. (447,400 sq. km.)
Population (2005): 26,593,000
GNP per capita (2004): U.S.$460
Principal exports (2000): cotton fiber 27.5%, energy products 10.3%, gold 6.6%, food products 5.4% *to:* Russia 26.2%; Ukraine 7.0%; Turkey 6.3%; Tajikistan 5.8%; Kazakhstan 3.9%

Ethnic Composition

Other 10.4%
Tajik 4.7%
Kazakh 4.1%
Russian 2.5%
Uzbek 78.3%

The flag of the former Soviet republic was legalized on Nov. 18, 1991. The blue is for water but also recalls the 14th-century ruler Timur. The green is for nature, fertility, and new life. The white is for peace and purity; red is for human life force. The stars are for the months and the Zodiac, while the moon is for the new republic and Islam.

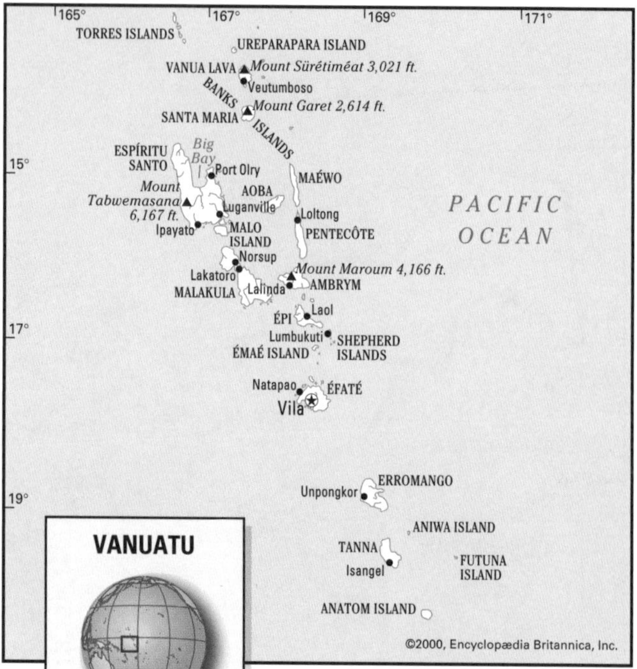
165°
167°
169°
171°
15°
17°
19°
TORRES ISLANDS
UREPARAPARA ISLAND
VANUA LAVA
Mount Sürétiméat 3,021 ft.
Veutumboso
BANKS ISLANDS
Mount Garet 2,614 ft.
SANTA MARIA
ESPÍRITU SANTO
Big Bay
Port Olry
MAÉWO
Mount Tabwemasana 6,167 ft.
AOBA
Luganville
Loltong
Ipayato
MALO ISLAND
PENTECÔTE
PACIFIC OCEAN
Norsup
Lakatoro
Mount Maroum 4,166 ft.
MALAKULA
Lalinda
AMBRYM
ÉPI
Laol
Lumbukuti
SHEPHERD ISLANDS
ÉMAÉ ISLAND
Natapao
ÉFATÉ
Vila
ERROMANGO
Unpongkor
ANIWA ISLAND
TANNA
Isangel
FUTUNA ISLAND
ANATOM ISLAND
©2000, Encyclopædia Britannica, Inc.
VANUATU
Scale 1: 11,818,000
0
50
100 mi
0
80
160 km

Official name: Republic of Vanuatu
Head of government: Prime Minister
Official languages: Bislama; French; English
Monetary unit: vatu
Area: 4,707 sq. mi. (12,190 sq. km.)
Population (2004): 202,000
GNP per capita (2004): U.S.$1,340
Principal exports (2004): coconut oil 24.1%, copra 10.5%, kava 10.3%, beef 6.7%, timber 5.8% *to:* E.U. countries 44.9%; Australia 12.1%; Japan 6.8%; New Caledonia 4.6%; Singapore 2.9%

Religious Affiliation

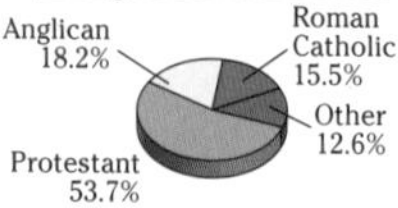
Anglican 18.2%
Roman Catholic 15.5%
Other 12.6%
Protestant 53.7%

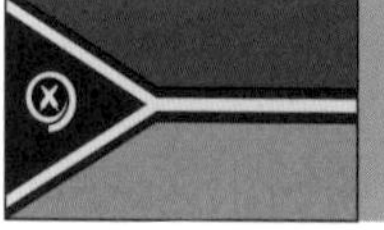

The flag was hoisted upon independence from France and Britain, on July 30, 1980. Black is for the soil and the people, green for vegetation, and red for local religious traditions such as the sacrifice of pigs. On the triangle are two crossed branches and a full-round pig's tusk, a holy symbol. The horizontal "Y" is for peace and Christianity.

VENEZUELA

Scale 1: 24,004,000

0 100 200 mi

0 150 300 km

Ethnic Composition

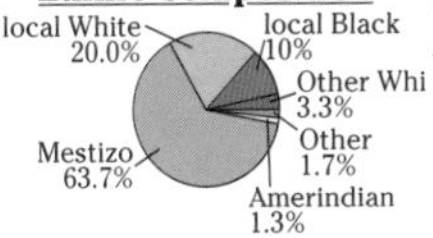

local White 20.0%
local Black 10%
Other Whi 3.3%
Other 1.7%
Amerindian 1.3%
Mestizo 63.7%

Official name: Bolivarian Republic of Venezuela
Head of government: President
Official language: Spanish
Monetary unit: bolívar
Area: 353,841 sq. mi. (916,445 sq. km.)
Population (2005): 26,749,000
GNP per capita (2004): U.S.$4,020
Principal exports (2003): crude petroleum and petroleum products 81.9%, iron and steel 3.1%, aluminum 3.0% *to* (2004): U.S. 55.0%; Netherlands Antilles 4.7%; Dominican Republic 2.8%; Canada 2.3%; Columbia 2.0%

This flag was adopted March 7, 2006. Yellow stands for the gold of the New World, separated by the blue of the Atlantic Ocean from "bloody Spain," symbolized by red. The stars are for the original seven provinces plus the eighth for Guyana. In the upper hoist corner, the national arms are added to flags flown on government buildings.

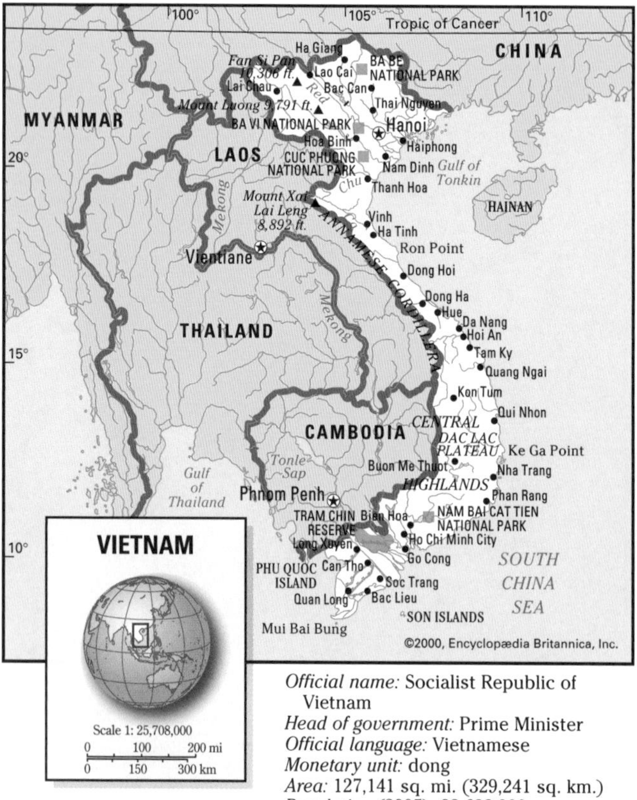

VIETNAM

Scale 1: 25,708,000
0 100 200 mi
0 150 300 km

Official name: Socialist Republic of Vietnam
Head of government: Prime Minister
Official language: Vietnamese
Monetary unit: dong
Area: 127,141 sq. mi. (329,241 sq. km.)
Population (2005): 82,628,000
GNP per capita (2004): U.S.$550
Principal exports (2002): crude petroleum 19.6%, garments 16.5%, fish and fish products 12.1%, footwear 11.2%, rice 4.3% *to* (2004): U.S. 18.8%; Japan 13.2%; China 10.3%; Australia 6.9%; Singapore 5.2%

Religious Affiliation

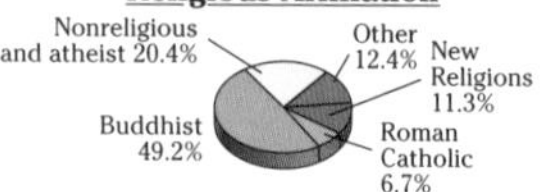

On Sept. 29, 1945, Vietnamese communists adopted the red flag in use today. On July 4, 1976, following the defeat of the American-sponsored government in the south, the flag became official throughout the nation. The five points of the star are said to stand for the proletariat, peasantry, military, intellectuals, and petty bourgeoisie.

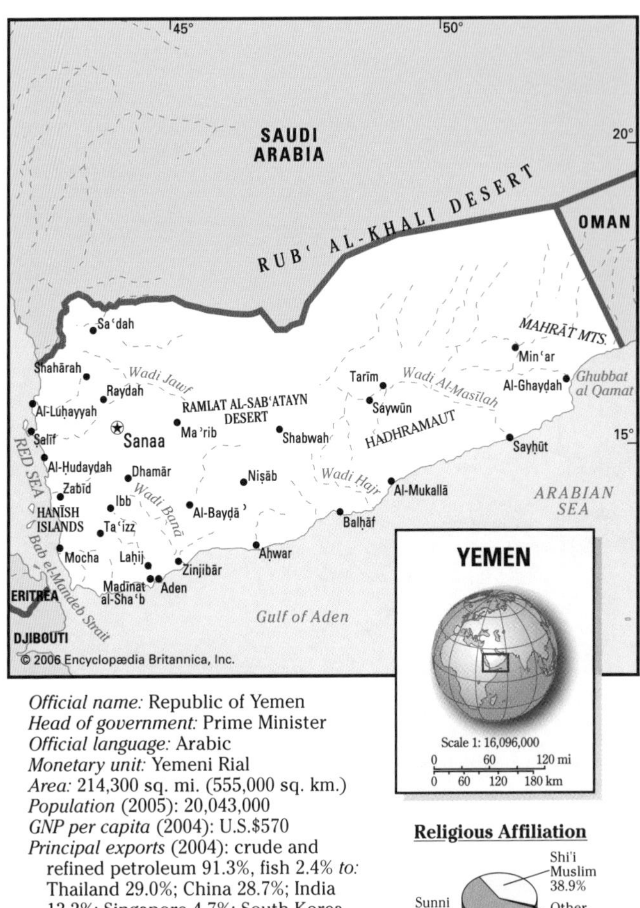

Official name: Republic of Yemen
Head of government: Prime Minister
Official language: Arabic
Monetary unit: Yemeni Rial
Area: 214,300 sq. mi. (555,000 sq. km.)
Population (2005): 20,043,000
GNP per capita (2004): U.S.$570
Principal exports (2004): crude and refined petroleum 91.3%, fish 2.4% *to:* Thailand 29.0%; China 28.7%; India 13.2%; Singapore 4.7%; South Korea 3.2%

Religious Affiliation

Revolutions broke out in North Yemen in 1962 and in South Yemen in 1967. In 1990 the two states unified, and that May 23 the tricolor was adopted, its design influenced by the former United Arab Republic. The black is for the dark days of the past, white for the bright future, and red for the blood shed for independence and unity.

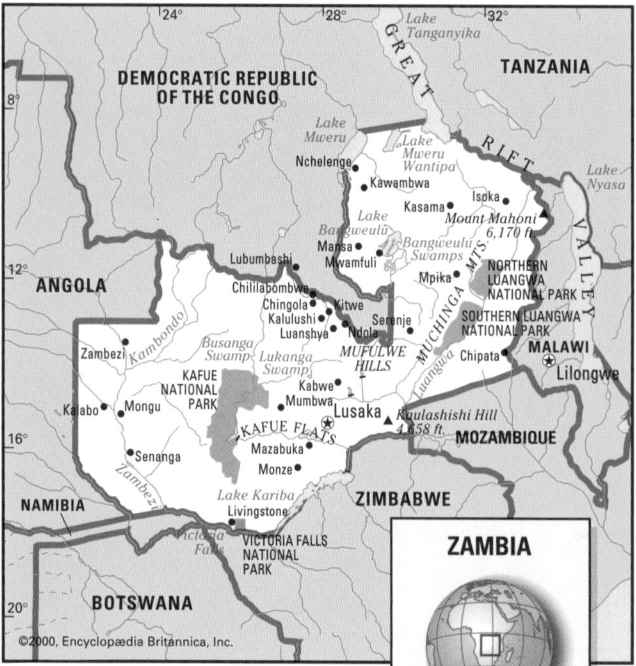

ZAMBIA

Scale 1: 23,251,000

0 100 200 mi

0 150 300 km

Official name: Republic of Zambia
Head of government: President
Official language: English
Monetary unit: Zambian kwacha
Area: 290,585 sq. mi. (752,612 sq. km.)
Population (2005): 11,262,000
GNP per capita (2004): U.S.$450
Principal exports (2002): refined copper 50.0%, other base metals including cobalt 8.9%, food 7.3% *to:* U.K. 42.3%; South Africa 23.0%; Tanzania 7.6%; Switzerland 6.1%

Religious Affiliation

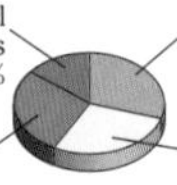

Traditional beliefs 14.3%
Roman Catholic 29.7%
Other 27.8%
Protestant 28.2%

Zambia separated from Britain on Oct. 24, 1964. Its flag, based on the flag of the United National Independence Party, has a green background for agriculture, red for the freedom struggle, black for the African people, and orange for copper. The orange eagle appeared in the colonial coat of arms of 1939. It symbolizes freedom and success.

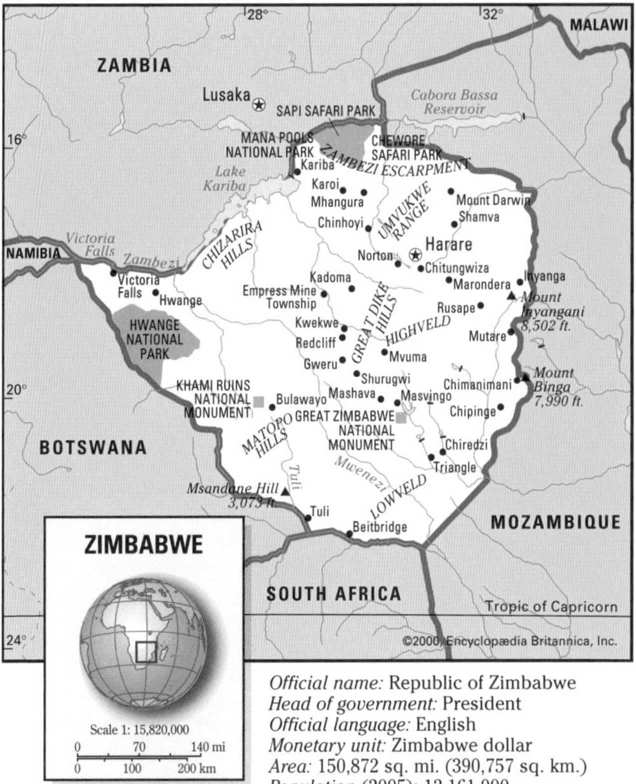

ZIMBABWE

Scale 1: 15,820,000

0 70 140 mi

0 100 200 km

©2000 Encyclopædia Britannica, Inc.

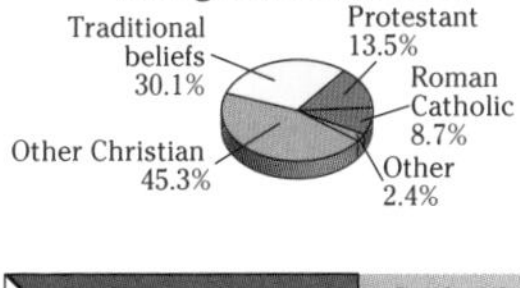

Official name: Republic of Zimbabwe
Head of government: President
Official language: English
Monetary unit: Zimbabwe dollar
Area: 150,872 sq. mi. (390,757 sq. km.)
Population (2005): 12,161,000
GNP per capita (2002): U.S.$480
Principal exports (2003): tobacco 21.2%, gold sales 11.2%, horticultural products 9.6%, ferroalloys 8.6%, nickel metal 6.4%, platinum 5.1%, sugar 4.5% *to:* South Africa 11.4%; Japan 9.5%; Switzerland 8.2%; U.K. 7.9%; Germany 7.5%; Zambia 6.2%

Religious Affiliation

Traditional beliefs 30.1%
Protestant 13.5%
Roman Catholic 8.7%
Other 2.4%
Other Christian 45.3%

On April 18, 1980, elections brought the black majority to power under the current flag. The black color is for the ethnic majority, while red is for blood, green for agriculture, yellow for mineral wealth, and white for peace and progress. At the hoist is a red star (for socialism) and the ancient "Zimbabwe Bird" from the Great Zimbabwe ruins.

States of the United States

ALABAMA

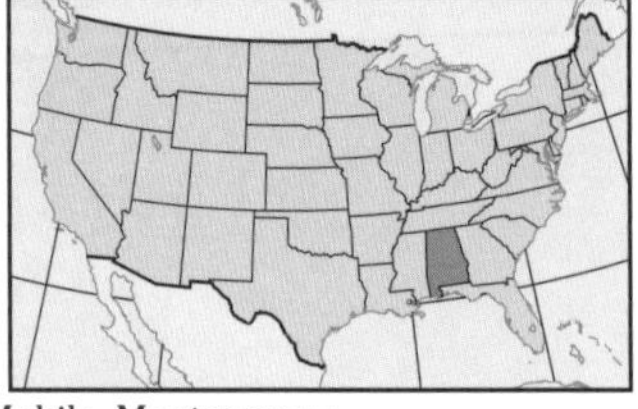

Official name: State of Alabama
Nickname: Heart of Dixie
State Capital: Montgomery
State flower: Camellia
Motto: We Dare Defend Our Rights
Admitted to the Union: 1819 (22nd)
Total area (2000): 51,419 sq. mi. (135,765 sq. km.) (ranks 30th)
Population (2004): 4,530,182. (ranks 23rd)
Chief cities: Birmingham, Huntsville, Mobile, Montgomery
Chief products/industries: Corn, soybeans, peanuts, livestock, coal, iron ore, limestone, petroleum, iron and steel, chemicals, textiles, historically notable cotton production.
Highest point: Cheaha Mountain 2405 ft. (733 m.)

State History

Original inhabitants were American Indians whose settlement sites and burial mounds are in evidence; the major groups were Cherokees, Chickasaws, Choctaws, and Creeks when area first explored by Spaniards, notably by Hernando de Soto 1539–40; first permanent settlement established 1711 by French at site of Mobile on Mobile Bay; became English 1763; southern part included in West Florida, retroceded to Spain in 1783 and claimed by U.S. as part of Louisiana Purchase 1803; rest of Alabama became part of U.S. 1783, with dividing line under dispute until 1795 when Spain ceded claim north of 31°; parts included in Territory South of the Ohio River 1790 and Mississippi Territory 1798 ff.; organized as a territory 1817; southern tip formally ceded to U.S. 1819; first constitutional convention July 1819; admitted to Union Dec. 14, 1819; 2nd constitutional convention Jan. 7–Mar. 20, 1861 passed ordinance of secession Jan. 11, 1861; government of Confederate States of America organized at Montgomery Feb. 4, 1861; 3rd constitutional convention Sept. 12–30, 1865 declared secession null and void, and abolished slavery; readmitted to Union 1868; present constitution, formulated by 6th constitutional convention, adopted 1901.

In the Civil War, the flag of the short-lived (Jan. 11–Feb. 8, 1861) Republic of Alabama showed the goddess of liberty with a sword and a single-starred flag, and the motto, "Independent Now and Forever." The present flag, adopted in 1895, recalls the Confederate battle flag, and so is usually square, not rectangular, but the law does not specify its dimensions.

88°
87°
86°
85°
35°
34°
33°
32°
31°
30°
TENNESSEE
MISSISSIPPI
GEORGIA
FLORIDA
Florence
Athens
Huntsville
Tuscumbia
Decatur
Scottsboro
Fort Payne
Russellville
Moulton
Guntersville
Cullman
Hamilton
Centre
Double Springs
Gadsden
Oneonta
Jasper
Ashville
Vernon
Heflin
Berry
Pell City
Anniston
Birmingham
Talladega
Carrollton
Columbiana
Ashland
Wedowee
Tuscaloosa
Centreville
Rockford
Lafayette
Eutaw
Dadeville
Clanton
Greensboro
Opelika
Marion
Wetumpka
Livingston
Selma
Prattville
Tuskegee
Phenix City
Montgomery
Linden
Union Springs
Hayneville
Butler
Camden
Clayton
Greenville
Luverne
Troy
Grove Hill
Abbeville
Monroeville
Elba
Ozark
Chatom
Evergreen
Dothan
Andalusia
Brewton
Geneva
Bay Minette
Mobile
Mobile Bay
Pensacola Bay
Choctawhatchee Bay
Perdido Bay
Gulf of Mexico
0 20 40 mi
0 30 60 km
© 2003 Encyclopædia Britannica, Inc.

ALASKA

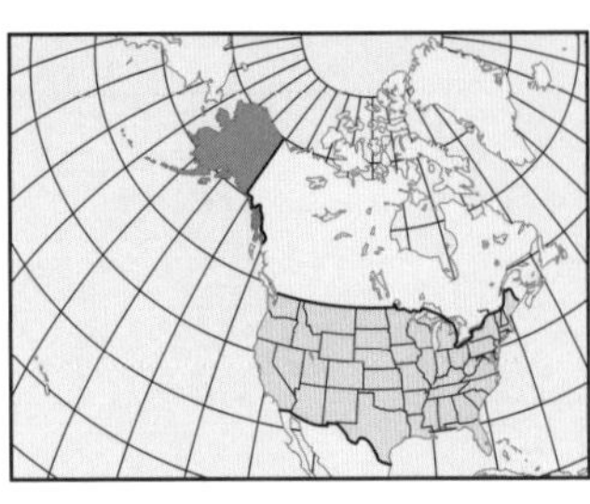

Official name: State of Alaska
Nickname: The Last Frontier
State Capital: Juneau
State flower: Forget-me-not
Motto: North to the Future (unofficial)
Admitted to the Union: 1959 (49th)
Total area (2000): 663,267 sq. mi. (1,717,854 sq. km.) (ranks 1st)
Population (2004): 655,435 (ranks 47th)
Chief cities: Anchorage, Fairbanks, Juneau
Principal products/industries: Oil extraction, quarrying (sand and gravel), fishing, timber, tourism
Highest point: Mt. McKinley 20,320 ft. (6198 m.)

State History

Original inhabitants (American Indians and Inuits) thought to have immigrated over Beringia as well as from the Arctic area. Explored by Russian voyages, especially of Vitus Bering 1741; their first permanent settlement on Kodiak Island 1792; visited by British explorers James Cook, George Vancouver, and Sir Alexander Mackenzie and by Hudson Bay traders 1778–1847; under trade monopoly of Russian-American Fur Company 1799–1861, first managed by Aleksandr Baranov; ownership claimed by Russia; region south to 54°40′ ceded by Russia to U.S. for $7,200,000 by treaty of 1867 negotiated by Secretary of State William H. Seward (hence early nickname of Alaska, "Seward's Folly"); organized 1884; received final U.S. territorial status 1912; gold discoveries, including Klondike 1896; disputed boundary with British Columbia arbitrated in favor of U.S. 1903; restriction of seal fisheries by treaties with Great Britain, Russia, and Japan 1911; in WWII Aleutian islands of Attu and Kiska occupied by Japanese June 1942–Aug. 1943; present constitution adopted 1956; was granted statehood 1959; suffered severe earthquake damage 1964; large oil reserves discovered 1968; crude-oil pipeline south from North Slope to Valdez begun 1975, opened 1977.

Alaska held a territorial flag design competition in 1926, and the winning design was created by 13-year-old Benny Benson, who lived in an orphanage. The dark blue represents the Alaskan sky and the Big Dipper points to the North Star, for Alaska's being the northernmost part of the U.S.

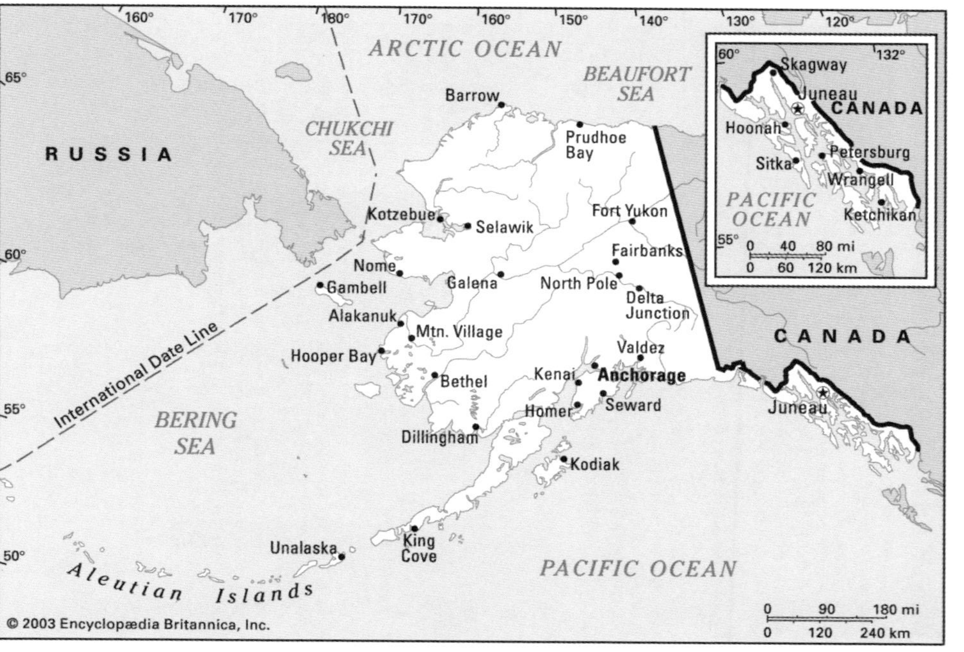

ARCTIC OCEAN
BEAUFORT SEA
CHUKCHI SEA
RUSSIA
CANADA
International Date Line
BERING SEA
PACIFIC OCEAN
Aleutian Islands
Barrow
Prudhoe Bay
Kotzebue
Selawik
Fort Yukon
Fairbanks
Nome
Gambell
Galena
North Pole
Delta Junction
Alakanuk
Mtn. Village
Hooper Bay
Valdez
Kenai
Anchorage
Bethel
Homer
Seward
Dillingham
Kodiak
Unalaska
King Cove
Juneau
Skagway
Hoonah
Sitka
Petersburg
Wrangell
Ketchikan
PACIFIC OCEAN
0 40 80 mi
0 60 120 km
0 90 180 mi
0 120 240 km
© 2003 Encyclopædia Britannica, Inc.

ARIZONA

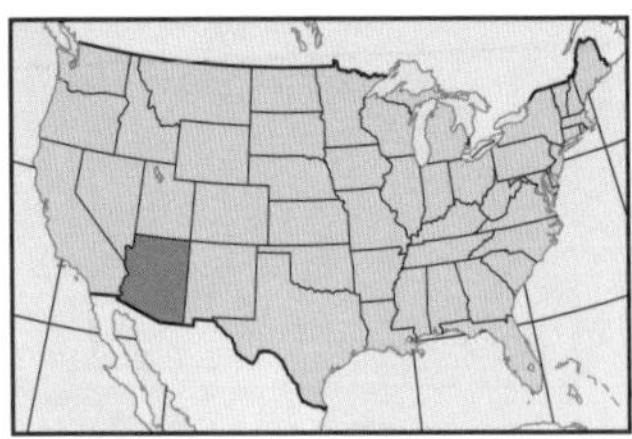

Official name: State of Arizona
Nickname: Grand Canyon State
State Capital: Phoenix
State Flower: Saguaro cactus
Motto: Ditat Deus (God Enriches)
Admitted to the Union: 1912 (48th)
Total area (2000): 113,998 sq. mi. (295,254 sq. km.) (ranks 6th)
Population (2004): 5,743,834 (ranks 18th)
Chief Cities: Glendale, Mesa, Phoenix, Scottsdale, Tempe, Tucson
Principal products/industries: Cotton, citrus fruit, copper, molybdenum, gold, electronic equipment, food processing, tourism
Highest point: Humphreys Peak 12,633 ft. (3853 m.)

State History

Inhabited probably from 25,000 B.C. Notable early cultures Hohokum 300 B.C.–1400 A.D. and Anasazi after 100 A.D. Apache and Navajo came later c. 1300. Spanish exploration began with expedition of Franciscan friar Marcos de Niza 1539; Coronado followed 1540; ruled by Spain as part of New Spain 1598–1821; inauguration of Spanish missions to Hopis 1638; region acquired by U.S. by Treaty of Guadalupe Hidalgo 1848 and Gadsden Purchase 1853; included in New Mexico Territory 1850; organized as territory of Arizona 1863; Apache wars continued up to latter part of 19th century until Geronimo finally surrendered 1886; with New Mexico refused statehood 1906; submitted a constitution for congressional approval 1911; congressional resolution accepting this constitution vetoed by President William Howard Taft chiefly because of provision allowing recall of judges by popular vote; after objectionable matter withdrawn from constitution, admitted to Union Feb. 14, 1912; by state constitutional amendment restored the provision allowing recall of judges Nov. 1912.

Five years after attaining statehood, Arizona adopted its state flag. The rays suggest a colorful Arizona sunset over a desert in shadow, and the central star represents the state as a rich copper-producing area. The red and yellow are colors from the Spanish flag, recalling early explorers; the red and blue suggest the Stars and Stripes.

38°
114°
112°
110°
0
50
100 mi
0
70
140 km
UTAH
NEVADA
COLORADO
Four Corners:
Only point in
the United
States common
to four states.
Page
Kayenta
36°
Tuba City
Grand
Canyon
Window Rock
Kingman
Williams
Flagstaff
Bullhead City
Winslow
NEW MEXICO
CALIFORNIA
Chino Valley
Sedona
Holbrook
Lake Havasu
City
Cottonwood
Snowflake
Prescott
St. Johns
34°
Parker
Payson
Show Low
Wickenburg
Eagar
Colorado
Sun City
Glendale
Scottsdale
Phoenix
Mesa
Globe
Tempe
Chandler
Superior
Florence
Clifton
Gila Bend
Yuma
Casa Grande
Coolidge
Wellton
Thatcher
Safford
Somerton
Tucson
Willcox
32°
Benson
Sierra
Vista
Tombstone
Tubac
Bisbee
Douglas
Nogales
Gulf of
California
MEXICO
© 2003 Encyclopædia Britannica, Inc.

ARKANSAS

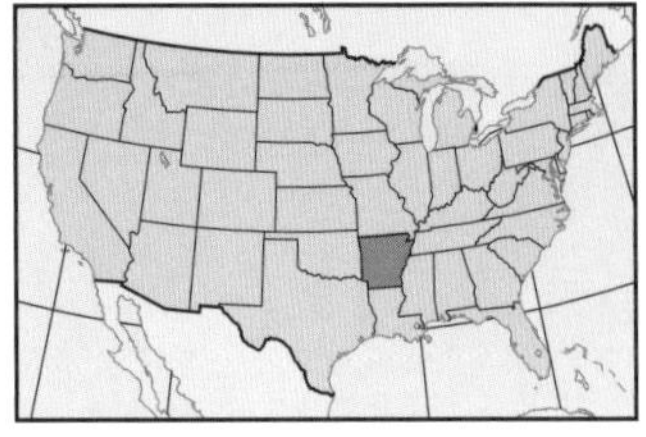

Official name: State of Arkansas
Nickname: The Natural State
State Capital: Little Rock
State Flower: Apple blossom
Motto: Regnat Populus (The People Rule)
Admitted to the Union: 1836 (25th)
Total area (2000): 53,179 sq. mi. (137,732 sq. km.) (ranks 29th)
Population (2004): 2,752,629 (ranks 32nd)
Chief Cities: Fort Smith, Little Rock, North Little Rock, Pine Bluff
Principal products/industries: Soybeans, cotton, rice, livestock, bauxite, machinery, food processing
Highest point: Magazine Mountain 2753 ft. (840 m.)

State History

Early inhabitants, American Indians c. 500 A.D.; among first European explorers, Hernando de Soto 1541, Jacques Marquette and Louis Joliet 1673, Sieur de La Salle and Henry de Tonti 1682; Arkansas Post first permanent settlement (1686); in region claimed by France and yielded to Spain 1762; retroceded to France 1800; included in Louisiana Purchase 1803, Louisiana Territory 1805, and Missouri Territory 1812; Arkansas Territory organized 1819, which included current state plus most of what is now Oklahoma (except a strip along the northern boundary), and which was reduced to the current state's boundaries by 1828; adopted first constitution 1836 and admitted to Union June 15 of same year; seceded 1861; capture of Arkansas Post from Confederates 1863; readmitted into Union 1868; implementation of strict Jim Crow laws ensued; federal troops sent to Little Rock 1957 to enforce school desegregation laws.

The three stars originally appearing in the center recalled that Arkansas was the third state created from the Louisiana Territory and that it had been ruled by three different countries (France, Spain, and the U.S.). The flag was modified in 1923 by the addition of a fourth star to stand for the Confederate States of America.

95°
94°
93°
MISSOURI
92°
91°
90°
KENTUCKY
Bentonville
Eureka Springs
Rogers
Mountain Home
Piggott
Pocahontas
Siloam Springs
Springdale
Harrison
Paragould
36°
Fayetteville
Jasper
Mountain View
Jonesboro
Blytheville
Trumann
Osceola
TENNESSEE
Batesville
Clinton
Newport
Van Buren
Ozark
Clarksville
Heber Springs
Fort Smith
Russellville
West Memphis
Searcy
Booneville
Morrilton
Wynne
Dardanelle
Conway
35°
Waldron
Jacksonville
Forrest City
OKLAHOMA
0 30 60 mi
0 40 80 km
N. Little Rock
Marianna
Little Rock
W. Helena
Mena
Hot Springs
Benton
Helena
Stuttgart
Malvern
Pine Bluff
DeWitt
Arkadelphia
MISSISSIPPI
De Queen
34°
Murfreesboro
Star City
Fordyce
Dumas
Mississippi
Ashdown
Hope
Warren
Monticello
Camden
Hampton
Texarkana
Magnolia
Lake Village
TEXAS
El Dorado
33°
Crossett
LOUISIANA

CALIFORNIA

Official name: State of California
Nickname: Golden State
State Capital: Sacramento
State Flower: Golden poppy
Motto: Eureka (I Have Found It)
Admitted to the Union: 1850 (31st)
Total area (2000): 163,696 sq. mi. (423,970 sq. km.) (ranks 3rd)
Population (2004): 35,893,799 (ranks 1st)
Chief Cities: Anaheim, Fresno, Long Beach, Los Angeles, Oakland, Sacramento, San Diego, San Francisco, San Jose, Santa Ana

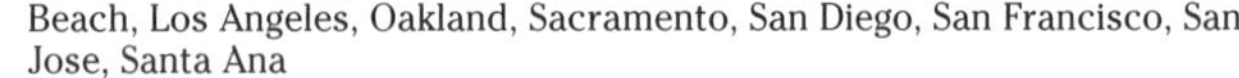

Principal products/industries: Tomatoes, lettuce, broccoli, strawberries, grapes, oranges, and other fruits and vegetables, cotton, rice, flowers, oil, natural gas, gypsum, transportation equipment, electrical machinery, electronics, movie and television industries, tourism
Highest point: Mt. Whitney 14,494 ft. (4419 m.)

State History

Inhabited originally by American Indians; first European coastal exploration by voyage of Spanish emissaries Juan Rodríguez Cabrillo and Bartolomé Ferrelo who established Spanish claim to region 1542–43; coast reached by English mariner Sir Francis Drake 1579; first Franciscan mission established by Junípero Serra at San Diego 1769; remained under Spanish control and later under Mexican control until conquered by U.S. forces during Mexican War (1846–47); ceded to U.S. by Treaty of Guadalupe Hidalgo 1848; settlement by Americans begun in 1841, greatly accelerated after discovery of gold at Coloma (Sutter's Mill) in 1848 which brought influx of miners and adventurers; admitted to Union Sept. 9, 1850 as a free state under Missouri Compromise; present constitution (many times amended) drawn up by constitutional convention 1878–79, ratified by people, and in force Jan. 1, 1880; with an already expanding population, state in 20th century grew even more with advent of the automobile; has more miles of freeway than any other state in U.S.; economy largest of all states in U.S.; subject to earthquakes, state suffered severe ones in north around San Francisco especially 1906 and 1989 and in south around Los Angeles 1994.

In 1846, during the Mexican-American War, Mexican-ruled California proclaimed independence and raised the original Bear Flag (June 14, 1846), featuring the now-extinct California grizzly bear. In 1911 the flag of the short-lived California Republic became the state flag. It is unusual in featuring a design used by a formerly independent country.

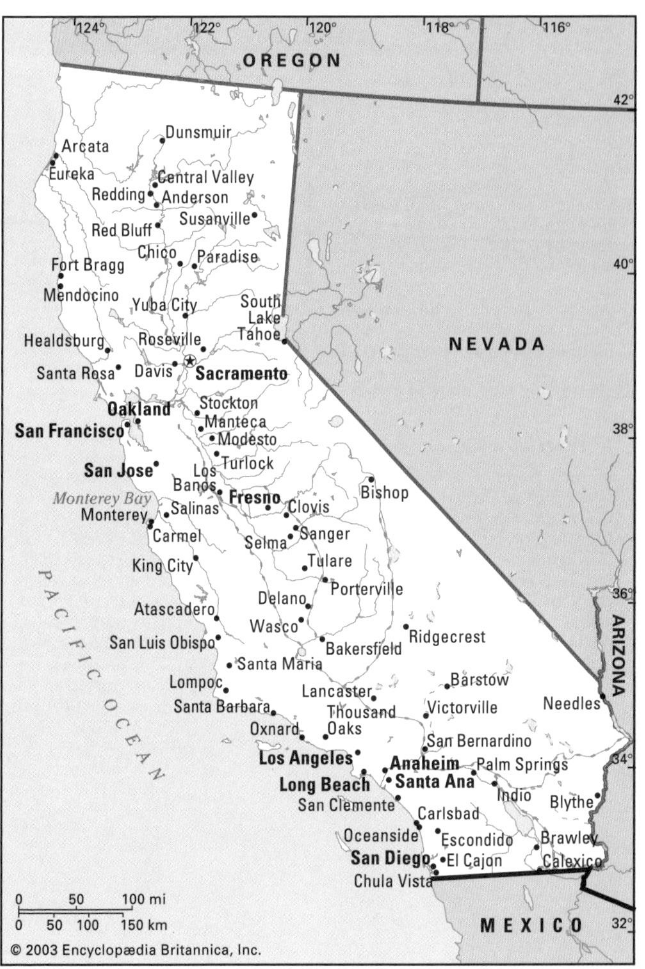

124°
122°
120°
118°
116°
OREGON
42°
40°
38°
36°
34°
32°
NEVADA
ARIZONA
MEXICO
PACIFIC OCEAN
Monterey Bay
Dunsmuir
Arcata
Eureka
Central Valley
Redding
Anderson
Susanville
Red Bluff
Chico
Paradise
Fort Bragg
Mendocino
Yuba City
South Lake Tahoe
Healdsburg
Roseville
Santa Rosa
Davis
Sacramento
Oakland
Stockton
San Francisco
Manteca
Modesto
Turlock
San Jose
Los Banos
Fresno
Bishop
Monterey
Salinas
Clovis
Carmel
Selma
Sanger
King City
Tulare
Porterville
Delano
Atascadero
Wasco
Ridgecrest
San Luis Obispo
Bakersfield
Santa Maria
Barstow
Lompoc
Lancaster
Santa Barbara
Thousand Oaks
Victorville
Needles
Oxnard
San Bernardino
Los Angeles
Anaheim
Palm Springs
Long Beach
Santa Ana
Indio
San Clemente
Blythe
Carlsbad
Oceanside
Escondido
Brawley
San Diego
El Cajon
Calexico
Chula Vista
0 50 100 mi
0 50 100 150 km

COLORADO

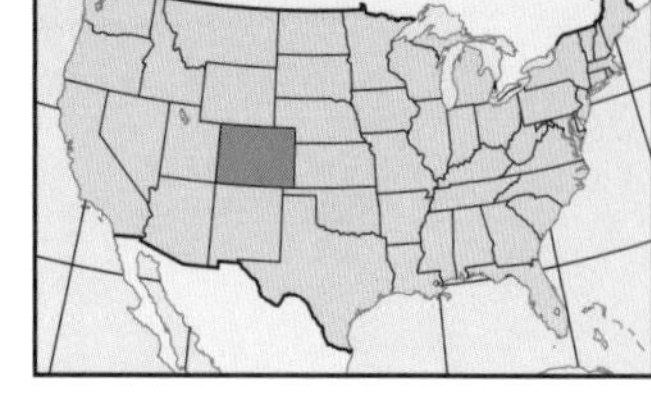

Official name: State of Colorado
Nickname: Centennial State
State Capital: Denver
State Flower: Columbine
Motto: Nil Sine Numine (Nothing Without Providence)
Admitted to the Union: 1876 (38th)
Total area (2000): 104,094 sq. mi. (269,601 sq. km.) (ranks 8th)
Population (2004): 4,601,403 (ranks 22nd)
Chief Cities: Aurora, Colorado Springs, Denver
Principal products/industries: Wheat, sugar beets, corn, livestock, oil, molybdenum, coal, food processing, printing, tourism, outdoor recreation
Highest point: Mt. Elbert 14,433 ft. (4402 m.)

State History

In early times, southwestern part of state inhabited by the Anasazi; when Europeans arrived, plains inhabited primarily by the Arapaho, Cheyenne, Comanche, and Kiowa; mountains inhabited mainly by the Utes; explored chiefly by 18th century Spaniards; claimed by Spain and also France; eastern part acquired by U.S. in Louisiana Purchase 1803, rest in territory yielded by Mexico 1845–48; explored for U.S. government by Zebulon Pike 1806, Stephen Long 1820, and John Frémont 1842; additional exploration by a host of fur trappers and traders; parts included in Louisiana, Missouri, Utah, New Mexico, Kansas, and Nebraska territories 1805–61; gold, discovered at Cherry Creek (in present-day Denver) in 1858, attracted American settlers; organized as territory of Colorado 1861; admitted as state Aug. 1, 1876; constitution adopted 1876.

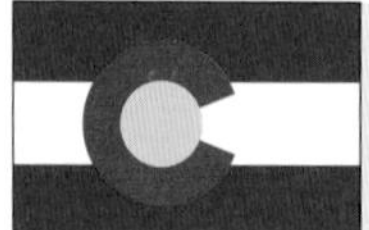

The red C stands not only for the name of the state but also for the state flower (columbine) and the state nickname ("Centennial State"). Colorado became a state in 1876, when the country was celebrating the centennial of its independence. The red, white, and blue suggest the U.S. flag; the blue, yellow, and white, the columbine colors.

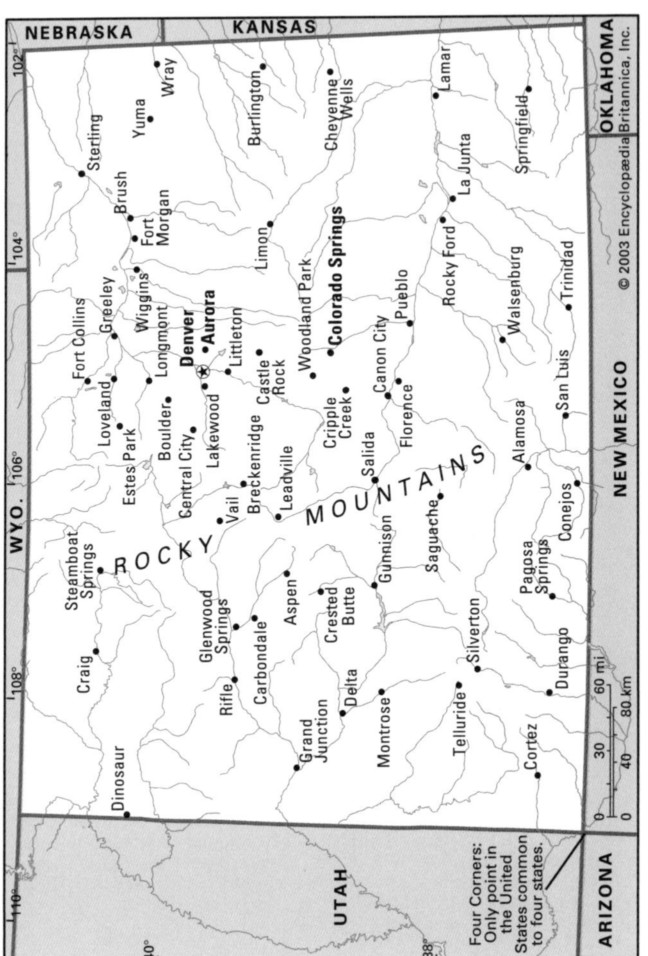
NEBRASKA
KANSAS
OKLAHOMA
WYO.
UTAH
NEW MEXICO
ARIZONA
ROCKY MOUNTAINS
Sterling
Yuma
Wray
Burlington
Cheyenne Wells
Lamar
Springfield
Brush
Fort Morgan
Limon
La Junta
Rocky Ford
Fort Collins
Greeley
Wiggins
Longmont
Denver
Aurora
Littleton
Castle Rock
Woodland Park
Colorado Springs
Pueblo
Canon City
Walsenburg
Trinidad
Loveland
Estes Park
Boulder
Central City
Lakewood
Breckenridge
Leadville
Cripple Creek
Florence
Salida
Alamosa
San Luis
Vail
Saguache
Conejos
Steamboat Springs
Glenwood Springs
Carbondale
Aspen
Crested Butte
Gunnison
Pagosa Springs
Craig
Rifle
Delta
Silverton
Durango
Grand Junction
Montrose
Telluride
Cortez
Dinosaur
Four Corners: Only point in the United States common to four states.
102°
104°
106°
108°
110°
40°
38°
0 30 60 mi
0 40 80 km
© 2003 Encyclopædia Britannica, Inc.

CONNECTICUT

Official name: State of Connecticut
Nicknames: Constitution State, Nutmeg State
State Capital: Hartford
State Flower: Mountain laurel
Motto: Qui Transtulit Sustinet (He Who Transplanted Still Sustains)
Admitted to the Union: 1788; 5th of the original 13 colonies to ratify the U.S. Constitution
Total area (2000): 5543 sq. mi. (14,357 sq. km.) (ranks 48th)
Population (2004): 3,503,604 (ranks 29th)
Chief Cities: Bridgeport, Hartford, New Haven, Stamford, Waterbury
Principal products/industries: Dairy products, shade-grown tobacco for cigar wrappers, jet engines, helicopters, submarines, guns and ammunition, insurance
Highest point: Mt. Frissell 2380 ft. (726 m.)

State History

Originally inhabited by the Algonquin Indians. Connecticut River explored 1614 by Dutch navigator Adriaen Block, and again 1632 by Edward Winslow of Plymouth; posts established 1633 by the Dutch at Hartford and by a Plymouth contingent at Windsor; a 3rd post established at Wethersfield 1634 following 1633 exploration of the area by John Oldham of Massachusetts Bay Colony; permanent settlements established at the three river towns of Hartford, Windsor, and Wethersfield 1635–36, primarily by colonists from Massachusetts Bay; Saybrook Colony established 1635; Pequot tribe nearly extinguished in Pequot War 1636–37; New Haven Colony established 1638; three river towns formed Connecticut Colony and adopted Fundamental Orders, considered by some to be the first American constitution based on the consent of the governed, 1638–39; in New England Confederation 1643–84; Connecticut Colony absorbed Saybrook Colony 1644; received charter 1662 which united Connecticut and New Haven colonies and granted strip of land extending to Pacific; included in Dominion of New England, the government of Connecticut was briefly taken over by British colonial governor Sir Edmund Andros 1687–89; relinquished claims to western lands 1786 except for Western Reserve (situated in what is now Ohio) to which it abandoned jurisdiction 1800; participated in Hartford Convention 1814–15; adopted state constitution 1818, in force until 1965, when it was replaced by another.

The coat of arms is based on the 1711 seal of the colony of Connecticut. Its three grapevines are thought to represent either the colonies of Connecticut, New Haven, and Saybrook or the first three area towns established by Europeans (Hartford, Wethersfield, and Windsor).

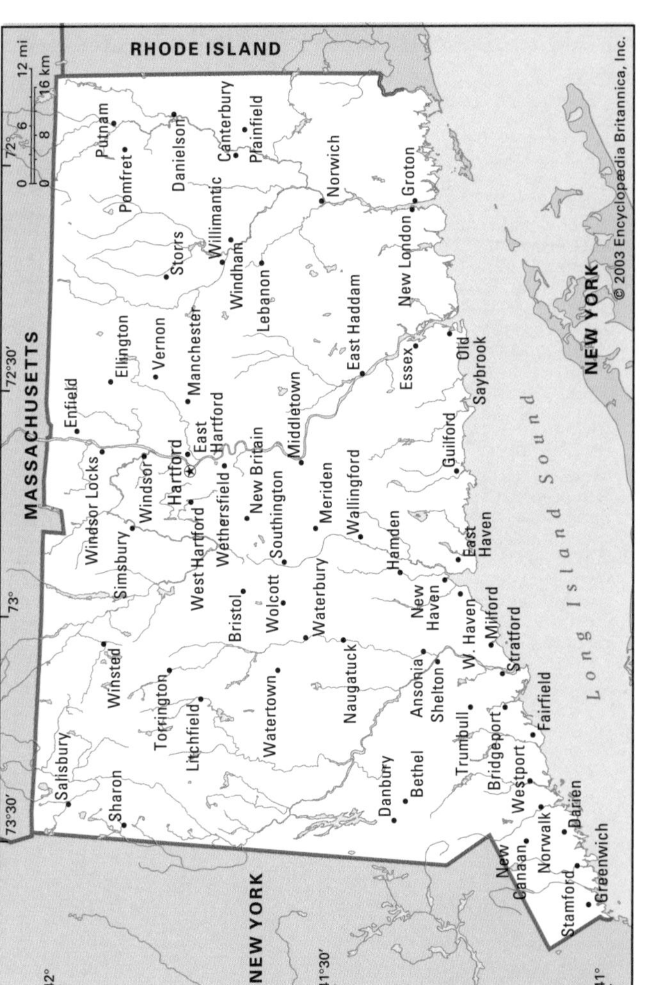
RHODE ISLAND
MASSACHUSETTS
NEW YORK
NEW YORK
Long Island Sound
© 2003 Encyclopædia Britannica, Inc.
0 6 12 mi
0 8 16 km
42°
41°30′
41°
73°30′
73°
72°30′
72°
Putnam
Pomfret
Danielson
Canterbury
Plainfield
Storrs
Willimantic
Windham
Norwich
Lebanon
Groton
New London
East Haddam
Essex
Old Saybrook
Enfield
Ellington
Vernon
Manchester
East Hartford
Hartford
Windsor Locks
Windsor
Wethersfield
West Hartford
New Britain
Middletown
Southington
Meriden
Wallingford
Guilford
Simsbury
Hamden
East Haven
New Haven
W. Haven
Milford
Stratford
Bristol
Wolcott
Waterbury
Naugatuck
Winsted
Torrington
Litchfield
Watertown
Ansonia
Shelton
Trumbull
Bridgeport
Fairfield
Westport
Salisbury
Sharon
Danbury
Bethel
Norwalk
Darien
New Canaan
Stamford
Greenwich

DELAWARE

Official name: State of Delaware
Nicknames: First State, Diamond State
State Capital: Dover
State Flower: Peach blossom
Motto: Liberty and Independence
Admitted to the Union: 1787; 1st of the original 13 colonies to ratify the U.S. Constitution
Total area (2000): 2489 sq. mi. (6447 sq. km.) (ranks 49th)
Population (2004): 830,364 (ranks 45th)
Chief Cities: Dover, Newark, Wilmington
Principal products/industries: Chemicals, food processing, poultry, fishing, soybeans, corn
Highest point: New Castle County 448 ft. (137 m.)

State History

Region originally inhabited by several Algonquian tribes; earliest European settlements made by Dutch 1631 at present site of Lewes; first permanent settlements made by Swedes 1638; New Sweden captured by Dutch 1655 and, as part of New Netherland, by English 1664; part of New York until it became part of a grant made to William Penn 1682; in 1704 received right to separate legislative assembly, but remained under governor of Pennsylvania until 1776; active in American Revolution; formulated first state constitution 1776, adopted present constitution 1897; remained in Union during Civil War.

The diamond shape may represent the nickname "Diamond State." The coat of arms incorporates symbols appropriate for the late 18th century—a soldier, a farmer, agricultural produce (a sheaf of wheat and an ear of corn), an ox, and a ship.

76°
75°30′
75°
PENNSYLVANIA
NEW JERSEY
MARYLAND
Arden
Claymont
Hockessin
Bellefonte
Elsmere
Edgemoor
Marshallton
Wilmington
Newport
Newark
New Castle
Bear
Glasgow
Delaware City
Port Penn
Odessa
Middletown
39°30′
Chesapeake Bay
Smyrna
Clayton
Leipsic
Cheswold
Dupont Manor
Dover
Rodney Village
Kent Acres
Camden
Highland Acres
Rising Sun
Delaware Bay
39°
Felton
Frederica
Harrington
Houston
Milford
Lincoln
Ellendale
Greenwood
Milton
Lewes
Bridgeville
Rehoboth Beach
Georgetown
ATLANTIC OCEAN
Rehoboth Bay
Seaford
Indian River Inlet
Millsboro
Laurel
Ocean View
Bethany Beach
38°30′
Delmar
Selbyville
Fenwick Island
0 6 12 mi
0 5 10 15 km
© 2003 Encyclopædia Britannica, Inc.

FLORIDA

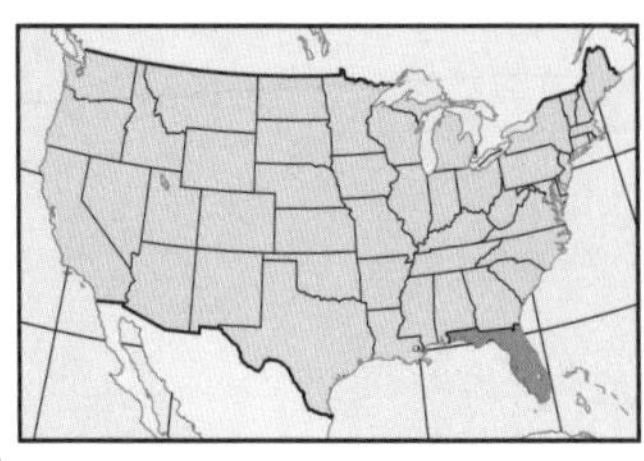

Official name: State of Florida
Nickname: Sunshine State
State Capital: Tallahassee
State Flower: Orange blossom
Motto: In God We Trust
Admitted to the Union: 1845 (27th)
Total area (2000): 65,755 sq. mi. (170,304 sq. km.) (ranks 22nd)
Population (2004): 17,397,161 (ranks 4th)
Chief Cities: Fort Lauderdale, Hialeah, Jacksonville, Miami, Orlando, St. Petersburg, Tampa
Principal products/industries: Citrus fruits, vegetables, dairy products, cattle, phosphates, electronic equipment, tourism
Highest point: Walton County 345 ft. (105 m.)

State History

Spanish Florida, which included southeastern part of present U.S., sighted and explored by Juan Ponce de León 1513; St. Augustine settled 1565; following Seven Years' War, ceded to England by Spain in exchange for Havana 1763; divided into two provinces (known as the Floridas), East and West Florida; retroceded to Spain 1783; West Florida claimed by U.S. as part of Louisiana Purchase 1803; border crossed by Gen. Andrew Jackson who captured Pensacola 1814 and 1818; purchased for $5,000,000 by U.S. under Adams-Onís Treaty 1819; organized as territory of Florida 1822; most Seminole natives relocated to Indian Territory (now Oklahoma) following war (1835–42); admitted to Union as slave state Mar. 3, 1845; passed ordinance of secession Jan. 10, 1861; annulled ordinance of secession Oct. 28, 1865 and abolished slavery; readmitted to Union 1868; present constitution adopted 1885, much amended 1968.

After the Civil War, Florida designated the state seal to appear in the center of a white flag; the design showed an American Indian woman on a promontory extending into water where a steamboat was sailing. Later, a red saltire (similar to that of the Confederate Battle Flag) was added so that it would not resemble a flag of surrender.

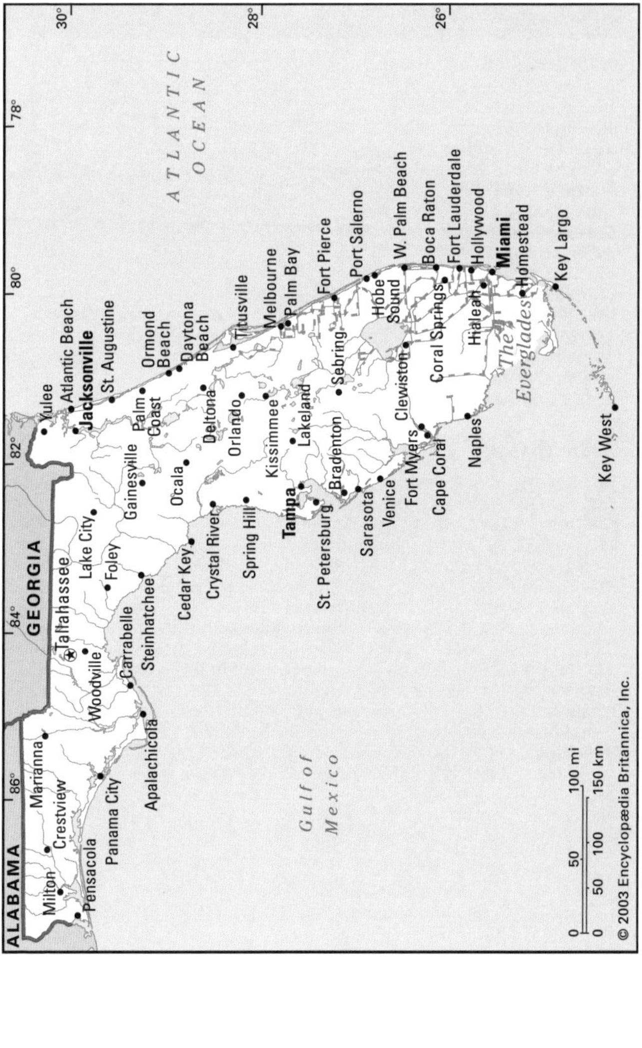
ALABAMA
GEORGIA
ATLANTIC OCEAN
Gulf of Mexico
The Everglades
30°
28°
26°
78°
80°
82°
84°
86°
Yulee
Atlantic Beach
Jacksonville
St. Augustine
Palm Coast
Ormond Beach
Daytona Beach
Deltona
Titusville
Orlando
Kissimmee
Melbourne
Palm Bay
Fort Pierce
Port Salerno
Hobe Sound
W. Palm Beach
Boca Raton
Coral Springs
Fort Lauderdale
Hollywood
Hialeah
Miami
Homestead
Key Largo
Key West
Naples
Clewiston
Sebring
Lakeland
Tampa
St. Petersburg
Bradenton
Sarasota
Venice
Fort Myers
Cape Coral
Spring Hill
Crystal River
Cedar Key
Ocala
Gainesville
Lake City
Foley
Steinhatchee
Carrabelle
Tallahassee
Woodville
Apalachicola
Marianna
Panama City
Crestview
Milton
Pensacola
0 50 100 mi
0 50 100 150 km
© 2003 Encyclopædia Britannica, Inc.

GEORGIA

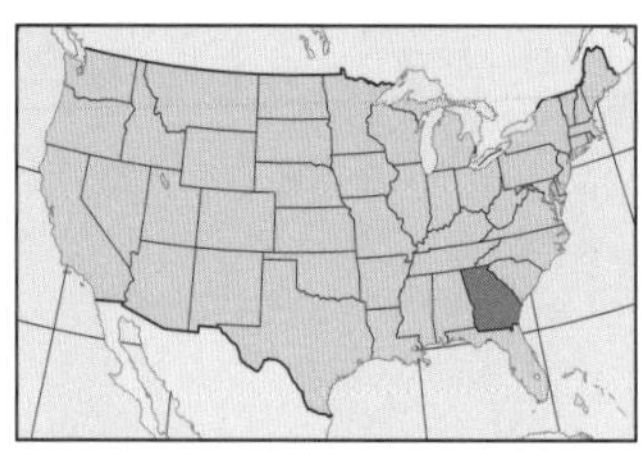

Official name: State of Georgia
Nicknames: Empire State of the South, Peach State
State Capital: Atlanta
State Flower: Cherokee rose
Motto: Wisdom, Justice, Moderation
Admitted to the Union: 1788; 4th of the original 13 colonies to ratify the U.S. Constitution
Total area (2000): 59,425 sq. mi. (153,909 sq. km.) (ranks 24th)
Population (2004): 8,829,383 (ranks 9th)
Chief Cities: Albany, Atlanta, Augusta, Columbus, Macon, Savannah
Principal products/industries: Processed foods, peanuts, pecans, peaches, tobacco, poultry, livestock, clays, textiles, pulp, carpets and rugs, automobile assembly
Highest point: Brasstown Bald 4784 ft. (1459 m.)

State History

Inhabited by Creek and Cherokee peoples when explored by Spanish and penetrated by Spanish missions 16th century; English colony, last of original 13 colonies to be founded, chartered 1732 and settled 1733 at Savannah by English philanthropist James E. Oglethorpe as refuge for debtors and as buffer state between Spanish Florida and the Carolinas; surrendered charter to crown 1752; became royal colony 1754; Savannah held by British 1778–82; chartered University of Georgia 1785, the oldest state university; first southern state to ratify U.S. Constitution Jan. 2, 1788; ceded claims to western lands (now Alabama and Mississippi) 1802; Creek and Cherokee tribes forcibly removed to Indian Territory 1830s; seceded from Union Jan. 19, 1861; scene of battle of Chickamauga 1863, campaign between Chattanooga and Atlanta, and Gen. William T. Sherman's "March to the Sea" 1864; ordinance of secession repealed Oct. 30, 1865 and slavery abolished; last state to be readmitted to Union July 15, 1870; adopted present constitution 1945.

Approved in March 2004, Georgia's flag is reminiscent of the Confederate Stars and Bars, with three broad red-white-red stripes and a blue canton. The state coat of arms (from the seal) and the motto "In God we trust" below it in yellow within the canton are surrounded by a circle of 13 white stars, symbolizing Georgia's position as one of the 13 original U.S. states.

85°
84°
83°
82°
81°
35°
34°
33°
32°
31°
30°
TENNESSEE
NORTH CAROLINA
SOUTH CAROLINA
ALABAMA
FLORIDA
ATLANTIC OCEAN
Gulf of Mexico
Savannah River
Dalton
Blue Ridge
Blairsville
Clayton
Ellijay
La Fayette
Cleveland
Calhoun
Dahlonega
Toccoa
Jasper
Summerville
Dawsonville
Homer
Hartwell
Rome
Cartersville
Canton
Gainesville
Jefferson
Elberton
Cedartown
Roswell
Winder
Athens
Marietta
Lexington
Smyrna
Monroe
Lincolnton
Buchanan
Atlanta
Decatur
Washington
Madison
Carrollton
East Point
Greensboro
Martinez
Covington
Thomson
Augusta
Newnan
Jackson
Sparta
Griffin
Eatonton
Waynesboro
Milledgeville
Zebulon
Gray
La Grange
Barnesville
Louisville
Thomaston
Sandersville
Macon
Irwinton
Sylvania
Wrightsville
Talbotton
Warner Robins
Swainsboro
Butler
Columbus
Fort Valley
Dublin
Statesboro
Buena Vista
Perry
Cochran
Metter
Springfield
Cusseta
Oglethorpe
Vidalia
Lyons
Claxton
Andersonville
Eastman
Vienna
Savannah
Reidsville
Lumpkin
Americus
McRae
Cordele
Abbeville
Hinesville
Hazlehurst
Cuthbert
Fitzgerald
Baxley
Dawson
Leesburg
Ludowici
Jesup
Fort Gaines
Albany
Sylvester
Douglas
Alma
Tifton
Darien
Pearson
Blackshear
Newton
Camilla
Moultrie
Nashville
Brunswick
Colquitt
Waycross
Nahunta
Adel
Woodbine
Lakeland
Homerville
Bainbridge
Thomasville
Cairo
Valdosta
Folkston
Quitman
Statenville
0 20 40 mi
0 30 60 km
© 2003 Encyclopædia Britannica, Inc.

HAWAII

Official name: State of Hawaii
Nickname: Aloha State
State Capital: Honolulu
State Flower: Yellow hibiscus
Motto: Ua Mau Ke Ea O Ka Aina I Ka Pono (The Life of the Land is Perpetuated in Righteousness)
Admitted to the Union: 1959 (50th)
Total area (2000): 10,931 sq. mi. (28,311 sq. km.) (ranks 43rd)
Population (2004): 1,262,840 (ranks 42nd)
Chief Cities/settlements: Hilo (on island of Hawaii), Honolulu (on island of Oahu), Lihue (on island of Kauai), Wailuku (on island of Maui)
Principal products/industries: Sugarcane production, food processing, tourism, military bases
Highest point: Mauna Kea 13,796 ft. (4208 m.) on island of Hawaii

State History

Original settlers came from the Marquesas Islands c. 400 A.D.; groups from Tahiti arrived c. 900–1000 A.D.; first European encounter 1778 with English Capt. James Cook who named it the Sandwich Islands and was killed here 1779; most of island group united under rule (1795–1819) of King Kamehameha I; frequented by American whalers from early 19th century; first visited by Christian missionaries from New England 1820; recognized as independent by U.S., Great Britain, and France 1840s; secured reciprocity treaty with U.S. 1875; Queen Liliuokalani overthrown and provisional government established with U.S. assistance 1893; declared republic 1894; annexed to U.S. by joint resolution 1898; established as U.S. territory 1900; scene of Japanese attack on Pearl Harbor Dec. 7, 1941; admitted as a state Aug. 21, 1959.

In 1793 Captain George Vancouver from Great Britain presented the Union Jack to the conquering king Kamehameha I, who was then uniting the islands into a single state; the Union Jack flew unofficially as the flag of Hawaii until 1816, when red, white, and blue stripes were added.

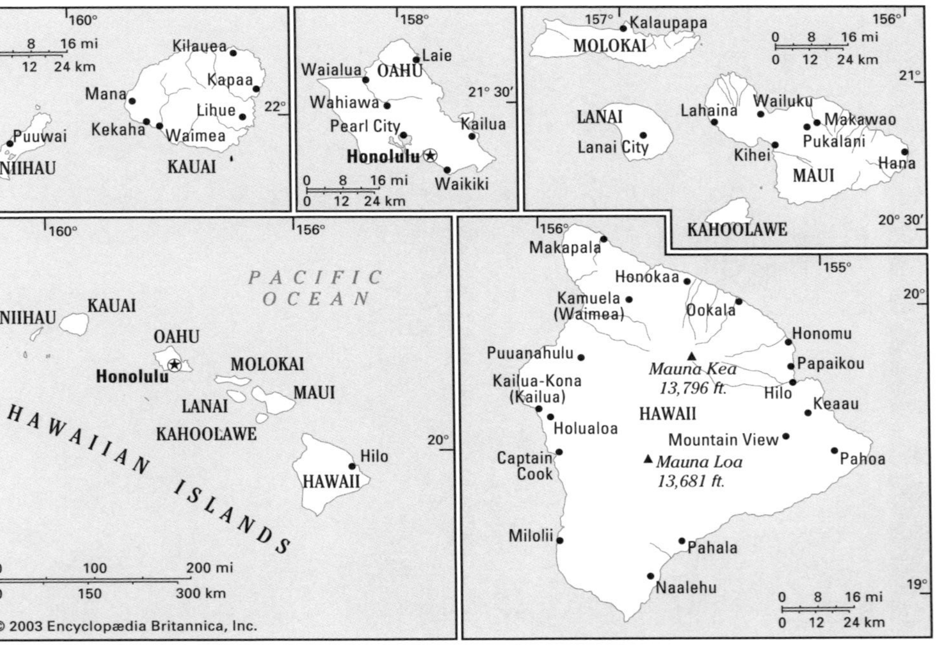
160°
0 8 16 mi
0 12 24 km
Kilauea
Kapaa
Mana
Lihue
22°
Kekaha
Waimea
Puuwai
NIIHAU
KAUAI
158°
Laie
Waialua
OAHU
21° 30′
Wahiawa
Pearl City
Kailua
Honolulu
Waikiki
0 8 16 mi
0 12 24 km
157°
Kalaupapa
156°
MOLOKAI
0 8 16 mi
0 12 24 km
21°
LANAI
Lanai City
Lahaina
Wailuku
Makawao
Pukalani
Kihei
Hana
MAUI
KAHOOLAWE
20° 30′
160°
156°
PACIFIC OCEAN
NIIHAU
KAUAI
OAHU
Honolulu
MOLOKAI
MAUI
LANAI
KAHOOLAWE
20°
Hilo
HAWAII
HAWAIIAN ISLANDS
0 100 200 mi
0 150 300 km
© 2003 Encyclopædia Britannica, Inc.
156°
Makapala
155°
Honokaa
Kamuela (Waimea)
Ookala
20°
Honomu
Puuanahulu
Papaikou
Mauna Kea 13,796 ft.
Kailua-Kona (Kailua)
Hilo
Keaau
HAWAII
Holualoa
Mountain View
Captain Cook
Mauna Loa 13,681 ft.
Pahoa
Milolii
Pahala
Naalehu
19°
0 8 16 mi
0 12 24 km

IDAHO

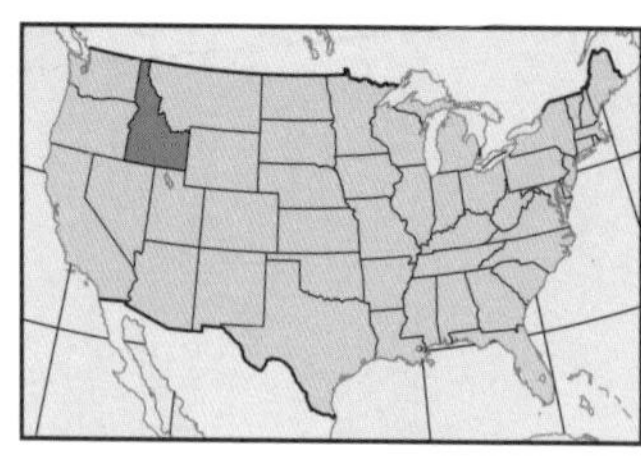

Official name: State of Idaho
Nickname: Gem State
State Capital: Boise
State Flower: Syringa
Motto: Esto Perpetua (Let It Be Perpetual)
Admitted to the Union: 1890 (43rd)
Total area (2000): 83,570 sq. mi. (216,446 sq. km.) (ranks 14th)
Population (2004): 1,393,262 (ranks 39th)
Chief Cities: Boise, Idaho Falls, Lewiston, Nampa, Pocatello, Twin Falls
Principal products/industries: Potatoes, sugar beets, wheat, cattle, antimony, silver, phosphates, lead, wood products, chemicals, food products, fishing, hunting, outdoor recreation
Highest point: Borah Peak, 12,662 ft. (3862 m.)

State History

First inhabited by American Indians; explored by Lewis and Clark expedition 1805; part of Oregon Country; ceded to U.S. by British 1846; included in Oregon Territory 1848; became part of Washington Territory in 1850s, and part of Idaho Territory 1863; gold discovered 1860; crossed by Oregon Trail; admitted to Union July 3, 1890.

On March 5, 1866, Idaho Territory adopted its first official seal, representing mountains below a new moon, a steamer on the Shoshone River, figures of Liberty and Peace, an elk's head, and agricultural produce. A similar seal was adopted for the new state on March 14, 1891.

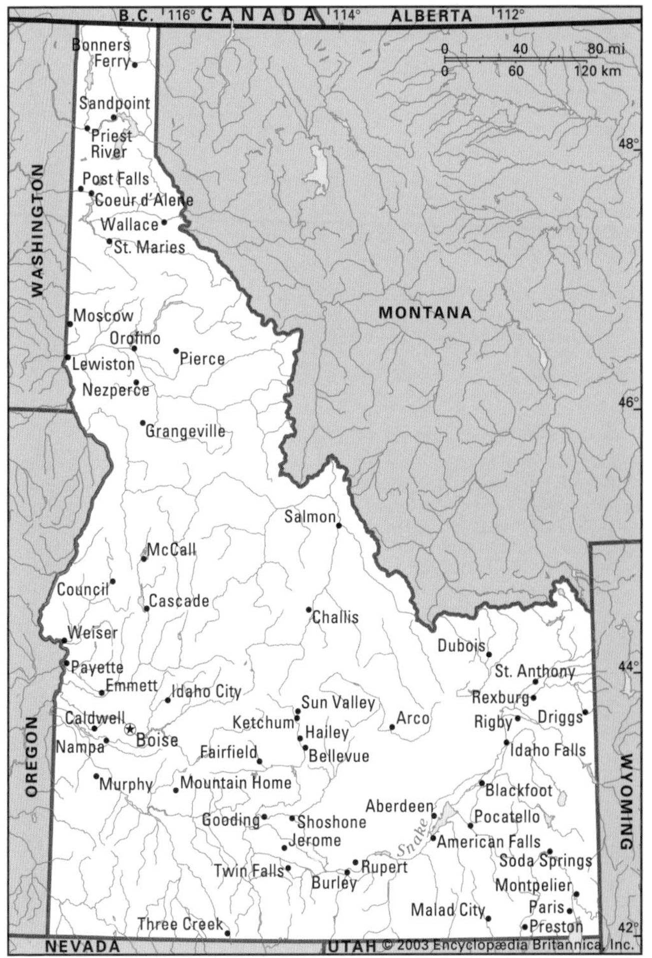
B.C.
116°
CANADA
114°
ALBERTA
112°
0
40
80 mi
0
60
120 km
48°
46°
44°
42°
WASHINGTON
OREGON
MONTANA
WYOMING
NEVADA
UTAH
Bonners Ferry
Sandpoint
Priest River
Post Falls
Coeur d'Alene
Wallace
St. Maries
Moscow
Orofino
Pierce
Lewiston
Nezperce
Grangeville
Salmon
McCall
Council
Cascade
Challis
Weiser
Payette
Emmett
Idaho City
Caldwell
Nampa
Boise
Murphy
Mountain Home
Fairfield
Ketchum
Sun Valley
Hailey
Bellevue
Arco
Dubois
St. Anthony
Rexburg
Rigby
Driggs
Idaho Falls
Blackfoot
Aberdeen
Pocatello
American Falls
Snake
Gooding
Shoshone
Jerome
Twin Falls
Rupert
Burley
Soda Springs
Montpelier
Paris
Preston
Malad City
Three Creek
© 2003 Encyclopædia Britannica, Inc.

ILLINOIS

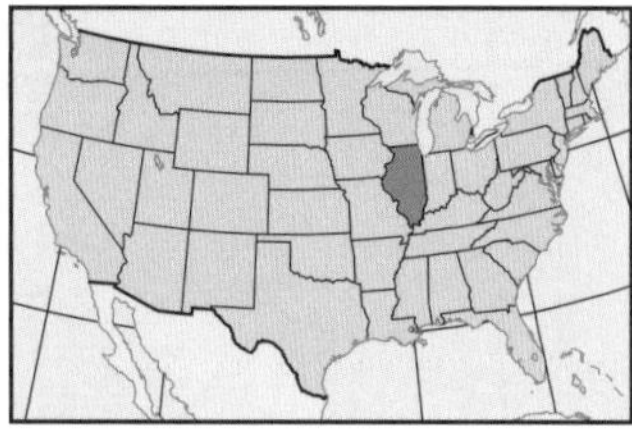

Official name: State of Illinois
Nickname: Prairie State
State Capital: Springfield
State Flower: Violet
Motto: State Sovereignty—National Union
Admitted to the Union: 1818 (21st)
Total area (2000): 57,914 sq. mi. (149,998 sq. km.) (ranks 25th)
Population (2004): 12,713,364 (ranks 5th)
Chief Cities: Aurora, Chicago, Peoria, Rockford, Springfield
Principal products/industries: Corn, soybeans, dairy products, livestock, oil, coal, machinery, chemicals, metal products, food products, printing and publishing
Highest point: Charles Mound, 1235 ft. (377 m.)

State History

Explored by Père Jacques Marquette and Louis Jolliet 1673 and by René-Robert Cavelier de La Salle who erected Fort Crèvecœur on Illinois River 1680; included in French Louisiana; ceded by France to England 1763 and by England to U.S. 1783; Virginia claims to territory given up by 1786; part of Northwest Territory 1787, of Indiana Territory 1800, and of Illinois Territory 1809; admitted to the Union Dec. 3, 1818 with capital at Kaskaskia (capital transferred to Vandalia 1820 and to Springfield 1837); adopted present constitution 1970.

On July 6, 1915, the legislature adopted a flag that had been developed in a contest. The flag showed design elements from the state seal—a rock on a stretch of land with water and the rising sun behind it, plus a shield bearing the national stars and stripes in the claws of a bald eagle.

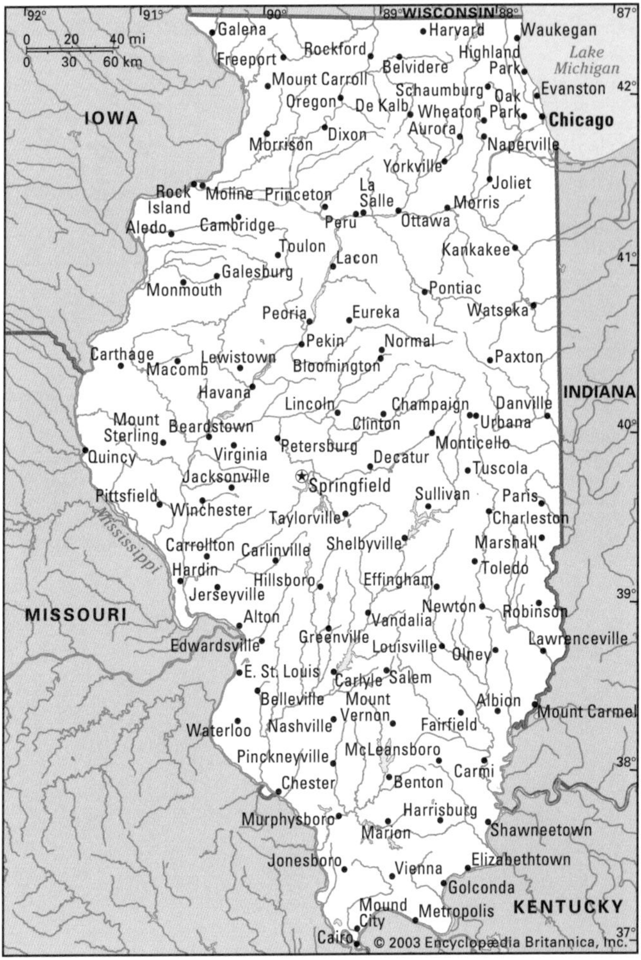
92°
91°
90°
89°
WISCONSIN
88°
87°
0 20 40 mi
0 30 60 km
IOWA
Galena
Harvard
Waukegan
Lake Michigan
Freeport
Rockford
Highland Park
Belvidere
Mount Carroll
Schaumburg
Oak Park
Evanston
42°
Oregon
De Kalb
Wheaton
Chicago
Aurora
Morrison
Dixon
Naperville
Yorkville
Joliet
Rock Island
Moline
Princeton
La Salle
Morris
Peru
Ottawa
Aledo
Cambridge
Toulon
Kankakee
Lacon
41°
Galesburg
Monmouth
Pontiac
Peoria
Eureka
Watseka
Pekin
Normal
Carthage
Macomb
Lewistown
Bloomington
Paxton
Havana
INDIANA
Lincoln
Champaign
Danville
Mount Sterling
Beardstown
Clinton
Urbana
40°
Quincy
Virginia
Petersburg
Monticello
Decatur
Tuscola
Jacksonville
Springfield
Pittsfield
Winchester
Sullivan
Paris
Taylorville
Charleston
Mississippi
Carrollton
Carlinville
Shelbyville
Marshall
Hardin
Toledo
Hillsboro
Effingham
Jerseyville
39°
Newton
Robinson
MISSOURI
Alton
Vandalia
Greenville
Lawrenceville
Edwardsville
Louisville
Olney
E. St. Louis
Carlyle
Salem
Belleville
Mount Vernon
Albion
Mount Carmel
Waterloo
Nashville
Fairfield
Pinckneyville
McLeansboro
38°
Carmi
Chester
Benton
Murphysboro
Harrisburg
Marion
Shawneetown
Jonesboro
Elizabethtown
Vienna
Golconda
Mound City
Metropolis
KENTUCKY
37°
Cairo
© 2003 Encyclopædia Britannica, Inc.

INDIANA

Official name: State of Indiana
Nickname: Hoosier State
State Capital: Indianapolis
State Flower: Peony
Motto: The Crossroads of America
Admitted to the Union: 1816 (19th)
Total area (2000): 36,418 sq. mi. (94,321 sq. km.) (ranks 38th)
Population (2004): 6,237,569 (ranks 14th)
Chief Cities: Evansville, Fort Wayne, Gary, Indianapolis, South Bend
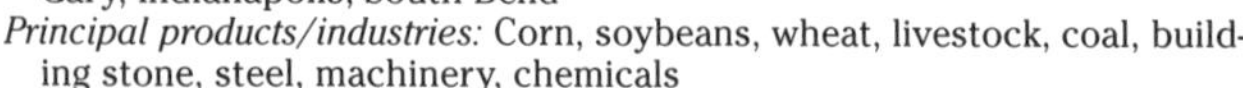
Principal products/industries: Corn, soybeans, wheat, livestock, coal, building stone, steel, machinery, chemicals
Highest point: Franklin township 1257 ft. (383 m.)

State History

Inhabited early perhaps by Mound Builders; the Miami, among other American Indians in area when Europeans first arrived; French settlement at Vincennes c. 1700; included in territory ceded by France to England 1763; ceded by England to U.S. by Treaty of Paris 1783; included in Northwest Territory 1787 and Indiana Territory 1800; admitted to the Union Dec. 11, 1816; capital removed from Corydon to Indianapolis 1825; adopted present constitution 1851.

In 1916, celebrating Indiana's centennial, a competition yielded this "state banner," approved on May 31, 1917. The torch is symbolic of enlightenment and liberty. A total of 19 stars ring the torch, recalling that the state was the 19th to join the Union. In 1955 the General Assembly changed its classification from state banner to state flag.

Lake Michigan
MICHIGAN
ILLINOIS
OHIO
KENTUCKY
88°
87°
86°
85°
42°
41°
40°
39°
38°
Michigan City
South Bend
Elkhart
Angola
Gary
Hammond
Portage
La Porte
Mishawaka
Lagrange
Goshen
Hobart
Valparaiso
Nappanee
Albion
Auburn
Crown Point
Knox
Plymouth
Warsaw
Columbia City
Rochester
Fort Wayne
Rensselaer
Winamac
Huntington
Decatur
Kentland
Logansport
Wabash
Monticello
Peru
Bluffton
Fowler
Delphi
Kokomo
Marion
Geneva
West Lafayette
Lafayette
Hartford City
Portland
Williamsport
Tipton
Frankfort
Muncie
Winchester
Covington
Lebanon
Anderson
Crawfordsville
Noblesville
Carmel
New Castle
Newport
Indianapolis
Greenfield
Richmond
Danville
Rockville
Greenwood
Rushville
Connersville
Greencastle
Brazil
Franklin
Shelbyville
Terre Haute
Martinsville
Greensburg
Brookville
Spencer
Nashville
Columbus
Lawrenceburg
Sullivan
Bloomington
North Vernon
Seymour
Rising Sun
Bloomfield
Brownstown
Bedford
Vevay
Madison
Vincennes
Shoals
Scottsburg
Washington
Paoli
Salem
French Lick
Charlestown
Jasper
English
New Albany
Clarksville
Princeton
Huntingburg
Jeffersonville
New Harmony
Corydon
Boonville
Evansville
Mt. Vernon
Tell City
Newburgh
Ohio
0 20 40 mi
0 30 60 km
© 2003 Encyclopædia Britannica, Inc.

IOWA

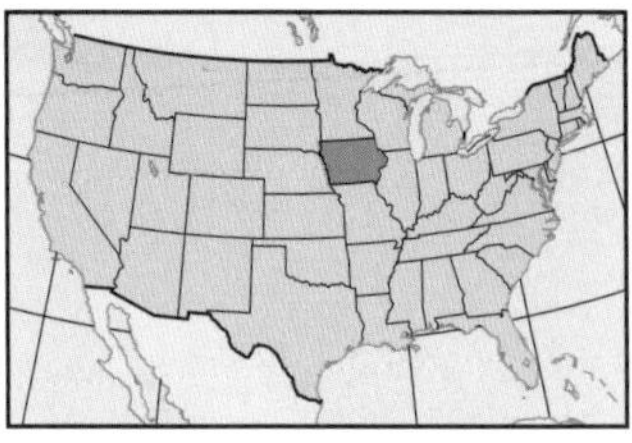

Official name: State of Iowa
Nickname: Hawkeye State
State Capital: Des Moines
State Flower: Wild rose
Motto: Our Liberties We Prize, and Our Rights We Will Maintain
Admitted to the Union: 1846 (29th)
Total area (2000): 56,272 sq. mi. (145,743 sq. km.) (ranks 26th)
Population (2004): 2,954,451 (ranks 30th)
Chief Cities: Cedar Rapids, Davenport, Des Moines, Sioux City, Waterloo
Principal products/industries: Corn, soybeans, oats, hay, cattle, hogs, cement, food products, farm machinery, chemicals
Highest point: Ocheyedan Mound 1670 ft. (509 m.)

State History

Traces found of early inhabitation by Mound Builders, among others; French explorers Louis Jolliet and Jacques (Père) Marquette among first Europeans to visit 1673; became part of U.S. by Louisiana Purchase 1803; part of Louisiana Territory 1805, of Missouri Territory 1812, unorganized territory c. 1821–34, of Michigan Territory 1834, of Wisconsin Territory 1836, and of Iowa Territory 1838; first permanent settlement made 1833 at Dubuque; held first constitutional convention 1844; present constitution dates from 1857. Admitted to Union Dec. 28, 1846; capital moved from Iowa City to Des Moines 1857.

In 1921 the legislature approved a state banner—rather than a state flag—with a blue stripe along the hoist and a red stripe in the fly, recalling the French Tricolor, which had flown over Iowa before the Louisiana Purchase of 1803. In the center is a flying bald eagle and a ribbon emblazoned with the state motto.

MINNESOTA
SOUTH DAKOTA
WISCONSIN
NEBRASKA
ILLINOIS
MISSOURI
KANSAS
Mississippi
Missouri
97°
96°
95°
94°
93°
92°
91°
90°
43°
42°
41°
40°
Northwood
Cresco
Decorah
Spirit Lake
Estherville
Sioux Center
Clear Lake
Mason City
New Hampton
Spencer
Algona
Charles City
West Union
Le Mars
Cherokee
Pocahontas
Clarion
Waverly
Cedar Falls
Dubuque
Sioux City
Storm Lake
Fort Dodge
Webster City
Waterloo
Independence
Ida Grove
Eldora
Vinton
Anamosa
Maquoketa
Onawa
Carroll
Boone
Ames
Marshalltown
Cedar Rapids
Clinton
Denison
Des Moines
Grinnell
Audubon
Newton
Iowa City
Bettendorf
Davenport
Harlan
Adel
Muscatine
Council Bluffs
Atlantic
Indianola
Pella
Oskaloosa
Washington
Winterset
Knoxville
Creston
Osceola
Ottumwa
Fairfield
Mt. Pleasant
Glenwood
Red Oak
Mount Ayr
Shenandoah
Clarinda
Centerville
Keosauqua
Fort Madison
Burlington
Lamoni
Keokuk
0
30
60 mi
0
40
80 km
© 2003 Encyclopædia Britannica, Inc.

KANSAS

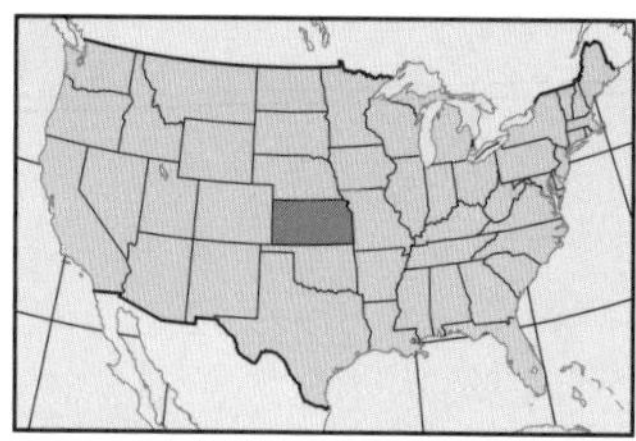

Official name: State of Kansas
Nickname: Sunflower State
State Capital: Topeka
State Flower: Sunflower
Motto: Ad Astra per Aspera (To the Stars Through Difficulty)
Admitted to the Union: 1861 (34th)
Total area (2000): 82,277 sq. mi. (213,096 sq. km.) (ranks 15th)
Population (2004): 2,735,502 (ranks 33rd)
Chief Cities: Kansas City, Overland Park, Topeka, Wichita
Principal products/industries: Wheat, sorghum, corn, cattle, oil, salt, transportation equipment, machinery, chemicals
Highest point: Mt. Sunflower 4039 ft. (1232 m.)

State History

Before coming of Europeans, inhabited sparsely by both nomadic and settled American Indians, among them, the Kansa; probably entered by Spanish explorer Francisco de Coronado's expedition 1541; came to U.S. as part of Louisiana Purchase 1803; included in Louisiana Territory 1805 and Missouri Territory 1812; southwestern corner lost to Spanish in 1819 treaty; in unorganized territory c. 1821–54; regained southwestern corner with annexation of Texas 1845; by Kansas-Nebraska Act 1854, Kansas Territory organized, including Kansas and central portion of eastern Colorado; admitted to Union with present boundaries as free state Jan. 29, 1861.

In the center of the Kansas flag is a version of the seal, the original of which is dated 1861. Some of the state's features are: commerce, shown by the river and boat; agriculture, by the plowing farmer; and westward settlement, by the wagon train and the homesteader's cabin (which stopped pouring chimney smoke in 1985). The sunflower became the state flower in 1903.

102°
101°
100°
99°
98°
97°
96°
95°
IOWA
94°
NEBRASKA
Missouri
40°
39°
38°
37°
36°
COLORADO
MISSOURI
OKLAHOMA
TEXAS
Oberlin
Norton
St. Francis
Phillipsburg
Marysville
Hiawatha
Concordia
Atchison
Colby
Stockton
Clay Center
Holton
Leavenworth
Goodland
Hill City
Osborne
Manhattan
Kansas City
Topeka
Lawrence
Oakley
Wa Keeney
Lincoln
Abilene
Junction City
Olathe
Overland Park
Gove
Hays
Russell
Salina
Lyndon
Ottawa
Ness City
La Crosse
Leoti
Scott City
McPherson
Marion
Emporia
Garnett
Great Bend
Syracuse
Garden City
Newton
Burlington
Fort Scott
Hutchinson
Iola
Kinsley
El Dorado
Dodge City
Kingman
Chanute
Ulysses
Pratt
Wichita
Fredonia
Parsons
Meade
Ashland
Wellington
Independence
Pittsburg
Hugoton
Medicine Lodge
Winfield
Liberal
Arkansas City
Coffeyville
0 30 60 mi
0 40 80 km
© 2003 Encyclopædia Britannica, Inc.

KENTUCKY

Official name: Commonwealth of Kentucky
Nickname: Bluegrass State
State Capital: Frankfort
State Flower: Goldenrod
Motto: United We Stand, Divided We Fall
Admitted to the Union: 1792 (15th)
Total area (2000): 40,409 sq. mi. (104,659 sq. km.) (ranks 37th)
Population (2004): 4,145,922 (ranks 26th)
Chief Cities: Bowling Green, Covington, Lexington, Louisville, Owensboro
Principal products/industries: Tobacco, corn, wheat, thoroughbred horses, cattle, hogs, oil, natural gas, coal, bourbon whiskey, farm equipment, chemicals
Highest point: Black Mt. 4139 ft. (2162 m.)

State History

Inhabited by American Indian peoples before arrival of European explorers; entered by American explorer Thomas Walker 1750; included in territory ceded by French 1763; explored by expeditions under American pioneer Daniel Boone from 1769; first permanent English settlement at Boonesborough made by Transylvania Company 1775; because of its many Indian wars known as the "Dark and Bloody Ground"; organized as county of Virginia 1776; included in territory of U.S. by Treaty of Paris 1783; received consent of Virginia to statehood 1789; admitted to Union June 1, 1792; as border state during Civil War torn between North and South, providing troops to both sides; despite an attempt to be neutral, invaded by Confederate troops 1862; suffered skirmishes thereafter but remained in Union; adopted present constitution 1891.

At the time of its admission to the Union in 1792, Kentucky was considered the nation's western frontier, and this was reflected in the symbolism of the state seal: two men embracing, one a frontiersman in buckskins and the other a gentleman in formal frock coat, suggesting Westerners and Easterners in national unity.

88°
87°
86°
85°
84°
83°
82°
89°
88°
39°
38°
37°
37°
MISSOURI
ILLINOIS
Ohio
Morganfield
Marion
Princeton
Paducah
Wickliffe
Mayfield
Cadiz
Clinton
Hickman
Murray
TENNESSEE
INDIANA
OHIO
WEST VIRGINIA
VIRGINIA
ILLINOIS
TENNESSEE
Ohio
Covington
Independence
Alexandria
Carrollton
Wiliamstown
Maysville
Vanceburg
Ashland
La Grange
Cynthiana
Flemingsburg
Frankfort
Paris
Morehead
Louisa
Louisville
Shelbyville
Lexington
Brandenburg
Lawrenceburg
Winchester
West Liberty
Paintsville
Radcliff
Richmond
Salyersville
Prestonsburg
Henderson
Owensboro
Danville
Berea
Jackson
Pikeville
Morganfield
Elizabethtown
Stanford
Madisonville
Leitchfield
Campbellsville
Mount Vernon
Hazard
Marion
Greenville
Morgantown
London
Manchester
Whitesburg
Columbia
Somerset
Princeton
Bowling Green
Corbin
Barbourvillle
Glasgow
Hopkinsville
Russellville
Monticello
Elkton
Franklin
Tompkinsville
Williamsburg
Middlesboro
Murray
0
20
40 mi
0
30
60 km
© 2003 Encyclopædia Britannica, Inc.

LOUISIANA

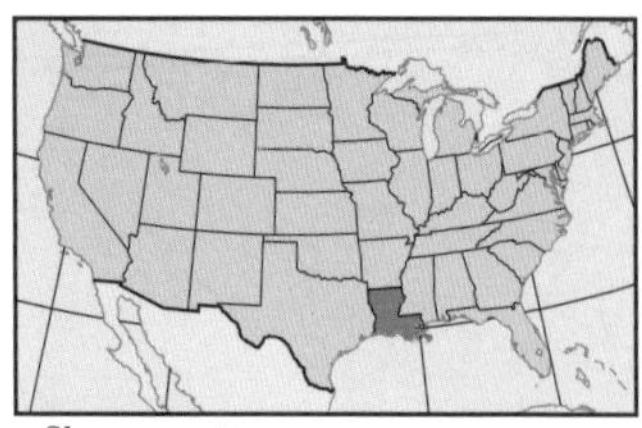

Official name: State of Louisiana
Nickname: Pelican State
State Capital: Baton Rouge
State Flower: Magnolia
Motto: Union, Justice, Confidence
Admitted to the Union: 1812 (18th)
Total area (2000): 51,840 sq. mi. (134,264 sq. km.) (ranks 31st)
Population (2004): 4,515,770 (ranks 24th)
Chief Cities: Baton Rouge, New Orleans, Shreveport
Principal products/industries: Rice, soybeans, cotton, sugarcane, seafood, oil, natural gas, sulfur, salt, chemicals, transportation equipment, lumber, tourism
Highest point: Driskill Mt. 535 ft. (163 m.)

State History

Inhabited by native peoples for thousands of years prior to European exploration, which began in the 16th century; name "Louisiana" originally applied to entire Mississippi River basin, claimed for France by explorer René-Robert Cavelier, Sieur de La Salle 1682; Natchitoches, first settlement within area of present state, founded 1714; New Orleans founded 1718; except for New Orleans, region east of Mississippi River ceded by France to Great Britain 1763; West Florida (incl. portion of present state of Louisiana east of Mississippi River north of Lake Pontchartrain) returned to Spain 1783 and claimed by U.S. as part of Louisiana Purchase 1803; New Orleans and region west of Mississippi River ceded to Spain 1762–63; returned to France 1800–03, and sold to U.S. in Louisiana Purchase; Orleans Territory organized 1804 and admitted to Union Apr. 30, 1812 as state of Louisiana, the first to be carved out of Louisiana Purchase; passed ordinance of secession Jan. 26, 1861; abolished slavery 1864; readmitted to Union 1868; present constitution adopted 1974.

A pelican tearing at its breast to feed its young is the central emblem of the flag. Real pelicans never perform this activity, but from the Middle Ages this symbol has represented the spirit of self-sacrifice and dedication to progeny. As early as 1812 the pelican was used as a Louisiana symbol.

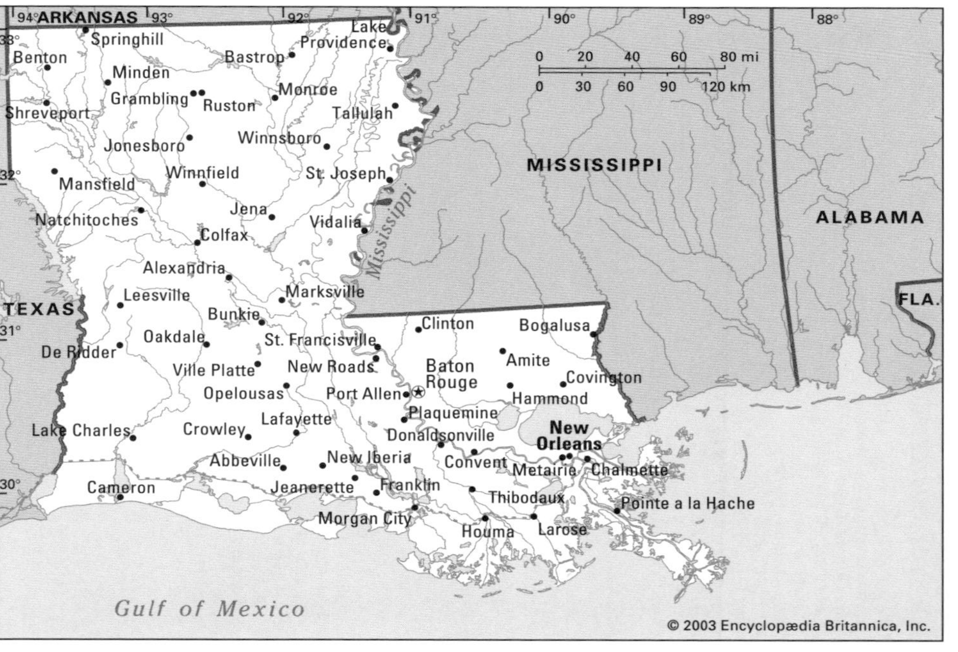
ARKANSAS
MISSISSIPPI
ALABAMA
FLA.
TEXAS
Gulf of Mexico
Mississippi
0 20 40 60 80 mi
0 30 60 90 120 km
94°
93°
92°
91°
90°
89°
88°
33°
32°
31°
30°
Springhill
Benton
Minden
Grambling
Ruston
Shreveport
Bastrop
Lake Providence
Monroe
Tallulah
Jonesboro
Winnsboro
Winnfield
Mansfield
St. Joseph
Jena
Natchitoches
Vidalia
Colfax
Alexandria
Leesville
Marksville
Bunkie
Oakdale
St. Francisville
De Ridder
Ville Platte
New Roads
Opelousas
Port Allen
Clinton
Bogalusa
Amite
Baton Rouge
Covington
Hammond
Plaquemine
Lake Charles
Crowley
Lafayette
Donaldsonville
New Orleans
Abbeville
New Iberia
Convent
Metairie
Chalmette
Cameron
Jeanerette
Franklin
Thibodaux
Pointe a la Hache
Morgan City
Houma
Larose
© 2003 Encyclopædia Britannica, Inc.

MAINE

Official name: State of Maine
Nickname: Pine Tree State
State Capital: Augusta
State Flower: White pine cone and tassel
Motto: Dirigo (I Direct)
Admitted to the Union: 1820 (23rd)
Total area (2000): 35,385 sq. mi. (91,646 sq. km.) (ranks 39th)
Population (2004): 1,317,253 (ranks 40th)

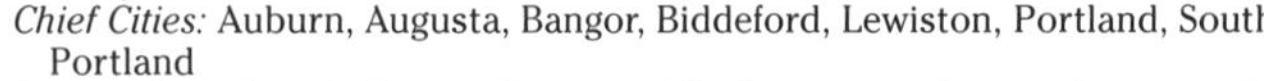

Chief Cities: Auburn, Augusta, Bangor, Biddeford, Lewiston, Portland, South Portland
Principal products/industries: Potatoes, blueberries, apples, poultry, gravel, tourism, fishing (esp. lobstering), food products, leather goods, paper, wood products
Highest point: Mt. Katahdin 5267 ft. (1606 m.)

State History

Evidence of prehistoric inhabitants; inhabited by Algonquians (especially Penobscot and Passamaquoddy tribes) at time of European settlement; claimed and settled by both English and French; included in grant to Plymouth Company 1606; first settlement by English at mouth of the Sagadahoc (Kennebec) 1607 failed, but city of Saco and Monhegan Island were settled c. 1622; through series of grants, beginning in 1622, claimed by Massachusetts Bay Colony and English proprietor Sir Ferdinando Gorges; annexed to Massachusetts (1652) which bought out Gorges's claim 1677; northern parts frequently attacked by French 17th–18th centuries; a district of Massachusetts until 1820; admitted to Union as free state as part of Missouri Compromise Mar. 15, 1820; boundary with Canada settled by treaty with Great Britain 1842.

Until 1820 Maine was a district of Massachusetts, and its early symbols were based on that connection. The pine tree emblem was used for the Massachusetts naval flag in 1776. The current state flag, established in 1909, has its coat of arms showing a moose-and-pine tree emblem on a shield supported by a farmer and a sailor.

71°
70°
69°
68°
67°
47°
46°
45°
44°
43°
0 20 40 mi
0 32 64 km
St. Lawrence River
QUEBEC
CANADA
NEW BRUNSWICK
CANADA
NEW HAMPSHIRE
MASS.
Frenchville
Fort Kent
Van Buren
Eagle Lake
Caribou
Washburn
Presque Isle
Monticello
Houlton
Millinocket
Danforth
Moosehead Lake
Greenville
Lincoln
Brownville
Dover-Foxcroft
Bingham
Dexter
Old Town
Orono
Bangor
Calais
Eastport
Lubec
Madison
Farmington
Skowhegan
Pittsfield
Machias
Rumford
Waterville
Ellsworth
Belfast
Castine
Bar Harbor
Augusta
Norway
Gardiner
MT. DESERT ISLAND
Lewiston
Bridgton
Rockland
Camden
Auburn
Vinalhaven
Wiscasset
Brunswick
Bath
Freeport
Boothbay Harbor
Westbrook
Portland
South Portland
Sanford
Saco
Biddeford
Kennebunk
Kennebunkport
Ogunquit
Kittery
ATLANTIC OCEAN
© 2003 Encyclopædia Britannica, Inc.

MARYLAND

Official name: State of Maryland
Nickname: Old Line State
State Capital: Annapolis
State Flower: Black-eyed Susan
Motto: Fatti Maschii, Parole Femine (Manly Deeds, Womanly Words)
Admitted to the Union: 1788; 7th of the original 13 colonies to ratify the U.S. Constitution
Total area (2000): 12,407 sq. mi. (32,133 sq. km.) (ranks 42nd)
Population (2004): 5,558,058 (ranks 19th)
Chief Cities: Annapolis, Baltimore
Principal products/industries: Dairy products, food products, corn, tobacco, chickens and other livestock, fishing especially for crabs, stone, sand and gravel, tourism, primary metals, transportation equipment, chemicals, electrical equipment
Highest point: Backbone Mt. 3360 ft. (1025 m.)

State History

Originally inhabited by American Indians; English first visited early 17th century; granted to George Calvert (Lord Baltimore) as proprietary colony 1632; first American colony to achieve religious freedom; first settled at St. Marys 1634, which was its capital 1634–94; colony under rule of British crown 1689–1715; its long-standing boundary dispute with Pennsylvania settled by drawing of Mason-Dixon Line 1760s; first state constitution adopted 1776; adopted Articles of Confederation 1781; ceded territory for District of Columbia; during Civil War remained in the Union, but was subjected to suspension of habeas corpus; invaded by Confederate forces 1862; abolished slavery 1864; adopted present constitution 1867.

Maryland has a state flag that was flown when the colony was under British rule: the personal banner of Sir George Calvert, the first Lord Baltimore. It has six vertical yellow and black stripes, with a matching diagonal. It is combined with the arms of the Crossland family (maternal family of Sir George Calvert): a quartered white-and-red shield.

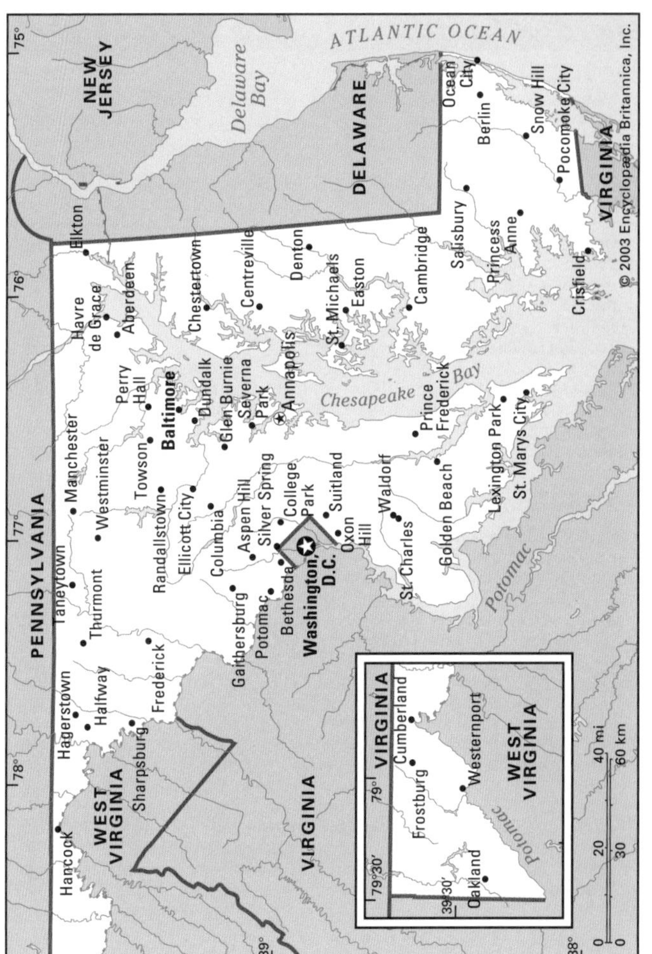

PENNSYLVANIA
NEW JERSEY
DELAWARE
VIRGINIA
WEST VIRGINIA
ATLANTIC OCEAN
Delaware Bay
Chesapeake Bay
Potomac
Washington, D.C.
Baltimore
Annapolis
Elkton
Havre de Grace
Aberdeen
Chestertown
Centreville
Denton
St. Michaels
Easton
Cambridge
Salisbury
Princess Anne
Crisfield
Berlin
Ocean City
Snow Hill
Pocomoke City
Manchester
Westminster
Towson
Perry Hall
Dundalk
Glen Burnie
Severna Park
Randallstown
Ellicott City
Columbia
Aspen Hill
Silver Spring
College Park
Suitland
Oxon Hill
Waldorf
St. Charles
Golden Beach
Prince Frederick
Lexington Park
St. Marys City
Taneytown
Thurmont
Frederick
Gaithersburg
Potomac
Bethesda
Hagerstown
Halfway
Sharpsburg
Hancock
Cumberland
Frostburg
Westernport
Oakland
75°
76°
77°
78°
79°
79°30'
39°30'
39°
38°
0 20 40 mi
0 30 60 km
© 2003 Encyclopædia Britannica, Inc.

MASSACHUSETTS

Official name: Commonwealth of Massachusetts
Nickname: Bay State
State Capital: Boston
State Flower: Mayflower
Motto: Ense Petit Placidam Sub Libertate Quietem (By the Sword We Seek Peace, but Peace Only Under Liberty)
Admitted to the Union: 1788; 6th of the original 13 colonies to ratify the U.S. Constitution
Total area (2000): 10,555 sq. mi. (27,336 sq. km.) (ranks 44th)
Population (2004): 6,416,505 (ranks 13th)
Chief Cities: Boston, Springfield, Worcester
Principal products/industries: Dairy products, cranberries and other fruit, vegetables, electronic equipment, electrical equipment, printing and publishing, tourism, education, fishing
Highest point: Mt. Greylock 3487 ft. (1064 m.)

State History

Perhaps explored by Norse c. 11th century; coast skirted by Florentine explorer Giovanni da Verrazano 1524; Cape Cod discovered by Englishman Bartholomew Gosnold 1602 who made first (temporary) European settlement within present limits of state; at time of European settlement, region inhabited by several Algonquin tribes; Plymouth settled by Pilgrims 1620; Massachusetts Bay Colony, founded and governed by Massachusetts Bay Company 1629–84; Harvard College founded 1636; joined New England Confederation 1643; acquired province of Maine 1652; after loss of first charter 1684, governed as part of Dominion of New England 1686; by its 2nd charter 1691, received jurisdiction over Maine and Plymouth colonies; in 18th century, gradually became a center of resistance to imperial colonial policy; British troops withdrawn to Boston after colonial uprisings at Lexington and Concord 1775; battle of Bunker Hill 1775; British evacuated Boston 1776; gave up claims to western lands 1785–86; western Massachusetts scene of Shays' Rebellion, an uprising in protest of harsh government economic policies 1786–87; eastern Massachusetts early center of American cotton manufacture. Maine became separate state 1820.

The seal of the Massachusetts Bay Colony of 1629 showed an Indian and pine trees, and both of these symbols have continued to be used up to the present time. The Indian appears in gold on a blue shield together with a silver star indicative of statehood.

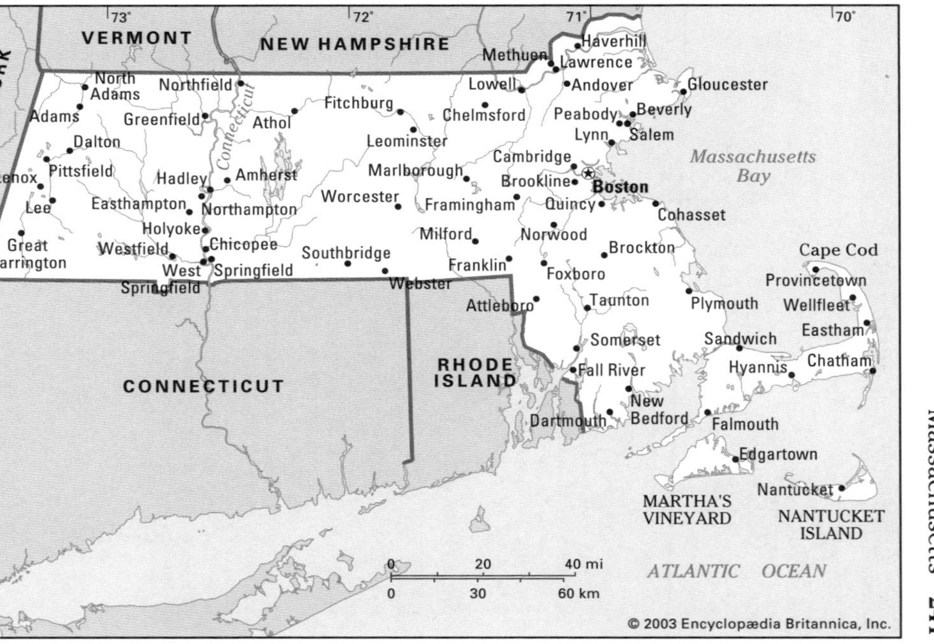

VERMONT
NEW HAMPSHIRE
NEW YORK
CONNECTICUT
RHODE ISLAND
Massachusetts Bay
Cape Cod
MARTHA'S VINEYARD
NANTUCKET ISLAND
ATLANTIC OCEAN
Connecticut
73°
72°
71°
70°
42°
41°
0
20
40 mi
0
30
60 km
North Adams
Adams
Pittsfield
Dalton
Lenox
Lee
Great Barrington
Northfield
Greenfield
Hadley
Easthampton
Westfield
Holyoke
Northampton
Amherst
Chicopee
Springfield
West Springfield
Athol
Fitchburg
Leominster
Worcester
Southbridge
Webster
Marlborough
Framingham
Milford
Franklin
Chelmsford
Lowell
Methuen
Haverhill
Lawrence
Andover
Peabody
Lynn
Salem
Beverly
Gloucester
Cambridge
Brookline
Boston
Quincy
Norwood
Foxboro
Attleboro
Cohasset
Brockton
Taunton
Somerset
Fall River
New Bedford
Dartmouth
Plymouth
Sandwich
Falmouth
Hyannis
Chatham
Eastham
Wellfleet
Provincetown
Edgartown
Nantucket
© 2003 Encyclopædia Britannica, Inc.

MICHIGAN

Official name: State of Michigan
Nickname: Wolverine State
State Capital: Lansing
State Flower: Apple blossom
Motto: Si Quaeris Paeninsulam Amoenam Circumspice (If You Seek a Beautiful Peninsula, Look Around You)
Admitted to the Union: 1837 (26th)
Total area (2000): 96,716 sq. mi. (250,494 sq. km.) (ranks 11th)
Population (2004): 10,112,620 (ranks 8th)
Chief Cities: Ann Arbor, Detroit, Flint, Grand Rapids, Lansing, Livonia, Sterling Heights, Warren
Principal products/industries: Dairy products, fruit, iron ore, limestone, copper, natural gas, motor vehicles and parts, tourism
Highest point: Mt. Arvon 1979 ft. (604 m.)

State History

Inhabited especially by Algonquian tribes prior to arrival of Europeans; first European to visit the region was French adventurer Étienne Brulé in early 17th century; first settled at Sault Sainte Marie by French explorer and missionary Père Marquette 1668; military post of Detroit founded 1701; ceded to England 1763 following French and Indian War and to U.S. 1783; included in Northwest Territory 1787 and in Indiana Territory 1800, 1803; Michigan Territory organized on the Lower Peninsula, 1805; boundaries extended 1818 to include Upper Peninsula and beyond; Upper Peninsula briefly included in Wisconsin Territory 1836; boundary dispute with Ohio (Toledo War) settled by U.S. Congress in favor of Ohio, with Michigan receiving as compensation the Upper Peninsula and statehood (admitted as free state Jan. 26, 1837); Lansing became capital 1847; adopted present constitution 1963.

The bald eagle of the U.S. serves as a crest to the state shield, while an elk and a moose, supposedly based on the coat of arms of the Hudson's Bay Company, serve as supporters. The central design of the shield shows a man with a rifle standing on a peninsula and the sun setting over surrounding waters.

Lake Superior
ISLE ROYALE
Lake Huron
Lake Michigan
Lake Erie
CANADA
ONTARIO
WISCONSIN
ILLINOIS
INDIANA
OHIO
Eagle River
Calumet
Houghton
L'Anse
Marquette
Ishpeming
Munising
Grand Marais
Newberry
Sault Ste. Marie
Crystal Falls
Iron Mountain
Gladstone
Escanaba
Manistique
St. Ignace
Mackinaw City
Cheboygan
Rogers City
Petoskey
Charlevoix
Menominee
Leland
Bellaire
Gaylord
Atlanta
Alpena
Traverse City
Kalkaska
Mio
Harrisville
Frankfort
Beulah
Grayling
Manistee
Cadillac
Lake City
West Branch
Tawas City
Harrison
Gladwin
Ludington
Reed City
Clare
Bad Axe
Baldwin
Big Rapids
Midland
Bay City
Hart
Mt. Pleasant
Caro
Sandusky
Whitehall
Alma
Saginaw
Frankenmuth
Muskegon
Grand Rapids
Greenville
St. Johns
Owosso
Lapeer
Grand Haven
Ionia
Flint
Port Huron
Wyoming
Corunna
Waterford
Holland
Lansing
East Lansing
Sterling Heights
Pontiac
Hastings
Charlotte
South Haven
Battle Creek
Mason
Livonia
Warren
Kalamazoo
Ann Arbor
Detroit
Benton Harbor
Marshall
Jackson
Portage
Tecumseh
Monroe
St. Joseph
Dowagiac
Coldwater
Three Rivers
Sturgis
Hillsdale
Adrian
Niles
Ontonagon
Bessemer
Ironwood
Iron River
0 20 40 60 80 mi
0 30 60 90 120 km
88° 87° 86° 85° 84° 83° 82°
47° 46° 45° 44° 43° 42°
© 2003 Encyclopædia Britannica, Inc.

MINNESOTA

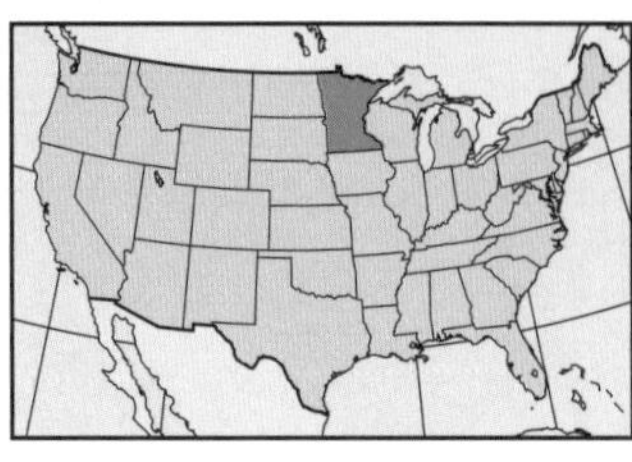

Official name: State of Minnesota
Nicknames: North Star State, Gopher State
State Capital: St. Paul
State Flower: Pink and white moccasin flower
Motto: L'étoile du Nord (Star of the North)
Admitted to the Union: 1858 (32nd)
Total area (2000): 86,939 sq. mi. (225,171 sq. km.) (ranks 12th)
Population (2004): 5,100,958 (ranks 21st)
Chief Cities: Bloomington, Duluth, Minneapolis, Rochester, St. Paul
Principal products/industries: Oats, corn, soybeans, sugar beets, wild rice, turkeys, hogs, dairy products, iron ore, granite, limestone, electronic equipment, pulp and paper products, food processing, tourism
Highest point: Eagle Mt. 2301 ft. (702 m.)

State History

Evidence of prehistoric habitation; at time of European arrival, inhabited by Algonquian Ojibwa and Siouan Dakota American Indian tribes; probably visited by French explorers Pierre Radisson and Seigneur Chouart des Groseilliers 1654–60; Upper Mississippi Valley explored by Frenchmen René-Robert, Sieur de La Salle and Louis Hennepin 1680, and became extensive fur-trading region under the French; part northeast of the Mississippi ceded to British 1763 and to U.S. 1783, and included in Northwest Territory 1787; southwestern part acquired by U.S. in Louisiana Purchase 1803; northwestern part ceded to U.S. in border treaty with British 1818; Fort Snelling, first U.S. outpost in the region, established 1819; included in various territories before organization of Minnesota Territory Mar. 3, 1849, which included present Minnesota and the parts of North and South Dakota that lie east of the Missouri River; admitted to Union (with present boundaries) May 11, 1858; Sioux uprising occurred in southern Minnesota 1862; an early center of the Grange movement from 1867 on.

The central design of the flag has the state seal in circular form. Around the seal are 19 gold stars (arranged in 5 groups) symbolizing Minnesota as the 19th state to follow the original 13, and a border of lady's slipper flowers. Inside is a mounted Indian, a representation of St. Anthony Falls, and a setting sun.

MANITOBA
CANADA
ONTARIO
NORTH DAKOTA
SOUTH DAKOTA
WISCONSIN
IOWA
Lake Superior
Mississippi
Angle Inlet
Grand Portage
Grand Marais
Hallock
Roseau
Baudette
International Falls
Warren
Thief River Falls
Big Falls
Red Lake Falls
Crookston
Ely
Tower
Virginia
Chisolm
Hibbing
Bagley
Bemidji
Ada
Mahnomen
Grand Rapids
Two Harbors
Walker
Moorhead
Detroit Lakes
Park Rapids
Proctor
Duluth
Carlton
Aitkin
Wadena
Brainerd
Fergus Falls
Breckenridge
Elbow Lake
Long Prairie
Little Falls
Hinckley
Alexandria
Mora
Pine City
Wheaton
Sauk Centre
Foley
Morris
Glenwood
St. Cloud
Cambridge
Elk River
Ortonville
Benson
Coon Rapids
Willmar
Litchfield
Buffalo
Madison
Minneapolis
St. Paul
Granite Falls
Hutchinson
Montevideo
Chaska
Bloomington
Olivia
Glencoe
Shakopee
Hastings
Canby
Gaylord
Red Wing
Redwood Falls
Le Sueur
St. Peter
Ivanhoe
Marshall
Northfield
Wabasha
New Ulm
Faribault
Mankato
Owatonna
Winona
Slayton
Waseca
Pipestone
St. James
Rochester
Windom
Luverne
Albert Lea
Preston
Caledonia
Worthington
Fairmont
Blue Earth
Austin
0 20 40 60 80 mi
0 30 60 90 120 km
© 2003 Encyclopædia Britannica, Inc.

MISSISSIPPI

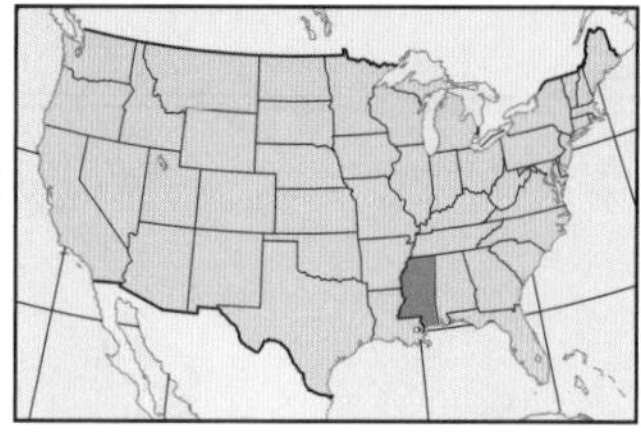

Official name: State of Mississippi
Nickname: Magnolia State
State Capital: Jackson
State Flower: Magnolia
Motto: Virtute et Armis (By Valor and Arms)
Admitted to the Union: 1817 (20th)
Total area (2000): 48,430 sq. mi. (125,434 sq. km.) (ranks 32nd)
Population (2004): 2,902,966 (ranks 31st)
Chief Cities: Biloxi, Greenville, Gulfport, Hattiesburg, Jackson, Meridian,
Principal Products: Cotton, soybeans, grains, livestock, petroleum, natural gas, chemicals, apparel, wood products
Highest point: Woodall Mt. 806 ft. (246 m.)

State History

Evidence of prehistoric inhabitants (Mound Builders); prior to European settlement inhabited by several tribes including the Choctaw, Natchez, and Chickasaw; became part of French-controlled Louisiana; Biloxi settled by French colonist Pierre Le Moyne d'Iberville 1699; except for southern part (British West Florida), region ceded to U.S. 1783; northern section included in Territory South of the Ohio River 1790; southern part included in Mississippi Territory 1798, which was expanded 1804 to include most of current state; western part of the territory admitted to the Union with its present boundaries Dec. 10, 1817 as state of Mississippi, but its southernmost strip of land not formally ceded by Spain until 1819; seceded Jan. 9, 1861; scene of important battles during Civil War; readmitted to Union Feb. 23, 1870; adopted present constitution 1890.

After the Civil War, a new state constitution was adopted, the product of a white majority that wished to minimize the influence in state affairs of local blacks and of the federal government. The new flag, still in use, has three stripes that recall the Stars and Bars of the Confederacy, and the Confederate Battle Flag as its canton.

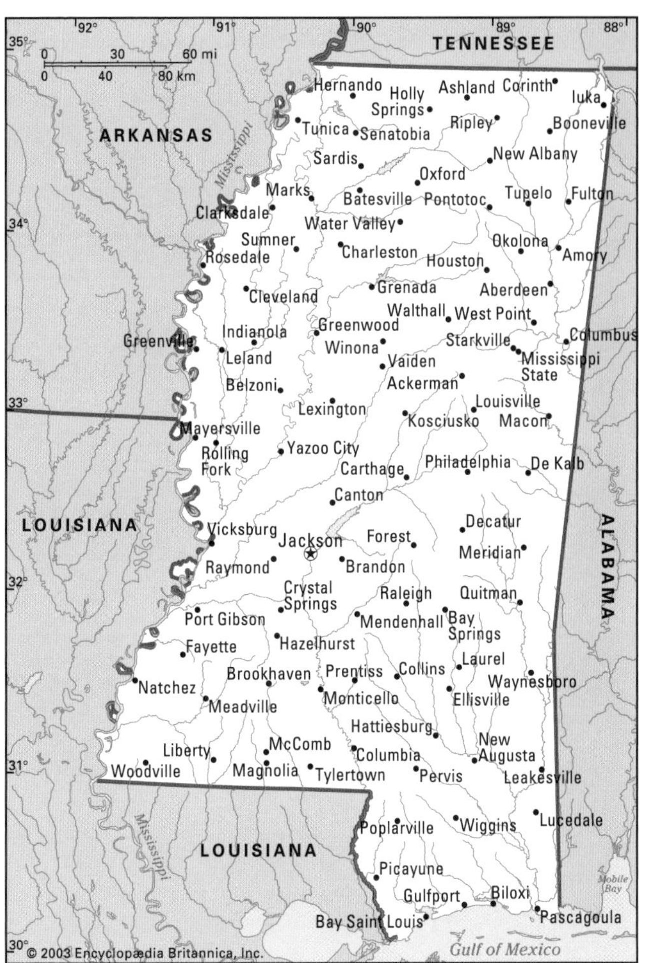

TENNESSEE
ARKANSAS
LOUISIANA
LOUISIANA
ALABAMA
Mississippi
Mississippi
Gulf of Mexico
Mobile Bay
0 30 60 mi
0 40 80 km
92°
91°
90°
89°
88°
35°
34°
33°
32°
31°
30°
Hernando
Holly Springs
Ashland
Corinth
Iuka
Tunica
Senatobia
Ripley
Booneville
Sardis
New Albany
Oxford
Marks
Batesville
Pontotoc
Tupelo
Fulton
Clarksdale
Water Valley
Sumner
Charleston
Okolona
Amory
Rosedale
Houston
Grenada
Aberdeen
Cleveland
Walthall
West Point
Greenwood
Indianola
Columbus
Greenville
Winona
Starkville
Leland
Vaiden
Mississippi State
Belzoni
Ackerman
Louisville
Lexington
Kosciusko
Macon
Mayersville
Rolling Fork
Yazoo City
Carthage
Philadelphia
De Kalb
Canton
Decatur
Vicksburg
Jackson
Forest
Meridian
Raymond
Brandon
Crystal Springs
Raleigh
Quitman
Port Gibson
Mendenhall
Bay Springs
Hazelhurst
Fayette
Laurel
Brookhaven
Prentiss
Collins
Waynesboro
Natchez
Monticello
Ellisville
Meadville
Hattiesburg
New Augusta
Liberty
McComb
Columbia
Woodville
Magnolia
Tylertown
Pervis
Leakesville
Poplarville
Wiggins
Lucedale
Picayune
Gulfport
Biloxi
Bay Saint Louis
Pascagoula

MISSOURI

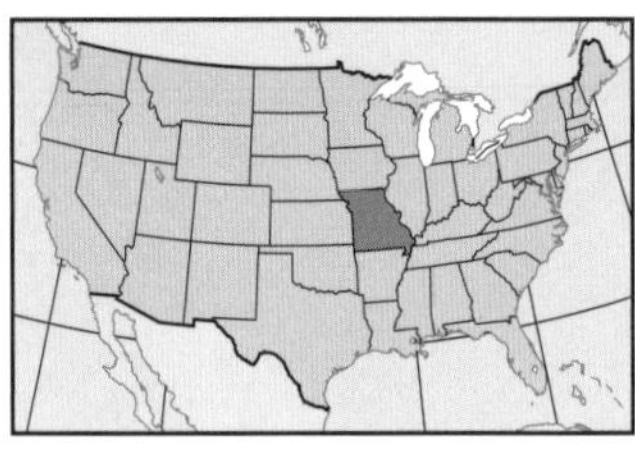

Official name: State of Missouri
Nickname: Show Me State
State Capital: Jefferson City
State Flower: Hawthorn
Motto: Salus Populi Suprema Lex Esto (Let the Welfare of the People Be the Supreme Law)
Admitted to the Union: 1821 (24th)
Total area (2000): 69,704 sq. mi. (180,533 sq. km.) (ranks 21st)
Population (2004): 5,754,618 (ranks 17th)
Chief Cities: Independence, Kansas City, Springfield, St. Louis
Principal products/industries: Soybeans, corn, wheat, cotton, livestock, cement, lead, iron ore, coal, transportation and aerospace equipment, chemicals, fabricated metal products
Highest point: Taum Sauk Mt. 1772 ft. (540 m.)

State History

Evidence of prehistoric inhabitants (Mound Builders); prior to European settlement inhabited by several Algonquian and Siouan tribes, including the Osage and the Missouri; visited by French explorers Père Marquette 1673 and Louis Jolliet 1683; probably first settled by French at Ste. Genevieve 1735; part of Louisiana Purchase 1803; included in Louisiana Territory 1805, and in Missouri Territory 1812; Missouri's application for admission as slave state 1817 caused bitter controversy which was settled by Missouri Compromise 1820 (Missouri admitted as slave state Aug. 10, 1821, Maine as free, no slavery above 36°30′—later repealed); did not secede from Union 1861; scene of fighting during Civil War 1861–64; adopted present constitution 1945.

The flag has the state coat of arms, which is divided vertically, with the arms of the United States on one side and a crescent and bear on the other. The crescent, a traditional symbol in heraldry of a 2nd son, was intended to indicate that Missouri was the 2nd state carved out of the Louisiana Territory.

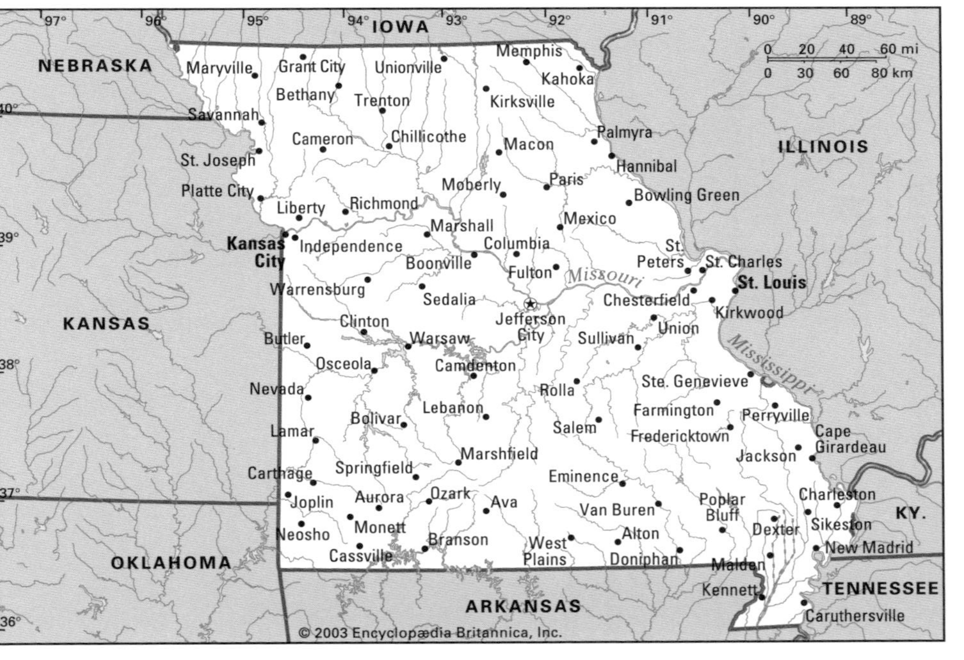
IOWA
NEBRASKA
ILLINOIS
KANSAS
OKLAHOMA
ARKANSAS
TENNESSEE
KY.
Missouri
Mississippi
0 20 40 60 mi
0 30 60 80 km
97° 96° 95° 94° 93° 92° 91° 90° 89°
40° 39° 38° 37° 36°
Maryville
Grant City
Unionville
Memphis
Kahoka
Bethany
Trenton
Kirksville
Savannah
Cameron
Chillicothe
Macon
Palmyra
St. Joseph
Hannibal
Moberly
Paris
Platte City
Liberty
Richmond
Bowling Green
Mexico
Marshall
Kansas City
Independence
Columbia
St. Peters
St. Charles
Boonville
Fulton
St. Louis
Warrensburg
Sedalia
Chesterfield
Kirkwood
Jefferson City
Clinton
Union
Butler
Warsaw
Sullivan
Osceola
Camdenton
Ste. Genevieve
Nevada
Rolla
Lebanon
Farmington
Perryville
Bolivar
Salem
Fredericktown
Cape Girardeau
Lamar
Marshfield
Jackson
Carthage
Springfield
Eminence
Joplin
Aurora
Ozark
Ava
Poplar Bluff
Charleston
Van Buren
Dexter
Sikeston
Neosho
Monett
Branson
West Plains
Alton
New Madrid
Cassville
Doniphan
Malden
Kennett
Caruthersville
© 2003 Encyclopædia Britannica, Inc.

MONTANA

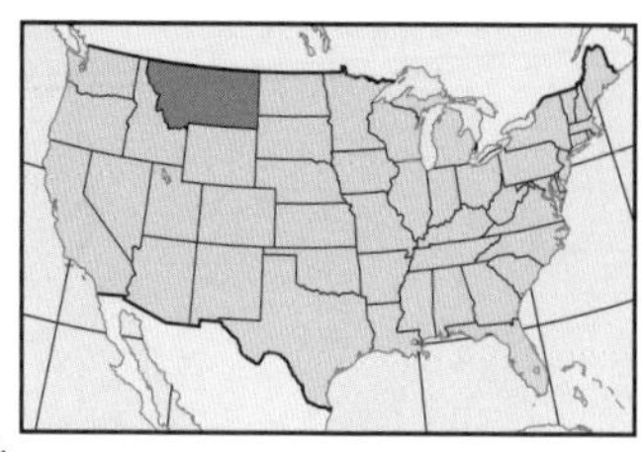

Official name: State of Montana
Nickname: Treasure State
State Capital: Helena
State Flower: Bitterroot
Motto: Oro y Plata (Gold and Silver)
Admitted to the Union: 1889 (41st)
Total area (2000): 147,042 sq. mi. (380,838 sq. km.) (ranks 4th)
Population (2004): 926,865 (ranks 44th)
Chief Cities: Billings, Bozeman, Butte, Great Falls, Helena, Missoula
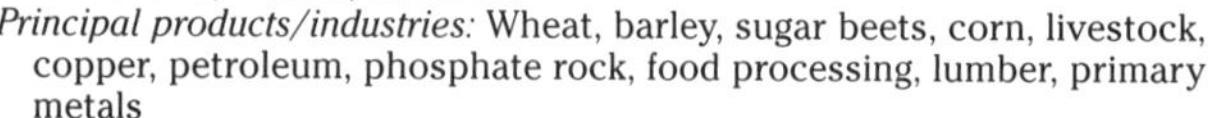
Principal products/industries: Wheat, barley, sugar beets, corn, livestock, copper, petroleum, phosphate rock, food processing, lumber, primary metals
Highest point: Granite Peak 12,799 ft. (3904 m.)

State History

Inhabited by several native tribes prior to European settlement, including Blackfoot, Cheyenne, Arapaho, and Flathead Indians; all except a small area in northwest was part of Louisiana Purchase 1803; crossed by American explorers Meriwether Lewis and William Clark 1805–06; its boundary with Canada settled by treaties 1818 and 1846; part west of the Rocky Mountains acquired in Oregon Country; parts included in various territories of the U.S. prior to organization of territory of Montana 1864; first crossed by rail (Northern Pacific) 1883; admitted to Union Nov. 8, 1889; adopted new state constitution 1972.

The state flag has at its center a seal that includes a representation of the Rocky Mountains, fundamental to the state's topography and to its name, from the Spanish montaña ("mountain"). The seal also depicts a river and forests and Great Falls, a distinctive landmark.

CANADA
BRITISH COLUMBIA
ALBERTA
SASKATCHEWAN
NORTH DAKOTA
SOUTH DAKOTA
WYOMING
IDAHO
Libby
Whitefish
Columbia Falls
Kalispell
Polson
Ronan
Superior
Missoula
Hamilton
Deer Lodge
Anaconda
Butte
Helena
Dillon
Lima
Cut Bank
Shelby
Conrad
Choteau
Great Falls
Chester
Havre
Chinook
Big Sandy
Fort Benton
White Sulphur Springs
Townsend
Bozeman
Gardiner
West Yellowstone
Winifred
Lewistown
Winnett
Roundup
Harlowton
Big Timber
Livingston
Billings
Laurel
Red Lodge
Malta
Glasgow
Opheim
Plentywood
Culbertson
Wolf Point
Circle
Jordan
Sidney
Glendive
Wibaux
Terry
Miles City
Baker
Hysham
Forsyth
Ekalaka
Colstrip
Hardin
Broadus
Hammond
50°
116°
114°
112°
110°
108°
106°
104°
48°
46°
44°
0 40 80 mi
0 60 120 km
© 2003 Encyclopædia Britannica, Inc.

NEBRASKA

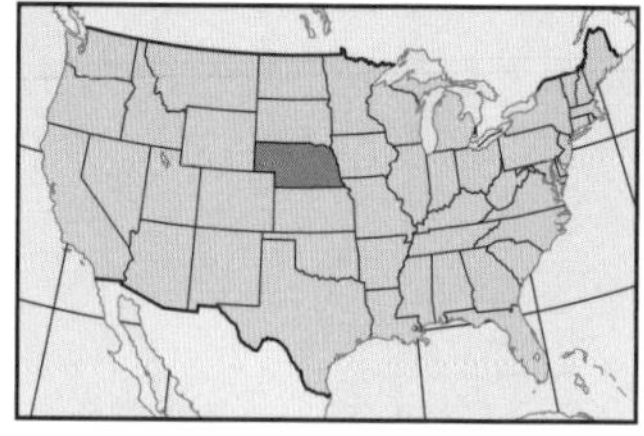

Official name: State of Nebraska
Nickname: Cornhusker State
State Capital: Lincoln
State Flower: Goldenrod
Motto: Equality Before the Law
Admitted to the Union: 1867 (37th)
Total area (2000): 77,354 sq. mi. (200,345 sq. km.) (ranks 16th)
Population (2004): 1,747,214 (ranks 38th)
Chief Cities: Lincoln, Omaha
Principal products/industries: Corn, wheat, livestock, oil, food processing, machinery, fabricated metal products
Highest point: Johnson Township 5424 ft. (1654 m.)

State History

Part of Louisiana Purchase 1803, of Louisiana Territory 1805, and of Missouri Territory 1812; part of unorganized U.S. territory c. 1821–54; part of Nebraska Territory organized 1854 as result of Kansas-Nebraska Act; territory reduced to area of present state by 1863; held first constitutional convention 1866; admitted to Union Mar. 1, 1867; established one-house legislature, the nation's only one, 1937.

In 1925, Nebraska became the last of the conterminous 48 states to adopt a flag of its own. In the design is the seal, which shows the Missouri River with a steamboat, a blacksmith in the foreground, a settler's cabin surrounded by wheat sheaves and growing corn, and a railroad train heading toward the Rocky Mountains.

SOUTH DAKOTA
Missouri
WYOMING
IOWA
MO.
COLORADO
KANSAS
Platte
Chadron
Harrison
Rushville
Valentine
Springview
Butte
Ainsworth
Bassett
O'Neill
Hartington
Dakota City
Pierce
Wayne
Neligh
Norfolk
West Point
Madison
Alliance
Scottsbluff
Gering
Hyannis
Mullen
Thedford
Taylor
Ord
Blair
Bridgeport
Arthur
Tryon
Broken Bow
Greeley
Columbus
Fremont
Omaha
Kimball
Sidney
Oshkosh
North Platte
Loup City
Central City
Papillion
Bellevue
Ogallala
Gothenburg
Grand Island
Seward
Lincoln
Grant
Lexington
Kearney
Aurora
York
Nebraska City
Imperial
Hastings
Crete
Holdrege
Minden
Auburn
McCook
Beatrice
Beaver City
Benkelman
Red Cloud
Fairbury
Falls City
104
103
102
101
100
99
98
97
96
95
43
42
41
40
39
0 20 40 60 80 mi
0 30 60 90 120 km
© 2003 Encyclopædia Britannica, Inc.

NEVADA

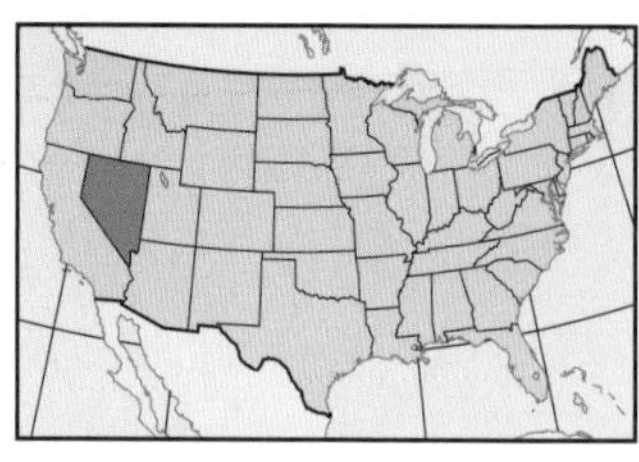

Official name: State of Nevada
Nickname: Silver State; Sagebrush State
State Capital: Carson City
State Flower: Sagebrush
Motto: All For Our Country
Admitted to the Union: 1864 (36th)
Total area (2000): 110,561 sq. mi. (286,351 sq. km.) (ranks 7th)
Population (2004): 2,334,771 (ranks 35th)
Chief Cities: Carson City, Las Vegas, Reno
Principal products/industries: Wheat, livestock, gold, barite, mercury, lumber and wood products, chemicals, tourism and gambling
Highest point: Boundary Peak 13,140 ft. (4007 m.)

State History

Evidence of prehistoric inhabitants in the region (since about 20,000 years ago) includes projectile points, rock art, and dwelling remains; some Anasazi sites in southeast; at time of European contact (c. 18th century) region inhabited by several Indian tribes including Shoshoni and Paiute; some exploration by Spanish (18th century), fur traders (1820s), and others; major exploration and mapping by John C. Frémont and Kit Carson 1843–45; included in region ceded by Mexico to U.S. 1848; included in Utah Territory 1850–61; first permanent settlement made c. 1850 at Mormon Station (now Genoa); settlement increased after discovery of Comstock Lode 1859; organized as Territory of Nevada 1861; admitted to Union as state Oct. 31, 1864; enlarged slightly 1866 to present boundaries.

An early state flag, honoring the mining industry in the state, had silver and gold stars and the words "silver," "Nevada," and "gold" on a blue field. Today's flag features a wreath of sagebrush surrounding a silver star and the motto "Battle Born," honoring Nevada's admission to the Union during the Civil War.

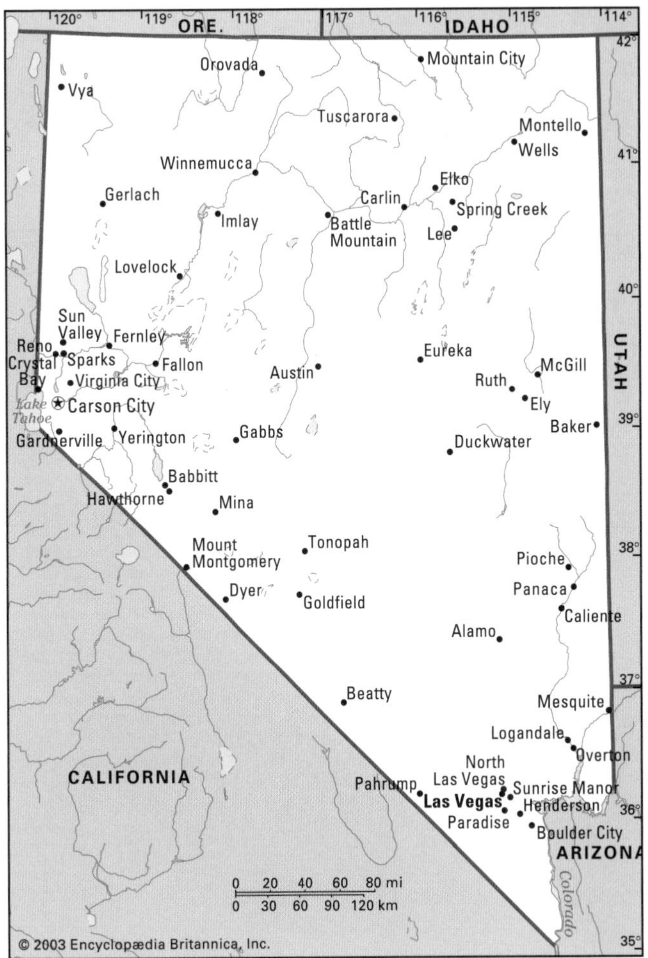
ORE.
IDAHO
UTAH
ARIZONA
CALIFORNIA
120°
119°
118°
117°
116°
115°
114°
42°
41°
40°
39°
38°
37°
36°
35°
Orovada
Mountain City
Vya
Tuscarora
Montello
Wells
Winnemucca
Elko
Gerlach
Carlin
Spring Creek
Imlay
Battle Mountain
Lee
Lovelock
Sun Valley
Fernley
Reno
Crystal Bay
Sparks
Fallon
Virginia City
Eureka
McGill
Austin
Ruth
Ely
Lake Tahoe
Carson City
Baker
Gardnerville
Yerington
Gabbs
Duckwater
Babbitt
Hawthorne
Mina
Mount Montgomery
Tonopah
Pioche
Panaca
Dyer
Goldfield
Caliente
Alamo
Beatty
Mesquite
Logandale
Overton
North Las Vegas
Pahrump
Sunrise Manor
Las Vegas
Henderson
Paradise
Boulder City
Colorado
0 20 40 60 80 mi
0 30 60 90 120 km
© 2003 Encyclopædia Britannica, Inc.

NEW HAMPSHIRE

Official name: State of New Hampshire
Nickname: Granite State
State Capital: Concord
State Flower: Purple lilac
Motto: Live Free Or Die
Admitted to the Union: 1788; 9th of the original 13 colonies to ratify the U.S. Constitution
Total area (2000): 9,350 sq. mi. (24,216 sq. km.) (ranks 46th)
Population (2004): 1,299,500 (ranks 41st)
Chief Cities: Concord, Manchester, Nashua

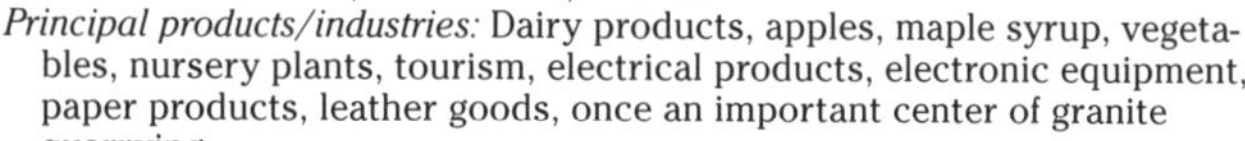

Principal products/industries: Dairy products, apples, maple syrup, vegetables, nursery plants, tourism, electrical products, electronic equipment, paper products, leather goods, once an important center of granite quarrying
Highest point: Mt. Washington 6288 ft. (1918 m.)

State History

Prior to European settlement, inhabited by numerous Algonquin tribes, especially of the Pennacook confederacy; coast explored by several English explorers early 17th century; area east of the Merrimack River included in grant to John Mason and Sir Ferdinando Gorges 1622 and in New Hampshire grant to Mason 1629; first settled by English near Portsmouth 1623; controlled by Massachusetts 1641–79; made a separate royal province 1679 but under same governor as Massachusetts 1699–1741; area of Vermont settled under New Hampshire jurisdiction, which New York disputed; area of Vermont awarded 1764 by royal order to jurisdiction of New York (final claims to area not relinquished by New Hampshire until 1782); first colony to declare independence from Great Britain 1776; adopted first constitution 1776, present constitution 1784 which later was frequently amended; Dartmouth College case decided 1819 in U.S. Supreme Court, confirming right of private corporations against excessive state regulation.

The 1909 flag law provided for the state seal in the center, framed by a wreath of laurel with nine stars interspersed, signifying the rank of New Hampshire as the ninth state to ratify the U.S. Constitution. The seal, modified in 1931, features the frigate Raleigh being built at Portsmouth in 1776.

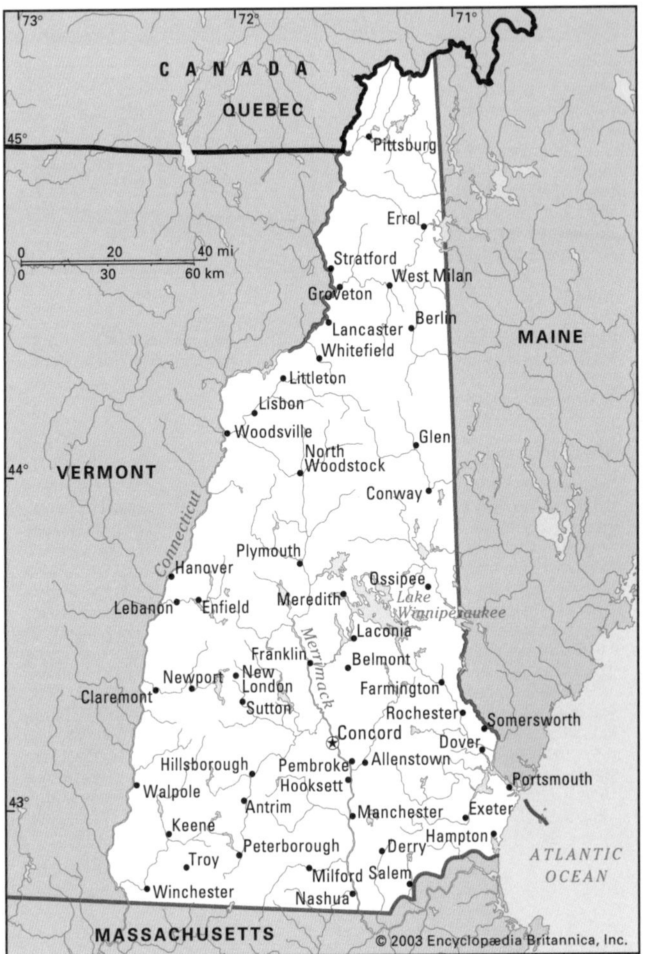

73°
72°
71°
CANADA
QUEBEC
45°
Pittsburg
Errol
0
20
40 mi
0
30
60 km
Stratford
West Milan
Groveton
Berlin
Lancaster
MAINE
Whitefield
Littleton
Lisbon
Woodsville
Glen
North
Woodstock
44°
VERMONT
Conway
Connecticut
Plymouth
Hanover
Ossipee
Lake
Winnipesaukee
Lebanon
Enfield
Meredith
Merrimack
Laconia
Franklin
Belmont
New
London
Newport
Farmington
Claremont
Sutton
Rochester
Somersworth
Concord
Dover
Hillsborough
Pembroke
Allenstown
Portsmouth
Hooksett
Walpole
43°
Antrim
Manchester
Exeter
Keene
Hampton
Peterborough
Derry
ATLANTIC
OCEAN
Troy
Milford
Salem
Winchester
Nashua
MASSACHUSETTS
© 2003 Encyclopædia Britannica, Inc.

NEW JERSEY

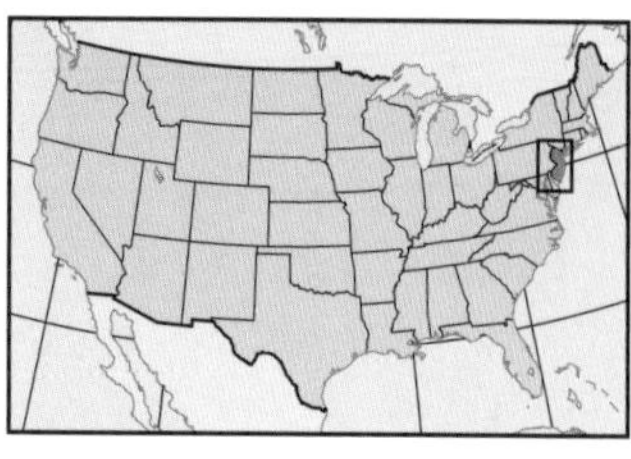

Official name: State of New Jersey
Nickname: Garden State
State Capital: Trenton
State Flower: Violet
Motto: Liberty and Prosperity
Admitted to the Union: 1787; 3rd of the original 13 colonies to ratify the U.S. Constitution
Total area (2000): 8,721 sq. mi. (22,588 sq. km.) (ranks 47th)
Population (2004): 8,698,879 (ranks 10th)
Chief Cities: Elizabeth, Jersey City, Newark, Paterson
Principal products/industries: Corn, cranberries, peppers, tomatoes, nursery plants, chemicals, electronic equipment, apparel, electrical machinery
Highest point: High Point 1803 ft. (550 m.)

State History

Prior to European colonization, region inhabited especially by Delaware tribes; sighted by Florentine navigator Giovanni da Verrazano 1524 and English navigator Henry Hudson 1609; first settled by Dutch and along Delaware River by Swedes; ceded to English as part of New Netherland 1664 and given the Latin name of Nova Caesarea; its eastern and northern part (East Jersey) became a proprietary colony regranted by Duke of York to Sir George Carteret and was sold to William Penn and associates 1682; its western and southern part (West Jersey), or the lower counties on Delaware River, held by William Penn 1676–1702; became royal province 1702; governed by governor of New York until 1738; declared independence from England and adopted first state constitution 1776; scene of numerous battles during the Revolutionary War, especially the important battles at Trenton, Princeton, and Monmouth; delegates to Constitutional Convention 1787 forwarded New Jersey Plan for small states; Trenton became state capital 1790; adopted new state constitution 1844 which included several democratic reforms; present constitution adopted 1947.

The state flag was adopted in 1896. The coat of arms depicts three plows that stand for agriculture, which is also represented by the goddess Ceres (one of the supporters). The other supporter is Liberty. The horse's head in the crest was shown on early New Jersey coins.

76°
75°30′
75°
74°30′
74°
NEW YORK
Hudson
41°
40°30′
40°
39°30′
39°
PENNSYLVANIA
MARYLAND
DELAWARE
Delaware
Delaware Bay
ATLANTIC OCEAN
Newton
Wanaque
Hopatcong
Paterson
Dover
Passaic
Hackensack
Hackettstown
Montclair
Bloomfield
Belvidere
Morristown
East Orange
Newark
Phillipsburg
Jersey City
High Bridge
Union
Elizabeth
Plainfield
Somerville
Piscataway
Flemington
Edison
Perth Amboy
New Brunswick
Sayreville
Rosemont
Rumson
Hopewell
Middletown
Long Branch
Princeton
Freehold
Trenton
Asbury Park
Neptune
Candlewood
Manasquan
Burlington
Willingboro
Mantoloking
Camden
Mount Holly
Toms River
Seaside Heights
Collingswood
Cherry Hill
Paulsboro
Woodbury
Gibbstown
Clementon
Glassboro
Batsto
Hammonton
Ship Bottom
Salem
Alloway
Beach Haven
Vineland
Mays Landing
Bridgeton
Pleasantville
Millville
Atlantic City
Port Norris
Ocean City
Cape May Court House
Sea Isle City
Avalon
Wildwood
Cape May
0 5 10 15 20 mi
0 10 20 km
© 2003 Encyclopædia Britannica, Inc.

NEW MEXICO

Official name: State of New Mexico
Nickname: Land of Enchantment
State Capital: Santa Fe
State Flower: Yucca
Motto: Crescit Eundo (It Grows As It Goes)
Admitted to the Union: 1912 (47th)
Total area (2000): 121,590 sq. mi. (314,915 sq. km.) (ranks 5th)
Population (2004): 1,903,289 (ranks 36th)
Chief Cities: Albuquerque, Las Cruces, Santa Fe
Principal products/industries: Livestock, oil, natural gas, potash, copper, uranium, food processing, chemicals
Highest point: Wheeler Peak 13,161 ft. (4014 m.)

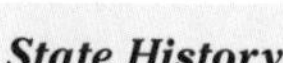

State History

Evidence of prehistoric inhabitants, especially Mogollon and Anasazi peoples; at time of European arrival inhabited mainly by Pueblo tribes (such as the Zuni) and Athabascan tribes (such as the Apache and the Navajo); first European visitor to area was missionary Marcos de Niza sent from Mexico (New Spain) 1539; explored by Spanish explorer Francisco Vásquez de Coronado's expedition 1540–42; Spanish settlement begun by explorer Juan de Oñate 1598; Santa Fe founded in 1609–10; governed by Mexico after 1821; part east of Rio Grande included in annexation of Texas 1845; rest ceded to U.S. by Mexico 1848 (Treaty of Guadalupe Hidalgo) except for southern strip which was included in Gadsden Purchase 1853; first bid for statehood 1850 denied in favor of organization of New Mexico Territory; territory reduced to area of present state by 1863; held several constitutional conventions before finally being admitted to Union as state Jan. 6, 1912.

The flag was officially adopted in March 1925 as a result of a design competition. The colors are based on the flag of Spain, which had ruled New Mexico until the early 19th century. Today the Zia sun is widely recognized as a state symbol, and the design of the capitol building of New Mexico was influenced by its shape.

108°
106°
104°
38°
36°
34°
32°
COLORADO
UTAH
ARIZONA
OKLA.
TEXAS
MEXICO
Four Corners: Only point in the United States common to four states.
Shiprock
Aztec
Farmington
Bloomfield
Chama
Tierra Amarilla
Raton
Clayton
Taos
El Rito
Espanola
Chimayo
Mora
Los Alamos
Mosquero
Las Vegas
Santa Fe
Gallup
Rio Rancho
Bernalillo
Milan
Grants
Tucumcari
Zuni
Armijo
Albuquerque
Santa Rosa
Los Lunas
Estancia
Belen
Vaughn
Mountainair
Clovis
Pie Town
Fort Sumner
Gran Quivira
Portales
Socorro
Reserve
Carrizozo
Rio Grande
Roswell
Truth or Consequences
Ruidoso
Dexter
Tularosa
Hagerman
Lovington
Alamogordo
Artesia
Hobbs
Silver City
Bayard
Hatch
Eunice
Deming
Las Cruces
Carlsbad
Lordsburg
Mesilla
University Park
Jal
La Mesa
Anthony
0 40 80 mi
0 60 120 km

NEW YORK

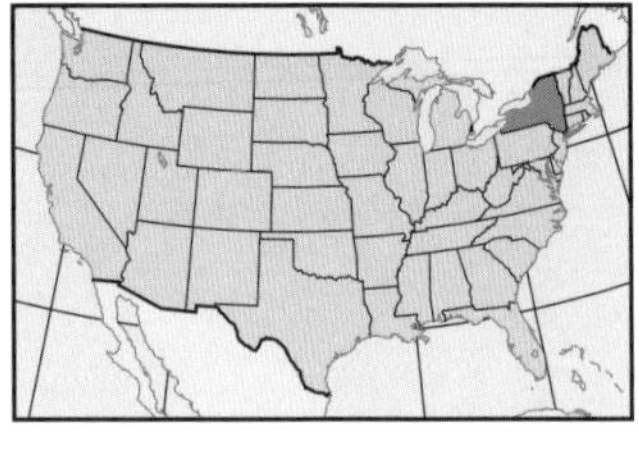

Official name: State of New York
Nickname: Empire State
State Capital: Albany
State Flower: Rose
Motto: Excelsior (Ever Upward)
Admitted to the Union: 1788; 11th of the original 13 colonies to ratify the U.S. Constitution
Total area (2000): 54,556 sq. mi. (141,299 sq. km.) (ranks 27th)
Population (2004): 19,227,088 (ranks 3rd)
Chief Cities: Albany, Buffalo, New York City, Rochester, Syracuse, Yonkers
Principal products/industries: Vegetables, fruit, dairy products, zinc, gravel, salt, apparel, primary metals, electrical machinery, chemicals, finance, printing and publishing, food processing
Highest point: Mt. Marcy 5344 ft. (1630 m.)

State History

Prior to European colonization inhabited by Algonquins (Mahican, Wappinger) and Iroquois (Mohawk, Oneida, Onondaga, Cayuga, and Seneca); New York Bay visited by Florentine navigator Giovanni da Verrazano 1524; explored 1609 by English navigator Henry Hudson (Hudson River) and French explorer Samuel de Champlain (northern New York to Lake Champlain); Dutch trading posts, established on Manhattan Island and at Fort Nassau, were taken over by Dutch West India Company under which early colonization occurred; opened 1629 to patroon colonization for several years; formed part of Dutch colony of New Netherland, surrendered without resistance to English 1664 and renamed New York after its proprietor, Duke of York; briefly recaptured by Dutch 1673–74; scene of much fighting during French and Indian War, in which the Iroquois Confederacy became allied with the British; after ratifying Declaration of Independence, held first state constitutional convention 1776, adopted first state constitution 1777; scene of numerous engagements of the American Revolution including Ticonderoga, Long Island, White Plains, Saratoga, and Kingston, and also of Benedict Arnold's treason at West Point; ratified U.S. Constitution 1788; state capital moved 1797 from New York City to Albany; Canadian frontier scene of several engagements during War of 1812; opening of Erie Canal 1825 spurred development of western New York; adopted present constitution 1894.

The coat of arms features a sun symbol, two supporters, and the state motto. The scene depicted under the sun is a view of the Hudson River. The supporters of the shield are Liberty (with her liberty cap on a staff) and Justice. An American eagle surmounts the globe at the top.

80°
79°
78°
77°
76°
75°
74°
45°
44°
43°
42°
41°
73°
72°
QUEBEC
VERMONT
MASS.
CONN.
CANADA
ONTARIO
PENNSYLVANIA
CONNECTICUT
NEW JERSEY
PA.
Long Island Sound
ATLANTIC OCEAN
Lake Ontario
Lake Erie
Newburgh
Peekskill
New City
Ossining
White Plains
Yonkers
Brentwood
Stony Brook
Montauk
Hampton Bays
New York City
Levittown
Hempstead
Massena
Malone
Plattsburgh
Ogdensburg
Potsdam
Canton
Keeseville
Saranac Lake
Gouverneur
Tupper Lake
Clayton
Brownville
Carthage
Watertown
Ticonderoga
Adams
Lowville
Big Moose
Pulaski
Boonville
Lake George
Glens Falls
Oswego
Lake Pleasant
Camden
Wilson
Fulton
Rome
Saratoga Springs
Lockport
Rochester
Greece
Oneida
Utica
Gloversville
Niagara Falls
Tonawanda
Newark
Syracuse
Amsterdam
Ilion
Buffalo
Cheektowaga
Canandaigua
Auburn
Schenectady
Watervliet
Lackawana
West Seneca
Geneva
Cooperstown
Troy
Geneseo
Albany
Cortland
Penn Yan
Ovid
Cobleskill
Norwich
Ravena
Dunkirk
Fredonia
Franklinville
Ithaca
Oneonta
Hudson
Alfred
Bath
Sidney
Delhi
Mayville
Salamanca
Catskill
Corning
Owego
Olean
Wellsville
Jamestown
Elmira
Binghamton
Kingston
Liberty
Poughkeepsie
New Paltz
Newburgh
Beacon
0 20 40 mi
0 20 40 60 km
© 2003 Encyclopædia Britannica, Inc.

NORTH CAROLINA

Official name: State of North Carolina
Nicknames: Tar Heel State, Old North State
State Capital: Raleigh
State Flower: Dogwood
Motto: To Be Rather Than To Seem
Admitted to the Union: 1789; 12th of the original 13 colonies to ratify the U.S. Constitution
Total area (2000): 53,819 sq. mi. (139,389 sq. km.) (ranks 28th)

Population (2004): 8,541,221 (ranks 11th)
Chief Cities: Charlotte, Durham, Greensboro, Raleigh, Winston-Salem
Principal products/industries: Tobacco, corn, soybeans, peanuts, livestock, gravel, feldspar, tourism, textiles, cigarettes, food products, chemicals, furniture
Highest point: Mt. Mitchell 6684 ft. (2039 m.)

State History

Inhabited by several Algonquin, Siouan, and Iroquoian tribes prior to European contact, especially the Cherokee, Catawba, and Tuscarora; coast explored by Florentine navigator Giovanni da Verrazano (under French employ) 1524, and others; first English settlement in the New World established 1585 at Roanoke Island; region of Albemarle Sound settled mid-17th century by Virginia colonists; formed a part of Carolina grant given 1663 (expanded 1665) by King Charles II to eight noblemen of his court; governed largely separately from South Carolina from late 17th century, and officially separated 1712; Regulator movement (1768–71) against excessive taxation and government corruption suppressed by colonial forces at Alamance 1771; first Revolutionary battle in the state occurred at "Moores Creek Bridge" Feb. 27, 1776; Provincial Congress adopted Apr. 12, 1776 the Halifax Resolves that authorized the delegates for North Carolina to the Continental Congress "to concur with the delegates of the other colonies in declaring independency"—the first explicit sanction of independence by an American colony; adopted state constitution 1776; passed ordinance of secession May 20, 1861; secession ordinance annulled and slavery abolished 1865; new state constitution 1868; readmitted to Union July 11, 1868; latest state constitution 1971.

One of the ribbons in the flag has "May 20th, 1775," the date on which some local citizens were supposedly first to proclaim their independence from Great Britain. The other ribbon has "April 12th, 1776," date of the Halifax Resolves, authorizing North Carolina delegates to approve the U.S. Declaration of Independence.

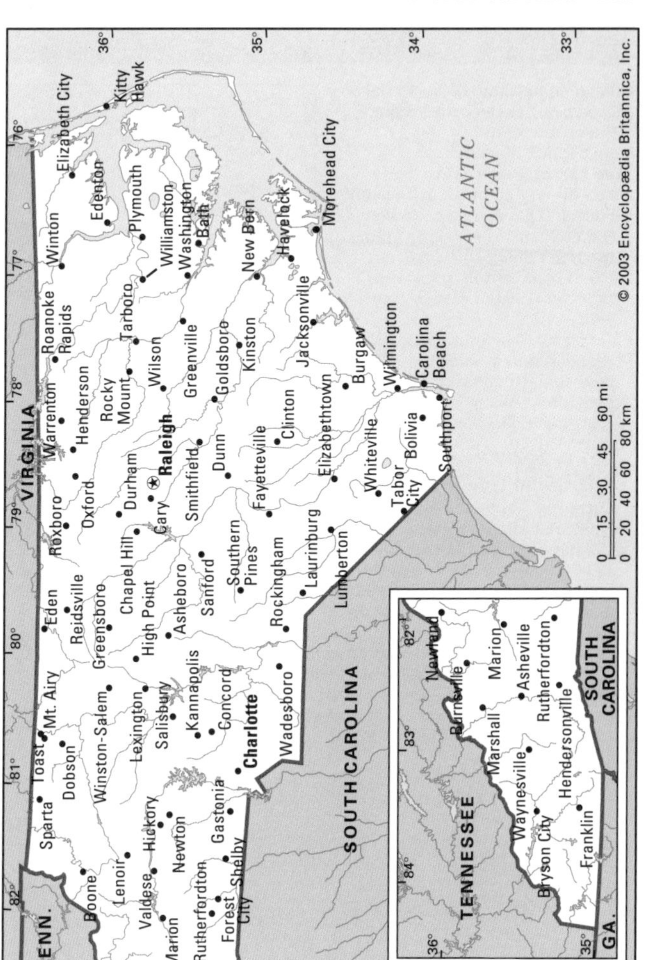
VIRGINIA
TENN.
SOUTH CAROLINA
ATLANTIC OCEAN
Elizabeth City
Kitty Hawk
Edenton
Plymouth
Winton
Williamston
Washington
Bath
New Bern
Havelock
Morehead City
Roanoke Rapids
Tarboro
Greenville
Kinston
Goldsboro
Jacksonville
Rocky Mount
Wilson
Henderson
Warrenton
Raleigh
Smithfield
Dunn
Clinton
Fayetteville
Elizabethtown
Burgaw
Wilmington
Carolina Beach
Southport
Bolivia
Whiteville
Tabor City
Lumberton
Laurinburg
Rockingham
Southern Pines
Sanford
Cary
Durham
Oxford
Roxboro
Chapel Hill
Eden
Reidsville
Greensboro
High Point
Asheboro
Wadesboro
Concord
Kannapolis
Salisbury
Lexington
Winston-Salem
Mt. Airy
Toast
Dobson
Sparta
Charlotte
Gastonia
Hickory
Newton
Lenoir
Boone
Valdese
Marion
Rutherfordton
Forest City
Shelby
76°
77°
78°
79°
80°
81°
82°
36°
35°
34°
33°
0 15 30 45 60 mi
0 20 40 60 80 km
TENNESSEE
SOUTH CAROLINA
GA.
Newland
Burnsville
Marion
Marshall
Asheville
Rutherfordton
Waynesville
Hendersonville
Bryson City
Franklin
82°
83°
84°
36°
35°
© 2003 Encyclopædia Britannica, Inc.

NORTH DAKOTA

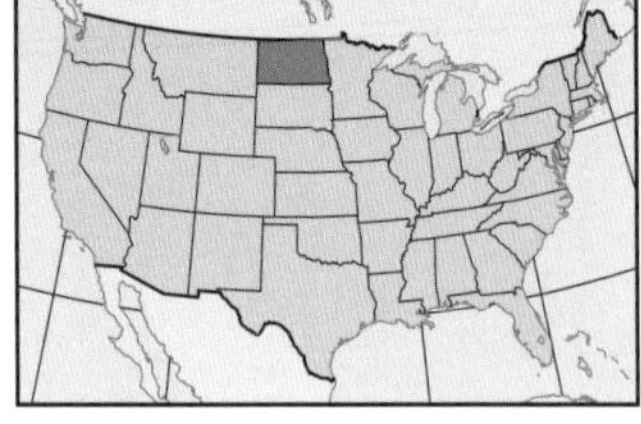

Official name: State of North Dakota
Nicknames: Peace Garden State, Flickertail State
State Capital: Bismarck
State Flower: Wild prairie rose
Motto: Liberty and Union, Now and Forever, One and Inseparable
Admitted to the Union: 1889 (39th)
Total area (2000): 70,700 sq. mi. (183,112 sq. km.) (ranks 19th)
Population (2004): 634,366 (ranks 48th)
Chief Cities: Bismarck, Fargo, Grand Forks, Minot
Principal products/industries: Wheat, barley, flaxseed, oats, livestock, oil, coal, food processing
Highest point: White Butte 3506 ft. (1069 m.)

State History

Evidence of prehistoric inhabitants throughout the state; at time of European contact was inhabited by native Algonquin (Cheyenne and Ojibwa), Caddoan (Arikara), and especially Siouan (Assiniboin, Dakota, Hidatsa, and Mandan) peoples; first visited by La Vérendrye brothers 1742–43; greater part included in Louisiana Purchase 1803; northern limit of northeast section determined by treaty with Great Britain 1818; parts included in several U.S. territories 1805–61; Dakota Territory (capital Yankton 1861–83, Bismark 1883–89) organized Mar. 2, 1861 including North and South Dakota and much of Wyoming and Montana; reduced in 1868 to area of present two states of North and South Dakota; settlement hastened by discovery of gold c. 1874 in the Black Hills; separated from South Dakota and admitted to Union as state Nov. 2, 1889; constitution passed 1889.

In the late 19th century the Dakota Territorial Guard displayed a blue flag with the coat of arms of the U.S. in the center. After North Dakota joined the Union in 1889, a similar design was used by the state's National Guard. In 1911 the design was approved for the official state flag.

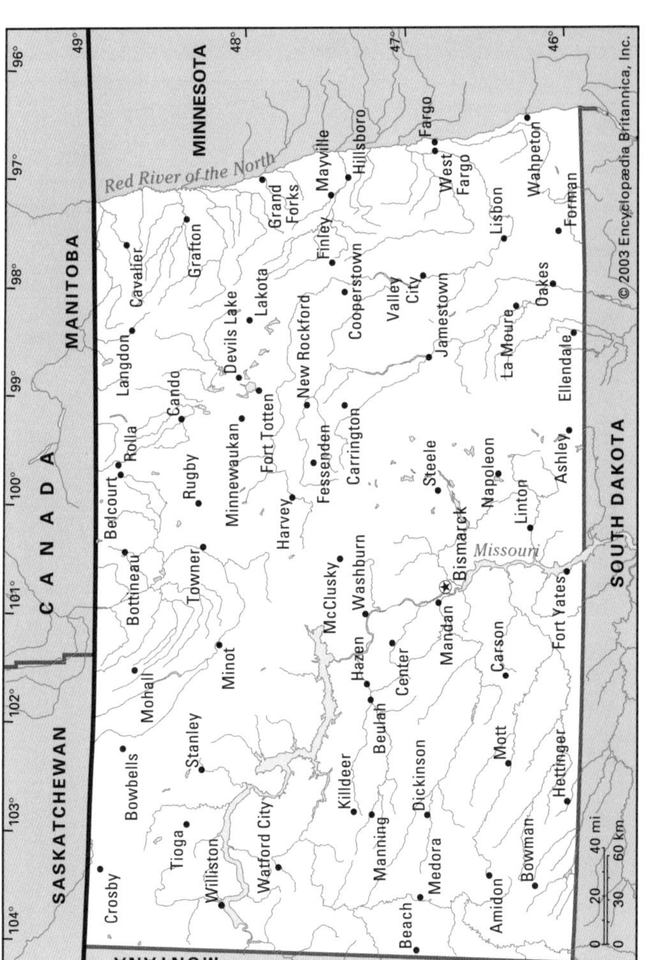
CANADA
MANITOBA
SASKATCHEWAN
MINNESOTA
MONTANA
SOUTH DAKOTA
Red River of the North
Missouri
96°
97°
98°
99°
100°
101°
102°
103°
104°
49°
48°
47°
46°
Crosby
Bowbells
Tioga
Williston
Stanley
Mohall
Minot
Bottineau
Towner
Belcourt
Rolla
Rugby
Cando
Langdon
Cavalier
Grafton
Devils Lake
Minnewaukan
Fort Totten
Lakota
Grand Forks
Mayville
Hillsboro
Finley
Cooperstown
New Rockford
Fessenden
Carrington
Harvey
McClusky
Washburn
Watford City
Killdeer
Manning
Beulah
Hazen
Center
Mandan
Bismarck
Steele
Jamestown
Valley City
Fargo
West Fargo
Lisbon
Wahpeton
Forman
Oakes
La Moure
Ellendale
Ashley
Napoleon
Linton
Fort Yates
Carson
Mott
Hettinger
Dickinson
Medora
Beach
Amidon
Bowman
0 20 40 mi
0 30 60 km
© 2003 Encyclopædia Britannica, Inc.

OHIO

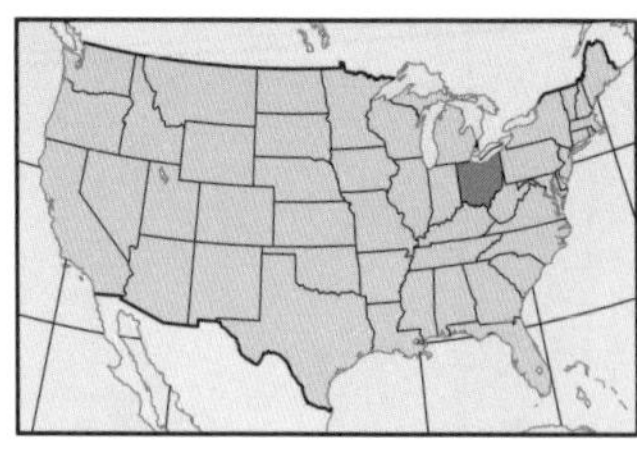

Official name: State of Ohio
Nickname: Buckeye State
State Capital: Columbus
State Flower: Scarlet carnation
Motto: With God, All Things Are Possible
Admitted to the Union: 1803 (17th)
Total area (2000): 44,825 sq. mi. (116,096 sq. km.) (ranks 34th)
Population (2004): 11,459,011 (ranks 7th)
Chief Cities: Akron, Cincinnati, Cleveland, Columbus, Dayton, Toledo
Principal products/industries: Corn, soybeans, oats, livestock, natural gas, coal, iron and steel, rubber products, machinery
Highest point: Campbell Hill 1549 ft. (472 m.)

State History

Has many earthwork mounds of prehistoric Mound Builders; inhabited by various Indian tribes (including Miami, Shawnee, Delaware, and Wyandot) when Europeans began settling the area; claimed by both France and Britain in colonial times; ceded to Britain 1763 following French and Indian War; became part of U.S. by Treaty of Paris 1783 following American Revolution; included 1787 in Northwest Territory; first permanent white settlement at Marietta 1788; western boundary with Indian lands determined by Maj. Gen. Anthony Wayne's defeat of Indians 1794 at Fallen Timbers and by Treaty of Greenville 1795; Western Reserve incorporated 1800; first constitution 1802; unofficially entered Union Feb. 19, 1803. In 1953, by resolution of U.S. Congress, Mar. 1, 1803 declared official day of admission to Union.

The red disk at the hoist end suggests the seed of the buckeye, the official state tree. The white O is the initial letter of the state name, while the use of stars and stripes and the colors red, white, and blue clearly honor the national flag. The 17 stars in the flag recall that Ohio was the 17th state to join the Union.

CANADA
ONTARIO
MICHIGAN
Lake Erie
PENNSYLVANIA
INDIANA
WEST VIRGINIA
KENTUCKY
Ohio River
Ohio
85°
84°
83°
82°
81°
42°
41°
40°
39°
38°
Conneaut
Ashtabula
Painesville
Jefferson
Chardon
Cleveland
Toledo
Wauseon
Port Clinton
Sandusky
Lorain
Parma
Bryan
Napoleon
Bowling Green
Fremont
Elyria
Warren
Niles
Defiance
Clyde
Norwalk
Cuyahoga Falls
Ravenna
New Bavaria
Medina
Tiffin
Youngstown
Paulding
Findlay
Willard
Akron
Barberton
Ottawa
Alliance
Salem
Van Wert
Shelby
Ashland
Upper Sandusky
Bucyrus
Canton
Delphos
Lima
Lisbon
Wooster
Massillon
Galion
Mansfield
Kenton
East Liverpool
Millersburg
Celina
Marion
Mount Gilead
Dover
New Philadelphia
Wapakoneta
Mount Vernon
Steubenville
Bellefontaine
Cadiz
Delaware
Marysville
Coshocton
Martins Ferry
Sidney
Upper Arlington
Newark
St. Clairsville
Greenville
Urbana
Troy
Columbus
Zanesville
Cambridge
London
Grove City
New Lexington
Springfield
Caldwell
Dayton
Lancaster
Woodsfield
Kettering
Xenia
Washington Court House
Circleville
McConnelsville
Middletown
Logan
Marietta
Hamilton
Lebanon
Wilmington
Chillicothe
Athens
Fairfield
McArthur
Hillsboro
Cincinnati
Waverly
Pomeroy
Batavia
Jackson
Georgetown
Gallipolis
West Union
Portsmouth
Ironton
South Point
0 20 40 mi
0 30 60 km
© 2003 Encyclopædia Britannica, Inc.

OKLAHOMA

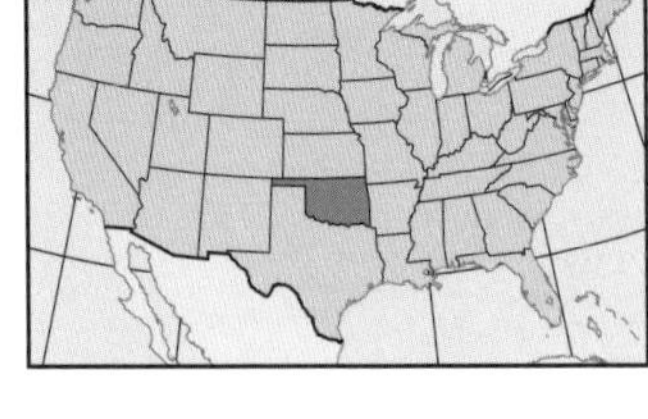

Official name: State of Oklahoma
Nickname: Sooner State
State Capital: Oklahoma City
State Flower: Mistletoe
Motto: Labor Omnia Vincit (Labor Conquers All Things)
Admitted to the Union: 1907 (46th)
Total area (2000): 69,898 sq. mi. (181,036 sq. km.) (ranks 20th)
Population (2004): 3,523,553 (ranks 28th)
Chief Cities: Oklahoma City, Tulsa
Principal products/industries: Wheat, cotton, sorghum, beef cattle, gas and petroleum, food processing, fabricated-metal products
Highest point: Black Mesa 4973 ft. (1517 m.)

State History

Except for Panhandle, formed part of Louisiana Purchase 1803; southern part nominally included in Arkansas Territory 1819–28; settled by Indians as unorganized Indian Territory c. 1820–40, especially following the 1830 Indian Removal Act and subsequent forced migration of tribes from the East; part opened to white settlement 1889; western part organized as Oklahoma Territory 1890; rest gradually opened to whites; on Nov. 16, 1907, Indian Territory and Oklahoma Territory were merged and admitted to Union as state.

The blue background symbolizes loyalty and devotion; the traditional bison-hide shield of the Osage Indians suggests the defense of the state. The shield has small crosses, standing for stars (common in Native American art), and an olive branch and calumet as emblems of peace for whites and Native Americans.

KANSAS
MISSOURI
ARKANSAS
TEXAS
TEXAS
Red
101°
100°
99°
98°
97°
96°
95°
37°
36°
35°
34°
Beaver
Buffalo
Alva
Cherokee
Blackwell
Newkirk
Ponca City
Bartlesville
Pawhuska
Miami
Vinita
Jay
Woodward
Fairview
Enid
Perry
Pawnee
Claremore
Pryor
Arnett
Taloga
Stillwater
Tulsa
Broken Arrow
Sapulpa
Wagoner
Tahlequah
Kingfisher
Guthrie
Watonga
Chandler
Muskogee
Stilwell
Edmond
Cheyenne
Clinton
Weatherford
Oklahoma City
Okmulgee
Sallisaw
Elk City
El Reno
Moore
Shawnee
Henryetta
Stigler
Sayre
Cordell
Norman
Wewoka
Holdenville
Poteau
Anadarko
Chickasha
Magnum
Hobart
McAlester
Wilburton
Pauls Valley
Ada
Hollis
Altus
Lawton
Duncan
Sulphur
Coalgate
Atoka
Frederick
Walters
Graham
Tishomingo
Antlers
Ardmore
Waurika
Madill
Durant
Hugo
Idabel
103°
COLO.
102°
KANSAS
101°
100°
37°
N. MEX.
Boise City
Guymon
Beaver
TEXAS
0
30
60 mi
0
40
80 km
© 2003 Encyclopædia Britannica, Inc.

OREGON

Official name: State of Oregon
Nickname: Beaver State
State Capital: Salem
State Flower: Oregon grape
Motto: Alis Volat Propriis (She Flies With Her Own Wings)
Admitted to the Union: 1859 (33rd)
Total area (2000): 98,381 sq. mi. (254,805 sq. km.) (ranks 9th)
Population (2004): 3,594,586 (ranks 27th)
Chief Cities: Eugene, Portland, Salem
Principal products/industries: Wheat, fruit, vegetables, livestock, dairy products, lumber, fishing, gravel, plywood, primary-metal products, high-tech industries, tourism
Highest point: Mt. Hood 11,239 ft. (3428 m.)

State History

Inhabited by numerous American Indian peoples when Europeans arrived; coast first sighted by Spanish sailors; region claimed for England by Sir Francis Drake 1579; visited by Capt. James Cook 1778; Columbia River explored by Capt. Robert Gray of Boston 1792, giving U.S. a claim to the region; mouth of Columbia River reached by Meriwether Lewis and William Clark's overland expedition 1805; for a time jointly occupied by England and U.S.; first white settlement founded at Astoria by American fur trader John Jacob Astor 1811, but lost to British during War of 1812; region dominated by Britain's Hudson's Bay Company under John McLoughlin (often called "the father of Oregon") 1820s through 1840s; first permanent settlement in the Willamette Valley established 1834 by Methodist missionaries; settlement accelerated from c. 1843 with mass migration of Americans over the Oregon Trail; Great Britain relinquished claim to region 1846; part of Oregon Territory 1848; admitted to Union with present boundaries Feb. 14, 1859.

The elements in the seal are ships, mountains, and symbols of agriculture, as well as a pioneer covered wagon and the phrase "The Union." The 33 stars correspond to Oregon's order of admission to the Union. A beaver symbol on the reverse recalls the importance of the animal to early trappers and hunters in the Pacific Northwest.

126°
124°
122°
120°
118°
46°
44°
42°
Columbia
WASHINGTON
0 20 40 60 80 mi
0 30 60 90 120 km
Astoria
Seaside
St. Helens
Hood River
The Dalles
Hermiston
Milton-Freewater
Arlington
Pendleton
Hillsboro
Portland
Tillamook
Beaverton
Moro
Heppner
Enterprise
Oregon City
Condon
La Grande
McMinnville
Woodburn
Kinzua
Lincoln City
Dallas
Salem
Fossil
Baker City
PACIFIC OCEAN
Independence
Albany
Madras
Newport
Lebanon
Bates
Corvallis
IDAHO
Sweet Home
Redmond
Prineville
Canyon City
Junction City
Ontario
Florence
Eugene
Springfield
Bend
Vale
Nyssa
Reedsport
Cottage Grove
Oakridge
La Pine
North Bend
Burns
Coos Bay
Oakland
Bandon
Coquille
Roseburg
Jordan Valley
Riddle
Port Orford
Grants Pass
Eagle Point
Gold Beach
Klamath Falls
Lakeview
Medford
Ashland
Brookings
NEVADA
CALIFORNIA
© 2003 Encyclopædia Britannica, Inc.

PENNSYLVANIA

Official name: Commonwealth of Pennsylvania
Nickname: Keystone State
State Capital: Harrisburg
State Flower: Mountain laurel
Motto: Virtue, Liberty, and Independence
Admitted to the Union: 1787; 2nd of the original 13 colonies to ratify the U.S. Constitution
Total area (2000): 46,055 sq. mi. (119,283 sq. km.) (ranks 33rd)
Population (2004): 12,406,292 (ranks 6th)
Chief Cities: Allentown, Erie, Harrisburg, Philadelphia, Pittsburgh
Principal products/industries: Corn, wheat, oats, dairy products, coal, iron ore, iron and steel, electrical machinery, apparel, chemicals, transportation equipment
Highest point: Mt. Davis 3213 ft. (980 m.)

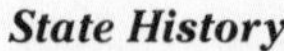

State History

French adventurer Étienne Brulé probably first European to visit this area 1615–16, inhabited principally by Delaware, Susquehanna, and Shawnee tribes; first European settlement made by Swedes on Tinicum Island 1643; rights to land granted by British crown to William Penn, who established Quaker colony 1682; first hospital in U.S. established in Philadelphia 1751; Pennsylvania-Maryland boundary line determined 1763–67; Declaration of Independence pronounced in Philadelphia 1776; delegation headed by Benjamin Franklin represented Pennsylvania in Constitutional Convention in Philadelphia 1787; ratified U.S. Constitution Dec. 12, 1787; flood disaster at Johnstown May 31, 1889.

Agriculture and commerce are represented in the coat of arms by the ship and the wheat sheaves, the plow, the wreath of corn and olive, and the horses in harness. The state motto, "Virtue, Liberty, and Independence," is inscribed on the ribbon below the arms.

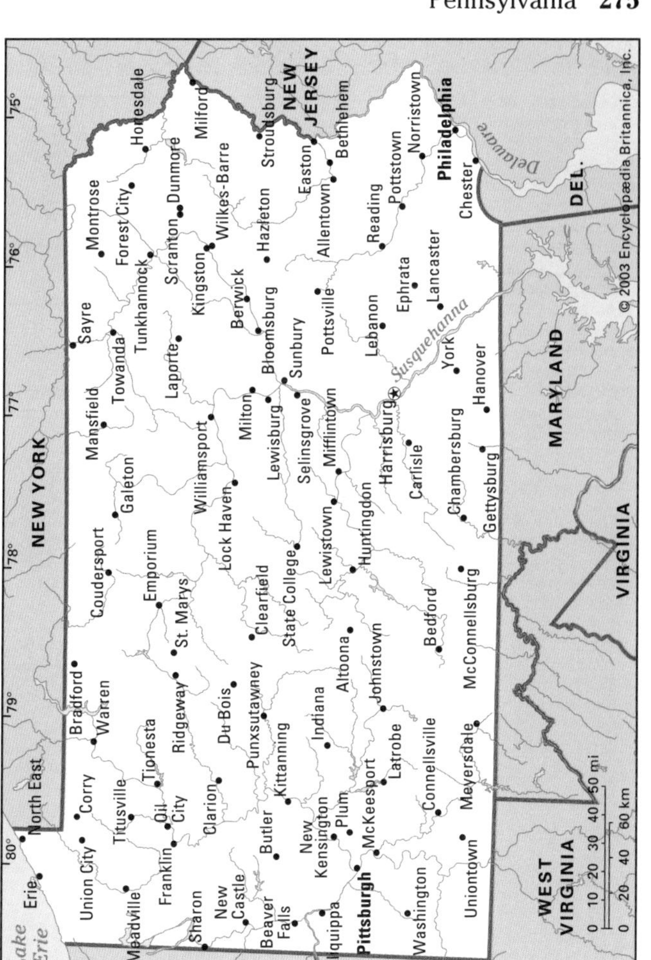
NEW YORK
NEW JERSEY
DEL.
MARYLAND
VIRGINIA
WEST VIRGINIA
OHIO
Lake Erie
Delaware
Susquehanna
North East
Erie
Union City
Corry
Meadville
Titusville
Warren
Bradford
Tionesta
Oil City
Franklin
Sharon
New Castle
Clarion
Ridgeway
St. Marys
Emporium
Coudersport
Galeton
Mansfield
Sayre
Towanda
Montrose
Forest City
Tunkhannock
Honesdale
Milford
Scranton
Dunmore
Wilkes-Barre
Kingston
Berwick
Hazleton
Stroudsburg
Easton
Bethlehem
Allentown
Laporte
Bloomsburg
Williamsport
Lock Haven
Milton
Lewisburg
Sunbury
Selinsgrove
Mifflintown
Pottsville
Reading
Pottstown
Norristown
Philadelphia
Chester
Lebanon
Ephrata
Lancaster
York
Hanover
Harrisburg
Carlisle
Chambersburg
Gettysburg
Lewistown
Huntingdon
State College
Clearfield
Du Bois
Punxsutawney
Kittanning
Butler
New Kensington
Plum
Indiana
Altoona
Johnstown
Latrobe
McKeesport
Pittsburgh
Beaver Falls
Aliquippa
Washington
Uniontown
Connellsville
Meyersdale
Bedford
McConnellsburg
75°
76°
77°
78°
79°
80°
42°
41°
40°
39°
0 10 20 30 40 50 mi
0 20 40 60 km
© 2003 Encyclopædia Britannica, Inc.

RHODE ISLAND

Official name: State of Rhode Island and Providence Plantations
Nicknames: Ocean State, Little Rhody
State Capital: Providence
State Flower: Violet
Motto: Hope
Admitted to the Union: 1790; 13th of the original 13 colonies to ratify the U.S. Constitution
Total area (2000): 1545 sq. mi. (4002 sq. km.) (ranks 50th)
Population (2004): 1,080,632 (ranks 43rd)
Chief Cities: Cranston, Newport, Pawtucket, Providence, Warwick
Principal products/industries: Jewelry making, electronics, tourism, historically important textile industry
Highest point: Jerimoth Hill 812 ft. (248 m.)

State History

Originally settled by Narragansett Indians; Narragansett Bay explored by Florentine navigator Giovanni da Verrazano 1524; first permanent nonnative settlement founded by Roger Williams for religious dissenters at Providence 1636; scattered settlements united when charter granted by British King Charles II to Roger Williams 1663; charter provisions continued in effect until Dorr's Rebellion 1842, led by political activist Thomas Dorr, whose attempts to form an alternate government providing for extension of suffrage resulted in new state constitution 1843.

The Rhode Island legislature adopted an anchor for its colonial seal in 1647. The anchor was used on military flags by the time of the American Revolutionary War. The flag's anchor and motto were represented in Rococo style and encircled by stars corresponding to the number of original states in the Union.

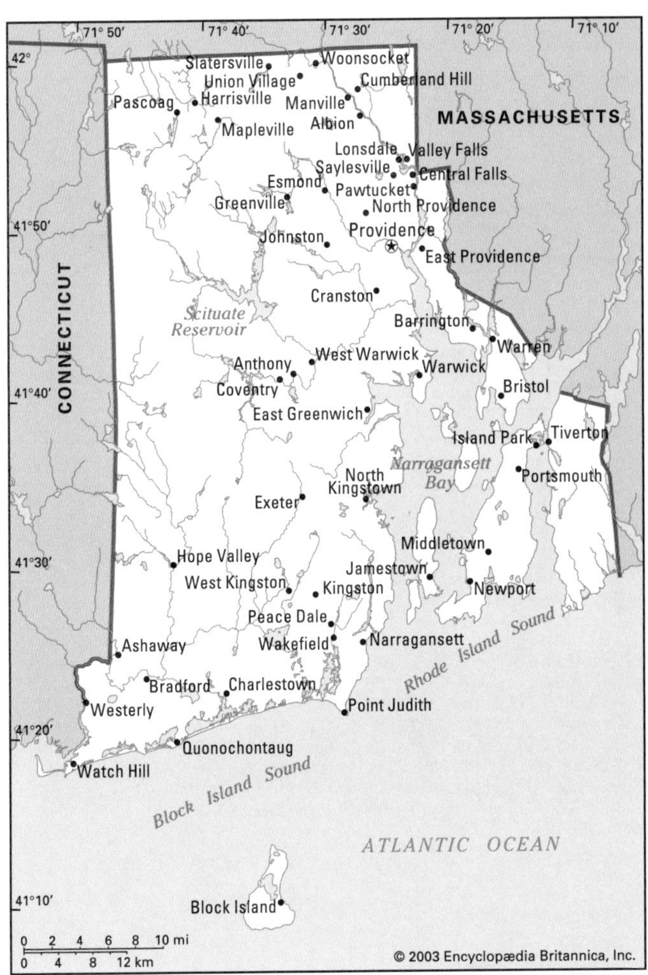
71° 50′
71° 40′
71° 30′
71° 20′
71° 10′
42°
41°50′
41°40′
41°30′
41°20′
41°10′
MASSACHUSETTS
CONNECTICUT
Slatersville
Woonsocket
Union Village
Cumberland Hill
Pascoag
Harrisville
Manville
Mapleville
Albion
Lonsdale
Valley Falls
Saylesville
Central Falls
Esmond
Pawtucket
Greenville
North Providence
Johnston
Providence
East Providence
Cranston
Scituate Reservoir
Barrington
Warren
West Warwick
Anthony
Warwick
Coventry
Bristol
East Greenwich
Island Park
Tiverton
Narragansett Bay
North Kingstown
Portsmouth
Exeter
Middletown
Hope Valley
Jamestown
West Kingston
Kingston
Newport
Peace Dale
Wakefield
Narragansett
Ashaway
Rhode Island Sound
Bradford
Charlestown
Westerly
Point Judith
Quonochontaug
Watch Hill
Block Island Sound
ATLANTIC OCEAN
Block Island
0 2 4 6 8 10 mi
0 4 8 12 km
© 2003 Encyclopædia Britannica, Inc.

SOUTH CAROLINA

Official name: State of South Carolina
Nickname: Palmetto State
State Capital: Columbia
State Flower: Yellow jessamine
Motto: Dum Spiro, Spero (While I Breathe, I Hope)
Admitted to the Union: 1788; 8th of the original 13 colonies to ratify the U.S. Constitution
Total area (2000): 32,020 sq. mi. (82,932 sq. km.) (ranks 40th)
Population (2004): 4,198,068 (ranks 25th)
Chief Cities: Charleston, Columbia
Principal products/industries: Tobacco, cotton, soybeans, fruit, peanuts, livestock, lumbering, sand, gravel, stone, textiles, chemicals, paper products, cement, clothing, tourism
Highest point: Sassafras Mt. 3560 ft. (1086 m.)

State History

Evidence of Mound Builder inhabitants in western part of state; at time of European contact, inhabited by Siouan, Iroquoian, and Muskogean Indians; coast explored by Spanish 1521; unsuccessful attempts at settlement made by Spanish and French 16th century; included in Carolina grant given 1663 by Charles II to eight noblemen of his court; Charleston founded 1670; English settlements harassed by Spanish and Indians 17th–18th centuries; overthrew proprietary rule 1719 in favor of rule as a crown province 1729; scene of several engagements during American Revolution, notably Kings Mountain, Cowpens, Eutaw Springs, Camden, and Guilford Courthouse; ceded western lands to U.S. 1787; ratified U.S. Constitution May 23, 1788; first state to secede from Union, passing ordinance of secession Dec. 20, 1860; Confederate forces attacked Fort Sumter Apr. 12, 1861, in the initial action of the Civil War; ordinance of secession repealed and slavery abolished 1865; readmitted to the Union June 25, 1868; adopted its present constitution 1895.

On September 13, 1775, a blue flag with a white crescent was raised by anti-British forces at a fort in Charleston Harbor. The fortification was protected by palmetto logs that caused British cannonballs to bounce off. Consequently the palmetto was adopted by South Carolinians as their chief state symbol.

NORTH CAROLINA
GEORGIA
ATLANTIC
OCEAN
Gaffney
York
Rock Hill
Greer
Spartanburg
Easley
Greenville
Chester
Clemson
Simpsonville
Union
Lancaster
Cheraw
Bennettsville
Anderson
Laurens
Clinton
Winnsboro
Dillon
Newberry
Darlington
Mullins
Abbeville
Greenwood
Camden
Florence
Marion
Columbia
Pamplico
McCormick
Saluda
Cayce
Oak Grove
Sumter
Lake City
North Myrtle Beach
Conway
Edgefield
St. Matthews
Manning
Kingstree
Myrtle Beach
North Augusta
Aiken
Orangeburg
Georgetown
Bamberg
St. George
Jackson
Barnwell
Moncks Corner
Allendale
Summerville
Walterboro
Hampton
North Charleston
Charleston
Mt. Pleasant
Estill
Ridgeland
Beaufort
Port Royal
Hilton Head Island
83°
82°
81°
80°
79°
78°
35°
34°
33°
32°
0
20
40 mi
0
30
60 km

SOUTH DAKOTA

Official name: State of South Dakota
Nickname: Mount Rushmore State
State Capital: Pierre
State Flower: Pasqueflower
Motto: Under God the People Rule
Admitted to the Union: 1889 (40th)
Total area (2000): 77,117 sq. mi. (199,731 sq. km.) (ranks 17th)
Population (2004): 770,883 (ranks 46th)
Chief Cities: Rapid City, Sioux Falls
Principal products/industries: Corn, wheat, oats, rye, flaxseed, livestock, gold, food processing, lumber and wood products, tourism
Highest point: Harney Peak 7242 ft. (2209 m.)

State History

Evidence of prehistoric Mound Builders' settlements; at time of European contact, inhabited by several Indian tribes, including especially the Arikara, who soon moved north, and several Dakota tribes; explored somewhat by French in 18th century; included in Louisiana Purchase 1803 and traversed by Lewis and Clark expedition 1804, 1806; fur trade with Indians conducted throughout 19th century until outbreak of Civil War; first permanent European settlement founded 1817, on future site of Fort Pierre, as a trading post; after several attempts, organized as part of Dakota Territory 1861 with capital at Yankton; latter 19th century characterized by conflict with Indians, several insect plagues, and Black Hills gold rush (discovery 1874); admitted to Union Nov. 2, 1889 upon division of Dakota Territory into two states; Pierre selected as state capital 1889; state constitution dates from 1889.

The South Dakota seal is represented over a sun in such a way that only the sun's rays are visible. The seal repeats the name of the state and the date of admission to the Union. Around the seal is the state name and nickname. The seal depicts a farmer, cattle, crops, a smelting furnace, and a steamship.

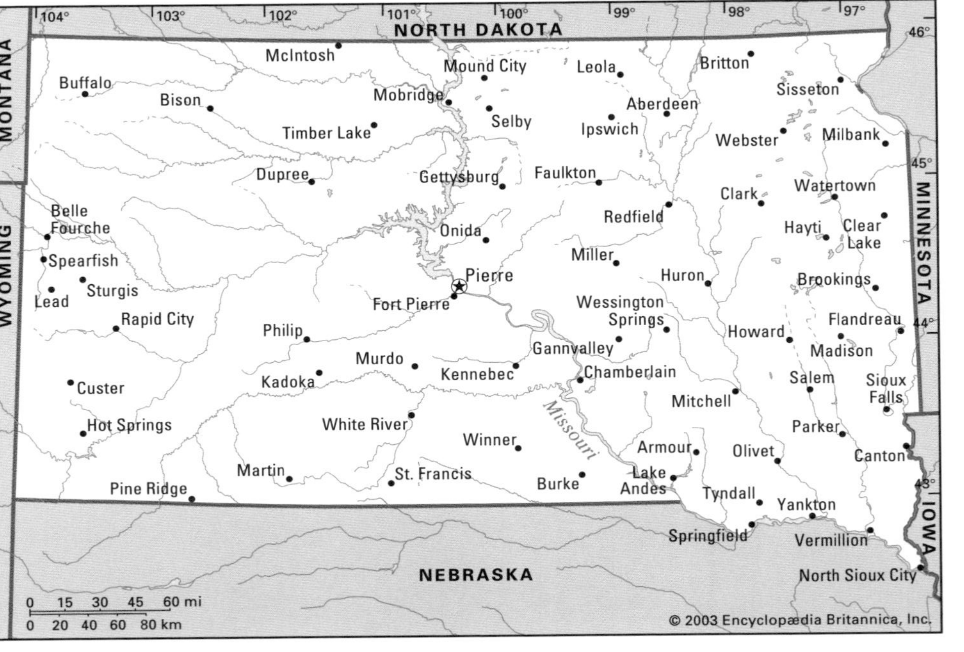
NORTH DAKOTA
MONTANA
WYOMING
MINNESOTA
IOWA
NEBRASKA
104°
103°
102°
101°
100°
99°
98°
97°
46°
45°
44°
43°
McIntosh
Mound City
Leola
Britton
Sisseton
Buffalo
Bison
Mobridge
Selby
Aberdeen
Ipswich
Webster
Milbank
Timber Lake
Dupree
Gettysburg
Faulkton
Clark
Watertown
Belle Fourche
Redfield
Hayti
Clear Lake
Onida
Spearfish
Miller
Sturgis
Lead
Pierre
Huron
Brookings
Fort Pierre
Wessington Springs
Rapid City
Flandreau
Philip
Howard
Madison
Gannvalley
Murdo
Kennebec
Chamberlain
Kadoka
Custer
Salem
Sioux Falls
Mitchell
Missouri
White River
Hot Springs
Parker
Winner
Armour
Olivet
Canton
Martin
St. Francis
Burke
Lake Andes
Pine Ridge
Tyndall
Yankton
Springfield
Vermillion
North Sioux City
0 15 30 45 60 mi
0 20 40 60 80 km
© 2003 Encyclopædia Britannica, Inc.

TENNESSEE

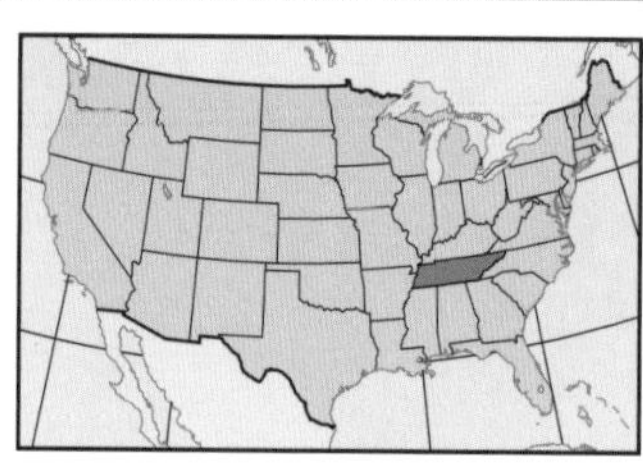

Official name: State of Tennessee
Nickname: Volunteer State
State Capital: Nashville
State Flower: Iris
Motto: Agriculture and Commerce
Admitted to the Union: 1796 (16th)
Total area (2000): 42,143 sq. mi. (109,151 sq. km.) (ranks 36th)
Population (2004): 5,900,962 (ranks 16th)
Chief Cities: Chattanooga, Knoxville, Memphis, Nashville
Principal products/industries: Tobacco, soybeans, corn, livestock, coal, phosphate rock, chemicals, textiles, cement, electrical machinery
Highest point: Clingmans Dome 6643 ft. (2026 m.)

State History

Original inhabitants included Chicksaw, Cherokee, and Shawnee, among others; region visited by Spanish explorer Hernando de Soto c. 1540; included in British charter of Carolina and in French Louisiana claim late 17th century; claim to region ceded by France to Great Britain after French and Indian War; first permanent settlements made in Watauga Valley c. 1770; acknowledged by Great Britain as a part of United States after Revolutionary War; temporary state of Franklin formed c. 1784; included in Territory South of the Ohio River after North Carolina relinquished claims 1790; admitted to Union with present boundaries June 1, 1796; passed ordinance of secession June 8, 1861; scene of battles in Civil War, notably Shiloh, Chattanooga, Stones River, Nashville; slavery abolished and ordinance of secession declared null and void 1865; first of seceding states to be reorganized and readmitted to Union (July 24, 1866). Constitution dates from 1870.

The current flag design features three stripes and three stars. These were said by the designer to refer to "the three grand divisions of the State," but they have also been said to represent the three presidents who lived in Tennessee (Andrew Jackson, James Polk, and Andrew Johnson).

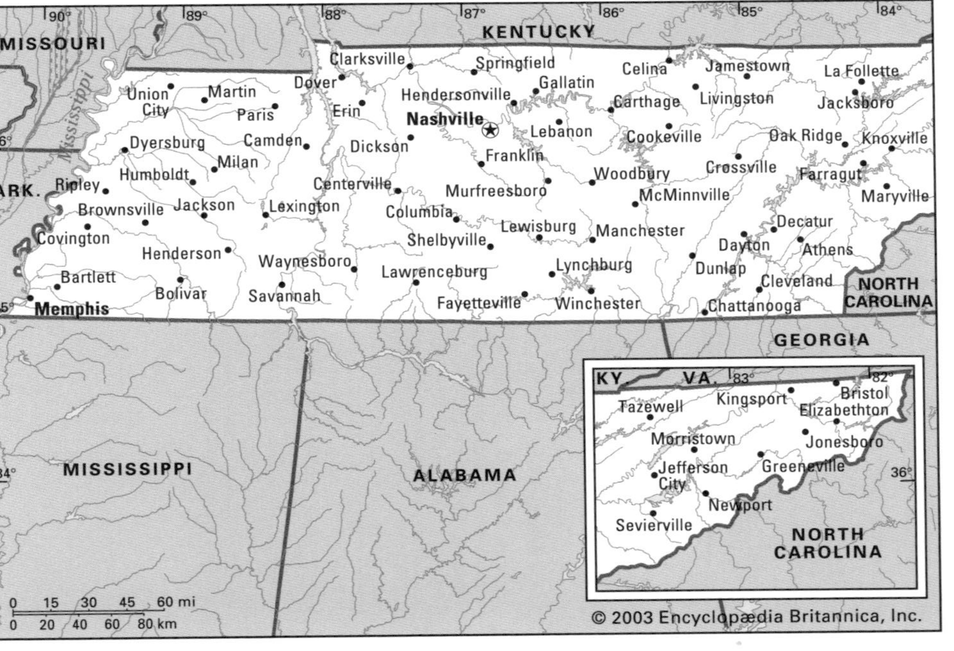
90°
89°
88°
87°
86°
85°
84°
MISSOURI
KENTUCKY
Clarksville
Springfield
Celina
Jamestown
La Follette
Dover
Union City
Martin
Hendersonville
Gallatin
Carthage
Livingston
Jacksboro
Paris
Erin
Nashville
Lebanon
36°
Dyersburg
Camden
Dickson
Cookeville
Oak Ridge
Knoxville
Franklin
Milan
Humboldt
Woodbury
Crossville
Farragut
ARK.
Ripley
Centerville
Murfreesboro
McMinnville
Maryville
Brownsville
Jackson
Lexington
Columbia
Lewisburg
Manchester
Decatur
Covington
Shelbyville
Dayton
Athens
Henderson
Waynesboro
Lynchburg
Dunlap
Lawrenceburg
Bartlett
Cleveland
NORTH CAROLINA
Bolivar
Savannah
Fayetteville
Winchester
Chattanooga
35°
Memphis
Mississippi
GEORGIA
KY.
VA.
83°
82°
Bristol
Tazewell
Kingsport
Elizabethton
Morristown
Jonesboro
Jefferson City
Greeneville
36°
Newport
Sevierville
NORTH CAROLINA
34°
MISSISSIPPI
ALABAMA
0 15 30 45 60 mi
0 20 40 60 80 km

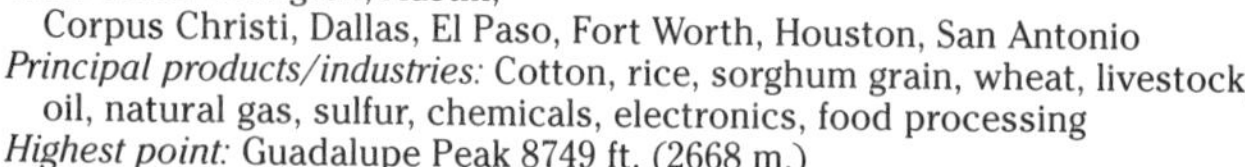

TEXAS

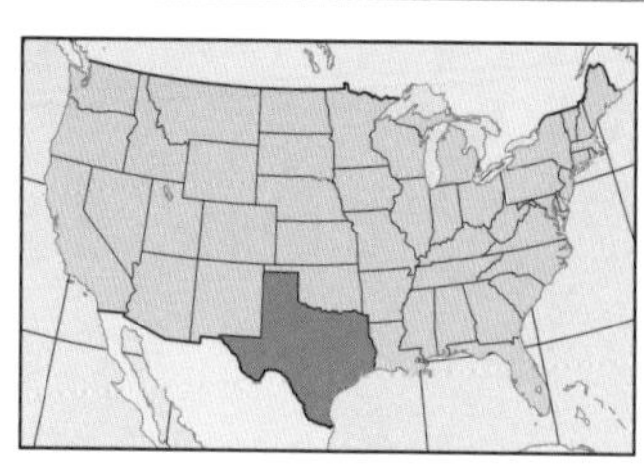

Official name: State of Texas
Nickname: Lone Star State
Capital: Austin
State flower: Bluebonnet
Motto: Friendship
Admitted to the Union: 1845 (28th)
Total area (2000): 268,581 sq. mi. (695,621 sq. km.) (ranks 2nd)
Population (2004): 22,490,022 (ranks 2nd)
Chief cities: Arlington, Austin, Corpus Christi, Dallas, El Paso, Fort Worth, Houston, San Antonio
Principal products/industries: Cotton, rice, sorghum grain, wheat, livestock, oil, natural gas, sulfur, chemicals, electronics, food processing
Highest point: Guadalupe Peak 8749 ft. (2668 m.)

State History

Originally inhabited by Indians including Apaches, several tribes of the Caddo group, and others; explored by Spaniards early 16th–late 17th centuries; French explorer René-Robert Cavelier, Sieur de La Salle, attempted settlement at Matagorda Bay 1685, laying basis for French claim to region as part of Louisiana; effective Spanish occupation began c. 1700; U.S. acquired French claim in Louisiana Purchase 1803; U.S. claim to Texas relinquished by treaty with Spain 1819; became part of Mexico after Mexico gained independence from Spain 1821; Declaration of Independence from Mexico Mar. 1836; Texan army under commander Sam Houston won decisive battle against Mexican forces at San Jacinto Apr. 1836, gaining independence for the Republic of Texas; sought annexation to U.S. and was admitted to Union Dec. 29, 1845; boundary with Mexico along the Rio Grande fixed after Mexican War by Treaty of Guadalupe Hidalgo 1848; passed ordinance of secession Feb. 1, 1861; readmitted to Union Mar. 30, 1870; adopted constitution 1876.

The first official (though nonnational) Texas flag was based on the green-white-red vertical tricolor of Mexico. The present state flag was originally adopted in 1839 as the second national flag of the Republic of Texas. There was no change when Texas became a state of the United States in 1845.

COLO.
KANSAS
MISSOURI
NEW MEXICO
OKLAHOMA
ARKANSAS
LOUISIANA
MEXICO
Gulf of Mexico
PADRE ISLAND
Rio Grande
Red
104°
102°
100°
98°
96°
94°
36°
34°
32°
30°
28°
26°
Dalhart
Spearman
Perryton
Canadian
Dumas
Borger
Pampa
Panhandle
Wheeler
Amarillo
Hereford
Canyon
Wellington
Dimmitt
Tulia
Memphis
Muleshoe
Childress
Quanah
Plainview
Vernon
Wichita Falls
Littlefield
Denison
Paris
Levelland
Lubbock
Benjamin
Gainesville
Sherman
New Boston
Texarkana
Seymour
Denton
Greenville
Atlanta
Aspermont
Brownfield
Post
Haskell
Graham
Fort Worth
Plano
Mt. Pleasant
Garland
Dallas
Marshall
Seminole
Snyder
Sweetwater
Mineral Wells
Weatherford
Arlington
Tyler
Longview
Lamesa
Andrews
Big Spring
Abilene
Stephenville
Corsicana
Athens
Henderson
Midland
Coleman
Hillsboro
Palestine
Nacogdoches
Mexia
Kermit
Robert Lee
Odessa
Brownwood
Waco
Crockett
Lufkin
Monahans
Marlin
Pecos
San Angelo
Gatesville
Jasper
Rankin
Big Lake
Brady
Killeen
Temple
Madisonville
Mason
Round Rock
Woodville
Fort Stockton
Ozona
Sonora
Llano
Caldwell
Bryan
Huntsville
Conroe
Orange
Fredericksburg
Austin
Alpine
San Marcos
Brenham
Kerrville
Liberty
Beaumont
Sanderson
Rocksprings
Lockhart
Houston
Pasadena
New Braunfels
Missouri City
Leakey
Texas City
Galveston
Seguin
Wharton
Angleton
Hondo
San Antonio
Del Rio
Uvalde
El Campo
Lake Jackson
Crystal City
Victoria
Bay City
Eagle Pass
Pearsall
Pleasanton
Port Lavaca
Carrizo Springs
Beeville
Refugio
Cotulla
Sinton
Aransas Pass
Alice
Corpus Christi
Laredo
Kingsville
Hebbronville
Falfurrias
Zapata
Edinburg
Rio Grande City
Harlingen
McAllen
Brownsville
N.M.
106°
104°
El Paso
Mentone
Sierra Blanco
Pecos
Van Horn
Fort Davis
Marfa
Alpine
29°30′
MEXICO
0 60 120 mi
0 80 160 km

UTAH

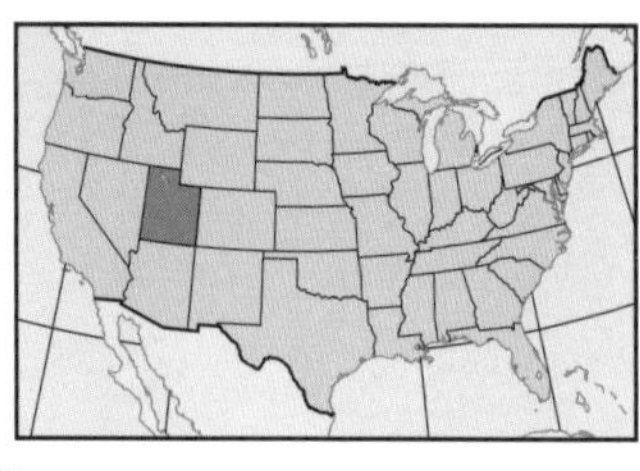

Official name: State of Utah
Nickname: Beehive State
State Capital: Salt Lake City
State Flower: Sego lily
Motto: Industry
Admitted to the Union: 1896 (45th)
Total area (2000): 84,899 sq. mi. (219,887 sq. km.) (ranks 13th)
Population (2004): 2,389,039 (ranks 34th)
Chief Cities: Ogden, Orem, Provo, Salt Lake City, Sandy, West Valley City
Principal products/industries: Wheat, hay, livestock, turkeys, dairy products, copper, gold, silver, molybdenum, high-tech products, food products, tourism
Highest point: Kings Peak 13,528 ft. (4126 m.)

State History

Originally inhabited by American Indian peoples including the Shoshoni, Ute, and Paiute. Possibly explored by Spaniards sent out by explorer Francisco Vásquez de Coronado 1540; visited by Spanish missionaries 1776; Great Salt Lake discovered by American pioneer James Bridger 1824; acquired by U.S. from Mexico in Treaty of Guadalupe Hidalgo 1848; first permanent white settlers were Mormons, led to valley of Great Salt Lake by Brigham Young, head of Mormon Church, in 1847; part of Utah Territory organized 1850; territory reduced to area of present state by 1868; conflict between Mormon authorities and U.S. government, known as Utah War (1857–58); admitted to Union Jan. 4, 1896.

The design carries the state seal, which features a bald eagle over a beehive and crossed U.S. flags to indicate the protection of the U.S. and Utah's loyalty to the nation. The dates 1847 and 1896 refer to the settlement of the original Mormon community at Salt Lake City and the achievement of statehood.

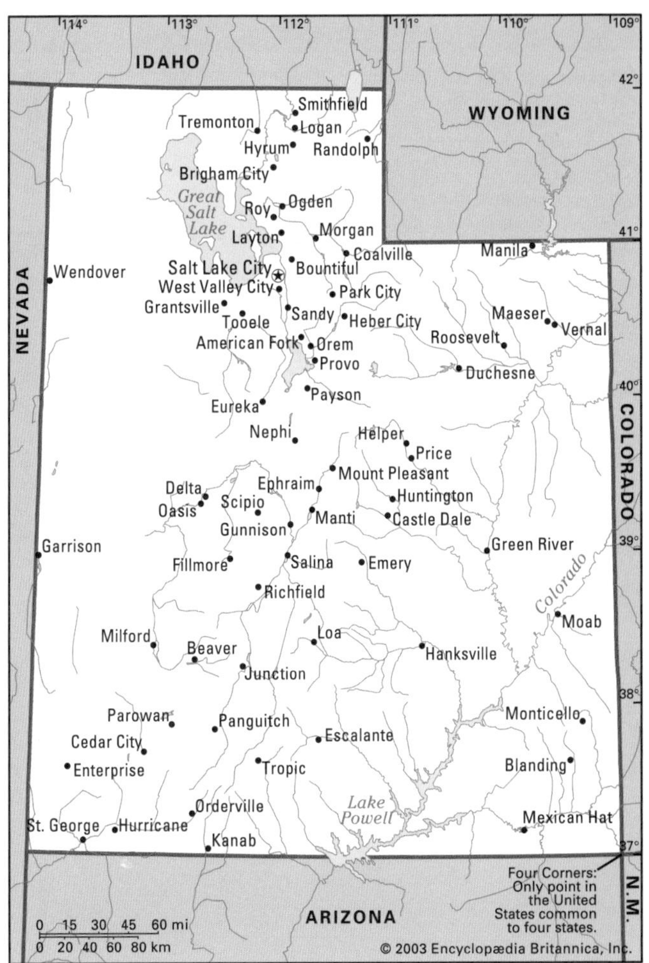
IDAHO
WYOMING
NEVADA
COLORADO
ARIZONA
N.M.
114°
113°
112°
111°
110°
109°
42°
41°
40°
39°
38°
37°
Smithfield
Tremonton
Logan
Hyrum
Randolph
Brigham City
Great Salt Lake
Ogden
Roy
Morgan
Layton
Coalville
Manila
Salt Lake City
Bountiful
Wendover
West Valley City
Park City
Grantsville
Tooele
Sandy
Heber City
Maeser
Vernal
American Fork
Orem
Roosevelt
Provo
Duchesne
Payson
Eureka
Nephi
Helper
Price
Mount Pleasant
Delta
Ephraim
Huntington
Oasis
Scipio
Manti
Castle Dale
Gunnison
Garrison
Green River
Fillmore
Salina
Emery
Richfield
Colorado
Moab
Milford
Loa
Beaver
Hanksville
Junction
Parowan
Monticello
Panguitch
Escalante
Cedar City
Enterprise
Tropic
Blanding
Lake Powell
Orderville
Mexican Hat
St. George
Hurricane
Kanab
Four Corners: Only point in the United States common to four states.
0 15 30 45 60 mi
0 20 40 60 80 km
© 2003 Encyclopædia Britannica, Inc.

VERMONT

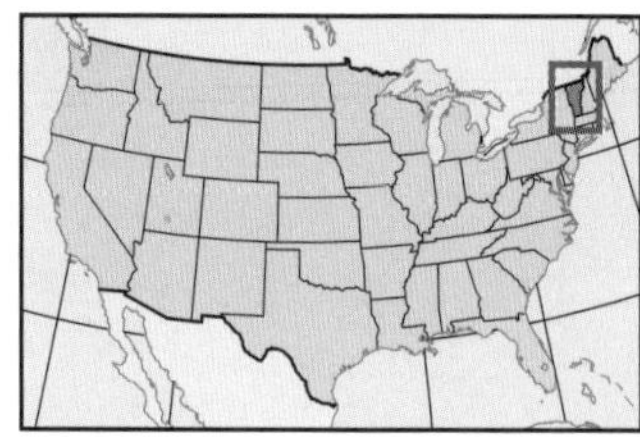

Official name: State of Vermont
Nickname: Green Mountain State
State Capital: Montpelier
State Flower: Red clover
Motto: Freedom and Unity
Admitted to the Union: 1791 (14th)
Total area (2000): 9,614 sq. mi. (24,901 sq. km.) (ranks 45th)
Population (2004): 621,394 (ranks 49th)
Chief Cities/Towns: Burlington, Essex, Rutland
Principal products/industries: Dairy products, maple syrup, apples, food products, marble, talc, metalworking, textiles, furniture, electronics, paper goods, tourism
Highest point: Mt. Mansfield 4393 ft. (1340 m.)

State History

Inhabited originally by American Indians, the Abnaki; explored 1609 by French expedition led by Samuel de Champlain, who discovered the lake now bearing his name; temporary settlement by French at Fort Ste. Anne on Isle La Motte 1666; English established Fort Dummer near site of present Brattleboro 1724; disputes arose between New Hampshire and New York concerning jurisdiction of area, New Hampshire having awarded grants to settlers; Green Mountain Boys organized by Ethan Allen 1770 to repel encroachers from west, New York having won its appeal to crown for rights to settle; when Revolutionary War intervened, Allen and Green Mountain Boys fighting for colonies captured Fort Ticonderoga from British 1775; declared itself independent republic 1777; claims to the region later dropped by New Hampshire and New York; admitted to Union Mar. 4, 1791; present constitution adopted 1793 (since amended).

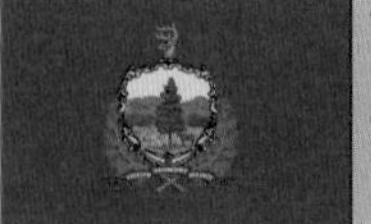

The flag design has the Vermont coat of arms which shows a pastoral scene with the Green Mountains in the background, a large pine tree in the foreground, wheat sheaves, and a cow. The inscription "Freedom and Unity," the word "Vermont," a wreath, and the head of a deer as the crest complete the design.

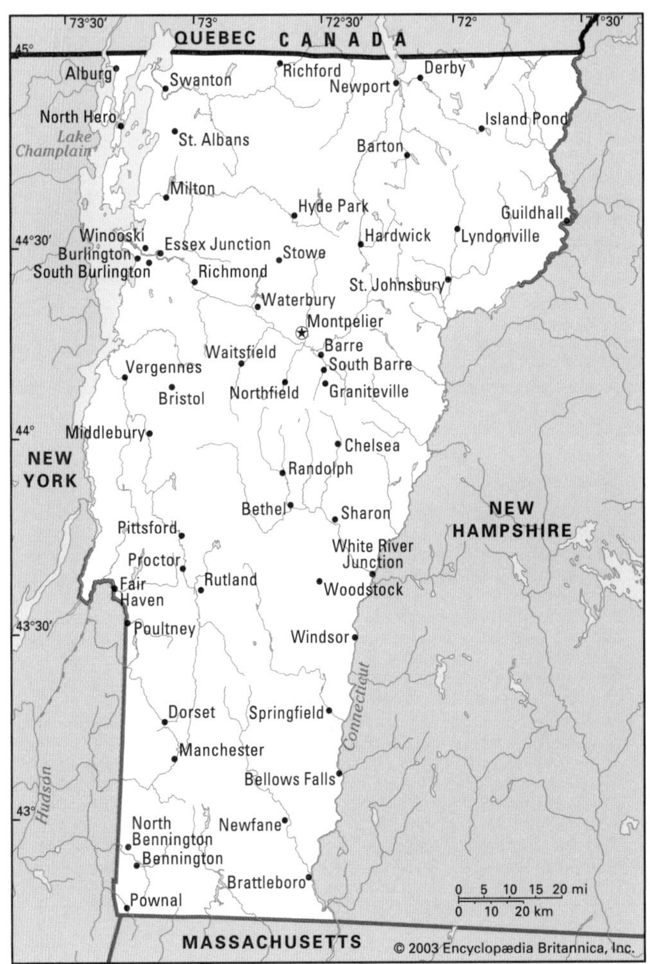
73°30′
73°
72°30′
72°
71°30′
45°
44°30′
44°
43°30′
43°
QUEBEC
CANADA
Alburg
Swanton
Richford
Newport
Derby
North Hero
Lake Champlain
St. Albans
Island Pond
Barton
Milton
Hyde Park
Guildhall
Winooski
Essex Junction
Burlington
South Burlington
Hardwick
Lyndonville
Stowe
Richmond
St. Johnsbury
Waterbury
Montpelier
Barre
Waitsfield
South Barre
Vergennes
Bristol
Northfield
Graniteville
Middlebury
Chelsea
NEW YORK
Randolph
Bethel
Sharon
NEW HAMPSHIRE
Pittsford
White River Junction
Proctor
Rutland
Fair Haven
Woodstock
Poultney
Windsor
Connecticut
Dorset
Springfield
Manchester
Bellows Falls
Hudson
North Bennington
Newfane
Bennington
Brattleboro
Pownal
0 5 10 15 20 mi
0 10 20 km
MASSACHUSETTS
© 2003 Encyclopædia Britannica, Inc.

VIRGINIA

Official name: Commonwealth of Virginia
Nickname: Old Dominion
State Capital: Richmond
State Flower: American dogwood
Motto: Sic Semper Tyrannis (Thus Always to Tyrants)
Admitted to the Union: 1788; 10th of the original 13 colonies to ratify the U.S. Constitution
Total area (2000): 42,774 sq. mi. (110,785 sq. km.) (ranks 35th)
Population (2004): 7,459,827 (ranks 12th)
Chief Cities: Norfolk, Richmond, Virginia Beach
Principal products/industries: Dairy products, tobacco, vegetables, livestock, coal, chemicals, food products, transportation equipment, electrical equipment, textiles, federal-government employment
Highest point: Mt. Rogers 5729 ft. (1747 m.)

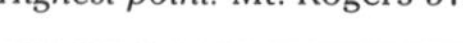

State History

Originally inhabited by American Indians when futile attempts were made by English navigator Sir Walter Raleigh to found settlements 1584–87; first royal charter to London (Virginia) Company followed by first permanent settlement, made by colonists sent out by this company, at Jamestown 1607; first popular assembly in America convened 1619; colony finally thrived primarily on successful tobacco cultivation introduced to settlers by Indians; one of the first colonies to express resistance to the Stamp Act and other British taxes 1765; active in movement for independence during the Revolution; scene of surrender of British Lord Charles Cornwallis at Yorktown 1781; northwestern part of western lands ceded to U.S. 1784, southern part admitted to the Union as the state of Kentucky 1792; ratified the U.S. Constitution June 25, 1788; although slavery had been outlawed, it continued to be important part of economy; tensions heightened between slaveholders and abolitionists during first half of 19th century; passed ordinance of secession 1861; western counties remained loyal to the Union, separated from Virginia 1861 and admitted to the Union as the state of West Virginia 1863; scene of many battles of the Civil War, among them Bull Run (first and second), Fair Oaks, Chancellorsville, Fredericksburg, the Wilderness, Cold Harbor, and many engagements in Shenandoah Valley; readmitted to Union Jan. 26, 1870. New constitution promulgated 1902, revised 1971.

The design of the seal features a woman personifying virtue and dressed as an Amazon. She wears a helmet and holds a spear and sword above the Latin motto "Sic semper tyrannis" ("Thus always to tyrants"). She is standing on the prostrate figure of a fallen king, his crown lying to one side.

KENTUCKY
WEST VIRGINIA
Grundy
Clintwood
Tazewell
Wise
Marion
Abingdon
Gate City
TENNESSEE
N.C.
83°
82°
37°
81°
80°
79°
78°
77°
76°
75°
PENNSYLVANIA
NEW JERSEY
MARYLAND
DELAWARE
39°
38°
37°
Potomac R.
Winchester
Leesburg
Front Royal
Reston
Washington, D.C.
Woodstock
Annandale
Arlington
Alexandria
Luray
Manassas
Dale City
Chesapeake Bay
Harrisonburg
Culpeper
Monterey
Fredericksburg
Orange
WEST VIRGINIA
Staunton
Waynesboro
Spotsylvania
Stuarts Draft
Charlottesville
Tappahannock
Lexington
Lancaster
Accomac
Hanover
Lovingston
Covington
Buena Vista
Richmond
Saluda
Powhatan
New Castle
Amherst
Eastville
Mathews
Appomattox
Hopewell
Lynchburg
Blacksburg
Farmville
Roanoke
Williamsburg
Radford
Petersburg
Hampton
Tazewell
Charlotte Court House
Christiansburg
Newport News
Lunenburg
Norfolk
Virginia Beach
Wytheville
Chatham
Portsmouth
Halifax
Chesapeake
Marion
Lawrenceville
Martinsville
Suffolk
Galax
Danville
Emporia
Franklin
South Boston
ATLANTIC OCEAN
0 30 60 mi
0 40 80 km
NORTH CAROLINA
© 2003 Encyclopædia Britannica, Inc.

WASHINGTON

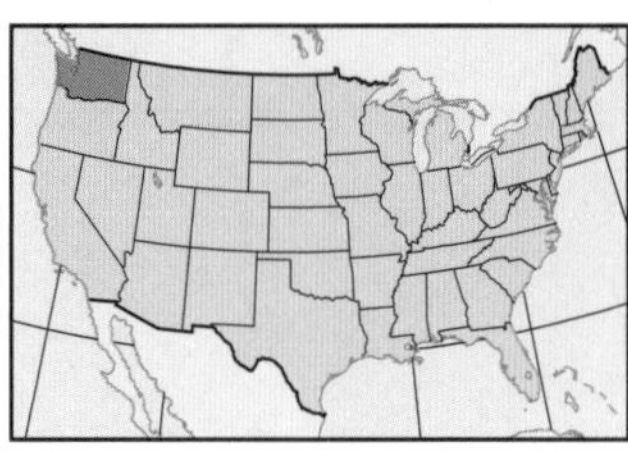

Official name: State of Washington
Nickname: Evergreen State
State Capital: Olympia
State Flower: Rhododendron
Motto: Alki (By and By)
Admitted to the Union: 1889 (42nd)
Total area (2000): 71,300 sq. mi. (184,665 sq. km.) (ranks 18th)
Population (2004): 6,203,788 (ranks 15th)
Chief Cities: Seattle, Spokane, Tacoma
Principal products/industries: Wheat, fruit, dairy products, fishing, zinc, lead, gravel, aircraft and other transportation equipment, lumber, chemicals
Highest point: Mt. Rainier 14,410 ft. (4395 m.)

State History

Area inhabited by Pacific coast Indians when region visited by Spanish, Russian, British, and French explorers 1543–1792 (short-lived settlement 1791 at Neah Bay); explored by Lewis and Clark, who sailed down Columbia River 1805; part of Oregon Country; occupied jointly by Great Britain and U.S. 1818–46; first permanent settlement at Tumwater 1845; by treaty with Great Britain 1846 northern boundary set at 49th parallel; part of Oregon Territory 1848; settlement at Seattle 1851, at Tacoma 1852; became part of Washington Territory 1853; territory reduced to area of present state 1863; admitted to Union as state Nov. 11, 1889.

The flag contains the state seal with the name of the state, the date of its admission to the Union, and a bust of George Washington. In 1915 a background of green for the flag of the "Evergreen State" was chosen.

BRITISH COLUMBIA
CANADA
IDAHO
OREGON
PACIFIC OCEAN
Puget Sound
Columbia
49°
48°
47°
46°
124°
122°
120°
118°
Neah Bay
La Push
Forks
Port Angeles
Ferndale
Lynden
Bellingham
Friday Harbor
Anacortes
Oak Harbor
Sedro-Woolley
Mount Vernon
Coupeville
Port Townsend
Everett
Quilcene
Shoreline
Seattle
Bellevue
Bremerton
Renton
Snoqualmie
Tacoma
Federal Way
Lakewood
Olympia
Shelton
Aberdeen
Hoquiam
Pacific Beach
South Bend
Centralia
Chehalis
Long Beach
Cathlamet
Longview
Kelso
Woodland
Vancouver
Camas
Washougal
Stevenson
White Salmon
Goldendale
Wenatchee
Leavenworth
Chelan
Waterville
Brewster
Okanogan
Omak
Republic
Colville
Chewelah
Newport
Coulee Dam
Grand Coulee
Ephrata
Quincy
Ellensburg
Selah
Yakima
Union Gap
Toppenish
Sunnyside
Grandview
Moses Lake
Othello
Richland
Pasco
Kennewick
Ritzville
Medical Lake
Spokane
Opportunity
Cheney
Colfax
Pullman
Pomeroy
Dayton
Walla Walla
Clarkston
Asotin
0 15 30 45 60 mi
0 20 40 60 80 km

WEST VIRGINIA

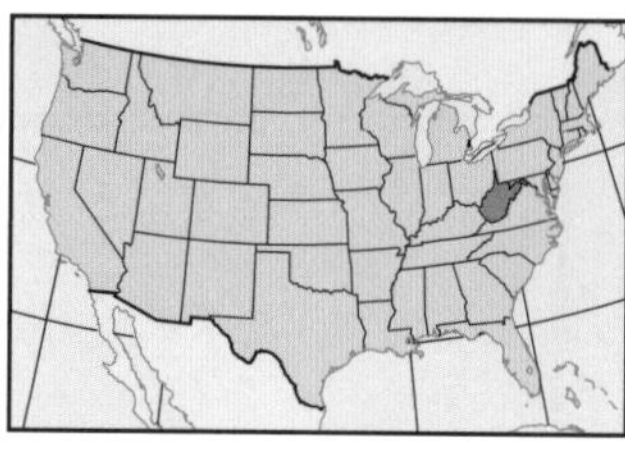

Official name: State of West Virginia
Nickname: Mountain State
State Capital: Charleston
State Flower: Rhododendron
Motto: Montani Semper Liberi (Mountaineers Are Always Free)
Admitted to the Union: 1863 (35th)
Total area (2000): 24,230 sq. mi. (62,755 sq. km.) (ranks 41st)
Population (2004): 1,815,354 (ranks 37th)
Chief Cities: Charleston, Huntington
Principal products/industries: Corn, tobacco, apples, dairy products, cattle, coal, stone, primary metals, chemicals, recreation
Highest point: Spruce Knob 4861 ft. (1483 m.)

State History

Inhabited originally by Mound Builders and later by other American Indian peoples; European arrival 17th–18th centuries brought conflicts among French, British, and Indians; although part of Virginia, rugged terrain restricted settlement; after American Revolution, concerns of inhabitants who were less likely to have slaves differed from those in eastern Virginia; dissatisfaction with Virginia government grew, as did sentiment for separation from eastern part of state; with outbreak of Civil War, residents from western Virginia voted against ordinance of secession May 1861; government loyal to U.S. federal government organized at Wheeling June 1861; population voted to create new state 1861 and a state constitution ratified 1862; admitted to Union June 20, 1863; state constitution adopted 1872 (since amended).

Last modified in 1929, West Virginia's flag shows a farmer, a miner and a rock with the date of statehood, June 20, 1863. The motto, "Mountaineers are always free," refers to the secession of the citizens of the mountains of western Virginia in 1861 when slave-holding Virginia joined the Confederacy.

82°
81°
80°
79°
78°
39°
38°
PENNSYLVANIA
MARYLAND
OHIO
VIRGINIA
KENTUCKY
Ohio
Moundsville
New Martinsville
Paden City
Morgantown
Fairmont
Kingwood
Ridgeley
Berkeley Springs
Martinsburg
Harpers Ferry
Ranson
Charles Town
Keyser
Romney
Vienna
St. Marys
Shinnston
Grafton
Parkersburg
Clarksburg
Philippi
Harrisville
Weston
Moorefield
Elizabeth
Buckhannon
Petersburg
Ravenswood
Glenville
Elkins
Ripley
Point Pleasant
Spencer
Pickens
Franklin
Sutton
Winfield
Sissonville
Durbin
Huntington
Cowen
Charleston
St. Albans
Cass
Summersville
South Charleston
Richwood
Hamlin
Wayne
Marlinton
Fayetteville
Madison
Oak Hill
Rainelle
Mt. Hope
Logan
Lewisburg
Williamson
Beckley
White Sulphur Springs
Hinton
Pineville
Mullens
Union
Welch
Princeton
War
Bluefield
Cucumber
0 10 20 30 40 mi
0 15 30 45 60 km
81°
40°30′
80° 30′
Weirton
OHIO
PENNSYLVANIA
Ohio
Wheeling
40°
Moundsville
© 2003 Encyclopædia Britannica, Inc.

WISCONSIN

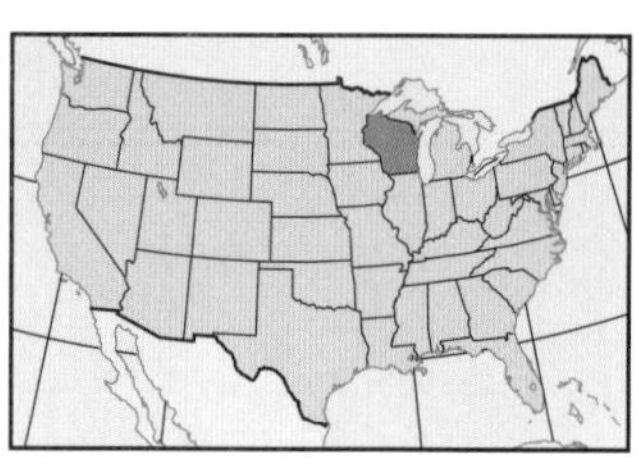

Official name: State of Wisconsin
Nickname: Badger State (unofficial)
State Capital: Madison
State Flower: Violet
Motto: Forward
Admitted to the Union: 1848 (30th)
Total area (2000): 65,498 sq. mi. (169,639 sq. km.) (ranks 23rd)
Population (2004): 5,509,026 (ranks 20th)
Chief Cities: Green Bay, Kenosha, Madison, Milwaukee, Racine
Principal products/industries: Dairy products, corn, cranberries, potatoes, livestock, machinery, paper products, metal products, recreation
Highest point: Timms Hill 1951 ft. (595 m.)

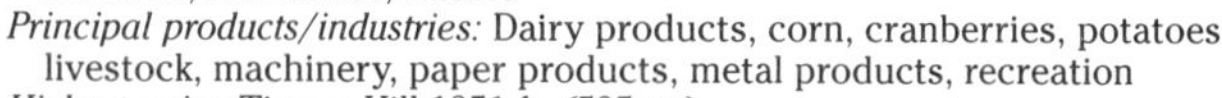

State History

Originally inhabited by prehistoric Mound Builders; by time of European arrival, several different Indian tribes were inhabiting the region; area visited by French explorer Jean Nicolet 1634; first permanent European settlement 1717; French settlement at Green Bay 1745; throughout 18th century some Indian tribes sided with French while others sided with English, provoking general unrest; French claim ceded to Great Britain 1763 after French and Indian War; recognized by Great Britain as part of U.S. 1783; claims relinquished during 1780s by Virginia, Massachusetts, and Connecticut; part of Northwest Territory 1787, Indiana Territory 1800, Illinois Territory 1809, and Michigan Territory 1818; conflicts between Indians and settlers continued into 19th century culminating in Black Hawk War 1832, in which Indians suffered massacre; included in Wisconsin Territory 1836; admitted to Union May 29, 1848; constitution ratified 1848 (since amended).

The flag features the U.S. motto and national shield in the center, surrounded by symbols of typical 19th-century occupations—farming, mining, manufacturing, and shipping. A miner and sailor serve as supporters to the shield, above which appears a badger as a crest honoring "the Badger State," a nickname referring to early miners.

93°
92°
91°
90°
89°
88°
87°
47°
46°
45°
44°
43°
42°
MINNESOTA
Lake Superior
MICHIGAN
MINNESOTA
IOWA
ILLINOIS
Lake Michigan
Green Bay
Mississippi River
Washburn
Superior
Ashland
Hurley
Hayward
Eagle River
Florence
Grantsburg
Shell Lake
Phillips
Rhinelander
Crandon
Balsam Lake
Rice Lake
Ladysmith
Barron
Merrill
Antigo
Medford
New Richmond
Peshtigo
Marinette
Sturgeon Bay
Wausau
Hudson
Chippewa Falls
Keshena
Oconto
Menomonie
Eau Claire
Shawano
Ellsworth
Marshfield
Algoma
Durand
Neillsville
Wisconsin Rapids
Stevens Point
Green Bay
Kewaunee
Plover
De Pere
Alma
Whitehall
Appleton
Kaukauna
Two Rivers
Black River Falls
Neenah
Manitowoc
Tomah
Wautoma
Oshkosh
Sparta
Berlin
Ripon
Fond du Lac
Sheboygan
La Crosse
Mauston
Wisconsin Dells
Waupun
Plymouth
Viroqua
Reedsburg
Portage
West Bend
Beaver Dam
Port Washington
Baraboo
Columbus
Richland Center
Watertown
Menomonee Falls
Spring Green
Madison
Milwaukee
Waukesha
Prairie du Chien
Dodgeville
Jefferson
West Allis
Stoughton
Whitewater
Lancaster
Platteville
Janesville
Elkhorn
Racine
Monroe
Beloit
Lake Geneva
Kenosha
0 40 80 mi
0 50 100 km
© 2003 Encyclopædia Britannica, Inc.

WYOMING

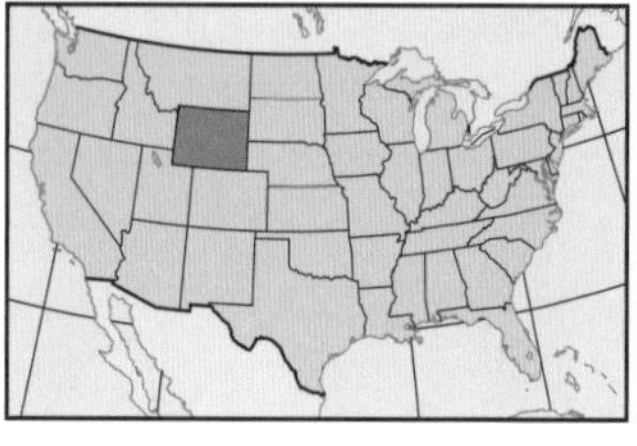

Official name: State of Wyoming
Nicknames: Equality State, Cowboy State
State Capital: Cheyenne
State Flower: Indian paintbrush
Motto: Equal Rights
Admitted to the Union: 1890 (44th)
Total area (2000): 97,814 sq. mi. (253,336 sq. km.) (ranks 10th)
Population (2004): 506,529 (ranks 50th)
Chief Cities: Casper, Cheyenne, Laramie
Principal products/industries: Sugar beets, beans, barley, hay, wheat, livestock, oil, natural gas, uranium, coal, oil refining, tourism
Highest point: Gannett Peak 13,804 ft. (4210 m.)

State History

Inhabited by Plains Indians when first visited by white explorers during 18th century; originally a part of Louisiana region claimed by France; greater part acquired by U.S. in Louisiana Purchase 1803; remainder acquired with annexation of Texas 1845, British cession of Oregon Country 1846, and cession of Mexican territory to U.S. 1848; included in several U.S. territories prior to organization of Wyoming 1868; adopted women's suffrage, first instance in U.S., 1869; admitted to Union July 10, 1890; constitution adopted 1890; Nellie Tayloe Ross governor 1925–27, first woman governor of a U.S. state.

The seal, adopted in 1893, includes the motto, "Equal rights," recalling that in 1869 Wyoming was first to give equal voting and office-holding rights to women. Adopted on January 31, 1917, the design's white is said to stand for purity and uprightness, and blue for sky, fidelity, justice, and virility. The red is for the blood shed by both early pioneers and the original native population.

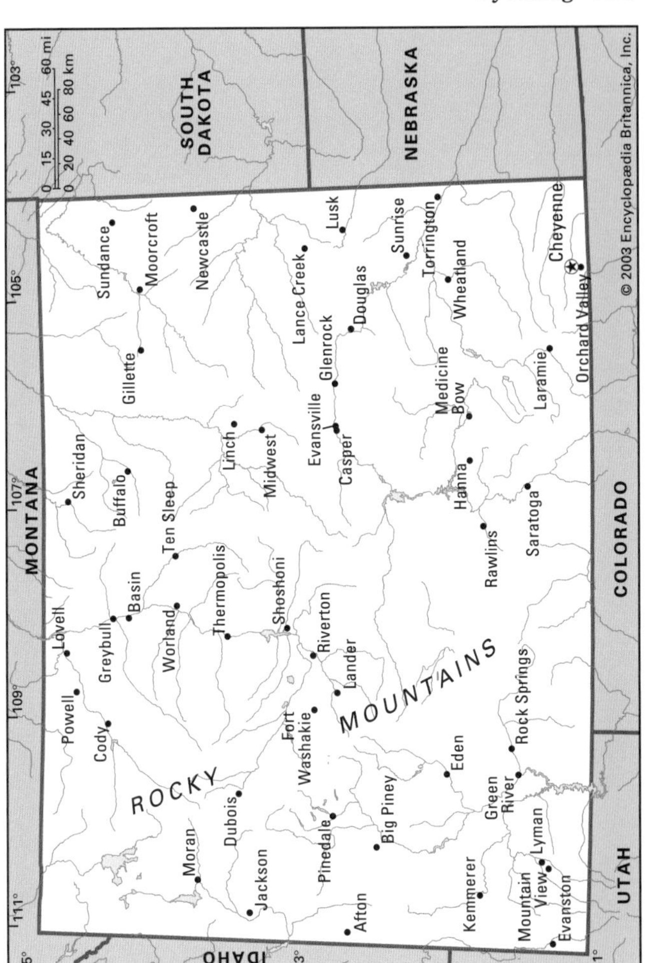
MONTANA
SOUTH DAKOTA
NEBRASKA
COLORADO
UTAH
IDAHO
ROCKY MOUNTAINS
0 15 30 45 60 mi
0 20 40 60 80 km
45°
43°
41°
111°
109°
107°
105°
103°
Sundance
Moorcroft
Newcastle
Gillette
Lusk
Lance Creek
Sunrise
Torrington
Douglas
Wheatland
Glenrock
Cheyenne
Orchard Valley
Laramie
Medicine Bow
Evansville
Casper
Linch
Midwest
Sheridan
Buffalo
Ten Sleep
Hanna
Saratoga
Rawlins
Thermopolis
Shoshoni
Basin
Worland
Lovell
Greybull
Riverton
Lander
Powell
Cody
Fort Washakie
Rock Springs
Eden
Dubois
Big Piney
Green River
Pinedale
Moran
Jackson
Lyman
Mountain View
Evanston
Kemmerer
Afton
© 2003 Encyclopædia Britannica, Inc.

The District of Columbia and the Territories of the United States

THE DISTRICT OF COLUMBIA

Official name: District of Columbia
Nickname: D.C.
State Flower: American beauty rose
Motto: Justice to all
Admitted to the Union: February 21, 1871 (as a municipal corporation)
Total area: 68 sq. mi. (176 sq. km.)
Population (2005): 550,521
Principal industries: government and tourism
Highest point: Tenleytown 410 ft. (125 m.)

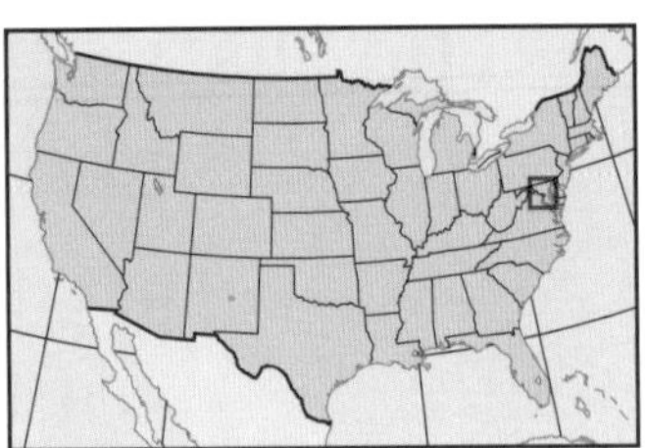

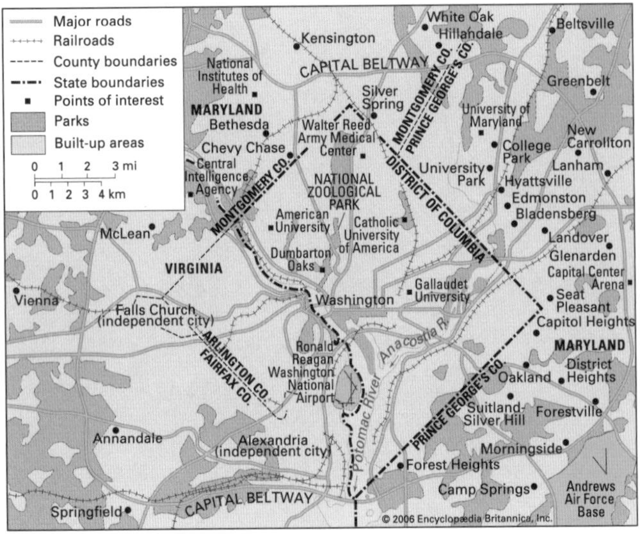

First flown on October 23, 1938, the District's flag was adapted by designer Charles Dunn from the coat of arms of George Washington's family, dating to the 1500s in England. Speculation is that the three stars stand for the three commissioners who once ran the District, and that the Washington family arms' design (with its blue stars, not red) inspired the Stars and Stripes.

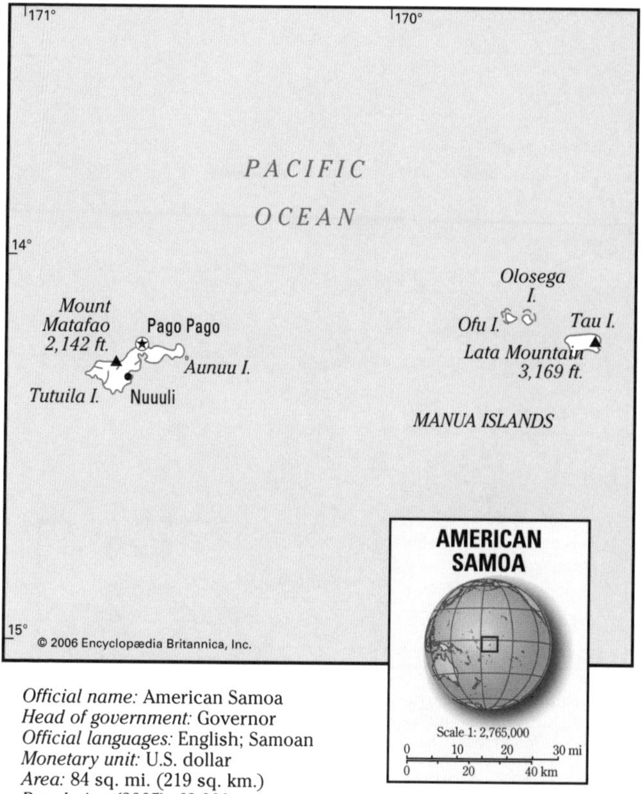

171°
170°
PACIFIC
OCEAN
14°
15°
Mount
Matafao
2,142 ft.
Pago Pago
Aunuu I.
Tutuila I.
Nuuuli
Olosega
I.
Ofu I.
Tau I.
Lata Mountain
3,169 ft.
MANUA ISLANDS
AMERICAN
SAMOA
Scale 1: 2,765,000
0 10 20 30 mi
0 20 40 km

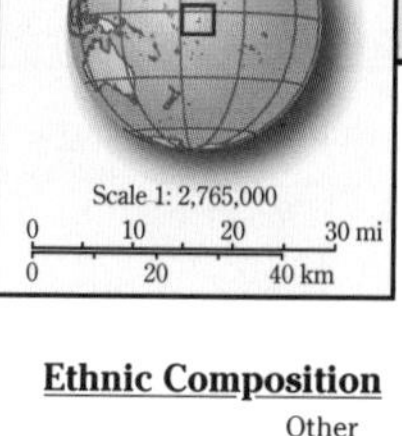

Official name: American Samoa
Head of government: Governor
Official languages: English; Samoan
Monetary unit: U.S. dollar
Area: 84 sq. mi. (219 sq. km.)
Population (2005): 63,900
GNP per capita (1997): U.S.$4,300
Principal exports (2001): tuna 86.3%, fish meal 8.9%, pet food 4.8% *to:* United States 99.6%

Ethnic Composition

Samoan
88.2%
Other
6.2%
Asian
2.8%
Tongan
2.8%

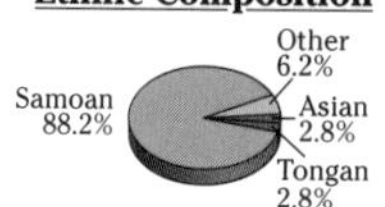

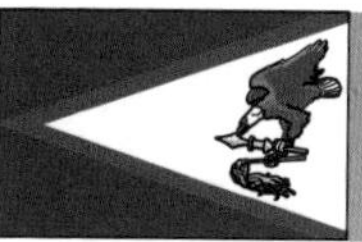

In 1900, part of Samoa became a U.S. territory. This flag, based on heraldric ideas by the Samoans, became official on April 27, 1960. The red, white, and blue are traditional in both Samoa and the United States. The eagle holds in its talons two Samoan emblems, a fly whisk, symbol of the wisdom of traditional chiefs, and a war club, representing state power.

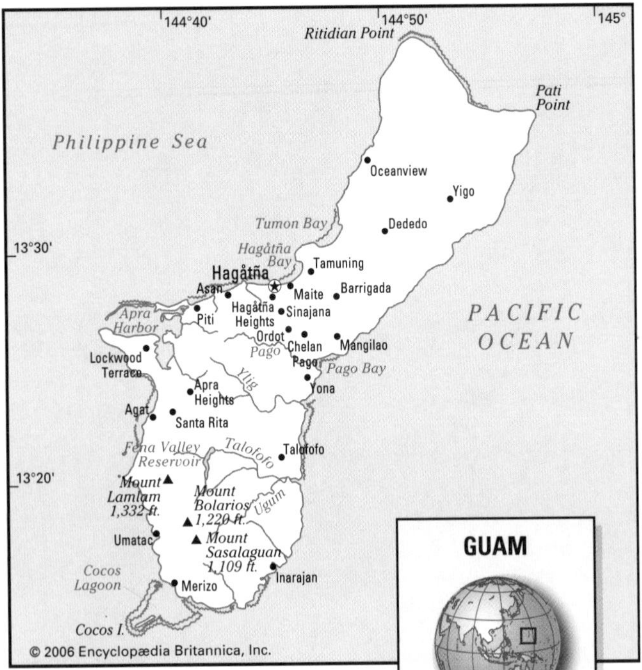
144°40'
144°50'
145°
Ritidian Point
Pati Point
Philippine Sea
Oceanview
Yigo
Tumon Bay
Dededo
13°30'
Hagåtña Bay
Tamuning
Hagåtña
Asan
Maite
Barrigada
PACIFIC OCEAN
Apra Harbor
Piti
Hagåtña Heights
Sinajana
Ordot
Chelan
Mangilao
Pago
Lockwood Terrace
Pago
Pago Bay
Ylig
Apra Heights
Yona
Agat
Santa Rita
Fena Valley Reservoir
Talofofo
Talofofo
13°20'
Mount Lamlam 1,332 ft.
Mount Bolarios 1,220 ft.
Ugum
Umatac
Mount Sasalaguan 1,109 ft.
Cocos Lagoon
Inarajan
Merizo
Cocos I.
© 2006 Encyclopædia Britannica, Inc.
GUAM

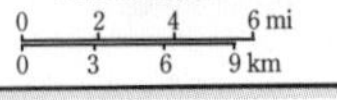
Scale 1: 722,700
0
2
4
6 mi
0
3
6
9 km

Official name: Territory of Guam
Head of government: Governor
Official languages: Chamorro; English
Monetary unit: U.S. dollar
Area: 209 sq. mi. (543 sq. km.)
Population (2005): 170,000
GDP per capita (2002): U.S.$15,440
Principal exports (2001): food 52.2%, petroleum and natural gas products 6.2%, perfumes 6.0%, tobacco 5.8% *to:* Japan 50.0%; Palau 9.4%; Hong Kong 7.4%; Taiwan 4.7%

Ethnic Composition

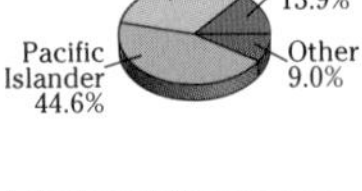
Asian 32.5%
Mixed 13.9%
Pacific Islander 44.6%
Other 9.0%

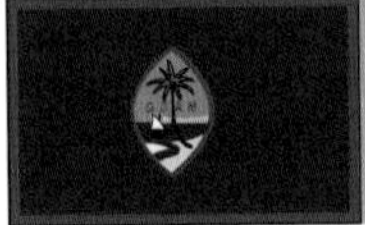

U.S. administered Guam after the 1898 Spanish-American War, and it became a territory in 1950. This flag was adopted in 1917, and reconfirmed in 1931. The lozenge's red border commemorates nearly three years of Japanese occupation endured in World War II, and the shape recalls stones used by ancient Chamorros for hunting. They used the type of canoe shown.

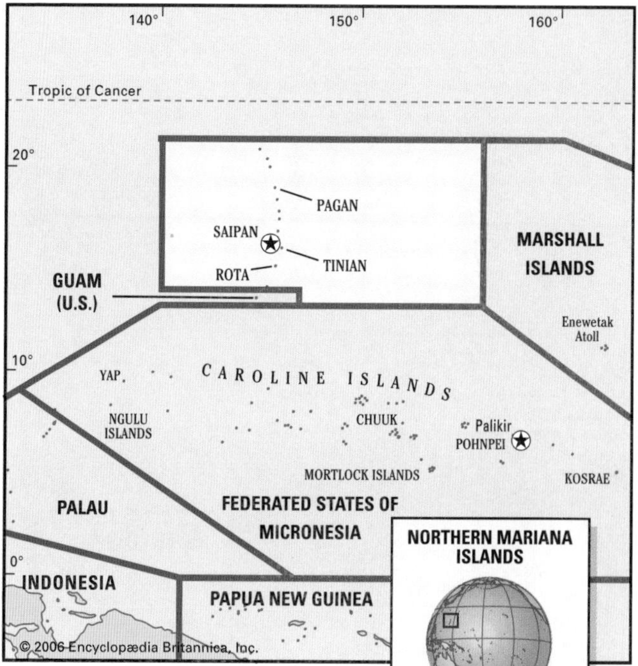
140°
150°
160°
Tropic of Cancer
20°
10°
0°
PAGAN
SAIPAN
ROTA
TINIAN
GUAM
(U.S.)
MARSHALL
ISLANDS
Enewetak
Atoll
YAP
CAROLINE ISLANDS
NGULU
ISLANDS
CHUUK
Palikir
POHNPEI
MORTLOCK ISLANDS
KOSRAE
PALAU
FEDERATED STATES OF
MICRONESIA
INDONESIA
PAPUA NEW GUINEA
© 2006 Encyclopædia Britannica, Inc.

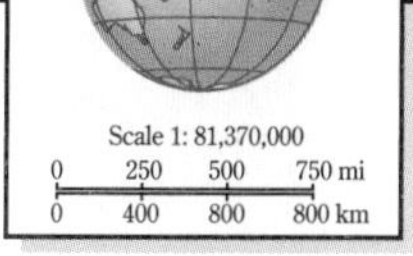
NORTHERN MARIANA
ISLANDS
Scale 1: 81,370,000
0 250 500 750 mi
0 400 800 800 km

Official name: Commonwealth of the Northern Mariana Islands
Head of government: Governor
Official languages: Chamorro; Carolinian; English
Monetary unit: U.S. dollar
Area: 177 sq. mi. (457 sq. km.)
Population (2005): 80,400
GDP per capita (2004): U.S.$8,040
Principal exports (2004): garments 37.0%, food 9.6%, petroleum products 8.2%, transport equipment 5.0% *to:* U.S. about 100%

Ethnic Composition

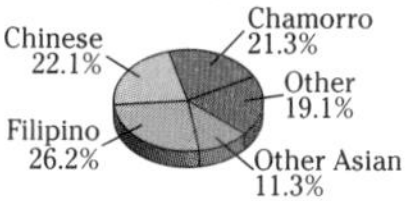
Chinese
22.1%
Chamorro
21.3%
Other
19.1%
Filipino
26.2%
Other Asian
11.3%

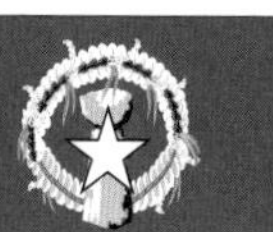

Once the Ladrone Islands, these 15 islands were under Japan from 1914. The U.S. occupied them in 1944, and in 1986 they became a U.S. commonwealth. The latte stones, used as housing supports and burial markers, are revered. The original flag, adopted March 31, 1972, lacked the wreath, added in 1981; the current flag was adopted in the mid-1990s.

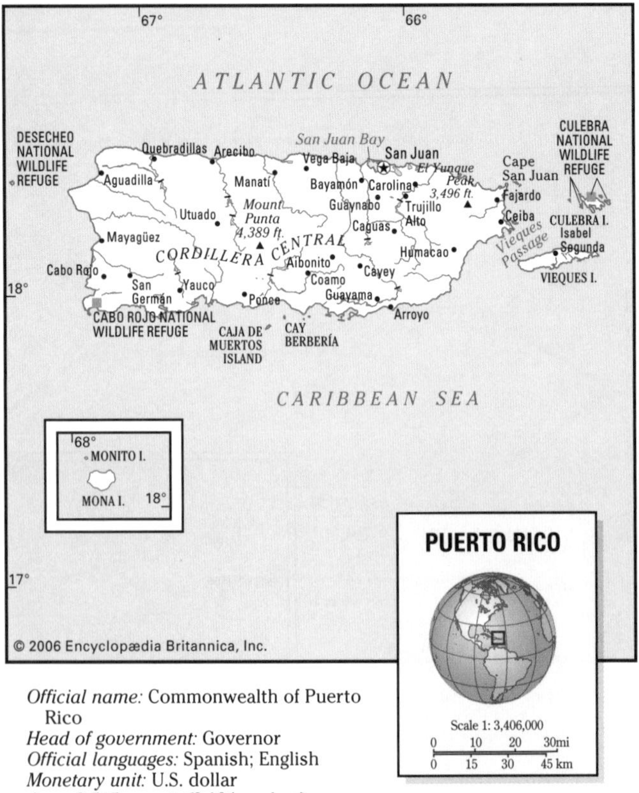

67°
66°
ATLANTIC OCEAN
DESECHEO NATIONAL WILDLIFE REFUGE
Quebradillas
Arecibo
San Juan Bay
Vega Baja
San Juan
CULEBRA NATIONAL WILDLIFE REFUGE
Cape San Juan
Aguadilla
Manatí
Bayamón
Carolina
El Yunque Peak 3,496 ft.
Fajardo
Guaynabo
Trujillo Alto
Utuado
Mount Punta 4,389 ft.
Caguas
Ceiba
CULEBRA I.
Isabel Segunda
Mayagüez
CORDILLERA CENTRAL
Humacao
Vieques Passage
Cabo Rojo
Aibonito
Cayey
VIEQUES I.
18°
San Germán
Yauco
Coamo
Ponce
Guayama
Arroyo
CABO ROJO NATIONAL WILDLIFE REFUGE
CAJA DE MUERTOS ISLAND
CAY BERBERÍA
CARIBBEAN SEA
68°
MONITO I.
MONA I.
18°
17°
PUERTO RICO
Scale 1: 3,406,000
0 10 20 30mi
0 15 30 45 km

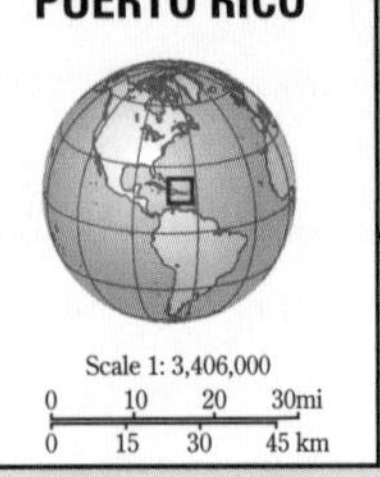

Official name: Commonwealth of Puerto Rico
Head of government: Governor
Official languages: Spanish; English
Monetary unit: U.S. dollar
Area: 3,515 sq. mi. (9,104 sq. km.)
Population (2005): 3,911,000
GNP per capita (2004): U.S.$12,920
Principal exports (2003): pharmaceutical and chemical products 71.8%, electronic and electrical products 12.5%
to: U.S. 86.4%; The Netherlands 2.1%

Ethnic Composition

White 72.1%
Black 15.0%
Mulatto 12.9%

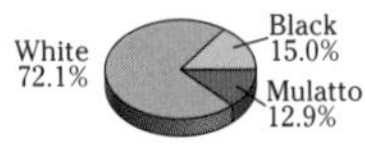

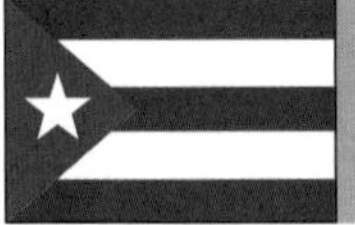

The flag chosen by exiled Puerto Ricans in 1895 was the Cuban flag with red and blue reversed. Raised on July 25, 1952, when Puerto Rico became a U.S. commonwealth, the star is for the commonwealth; the white stripes are for individual rights and freedom. The red stripes, as well as the corners of the triangle, correspond to the three branches of government.

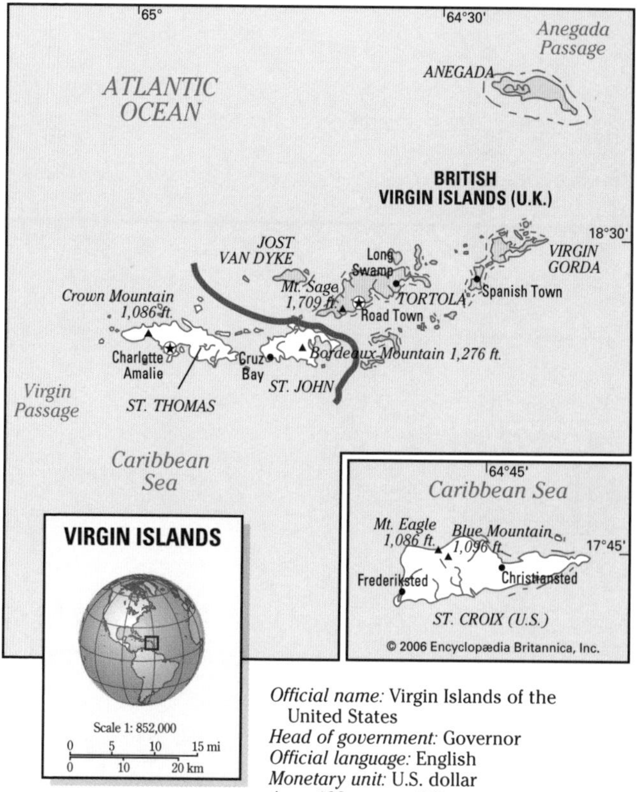

65°
64°30'
Anegada Passage
ANEGADA
ATLANTIC OCEAN
BRITISH VIRGIN ISLANDS (U.K.)
18°30'
JOST VAN DYKE
Long Swamp
VIRGIN GORDA
Mt. Sage 1,709 ft.
TORTOLA
Spanish Town
Crown Mountain 1,086 ft.
Road Town
Charlotte Amalie
Cruz Bay
Bordeaux Mountain 1,276 ft.
ST. JOHN
Virgin Passage
ST. THOMAS
Caribbean Sea
64°45'
Caribbean Sea
Mt. Eagle 1,086 ft.
Blue Mountain 1,096 ft.
17°45'
Frederiksted
Christiansted
ST. CROIX (U.S.)
© 2006 Encyclopædia Britannica, Inc.
VIRGIN ISLANDS
Scale 1: 852,000
0 5 10 15 mi
0 10 20 km

Official name: Virgin Islands of the United States
Head of government: Governor
Official language: English
Monetary unit: U.S. dollar
Area: 138 sq. mi. (353 sq. km.)
Population (2005): 109,000
GDP per capita (2004): U.S.$24,100
Principal exports (2003): refined petroleum 93.1% *to:* United States 93.2%; other countries 6.8%

Ethnic Composition

White 15.0%
Black 61.1%
Puerto Rican 12.0%
Other 11.9%

V
I

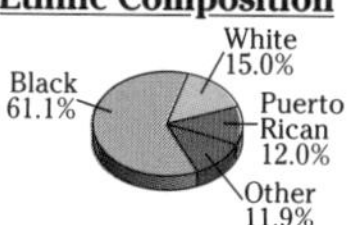

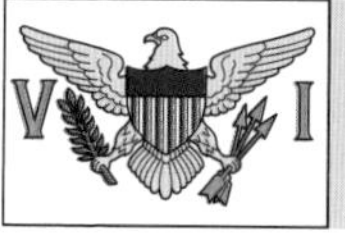

The islands, bought by the U.S. in 1917, flew the U.S. flag until May 17, 1921, when the territorial governor authorized this flag. The arrows are thought to represent the main islands of Saint Croix, Saint John, and Saint Thomas. In 1493, Columbus named the islands for St. Ursula, the legendary 4th-century leader of virgins who reputedly were martyred in Germany by the Huns.

List of Selected Cities

AFGHANISTAN . . . . page 1

Adraskan	33°39' N,	062°16' E
Almār	35°50' N,	064°32' E
Anār Darreh	32°46' N,	061°39' E
Andkhvoy	36°56' N,	065°08' E
Āqchah	36°56' N,	066°11' E
Baghlān	36°13' N,	068°46' E
Bāghrān	33°04' N,	065°05' E
Bagrām	34°58' N,	069°17' E
Bālā Bolūk	32°38' N,	062°28' E
Bāmīān (Bāmyān)	34°50' N,	067°50' E
Barg-e Matāl	35°40' N,	071°21' E
Bāzār-e Panjvā'i	31°32' N,	065°28' E
Chaghcharān	34°31' N,	065°15' E
Chahār Borjak	30°17' N,	062°03' E
Chakhānsūr	31°10' N,	062°04' E
Delārām	32°11' N,	063°25' E
Do Qal'eh	32°08' N,	061°27' E
Dowlātabād	36°26' N,	064°55' E
Dūrāj	37°56' N,	070°43' E
Eslām Qal'eh	34°40' N,	061°04' E
Farāh (Farrah, Ferah)	32°22' N,	062°07' E
Feyẕābād (Faizābād)	37°06' N,	070°34' E
Ghaznī	33°33' N,	068°26' E
Ghūrīān	34°21' N,	061°30' E
Gīzāb	33°23' N,	066°16' E
Golestān	32°37' N,	063°39' E
Golrān	35°06' N,	061°41' E
Gowmal Kalay	32°31' N,	068°51' E
Herāt (Harāt)	34°20' N,	062°12' E
Jabal os Sarāj	35°07' N,	069°14' E
Jalālābād	34°26' N,	070°28' E
Jaldak	31°58' N,	066°43' E
Jawand	35°04' N,	064°09' E
Kabul	34°31' N,	069°12' E
Kajakī	32°16' N,	065°03' E
Kandahār (Qandahār)	31°35' N,	065°45' E
Khadīr	33°55' N,	065°56' E
Khānābād	36°41' N,	069°07' E
Kholm	36°42' N,	067°41' E
Khowst	33°22' N,	069°57' E
Kondūz (Qonduz)	36°45' N,	068°51' E
Koshk	34°57' N,	062°15' E
Kūhestānāt	35°49' N,	065°52' E
Lashkar Gāh (Bust)	31°35' N,	064°21' E
Maḥmūd-e Rāqī	35°01' N,	069°20' E
Mazār-e Sharif	36°42' N,	067°06' E
Nāvor	33°53' N,	067°57' E
Orgūn	32°57' N,	069°11' E
Orūzgān	32°56' N,	066°38' E
Owbeh	34°22' N,	063°10' E
Palālak	30°14' N,	062°54' E
Pol-e 'Alam	33°59' N,	069°02' E
Porchaman	33°08' N,	063°51' E
Qalāt	32°07' N,	066°54' E
Qal'eh-ye Now	34°59' N,	063°08' E
Sar-e Pol	36°14' N,	065°55' E
Sayghān	35°11' N,	067°42' E
Shāh Jūy	32°31' N,	067°25' E
Shahrak	34°06' N,	064°18' E
Shīndand (Sabzevār)	33°18' N,	062°08' E
Shīr Khān	37°11' N,	068°36' E
Yangī Qal'eh	37°28' N,	069°36' E
Zaranj	30°58' N,	061°53' E

ALBANIA . . . . page 2

Berat	40°42' N,	019°57' E
Burrel	41°36' N,	020°01' E
Cërrik	41°02' N,	019°57' E
Çorovodë	40°30' N,	020°13' E
Durrës	41°19' N,	019°26' E
Elbasan	41°06' N,	020°05' E
Ersekë	40°22' N,	020°40' E
Fier	40°43' N,	019°34' E
Gjirokastër	40°05' N,	020°10' E
Gramsh	40°52' N,	020°11' E
Himarë	40°07' N,	019°44' E
Kavajë	41°11' N,	019°33' E
Korçë (Koritsa)	40°37' N,	020°46' E
Krujë	41°30' N,	019°48' E
Kukës	42°05' N,	020°24' E
Laç	41°38' N,	019°43' E
Lezhë	41°47' N,	019°39' E
Librazhd	41°11' N,	020°19' E
Lushnje	40°56' N,	019°42' E
Patos	40°38' N,	019°39' E
Përmet	40°14' N,	020°21' E
Peshkopi	41°41' N,	020°25' E
Pogradec	40°54' N,	020°39' E
Pukë	42°03' N,	019°54' E
Rrëshen	41°47' N,	019°54' E
Sarandë	39°52' N,	020°00' E
Shkodër (Scutari)	42°05' N,	019°30' E
Tepelenë	40°19' N,	020°01' E
Trana (Tirana)	41°20' N,	019°50' E
Vlorë	40°27' N,	019°30' E
Vorë	41°23' N,	019°40' E

ALGERIA . . . . page 3

Adrar (Timmi)	27°54' N,	000°17'W
Aïn Beïda (Daoud)	35°48' N,	007°24' E
Algiers (or Al-Jaza'ir)	36°47' N,	003°03' E
Annaba (Bone)	36°54' N,	007°46' E

Batna . . . 35°34' N, 006°11' E
Béchar (Colomb-Bechar) . . . 31°37' N, 002°13' W
Bejaïa (Bougie) . . . 36°45' N, 005°05' E
Beni Abbès . . . 30°08' N, 002°10' W
Biskra (Beskra) . . . 34°51' N, 005°44' E
Bordj Bou Arréridj . . . 36°04' N, 004°47' E
Chlef (El-Asnam or Orleansville) . . . 36°10' N, 001°20' E
Constantine (Qacentina) . . . 36°22' N, 006°37' E
Djelfa . . . 34°40' N, 003°15' E
El-Oued . . . 33°20' N, 006°53' E
Ghardaïa . . . 32°29' N, 003°40' E
In Salah (Aïn Salah) . . . 27°13' N, 002°28' E
Kenadsa . . . 31°34' N, 002°26' E
Médéa (Lemdiyya) . . . 36°16' N, 002°45' E
Mostaganem (Mestghanem) . . . 35°56' N, 000°05' E
Oran (Wahran) . . . 35°42' N, 000°38' W
Ouargla (Warqla) . . . 31°57' N, 005°20' E
Saïda . . . 34°50' N, 000°09' E
Sétif (Stif) . . . 36°12' N, 005°24' E
Sidi Bel Abbés . . . 35°12' N, 000°38' W
Skikda (Philippeville) . . . 36°52' N, 006°54' E
Souk-Ahras . . . 36°17' N, 007°57' E
Tamanrasset (Fort Laperrine) . . . 22°47' N, 005°31' W
Tébessa (Tbessa or Theveste) . . . 35°24' N, 008°07' E
Tiaret (Tihert or Tagdempt) . . . 35°22' N, 001°19' E
Tindouf . . . 27°42' N, 008°09' W
Tlemcen (Tlemsen) . . . 34°52' N, 001°19' W
Touggourt . . . 33°06' N, 006°04' E

ANDORRA . . . . page 4

Andorra la Vella . . . 42°30' N, 001°30' E
Canillo . . . 42°34' N, 001°35' E
Encamp . . . 42°32' N, 001°35' E
La Massana . . . 42°33' N, 001°31' E
Les Escaldes . . . 42°30' N, 001°32' E
Ordino . . . 42°34' N, 001°30' E
Sant Julià de Lòria . . . 42°28' N, 001°30' E
Soldeu . . . 42°35' N, 001°40' E

ANGOLA . . . . page 5

Benguela (São Félipe de Benguela) . . . 12°35' S, 013°24' E
Caála (Robert Williams) . . . 12°51' S, 015°34' E
Cabinda . . . 05°33' S, 012°12' E
Cacolo . . . 10°08' S, 019°16' E
Caconda . . . 13°44' S, 015°04' E
Caluquembe . . . 13°52' S, 014°26' E
Camacupa (General Machado) . . . 12°01' S, 017°29' E
Cangamba . . . 13°41' S, 019°52' E
Catumbela . . . 12°26' S, 013°33' E
Cubal . . . 13°02' S, 014°15' E
Cuchi . . . 14°39' S, 016°54' E
Damba . . . 06°41' S, 015°08' E
Gabela . . . 10°51' S, 014°22' E
Ganda (Mariano Machado) . . . 13°01' S, 014°38' E
Huambo (Nova Lisboa) . . . 12°46' S, 015°44' E
Kuito (Silva Porto) . . . 12°23' S, 016°56' E
Lobito . . . 12°21' S, 013°33' E
Luanda (São Paulo de Luanda) . . . 08°49' S, 013°15' E
Luau . . . 10°42' S, 022°14' E
Lubango (Sá da Bandeira) . . . 14°55' S, 013°30' E
Lucapa . . . 08°25' S, 020°45' E
Luena (Vila Luso) . . . 11°47' S, 019°55' E
Malanje . . . 09°32' S, 016°20' E
Mavinga . . . 15°48' S, 020°21' E
M'banza Congo (São Salvador) . . . 06°16' S, 014°15' E
Menongue (Serpa Pinto) . . . 14°40' S, 017°42' E
Namibe (Moçâmedes, or Mossamedes) . . . 15°10' S, 012°09' E
N'dalatando (Dalatando, or Salazar) . . . 09°18' S, 014°55' E
Negage . . . 07°46' S, 015°16' E
Nóqui . . . 05°51' S, 013°26' E
Ondjiva . . . 17°04' S, 015°44' E
Porto Amboin . . . 10°44' S, 013°45' E
Quimbele . . . 06°31' S, 016°13' E
Saurimo (Henrique de Carvalho) . . . 09°39' S, 020°24' E
Soyo . . . 06°08' S, 012°22' E
Sumbe (Novo Redondo) . . . 11°12' S, 013°50' E
Tombua (Porto Alexandre) . . . 15°48' S, 011°51' E
Uige (Carmona) . . . 07°37' S, 015°03' E
Waku Kungo (Santa Comba) . . . 11°21' S, 015°07' E

ANTIGUA AND BARBUDA . . . . page 6

Codrington . . . 17°38' N, 061°50' W
St. John's . . . 17°06' N, 061°51' W

ARGENTINA . . . . page 7

Avellaneda . . . 29°07' S, 059°40' W
Bahía Blanca . . . 38°43' S, 062°17' W
Buenos Aires . . . 34°36' S, 058°27' W
Comodoro Rivadavia . . . 45°52' S, 067°30' W
Concordia . . . 31°24' S, 058°02' W
Córdoba . . . 31°24' S, 064°11' W
Corrientes . . . 27°28' S, 058°50' W
Formosa . . . 26°11' S, 058°11' W
La Plata . . . 34°55' S, 057°57' W
La Rioja . . . 29°26' S, 066°51' W
Luján . . . 34°34' S, 059°07' W
Mar del Plata . . . 38°00' S, 057°33' W
Mercedes . . . 33°40' S, 065°28' W

Neuquén . . . . 38°57' S, 068°04' W
Paraná . . . . 31°44' S, 060°32' W
Posadas . . . . 27°23' S, 055°53' W
Rawson . . . . 43°18' S, 065°06' W
Resistencia . . . . 27°27' S, 058°59' W
Río Gallegos . . . . 51°38' S, 069°13' W
Salta . . . . 24°47' S, 065°25' W
San Miguel de Tucumán . . . 26°49' S, 065°13' W
San Rafael . . . . 34°36' S, 068°20' W
Santa Fe . . . . 31°38' S, 060°42' W
Santa Rosa . . . . 36°37' S, 064°17' W
Santiago del Estero . . . . 27°47' S, 064°16' W
Tandil . . . . 37°19' S, 059°09' W
Tigre . . . . 34°25' S, 058°34' W
Ushuaia . . . . 54°48' S, 068°18' W
Viedma . . . . 40°48' S, 063°00' W
Villa María . . . . 32°25' S, 063°15' W

ARMENIA . . . . page 8

Abovyan . . . . 40°15' N, 044°35' E
Alaverdi . . . . 41°08' N, 044°39' E
Ararat . . . . 39°50' N, 044°42' E
Artashat (Artaxata) . . . . . . 39°57' N, 044°33' E
Artik . . . . 40°37' N, 043°59' E
Charentsavan . . . . 40°24' N, 044°38' E
Dilijan . . . . 40°44' N, 044°52' E
Ejmiadzin (Echmiadzin) . . . 40°10' N, 044°18' E
Goris (Geryusy) . . . . 39°30' N, 046°23' E
Gyumri (Kumayri, Alexandropol, or Leninakan) . . . . 40°48' N, 043°50' E
Hoktemberyan (Oktemberyan) . . . . 40°09' N, 044°02' E
Hrazdan (Razdan) . . . . 40°29' N, 044°46' E
Ijevan . . . . 40°51' N, 045°09' E
Kamo (Nor-Bayazet) . . . . . . 40°21' N, 045°08' E
Kapan . . . . 39°12' N, 046°24' E
Sevan . . . . 40°32' N, 044°56' E
Spitak . . . . 40°49' N, 044°16' E
Stepanavan . . . . 41°01' N, 044°23' E
Vanadzor . . . . 40°48' N, 044°30' E
Yerevan (Erevan) . . . . 40°11' N, 044°30' E

AUSTRALIA . . . . page 9

Adelaide . . . . 34°56' S, 138°36' E
Alice Springs . . . . 23°42' S, 133°53' E
Bowral . . . . 34°28' S, 150°25' E
Brisbane . . . . 27°30' S, 153°01' E
Broken Hill . . . . 31°57' S, 141°26' E
Bunbury . . . . 33°20' S, 115°38' E
Bundaberg . . . . 24°51' S, 152°21' E
Cairns . . . . 16°55' S, 145°46' E
Canberra . . . . 35°20' S, 149°10' E
Darwin . . . . 12°28' S, 130°50' E
Devonport . . . . 41°10' S, 146°21' E
Geelong . . . . 38°09' S, 144°21' E
Geraldton . . . . 28°46' S, 114°36' E
Gladstone . . . . 23°51' S, 151°15' E
Gold Coast . . . . 28°06' S, 153°27' E
Goulburn . . . . 34°45' S, 149°43' E
Hobart . . . . 42°55' S, 147°20' E
Kalgoorlie-Boulder . . . . 30°45' S, 121°28' E
Lismore . . . . 28°48' S, 153°16' E
Mackay . . . . 21°09' S, 149°12' E
Maryborough . . . . 25°32' S, 152°42' E
Melbourne . . . . 37°50' S, 145°00' E
Mount Gambier . . . . 37°50' S, 140°46' E
Mount Isa . . . . 20°44' S, 139°30' E
Newcastle . . . . 32°55' S, 151°45' E
Perth . . . . 31°56' S, 115°50' E
Port Macquarie . . . . 31°26' S, 152°55' E
Rockingham . . . . 32°17' S, 115°43' E
Sydney . . . . 33°53' S, 151°12' E
Toowoomba . . . . 27°33' S, 151°58' E
Warrnambool . . . . 38°23' S, 142°29' E
Whyalla . . . . 33°02' S, 137°35' E
Wollongong . . . . 34°25' S, 150°54' E

AUSTRIA . . . . page 10

Amstetten . . . . 48°07' N, 014°52' E
Baden . . . . 48°01' N, 016°14' E
Branau [am Inn] . . . . 48°16' N, 013°02' E
Bregenz . . . . 47°30' N, 009°46' E
Bruck [an der Leitha] . . . . . 47°25' N, 015°17' E
Dornbirn . . . . 47°25' N, 009°44' E
Eisenstadt . . . . 47°51' N, 016°31' E
Feldkirch . . . . 47°14' N, 009°36' E
Freistadt . . . . 48°30' N, 014°30' E
Fürstenfeld . . . . 47°03' N, 016°05' E
Gmünd . . . . 48°46' N, 014°59' E
Gmunden . . . . 47°55' N, 013°48' E
Graz . . . . 47°04' N, 015°27' E
Hallein . . . . 47°41' N, 013°06' E
Innsbruck . . . . 47°16' N, 011°24' E
Kapfenberg . . . . 47°26' N, 015°18' E
Klagenfurt . . . . 46°38' N, 014°18' E
Klosterneuburg . . . . 48°18' N, 016°19' E
Köflach . . . . 47°04' N, 015°05' E
Krems an der Donau . . . . . . 48°25' N, 015°36' E
Kufstein . . . . 47°35' N, 012°10' E
Laa [an der Thaya] . . . . 48°43' N, 016°23' E
Landeck . . . . 47°08' N, 010°34' E
Leibnitz . . . . 46°46' N, 015°32' E
Leoben (Donawitz) . . . . 47°23' N, 015°06' E
Leonding . . . . 48°16' N, 014°15' E
Liezen . . . . 47°34' N, 014°14' E
Linz . . . . 48°18' N, 014°18' E
Neunkirchen . . . . 47°43' N, 016°05' E
Oberwart . . . . 47°17' N, 016°12' E
Radenthein . . . . 46°48' N, 013°43' E
Salzburg . . . . 47°48' N, 013°02' E
Sankt Pölten . . . . 48°12' N, 015°38' E
Schrems . . . . 48°47' N, 015°04' E
Steyr . . . . 48°03' N, 014°25' E
Telfs . . . . 47°18' N, 011°04' E
Ternitz . . . . 47°43' N, 016°02' E
Traun . . . . 48°13' N, 014°14' E
Trofaiach . . . . 47°25' N, 015°00' E

Vienna (Wien)	48°12' N,	016°22' E
Villach	46°36' N,	013°50' E
Vöcklabruck	48°01' N,	013°39' E
Völkermarkt	46°39' N,	014°38' E
Weiner Neustadt	47°48' N,	016°15' E
Wolfsberg	46°50' N,	014°50' E

AZERBAIJAN . . . . . page 11

Ağcabädi	40°02' N,	047°28' E
Ağdam	39°59' N,	046°57' E
Ağstafa	41°07' N,	045°27' E
Ağsu	40°34' N,	048°24' E
Äli-Bayramli	39°55' N,	048°56' E
Astara	38°26' N,	048°53' E
Baku (Bakı)	40°23' N,	049°51' E
Balakän	41°43' N,	046°24' E
Bärdä	40°24' N,	047°10' E
Daškäsän	40°32' N,	046°07' E
Däväçi	41°12' N,	048°59' E
Füzuli	39°36' N,	047°09' E
Gäncä (Gyandzha, Gandzha, Kirovabad, or Yelizavetpol)	40°41' N,	046°22' E
Göyçay	40°39' N,	047°45' E
İmişli	40°47' N,	048°09' E
İsmayıllı	40°47' N,	048°09' E
Kürdämir	40°21' N,	048°11' E
Länkäran	38°45' N,	048°50' E
Masallı	39°03' N,	048°40' E
Mingäçevir (Mingechaur)	40°45' N,	047°03' E
Nakhichevan (Naxcivan)	39°12' N,	045°24' E
Neftçala	39°23' N,	049°16' E
Ordubad	38°54' N,	046°01' E
Qäbälä (Kutkashen)	40°58' N,	047°52' E
Qax	41°25' N,	046°55' E
Qazax	41°05' N,	045°22' E
Qazimämmäd	40°03' N,	048°56' E
Şäki (Sheki, Nukha)	41°12' N,	047°12' E
Salyan	39°35' N,	048°59' E
Şamaxı	40°38' N,	048°39' E
Şämkir	40°50' N,	046°02' E
Siyäzän	41°04' N,	049°02' E
Sumqayit	40°36' N,	049°38' E
Tovuz	40°59' N,	045°36' E
Ucar	40°31' N,	047°39' E
Xaçmaz	41°28' N,	048°48' E
Xankändi (Stepanakert)	39°50' N,	046°46' E
Xudat	41°38' N,	048°41' E
Yevlax	40°37' N,	047°09' E
Zaqatala	41°38' N,	046°39' E

BAHAMAS, THE . . page 12

Dunmore Town	25°30' N,	076°39' W
Freeport	26°32' N,	078°42' W
Matthew Town	20°57' N,	073°40' W
Nassau	25°05' N,	077°21' W
Old Bight	24°15' N,	075°21' W
West End	26°41' N,	078°58' W

BAHRAIN . . . . page 13

Ad Dūr	25°59' N,	050°37' E
Al-Ḥadd	26°15' N,	050°39' E
Al Jasrah	26°10' N,	050°27' E
Al Mālikīyah	37°10' N,	042°08' E
Al-Muharraq	26°16' N,	050°37' E
Ar-Rifa'	26°07' N,	050°33' E
Ar-Rifā'ash-Sharqī	26°07' N,	050°34' E
Ar-Rumaythah	25°55' N,	050°33' E
'Awāli	26°05' N,	050°33' E
Bārbaār	26°14' N,	050°29' E
Madīnat Ḥamad	26°08' N,	050°30' E
Madīnat 'Īsā	26°10' N,	050°33' E
Manama	26°13' N,	050°35' E

BANGLADESH . . . . page 14

Azmiriganj	24°33' N,	091°14' E
Bāgerhāt	22°40' N,	089°48' E
Bājitpur	24°13' N,	090°57' E
Barisāl	22°42' N,	090°22' E
Bhairab Bāzār	24°04' N,	090°58' E
Bogra	24°51' N,	089°22' E
Brāhmanbāria	23°59' N,	091°07' E
Chālna Port (Mongla Port)	22°28' N,	089°35' E
Chāndpur	23°13' N,	090°39' E
Chaumuhāni (Chowmohani)	22°56' N,	091°07' E
Chittagong	22°20' N,	091°50' E
Chuadānga	23°38' N,	088°51' E
Comilla (Kumillā)	23°27' N,	091°12' E
Cox's Bāzār	21°26' N,	091°59' E
Dhaka (Dacca or Dhakal)	23°43' N,	090°25' E
Dinājpur	25°38' N,	088°38' E
Farīdpur	23°36' N,	089°50' E
Gopālpur	24°50' N,	090°06' E
Ishurdi (Ishurda)	24°08' N,	089°05' E
Jamālpur	24°55' N,	089°56' E
Jessore	23°10' N,	089°13' E
Jhenida	23°33' N,	089°10' E
Khulna	22°48' N,	089°33' E
Kishorganj	24°26' N,	090°46' E
Kurigrām	25°49' N,	089°39' E
Kushtia	23°55' N,	089°07' E
Lākshām	23°14' N,	091°08' E
Lakshmipur	22°57' N,	090°50' E
Lālmanir Hāt (Lalmonirhat)	25°54' N,	089°27' E
Mādārīpur	23°10' N,	090°12' E
Mymensingh (Nasirābād)	24°45' N,	090°24' E
Naogaon	24°47' N,	088°56' E
Nārāyanganj	23°37' N,	090°30' E
Narsinghdi (Narsingdi)	23°55' N,	090°43' E
Nawābganj	24°36' N,	088°17' E
Noākhāli (Sudhárám)	22°49' N,	091°06' E
Pābna (Pubna)	24°00' N,	089°15' E
Patuākhāli	22°21' N,	090°21' E
Rājshāhi	24°22' N,	088°36' E
Rāngāmāti	22°38' N,	092°12' E

Rangpur . . . . . 25°45' N, 089°15' E
Saidpur . . . . . 25°47' N, 088°54' E
Sātkhira . . . . . 22°43' N, 089°06' E
Sherpur . . . . . 24°41' N, 089°25' E
Sherpur . . . . . 25°01' N, 090°01' E
Sirajganj (Seraganj) . . . . . 24°27' N, 089°43' E
Sylhet . . . . . 24°54' N, 091°52' E
Tangail . . . . . 24°15' N, 089°55' E

BARBADOS . . . . page 15

Bennetts . . . . . 13°10' N, 059°36' W
Bridgetown . . . . . 13°06' N, 059°37' W
Holetown . . . . . 13°11' N, 059°39' W
Marchfield . . . . . 13°07' N, 059°28' W
Massiah . . . . . 13°10' N, 059°29' W
Oistins . . . . . 13°04' N, 059°32' W
Portland . . . . . 13°16' N, 059°36' W
Prospect . . . . . 13°08' N, 059°36' W
Speightstown . . . . . 13°15' N, 059°39' W
Westmoreland . . . . . 13°13' N, 059°37' W

BELARUS . . . . page 16

Baranovichi . . . . . 53°08' N, 026°02' E
Beloözersk
(Beloozyorsk) . . . . . 52°28' N, 025°10' E
Bobruysk . . . . . 53°09' N, 029°14' E
Borisov (Barysaw) . . . . . 54°15' N, 028°30' E
Braslav . . . . . 55°38' N, 027°02' E
Brest (Brest-Litovsk) . . . . . 52°06' N, 023°42' E
Bykhov . . . . . 53°31' N, 030°15' E
Chashniki . . . . . 54°52' N, 029°10' E
Cherikov . . . . . 53°34' N, 031°23' E
Cherven . . . . . 53°42' N, 028°26' E
Dobrush . . . . . 52°25' N, 031°19' E
Dokshitsy . . . . . 54°54' N, 027°46' E
Drogichin . . . . . 52°11' N, 025°09' E
Dyatlovo . . . . . 53°28' N, 025°24' E
Dzerzhinsk . . . . . 53°41' N, 027°08' E
Gantsevichi . . . . . 52°45' N, 026°26' E
Glubokoye . . . . . 55°08' N, 027°41' E
Gorki . . . . . 54°17' N, 030°59' E
Gorodok . . . . . 55°28' N, 029°59' E
Grodno (Hrodna) . . . . . 53°41' N, 023°50' E
Homyel' (Gomel) . . . . . 52°25' N, 031°00' E
Kletsk . . . . . 53°04' N, 026°38' E
Klimovichi . . . . . 53°37' N, 031°58' E
Kobrin . . . . . 52°13' N, 024°21' E
Kossovo . . . . . 52°45' N, 025°09' E
Kostyukovichi . . . . . 53°20' N, 032°03' E
Lepel . . . . . 54°53' N, 028°42' E
Lida . . . . . 53°53' N, 025°18' E
Luninets . . . . . 52°15' N, 026°48' E
Mahilyow
(Mogilyov, Mahilyou) . . . 53°54' N, 030°21' E
Malorita . . . . . 51°47' N, 024°05' E
Minsk (Mensk) . . . . . 53°54' N, 027°34' E
Molodechno
(Maladzyechna) . . . . . 54°19' N, 026°51' E
Mosty . . . . . 53°25' N, 024°32' E
Mozyr (Mazyr) . . . . . 52°03' N, 029°16' E
Mstislavl . . . . . 54°02' N, 031°44' E
Narovlya . . . . . 51°48' N, 029°30' E
Nesvizh . . . . . 53°13' N, 026°40' E
Novolukomi . . . . . 54°39' N, 029°13' E
Orsha . . . . . 54°31' N, 030°26' E
Oshmyany . . . . . 54°25' N, 025°56' E
Osipovichi . . . . . 53°18' N, 028°38' E
Petrikov . . . . . 52°08' N, 028°30' E
Pinsk . . . . . 52°07' N, 026°07' E
Polotsk (Polatsk) . . . . . 55°29' N, 028°47' E
Pruzhany . . . . . 52°33' N, 024°28' E
Rechitsa (Rechytsa) . . . . . 52°22' N, 030°23' E
Slutsk . . . . . 53°01' N, 027°33' E
Soligorsk (Salihorsk) . . . . . 52°48' N, 027°32' E
Starye Dorogi . . . . . 53°02' N, 028°16' E
Stolbtsy . . . . . 53°29' N, 026°44' E
Stolin . . . . . 51°53' N, 026°51' E
Svetlogorsk
(Svetlahorsk) . . . . . 52°38' N, 029°46' E
Verkhnedvinsk . . . . . 55°47' N, 027°56' E
Vetka . . . . . 52°33' N, 031°10' E
Vileyka . . . . . 54°30' N, 026°55' E
Vitebsk (Vitsyebsk) . . . . . 55°12' N, 030°11' E
Volkovysk . . . . . 53°10' N, 024°28' E
Vysokoye . . . . . 52°22' N, 023°22' E
Yelsk . . . . . 51°48' N, 029°09' E
Zaslavl . . . . . 54°00' N, 027°17' E
Zhitkovichi . . . . . 52°14' N, 027°52' E
Zhodino . . . . . 54°06' N, 028°21' E

BELGIUM . . . . page 17

Aalst (Alost) . . . . . 50°56' N, 004°02' E
Aalter . . . . . 51°05' N, 003°27' E
Antwerp (Antwerpen,
Anvers) . . . . . 51°13' N, 004°25' E
Arlon (Aarlen) . . . . . 49°41' N, 005°49' E
Ath . . . . . 50°38' N, 003°47' E
Athus . . . . . 49°34' N, 005°50' E
Bastogne . . . . . 50°00' N, 005°43' E
Bouillon . . . . . 49°48' N, 005°04' E
Boussu . . . . . 50°26' N, 003°48' E
Braine-l'Alleud . . . . . 50°41' N, 004°22' E
Brecht . . . . . 51°21' N, 004°38' E
Bree . . . . . 51°08' N, 005°36' E
Brugge (Bruges) . . . . . 51°13' N, 003°14' E
Brussels (Brussel,
Bruxelles) . . . . . 50°50' N, 004°20' E
Charleroi . . . . . 50°25' N, 004°26' E
Ciney . . . . . 50°18' N, 005°06' E
Couvin . . . . . 50°03' N, 004°29' E
Dinant . . . . . 50°16' N, 004°55' E
Eeklo . . . . . 51°11' N, 003°34' E
Enghien (Edingen) . . . . . 50°42' N, 004°02' E
Eupen . . . . . 50°38' N, 006°02' E
Florenville . . . . . 49°42' N, 005°18' E
Geel (Gheel) . . . . . 51°10' N, 005°00' E
Genk (Genck) . . . . . 50°58' N, 005°30' E
Ghent (Gand, Gent) . . . . . 51°03' N, 003°43' E
Hasselt . . . . . 50°56' N, 005°20' E
Ixelles (Elsene) . . . . . 50°50' N, 004°22' E
Kapellen . . . . . 51°19' N, 004°26' E

Kortrijk (Courtrai) . . . . 50°50' N, 003°16' E
La Louviere . . . . 50°28' N, 004°11' E
Liège (Luttich) . . . . 50°38' N, 005°34' E
Louvain (Leuven) . . . . 50°53' N, 004°42' E
Marche-en-Famenne . . . . . . 50°12' N, 005°20' E
Mechelen (Malines) . . . . . . 51°02' N, 004°28' E
Mons (Bergen) . . . . 50°27' N, 003°56' E
Mouscron (Moeskroen) . . . 50°44' N, 003°13' E
Namur (Namen) . . . . 50°28' N, 004°52' E
Neerpelt. . . . . 51°13' N, 005°25' E
Ostend (Oostende). . . . . . . 51°13' N, 002°55' E
Peer . . . . 51°08' N, 005°28' E
Péruwelz . . . . 50°31' N, 003°35' E
Philippeville . . . . 50°12' N, 004°32' E
Riemst . . . . 50°48' N, 005°36' E
Roeselare (Roulers) . . . . . . 50°57' N, 003°08' E
Saint-Hubert . . . . 50°01' N, 005°23' E
Schaerbeek
(Schaarbeek) . . . . 50°51' N, 004°23' E
Seraing. . . . . 50°36' N, 005°29' E
Sint-Niklaas . . . . 51°10' N, 004°08' E
Spa. 50°30' N, 005°52' E
Spy. 50°29' N, 004°42' E
Staden . . . . 50°59' N, 003°01' E
Tessenderlo . . . . 51°04' N, 005°05' E
Thuin. . . . . 50°20' N, 004°17' E
Tienen . . . . 50°48' N, 004°57' E
Torhout. . . . . 51°04' N, 003°06' E
Tournai (Doornik) . . . . 50°36' N, 003°23' E
Turnhout. . . . . 51°19' N, 004°57' E
Uccle (Ukkel) . . . . 50°48' N, 004°19' E
Verviers. . . . . 50°35' N, 005°52' E
Wanze . . . . 50°32' N, 005°13' E
Waremme . . . . 50°41' N, 005°15' E
Waterloo . . . . 50°43' N, 004°23' E
Zwijndrecht. . . . . 51°13' N, 004°20' E

BELIZE . . . . page 18

Belize City. . . . . 17°30' N, 088°12' W
Belmopan . . . . 17°15' N, 088°46' W
Benque Viejo. . . . . 17°05' N, 089°08' W
Bermudian Landing . . . . . . 17°33' N, 088°31' W
Corozal . . . . 18°24' N, 088°24' W
Dangriga (Stann Creek) . . . 16°58' N, 088°13' W
Monkey River . . . . 16°22' N, 088°29' W
Orange Walk . . . . 18°06' N, 088°33' W
Pembroke Hall . . . . 18°17' N, 088°27' W
Punta Gorda . . . . 16°07' N, 088°48' W
San Ignacio (El Cavo) . . . . . 17°10' N, 89°04' W

BENIN . . . . page 19

Abomey. . . . . 07°11' N, 001°59' E
Cotonou. . . . . 06°21' N, 002°26' E
Djougou. . . . . 09°42' N, 001°40' E
Kandi . . . . 11°08' N, 002°56' E
Natitingou . . . . 10°19' N, 001°22' E
Parakou . . . . 09°21' N, 002°37' E
Porto-Novo . . . . 06°29' N, 002°37' E
Savalou . . . . 07°56' N, 001°58' E
Savé . . . . 08°02' N, 002°29' E

BHUTAN . . . . page 20

Bumthang (Byakar or
Jakar) . . . . 27°32' N, 090°43' E
Chhukha . . . . 27°04' N, 089°35' E
Chima Kothi . . . . 27°03' N, 089°35' E
Chirang . . . . 27°04' N, 090°06' E
Dagana (Taga). . . . . 27°03' N, 089°55' E
Deothang (Dewangiri) . . . . 26°52' N, 091°28' E
Domphu (Damphu). . . . . . . 27°01' N, 090°08' E
Gaylegphug (Gelekphu,
Hatisar or Hatsar) . . . . . . 26°51' N, 090°29' E
Ha . . . . 27°22' N, 089°17' E
Kanglung (Kanglum). . . . . . 27°16' N, 091°30' E
Lhuntsi . . . . 27°39' N, 091°09' E
Mongar . . . . 27°15' N, 091°12' E
Paro . . . . 27°26' N, 089°25' E
Pema Gatsel . . . . 26°59' N, 091°26' E
Phuntsholing. . . . . 26°52' N, 089°26' E
Punakha. . . . . 27°37' N, 089°52' E
Samchi (Tori Bari) . . . . 26°53' N, 089°07' E
Samdrup Jongkhar . . . . 26°47' N, 091°30' E
Shemgang . . . . 27°12' N, 090°38' E
Shompangkha (Sarbhang) . 26°52' N, 090°16' E
Sibsoo . . . . 27°01' N, 088°55' E
Tashigang . . . . 27°20' N, 091°32' E
Thimphu . . . . 27°28' N, 089°38' E
Tongsa. . . . . 27°31' N, 090°30' E
Wangdü Phodrang . . . . 27°29' N, 089°54' E

BOLIVIA . . . . page 21

Apolo. . . . . 14°43' S, 068°31' W
Benavides . . . . 12°38' S, 067°20' W
Bermejo. . . . . 22°44' S, 064°21' W
Camargo . . . . 20°39' S, 065°13' W
Camiri . . . . 20°03' S, 063°31' W
Caranavi . . . . 15°46' S, 067°36' W
Chulumani. . . . . 16°24' S, 067°31' W
Cobija . . . . 11°02' S, 068°44' W
Cochabamba. . . . . 17°24' S, 066°09' W
Concepción. . . . . 16°15' S, 062°04' W
Copacabana . . . . 16°10' S, 069°05' W
Corocoro. . . . . 17°12' S, 068°29' W
Cuevo . . . . 20°27' S, 063°32' W
El Carmen . . . . 18°49' S, 058°33' W
Fortaleza . . . . 10°37' S, 066°13' W
Guayaramerin . . . . 10°48' S, 065°23' W
Huacaya. . . . . 20°45' S, 063°43' W
Huachacalla. . . . . 18°45' S, 068°17' W
Ixiamas . . . . 13°45' S, 068°09' W
La Esperanza. . . . . 14°34' S, 062°10' W
La Horquilla . . . . 12°34' S, 064°25' W
La Paz . . . . 16°30' S, 068°09' W
Llallagua . . . . 18°25' S, 066°38' W
Llica. . . . . 19°52' S, 068°16' W
Loreto . . . . 15°13' S, 064°40' W

Magdalena	13°20' S,	064°08' W
Monteagudo	19°49' S,	063°59' W
Montero	17°20' S,	063°15' W
Oruro	17°59' S,	067°09' W
Porvenir	11°15' S,	068°41' W
Potosí	19°35' S,	065°45' W
Puerto Acosta	15°32' S,	069°15' W
Puerto Rico	11°05' S,	067°38' W
Punata	17°33' S,	065°50' W
Quetena	22°10' S,	067°25' W
Quillacollo	17°26' S,	066°17' W
Reyes	14°19' S,	067°23' W
Riberalta	10°59' S,	066°06' W
Roboré	18°20' S,	059°45' W
Samaipata	18°09' S,	063°52' W
San Ignacio	16°23' S,	060°59' W
San José	17°51' S,	060°47' W
San Matías	16°22' S,	058°24' W
San Pablo	15°41' S,	063°15' W
San Ramón	13°17' S,	064°43' W
Santa Cruz	17°48' S,	063°10' W
Santiago	19°22' S,	060°51' W
Siglo Veinte	18°22' S,	066°38' W
Sucre	19°02' S,	065°17' W
Tarabuco	19°10' S,	064°57' W
Tarija	21°31' S,	064°45' W
Tiahuanacu (Tiwanacu)	16°33' S,	068°42' W
Trinidad	14°47' S,	064°47' W
Tupiza	21°27' S,	065°43' W
Uyuni	20°28' S,	066°50' W
Villazón	22°06' S,	065°36' W
Yacuiba	22°02' S,	063°45' W

BOSNIA AND HERZEGOVINA . . . page 22

Banja Luka	44°46' N,	017°10' E
Bihać	44°49' N,	015°52' E
Bijeljina	44°45' N,	019°13' E
Bosanska Gradiška	45°09' N,	017°15' E
Bosanski Šamac	45°04' N,	018°28' E
Brčko	44°52' N,	018°49' E
Derventa	44°59' N,	017°55' E
Goražde	43°40' N,	018°59' E
Jablanica	43°39' N,	017°45' E
Jajce	44°21' N,	017°17' E
Kladanj	44°14' N,	018°42' E
Ključ	44°32' N,	016°47' E
Konjic	43°39' N,	017°58' E
Mostar	43°21' N,	017°49' E
Prijedor	44°59' N,	016°42' E
Sanski Most	44°46' N,	016°40' E
Sarajevo	43°50' N,	018°25' E
Srebrenica	44°06' N,	019°18' E
Travnik	44°14' N,	017°40' E
Tuzla	44°33' N,	018°41' E
Vareš	44°10' N,	018°20' E
Zenica	44°13' N,	017°55' E

BOTSWANA . . . . . . page 23

Francistown	21°13' S,	027°31' E
Gaborone	24°40' S,	025°54' E
Ghanzi	21°34' S,	021°47' E
Kanye	24°59' S,	025°21' E
Kasane	17°49' S,	025°09' E
Letlhakane	21°25' S,	025°35' E
Lobatse	25°13' S,	025°40' E
Mahalapye	23°04' S,	026°50' E
Maun	19°59' S,	023°25' E
Mochudi	24°25' S,	026°09' E
Orapa	21°17' S,	025°22' E
Palapye (Palapye Road)	22°33' S,	027°08' E
Ramotswa	24°52' S,	025°49' E
Selebi-Phikwe	22°01' S,	027°50' E
Serowe	22°23' S,	026°43' E
Shashe	21°26' S,	027°27' E
Tlokweng	24°32' S,	025°58' E
Tshabong	26°03' S,	022°27' E
Tshane	24°05' S,	021°54' E

BRAZIL . . . . page 24

Aracaju	10°55' S,	037°04' W
Belém (Para)	01°27' S,	048°29' W
Belo Horizonte	19°55' S,	043°56' W
Boa Vista	02°49' N,	060°30' W
Brasília	15°47' S,	047°55' W
Campina Grande	07°13' S,	035°53' W
Campo Grande	20°27' S,	054°37' W
Canoas	29°56' S,	051°11' W
Caxias do Sul	29°10' S,	051°11' W
Curitiba	25°25' S,	049°15' W
Duque de Caxias	22°47' S,	043°18' W
Florianópolis	27°35' S,	048°34' W
Fortaleza	03°43' S,	038°30' W
Goiânia	16°40' S,	049°16' W
Itabuna	14°48' S,	039°16' W
João Pessoa	07°07' S,	034°52' W
Macapá	00°02' N,	051°03' W
Maceió	09°40' S,	035°43' W
Manaus	03°08' S,	060°01' W
Natal	05°47' S,	035°13' W
Nova Iguaçu	22°45' S,	043°27' W
Novo Hamburgo	29°41' S,	051°08' W
Passo Fundo	28°15' S,	052°24' W
Pôrto Alegre	30°04' S,	051°11' W
Pôrto Velho	08°46' S,	063°54' W
Recife	08°03' S,	034°54' W
Rio Branco	09°58' S,	067°48' W
Rio de Janeiro	22°54' S,	043°14' W
Rio Grande	32°02' S,	052°05' W
Salvador	12°59' S,	038°31' W
Santarém	02°26' S,	054°42' W
Santo André	23°40' S,	046°31' W
São Gonçalo	22°51' S,	043°04' W
São José do Rio Prêto	20°48' S,	049°23' W
São Luís	02°31' S,	044°16' W

São Paulo	23°32' S, 046°37' W
Tefé	03°22' S, 064°42' W
Teresina	05°05' S, 042°49' W
Vitória	20°19' S, 040°21' W

BRUNEI .... page 25

Badas	04°36' N, 114°27' E
Bandar Seri Begawan (Brunei)	04°53' N, 114°56' E
Bangar	04°43' N, 115°04' E
Kuala Belait	04°36' N, 114°14' E
Labi	04°23' N, 114°27' E
Labu	04°45' N, 115°11' E
Muara	05°02' N, 115°04' E
Seria	04°37' N, 114°19' E
Sukang	04°19' N, 114°37' E
Tutong	04°48' N, 114°39' E

BULGARIA .... page 26

Balchik	43°25' N, 028°10' E
Berkovitsa	43°14' N, 023°07' E
Blagoevgrad	42°01' N, 023°06' E
Burgas	42°30' N, 027°28' E
Dimitrovgrad	42°03' N, 025°36' E
Dobrich (Tolbukhin)	43°34' N, 027°50' E
Dulovo	43°49' N, 027°09' E
Gabrovo	42°52' N, 025°19' E
Grudovo	42°21' N, 027°10' E
Kazanlŭk	42°37' N, 025°24' E
Khaskovo	41°56' N, 025°33' E
Kŭrdzhali	41°39' N, 025°22' E
Kyustendil	42°17' N, 022°41' E
Lom	43°49' N, 023°14' E
Lovech	43°08' N, 024°43' E
Montana (Mikhaylovgrad)	43°25' N, 023°13' E
Nikopol	43°42' N, 024°54' E
Pazardzhik	42°12' N, 024°20' E
Pernik (Dimitrovo)	42°36' N, 023°02' E
Petrich	41°24' N, 023°13' E
Pleven	43°25' N, 024°37' E
Plovdiv	42°09' N, 024°45' E
Razgrad	43°32' N, 026°31' E
Ruse	43°50' N, 025°57' E
Shumen (Kolarovgrad)	43°16' N, 026°55' E
Silistra	44°07' N, 027°16' E
Sliven	42°40' N, 026°19' E
Sofia	42°41' N, 023°19' E
Stara Zagora	42°25' N, 025°38' E
Troyan	42°53' N, 024°43' E
Varna	43°13' N, 027°55' E
Veliko Tŭrnovo	43°04' N, 025°39' E
Velingrad	42°01' N, 024°00' E
Vidin	43°59' N, 022°52' E
Vratsa (Vraca)	43°12' N, 023°33' E
Vrŭv	44°11' N, 022°44' E
Yambol	42°29' N, 026°30' E

BURKINA FASO ... page 27

Banfora	10°38' N, 004°46' W
Bobo-Dioulasso	11°12' N, 004°18' W
Boulsa	12°39' N, 000°34' W
Dédougou	12°28' N, 003°28' W
Diébougou	10°58' N, 003°15' W
Dori	14°02' N, 000°02' W
Fada Ngourma	12°04' N, 000°21' W
Faramana	12°03' N, 004°40' W
Gaoua	10°20' N, 003°11' W
Kaya	13°05' N, 001°05' W
Koudougou	12°15' N, 002°22' W
Koupéla	12°11' N, 000°21' W
Léo	11°06' N, 002°06' W
Nouna	12°44' N, 003°52' W
Orodara	10°59' N, 004°55' W
Ouagadougou	12°22' N, 001°31' W
Ouahigouya	13°35' N, 002°25' W
Pô	11°10' N, 001°09' W
Réo	12°19' N, 002°28' W
Tenkodogo	11°47' N, 000°22' W
Yako	12°58' N, 002°16' W

BURUNDI .... page 28

Bubanza	03°06' S, 029°23' E
Bujumbura	03°23' S, 029°22' E
Bururi	03°57' S, 029°37' E
Gitega	03°26' S, 029°56' E
Muramvya	03°16' S, 029°37' E
Ngozi	02°54' S, 029°50' E
Nyanza-Lac	04°21' S, 029°36' E

CAMBODIA .... page 29

Ânlóng Vêng	14°14' N, 104°05' E
Bâ Kêv	13°42' N, 107°12' E
Battambang (Batdambang)	13°06' N, 103°12' E
Chbar	12°46' N, 107°10' E
Chŏâm Khsant	14°13' N, 104°56' E
Chŏng Kal	13°57' N, 103°35' E
Kâmpóng Cham	12°00' N, 105°27' E
Kâmpóng Chhnăng	12°15' N, 104°40' E
Kâmpóng Kdei	13°07' N, 104°21' E
Kâmpóng Saôm (Sihanoukville)	10°38' N, 103°30' E
Kâmpóng Spoe	11°27' N, 104°32' E
Kâmpóng Thum	12°42' N, 104°54' E
Kampot (Kâmpôt)	10°37' N, 104°11' E
Krâchéh (Kratie)	12°29' N, 106°01' E
Krâkôr	12°32' N, 104°12' E
Krŏng Kaôh Kŏng	11°37' N, 102°59' E
Lumphăt (Lomphat)	13°30' N, 106°59' E
Mémót	11°49' N, 106°11' E
Moŭng Roessei	12°46' N, 103°27' E
Ŏdŏngk	11°48' N, 104°45' E

Péam Prus . . . . 12°19' N, 103°09' E
Phnom Penh (Phnum Penh or Pnom Penh) . . . . 11°33' N, 104°55' E
Phnum Tbêng Méanchey. . . . . 13°49' N, 104°58' E
Phsar Réam (Ream) . . . . . . 10°30' N, 103°37' E
Prey Vêng . . . . 11°29' N, 105°19' E
Pursat (Poŭthĭsăt) . . . . 12°32' N, 103°55' E
Rôviĕng Tbong . . . . 13°21' N, 105°07' E
Sândăn. . . . . 12°42' N, 106°01' E
Senmonorom. . . . . 12°27' N, 107°12' E
Siĕmpang. . . . . 14°07' N, 106°23' E
Siem Reap (Siĕmréab) . . . . 13°22' N, 103°51' E
Sisŏphŏn . . . . 13°35' N, 102°59' E
Stoeng Trêng (Stung Treng) . . . . 13°31' N, 105°58' E
Svay Chék . . . . 13°48' N, 102°58' E
Takêv (Takéo). . . . . 10°59' N, 104°47' E
Tăng Krăsăng . . . . 12°34' N, 105°03' E
Virôchey . . . . 13°59' N, 106°49' E

CAMEROON . . . . . . page 30

Bafang . . . . 05°09' N, 010°11' E
Bafia. . . . . 04°45' N, 011°14' E
Bafoussam. . . . . 05°28' N, 010°25' E
Bamenda . . . . 05°56' N, 010°10' E
Banyo . . . . 06°45' N, 011°49' E
Batibo . . . . 05°50' N, 009°52' E
Batouri. . . . . 04°26' N, 014°22' E
Bertoua . . . . 04°35' N, 013°41' E
Bétaré-Oya . . . . 05°36' N, 014°05' E
Douala . . . . 04°03' N, 009°42' E
Ebolowa. . . . . 02°54' N, 011°09' E
Edéa. . . . . 03°48' N, 010°08' E
Eséka . . . . 03°39' N, 010°46' E
Foumban . . . . 05°43' N, 010°55' E
Garoua. . . . . 09°18' N, 013°24' E
Guider . . . . 09°56' N, 013°57' E
Kaélé . . . . 10°07' N, 014°27' E
Kribi. . . . . 02°57' N, 009°55' E
Kumba . . . . 04°38' N, 009°25' E
Loum . . . . 04°43' N, 009°44' E
Mamfe . . . . 05°46' N, 009°17' E
Maroua . . . . 10°36' N, 014°20' E
Mbalmayo . . . . 03°31' N, 011°30' E
Meiganga. . . . . 06°31' N, 014°18' E
Mora . . . . 11°03' N, 014°09 E
Ngaoundéré. . . . . 07°19' N, 013°35' E
Nkambe . . . . 06°38' N, 010°40' E
Nkongsamba . . . . 04°57' N, 009°56' E
Obala . . . . 04°10' N, 011°32' E
Sangmélima. . . . . 02°56' N, 011°59' E
Tcholliré . . . . 08°24' N, 014°10' E
Tibati . . . . 06°28' N, 012°38' E
Wum . . . . 06°23' N, 010°24' E
Yagoua. . . . . 10°20' N, 015°14' E
Yaoundé . . . . 03°52' N, 011°31' E
Yokadouma. . . . . 03°31' N, 015°03' E

CANADA . . . . page 31

Amos . . . . 48°35' N, 078°07' W
Arctic Bay . . . . 73°02' N, 085°11' W
Baie-Comeau . . . . 49°13' N, 068°09' W
Baker Lake. . . . . 64°15' N, 096°00' W
Banff . . . . 51°10' N, 115°34' W
Barrie. . . . . 44°24' N, 079°40' W
Battleford . . . . 52°44' N, 108°19' W
Beauport . . . . 46°52' N, 071°11' W
Bonavista . . . . 48°39' N, 053°07' W
Brandon. . . . . 49°50' N, 099°57' W
Bridgewater. . . . . 44°23' N, 064°31' W
Brooks . . . . 50°35' N, 111°53' W
Buchans. . . . . 48°49' N, 056°52' W
Burlington . . . . 43°19' N, 079°47' W
Burnaby. . . . . 49°16' N, 122°57' W
Calgary . . . . 51°03' N, 114°05' W
Cambridge Bay . . . . 69°03' N, 105°05' W
Camrose . . . . 53°01' N, 112°50' W
Carbonear . . . . 47°44' N, 053°13' W
Carmacks. . . . . 62°05' N, 136°17' W
Charlesbourg . . . . 46°51' N, 071°16' W
Charlottetown. . . . . 46°14' N, 063°08' W
Chatham . . . . 42°24' N, 082°11' W
Chibougamau . . . . 49°55' N, 074°22' W
Chicoutimi. . . . . 48°26' N, 071°04' W
Churchill . . . . 58°46' N, 094°10' W
Churchill Falls. . . . . 53°33' N, 064°01' W
Cranbrook. . . . . 49°30' N, 115°46' W
Dartmouth. . . . . 44°40' N, 063°34' W
Dauphin. . . . . 51°09' N, 100°03' W
Dawson . . . . 64°04' N, 139°26' W
Dawson Creek. . . . . 55°46' N, 120°14' W
Duck Lake . . . . 52°49' N, 106°14' W
Edmonton . . . . 53°33' N, 113°28' W
Elliot Lake . . . . 46°23' N, 082°42' W
Enderby. . . . . 50°33' N, 119°09' W
Eskimo Point . . . . 61°07' N, 094°03' W
Esterhazy . . . . 50°39' N, 102°05' W
Estevan . . . . 49°08' N, 102°59' W
Faro . . . . 62°14' N, 133°20' W
Fernie. . . . . 49°30' N, 115°04' W
Flin Flon. . . . . 54°46' N, 101°53' W
Fogo. . . . . 49°43' N, 054°17' W
Fort Liard . . . . 60°15' N, 123°28' W
Fort MacLeod . . . . 49°43' N, 113°25' W
Fort McMurray . . . . 56°44' N, 111°23' W
Fort McPherson . . . . 67°27' N, 134°53' W
Fort Qu'Appelle. . . . . 50°46' N, 103°48' W
Fort St. John . . . . 56°15' N, 120°51' W
Fort Smith . . . . 60°00' N, 111°53' W
Fredericton . . . . 45°58' N, 066°39' W
Gagnon . . . . 51°53' N, 068°10' W
Gander. . . . . 48°57' N, 054°37' W
Gaspe. . . . . 48°50' N, 064°29' W
Glace Bay . . . . 46°12' N, 059°57' W
Granby. . . . . 45°24' N, 072°43' W
Grand Bank . . . . 47°06' N, 055°46' W
Grande Prairie. . . . . 55°10' N, 118°48' W

Grand Falls . . . . 48°56' N, 055°40' W
Grimshaw . . . . 56°11' N, 117°36' W
Grise Fiord . . . . 76°25' N, 082°55' W
Haines Junction . . . . 60°45' N, 137°30' W
Halifax . . . . 44°39' N, 063°36' W
Hamilton . . . . 43°15' N, 079°51' W
Happy Valley-Goose Bay . . 53°19' N, 060°20' W
Harbour Grace . . . . 47°42' N, 053°13' W
Hay River. . . . . 60°49' N, 115°47' W
Inuvik. . . . . 68°21' N, 133°43' W
Iqaluit (Frobisher Bay). . . . 63°45' N, 068°31' W
Iroquois Falls . . . . 48°46' N, 080°41' W
Jasper . . . . 52°53' N, 118°05' W
Joliette. . . . . 46°01' N, 073°27' W
Jonquiere . . . . 48°25' N, 071°13' W
Kamloops . . . . 50°40' N, 120°19' W
Kapuskasing . . . . 49°25' N, 082°26' W
Kelowna. . . . . 49°53' N, 119°29' W
Kenora. . . . . 49°47' N, 094°29' W
Kindersley. . . . . 51°28' N, 109°10' W
Kirkland Lake . . . . 48°09' N, 080°02' W
Kitchener. . . . . 43°27' N, 080°29' W
Kuujjuaq (Fort-Chimo) . . . . 58°06' N, 068°25' W
La Baie. . . . . 48°20' N, 070°52' W
Labrador City . . . . 52°57' N, 066°55' W
La Tuque . . . . 47°26' N, 072°47' W
Lethbridge. . . . . 49°42' N, 112°49' W
Lewisporte . . . . 49°14' N, 055°03' W
Liverpool. . . . . 44°02' N, 064°43' W
Lloydminster. . . . . 53°17' N, 110°00' W
London . . . . 42°59' N, 081°14' W
Longueuil. . . . . 45°32' N, 073°30' W
Lynn Lake . . . . 56°51' N, 101°03' W
Maple Creek . . . . 49°55' N, 109°29' W
Marystown . . . . 47°10' N, 055°09' W
Mayo . . . . 63°36' N, 135°54' W
Medicine Hat. . . . . 50°03' N, 110°40' W
Mississauga. . . . . 43°35' N, 079°39' W
Moncton . . . . 46°07' N, 064°48' W
Montmagny . . . . 46°59' N, 070°33' W
Montreal . . . . 45°30' N, 073°36' W
Moose Jaw. . . . . 50°24' N, 105°32' W
Mount Pearl . . . . 47°31' N, 052°47' W
Nanaimo . . . . 49°10' N, 123°56' W
Nelson . . . . 49°30' N, 117°17' W
Nepean . . . . 45°16' N, 075°46' W
New Liskeard . . . . 47°30' N, 079°40' W
Niagara Falls . . . . 43°06' N, 079°04' W
Nickel Centre . . . . 46°34' N, 080°49' W
Nipawin . . . . 53°22' N, 104°00' W
North Battleford . . . . 52°47' N, 108°17' W
North Bay . . . . 46°19' N, 079°28' W
North West River . . . . 53°32' N, 060°08' W
Old Crow . . . . 67°34' N, 139°50' W
Oshawa . . . . 43°54' N, 078°51' W
Ottawa. . . . . 45°25' N, 075°42' W
Pangnirtung. . . . . 66°08' N, 065°43' W
Parry Sound . . . . 45°21' N, 080°02' W
Peace River . . . . 56°14' N, 117°17' W
Perce . . . . 48°32' N, 064°13' W
Peterborough . . . . 44°18' N, 078°19' W
Pine Point . . . . 60°50' N, 114°28' W
Portage la Prairie . . . . 49°59' N, 098°18' W
Port Alberni . . . . 49°14' N, 124°48' W
Port Hawkesbury . . . . 45°37' N, 061°21' W
Prince Albert. . . . . 53°12' N, 105°46' W
Prince George . . . . 53°55' N, 122°45' W
Prince Rupert . . . . 54°19' N, 130°19' W
Quebec . . . . 46°49' N, 071°14' W
Quesnel . . . . 53°00' N, 122°30' W
Rae-Edzo . . . . 62°50' N, 116°03' W
Rankin Inlet. . . . . 62°49' N, 092°05' W
Red Deer . . . . 52°16' N, 113°48' W
Regina . . . . 50°27' N, 104°37' W
Resolute Bay . . . . 74°41' N, 094°54' W
Revelstoke. . . . . 50°59' N, 118°12' W
Rimouski . . . . 48°26' N, 068°33' W
Roberval . . . . 48°31' N, 072°13' W
Ross River . . . . 61°59' N, 132°26' W
Sachs Harbour . . . . 72°00' N, 125°13' W
Saint Albert . . . . 53°38' N, 113°38' W
Sainte-Foy . . . . 46°47' N, 071°17' W
Saint John . . . . 45°16' N, 066°03' W
Saint John's . . . . 47°34' N, 052°43' W
Saskatoon . . . . 52°07' N, 106°38' W
Sault Ste. Marie. . . . . 46°31' N, 084°20' W
Scarborough . . . . 43°47' N, 079°15' W
Schefferville . . . . 54°48' N, 066°50' W
Selkirk . . . . 50°09' N, 096°52' W
Senneterre. . . . . 48°23' N, 077°14' W
Sept-Îles . . . . 50°12' N, 066°23' W
Shawinigan . . . . 46°33' N, 072°45' W
Shelburne . . . . 43°46' N, 065°19' W
Sherbrooke . . . . 45°25' N, 071°54' W
Snow Lake . . . . 54°53' N, 100°02' W
Springdale . . . . 49°30' N, 056°04' W
Sturgeon Falls . . . . 46°22' N, 079°55' W
Sudbury. . . . . 46°30' N, 081°00' W
Surrey . . . . 49°06' N, 122°47' W
Swan River . . . . 52°07' N, 101°16' W
Sydney. . . . . 46°09' N, 060°11' W
Teslin. . . . . 60°10' N, 132°43' W
The Pas . . . . 53°50' N, 101°15' W
Thompson. . . . . 55°45' N, 097°52' W
Thunder Bay . . . . 48°24' N, 089°19' W
Timmins . . . . 48°28' N, 081°20' W
Toronto . . . . 43°39' N, 079°23' W
Trois-Rivieres . . . . 46°21' N, 072°33' W
Truro . . . . 45°22' N, 063°16' W
Tuktoyaktuk . . . . 69°27' N, 133°02' W
Val-d'Or . . . . 48°06' N, 077°47' W
Vancouver. . . . . 49°15' N, 123°07' W
Vernon. . . . . 50°16' N, 119°16' W
Victoria . . . . 48°26' N, 123°22' W
Wabush . . . . 52°55' N, 066°52' W
Watson Lake . . . . 60°04' N, 128°42' W
Weyburn . . . . 49°40' N, 103°51' W
Whitehorse . . . . 60°43' N, 135°03' W
Williams Lake . . . . 52°08' N, 122°09' W
Windsor. . . . . 42°18' N, 083°01' W
Windsor. . . . . 44°59' N, 064°08' W
Winnipeg . . . . 49°53' N, 097°09' W

Yarmouth . . . . 43°50' N, 066°07' W
Yellowknife . . . . 62°27' N, 114°22' W
Yorkton . . . . 51°13' N, 102°28' W

CAPE VERDE . . . . . page 32

Mindelo . . . . 16°53' N, 025°00' W
Porto Novo . . . . 17°01' N, 025°04' W
Praia . . . . 14°55' N, 023°31' W
São Filipe . . . . 14°54' N, 024°31' W

CENTRAL AFRICAN REPUBLIC . . . . page 33

Alindao . . . . 05°02' N, 021°13' E
Baboua . . . . 05°48' N, 014°49' E
Bambari . . . . 05°45' N, 020°40' E
Bangassou . . . . 04°44' N, 022°49' E
Bangui . . . . 04°22' N, 018°35' E
Batangafo . . . . 07°18' N, 018°18' E
Berbérati . . . . 04°16' N, 015°47' E
Bimbo . . . . 04°18' N, 018°33' E
Birao . . . . 10°17' N, 022°47' E
Boda . . . . 04°19' N, 017°28' E
Bossangoa . . . . 06°29' N, 017°27' E
Bossembélé . . . . 05°16' N, 017°39' E
Bouar . . . . 05°57' N, 015°36' E
Bouca . . . . 06°30' N, 018°17' E
Bozoum . . . . 06°19' N, 016°23' E
Bria . . . . 06°32' N, 021°59' E
Carnot . . . . 04°56' N, 015°52' E
Dekóa . . . . 06°19' N, 019°04' E
Ippy . . . . 06°15' N, 021°12' E
Kaga Bandoro . . . . 06°59' N, 019°11' E
Mbaïki . . . . 03°53' N, 018°00' E
Mobaye . . . . 04°19' N, 021°11' E
Mouka . . . . 07°16' N, 021°52' E
Ndélé . . . . 08°24' N, 020°39' E
Nola . . . . 03°32' N, 016°04' E
Obo . . . . 05°24' N, 026°30' E
Ouadda . . . . 08°04' N, 022°24' E
Ouanda Djallé . . . . 08°54' N, 022°48' E
Sibut . . . . 05°44' N, 019°05' E
Zinga . . . . 03°43' N, 018°35' E

CHAD . . . . page 34

Abéché . . . . 13°49' N, 020°49' E
Adre . . . . 13°28' N, 022°12' E
Am Dam . . . . 12°46' N, 020°29' E
Am Timan . . . . 11°02' N, 020°17' E
Am Zoer . . . . 14°13' N, 021°23' E
Aozou . . . . 21°49' N, 017°25' E
Arada . . . . 15°01' N, 020°40' E
Ati . . . . 13°13' N, 018°20' E
Biltine . . . . 14°32' N, 020°55' E
Bol . . . . 13°28' N, 014°43' E
Bongor . . . . 10°17' N, 015°22' E
Doba . . . . 08°39' N, 016°51' E
Gélengdeng . . . . 10°56' N, 015°32' E
Goré . . . . 07°55' N, 016°38' E
Goz Beïda . . . . 12°13' N, 021°25' E
Koro Toro . . . . 16°05' N, 018°30' E
Laï . . . . 09°24' N, 016°18' E
Largeau (Faya-Largeau) . . . 17°55' N, 019°07' E
Mao . . . . 14°07' N, 015°19' E
Massenya . . . . 11°24' N, 016°10' E
Mongo . . . . 12°11' N, 018°42' E
Moundou . . . . 08°34' N, 016°05' E
N'Djamena (Fort Lamy) . . . 12°07' N, 015°03' E
Pala . . . . 09°22' N, 014°54' E
Sarh (Fort-Archambault) . . 09°09' N, 018°23' E

CHILE . . . . page 35

Antofagasta . . . . 23°39' S, 070°24' W
Arica . . . . 18°29' S, 070°20' W
Castro . . . . 42°29' S, 073°46' W
Chillán . . . . 36°36' S, 072°07' W
Chuquicamata . . . . 22°19' S, 068°56' W
Coihaique . . . . 45°34' S, 072°04' W
Concepción . . . . 36°50' S, 073°03' W
Copiapó . . . . 27°22' S, 070°20' W
Coquimbo . . . . 29°58' S, 071°21' W
Iquique . . . . 20°13' S, 070°10' W
La Serena . . . . 29°54' S, 071°16' W
Porvenir . . . . 53°18' S, 070°22' W
Potrerillos . . . . 26°26' S, 069°29' W
Puerto Aisén . . . . 45°24' S, 072°42' W
Puerto Montt . . . . 41°28' S, 072°57' W
Punta Arenas . . . . 53°09' S, 070°55' W
Purranque . . . . 40°55' S, 073°10' W
San Pedro . . . . 33°54' S, 071°28' W
Santiago . . . . 33°27' S, 070°40' W
Talca . . . . 35°26' S, 071°40' W
Talcahuano . . . . 36°43' S, 073°07' W
Temuco . . . . 38°44' S, 072°36' W
Tocopilla . . . . 22°05' S, 070°12' W
Valdivia . . . . 39°48' S, 073°14' W
Valparaíso . . . . 33°02' S, 071°38' W
Viña del Mar . . . . 33°02' S, 071°34' W

CHINA . . . . page 36-7

Anshan . . . . 41°07' N, 122°57' E
Beijing . . . . 39°56' N, 116°24' E
Changchun . . . . 43°52' N, 125°21' E
Changsha . . . . 28°12' N, 112°58' E
Chengdu . . . . 30°40' N, 104°04' E
Chongqing
(locally Yuzhou) . . . . 29°34' N, 106°35' E
Dalian (Lüda) . . . . 38°55' N, 121°39' E
Fushun . . . . 41°52' N, 123°53' E
Fuzhou . . . . 26°05' N, 119°18' E
Guangzhou . . . . 23°07' N, 113°15' E
Guiyang . . . . 26°35' N, 106°43' E
Haikou . . . . 20°03' N, 110°19' E
Hangzhou . . . . 30°15' N, 120°10' E

Harbin . . . . 45°45' N, 126°39' E
Hefei . . . . 31°51' N, 117°17' E
Hohhot . . . . 40°47' N, 111°37' E
Jinan . . . . 36°40' N, 117°00' E
Kunming . . . . 25°04' N, 102°41' E
Lanzhou. . . . . 36°03' N, 103°41' E
Lhasa . . . . 29°39' N, 091°06' E
Nanchang . . . . 28°41' N, 115°53' E
Nanjing . . . . 32°03' N, 118°47' E
Nanning . . . . 22°49' N, 108°19' E
Qingdao. . . . . 36°04' N, 120°19' E
Shanghai . . . . 31°14' N, 121°28' E
Shaoxing . . . . 30°00' N, 120°35' E
Shenyang. . . . . 41°48' N, 123°27' E
Shijiazhuang . . . . 38°03' N, 114°29' E
Tai'an. . . . . 36°12' N, 117°07' E
Taiyuan . . . . 37°52' N, 112°33' E
Tianjin . . . . 39°08' N, 117°12' E
Ürümqi . . . . 43°48' N, 087°35' E
Wuhan . . . . 30°35' N, 114°16' E
Xi'an. . . . . 34°16' N, 108°54' E
Xining . . . . 36°37' N, 101°46' E
Yinchuan . . . . 38°28' N, 106°19' E
Zhengzhou . . . . 34°45' N, 113°40' E

COLOMBIA . . . . page 38

Armenia. . . . . 04°31' N, 075°41' W
Barranquilla . . . . 10°59' N, 074°48' W
Bello. . . . . 06°20' N, 075°33'W
Bisinaca. . . . . 04°30' N, 069°40' W
Bogotá. . . . . 04°36' N, 074°05' W
Bolívar. . . . . 01°50' N, 076°58' W
Bucaramanga . . . . 07°08' N, 073°09' W
Buenaventura . . . . 03°53' N, 077°04' W
Cali. 03°27' N, 076°31'W
Caranacoa . . . . 02°25' N, 068°57' W
Cartagena . . . . 10°25' N, 075°32' W
Cúcuta . . . . 07°54' N, 072°31' W
Duitama. . . . . 05°50' N, 073°02' W
El Dorado . . . . 01°11' N, 071°52' W
El Yopal. . . . . 05°21' N, 072°23' W
Florencia . . . . 01°36' N, 075°36' W
Ibagué . . . . 04°27' N, 075°14' W
Macujer . . . . 00°24' N, 073°07' W
Magangué . . . . 09°14' N, 074°45' W
Manizales . . . . 05°05' N, 075°32' W
Matarca . . . . 00°30' S, 072°38' W
Medellín. . . . . 06°15' N, 075°35' W
Mitú . . . . 01°08' N, 070°03' W
Montería . . . . 08°46' N, 075°53' W
Ocaña . . . . 08°15' N, 073°20' W
Palmira . . . . 03°32' N, 076°16' W
Pasto . . . . 01°13' N, 077°17' W
Pereira. . . . . 04°49' N, 075°43' W
Popayán . . . . 02°27' N, 076°36' W
Puerto Berrío . . . . 06°29' N, 074°24' W
Puerto Carreño . . . . 06°12' N, 067°22' W
Puerto Inírida . . . . 03°51' N, 067°55' W
Quibdó. . . . . 05°42' N, 076°40' W
Ríohacha . . . . 11°33' N, 072°55' W
San José de Guaviare . . . . . 02°35' N, 072°38' W
San Martín. . . . . 03°42' N, 073°42' W
Santa Marta. . . . . 11°15' N, 074°13' W
Sincelejo . . . . 09°18' N, 075°24' W
Sogamoso . . . . 05°43' N, 072°56' W
Tuluá . . . . 04°06' N, 076°11' W
Tumaco . . . . 01°49' N, 078°46' W
Tunja . . . . 05°31' N, 073°22' W
Urrao . . . . 06°20' N, 076°11'W
Valledupar. . . . . 10°29' N, 073°15' W
Villa Rosario . . . . 07°50' N, 072°28' W
Villavicencio . . . . 04°09' N, 073°37' W
Zipaquirá. . . . . 05°02' N, 074°00' W

COMOROS . . . . . . page 39

Fomboni . . . . 12°18' S, 043°46' E
Mitsamiouli . . . . 11°22' S, 043°21' E
Moroni. . . . . 11°41' S, 043°16' E
Mutsamudu . . . . 12°10' S, 044°25' E

CONGO, DEMOCRATIC REPUBLIC OF THE page 40

Aketi . . . . 02°44' N, 023°46' E
Banana. . . . . 06°01' S, 012°24' E
Bandundu . . . . 03°19' S, 017°22' E
Beni . . . . 00°30' N, 029°28' E
Boende . . . . 00°13' S, 020°52' E
Boma . . . . 05°51' S, 013°03' E
Buta . . . . 02°48' N, 024°44' E
Butembo . . . . 00°09' N, 029°17' E
Gandajika . . . . 06°45' S, 023°57' E
Gemena . . . . 03°15' N, 019°46' E
Ilebo. . . . . 04°19' S, 020°35' E
Isiro . . . . 02°46' N, 027°37' E
Kabinda . . . . 06°08' S, 024°29' E
Kalemi (Albertville) . . . . . . 05°56' S, 029°12' E
Kamina . . . . 08°44' S, 025°00' E
Kananga
(Luluabourg) . . . . 05°54' S, 022°25' E
Kikwit . . . . 05°02' S, 018°49' E
Kindu . . . . 02°57' S, 025°56' E
Kinshasa
(Leopoldville) . . . . 04°18' S, 015°18' E
Kisangani
(Stanleyville) . . . . 00°30' N, 025°12' E
Kolwezi . . . . 10°43' S, 025°28' E
Kutu . . . . 02°44' S, 018°09' E
Likasi . . . . 10°59' S, 026°44' E
Lubumbashi
(Elisabethville) . . . . 11°40' N, 027°28' E
Manono . . . . 07°18' S, 027°25' E
Matadi . . . . 05°49' S, 013°27' E
Mbandaka . . . . 00°04' N, 018°16' E
Mbanza-Ngungu . . . . 05°15' S, 014°52' E
Mbuji-Mayi . . . . 06°09' S, 023°36' E
Mwene-Ditu . . . . 07°03' S, 023°27' E

Samba . . . . 04°38' S, 026°22' E
Tshikapa . . . . 06°25' S, 020°48' E
Yangambi . . . . 00°47' N, 024°28' E

CONGO, REPUBLIC OF THE . . . . page 41

Brazzaville. . . . . 04°16' S, 015°17' E
Djambala . . . . 02°33' S, 014°45' E
Gamboma . . . . 01°53' S, 015°51' E
Impfondo. . . . . 01°37' N, 018°04' E
Kayes. . . . . 04°25' S, 011°41' E
Liranga . . . . 00°40' S, 017°36' E
Loubomo. . . . . 04°12' N, 012°41' E
Madingou . . . . 04°09' S, 013°34' E
Makabana . . . . 02°48' S, 012°29' E
Makoua . . . . 00°01' N, 015°39' E
Mossendjo. . . . . 02°57' S, 012°44' E
Mpouya . . . . 02°37' S, 16°013' E
Nkayi . . . . 04°11' S, 013°18' E
Ouesso. . . . . 01°37' N, 016°04' E
Owando. . . . . 00°29' S, 015°55' E
Pointe-Noire . . . . 04°48' S, 011°51' E
Sibiti . . . . 03°41' S, 013°21' E
Souanké. . . . . 02°05' N, 014°03' E
Zanaga. . . . . 02°15' S, 013°50' E

COSTA RICA . . . . . page 42

Alajuela . . . . 10°01' N, 084°13' W
Cañas. . . . . 10°26' N, 085°06' W
Desamparados . . . . 09°54' N, 084°05' W
Golfito . . . . 08°39' N, 083°09' W
Heredia . . . . 10°00' N, 084°07' W
Ipís. . . . . 09°58' N, 084°01' W
La Cruz . . . . 11°04' N, 085°38' W
Liberia . . . . 10°38' N, 085°26' W
Miramar. . . . . 10°06' N, 084°44' W
Nicoya . . . . 10°09' N, 085°27' W
Puerto Limón
(Limón) . . . . 10°00' N, 083°02' W
Puntarenas . . . . 09°58' N, 084°50' W
Quesada . . . . 10°20' N, 084°26' W
San Isidro . . . . 09°23' N, 083°42' W
San José. . . . . 09°56' N, 084°05' W
San Ramón . . . . 10°05' N, 084°28' W
Santa Cruz. . . . . 10°16' N, 085°35' W
Siquirres . . . . 10°06' N, 083°31' W
Tilarán. . . . . 10°28' N, 084°58' W

COTE D´IVOIRE . . page 43

Abengourou . . . . 06°44' N, 003°29' W
Abidjan . . . . 05°19' N, 004°02' W
Aboisso . . . . 05°28' N, 003°12' W
Adzopé . . . . 06°06' N, 003°52' W
Agboville. . . . . 05°56' N, 004°13' W
Anyama . . . . 05°30' N, 004°03' W
Arrah . . . . 06°40' N, 003°58' W
Biankouma . . . . 07°44' N, 007°37' W
Bondoukou . . . . 08°02' N, 002°48' W
Bouaflé . . . . 06°59' N, 005°45' W
Bouaké. . . . . 07°41' N, 005°02' W
Bouna . . . . 09°16' N, 003°00' W
Boundiali. . . . . 09°31' N, 006°29' W
Daloa . . . . 06°53' N, 006°27' W
Daoukro. . . . . 07°03' N, 003°58' W
Dimbokro . . . . 06°39' N, 004°42' W
Divo . . . . 05°50' N, 005°22' W
Duékoué . . . . 06°45' N, 007°21' W
Ferkéssédougou . . . . 09°36' N, 005°12' W
Gagnoa . . . . 06°08' N, 005°56' W
Grand-Bassam. . . . . 05°12' N, 003°44' W
Guiglo . . . . 06°33' N, 007°29' W
Katiola . . . . 08°08' N, 005°06' W
Kong . . . . 09°09' N, 004°37' W
Korhogo . . . . 09°27' N, 005°38' W
Lakota . . . . 05°51' N, 005°41' W
Man . . . . 07°24' N, 007°33' W
Odienné. . . . . 09°30' N, 007°34' W
Oumé. . . . . 06°23' N, 005°25' W
San-Pédro . . . . 04°44' N, 006°37' W
Sassandra . . . . 04°57' N, 006°05' W
Séguéla . . . . 07°57' N, 006°40' W
Sinfra . . . . 06°37' N, 005°55' W
Tabou . . . . 04°25' N, 007°21' W
Tengréla . . . . 10°26' N, 006°20' W
Tortiya. . . . . 08°46' N, 005°41' W
Yamoussoukro . . . . 06°49' N, 005°17' W

CROATIA . . . . page 44

Bjelovar. . . . . 45°54' N, 016°51' E
Đakovo . . . . 45°19' N, 018°25' E
Dubrovnik . . . . 42°39' N, 018°07' E
Jasenovav . . . . 45°16' N, 016°54' E
Karlovac . . . . 45°29' N, 015°33' E
Knin . . . . 44°02' N, 016°12' E
Makarska. . . . . 43°18° N, 017°02' E
Nin . . . . 44°14' N, 015°11' E
Opatija. . . . . 45°20' N, 014°19' E
Osijek. . . . . 45°33' N, 018°42' E
Ploče . . . . 43°04' N, 017°26' E
Pula . . . . 44°52' N, 013°50' E
Sesvete . . . . 45°50' N, 016°10' E
Rijeka. . . . . 45°21' N, 014°24' E
Sisak . . . . 45°29' N, 016°22' E
Slavonski Brod . . . . 45°09' N, 018°02' E
Slavonska Požega
(Požega). . . . . 45°20' N, 017°41' E
Split . . . . 43°31' N, 016°26' E
Trogir . . . . 43°32' N, 016°15' E
Varaždin . . . . 46°18' N, 016°20' E
Vinkovci . . . . 45°17' N, 018°49' E
Vukovar. . . . . 45°21' N, 019°00' E
Zadar . . . . 44°07' N, 015°15' E
Zagreb . . . . 45°48' S, 016°00' E

CUBA . . . . page 45

Banes . . . . 20°58' N, 075°43' W
Baracoa . . . . 20°21' N, 074°30' W
Bayamo . . . . 20°23' N, 076°39' W
Camagüey . . . . 21°23' N, 077°55' W
Cárdenas . . . . 23°02' N, 081°12' W
Ciego de Avila . . . . 21°51' N, 078°46' W
Cienfuegos . . . . 22°09' N, 080°27' W
Colón . . . . 22°43' N, 080°54' W
Florida . . . . 21°32' N, 078°14' W
Guantánamo . . . . 20°08' N, 075°12' W
Güines . . . . 22°50' N, 082°02' W
Havana (La Habana) . . . . . 23°08' N, 082°22' W
Holguín . . . . 20°53' N, 076°15' W
Jagüey Grande . . . . 22°32' N, 081°08' W
Jovellanos . . . . 22°48' N, 081°12' W
Las Tunas . . . . 20°58' N, 076°57' W
Manzanillo . . . . 20°21' N, 077°07' W
Matanzas . . . . 23°03' N, 081°35' W
Mayarí . . . . 20°40' N, 075°41' W
Morón . . . . 22°06' N, 078°38' W
Nueva Gerona . . . . 21°53' N, 082°48' W
Nuevitas . . . . 21°33' N, 077°16' W
Palma Soriano . . . . 20°13' N, 076°00' W
Pinar del Río . . . . 22°25' N, 083°42' W
Placetas . . . . 22°19' N, 079°40' W
Puerto Padre . . . . 21°12' N, 076°36' W
Sagua la Grande . . . . 22°49' N, 080°05' W
San Antonio
de los Baños . . . . 22°53' N, 082°30' W
Sancti Spíritus . . . . 21°56' N, 079°27' W
Santa Clara . . . . 22°24' N, 079°58' W
Santa Cruz del Sur . . . . 20°43' N, 078°00' W
Santiago de Cuba . . . . 20°01' N, 075°49' W

CYPRUS . . . . page 46

Akanthou . . . . 35°22' N, 033°45' E
Akrotiri . . . . 34°36' N, 032°57' E
Athna . . . . 35°03' N, 033°47' E
Ayios Amvrosios . . . . 35°20' N, 033°35' E
Ayios Theodhoros . . . . 34°48' N, 033°23' E
Famagusta . . . . 35°07' N, 033°57' E
Kalokhorio . . . . 34°55' N, 033°32' E
Kouklia . . . . 34°42' N, 032°34' E
Kyrenia . . . . 35°20' N, 033°19' E
Larnaca . . . . 34°55' N, 033°38' E
Laxia . . . . 35°06' N, 033°22' E
Leonarisso . . . . 35°28' N, 034°08' E
Limassol . . . . 34°40' N, 033°02' E
Livadhia . . . . 35°24' N, 034°02' E
Liveras . . . . 35°23' N, 032°57' E
Mari . . . . 34°44' N, 033°18' E
Morphou . . . . 35°12' N, 032°59' E
Nicosia (Lefkosia) . . . . 35°10' N, 033°22' E
Ora . . . . 34°51' N, 033°12' E
Ormidhia . . . . 34°59' N, 033°47' E
Pakhna . . . . 34°46' N, 032°48' E
Pano Lakatamia . . . . 35°06' N, 033°18' E
Paphos . . . . 34°45' N, 032°25' E
Paralimni . . . . 35°02' N, 033°59' E
Patriki . . . . 35°22' N, 033°59' E
Perivolia . . . . 34°49' N, 033°35' E
Pomos . . . . 35°09' N, 032°33' E
Prastio . . . . 35°10' N, 033°45' E
Trikomo . . . . 35°17' N, 033°52' E
Tsadha . . . . 34°50' N, 032°28' E
Varosha . . . . 35°06' N, 033°57' E
Vroisha . . . . 35°04' N, 032°40' E
Yialoussa . . . . 35°32' N, 034°11' E

CZECH REPUBLIC . . . . page 47

Břeclav . . . . 48°46' N, 016°53' E
Brno . . . . 49°12' N, 016°38' E
Česká Lípa . . . . 50°41' N, 014°33' E
České Budějovice . . . . 48°59' N, 014°28' E
Český Těšín . . . . 49°45' N, 018°37' E
Cheb . . . . 50°04' N, 012°22' E
Chomutov . . . . 50°27' N, 013°26' E
Děčín . . . . 50°47' N, 014°13' E
Frýdek Místek . . . . 49°41' N, 018°21' E
Havířov . . . . 49°47' N, 018°22' E
Havlíčkův Brod . . . . 49°37' N, 015°35' E
Hodonín . . . . 48°52' N, 017°08' E
Hradec Králové . . . . 50°13' N, 015°50' E
Jablonec . . . . 50°43' N, 015°11' E
Jihlava . . . . 49°24' N, 015°35' E
Karlovy Vary . . . . 50°13' N, 012°54' E
Karviná . . . . 49°52' N, 018°33' E
Kladno . . . . 50°09' N, 014°06' E
Kolín . . . . 50°02' N, 015°12' E
Krnov . . . . 50°06' N, 017°43' E
Kroměříž . . . . 49°18' N, 017°24' E
Liberec . . . . 50°47' N, 015°03' E
Litvínov . . . . 50°36' N, 013°37' E
Mladá Boleslav . . . . 50°25' N, 014°54' E
Most . . . . 50°32' N, 013°39' E
Nový Jičín . . . . 49°36' N, 018°01' E
Olomouc . . . . 49°35' N, 017°15' E
Opava . . . . 49°57' N, 017°55' E
Orlová . . . . 49°51' N, 018°25' E
Ostrava . . . . 49°50' N, 018°17' E
Pardubice . . . . 50°02' N, 015°47' E
Písek . . . . 49°18' N, 014°09' E
Plzeň . . . . 49°45' N, 013°22' E
Prague (Praha) . . . . 50°05' N, 014°28' E
Přerov . . . . 49°27' N, 017°27' E
Příbřam . . . . 49°42' N, 014°01' E
Prostějov . . . . 49°28' N, 017°07' E
Šumperk . . . . 49°58' N, 016°58' E
Tábor . . . . 49°25' N, 014°40' E
Teplice . . . . 50°38' N, 013°50' E
Třebíč . . . . 49°13' N, 015°53' E
Trinec . . . . 49°41' N, 018°39' E
Trutnov . . . . 50°34' N, 015°54' E
Uherské Hradiště . . . . 49°04' N, 017°27' E
Ústí nad Labem . . . . 50°40' N, 014°02' E

Valašské Meziříči . . . . 49°28' N, 017°58' E
Vsetín . . . . 49°20' N, 018°00' E
Žd'ár nad Sázavou . . . . 49°35' N, 015°56' E
Zlín. 49°13' N, 017°40' E
Znojmo . . . . 48°51' N, 016°03' E

DENMARK . . . . page 48

Ålborg (Aalborg). . . . . 57°03' N, 009°56' E
Århus (Aarhus). . . . . 56°09' N, 010°13' E
Års . . . . 56°48' N, 009°32' E
Brønderslev . . . . 57°16' N, 009°58' E
Brørup. . . . . 55°29' N, 009°01' E
Copenhagen (København) . 55°40' N, 012°35' E
Esbjerg . . . . 55°28' N, 008°27' E
Fakse . . . . 55°15' N, 012°08' E
Fredericia . . . . 55°35' N, 009°46' E
Frederiksberg . . . . 55°41' N, 012°32' E
Frederikshavn. . . . . 57°26' N, 010°32' E
Gilleleje . . . . 56°07' N, 012°19' E
Give . . . . 55°51' N, 009°15' E
Grenå. . . . . 56°25' N, 010°53' E
Hadsund . . . . 56°43' N, 010°07' E
Helsingør . . . . 56°02' N, 012°37' E
Herning . . . . 56°08' N, 008°59' E
Hillerød . . . . 55°56' N, 012°19' E
Hirtshals . . . . 57°35' N, 009°58' E
Hjørring. . . . . 57°28' N, 009°59' E
Holstebro . . . . 56°21' N, 008°38' E
Hornslet. . . . . 56°19' N, 010°20' E
Horsens . . . . 55°52' N, 009°52' E
Jyderup . . . . 55°40' N, 011°26' E
Klarup . . . . 57°01' N, 010°03' E
Køge. . . . . 55°27' N, 012°11' E
Kolding . . . . 55°29' N, 009°29' E
Lemvig. . . . . 56°32' N, 008°18' E
Løgstør . . . . 56°58' N, 009°15' E
Næstved . . . . 55°14' N, 011°46' E
Nakskov. . . . . 54°50' N, 011°09' E
Nykøbing. . . . . 54°46' N, 011°53' E
Nykøbing. . . . . 55°55' N, 011°41' E
Nykøbing. . . . . 56°48' N, 008°52' E
Odense . . . . 55°24' N, 010°23' E
Ølgod . . . . 55°49' N, 008°37' E
Otterup . . . . 55°31' N, 010°24' E
Padborg. . . . . 54°49' N, 009°22' E
Randers . . . . 56°28' N, 010°03' E
Ribe . . . . 55°21' N, 008°46' E
Ringkøbing . . . . 56°05' N, 008°15' E
Rønne. . . . . 55°06' N, 014°42' E
Roskilde. . . . . 55°39' N, 012°05' E
Rudkøbing. . . . . 54°56' N, 010°43' E
Skagen . . . . 57°44' N, 010°36' E
Skive . . . . 56°34' N, 009°02' E
Skjern. . . . . 55°57' N, 008°30' E
Slagelse . . . . 55°24' N, 011°22' E
Sønderborg . . . . 54°55' N, 009°47' E
Struer. . . . . 56°29' N, 008°37' E
Svendborg. . . . . 55°03' N, 010°37' E
Thisted . . . . 56°57' N, 008°42' E
Tilst . . . . 56°12' N, 010°07' E
Toftlund. . . . . 55°11' N, 009°04' E
Tønder. . . . . 54°56' N, 008°54' E
Varde. . . . . 55°38' N, 008°29' E
Vejle. . . . . 55°42' N, 009°32' E
Viborg . . . . 56°26' N, 009°24' E
Vodskov . . . . 57°06' N, 010°02' E
Vordingborg . . . . 55°01' N, 011°55' E

DJIBOUTI . . . . page 49

Ali Sabih . . . . 11°10' N, 042°42' E
Dikhil . . . . 11°06' N, 042°23' E
Djibouti . . . . 11°36' N, 043°09' E
Tadjoura . . . . 11°47' N, 042°53' E

DOMINICA . . . . page 50

Castle Bruce . . . . 15°26' N, 061°16' W
Colihaut. . . . . 15°30' N, 061°29' W
La Plaine . . . . 15°20' N, 061°15' W
Marigot . . . . 15°32' N, 061°18' W
Portsmouth . . . . 15°35' N, 061°28' W
Rosalie. . . . . 15°22' N, 061°16' W
Roseau. . . . . 15°18' N, 061°24' W
Saint Joseph . . . . 15°24' N, 061°26 W
Salibia . . . . 15°29' N, 061°16' W
Soufrière . . . . 15°13' N, 061°22' W
Vieille Case . . . . 15°36' N, 061°24' W

DOMINICAN REPUBLIC . . . . page 51

Azua. . . . . 18°27' N, 070°44' W
Baní . . . . 18°17' N, 070°20' W
Barahona. . . . . 18°12' N, 071°06' W
Bayaguana. . . . . 18°58' N, 069°00' W
Bonao . . . . 18°56' N, 070°25' W
Cotuí . . . . 19°03' N, 070°09' W
Dajabón . . . . 19°33' N, 071°42' W
Duvergé. . . . . 18°22' N, 071°31' W
El Seibo . . . . 18°46' N, 069°02' W
Enriquillo. . . . . 17°54' N, 071°14' W
Higüey . . . . 18°37' N, 068°42' W
Jimaní . . . . 18°28' N, 071°51' W
La Romana . . . . 18°25' N, 068°58' W
La Vega . . . . 19°13' N, 070°31' W
Las Matas . . . . 18°52' N, 071°31' W
Mao . . . . 19°34' N, 071°05' W
Miches. . . . . 18°59' N, 069°03' W
Moca . . . . 19°24' N, 070°31' W
Montecristi . . . . 19°52' N, 071°39' W
Nagua (Julia Molina). . . . . . 19°23' N, 069°50' W
Neiba . . . . 18°28' N, 071°25' W
Pedernales . . . . 18°02' N, 071°45' W
Puerto Plata . . . . 19°48' N, 070°41' W
Sabaneta . . . . 19°28' N, 071°20' W
Salcedo . . . . 19°23' N, 070°25' W

Samaná	19°13' N, 069°19' W
San Cristóbal	18°25' N, 070°06' W
San Francisco de Macorís	19°18' N, 070°15' W
San Juan	18°48' N, 071°14' W
San Pedro de Macorís	18°27' N, 069°18' W
Sánchez	19°14' N, 069°36' W
Santiago	19°27' N, 070°42' W
Santo Domingo	18°28' N, 069°54' W

EAST TIMOR . . . . . page 52

Dili	08°33' S, 125°35' E
Manatuto	08°30' S, 126°01' E
Viqueque	08°52' S, 126°22' E

ECUADOR . . . . page 53

Ambato	01°15' S, 078°37' W
Azogues	02°44' S, 078°50' W
Babahoyo	01°49' S, 079°31' W
Balzar	01°22' S, 079°54' W
Cuenca	02°53' S, 078°59' W
Esmeraldas	00°59' N, 079°42' W
General Leonidas Plaza Gutiérrez	02°58' S, 078°25' W
Girón	03°10' S, 079°08' W
Guayaquil	02°10' S, 079°54' W
Huaquillas	03°29' S, 080°14' W
Ibarra	00°21' N, 078°07' W
Jipijapa	01°20' S, 080°35' W
Latacunga	00°56' S, 078°37' W
Loja	04°00' S, 079°13' W
Macará	04°23' S, 079°57' W
Macas	02°19' S, 078°07' W
Machala	03°16' S, 079°58' W
Manta	00°57' S, 080°44' W
Milagro	02°07' S, 079°36' W
Muisne	00°36' N, 080°02' W
Naranjal	02°40' S, 079°37' W
Otavalo	00°14' N, 078°16' W
Pasaje	03°20' S, 079°49' W
Piñas	03°40' S, 079°39' W
Portoviejo	01°03' S, 080°27' W
Puerto Francisco de Orellana (Coca)	00°28' S, 076°58' W
Puyo	01°28' S, 077°59' W
Quevedo	01°02' S, 079°27' W
Quito	00°13' S, 078°30' W
Riobamba	01°40' S, 078°38' W
Salinas	02°13' S, 080°58' W
San Gabriel	00°36' N, 077°49' W
San Lorenzo	01°17' N, 078°50' W
Santo Domingo de los Colorados (Santo Domingo)	00°15' S, 079°09' W
Tena	00°59' S, 077°49' W
Tulcán	00°48' N, 077°43' W
Valdez	01°15' N, 079°00' W
Yantzaza	03°51' S, 078°45' W
Zamora	04°04' S, 078°58' W
Zaruma	03°41' S, 079°37' W

EGYPT . . . . page 54

Akhmīm	26°34' N, 031°44' E
Al-ʿArish	31°08' N, 033°48' E
Alexandria (Al-Iskandariyah)	31°12' N, 029°54' E
Al-Fayyûm	29°19' N, 030°50' E
Al-Khārijah	25°26' N, 030°33' E
Al-Maḥallah Al-Kubrā	30°58' N, 031°10' E
Al-Manṣūrah	31°03' N, 031°23' E
Al-Maʿṣarah	25°30' N, 029°04' E
Al-Minyā	28°06' N, 030°45' E
Aswān	24°05' N, 032°53' E
Asyut	27°11' N, 031°11' E
Aṭ-Ṭur	28°14' N, 033°37' E
Az-Zāqaziq	30°35' N, 031°31' E
Banhā	30°28' N, 031°11' E
Bani Suwayf	29°05' N, 031°05' E
Cairo (Al-Qahirah)	30°03' N, 031°15' E
Damanhūr	31°02' N, 030°28' E
Damietta (Dumyāṭ)	31°25' N, 031°48' E
Giza (Al-Jīzah)	30°01' N, 031°13' E
Jirjā	26°20' N, 031°53' E
Luxor (Al-Uqsur)	25°41' N, 032°39' E
Mallawī	27°44' N, 030°50' E
Matruh	31°21' N, 027°14' E
Port Said (Bur Sa'id)	31°16' N, 032°18' E
Qinā	26°10' N, 032°43' E
Sawhāj	26°33' N, 031°42' E
Shibīn al-Kawm	30°33' N, 031°01' E
Suez (As-Suways)	29°58' N, 032°33' E
Ṭanṭā	30°47' N, 031°00' E

EL SALVADOR . . . page 55

Acajutla	13°35' N, 089°50' W
Chalatenango	14°02' N, 088°56' W
Chalchuapa	13°59' N, 089°41' W
Cojutepeque	13°43' N, 088°56' W
Ilobasco	13°51' N, 088°51' W
Izalco	13°45' N, 089°40' W
La Unión	13°20' N, 087°51' W
Nueva San Salvador (Santa Tecla)	13°41' N, 089°17' W
San Francisco (San Francisco Gotera)	13°42' N, 088°06' W
San Miguel	13°29' N, 088°11' W
San Salvador	13°42' N, 089°12' W
Santa Ana	13°59' N, 089°34' W
San Vincente	13°38' N, 088°48' W
Sensuntepeque	13°52' N, 088°38' W
Sonsonate	13°43' N, 089°44' W
Usulatán	13°21' N, 088°27' W
Zacatecoluca	13°20' N, 088°52' W

EQUATORIAL GUINEA . . . . page 56

Bata . . . . 01°51' N, 009°45' E
Kogo . . . . 01°05' N, 009°42' E
Malabo (Santa Isabel). . . . . 03°21' N, 008°40' E
Mbini . . . . 01°34' N, 009°37' E
Mikomeseng . . . . 02°08' N, 010°37' E
Niefang . . . . 01°51' N, 010°15' E
San Antonio de Ureca. . . . . 03°16' N, 008°32' E

ERITREA . . . . page 57

Akordat . . . . 15°33' N, 037°53' E
Aseb (Assab). . . . . 13°00' N, 042°44' E
Asmara (Asmera) . . . . 15°20' N, 038°56' E
Keren . . . . 15°47' N, 038°28' E
Massawa (Mitsiwa) . . . . . . 15°36' N, 039°28' E
Nakfa . . . . 16°40' N, 038°29' E

ESTONIA . . . . page 58

Abja-Paluoja . . . . 58°08' N, 025°21' E
Ambla . . . . 59°11' N, 025°51' E
Antsla . . . . 57°50' N, 026°32' E
Haapsalu . . . . 58°56' N, 023°33' E
Järva-Jaani. . . . . 59°02' N, 025°53' E
Järvakandi. . . . . 58°47' N, 024°49' E
Jõgeva . . . . 58°45' N, 026°24' E
Käina . . . . 58°50' N, 022°47' E
Kallaste . . . . 58°39' N, 027°09' E
Kärdla . . . . 59°00' N, 022°45' E
Kehra. . . . . 59°20' N, 025°20' E
Keila. . . . . 59°18' N, 024°25' E
Kilingi-Nõmme. . . . . 58°09' N, 024°58' E
Kiviõli . . . . 59°21' N, 026°57' E
Kohtla-Järve . . . . 59°24' N, 027°15' E
Kunda . . . . 59°29' N, 026°32' E
Kuressaare (Kingissepa) . . 58°15' N, 022°28' E
Lavassaare . . . . 58°31' N, 024°22' E
Lĭhula (Lihula) . . . . 58°41' N, 023°50' E
Loksa . . . . 59°35' N, 025°42' E
Maardu . . . . 59°25' N, 024°59' E
Märjamaa . . . . 58°54' N, 024°26' E
Mõisaküla . . . . 58°06' N, 025°11' E
Mustla . . . . 58°14' N, 025°52' E
Narva. . . . . 59°23' N, 028°12' E
Nuia . . . . 58°06' N, 025°33' E
Orissaare. . . . . 58°34' N, 023°05' E
Otepää. . . . . 58°03' N, 026°30' E
Paide . . . . 58°54' N, 025°33' E
Paldiski . . . . 59°20' N, 024°06' E
Pärnu. . . . . 58°24' N, 024°32' E
Põlva . . . . 58°03' N, 027°03' E
Püssi . . . . 59°22' N, 027°03' E
Rakvere . . . . 59°22' N, 026°20' E
Räpina . . . . 58°06' N, 027°27' E
Rapla . . . . 59°01' N, 024°47' E
Saue . . . . 59°18' N, 024°34' E
Sindi. . . . . 58°24' N, 024°40' E
Suure-Jaani . . . . 58°33' N, 025°28' E
Tallinn . . . . 59°25' N, 024°45' E
Tapa. . . . . 59°16' N, 025°58' E
Tartu . . . . 58°23' N, 026°43' E
Tootsi . . . . 58°34' N, 024°49' E
Tõrva. . . . . 58°00' N, 025°56' E
Türi . . . . 58°48' N, 025°26' E
Valga . . . . 57°47' N, 026°02' E
Viivikonna . . . . 59°19' N, 027°42' E
Viljandi . . . . 58°24' N, 025°36' E
Võsu. . . . . 59°35' N, 025°58' E

ETHIOPIA . . . . page 59

Addis Ababa (Adis Abeba). 09°02' N, 038°42' E
Adigrat. . . . . 14°17' N, 039°28' E
Adwa (Adowa or Aduwa). . 14°10' N, 038°54' E
Agaro . . . . 07°51' N, 036°39' E
Akaki . . . . 09°05' N, 039°00' E
Aksum . . . . 14°08' N, 038°43' E
Alamata . . . . 12°25' N, 039°33' E
Arba Minch (Arba Mench). 06°02' N, 037°33' E
Bahir Dar. . . . . 11°36' N, 037°23' E
Debre Markos . . . . 10°21' N, 037°44' E
Debre Zeyit . . . . 08°45' N, 038°59' E
Dembidollo . . . . 08°32' N, 038°48' E
Dese (Dase). . . . . 11°08' N, 039°38' E
Dire Dawa . . . . 09°35' N, 041°52' E
Finchaa . . . . 09°33' N, 037°21' E
Gonder. . . . . 12°36' N, 037°28' E
Gore. . . . . 08°09' N, 035°32' E
Harer (Harar) . . . . 09°19' N, 042°07' E
Jijiga. . . . . 09°21' N, 042°48' E
Jima (Jimma). . . . . 07°40' N, 036°50' E
Kembolcha (Kombolcha) . . 11°05' N, 039°44' E
Kibre Mengist . . . . 05°53' N, 038°59' E
Lalibela . . . . 12°02' N, 039°02' E
Mekele. . . . . 13°30' N, 039°28' E
Metu . . . . 08°18' N, 035°35' E
Nazret . . . . 08°33' N, 039°16' E
Nekemte . . . . 09°05' N, 036°33' E
Sodo. . . . . 06°54' N, 037°45' E
Weldya. . . . . 11°50' N, 039°41' E
Yirga Alem. . . . . 06°45' N, 038°25' E

FIJI . . . . page 60

Ba. 17°33' S, 177°41' E
Lami. . . . . 18°07' S, 178°25' E
Lautoka . . . . 17°37' S, 177°28' E
Nadi . . . . 17°48' S, 177°25' E
Suva. . . . . 18°08' S, 178°25' E

FINLAND . . . . page 61

Espoo (Esbo) . . . . 60°13' N, 024°40' E
Forssa . . . . 60°49' N, 023°38' E

Hämeenlinna (Tavastehus). 61°00' N, 024°27' E
Hanko . . . . . 59°50' N, 022°57' E
Haukipudas . . . . . 65°11' N, 025°21' E
Heinola . . . . . 61°13' N, 026°02' E
Helsinki . . . . . 60°10' N, 024°58' E
Ilmajoki . . . . . 62°44' N, 022°34' E
Ivalo . . . . . 68°39' N, 027°36' E
Jämsä . . . . . 61°52' N, 025°12' E
Joensuu . . . . . 62°36' N, 029°46' E
Jyväskylä . . . . . 62°14' N, 025°44' E
Kangasala . . . . . 61°28' N, 024°05' E
Kaskinen . . . . . 62°23' N, 021°13' E
Kemi . . . . . 65°44' N, 024°34' E
Kittilä . . . . . 67°40' N, 024°54' E
Kotka . . . . . 60°28' N, 026°55' E
Kouvola . . . . . 60°52' N, 026°42' E
Kuhmo . . . . . 64°08' N, 029°31' E
Kuopio . . . . . 62°54' N, 027°41' E
Lahti . . . . . 60°58' N, 025°40' E
Lappeenranta
(Villmanstrand) . . . . . 61°04' N, 028°11' E
Lapua . . . . . 62°57' N, 023°00' E
Lohja . . . . . 60°15' N, 024°05' E
Mariehamn
(Maarianhamina) . . . . . 60°06' N, 019°57' E
Mikkeli (Sankt Michel) . . . . 61°41' N, 027°15' E
Nivala . . . . . 63°55' N, 024°58' E
Nurmes . . . . . 63°33' N, 029°07' E
Oulu (Uleåborg) . . . . . 65°01' N, 025°28' E
Pello . . . . . 66°47' N, 023°55' E
Pietarsaari . . . . . 63°40' N, 022°42' E
Pori (Björneborg) . . . . . 61°29' N, 021°47' E
Posio . . . . . 66°06' N, 028°09' E
Raahe . . . . . 64°41' N, 024°29' E
Rauma . . . . . 61°08' N, 021°30' E
Rovaniemi . . . . . 66°30' N, 025°43' E
Salla . . . . . 66°50' N, 028°40' E
Salo . . . . . 60°23' N, 023°08' E
Sotkamo . . . . . 64°08' N, 028°25' E
Tampere (Tammerfors) . . . 61°30' N, 023°45' E
Turku (Åbo) . . . . . 60°27' N, 022°17' E
Vaasa (Vasa) . . . . . 63°06' N, 021°36' E
Vantaa (Vanda) . . . . . 60°18' N, 024°51' E

FRANCE . . . . page 62

Ajaccio . . . . . 41°55' N, 008°44' E
Amiens . . . . . 49°54' N, 002°18' E
Angers . . . . . 47°28' N, 000°33' W
Annecy . . . . . 45°54' N, 006°07' E
Auch . . . . . 43°39' N, 000°35' E
Aurillac . . . . . 44°55' N, 002°27' E
Auxerre . . . . . 47°48' N, 003°34' E
Avignon . . . . . 43°57' N, 004°49' E
Bar-le-Duc . . . . . 48°47' N, 005°10' E
Bastia . . . . . 42°42' N, 009°27' E
Beauvais . . . . . 49°26' N, 002°05' E
Belfort . . . . . 47°38' N, 006°52' E
Bonifacio . . . . . 41°23' N, 009°09' E
Bordeaux . . . . . 44°50' N, 000°34' W
Bourges . . . . . 47°05' N, 002°24' E
Brest . . . . . 48°24' N, 004°29' W
Caen . . . . . 49°11' N, 000°21' W
Cahors . . . . . 44°26' N, 001°26' E
Calais . . . . . 50°57' N, 001°50' E
Charleville-Mézières . . . . . 49°46' N, 004°43' E
Chartres . . . . . 48°27' N, 001°30' E
Clermont-Ferrand . . . . . 45°47' N, 003°05' E
Colmar . . . . . 48°05' N, 007°22' E
Dijon . . . . . 47°19' N, 005°01' E
Dunkirk (Dunkerque) . . . . . 51°03' N, 002°22' E
Épinal . . . . . 48°11' N, 006°27' E
Grenoble . . . . . 45°10' N, 005°43' E
Guéret . . . . . 46°10' N, 001°52' E
La Rochelle . . . . . 46°10' N, 001°09' W
Le Havre . . . . . 49°30' N, 000°08' E
Le Mans . . . . . 48°00' N, 000°12' E
Lille . . . . . 50°38' N, 003°04' E
Limoges . . . . . 45°45' N, 001°20' E
Lyon . . . . . 45°45' N, 004°51' E
Marseille . . . . . 43°18' N, 005°24' E
Metz . . . . . 49°08' N, 006°10' E
Mont-de-Marsan . . . . . 43°53' N, 000°30' W
Moulins . . . . . 46°34' N, 003°20' E
Nancy . . . . . 48°41' N, 006°12' E
Nantes . . . . . 47°13' N, 001°33' W
Nevers . . . . . 46°59' N, 003°10' E
Nice . . . . . 43°42' N, 007°15' E
Nîmes . . . . . 43°50' N, 004°21' E
Niort . . . . . 46°19' N, 000°28' W
Orléans . . . . . 47°55' N, 001°54' E
Paris . . . . . 48°52' N, 002°20' E
Pau . . . . . 43°18' N, 000°22' W
Périgueux . . . . . 45°11' N, 000°43' E
Perpignan . . . . . 42°41' N, 002°53' E
Poitiers . . . . . 46°35' N, 000°20' E
Quimper . . . . . 48°00' N, 004°06' W
Rennes . . . . . 48°05' N, 001°41' W
Saint-Brieuc . . . . . 48°31' N, 002°47' W
Strasbourg . . . . . 48°35' N, 007°45' E
Tarbes . . . . . 43°14' N, 000°05' E
Toulon . . . . . 43°07' N, 005°56' E
Toulouse . . . . . 43°36' N, 001°26' E
Tours . . . . . 47°23' N, 000°41' E
Troyes . . . . . 48°18' N, 004°05' E
Tulle . . . . . 45°16' N, 001°46' E
Valence . . . . . 44°56' N, 004°54' E
Vannes . . . . . 47°40' N, 002°45' W
Versailles . . . . . 48°48' N, 002°08' E
Vesoul . . . . . 47°38' N, 006°10' E

GABON . . . . page 63

Bitam . . . . . 02°05' N, 011°29' E
Booué . . . . . 00°06' S, 011°56' E
Fougamou . . . . . 01°13' S, 010°36' E
Franceville . . . . . 01°38' S, 013°35' E
Kango . . . . . 00°09' N, 010°08' E
Koula-Moutou . . . . . 01°08' S, 012°29' E
Lambaréné . . . . . 00°42' S, 010°13' E
Lastoursville . . . . . 00°49' S, 012°42' E

Léconi . . . . . 01°35' S, 014°14' E
Libreville . . . . . 00°23' N, 009°27' E
Makokou . . . . . 00°34' N, 012°52' E
Mayumba . . . . . 03°25' S, 010°39' E
Mekambo . . . . . 01°01' N, 013°56' E
Mimongo . . . . . 01°38' S, 011°39' E
Minvoul . . . . . 02°09' N, 012°08' E
Mitzic . . . . . 00°47' N, 011°34' E
Mouila . . . . . 01°52' S, 011°01' E
Ndjolé . . . . . 00°11' S, 010°45' E
Okondja . . . . . 00°41' S, 013°47' E
Omboué . . . . . 01°34' S, 009°15' E
Ovendo . . . . . 00°17' N, 009°30' E
Oyem . . . . . 01°37' N, 011°35' E
Port-Gentil . . . . . 00°43' S, 008°47' E
Setté Cama . . . . . 02°32' S, 009°45' E
Tchibanga . . . . . 02°51' S, 011°02' E

GAMBIA, THE . . . . page 64

Banjul . . . . . 13°27' N, 016°35' W
Basse Santa Su . . . . . 13°19' N, 014°13' W
Brikama . . . . . 13°16' N, 016°39' W
Georgetown . . . . . 13°32' N, 014°46' W
Mansa Konko . . . . . 13°28' N, 015°33' W
Serekunda . . . . . 13°26' N, 016°34' W
Yundum . . . . . 13°20' N, 016°41' W

GEORGIA . . . . page 65

Akhalk'alak'i . . . . . 41°24' N, 043°29' E
Batumi . . . . . 41°38' N, 041°38' E
Chiat'ura . . . . . 42°19' N, 043°18' E
Gagra . . . . . 43°20' N, 040°15' E
Gardabani . . . . . 41°28' N, 045°05' E
Gori . . . . . 41°58' N, 044°07' E
Gudaut'a . . . . . 43°06' N, 040°38' E
Khashuri . . . . . 41°59' N, 043°36' E
K'obulet'i . . . . . 41°50' N, 041°45' E
Kutaisi . . . . . 42°15' N, 042°40' E
Marneuli . . . . . 41°27' N, 044°48' E
Och'amch'ire . . . . . 42°43' N, 041°28' E
Pot'i . . . . . 42°09' N, 041°40' E
Rustari . . . . . 41°33' N, 045°03' E
Samtredia . . . . . 42°11' N, 042°20' E
Sokhumi . . . . . 43°00' N, 041°02' E
Tbilisi (Tiflis) . . . . . 41°42' N, 044°45' E
T'elavi . . . . . 41°55' N, 045°28' E
Tqibuli . . . . . 42°22' N, 042°59' E
Tqvarch'eli (Tkvarchely) . . 42°51' N, 041°41' E
Ts'khinvali (Staliniri) . . . . . 42°14' N, 043°58' E
Tsqaltubo . . . . . 42°20' N, 042°34' E
Zugdidi . . . . . 42°30' N, 041°53' E

GERMANY . . . . page 66

Aachen . . . . . 50°46' N, 006°06' E
Augsburg . . . . . 48°22' N, 010°53' E
Aurich . . . . . 53°28' N, 007°29' E
Baden-Baden . . . . . 48°45' N, 008°15' E
Berlin . . . . . 52°30' N, 013°22' E
Bielefeld . . . . . 52°02' N, 008°32' E
Bonn . . . . . 50°44' N, 007°06' E
Brandenburg . . . . . 52°25' N, 012°33' E
Bremen . . . . . 53°05' N, 008°48' E
Bremerhaven . . . . . 53°33' N, 008°35' E
Chemnitz
(Karl-Marx-Stadt) . . . . . 50°50' N, 012°55' E
Cologne (Köln) . . . . . 50°56' N, 006°57' E
Cottbus . . . . . 51°46' N, 014°20' E
Dessau . . . . . 51°50' N, 012°15' E
Dortmund . . . . . 51°31' N, 007°27' E
Dresden . . . . . 51°03' N, 013°45' E
Duisburg . . . . . 51°26' N, 006°45' E
Düsseldorf . . . . . 51°13' N, 006°46' E
Erfurt . . . . . 50°59' N, 011°02' E
Erlangen . . . . . 49°36' N, 011°01' E
Essen . . . . . 51°27' N, 007°01' E
Frankfurt am Main . . . . . 50°07' N, 008°41' E
Freiburg . . . . . 48°00' N, 007°51' E
Göttingen . . . . . 51°32' N, 009°56' E
Halle . . . . . 51°30' N, 012°00' E
Hamburg . . . . . 53°33' N, 010°00' E
Hannover . . . . . 52°22' N, 009°43' E
Heidelberg . . . . . 49°25' N, 008°42' E
Jena . . . . . 50°56' N, 011°35' E
Kassel . . . . . 51°19' N, 009°30' E
Kiel . . . . . 54°20' N, 010°08' E
Leipzig . . . . . 51°18' N, 012°20' E
Lübeck . . . . . 53°52' N, 010°42' E
Magdeburg . . . . . 52°10' N, 011°40' E
Mainz . . . . . 50°00' N, 008°15' E
Mannheim . . . . . 49°29' N, 008°28' E
Munich . . . . . 48°09' N, 011°35' E
Nürnberg (Nuremberg) . . . 49°27' N, 011°05' E
Oldenburg . . . . . 54°18' N, 010°53' E
Osnabrück . . . . . 52°16' N, 008°03' E
Potsdam . . . . . 52°24' N, 013°04' E
Regensburg . . . . . 49°01' N, 012°06' E
Rostock . . . . . 54°05' N, 012°08' E
Saarbrücken . . . . . 49°14' N, 007°00' E
Schwerin . . . . . 53°38' N, 011°23' E
Siegen . . . . . 50°52' N, 008°02' E
Stuttgart . . . . . 48°46' N, 009°11' E
Ulm . . . . . 48°24' N, 010°00' E
Wiesbaden . . . . . 50°05' N, 008°15' E
Würzburg . . . . . 49°48' N, 009°56' E
Zwickau . . . . . 50°44' N, 012°30'E

GHANA . . . . page 67

Accra . . . . . 05°33' N, 000°13' E
Anloga . . . . . 05°48' N, 000°54' E
Awaso . . . . . 06°14' N, 002°16' W
Axim . . . . . 04°52' N, 002°14' W
Bawku . . . . . 11°03' N, 000°15' W
Bolgatanga . . . . . 10°47' N, 000°51' W
Cape Coast . . . . . 05°06' N, 001°15' W
Damongo . . . . . 09°05' N, 001°49' W
Dunkwa . . . . . 05°58' N, 001°47' W

Koforidua . . . . 05°14' N, 001°20' W
Kumasi. . . . . 06°41' N, 001°37' W
Mampong . . . . 07°04' N, 001°24' W
Obuasi . . . . 06°12' N, 001°40' W
Prestea . . . . 05°26' N, 002°09' W
Salaga . . . . 08°33' N, 000°31' W
Sekondi-Takoradi . . . . 04°53' N, 001°45' W
Sunyani . . . . 07°20' N, 002°20' W
Swedru . . . . 05°32' N, 000°42' W
Tamale. . . . . 09°24' N, 000°50' W
Tarkwa. . . . . 05°18' N, 001°59' W
Tema . . . . 05°37' N, 000°01' W
Wa . . . . 10°03' N, 002°29' W
Yendi . . . . 09°26' N, 000°01' W

GREECE . . . . page 68

Alexandroúpolis
(Alexandhroupolis). . . . . 40°51' N, 025°52' E
Ándros. . . . . 37°50' N, 024°56' E
Árgos . . . . 37°38' N, 022°44' E
Árta . . . . 39°09' N, 020°59' E
Áyios Nikólaos . . . . 35°11' N, 025°43' E
Drama . . . . 41°09' N, 024°09' E
Edessa (Edhessa) . . . . 40°48' N, 022°03' E
Ermoúpolis
(Hermoúpolìs) . . . . 37°27' N, 024°56' E
Flórina . . . . 40°47' N, 021°24' E
Hydra (Ídhra) . . . . 37°21' N, 023°28' E
Igoumenítsa. . . . . 39°30' N, 020°16' E
Ioánnina (Yannina). . . . . . . 39°40' N, 020°50' E
Ios . . . . 36°44' N, 025°17' E
Iráklion
(Candia or Heraklion) . . . 35°20' N, 025°08' E
Kalamariá . . . . 40°35' N, 022°58' E
Kalamata (Kalámai) . . . . . . 37°02' N, 022°07' E
Kálimnos . . . . 36°57' N, 026°59' E
Karditsa. . . . . 39°22' N, 021°55' E
Kariaí. . . . . 40°15' N, 024°15' E
Karpenísion. . . . . 38°55' N, 021°47' E
Kateríni . . . . 40°16' N, 022°30' E
Kavála
(Kaválla or Neapolis) . . . 40°56' N, 024°25' E
Kéa. 37°38' N, 024°21' E
Kérkira. . . . . 39°36' N, 019°55' E
Khalkís (Chalcis). . . . . 38°28' N, 023°36' E
Khaniá (Canea) . . . . 35°31' N, 024°02' E
Khíos (Chios) . . . . 38°22' N, 026°08' E
Kilkís . . . . 41°00' N, 022°52' E
Komotiní . . . . 41°07' N, 025°24' E
Lamía. . . . . 38°54' N, 022°26' E
Larissa (Lárisa) . . . . 39°38' N, 022°25' E
Laurium (Lávrion) . . . . 37°43' N, 024°03' E
Mégara. . . . . 38°00' N, 023°21' E
Mesolóngion
(Missolonghi) . . . . 38°22' N, 021°26' E
Mitilíni (Mytilene). . . . . 39°06' N, 026°33' E
Monemvasía . . . . 36°41' N, 023°03' E
Náuplia(Navplion) . . . . 37°34' N, 022°48' E
Náxos. . . . . 37°06' N, 025°23' E
Néa Ionía . . . . 38°02' N, 023°45' E
Pátrai. . . . . 38°15' N, 021°44' E
Piraeus (Piraievs) . . . . 37°57' N, 028°38' E
Préveza . . . . 38°57' N, 020°45' E
Pylos (Pílos) . . . . 36°55' N, 021°42' E
Pyrgos (Pírgos). . . . . 37°41' N, 021°27' E
Réthimnon. . . . . 35°22' N, 024°28' E
Rhodes (Ródhos) . . . . 36°26' N, 028°13' E
Sámos . . . . 37°45' N, 026°58' E
Samothráki . . . . 40°29' N, 025°31' E
Sérrai. . . . . 41°05' N, 023°33' E
Sparta (Spárti) . . . . 37°05' N, 022°26' E
Thásos. . . . . 40°47' N, 024°43' E
Thebes (Thívai) . . . . 38°19' N, 023°19' E
Thessaloníki
(Salonika). . . . . 40°38' N, 022°56' E
Tríkala . . . . 39°33' N, 021°46' E
Trípolis . . . . 37°31' N, 022°22' E
Vólos . . . . 39°22' N, 022°57' E
Yithion (Githion) . . . . 36°45' N, 022°34' E
Xánthi . . . . 41°08' N, 024°53' E
Zákinthos . . . . 37°47' N, 020°54' E

GRENADA . . . . page 69

Birch Grove. . . . . 12°07' N, 061°40' W
Concord. . . . . 12°07' N, 061°44' W
Corinth . . . . 12°02' N, 061°40' W
Gouyave . . . . 12°10' N, 061°44 W
Grand Anse . . . . 12°01' N, 061°45' W
Grenville . . . . 12°07' N, 061°37' W
Hillsborough . . . . 12°29' N, 061°28' W
La Poterie . . . . 12°10' N, 061°36' W
Rose Hill . . . . 12°12' N, 061°37' W
St. George's . . . . 12°03' N, 061°45' W
Sauteurs . . . . 12°14' N, 061°38' W
Victoria . . . . 12°12' N, 061°42' W

GUATEMALA . . . . . page 70

Amatitlán. . . . . 14°29' N, 090°37' W
Antigua Guatemala
(Antigua) . . . . 14°34' N, 090°44' W
Champerico. . . . . 14°18' N, 091°55' W
Coatepeque. . . . . 14°42' N, 091°52' W
Cobán . . . . 15°29' N, 090°22' W
Cuilapa
(Cuajiniquilapa). . . . . 14°17' N, 090°18' W
El Estor . . . . 15°32' N, 089°21' W
Escuintla . . . . 14°18' N, 090°47' W
Esquipulas. . . . . 14°34' N, 089°21' W
Flores. . . . . 16°56' N, 089°53' W
Gualán . . . . 15°08' N, 089°22' W
Guatemala City
(Guatemala). . . . . 14°38' N, 090°31' W
Huehuetenango . . . . 15°20' N, 091°28' W
Jalapa . . . . 14°38' N, 089°59' W
Jutiapa. . . . . 14°17' N, 089°54' W
Mazatenango. . . . . 14°32' N, 091°30' W
Poptún. . . . . 16°21' N, 089°26' W

Pueblo Nuevo Tiquisate	14°17' N,	091°22' W
Puerto Barrios	15°43' N,	088°36' W
Puerto San José	13°55' N,	090°49' W
Quezaltenango	14°50' N,	091°31' W
Salamá	15°06' N,	090°16' W
San Benito	16°55' N,	089°54' W
San Cristóbal Verapaz	15°23' N,	090°24' W
Santa Cruz del Quiché	15°02' N,	091°08' W
Sololá	14°46' N,	091°11' W
Todos Santos Cuchumatán	15°31' N,	091°37' W
Villa Nueva	14°31' N,	090°35' W
Zacapa	14°58' N,	089°32' W
Zunil	14°47' N,	091°29' W

GUINEA .... page 71

Beyla	08°41' N,	008°38' W
Boffa	10°10' N,	014°02' W
Boké	10°56' N,	014°18' W
Conakry	09°31' N,	013°43' W
Dabola	10°45' N,	011°07' W
Dalaba	10°42' N,	012°15' W
Dinguiraye	11°18' N,	010°43' W
Faranah	10°02' N,	010°44' W
Forécariah	09°26' N,	013°06' W
Fria	10°27' N,	013°32' W
Gaoual	11°45' N,	013°12' W
Guéckédou	08°33' N,	010°09' W
Kankan	10°23' N,	009°18' W
Kérouané	09°16' N,	009°01' W
Kindia	10°04' N,	012°51' W
Kissidougou	09°11' N,	010°06' W
Kouroussa	10°39' N,	009°53' W
Labé	11°19' N,	012°17' W
Macenta	08°33' N,	009°28' W
Mamou	10°23' N,	012°05' W
Nzérékoré	07°45' N,	008°49' W
Pita	11°05' N,	012°24' W
Siguiri	11°25' N,	009°10' W
Télimélé	10°54' N,	013°02' W
Tougué	11°27' N,	011°41' W

GUINEA-BISSAU .. page 72

Bafatá	12°10' N,	014°40' W
Bambadinca	12°02' N,	014°52' W
Bedanda	11°21' N,	015°07' W
Béli	11°51' N,	013°56' W
Bissau	11°51' N,	015°35' W
Bissorã	12°03' N,	015°26' W
Bolama	11°35' N,	015°28' W
Buba	11°35' N,	015°00' W
Bula	12°07' N,	015°43' W
Buruntuma	12°26' N,	013°39' W
Cacheu	12°16' N,	016°10' W
Catió	11°17' N,	015°15' W
Empada	11°33' N,	015°14' W
Farim	12°29' N,	015°13' W
Fulacunda	11°46' N,	015°10' W
Gabú (Nova Lamego)	12°17' N,	014°13' W
Galomaro	11°57' N,	014°38' W
Jolmete	12°13' N,	015°52' W
Madina do Boé	11°45' N,	014°13' W
Mansôa	12°04' N,	015°19' W
Nhacra	11°58' N,	015°33' W
Piche	12°20' N,	013°57' W
Pirada	12°40' N,	014°10' W
Quebo	11°20' N,	014°56' W
Quinhámel	11°53' N,	015°51' W
Safim	11°57' N,	015°39' W
Sangonhá	11°10' N,	014°53' W
São Domingos	12°24' N,	016°12' W
Teixeira Pinto	12°04' N,	016°02' W
Tite	11°47' N,	015°24' W
Xitole	11°44' N,	014°49' W

GUYANA .... page 73

Apoteri	04°02' N,	058°34' W
Bartica	06°24' N,	058°37' W
Charity	07°24' N,	058°36' W
Corriverton	05°52' N,	057°10' W
Georgetown	06°48' N,	058°10' W
Isherton	02°19' N,	059°22' W
Ituni	05°30' N,	058°14' W
Karasabai	04°02' N,	059°32' W
Karmuda Village	05°38' N,	060°18' W
Lethem	03°23' N,	059°48' W
Linden	06°00' N,	058°18' W
Mabaruma	08°12' N,	059°47' W
Mahaicony Village	06°36' N,	057°48' W
Matthews Ridge	07°30' N,	060°10' W
New Amsterdam	06°15' N,	057°31' W
Orinduik	04°42' N,	060°01' W
Parika	06°52' N,	058°25' W
Port Kaituma	07°44' N,	059°53' W
Rose Hall	06°16' N,	057°21' W
Suddie	07°07' N,	058°29' W
Vreed en Hoop	06°48' N,	058°11' W

HAITI .... page 74

Anse-d'Hainault	18°30' N,	074°27' W
Cap-Haïtien	19°45' N,	072°12' W
Desdunes	19°17' N,	072°39' W
Gonaïves	19°27' N,	072°41' W
Grand Goâve	18°26' N,	072°46' W
Hinche	19°09' N,	072°01' W
Jean Rabel	18°15' N,	072°40' W
Lascahobas	18°50' N,	071°56' W
Léogâne	18°31' N,	072°38' W
Limbé	19°42' N,	072°24' W
Miragoâne	18°27' N,	073°06' W
Mirebalais	18°55' N,	072°06' W
Môle Saint-Nicolas	19°48' N,	073°23' W
Ouanaminthe	19°33' N,	071°44' W
Pètionville	18°31' N,	072°17' W

Petite Rivière de l'Artibonite . . . . 19°08' N, 072°29' W
Port-au-Prince . . . . 18°32' N, 072°20' W
Roseaux . . . . 18°36' N, 074°01' W
Saint-Louis du Nord . . . . . . 19°56' N, 072°43' W
Saint-Michel de l'Atalaye . . 19°22' N, 072°20' W
Thomasique . . . . 19°05' N, 071°50' W
Trou du Nord . . . . 19°38' N, 072°01' W
Verrettes . . . . 19°03' N, 072°28' W

HONDURAS . . . . . . page 75

Amapala . . . . 13°17' N, 087°39' W
Catacamas . . . . 14°48' N, 085°54' W
Choloma . . . . 15°37' N, 087°57' W
Choluteca . . . . 13°18' N, 087°12' W
Comayagua . . . . 14°27' N, 087°38' W
Danlí . . . . 14°02' N, 086°35' W
El Paraíso . . . . 15°01' N, 088°59' W
El Progreso . . . . 15°24' N, 087°48' W
Gracias . . . . 14°35' N, 088°35' W
Guaimaca . . . . 14°32' N, 086°49' W
Intibucá . . . . 14°19' N, 088°10' W
Juticalpa . . . . 14°39' N, 086°12' W
La Ceiba . . . . 15°47' N, 086°48' W
La Esperanza . . . . 14°18' N, 088°11' W
La Lima . . . . 15°26' N, 087°55' W
La Paz . . . . 14°19' N, 087°41' W
Morazán . . . . 15°19' N, 087°36' W
Nacaome . . . . 13°32' N, 087°29' W
Olanchito . . . . 15°30' N, 086°34' W
Puerto Cortés . . . . 15°50' N, 087°50' W
Puerto Lempira . . . . 15°16' N, 083°46' W
San Lorenzo . . . . 13°25' N, 087°27' W
San Marcos de Colón . . . . . 13°26' N, 086°48' W
San Pedro Sula . . . . 15°30' N, 088°02' W
Santa Bárbara . . . . 14°55' N, 088°14' W
Santa Rita . . . . 15°12' N, 087°53' W
Signatapeque . . . . 14°36' N, 087°57' W
Talanga . . . . 14°24' N, 087°05' W
Tegucigalpa . . . . 14°06' N, 087°13' W
Trujillo . . . . 15°55' N, 86°00' W
Yoro . . . . 15°08' N, 087°08' W
Yuscarán . . . . 13°56' N, 086°51' W

HUNGARY . . . . page 76

Baja . . . . 46°11' N, 018°58' E
Balmazújváros . . . . 47°37' N, 021°21' E
Barcs . . . . 45°58' N, 017°28' E
Békéscsaba . . . . 46°41' N, 021°06' E
Berettyóújfalu . . . . 47°13' N, 021°33' E
Budapest . . . . 47°30' N, 019°05' E
Cegléd . . . . 47°10' N, 019°48' E
Debrecen . . . . 47°32' N, 021°38' E
Dunaújváros (Sztálinváros) . . . . 46°59' N, 018°56' E
Eger . . . . 47°54' N, 020°23' E
Esztergom . . . . 47°48' N, 018°45' E
Fertőd
(Eszterháza) . . . . 47°37' N, 016°52' E
Gyomaendrőd . . . . 46°56' N, 020°50' E
Gyöngyös . . . . 47°47' N, 019°56' E
Gyor . . . . 47°41' N, 017°38' E
Gyula . . . . 46°39' N, 021°17' E
Hódmezovásárhely . . . . 46°25' N, 020°20' E
Kalocsa . . . . 46°32' N, 019°00' E
Kaposvár . . . . 46°22' N, 017°48' E
Kazincbarcika . . . . 48°15' N, 020°38' E
Kecskemét . . . . 46°54' N, 019°42' E
Keszthely . . . . 46°46' N, 017°15' E
Kisvárda . . . . 48°13' N, 022°05' E
Körmend . . . . 47°01' N, 016°36' E
Kőszeg . . . . 47°23' N, 016°33' E
Lenti . . . . 46°37' N, 016°33' E
Makó . . . . 46°13' N, 020°29' E
Marcali . . . . 46°35' N, 017°25' E
Miskolc . . . . 48°06' N, 020°47' E
Mohács . . . . 45°59' N, 018°42' E
Nagyatád . . . . 46°13' N, 017°22' E
Nagykanizsa . . . . 46°27' N, 016°59' E
Nagykőrös . . . . 47°02' N, 019°47' E
Nyirbátor . . . . 47°50' N, 022°08' E
Nyíregyháza . . . . 47°57' N, 021°43' E
Orosháza . . . . 46°34' N, 020°40' E
Ózd . . . . 48°13' N, 020°18' E
Paks . . . . 46°38' N, 018°52' E
Pápa . . . . 47°20' N, 017°28' E
Pécs . . . . 46°05' N, 018°14' E
Salgótarján . . . . 48°07' N, 019°49' E
Sarkad . . . . 46°45' N, 021°23' E
Sárospatak . . . . 48°19' N, 021°35' E
Sátoraljaújhely . . . . 48°24' N, 021°40' E
Siklós . . . . 45°51' N, 018°18' E
Sopron . . . . 47°41' N, 016°36' E
Szeged . . . . 46°15' N, 020°10' E
Szeghalom . . . . 47°02' N, 021°10' E
Székesfehérvár . . . . 47°12' N, 018°25' E
Szekszárd . . . . 46°21' N, 018°43' E
Szigetvár . . . . 46°03' N, 017°48' E
Szolnok . . . . 47°11' N, 020°12' E
Szombathely . . . . 47°14' N, 016°37' E
Tamási . . . . 46°38' N, 018°17' E
Tatabánya . . . . 47°34' N, 018°25' E
Vác . . . . 47°47' N, 019°08' E
Veszprém . . . . 47°06' N, 017°55' E
Zalaegerszeg . . . . 46°50' N, 016°51' E

ICELAND . . . . page 77

Akureyri . . . . 65°40' N, 018°06' W
Reykjavík . . . . 64°09' N, 021°57' W
Vestmannaeyjar . . . . 62°26' N, 020°16' W

INDIA . . . . page 78

Agra . . . . 27°11' N, 078°01' E
Ahmadabad (Ahmedabad) . . . . 23°02' N, 072°37' E
Ahmadnāgār (Ahmednagar) . . . . 19°05' N, 074°44' E
Allahabad . . . . 25°27' N, 081°51' E

Amritsar . . . . 31°35' N, 074°53' E
Āsānsol . . . . 23°41' N, 086°59' E
Balurghat. . . . . 25°13' N, 088°46' E
Bangalore . . . . 12°59' N, 077°35' E
Baroda (Vadodara). . . . . . . 22°18' N, 073°12' E
Bathinda (Bhatinda). . . . . . 30°12' N, 074°57' E
Bhilwara . . . . 25°21' N, 074°38' E
Bhiwandi . . . . 19°18' N, 073°04' E
Bhopal. . . . . 23°16' N, 077°24' E
Bombay (Mumbai) . . . . 18°58' N, 072°50' E
Calcutta . . . . 22°32' N, 088°22' E
Coimbatore . . . . 11°00' N, 076°58' E
Cuddapah . . . . 14°28' N, 078°49' E
Dehra Dun . . . . 30°19' N, 078°02' E
Delhi . . . . 28°40' N, 077°13' E
Eluru (Ellore) . . . . 16°42' N, 081°06' E
Gangānagar
(Sri Gangānagar) . . . . 29°55' N, 073°53' E
Guntur . . . . 16°18' N, 080°27' E
Gwalior . . . . 26°13' N, 078°10' E
Howrah (Haora) . . . . 22°35' N, 088°20' E
Hubli-Dharwad . . . . 15°21' N, 075°10' E
Hyderabad. . . . . 17°23' N, 078°28' E
Imphal . . . . 24°49' N, 093°57' E
Indore . . . . 22°43' N, 075°50' E
Jabalpur
(Jubbulpore) . . . . 23°10' N, 079°57' E
Jaipur. . . . . 26°55' N, 075°49' E
Jammu. . . . . 32°44' N, 074°52' E
Jamnagar. . . . . 22°28' N, 070°04' E
Jodhpur. . . . . 26°17' N, 073°02' E
Jūnāgadh. . . . . 21°31' N, 070°28' E
Kanpur (Cawnpore) . . . . . . 26°28' N, 080°21' E
Khambhat (Cambay) . . . . . 22°18' N, 072°37' E
Kochi . . . . 09°58' N, 076°14' E
Kota (Kotah) . . . . 25°11' N, 075°50' E
Longju . . . . 28°45' N, 093°35' E
Lucknow . . . . 26°51' N, 080°55' E
Ludhiana . . . . 30°54' N, 075°51' E
Madras (Chennai). . . . . 13°05' N, 080°17' E
Madurai (Madura) . . . . 09°56' N, 078°07' E
Malegaon. . . . . 20°33' N, 074°32' E
Meerut. . . . . 28°59' N, 077°42' E
Nagpur. . . . . 21°09' N, 079°06' E
New Delhi . . . . 28°36' N, 077°12' E
Patna . . . . 25°36' N, 085°07' E
Pune (Poona) . . . . 18°32' N, 073°52' E
Puri . . . . 19°48' N, 085°51' E
Quilon . . . . 08°53' N, 076°36' E
Raipur . . . . 21°14' N, 081°38' E
Rajkot . . . . 22°18' N, 070°47' E
Sambalpur. . . . . 21°27' N, 083°58' E
Shiliguri (Siliguri) . . . . 26°42' N, 088°26' E
Sholapur (Solapur). . . . . . . 17°41' N, 075°55' E
Sibsāgar. . . . . 26°59' N, 094°38' E
Srinagar . . . . 34°05' N, 074°49' E
Surat . . . . 21°10' N, 072°50' E
Thanjavur (Tanjore). . . . . . 10°48' N, 079°09' E
Tiruppur (Tirupper). . . . . . 11°06' N, 077°21' E
Vadodara (Baroda). . . . . . . 22°18' N, 073°12' E
Vārānasi (Banāras,
Benares). . . . . 25°20' N, 083°00' E
Vishākhapatnam
(Visākhāpatam). . . . . 17°42' N, 083°18' E

INDONESIA . . . . page 79

Ambon. . . . . 03°43' S, 128°12' E
Balikpapan . . . . 01°17' S, 116°50' E
Banda Aceh
(Kuta Raja). . . . . 05°34' N, 095°20' E
Bandung . . . . 06°54' S, 107°36' E
Banjarmasin . . . . 03°20' S, 114°35' E
Cilacap. . . . . 07°44' S, 109°00' E
Jakarta. . . . . 06°10' S, 106°48' E
Jambi . . . . 01°36' S, 103°37' E
Kendari . . . . 03°57' S, 122°35' E
Kupang . . . . 10°10' S, 123°35' E
Malang. . . . . 07°59' S, 112°37' E
Manado . . . . 01°29' N, 124°51' E
Mataram . . . . 08°35' S, 116°07' E
Medan . . . . 03°35' N, 098°40' E
Padang. . . . . 00°57' S, 100°21' E
Palembang. . . . . 02°55' S, 104°45' E
Palu . . . . 00°53' S, 119°53' E
Samarinda . . . . 00°30' S, 117°09' E
Semarang. . . . . 06°58' S, 110°25' E
Surabaya . . . . 07°15' S, 112°45' E
Ujungpandang. . . . . 05°07' S, 119°24' E

IRAN . . . . page 80

Ahvāz. . . . . 31°19' N, 048°42' E
Āmol . . . . 36°28' N, 052°21' E
Arāk. . . . . 34°05' N, 049°41' E
Ardabīl. . . . . 38°15' N, 048°18' E
Bakhtarān . . . . 34°19' N, 047°04' E
Bandar 'Abbās. . . . . 27°11' N, 056°17' E
Behbahān . . . . 30°35' N, 050°14' E
Bīrjand. . . . . 32°53' N, 059°13' E
Būshehr. . . . . 28°59' N, 050°50' E
Dārāb. . . . . 28°45' N, 054°34' E
Dezfūl. . . . . 32°23' N, 048°24' E
Eṣfahān . . . . 32°40' N, 051°38' E
Gorgān. . . . . 36°50' N, 054°29' E
Hamadān . . . . 34°48' N, 048°30' E
Kāshān. . . . . 33°59' N, 051°29' E
Kāzerūn . . . . 29°37' N, 051°38' E
Kermān . . . . 30°17' N, 057°05' E
Khorramābād . . . . 33°30' N, 048°20' E
Khvoy . . . . 38°33' N, 044°58' E
Mahābād . . . . 36°45' N, 045°43' E
Mashhad . . . . 36°18' N, 059°36' E
Orūmīyeh . . . . 37°33' N, 045°04' E
Qā'en. . . . . 33°44' N, 059°11' E
Qom. . . . . 34°39' N, 050°54' E
Quchan . . . . 37°06' N, 058°30' E
Rafsanjān. . . . . 30°24' N, 056°00' E
Rasht . . . . 37°16' N, 049°36' E
Sanandaj . . . . 35°19' N, 047°00' E
Shīrāz. . . . . 29°36' N, 052°32' E
Tabrīz . . . . 38°05' N, 046°18' E
Tehran. . . . . 35°40' N, 051°26' E

Yazd . . . . 31°53' N, 054°22' E
Zāhedān . . . . 29°30' N, 060°52' E
Zanjān . . . . 36°40' N, 048°29' E

IRAQ . . . . page 81

Ad-Diwaniyah . . . . 31°59' N, 044°56' E
Al-'Amarah . . . . 31°50' N, 047°09' E
Al-Gharrāf . . . . 31°21' N, 046°17' E
Al-Hillah . . . . 32°29' N, 044°25' E
Al-Khāliṣ . . . . 33°49' N, 044°32' E
Al-Kūt . . . . 32°30' N, 045°49' E
Al-Maḥmūdiya . . . . 33°03' N, 044°21' E
Al-Majarr al-Kabir . . . . 31°34' N, 047°00' E
'Ānah . . . . 34°28' N, 041°56' E
An-Najaf . . . . 31°59' N, 044°20' E
An-Nashwah . . . . 30°49' N, 047°36' E
An-Nasiriyah . . . . 31°02' N, 046°16' E
Ar-Ramādī . . . . 33°25' N, 043°17' E
Ar-Ruṭbah . . . . 33°02' N, 040°17' E
As-Samawah . . . . 31°18' N, 045°17' E
As-Sulaymaniyah . . . . 35°33' N, 045°26' E
Aṣ-Ṣuwayrah . . . . 32°55' N, 044°47' E
Baghdad . . . . 33°21' N, 044°25' E
Ba'qubah . . . . 33°45' N, 044°38' E
Barzān . . . . 36°55' N, 044°03' E
Basra (Al-Basrah) . . . . 30°30' N, 047°47' E
Dibs . . . . 35°40' N, 044°04' E
Hīt . . . . 33°38' N, 042°49' E
Irbil
(Arbela, Arbil, or Erbil) . . 36°11' N, 044°01' E
Jalūlā' . . . . 34°16' N, 045°10' E
Karbala' . . . . 32°36' N, 044°02' E
Khānaqin . . . . 34°21' N, 045°22' E
Kirkuk . . . . 35°28' N, 044°23' E
Mosul (Al-Mawsil) . . . . 36°20' N, 043°08' E
Qal'at Dizah . . . . 36°11' N, 045°07' E
Sinjār . . . . 36°19' N, 041°52' E
Tall Kayf . . . . 36°29' N, 043°08' E
Tikrīt . . . . 34°36' N, 043°42' E
Ṭūz Khurmātū
(Touz Hourmato) . . . . . . 34°53' N, 044°38' E
Zummār . . . . 36°47' N, 042°38' E

IRELAND . . . . page 82

Arklow
(An tinbhear Mor) . . . . . . 52°48' N, 006°09' W
Athlone . . . . 53°26' N, 007°57' W
Ballina . . . . 54°07' N, 009°10' W
Ballycastle . . . . 54°17' N, 009°22' W
Ballycotton . . . . 51°50' N, 008°01' W
Ballymote . . . . 54°05' N, 008°31' W
Ballyvaghan . . . . 53°07' N, 009°09' W
Bandon
(Droichead na Bandan) . . 51°45' N, 008°44' W
Bantry . . . . 51°41' N, 009°27' W
Belmullet . . . . 54°13' N, 010°00' W
Blarney . . . . 51°56' N, 008°34' W
Boyle . . . . 53°58' N, 008°18' W
Bray (Bre) . . . . 53°12' N, 006°06' W
Buncrana . . . . 55°08' N, 007°27' W
Carlow (Ceatharlach) . . . . . 52°50' N, 006°56' W
Carndonagh . . . . 55°15' N, 007°16' W
Carrick on Shannon . . . . . . 53°57' N, 008°05' W
Castlebar . . . . 53°51' N, 009°18' W
Castletownbere . . . . 51°39' N, 009°55' W
Cavan (Cabhan, An) . . . . . . 54°00' N, 007°22' W
Charleville (Rath Luirc) . . . 52°21' N, 008°41' W
Clifden . . . . 53°29' N, 010°01' W
Clonakilty . . . . 51°37' N, 008°53' W
Clonmel (Cluain Meala) . . . 52°21' N, 007°42' W
Cobh . . . . 51°51' N, 008°17' W
Cork (Corcaigh) . . . . 51°54' N, 008°28' W
Dingle . . . . 52°08' N, 010°15' W
Donegal . . . . 54°39' N, 008°07' W
Drogheda
(Droichead Atha) . . . . . . 53°43' N, 006°21' W
Dublin . . . . 53°20' N, 006°15' W
Dundalk (Dun Dealgan) . . . 54°00' N, 006°25' W
Dungarvan . . . . 52°05' N, 007°37' W
Ennis (Inis) . . . . 52°51' N, 008°59' W
Enniscorthy . . . . 52°30' N, 006°34' W
Ennistimon . . . . 52°56' N, 009°18' W
Galway (Gaillimh) . . . . 53°17' N, 009°03' W
Gort . . . . 53°04' N, 008°49' W
Kenmare . . . . 51°53' N, 009°35' W
Kilkee . . . . 52°41' N, 009°38' W
Kilkenny (Cill Chainnigh) . . 52°39' N, 007°15' W
Killarney (Cill Airne) . . . . . . 52°03' N, 009°31' W
Letterkenny . . . . 54°57' N, 007°44' W
Lifford . . . . 54°50 N, 007°29' W
Limerick (Luimneach) . . . . 52°40' N, 008°37' W
Listowel . . . . 52°27' N, 009°29' W
Longford . . . . 53°44' N, 007°48' W
Loughrea . . . . 53°12' N, 008°34' W
Mallow . . . . 52°08' N, 008°38' W
Monaghan . . . . 54°15' N, 006°58' W
Naas (Nas, An) . . . . 53°13' N, 006°40' W
New Ross (Ros Mhic
Thriuin) . . . . 52°23' N, 006°56' W
Portlaoise (Maryborough,
Portlaoighise) . . . . 53°02' N, 007°18' W
Portumna . . . . 53°05' N, 008°13' W
Roscommon . . . . 53°38' N, 008°11' W
Rosslare . . . . 52°17' N, 006°23' W
Shannon . . . . 52°42' N, 008°52' W
Sligo . . . . 54°16' N, 008°29' W
Swords . . . . 53°27' N, 006°13' W
Tralee . . . . 52°16' N, 009°43' W
Trim . . . . 53°33' N, 006°48' W
Tullamore . . . . 53°16' N, 007°29' W
Waterford (Port Lairge) . . . 52°15' N, 007°06' W
Westport . . . . 53°48' N, 009°31' W
Wexford (Loch Garman) . . 52°20' N, 006°28' W
Wicklow (Cill Mhantain) . . . 52°59' N, 006°03' W
Youghal . . . . 51°57' N, 007°51' W

ISRAEL . . . . page 83

'Arad . . . . 31°15' N, 035°13' E
Ashdod . . . . 31°49' N, 034°39' E

Ashqelon	31°40' N,	034°35' E
Bat Yam	32°01' N,	034°45' E
Beersheba (Be'er Sheva')	31°14' N,	034°47' E
Bet She'an	32°30' N,	035°30' E
Bet Shemesh	31°45' N,	035°00' E
Dimona	31°04' N,	035°02' E
Elat	29°33' N,	034°57' E
'En Yahav	30°38' N,	035°11' E
H̱adera	32°26' N,	034°55' E
Haifa (H̱efa)	32°50' N,	035°00' E
Haẕeva	30°48' N,	035°15' E
Herzliyya	32°10' N,	034°51' E
H̱olon	32°01' N,	034°46' E
Jerusalem (Yerushalayim)	31°46' N,	035°14' E
Karmi'el	32°55' N,	035°18' E
Nazareth (Naẕerat)	32°42' N,	035°18' E
Netanya	32°20' N,	034°51' E
Nir Yizẖaq	31°14' N,	034°22' E
Petaẖ Tiqwa	32°05' N,	034°53' E
Qiryat Ata	32°48' N,	035°06' E
Qiryat Shemona	33°13' N,	035°34' E
Rama	32°56' N,	035°22' E
Reẖovot	31°54' N,	034°49' E
Tel Aviv-Yafo	32°04' N,	034°46' E

ITALY . . . . page 84

Agrigento (Girgenti)	37°19' N,	013°34' E
Ancona	43°38' N,	013°30' E
Aosta	45°44' N,	007°20' E
Arezzo	43°25' N,	011°53' E
Bari	41°08' N,	016°51' E
Bologna	44°29' N,	011°20' E
Bolzano	46°31' N,	011°22' E
Brescia	45°33' N,	010°15' E
Cagliari	39°13' N,	009°07' E
Catania	37°30' N,	015°06' E
Catanzaro	38°54' N,	016°35' E
Crotone	39°05' N,	017°08' E
Cuneo (Coni)	44°23' N,	007°32' E
Fermo	43°09' N,	013°43' E
Florence (Firenze or Florentia)	43°46' N,	011°15' E
Foggia	41°27' N,	015°34' E
Genoa (Genova)	44°25' N,	008°57' E
Grosseto	42°46' N,	011°08' E
Iglesias	39°19' N,	008°32' E
Latina	41°28' N,	012°52' E
Manfredonia	41°38' N,	015°55' E
Marsala	37°48' N,	012°26' E
Milan (Milano)	45°28' N,	009°12' E
Naples (Napoli or Neapolis)	40°50' N,	014°15' E
Oristano	39°54' N,	008°36' E
Padua (Padova)	45°25' N,	011°53' E
Palermo	38°07' N,	013°22' E
Perugia (Perusia)	43°08' N,	012°22' E
Pescara	42°28' N,	014°13' E
Piombino	42°55' N,	010°32' E
Pisa	43°43' N,	010°23' E
Porto Torres	40°50' N,	008°24' E
Potenza	40°38' N,	015°48' E
Ragusa	36°55' N,	014°44' E
Ravenna	44°25' N,	012°12' E
Rome (Roma)	41°54' N,	012°29' E
Salerno	40°41' N,	014°47' E
San Remo	43°49' N,	007°46' E
Sassari	40°43' N,	008°34' E
Siena	43°19' N,	011°21' E
Syracuse (Siracusa)	37°04' N,	015°18' E
Taranto (Taras or Tarentum)	40°28' N,	017°14' E
Trapani	38°01' N,	012°29' E
Trento	46°04' N,	011°08' E
Trieste	45°40' N,	013°46' E
Turin (Torino)	45°03' N,	007°40' E
Udine	46°03' N,	013°14' E
Venice (Venezia)	45°27' N,	012°21' E
Verona	45°27' N,	011°00' E

JAMAICA . . . . page 85

Annotto Bay	18°16' N,	076°46' W
Kingston	17°58' N,	076°48' W
Lucea	18°27' N,	078°10' W
Mandeville	18°02' N,	077°30' W
May Pen	17°58' N,	077°14' W
Montego Bay	18°28' N,	077°55' W
Port Antonio	18°11' N,	076°28' W
St. Ann's Bay	18°26' N,	077°08' W
Savanna-la-Mar	18°13' N,	078°08' W
Spanish Town	17°59' N,	076°57' W

JAPAN . . . . page 86-7

Akita	39°43' N,	140°07' E
Aomori	40°49' N,	140°45' E
Asahikawa	43°46' N,	142°22' E
Chiba	35°36' N,	140°07' E
Fukui	36°04' N,	136°13' E
Fukuoka	33°35' N,	130°24' E
Fukushima	37°45' N,	140°28' E
Funabashi	35°42' N,	139°59' E
Gifu	35°25' N,	136°45' E
Hachinohe	40°30' N,	141°29' E
Hakodate	41°45' N,	140°43' E
Hiroshima	34°24' N,	132°27' E
Hofu	34°03' N,	131°34' E
Iwaki	37°05' N,	140°50' E
Kagoshima	31°36' N,	130°33' E
Kanazawa	36°34' N,	136°39' E
Kawasaki	35°32' N,	139°43' E
Kita-Kyushu	33°50' N,	130°50' E
Kōbe	34°41' N,	135°10' E
Kōchi	33°33' N,	133°33' E
Kumamoto	32°48' N,	130°43' E
Kushiro	42°58' N,	144°23' E
Kutchan	42°54' N,	140°45' E
Kyōto	35°00' N,	135°45' E

Matsue . . . . 35°28' N, 133°04' E
Matsuyama . . . . 33°50' N, 132°45' E
Mito . . . . 36°22' N, 140°28' E
Miyazaki . . . . 31°52' N, 131°25' E
Morioka . . . . 39°42' N, 141°09' E
Muroran . . . . 42°18' N, 140°59' E
Nagano . . . . 36°39' N, 138°11' E
Nagasaki . . . . 32°48' N, 129°55' E
Nagoya . . . . 35°10' N, 136°55' E
Naha . . . . 26°13' N, 127°40' E
Niigata . . . . 37°55' N, 139°03' E
Obihiro . . . . 42°55' N, 143°12' E
Okayama . . . . 34°39' N, 133°55' E
Ōsaka . . . . 34°40' N, 135°30' E
Otaru . . . . 43°13' N, 141°00' E
Sakai . . . . 34°35' N, 135°28' E
Sapporo . . . . 43°03' N, 141°21' E
Sendai . . . . 31°49' N, 130°18' E
Shizuoka . . . . 34°58' N, 138°23' E
Tokyo . . . . 35°42' N, 139°46' E
Tomakomai . . . . 42°38' N, 141°36' E
Tottori . . . . 35°30' N, 134°14' E
Toyama . . . . 36°41' N, 137°13' E
Utsunomiya . . . . 36°33' N, 139°52' E
Wakayama . . . . 34°13' N, 135°11' E
Wakkanai . . . . 45°25' N, 141°40' E
Yaizu . . . . 34°52' N, 138°20' E
Yamagata . . . . 38°15' N, 140°20' E
Yokohama . . . . 35°27' N, 139°39' E

JORDAN . . . . page 88

Adir . . . . 31°12' N, 035°46' E
Al-'Aqabah . . . . 29°31' N, 035°00' E
Al-Fayḍah . . . . 32°35' N, 038°13' E
Al-Ḥiṣn . . . . 32°29' N, 035°53' E
Al-Karak . . . . 31°11' N, 035°42' E
Al-Mafraq . . . . 32°21' N, 036°12' E
Al-Mazra'ah . . . . 31°16' N, 035°31' E
Al-Mudawwarah . . . . 29°19' N, 035°59' E
Al-Qaṭrānah . . . . 31°15' N, 036°03' E
Amman ('Ammān) . . . . 31°57' N, 035°56' E
Ar-Ramthā . . . . 32°34' N, 036°00' E
Ash-Shawbak . . . . 30°32' N, 035°34' E
Aṣ Ṣalt . . . . 32°03' N, 035°44' E
At-Ṭafilah . . . . 30°50' N, .035°36' E
Az-Zarqā` . . . . 32°05' N, 036°06' E
Bā'ir . . . . 30°46' N, 036°41' E
Dhāt Ra's . . . . 31°00' N, 035°46' E
Irbid . . . . 32°33' N, 035°51' E
Ma'ān . . . . 30°12' N, 035°44' E
Ma'dabā . . . . 31°43' N, 035°48' E
Maḥaṭṭat al-Ḥafif . . . . 32°12' N, 037°08' E
Maḥaṭṭat al-Jufūr . . . . 32°30' N, 038°12' E
Ṣuwayliḥ . . . . 32°02' N, 035°50' E

KAZAKHSTAN . . . . page 89

Almaty (Alma-Ata) . . . . 43°15' N, 076°57' E
Aqtau (Aktau, or
Shevchenko) . . . . 43°39' N, 051°12' E
Aqtöbe (Aktyubinsk) . . . . . 50°17' N, 057°10' E
Arqalyq . . . . 50°13' N, 066°50' E
Astana (Akmola,
Akmolinsk, Aqmola,
or Tselinograd) . . . . 51°10' N, 071°30' E
Atyraū (Atenau, Gurjev, or
Guryev) . . . . 47°07' N, 051°53' E
Ayaguz . . . . 47°56' N, 080°23' E
Balqash (Balkhash or
Balchas) . . . . 46°49' N, 075°00' E
Dzhezkazgan . . . . 47°47' N, 067°46' E
Kokchetav . . . . 53°17' N, 069°30' E
Leningor (Leninogorsk
or Ridder) . . . . 50°22' N, 083°32' E
Oral (Uralsk) . . . . 51°14' N, 051°22' E
Öskemen
(Ust-Kamenogorsk) . . . . . 49°58' N, 082°40' E
Panfīlov (Zharkent) . . . . . . 44°10' N, 080°01' E
Pavlodar . . . . 52°18' N, 076°57' E
Petropavl
(Petropavlovsk) . . . . 54°52' N, 069°06' E
Qaraghandy
(Karaganda) . . . . 49°50' N, 073°10' E
Qostanay (Kustanay) . . . . . 53°10' N, 063°35' E
Qyzylorda(Kzyl-Orda) . . . . 44°48' N, 065°28' E
Rūdnyy (Rudny) . . . . 52°57' N, 063°07' E
Semey
(Semipalatinsk . . . . 50°28' N, 080°13' E
Shchūchinsk . . . . 52°56' N, 070°12' E
Shymkent (Chimkent or
Cimkent) . . . . 42°18' N, 069°36' E
Taldyqorghan (Taldy
-Kurgan) . . . . 45°00' N, 078°24' E
Talghar . . . . 43°19' N, 077°15' E
Termirtaū
(Samarkand) . . . . 50°05' N, 072°56' E
Türkistan . . . . 43°20' N, 068°15' E
Tyuratam (Turaram or
Leninsk) . . . . 45°40' N, 063°20' E
Zhambyl (Dzhambul) . . . . . 42°54' N, 071°22' E
Zhangatas . . . . 43°34' N, 069°45' E
Zhetiqara . . . . 52°11' N, 061°12' E
Zhezqazghan . . . . 47°47' N, 067°46' E
Zyryan . . . . 49°43' N, 084°20' E

KENYA . . . . page 90

Bungoma . . . . 00°34' N, 034°34' E
Busia . . . . 00°28' N, 034°06' E
Eldoret . . . . 00°31' N, 035°17' E
Embu . . . . 00°32' S, 037°27' E
Garissa . . . . 00°28' S, 039°38' E
Isiolo . . . . 00°21' N, 037°35' E
Kisii . . . . 00°41' S, 034°46' E
Kisumu . . . . 00°06' S, 034°45' E
Lamu . . . . 02°16' S, 040°54' E
Lodwar . . . . 03°07' N, 035°36' E
Machakos . . . . 01°31' S, 037°16' E
Malindi . . . . 03°13' S, 040°07' E
Mandera . . . . 03°56' N, 041°52' E

Maralal . . . . 01°06' N, 036°42' E
Marsabit . . . . 02°20' N, 037°59' E
Meru . . . . 00°03' N, 037°39' E
Mombasa. . . . . 04°03' N, 039°40' E
Murang'a . . . . 00°43' N, 037°09' E
Nairobi. . . . . 01°17' S, 036°49' E
Nakuru. . . . . 00°17' S, 036°04' E
Nanyuki . . . . 00°01' N, 037°04' E
Wajir . . . . 01°45' N, 040°04' E

KIRIBATI . . . . page 91

Bairiki . . . . 01°20' N, 173°01' E

KUWAIT . . . . page 92

Al-Aḥmadī . . . . 29°05' N, 048°04' E
Al-Jahrah . . . . 29°20' N, 047°40' E
Ash-Shuʿaybah . . . . 29°03' N, 048°08' E
Ḥawallī. . . . . 29°19' N, 048°02' E
Kuwait . . . . 29°20' N, 047°59' E

KYRGYZSTAN . . . . page 93

Bishkek (Frunze). . . . . 42°54' N, 074°36' E
Dzhalal-Abad. . . . . 40°56' N, 073°00' E
Irkeshtam . . . . 39°41' N, 073°55' E
Kara-Balta . . . . 42°50' N, 073°52' E
Karakol (Przhevalsk) . . . . . 42°33' N, 078°18' E
Kök-Janggak . . . . 41°02' N, 073°12' E
Kyzyl-Kyya. . . . . 40°16' N, 072°08' E
Mayly-Say . . . . 41°17' N, 072°24' E
Naryn. . . . . 41°26' N, 075°58' E
Osh . . . . 40°32' N, 072°48' E
Sülüktü . . . . 39°56' N, 069°34' E
Talas . . . . 42°32' N, 072°14' E
Tash-Kömür . . . . 41°21' N, 072°14' E
Tokmok . . . . 42°52' N, 075°18' E
Ysyk-Kül (Rybachye) . . . . . 42°26' N, 076°12' E

LAOS . . . . page 94

Attapu . . . . 14°48' N, 106°50' E
Ban Houayxay. . . . . 20°18' N, 100°26' E
Champasak . . . . 14°53' N, 105°52' E
Louang Namtha. . . . . 20°57' N, 101°25' E
Louangphrabang. . . . . 19°52' N, 102°08' E
Muang Khammouan
(Muang Thakhek) . . . . . . 17°24' N, 104°48' E
Muang Pek. . . . . 19°35' N, 103°19' E
Muang Xaignabouri
(Sayaboury). . . . . 19°15' N, 101°45' E
Muang Xay . . . . 20°42' N, 101°59' E
Pakxé. . . . . 15°07' N, 105°47' E
Phôngsali. . . . . 21°41' N, 102°06' E
Saravan . . . . 15°43' N, 106°25' E
Savannakhét . . . . 16°33' N, 104°45' E
Vientiane
(Viangchan). . . . . 17°58' N, 102°36' E
Xam Nua . . . . 20°25' N, 104°02' E

LATVIA . . . . page 95

Aizpute . . . . 56°43' N, 021°36' E
Alūksne . . . . 57°25' N, 027°03' E
Auce. . . . . 56°28' N, 022°53' E
Balvi. . . . . 57°08' N, 027°15' E
Bauska. . . . . 56°24' N, 024°11' E
Cēsis . . . . 57°18' N, 025°15' E
Daugavpils. . . . . 55°53' N, 026°32' E
Dobele . . . . 56°37' N, 023°16' E
Gulbene . . . . 57°11' N, 026°45' E
Ilūkste . . . . 55°58' N, 026°18' E
Jaunjelgava . . . . 56°37' N, 025°05' E
Jēkabpils . . . . 56°29' N, 025°51' E
Jelgava. . . . . 56°39' N, 023°42' E
Jūrmala . . . . 56°58' N, 023°34' E
Kandava . . . . 57°02' N, 022°46' E
Kārsava . . . . 56°47' N, 027°40' E
Ķegums . . . . 56°44' N, 024°43' E
Krāslava . . . . 55°54' N, 027°10' E
Liepāja. . . . . 56°31' N, 021°01' E
Limbaži . . . . 57°31' N, 024°42' E
Ludza. . . . . 56°33' N, 027°43' E
Malta . . . . 56°23' N, 027°07' E
Mazsalace . . . . 57°52' N, 025°03' E
Ogre. . . . . 56°49' N, 024°36' E
Piltene . . . . 57°13' N, 021°40' E
Preili . . . . 56°18' N, 026°43' E
Priekulė. . . . . 55°33' N, 021°19' E
Rēzekne. . . . . 56°30' N, 027°19' E
Riga (Rīga). . . . . 56°57' N, 024°06' E
Rujiena . . . . 57°54' N, 025°19' E
Sabile. . . . . 57°03' N, 022°35' E
Salacgrīva . . . . 57°45' N, 024°21' E
Saldus . . . . 56°40' N, 022°30' E
Sigulda. . . . . 57°09' N, 024°51' E
Stučka . . . . 56°35' N, 025°12' E
Talsi. . . . . 57°15' N, 022°36' E
Valdemārpils. . . . . 57°22' N, 022°35' E
Valmiera . . . . 57°33' N, 025°24' E
Ventspils . . . . 57°24' N, 021°31' E
Viesīte . . . . 56°21' N, 025°33' E
Viļaka. . . . . 57°11' N, 027°41' E
Viļāni . . . . 56°33' N, 026°57' E
Zilupe. . . . . 56°23' N, 028°07' E

LEBANON . . . . page 96

Ad-Dāmūr . . . . 33°44' N, 035°27' E
Al-ʿAbdah . . . . 34°31' N, 035°58' E
Al-Batrūn . . . . 34°15' N, 035°39' E
Al-Hirmīl . . . . 34°23' N, 036°23' E
Al-Labwah . . . . 34°12' N, 036°21' E
Al-Qubayyāt . . . . 34°34' N, 036°17' E
Amyūn . . . . 34°18' N, 035°49' E
An-Nabaṭīyah at-Taḥtā . . . . 33°23' N, 035°29' E

Aṣ-Ṣarafand . . . . . 33°27' N, 035°18' E
Baalbek (Ba'labakk) . . . . . 34°00' N, 036°12' E
B'aqlīn . . . . . 33°41' N, 035°33' E
Beirut (Bayrut) . . . . . 33°53' N, 035°30' E
Bḥamdūn . . . . . 33°48' N, 035°39' E
Bint Jubayl . . . . . 33°07' N, 035°26' E
Bsharri . . . . . 34°15' N, 036°01' E
En-Nāqūrah . . . . . 33°07' N, 035°08' E
Ghazir . . . . . 34°01' N, 035°40' E
Ghazzah . . . . . 33°40' N, 035°49' E
Ghūmāh . . . . . 34°13' N, 035°42' E
Halbā . . . . . 34°33' N, 036°05' E
Ḥaṣbayya . . . . . 33°24' N, 035°41' E
Ḥimlāyā . . . . . 33°56' N, 035°42' E
Ihdin . . . . . 34°17' N, 035°58' E
Jubayl (Byblos) . . . . . 34°07' N, 035°39' E
Jubb Jannin . . . . . 33°37' N, 035°47' E
Jūniyah . . . . . 33°59' N, 035°58' E
Jwayyā . . . . . 33°14' N, 035°19' E
Khaldah . . . . . 33°47' N, 035°29' E
Marj 'Uyūn . . . . . 33°22' N, 035°35' E
Shḥim . . . . . 33°37' N, 035°29' E
Shikkā . . . . . 34°20' N, 035°44' E
Sidon (Sayda) . . . . . 33°33' N, 035°22' E
Tripoli (Tarabulus) . . . . . 34°26' N, 035°51' E
Tyre (Ṣūr) . . . . . 33°16' N, 035°11' E
Zaḥlah . . . . . 33°51' N, 035°53' E
Zghartā . . . . . 34°24' N, 035°54' E

LESOTHO . . . . page 97

Butha-Butha . . . . . 28°45' S, 028°15' E
Libono . . . . . 28°38' S, 028°35' E
Mafeteng . . . . . 29°49' S, 027°15' E
Maseru . . . . . 29°19' S, 027°29' E
Mohales Hoek . . . . . 30°09' S, 027°28' E
Mokhotlong . . . . . 29°22' S, 029°02' E
Qacha's Nek . . . . . 30°08' S, 028°41' E
Quthing . . . . . 30°24' S, 027°43' E
Roma . . . . . 29°27' S, 027°42' E
Teyateyaneng . . . . . 29°09' S, 027°44' E

LIBERIA . . . . page 98

Bentol . . . . . 06°26' N, 010°36' W
Bopolu . . . . . 06°54' N, 010°46' W
Buchanan
(Grand Bassa) . . . . . 05°53' N, 010°03' W
Careysburg . . . . . 06°24' N, 010°33' W
Gbarnga . . . . . 07°00' N, 009°29' W
Grand Cess
(Grand Sesters) . . . . . 04°34' N, 008°13' W
Greenville (Sino) . . . . . 05°00' N, 009°02' W
Harbel . . . . . 06°16' N, 010°21' W
Harper . . . . . 04°22' N, 007°23' W
Kle . . . . . 06°42' N, 010°53' W
Monrovia . . . . . 06°19' N, 010°48' W
Robertsport . . . . . 06°45' N, 011°22' W
Saniquellie
(Sangbui) . . . . . 07°22' N, 008°43' W
Tubmanburg
(Vaitown) . . . . . 06°52' N, 010°49' W
Voinjama . . . . . 08°25' N, 009°45' W
Yekepa . . . . . 07°35' N, 008°32' W
Zorzor . . . . . 07°47' N, 009°26' W
Zwedru (Tchien) . . . . . 06°04' N, 008°08' W

LIBYA . . . . page 99

Al-Bayḍā (Baida or
Zāwiyat al-Bayḍā) . . . . . 32°46' N, 021°43' E
Al-Kufrah . . . . . 24°10' N, 023°15' E
Al-Marj (Barce) . . . . . 32°30' N, 020°50' E
Al-'Uwaynāt
(Sardalas) . . . . . 25°48' N, 010°33' E
As-Sidrah (Es-Sidre) . . . . . 30°39' N, 018°22' E
Awbāri (Ubari) . . . . . 26°35' N, 012°46' E
Az-Zuwaytinah . . . . . 30°58' N, 020°07' E
Benghazi (Banghazi or
Bengasi) . . . . . 32°07' N, 020°04' E
Dahra . . . . . 29°30' N, 017°50' E
Darnah (Dērna) . . . . . 32°46' N, 022°39' E
Ghadāmis (Ghadāmes) . . . . 30°08' N, 009°30' E
Ghaddūwah (Goddua) . . . . 26°26' N, 014°18' E
Gharyān (Garian) . . . . . 32°10' N, 013°01' E
Ghāt . . . . . 24°58' N, 010°11' E
Marādah . . . . . 29°14' N, 019°13' E
Miṣrātah (Misurata) . . . . . 32°23' N, 015°06' E
Murzuq . . . . . 25°55' N, 013°55' E
Sabhā (Sebha) . . . . . 27°02' N, 014°26' E
Sarīr . . . . . 27°30' N, 022°30' E
Surt (Sirte) . . . . . 31°13' N, 016°35' E
Tarabulus, see Tripoli
Tāzirbū . . . . . 25°45' N, 021°00' E
Tobruk (Ṭubruq) . . . . . 32°05' N, 023°59' E
Tripoli (Ṭarābulus) . . . . . 32°54' N, 013°11' E
Waddān . . . . . 29°10' N, 016°08' E
Wāw al-Kabīr . . . . . 25°20' N, 016°43' E
Zalṭan (Zelten) . . . . . 32°57' N, 011°52' E
Zlīṭan (Zliten) . . . . . 32°28' N, 014°34' E
Zuwārah (Zuāra) . . . . . 32°56' N, 012°06' E

LIECHTENSTEIN page 100

Balzers . . . . . 47°04' N, 009°32' E
Eschen . . . . . 47°13' N, 009°32' E
Mauren . . . . . 47°13' N, 009°33' E
Schaan . . . . . 47°10' N, 009°31' E
Triesen . . . . . 47°07' N, 009°32' E
Vaduz . . . . . 47°09' N, 009°31' E

LITHUANIA . . . . . . page 101

Alytus . . . . . 54°24' N, 024°03' E
Anykščiai . . . . . 55°32' N, 025°06' E
Birštonas . . . . . 54°37' N, 024°02' E
Biržai . . . . . 56°12' N, 024°45' E
Druskininkai . . . . . 54°01' N, 023°58' E
Gargždai . . . . . 55°43' N, 021°24' E

Ignalina	55°21' N,	026°10' E
Jonava	55°05' N,	024°17' E
Joniškis	56°14' N,	023°37' E
Jurbarkas	55°04' N,	022°46' E
Kaunas	54°54' N,	023°54' E
Kazly Rūda	54°46' N,	023°30' E
Kėdainiai	55°17' N,	023°58' E
Kelmė	55°38' N,	022°56' E
Klaipėda	55°43' N,	021°07' E
Kuršėnai	56°00' N,	022°56' E
Lazdijai	54°14' N,	023°31' E
Marijampolė (Kapsukas)	54°34' N,	023°21' E
Mažeikiai	56°19' N,	022°20' E
Naujoji Akmenė	56°19' N,	022°54' E
Neringa	55°22' N,	021°04' E
Pagėgiai	55°09' N,	021°54' E
Pakruojis	58°58' N,	023°52' E
Palanga	55°55' N,	021°03' E
Pandėlys	56°01' N,	025°13' E
Panevėžys	55°44' N,	024°21' E
Pasvalys	56°04' N,	024°24' E
Plungė	55°55' N,	021°51' E
Priekulė	55°33' N,	021°19' E
Radviliškis	55°49' N,	023°32' E
Ramygala	55°31' N,	024°18' E
Raseiniai	55°22' N,	023°07' E
Rokiškis	55°58' N,	025°35' E
Šalčininkai	54°18' N,	025°23' E
Šiauliai	55°56' N,	023°19' E
Šilalė	55°28' N,	022°12' E
Šilutė	55°21' N,	021°29' E
Širvintos	55°03' N,	024°57' E
Skuodas	56°16' N,	021°32' E
Tauragė	55°15' N,	022°17' E
Telšiai	55°59' N,	022°15' E
Trakai	54°38' N,	024°56' E
Utena	55°30' N,	025°36' E
Varėna	54°13' N,	024°34' E
Vilkaviškis	54°39' N,	023°02' E
Vilkija	55°03' N,	023°35' E
Vilnius	54°41' N,	025°19' E
Zarasai	55°44' N,	026°15' E

LUXEMBOURG .. page 102

Bains (Modorf-les-Bains)	49°30' N,	006°17' E
Bettembourg	49°31' N,	006°06' E
Capellen	49°39' N,	005°59' E
Clervaux	50°03' N,	006°02' E
Diekirch	49°52' N,	006°10' E
Differdange	49°31' N,	005°53' E
Dudelange	49°28' N,	006°06' E
Echternach	49°49' N,	006°25' E
Esch-sur-Alzette	49°30' N,	005°59' E
Ettlebruck	49°51' N,	006°07' E
Grevenmacher	49°41' N,	006°27' E
Hesperange	49°34' N,	006°09' E
Junglinster	49°43' N,	006°15' E
Lorentzweiler	49°42' N,	006°09' E
Luxembourg	49°36' N,	006°08' E
Mamer	49°38' N,	006°02' E
Mersch	49°45' N,	006°06' E
Niederanven	49°39' N,	006°16' E
Pétange	49°33' N,	005°53' E
Rambrouch	49°50' N,	005°51' E
Redange	49°46' N,	005°53' E
Remich	49°32' N,	006°22' E
Sanem	49°33' N,	005°56' E
Schifflange	49°30' N,	006°01' E
Vianden	49°56' N,	006°13' E
Walfedange	49°39' N,	006°08' E
Wiltz	49°58' N,	005°56' E
Wincrange	50°03' N,	005°55' E
Wormeldange	49°37' N,	006°25' E

MACEDONIA .... page 103

Bitola	41°02' N,	021°20' E
Gostivar	41°48' N,	020°54' E
Kavadarci	41°26' N,	022°00' E
Kičevo	41°31' N,	020°57' E
Kočani	41°55' N,	022°25' E
Kruševo	41°22' N,	021°15' E
Kumanovo	42°08' N,	021°43' E
Ohrid	41°07' N,	020°48' E
Prilep	41°21' N,	021°34' E
Skopje (Skoplje)	42°00' N,	021°29' E
Štip	41°44' N,	022°12' E
Strumica	41°26' N,	022°39' E
Tetovo	42°01' N,	020°59' E
Tito Veles	41°42' N,	021°48' E

MADAGASCAR ... page 104

Ambanja	13°41' S,	048°27' E
Ambatondrazaka	17°50' S,	048°25' E
Andapa	14°39' S,	049°39' E
Ankarana (Sosumav)	13°05' S,	048°55' E
Antalaha	14°53' S,	050°17' E
Antananarivo (Tananarive)	18°55' S,	047°31' E
Antsirabe	19°51' S,	047°02' E
Antsirañana (Diégo-Suarez)	12°16' S,	049°17' E
Antsohihy	14°52' S,	047°59' E
Fianarantsoa	21°26' S,	047°05' E
Ihosy	22°24' S,	046°07' E
Maevatanana	16°57' S,	046°50' E
Mahabo	20°23' S,	044°40' E
Mahajanga (Majunga)	15°43' S,	046°19' E
Mahanoro	19°54' S,	048°48' E
Mananjary	21°13' S,	048°20' E
Maroantsetra	15°26' S,	049°44' E
Marovoay	16°06' S,	046°38' E
Morombe	21°44' S,	043°21' E
Morondava	20°17' S,	044°17' E
Port-Bergé (Boriziny)	15°33' S,	047°40' E
Toamasina (Tamatave)	18°10' S,	049°23' E

Tôlañaro (Faradofay, Fort-Dauphin or Taolanaro) . . . 25°02' S, 047°00' E
Toliara (Toliary or Tulear) . . . 23°21' S, 043°40' E
Vangaindrano . . . 23°21' S, 047°36' E
Vatomandry . . . 19°20' S, 048°59' E

MALAWI . . . . page 105

Balaka . . . 14°59' S, 034°57' E
Blantyre . . . 15°47' S, 035°00' E
Chikwawa . . . 16°03' S, 034°48' E
Cholo (Thyolo) . . . 16°04' S, 035°08' E
Dedza . . . 14°22' S, 034°20' E
Dowa . . . 13°39' S, 033°56' E
Karonga . . . 09°56' S, 033°56' E
Kasungu . . . 13°02' S, 033°29' E
Lilongwe . . . 13°59' S, 033°47' E
Mangoche (Fort Johnson) . 14°28' S, 035°16' E
Mchinji (Fort Manning) . . . 13°48' S, 032°54' E
Monkey Bay . . . 14°05' S, 034°55' E
Mzimba . . . 11°54' S, 033°36' E
Mzuzu . . . 11°27' S, 033°55' E
Nkhata Bay . . . 11°36' S, 034°18' E
Nkhota Kota (Kota Kota) . . . 12°55' S, 034°18' E
Nsanje (Port Herald) . . . 16°55' S, 035°16' E
Salima . . . 13°47' S, 034°26' E
Zomba . . . 15°23' S, 035°20' E

MALAYSIA . . . . . . page 106

Alor Setar . . . 06°07' N, 100°22' E
Batu Pahat . . . 01°51' N, 102°56' E
Bau . . . 01°25' N, 110°09' E
Bentong . . . 03°32' N, 101°55' E
Bintulu . . . 03°10' N, 113°02' E
Butterworth . . . 05°25' N, 100°24' E
George Town (Pinang) . . . 05°25' N, 100°20' E
Ipoh . . . 04°35' N, 101°05' E
Johor Baharu . . . 01°28' N, 103°45' E
Kangar . . . 06°26' N, 100°12' E
Kelang (Klang) . . . 03°02' N, 101°27' E
Keluang . . . 02°02' N, 103°19' E
Kota Baharu . . . 06°08' N, 102°15' E
Kota Kinabalu (Jesselton) . . . 05°59' N, 116°04' E
Kota Tinggi . . . 01°44' N, 103°54' E
Kuala Dungun (Dungun) . . . 04°47' N, 103°26' E
Kuala Lumpur . . . 03°10' N, 101°42' E
Kuala Terengganu . . . 05°20' N, 103°08' E
Kuantan . . . 03°48' N, 103°20' E
Kuching . . . 01°33' N, 110°20' E
Lundu . . . 01°40' N, 109°51' E
Melaka (Malacca) . . . 02°12' N, 102°15' E
Miri . . . 04°23' N, 113°59' E
Muar (Bandar Maharani) . . . 02°02' N, 102°34' E
Petaling Jaya . . . 03°05' N, 101°39' E
Sandakan . . . 05°50' N, 118°07' E
Sarikei . . . 02°07' N, 111°31' E
Seremban . . . 02°43' N, 101°56' E
Sibu . . . 02°18' N, 111°49' E
Song . . . 02°01' N, 112°33' E
Sri Aman (Simanggang) . . . 01°15' N, 111°26' E
Taiping . . . 04°51' N, 100°44' E
Tawau . . . 04°15' N, 117°54' E
Teluk Intan (Telok Anson) . . . 04°02' N, 101°01' E
Victoria (Labuan) . . . 05°17' N, 115°15' E

MALDIVES . . . . . . page 107

Male . . . 04°10' N, 073°30' E

MALI . . . . page 108

Ansongo . . . 15°40' N, 000°30' E
Bafoulabé . . . 13°48' N, 010°50' W
Bamako . . . 12°39' N, 008°00' W
Diamou . . . 14°05' N, 011°16' W
Diré . . . 16°16' N, 003°24' W
Gao . . . 16°16' N, 000°03' W
Goundam . . . 16°25' N, 003°40' W
Kalana . . . 10°47' N, 008°12' W
Kangaba . . . 11°56' N, 008°25' W
Kayes . . . 14°27' N, 011°26' W
Kolokani . . . 13°35' N, 008°02' W
Koro . . . 14°04' N, 003°05' W
Labbezanga . . . 14°57' N, 000°42' E
Ménaka . . . 15°55' N, 002°24' E
Mopti . . . 14°30' N, 004°12' W
Nara . . . 15°10' N, 007°17' W
Niafounké . . . 15°56' N, 004°00' W
Nioro Du Sahel . . . 15°14' N, 009°35' W
San . . . 13°18' N, 004°54' W
Ségou . . . 13°27' N, 006°16' W
Sikasso . . . 11°19' N, 005°40' W
Taoudenni . . . 22°40' N, 003°59' W
Timbuktu . . . 16°46' N, 003°01' W

MALTA . . . . page 109

Birkirkara . . . 35°54' N, 014°28' E
Hamrun . . . 35°53' N, 014°29' E
Mosta . . . 35°55' N, 014°26' E
Rabat . . . 35°53' N, 014°24' E
Valletta (Valetta) . . . 35°54' N, 014°31' E
Żabbar . . . 35°52' N, 014°32' E
Żebbug . . . 35°52' N, 014°26' E
Żejtun . . . 35°51' N, 014°32' E

MARSHALL ISLANDS . . . . page 110

Majuro . . . 07°09' N, 171°12' E

MAURITANIA . . . . page 111

Akjoujt	19°45' N,	014°23' W
Aleg	17°03' N,	013°55' W
Atar	20°31' N,	013°03' W
Ayoûn el 'Atroûs	16°40' N,	009°37' W
Bir Mogrein	25°14' N,	011°35' W
Bogué (Boghé)	16°35' N,	014°16' W
Boutilimit	17°33' N,	014°42' W
Chinguetti	20°27' N,	012°22' W
Fdérik	22°41' N,	012°43' W
Guérou	16°48' N,	011°50' W
Kaédi	16°09' N,	013°30' W
Kiffa	16°37' N,	011°24' W
Maghama	15°31' N,	012°51' W
M'Bout	16°02' N,	012°35' W
Mederdra	16°55' N,	015°39' W
Néma	16°37' N,	007°15' W
Nouadhibou	20°54' N,	017°04' W
Nouakchott	18°06' N,	015°57' W
Rosso	16°30' N,	015°49' W
Sélibaby	15°10' N,	012°11' W
Tichit	18°28' N,	009°30' W
Tidjikdja	18°33' N,	011°25' W
Timbédra	16°15' N,	008°10' W
Zouirât	22°42' N,	012°30' W

MAURITIUS. . . . . . page 112

Port Louis	20°10' S,	057°30' E

MEXICO . . . . page 113

Acapulco	16°51' N,	099°55' W
Aguascalientes	21°53' N,	102°18' W
Caborca	30°37' N,	112°06' W
Campeche	19°51' N,	090°32' W
Cananea	30°57' N,	110°18' W
Cancún	21°05' N,	086°46' W
Carmen	18°38' N,	091°50' W
Casas Grandes	30°22' N,	107°57' W
Chetumal	18°30' N,	088°18' W
Chihuahua	28°38' N,	106°05' W
Ciudad Acuña (Las Vacas)	29°18' N,	100°55' W
Ciudad Juárez	31°44' N,	106°29' W
Ciudad Obregón	27°29' N,	109°56' W
Ciudad Victoria	23°44' N,	099°08' W
Colima	19°14' N,	103°43' W
Culiacán	24°48' N,	107°24' W
Durango	24°02' N,	104°40' W
Guadalajara	20°40' N,	103°20' W
Guadalupe	25°41' N,	100°15' W
Guaymas	27°56' N,	110°54' W
Hermosillo	29°04' N,	110°58' W
Jiménez	27°08' N,	104°55' W
Juchitán	16°26' N,	095°01' W
La Paz	24°10' N,	110°18' W
León	21°07' N,	101°40' W
Matamoros	25°53' N,	097°30' W
Matehuala	23°39' N,	100°39' W
Mazatlán	23°13' N,	106°25' W
Mérida	20°58' N,	089°37' W
Mexicali	32°40' N,	115°29' W
Mexico City (Ciudad de Mexico)	19°24' N,	099°09' W
Minatitlán	17°59' N,	094°31' W
Monterrey	25°40' N,	100°19' W
Morelia	19°42' N,	101°07' W
Nuevo Laredo	27°30' N,	099°31' W
Oaxaca	17°03' N,	096°43' W
Poza Rica	20°33' N,	097°27' W
Puebla	19°03' N,	098°12' W
Saltillo	25°25' N,	101°00' W
San Felipe	31°00' N,	114°52' W
San Ignacio	27°27' N,	112°51' W
Tampico	22°13' N,	097°51' W
Tijuana	32°32' N,	117°01' W
Torreón	25°33' N,	103°26' W
Tuxtla	16°45' N,	093°07' W
Veracruz	19°12' N,	096°08' W
Villahermosa	17°59' N,	092°55' W
Zapopan	20°43' N,	103°24' W

MICRONESIA, FEDERATED STATES OF . . . . . . page 114

Colonia	09°31' N,	138°08' E
Kosrae	05°19' N,	162°59' E
Palikir	06°59' N,	158°08' E
Weno	07°26' N,	151°52' E

MOLDOVA . . . . . page 115

Bălţi	47°46' N,	027°56' E
Calaras	47°16' N,	028°19' E
Căuşeni	46°38' N,	029°25' E
Chişinău	47°00' N,	028°50' E
Ciadâr-Lunga	46°03' N,	028°50' E
Comrat (Komrat)	46°18' N,	028°39' E
Drochia	48°02' N,	027°48' E
Dubăsari	47°07' N,	029°10' E
Făleşti (Faleshty)	47°34' N,	027°42' E
Floreşti	47°53' N,	028°17' E
Hânceşti (Kotovsk)	46°50' N,	028°36' E
Kagul	45°54' N,	028°11' E
Leova (Leovo)	46°28' N,	028°15' E
Orhei (Orgeyev)	47°22' N,	028°49' E
Râbnita	47°45' N,	029°00' E
Rezina	47°45' N,	028°58' E
Soroca (Soroki)	48°09' N,	028°18' E
Tighina	46°49' N,	029°29' E
Tiraspol	46°50' N,	029°37' E
Ungheni	47°12' N,	027°48' E

MONACO. . . . . . page 116

Monaco	43°44' N,	007°25' E

MONGOLIA . . . . . . page 117

City	Latitude	Longitude
Altay	46°20' N,	096°18' E
Arvayheer	46°15' N,	102°48' E
Baruun-Urt	46°42' N,	113°15' E
Bulgan	48°45' N,	103°34' E
Choybalsan (Bayan Tumen)	48°04' N,	114°30' E
Choyr	46°20' N,	108°20' E
Dalandzadgad	43°34' N,	104°25' E
Darhan	49°29' N,	105°55' E
Dariganga	45°18' N,	113°52' E
Dzüünharaa	48°52' N,	106°28' E
Erdenet	49°02' N,	104°05' E
Ereen	49°15' N,	112°29' E
Hanh	51°30' N,	100°40' E
Hatgal	50°26' N,	100°09' E
Hovd (Jirgalanta)	48°01' N,	091°38' E
Mörön	49°38' N,	100°10' E
Öndörhaan (Tsetsen Khan)	47°19' N,	110°39' E
Saynshand	44°52' N,	110°09' E
Sühbaatar	50°15' N,	106°12' E
Tes	49°41' N,	095°48' E
Tosontsengel	48°47' N,	098°15' E
Tsetserleg	47°30' N,	101°27' E
Tümentsogt	47°27' N,	112°15' E
Ulaanbaatar	47°55' N,	106°53' E
Uliastay	47°45' N,	096°49' E

MONTENEGRO . . page 118

City	Latitude	Longitude
Bar	42°05' N,	019°06' E
Nikšić	42°46' N,	018°58' E
Podgorica (Titograd)	42°26' N,	019°16' E

MOROCCO . . . . . . page 119

City	Latitude	Longitude
Agadir	30°24' N,	009°36' W
Asilah (Arzila or Arcila)	35°28' N,	006°02' W
Beni Mellal	32°20' N,	006°21' W
Berkane	34°56' N,	002°20' W
Boudenib	31°57' N,	003°36' W
Boulemane	33°22' N,	004°45' W
Casablanca (Ad-Dār al-Bayḍā' or Dar el-Beida)	33°37' N,	007°35' W
El Jadida (Mazagan)	33°15' N,	008°30' W
El-Kelaa des Srarhna	32°03' N,	007°24' W
Er-Rachidia (Ksar es-Souk)	31°56' N,	004°26' W
Fès (Fez)	34°02' N,	004°59' W
Figuig	32°06' N,	001°14' W
Guelmim (Goulimine)	28°56' N,	010°04' W
Kenitra (Mina Hassan Tani or Port-Lyautey)	34°16' N,	006°36' W
Khouribga	32°53' N,	006°54' W
Larache (El-Araish)	35°12' N,	006°09' W
Marrakech	31°38' N,	008°00' W
Meknès	33°54' N,	005°33' W
Mohammedia (Fedala)	33°42' N,	007°24' W
Nador	35°11' N,	002°56' W
Ouarzazate	30°55' N,	006°55' W
Oued Zem	32°52' N,	006°34' W
Oujda	34°40' N,	001°54' W
Rabat (Ribat)	34°02' N,	006°50' W
Safi (Asfi)	32°18' N,	009°14' W
Salé (Sla)	34°04' N,	006°48' W
Settat	33°00' N,	007°37' W
Tangier (Tanger)	35°48' N,	005°48' W
Tan-Tan	28°26' N,	011°06' W
Taounate	34°33' N,	004°39' W
Tarfaya	27°57' N,	012°55' W
Tata	29°45' N,	007°59' W
Taza	34°13' N,	004°01' W
Tétouan (Tetuan)	35°34' N,	005°22' W
Zagora	30°19' N,	005°50' W

MOZAMBIQUE . . . page 120

City	Latitude	Longitude
Angoche	16°15' S,	039°54' E
Beira	19°50' S,	034°52' E
Chimoio (Vila Pery)	19°08' S,	033°29' E
Chokwe	24°32' S,	032°59' E
Inhambane	23°52' S,	035°23' E
Lichinga	13°18' S,	035°14' E
Maputo (Lourenço Marques)	25°58' S,	032°34' E
Massinga	23°20' S,	035°22' E
Memba	14°12' S,	040°32' E
Moçambique (Mozambique)	15°03' S,	040°45' E
Mocubúri	14°39' S,	038°54' E
Mopeia Velha	17°59' S,	035°43' E
Morrumbene	23°39' S,	035°20' E
Nacala	14°33' S,	040°40' E
Namapa	13°43' S,	039°50' E
Nampula	15°09' S,	039°18' E
Panda	24°03' S,	034°43' E
Pemba	12°57' S,	040°30' E
Quelimane	17°51' S,	036°52' E
Quissico	24°43' S,	034°45' E
Tete	16°10' S,	033°36' E
Vila da Manhiça	25°24' S,	032°48' E
Vila da Mocimboa da Praia	11°20' S,	040°21' E
Vila do Chinde (Chinde)	18°34' S,	036°27' E
Xai Xai (Joaõ Belo)	25°04' S,	033°39' E

MYANMAR . . . . . page 121

City	Latitude	Longitude
Allanmyo	19°22' N,	095°13' E
Bassein (Pathein)	16°47' N,	094°44' E
Bhamo	24°16' N,	097°14' E
Chauk	20°53' N,	094°49' E

Henzada	17°38' N,	095°28' E
Homalin	24°52' N,	094°55' E
Kale	16°05' N,	097°54' E
Katha	24°11' N,	096°21' E
Kawthaung	09°59' N,	098°33' E
Kēng Tung	21°17' N,	099°36' E
Kyaikkami	16°04' N,	097°34' E
Kyaukpyu (Ramree)	19°05' N,	093°52' E
Labutta	16°09' N,	094°46' E
Loi-kaw	19°41' N,	097°13' E
Magwe (Magwa)	20°09' N,	094°55' E
Mandalay	22°00' N,	096°05' E
Mergui	12°26' N,	098°36' E
Minbu	20°11' N,	094°53' E
Monywa	22°07' N,	095°08' E
Moulmein (Mawlamyine)	16°30' N,	097°38' E
Myitkyina	25°23' N,	097°24' E
Palaw	12°58' N,	098°39' E
Pegu (Bago)	17°20' N,	096°29' E
Prome (Pye)	18°49' N,	095°13' E
Putao	27°21' N,	097°24' E
Pyinmana	19°44' N,	096°13' E
Sagaing	21°52' N,	095°59' E
Shwebo	22°34' N,	095°42' E
Sittwe (Akyab)	20°09' N,	092°54' E
Syriam	16°46' N,	096°15' E
Taunggyi	20°47' N,	097°02' E
Tavoy (Dawei)	14°05' N,	098°12' E
Tenasserim	12°05' N,	099°01' E
Thaton	16°55' N,	097°22' E
Tonzang	23°36' N,	093°42' E
Toungoo	18°56' N,	096°26' E
Yangon (Rangoon)	16°47' N,	096°10' E

NAMIBIA . . . . page 122

Aranos	24°08' S,	019°07' E
Bagani	18°07' S,	021°38' E
Gobabis	22°27' S,	018°58' E
Grootfontein	19°34' S,	018°07' E
Karasburg	28°01' S,	018°45' E
Karibib	21°56' S,	015°50' E
Keetmanshoop	26°35' S,	018°08' E
Khorixas	20°22' S,	014°58' E
Lüderitz	26°38' S,	015°09' E
Maltahöhe	24°50' S,	016°59' E
Mariental	24°38' S,	017°58' E
Okahandja	21°59' S,	016°55' E
Omaruru	21°26' S,	015°56' E
Ondangwa (Ondangua)	17°55' S,	015°57' E
Opuwo	18°04' S,	013°51' E
Oranjemund	28°33' S,	016°26' E
Oshakati	17°47' S,	015°41' E
Otjimbingwe	22°21' S,	016°08' E
Otjiwarongo	20°27' S,	016°39' E
Outjo	20°07' S,	016°09' E
Rehoboth	23°19' S,	017°05' E
Rundu	17°56' S,	019°46' E
Swakopmund	22°41' S,	014°32' E
Tsumeb	19°14' S,	017°43' E
Usakos	22°00' S,	015°36' E
Walvis Bay	22°57' S,	014°30' E
Warmbad	28°27' S,	018°44' E
Windhoek	22°35' S,	017°05' E

NAURU . . . . page 123

Yaren	00°32' S,	166°55' E

NEPAL . . . . page 124

Bāglūṅg	28°16' N,	083°36' E
Banepa	27°38' N,	085°31' E
Bhairahawā	27°30' N,	083°27' E
Bhaktapur (Bhadgaon)	27°41' N,	085°25' E
Bhojpūr	27°10' N,	087°03' E
Biratnagar	26°29' N,	087°17' E
Birendranagar	28°46' N,	081°38' E
Birganj	27°00' N,	084°52' E
Dailekh	28°50' N,	081°44' E
Dandeldhūrā	29°18' N,	080°35' E
Ilām	26°54' N,	087°56' E
Jājarkot	28°42' N,	082°12' E
Jalésvar	26°38' N,	085°48' E
Jomosom	28°47' N,	083°44' E
Jumlā	29°17' N,	082°10' E
Kathmandu	27°43' N,	085°19' E
Lahān	26°43' N,	086°29' E
Lalitpur (Patan)	27°40' N,	085°20' E
Lumbini (Rummin-dei)	27°29' N,	083°17' E
Mahendranagar	28°55' N,	080°20' E
Mustāng	29°11' N,	083°58' E
Nepālganj	28°03' N,	081°37' E
Pokharā	28°14' N,	083°59' E
Sallyān	28°22' N,	082°10' E
Simikot	29°58' N,	081°50' E
Taplejūṅg	27°21' N,	087°40' E

NETHERLANDS, THE . . . . page 125

Alkmaar	52°38' N,	004°45' E
Almelo	52°21' N,	006°40' E
Amersfoort	52°09' N,	005°23' E
Amstelveen	52°18' N,	004°52' E
Amsterdam	52°21' N,	004°55' E
Apeldoorn	52°13' N,	005°58' E
Arnhem	51°59' N,	005°55' E
Assen	53°00' N,	006°33' E
Bergen op Zoom	51°30' N,	004°18' E
Breda	51°34' N,	004°48' E
Delft	52°00' N,	004°22' E
Den Helder	52°58' N,	004°46' E
Deventer	52°15' N,	006°12' E
Dordrecht (Dort or Dordt)	51°48' N,	004°40' E
Drachten	53°06' N,	006°06' E

City	Latitude	Longitude
Ede	52°02' N,	005°40' E
Eindhoven	51°27' N,	005°28' E
Emmen	52°47' N,	006°54' E
Enschede	52°13' N,	006°54' E
Geleen	50°58' N,	005°50' E
Gendringen	51°52' N,	006°23' E
Groningen	53°13' N,	006°33' E
Haarlem	52°22' N,	004°39' E
Heerenveen	52°57' N,	005°56' E
Heerlen	50°54' N,	005°59' E
Helmond	51°29' N,	005°40' E
Hengelo	52°16' N,	006°48' E
Hilversum	52°14' N,	005°11' E
Hoofddorp (Haarlemmermeer)	52°18' N,	004°42' E
Hoorn	52°39' N,	005°04' E
IJmuiden	52°28' N,	004°36' E
Langedijk	52°42' N,	004°49' E
Leeuwarden (Ljouwert)	53°12' N,	005°47' E
Leiden (Leyden)	52°09' N,	004°30' E
Lelystad	52°31' N,	005°29' E
Maastricht	50°51' N,	005°41' E
Meppel	52°42' N,	006°12' E
Middelburg	51°30' N,	003°37' E
Nieuwegein	52°02' N,	005°06' E
Nijmegen (Nimwegen)	51°50' N,	005°52' E
Ommen	52°31' N,	006°26' E
Oostburg	51°20' N,	003°30' E
Oss	51°46' N,	005°32' E
Purmerend	52°31' N,	004°57' E
Ridderkerk	51°52' N,	004°36' E
Roermond	51°12' N,	006°00' E
Roosendaal	51°32' N,	004°28' E
Rosmalen	51°43' N,	005°22' E
Rotterdam	51°55' N,	004°30' E
Schiedam	51°55' N,	004°24' E
's-Hertogenbosch (Den Bosch or Bois-le-Duc)	51°42' N,	005°19' E
Sneek (Snits)	53°02' N,	005°40' E
Soest	52°11' N,	005°18' E
Steenwijk	52°47' N,	006°07' E
Stein	50°58' N,	005°46' E
Terneuzen	51°20' N,	003°50' E
The Hague ('s-Gravenhage, Den Haag, or La Haye)	52°05' N,	004°18' E
Tholen	51°32' N,	004°13' E
Tilburg	51°33' N,	005°07' E
Utrecht	52°05' N,	005°08' E
Veenendaal	52°02' N,	005°33' E
Venlo	51°22' N,	006°10' E
Vlaardingen	51°55' N,	004°21' E
Vlissingen (Flushing)	51°27' N,	003°35' E
Zaanstad	52°27' N,	004°50' E
Zoetermeer	52°03' N,	004°30' E
Zwolle	52°30' N,	006°05' E

NEW ZEALAND . . page 126

City	Latitude	Longitude
Auckland	36°52' S,	174°46' E
Blenheim	41°31' S,	173°57' E
Cheviot	42°49' S,	173°16' E
Christchurch	43°32' S,	172°39' E
Dunedin	45°53' S,	170°29' E
East Coast Bays	36°45' S,	174°45' E
Gisborne	38°39' S,	178°01' E
Greymouth	42°27' S,	171°12' E
Hamilton	37°47' S,	175°16' E
Hastings	39°39' S,	176°50' E
Invercargill	46°25' S,	168°22' E
Lower Hutt	41°13' S,	174°56' E
Manukau	36°57' S,	174°56' E
Milford Sound	44°41' S,	167°55' E
Napier	39°31' S,	176°54' E
Nelson	41°17' S,	173°17' E
New Plymouth	39°04' S,	174°04' E
Oamaru	45°06' S,	170°58' E
Paeroa	37°23' S,	175°40' E
Palmerston North	40°21' S,	175°37' E
Porirua	41°08' S,	174°51' E
Rotorua	38°10' S,	176°14' E
Takapuna	36°47' S,	174°45' E
Tauranga	37°42' S,	176°08' E
Timaru	44°24' S,	171°14' E
Upper Hutt	41°08' S,	175°03' E
Waihi	37°24' S,	175°56' E
Wanganui	39°56' S,	175°02' E
Wellington	41°18' S,	174°47' E
Westport	41°45' S,	171°36' E
Whangarei	35°43' S,	174°20' E

NICARAGUA . . . . . page 127

City	Latitude	Longitude
Bluefields	12°00' N,	083°45' W
Chinandega	12°37' N,	087°09' W
Esquipulas	12°40' N,	085°47' W
Estelí	13°05' N,	086°21' W
Granada	11°56' N,	085°57' W
Juigalpa	12°05' N,	085°24' W
León	12°26' N,	086°53' W
Managua	12°09' N,	086°17' W
Masaya	11°58' N,	086°06' W
Matagalpa	12°55' N,	085°55' W
Nandaime	11°45' N,	086°03' W
Ocotal	13°38' N,	086°29' W
Puerto Cabezas	14°02' N,	083°23' W
San Carlos	11°07' N,	084°47' W
San Juan del Norte (Greytown)	10°55' N,	083°42' W
San Juan del Sur	11°15' N,	085°52' W
Somoto	13°29' N,	086°35' W
Waspam	14°44' N,	083°58' W

NIGER . . . . page 128

City	Latitude	Longitude
Agadez	16°58' N,	007°59' E
Ayorou	14°44' N,	000°55' E
Bilma	18°41' N,	012°56' E
Dakoro	14°31' N,	006°46' E
Diffa	13°19' N,	012°37' E
Dogondoutchi	13°38' N,	004°02' E

Dosso	13°03' N,	003°12' E
Filingué	14°21' N,	003°19' E
Gaya	11°53' N,	003°27' E
Gouré	13°58' N,	010°18' E
I-n-Gall	16°47' N,	006°56' E
Keïta	14°46' N,	005°46' E
Kolo	13°19' N,	002°20' E
Madaoua	14°06' N,	006°26' E
Magaria	13°00' N,	008°54' E
Maradi	13°29' N,	007°06' E
Mayahi	13°58' N,	007°40' E
Nguigmi	14°15' N,	013°07' E
Niamey	13°31' N,	002°07' E
Tahoua	14°54' N,	005°16' E
Tânout	14°58' N,	008°53' E
Zinder	13°48' N,	008°59' E

NIGERIA . . . . page 129

Aba	05°07' N,	007°22' E
Abuja	09°15' N,	006°56' E
Ado-Ekiti	07°38' N,	005°13' E
Asari	10°31' N,	012°18' E
Awka	06°13' N,	007°05' E
Azare	11°41' N,	010°12' E
Bauchi	10°19' N,	009°50' E
Benin City	06°20' N,	005°38' E
Bida	09°05' N,	006°01' E
Birnin Kebbi	12°28' N,	004°12' E
Biu	10°37' N,	012°12' E
Calabar	04°57' N,	008°19' E
Deba Habe	10°13' N,	011°23' E
Dikwa	12°02' N,	013°55' E
Dukku	10°49' N,	010°46' E
Ede	07°44' N,	004°26' E
Enugu	06°26' N,	007°29' E
Funtua	11°32' N,	007°19' E
Garko	11°39' N,	008°48' E
Gashua	12°52' N,	011°03' E
Gboko	07°19' N,	009°00' E
Gombe	10°17' N,	011°10' E
Gumel	12°38' N,	009°23' E
Gusau	12°10' N,	006°40' E
Ibadan	07°23' N,	003°54' E
Ibi	08°11' N,	009°45' E
Idah	07°06' N,	006°44' E
Ife	07°28' N,	004°34' E
Ifon	06°55' N,	005°46' E
Ikerre	07°30' N,	005°14' E
Ila	08°01' N,	004°54' E
Ilorin	08°30' N,	004°33' E
Iwo	07°38' N,	004°11' E
Jega	12°13' N,	004°23' E
Jimeta	09°17' N,	012°28' E
Jos	09°55' N,	008°54' E
Kaduna	10°31' N,	007°26' E
Kano	12°00' N,	008°31' E
Katsina	13°00' N,	007°36' E
Kaura Namoda	12°36' N,	006°35' E
Keffi	08°51' N,	007°52' E
Kishi	09°05' N,	003°51' E
Kumo	10°03' N,	011°13' E
Lafia	08°29' N,	008°31' E
Lafiagi	08°52' N,	005°25' E
Lagos	06°27' N,	003°23' E
Lere	09°43' N,	009°21' E
Mada	12°09' N,	006°56' E
Maiduguri	11°51' N,	013°09' E
Makurdi	07°44' N,	008°32' E
Minna	09°37' N,	006°33' E
Mubi	10°16' N,	013°16' E
Mushin	06°32' N,	003°22' E
Ngurtuwa	13°05' N,	013°34' E
Nguru	12°53' N,	010°28' E
Nsukka	06°52' N,	007°23' E
Ogbomosho	08°08' N,	004°16' E
Omoko	05°21' N,	006°39' E
Onitsha	06°10' N,	006°47' E
Opobo Town	04°31' N,	007°32' E
Oron	04°50' N,	008°14' E
Oshogbo	07°46' N,	004°34' E
Oyo	07°51' N,	003°56' E
Pindiga	09°59' N,	010°54' E
Port Harcourt	04°46' N,	007°01' E
Potiskum	11°43' N,	011°04' E
Sapele	05°55' N,	005°42' E
Shaki	08°40' N,	003°23' E
Sokoto	13°04' N,	005°15' E
Ugep	05°48' N,	008°05' E
Umuahia	05°32' N,	007°29' E
Uyo	05°03' N,	007°56' E
Warri	05°31' N,	005°45' E
Wukari	07°51' N,	009°47' E
Zaria	11°04' N,	007°42' E

NORTH KOREA . . page 130

Anju	39°36' N,	125°40' E
Ch'ŏngjin	41°46' N,	129°49' E
Cho'san	40°50' N,	125°48' E
Haeju	38°02' N,	125°42' E
Hamhŭng	39°54' N,	127°32' E
Hŭich'ŏn	40°10' N,	126°17' E
Hyangsan	40°03' N,	126°10' E
Hyesan	41°24' N,	128°10' E
Ich'ŏn	38°29' N,	126°53' E
Kaesŏng	37°58' N,	126°33' E
Kanggye	40°58' N,	126°36' E
Kimch'aek (Songjin)	40°41' N,	129°12' E
Kŭmch'ŏn	38°09' N,	126°29' E
Kusŏng	39°59' N,	125°15' E
Kyŏngwŏn	42°49' N,	130°09' E
Manp'o	41°09' N,	126°17' E
Myŏngch'ŏn	41°04' N,	129°26' E
Najin	42°15' N,	130°18' E
Namp'o	38°44' N,	125°24' E
P'anmunjŏm	37°57' N,	126°40' E
Puryŏng	42°04' N,	129°43' E
P'yŏngsŏng	39°15' N,	125°52' E
Pyŏngyang	39°01' N,	125°45' E
Sariwŏn	38°30' N,	125°45' E
Sinp'o	40°02' N,	128°12' E

Sinŭiju . . . . 40°06' N, 124°24' E
Songnim. . . . . 38°44' N, 125°38' E
Taegwan . . . . 40°13' N, 125°12' E
Tanch'ŏn . . . . 40°28' N, 128°55' E
Tŏkch'ŏn . . . . 39°45' N, 126°18' E
T'ongch'ŏn. . . . . 38°57' N, 127°52' E
Unggi . . . . 42°20' N, 130°24' E
Wŏnsan . . . . 39°10' N, 127°26' E

NORWAY . . . . page 131

Ålesund . . . . 62°28' N, 006°09' E
Alta . . . . 69°58' N, 023°15' E
Båtsfjord . . . . 70°38' N, 029°44' E
Bergen . . . . 60°23' N, 005°20' E
Bodø . . . . 67°17' N, 014°23' E
Brønnøysund . . . . 65°28' N, 012°13' E
Drammen. . . . . 59°44' N, 010°15' E
Elverum . . . . 60°53' N, 011°34' E
Evje . . . . 58°36' N, 007°51' E
Fauske . . . . 67°15' N, 015°24' E
Finnsnes . . . . 69°14' N, 017°59' E
Flekkefjord . . . . 58°17' N, 006°41' E
Hamar . . . . 60°48' N, 011°06' E
Hammerfest. . . . . 70°40' N, 023°42' E
Hareid . . . . 62°22' N, 006°02' E
Harstad . . . . 68°47' N, 016°33' E
Haugesund . . . . 59°25' N, 005°18' E
Hermansverk. . . . . 61°11' N, 006°51' E
Karasjok . . . . 69°27' N, 025°30' E
Kautokeino . . . . 68°59' N, 023°08' E
Kolsås . . . . 59°55' N, 010°31' E
Kongsvinger . . . . 60°12' N, 012°00' E
Kristiansund . . . . 63°07' N, 007°45' E
Lillehammer . . . . 61°08' N, 010°30' E
Måløy. . . . . 61°56' N, 005°07' E
Mandal. . . . . 58°02' N, 007°27' E
Molde. . . . . 62°44' N, 007°11' E
Mosjøen. . . . . 65°50' N, 013°12' E
Narvik . . . . 68°26' N, 017°25' E
Nordfold . . . . 67°46' N, 015°12' E
Oslo (Christiania,
Kristiania) . . . . 59°55' N, 010°45' E
Sandnessjøen . . . . 66°01' N, 012°38' E
Sarpsborg . . . . 59°17' N, 011°07' E
Skien . . . . 59°12' N, 009°36' E
Skjervøy. . . . . 70°02' N, 020°59' E
Stavanger . . . . 58°58' N, 005°45' E
Steinkjer . . . . 64°01' N, 011°30' E
Svolvær . . . . 68°14' N, 014°34' E
Tønsberg. . . . . 59°17' N, 010°25' E
Tromsø . . . . 69°40' N, 018°58' E
Trondheim . . . . 63°25' N, 010°25' E
Vadsø. . . . . 70°05' N, 029°46' E
Vardø. . . . . 70°22' N, 031°06' E

OMAN . . . . page 131

Al-Maṣna'ah. . . . . 23°47' N, 057°38' E
Ar-Rustaq . . . . 23°24' N, 057°26' E
Bahlā' (Bahlah) . . . . 22°58' N, 057°18' E
Barkā'. . . . . 23°43' N, 057°53' E
Ḍank. . . . . 23°33' N, 056°16' E
Duqm . . . . 19°39' N, 057°42' E
Haymā'. . . . . 19°56' N, 056°19' E
Ibrā' . . . . 22°43' N, 058°32' E
Khabura. . . . . 23°59' N, 057°08' E
Khaṣab. . . . . 26°12' N, 056°15' E
Khawr Rawrī (Khor Rori) . . 17°02' N, 054°27' E
Maṭraḥ. . . . . 23°37' N, 058°34' E
Mirbāṭ . . . . 17°00' N, 054°41' E
Muscat (Masqat). . . . . 23°37' N, 058°35' E
Nizwā (Nazwah). . . . . 22°56' N, 057°32' E
Qurayyāt . . . . 23°15' N, 058°54' E
Rakhyūt . . . . 16°44' N, 053°20' E
Ṣalalah . . . . 17°00' N, 054°06' E
Shināṣ . . . . 24°46' N, 056°28' E
Ṣuḥār . . . . 24°22' N, 056°45' E
Ṣūr . . . . 22°34' N, 059°32' E
Tāqah . . . . 17°02' N, 054°24' E
Thamarīt . . . . 17°39' N, 054°02' E

PAKISTAN . . . . page 133

Badīn . . . . 24°39' N, 068°50' E
Bahāwalnagar . . . . 29°59' N, 073°16' E
Bannu . . . . 32°59' N, 070°36' E
Chitrāl . . . . 35°51' N, 071°47' E
Dādu . . . . 26°44' N, 067°47' E
Dera Ghazi Khan. . . . . 30°03' N, 070°38' E
Dera Ismail Khan . . . . 31°50' N, 070°54' E
Faisalabad (Lyallpur) . . . . . 31°25' N, 073°05' E
Gujranwala . . . . 32°09' N, 074°11' E
Gwadar . . . . 25°07' N, 062°19' E
Hyderabad. . . . . 25°22' N, 068°22' E
Islamabad . . . . 33°42' N, 073°10' E
Karachi . . . . 24°52' N, 067°03' E
Khuzdār. . . . . 27°48' N, 066°37' E
Kotri. . . . . 25°22' N, 068°18' E
Larkana . . . . 27°33' N, 068°13' E
Las Bela. . . . . 26°14' N, 066°19' E
Loralai . . . . 30°22' N, 068°36' E
Mardan . . . . 34°12' N, 072°02' E
Mianwali . . . . 32°35' N, 071°33' E
Mīrpur Khās . . . . 25°32' N, 069°00' E
Multan . . . . 30°11' N, 071°29' E
Nawabshah . . . . 26°15' N, 068°25' E
Panjgūr . . . . 26°58' N, 064°06' E
Peshawar. . . . . 34°01' N, 071°33' E
Pishīn. . . . . 30°35' N, 067°00' E
Quetta . . . . 30°12' N, 067°00' E
Rahīmyār Khān . . . . 28°25' N, 070°18' E
Rawalpindi . . . . 33°36' N, 073°04' E
Sahiwal (Montgomery). . . . 30°40' N, 073°06' E
Sargodha . . . . 32°05' N, 072°40' E
Sūi . . . . 28°37' N, 069°19' E
Sukkur . . . . 27°42' N, 068°52' E
Thatta . . . . 24°45' N, 067°55' E
Turbat . . . . 25°59' N, 063°04' E
Wāh . . . . 33°48' N, 072°42' E
Zhob (Fort Sandeman) . . . . 31°20' N, 069°27' E

PALAU . . . . page 134

Airai . . . 07°22' N, 134°33' E
Klouklubed . . . 07°02' N, 134°15' E
Koror . . . 07°20' N, 134°29' E
Melekeok . . . 07°29' N, 134°38' E
Meyungs . . . 07°20' N, 134°27' E
Ngardmau . . . 07°37' N, 134°36' E

PANAMA . . . . page 135

Aguadulce . . . 08°15' N, 080°33' W
Almirante . . . 09°18' N, 082°24' W
Antón . . . 08°24' N, 080°16' W
Boquete . . . 08°47' N, 082°26' W
Cañazas . . . 09°06' N, 078°10' W
Capira . . . 08°45' N, 079°53' W
Changuinola . . . 09°26' N, 082°31' W
Chepo . . . 09°10' N, 079°06' W
Chitré . . . 07°58' N, 080°26' W
Colón . . . 09°22' N, 079°54' W
David . . . 08°26' N, 082°26' W
Guararé . . . 07°49' N, 080°17' W
La Chorrera . . . 08°53' N, 079°47' W
La Concepción . . . 08°31' N, 082°37' W
La Palma . . . 08°25' N, 078°09' W
Las Cumbres . . . 09°05' N, 079°32' W
Las Lajas . . . 08°15' N, 081°52' W
Las Tablas . . . 07°46' N, 080°17' W
Ocú . . . 07°57' N, 080°47' W
Panama City (Panama) . . . 08°58' N, 079°32' W
Pedregal . . . 09°04' N, 079°26' W
Penonomé . . . 08°31' N, 080°22' W
Portobelo (Puerto Bello) . . . 09°33' N, 079°39' W
Puerto Armuelles . . . 08°17' N, 082°52' W
San Miguelito . . . 09°02' N, 079°30' E
Santiago . . . 08°06' N, 080°59' W
Soná . . . 08°01' N, 081°19' W
Yaviza (Yavisa) . . . 08°11' N, 077°41' W

PAPUA NEW GUINEA . . . . page 136

Aitape . . . 03°08' S, 142°21' E
Alotau . . . 10°20' S, 150°25' E
Ambunti . . . 04°14' S, 142°50' E
Arawa . . . 06°13' S, 155°33' E
Baimuru . . . 07°30' S, 144°49' E
Balimo . . . 08°03' S, 142°57' E
Bogia . . . 04°16' S, 144°54' E
Buin . . . 06°50' S, 155°44' E
Bulolo . . . 07°12' S, 146°39' E
Bwagaoia . . . 10°42' S, 152°50' E
Daru . . . 09°05' S, 143°12' E
Finschhafen . . . 06°36' S, 147°51' E
Goroka . . . 06°05' S, 145°23' E
Kandrian . . . 06°13' S, 149°33' E
Kavieng . . . 02°34' S, 150°48' E
Kerema . . . 07°58' S, 145°46' E
Kikori . . . 07°25' S, 144°15' E
Kimbe . . . 05°33' S, 150°09' E
Kiunga . . . 06°07' S, 141°18' E
Kupiano . . . 10°05' S, 148°11' E
Lae . . . 06°44' S, 147°00' E
Lorengau . . . 02°01' S, 147°16' E
Losuia . . . 08°32' S, 151°04' E
Madang . . . 05°13' S, 145°48' E
Mt. Hagen . . . 05°52' S, 144°13' E
Namatanai . . . 03°40' S, 152°27' E
Popondetta . . . 08°46' S, 148°14' E
Port Moresby . . . 09°29' S, 147°11' E
Rabaul . . . 04°12' S, 152°11' E
Saidor . . . 05°38' S, 146°28' E
Samarai . . . 10°37' S, 150°40' E
Tari . . . 05°42' S, 142°57' E
Vanimo . . . 02°41' S, 141°18' E
Wewak . . . 03°33' S, 143°38' E

PARAGUAY . . . . . page 137

Asunción . . . 25°16' S, 057°40' W
Caacupé . . . 25°23' S, 057°09' W
Caaguazú . . . 25°26' S, 056°02' W
Caazapá . . . 26°09' S, 056°24' W
Capitán Pablo Lagerenza . . . 19°55' S, 060°47' W
Ciudad del Este (Puerto Presidente Stroessner) . . . 25°31' S, 054°37' W
Concepción . . . 23°25' S, 057°17' W
Encarnación . . . 27°20' S, 055°54' W
Filadelfia . . . 22°21' S, 060°02' W
Fuerto Olimpo . . . 21°02' S, 057°54' W
General Eugenio A. Garay . . . 20°31' S, 062°08' W
Luque . . . 25°16' S, 057°34' W
Mariscal Estigarribia . . . 22°02' S, 060°38' W
Paraguari . . . 25°38' S, 057°09' W
Pedro Juan Caballero . . . 22°34' S, 055°37' W
Pilar . . . 26°52' S, 058°23' W
Pozo Colorado . . . 23°26' S, 058°58' W
Salto del Guairá . . . 24°05' S, 054°20' W
San Juan Bautista . . . 26°38' S, 057°10' W
San Lázaro . . . 22°10' S, 057°58' W
Villarica . . . 25°45' S, 056°26' W

PERU . . . . page 138

Abancay . . . 13°35' S, 072°55' W
Acomayo . . . 13°55' S, 071°41' W
Arequipa . . . 16°24' S, 071°33' W
Ayabaca . . . 04°38' S, 079°43' W
Ayacucho . . . 13°07' S, 074°13' W
Ayaviri . . . 14°52' S, 070°35' W
Bagua . . . 05°40' S, 078°31' W
Barranca . . . 10°45' S, 077°46' W
Cajamarca . . . 07°10' S, 078°31' W
Callao . . . 12°04' S, 077°09' W
Castilla . . . 05°12' S, 080°38' W
Cerro de Pasco . . . 10°41' S, 076°16' W
Chiclayo . . . 06°46' S, 079°51' W

City	Latitude	Longitude
Chimbote	09°05' S,	078°36' W
Contamana	07°15' S,	074°54' W
Cuzco	13°31' S,	071°59' W
Espinar	14°47' S,	071°29' W
Huacho	11°07' S,	077°37' W
Huancayo	12°04' S,	075°14' W
Huánuco	09°55' S,	076°14' W
Huaraz	09°32' S,	077°32' W
Huarmey	10°04' S,	078°10' W
Ica	14°04' S,	075°42' W
Iñapari	10°57' S,	069°35' W
Iquitos	03°46' S,	073°15' W
Juliaca	15°30' S,	070°08' W
Lagunas	05°14' S,	075°38' W
Lima	12°03' S,	077°03' W
Macusani	14°05' S,	070°26' W
Miraflores	12°07' S,	077°02' W
Moquegua	17°12' S,	070°56' W
Moyobamba	06°03' S,	076°58' W
Nauta	04°32' S,	073°33' W
Pampas	12°24' S,	074°54' W
Pisco	13°42' S,	076°13' W
Piura	05°12' S,	080°38' W
Pucallpa	08°23' S,	074°32' W
Puerto Maldonado	12°36' S,	069°11' W
Puno	15°50' S,	070°02' W
Requena	04°58' S,	073°50' W
San Juan	15°21' S,	075°10' W
Tacna	18°01' S,	070°15' W
Tarapoto	06°30' S,	076°25' W
Trujillo	08°07' S,	079°02' W
Tumbes	03°34' S,	080°28' W

PHILIPPINES . . . . . page 139

City	Latitude	Longitude
Angeles	15°09' N,	120°35' E
Aparri	18°22' N,	121°39' E
Bacolod	10°40' N,	122°56' E
Balabac	07°59' N,	117°04' E
Batangas	13°45' N,	121°03' E
Bayombong	16°29' N,	121°09' E
Borongan	11°37' N,	125°26' E
Butuan	08°54' N,	125°35' E
Cagayan de Oro	08°29' N,	124°39' E
Caloocan	14°39' N,	120°58' E
Cavite	14°29' N,	120°55' E
Cebu	10°18' N,	123°54' E
Daet	14°05' N,	122°55' E
Dagupan	16°03' N,	120°20' E
Dipolog	08°35' N,	123°20' E
Dumaguete	09°18' N,	123°18' E
General Santos	06°07' N,	125°10' E
Iligan	08°14' N,	124°14' E
Iloilo City	10°42' N,	122°33' E
Isabela	06°42' N,	121°58' E
Jolo	06°03' N,	121°00' E
Laoag	12°34' N,	125°00' E
Lucena	13°56' N,	121°37' E
Manila	14°35' N,	121°00' E
Masbate	12°22' N,	123°36' E
Mati	06°57' N,	126°13' E
Naga (Nueva Caceres)	13°37' N,	123°11' E
Ormoc	11°00' N,	124°37' E
Ozamiz	08°08' N,	123°50' E
Pandan	14°03' N,	124°10' E
Puerto Princesa	09°44' N,	118°44' E
Quezon City	14°38' N,	121°00' E
Romblon	12°35' N,	122°15' E
Roxas (Capiz)	11°35' N,	122°45' E
Surigao	09°45' N,	125°30' E
Tagbilaran	09°39' N,	123°51' E
Tuguegarao	17°37' N,	121°44' E
Zamboanga	06°54' N,	122°04' E

POLAND . . . . page 140

City	Latitude	Longitude
Biała Podlaska	52°02' N,	023°08' E
Białystok	53°08' N,	023°09' E
Bielsko-Biała	49°49' N,	019°02' E
Bydgoszcz	53°09' N,	018°00' E
Ciechanów	52°53' N,	020°37' E
Częstochowa	50°48' N,	019°07' E
Dąbrova Górnicza	50°20' N,	019°12' E
Elbląg	54°10' N,	019°23' E
Gdańsk (Danzig)	54°21' N,	018°40' E
Gdynia	54°30' N,	018°33' E
Gorzów Wielkopolski	52°44' N,	015°14' E
Grudziądz	53°29' N,	018°46' E
Iława	53°36' N,	019°34' E
Inowrocław	52°48' N,	018°16' E
Kalisz	51°45' N,	018°05' E
Katowice	50°16' N,	019°01' E
Kielce	50°50' N,	020°40' E
Konin	52°13' N,	018°16' E
Koszalin	54°12' N,	016°11' E
Kraków	50°05' N,	019°55' E
Krosno	49°41' N,	021°47' E
Legnica	51°12' N,	016°12' E
Leszno	51°51' N,	016°35' E
Łódź	51°45' N,	019°28' E
Łomża	53°11' N,	022°05' E
Lublin	51°15' N,	022°34' E
Malbork	54°02' N,	019°03' E
Mogilno	52°40' N,	017°58' E
Nidzica	53°22' N,	020°26' E
Nowy Sącz	49°38' N,	020°43' E
Olsztyn	53°47' N,	020°29' E
Opole	50°40' N,	017°57' E
Ostrołęka	53°05' N,	021°34' E
Piła	53°09' N,	016°45' E
Pińczów	50°32' N,	020°32' E
Piotrków Trybunalski	51°24' N,	019°41' E
Pisz	53°38' N,	021°48' E
Poznań	52°25' N,	016°58' E
Radom	51°25' N,	021°09' E
Rybnik	50°07' N,	018°32' E
Rzeszów	50°03' N,	022°00' E
Siedlce	52°10' N,	022°18' E
Słupsk	54°27' N,	017°02' E
Suwałki	54°06' N,	022°56' E

Szczecin (Stettin)	53°25' N,	014°35' E
Tarnobrzeg	50°35' N,	021°41' E
Tarnów	50°01' N,	020°59' E
Tczew	54°06' N,	018°48' E
Tomaszów Mazowiecki	51°32' N,	020°01' E
Toruń	53°02' N,	018°36' E
Tuchola	53°35' N,	017°51' E
Tychy	50°08' N,	018°59' E
Wałbrzych	50°46' N,	016°17' E
Warsaw (Warszawa)	52°15' N,	021°00' E
Włocławek	52°39' N,	019°05' E
Wrocław (Breslau)	51°06' N,	017°02' E
Zabrze	50°19' N,	018°47' E
Zamość	50°43' N,	023°15' E
Zielona Góra	51°56' N,	015°30' E

PORTUGAL ...... page 141

Alcobaça	39°33' N,	008°59' W
Almada	38°41' N,	009°09' W
Amadora	38°45' N,	009°14' W
Aveiro	40°38' N,	008°39' W
Barreiro	38°40' N,	009°04' W
Batalha	39°39' N,	008°50' W
Beja	38°01' N,	007°52' W
Braga	41°33' N,	008°26' W
Bragança	41°49' N,	006°45' W
Castelo Branco	39°49' N,	007°30' W
Chaves	41°44' N,	007°28' W
Coimbra	40°12' N,	008°25' W
Elvas	38°53' N,	007°10' W
Évora	38°34' N,	007°54' W
Faro	37°01' N,	007°56' W
Fátima	39°37' N,	008°39' W
Figueira da Foz	40°09' N,	008°52' W
Guarda	40°32' N,	007°16' W
Guimarães	41°27' N,	008°18' W
Leiria	39°45' N,	008°48' W
Lisbon (Lisboa)	38°43' N,	009°08' W
Nazaré	39°36' N,	009°04' W
Odivelas	38°47' N,	009°11' W
Oeiras	38°41' N,	009°19' W
Portalegre	39°17' N,	007°26' W
Portimão (Vila Nova de Portimão)	37°08' N,	008°32' W
Porto (Oporto)	41°09' N,	008°37' W
Póvoa de Varzim	41°23' N,	008°46' W
Queluz	38°45' N,	009°15' W
Santarém	39°14' N,	008°41' W
Setúbal	38°32' N,	008°54' W
Sines	37°57' N,	008°52' W
Tomar	39°36' N,	008°25' W
Torres Vedras	39°06' N,	009°16' W
Urgeiriça	40°30' N,	007°53' W
Viana do Castelo	41°42' N,	008°50' W
Vila do Conde	41°21' N,	008°45' W
Vila Franca de Xira	38°57' N,	008°59' W
Vila Nova de Gaia	41°08' N,	008°37' W
Vila Real	41°18' N,	007°45' W
Viseu	40°39' N,	007°55' W

QATAR .... page 142

Al-Wakrah	25°10' N,	051°36' E
Al -Rayyān	25°18' N,	051°27' E
Ar-Ruways	26°08' N,	051°13' E
Doha (ad-Dawhah)	25°17' N,	051°32' E
Dukhān	25°25' N,	050°47' E
Musay'id	25°00' N,	051°33' E
Umm Bāb	25°09' N,	050°50' E

ROMANIA .... page 143

Alba Iulia (Gyulafehérvár)	46°04' N,	023°35' E
Alexandria	43°59' N,	025°20' E
Arad	46°11' N,	021°19' E
Bacău	46°34' N,	026°54' E
Baia Mare	47°40' N,	023°35' E
Bârlad	46°14' N,	027°40' E
Bistriţa	47°08' N,	024°29' E
Botoşani	47°45' N,	026°40' E
Brăila	45°16' N,	027°59' E
Braşov (Oraşul Stalin)	45°38' N,	025°35' E
Bucharest	44°26' N,	026°06' E
Buzău	45°09' N,	026°50' E
Calafat	43°59' N,	022°56' E
Călăraşi	44°12' N,	027°20' E
Cluj-Napoca	46°46' N,	023°36' E
Constanţa	44°11' N,	028°39' E
Craiova	44°19' N,	023°48' E
Dej	47°09' N,	023°52' E
Deva	45°53' N,	022°54' E
Drobeta-Turnu Severin	44°38' N,	022°40' E
Focşani	45°42' N,	027°11' E
Galaţi (Galatz)	45°27' N,	028°03' E
Giurgiu	43°53' N,	025°58' E
Hunedoara	45°45' N,	022°54' E
Iaşi (Jassy)	47°10' N,	027°36' E
Lugoj	45°41' N,	021°55' E
Mangalia	43°48' N,	028°35' E
Medgidia	44°15' N,	028°17' E
Mediaş	46°10' N,	024°21' E
Mizil	45°01' N,	026°27' E
Oneşti (Gheorghe Gheorghiu Dej)	46°15' N,	026°45' E
Oradea (Nagyvarad)	47°04' N,	021°56' E
Petroşani	45°25' N,	023°22' E
Piatra-Neamţ	46°55' N,	026°20' E
Piteşti	44°51' N,	024°52' E
Ploieşti (Ploeşti)	44°57' N,	026°01' E
Reşiţa	45°18' N,	021°55' E
Roman	46°55' N,	026°55' E
Satu Mare	47°48' N,	022°53' E
Sebeş	45°58' N,	023°34' E
Slatina	44°26' N,	024°22' E
Suceava	47°38' N,	026°15' E
Ţăndărei	44°39' N,	027°40' E
Târgovişte	44°56' N,	025°27' E
Targu Jiu	45°03' N,	023°17' E

City	Latitude	Longitude
Târgu Mureş	46°33' N	024°34' E
Tecuci	45°52' N	027°25' E
Timişoara	45°45' N	021°13' E
Tulcea	45°10' N	028°48' E
Turda	46°34' N	023°47' E
Vaslui	46°38' N	027°44' E
Zalau	47°12' N	023°03' E

RUSSIA . . . . page 144-5

City	Latitude	Longitude
Abakan	53°43' N	091°26' E
Aginskoye	51°06' N	114°32' E
Anadyr (Novo-Mariinsk)	64°45' N	177°29' E
Angarsk	52°34' N	103°54' E
Birobidzhan	48°48' N	132°57' E
Biysk (Biisk)	52°34' N	085°15' E
Cheboksary	56°09' N	047°15' E
Chelyabinsk	55°10' N	061°24' E
Cherepovets	59°08' N	037°54' E
Chita	52°03' N	113°30' E
Dudinka	69°25' N	086°15' E
Gorno-Altaysk (Ulala, or Oyrot-Tura)	51°58' N	085°58' E
Grozny	43°20' N	045°42' E
Izhevsk (Ustinov)	56°51' N	053°14' E
Kaluga	54°31' N	036°16' E
Kazan	55°45' N	049°08' E
Khanty-Mansiysk (Ostyako-Vogulsk)	61°00' N	069°06' E
Kirovsk	67°37' N	033°40' E
Komsomol'sk-na-Amure	50°35' N	137°02' E
Krasnoyarsk	56°01' N	092°50' E
Kudymkar	59°01' N	054°39' E
Kurgan	55°26' N	065°18' E
Kyzyl (Khem-Beldyr)	51°42' N	094°27' E
Magadan	59°34' N	150°48' E
Makhachkala	42°58' N	047°30' E
Maykop (Maikop)	44°35' N	040°10' E
Moscow (Moskva)	55°45' N	037°35' E
Murmansk	68°58' N	033°05' E
Nal'chik	43°29' N	043°37' E
Nar'yan-Mar	67°39' N	053°00' E
Nizhnekamsk	55°36' N	051°47' E
Nizhny Novgorod (Gorky)	56°20' N	044°00' E
Novgorod	58°31' N	031°17' E
Novokuznetsk (Kuznetsk, or Stalinsk)	53°45' N	087°06' E
Novosibirsk	55°02' N	082°55' E
Omsk	55°00' N	073°24' E
Orenburg (Chkalov)	51°45' N	055°06' E
Orsk	51°12' N	058°34' E
Palana	59°07' N	159°58' E
Penza	53°13' N	045°00' E
Perm' (Molotov)	58°00' N	056°15' E
Petropavlovsk-Kamchatsky	53°01' N	158°39' E
Petrozavodsk	61°49' N	034°20' E
Rostov-na-Donu (Rostov-on-Don)	47°14' N	039°42' E
St. Petersburg (Leningrad, or Sankt Peterburg)	59°55' N	030°15' E
Salavat	53°21' N	055°55' E
Salekhard	66°33' N	066°40' E
Samara (Kuybyshev)	53°12' N	050°09' E
Saransk	54°11' N	045°11' E
Saratov	51°34' N	046°02' E
Smolensk	54°47' N	032°03' E
Syktyvkar	61°40' N	050°48' E
Tomsk	56°30' N	084°58' E
Tver' (Kalinin)	56°52' N	035°55' E
Tyumen'	57°09' N	065°26' E
Ufa	55°45' N	055°56' E
Ulan-Ude	51°50' N	107°37' E
Ussuriysk	43°48' N	131°59' E
Ust'-Ordinsky	52°48' N	104°45' E
Vladimir	56°10' N	040°25' E
Vladivostok	43°08' N	131°54' E
Volgograd (Stalingrad, or Tsaritsyn)	48°45' N	044°25' E
Vologda	59°13' N	039°54' E
Voronezh	51°38' N	039°12' E
Yakutsk	62°00' N	129°40' E
Yaroslavl	57°37' N	039°52' E
Yekaterinburg (Sverdlovsk)	56°51' N	060°36' E
Yuzhno-Sakhalinsk	46°57' N	142°44' E

RWANDA . . . . . . page 146

City	Latitude	Longitude
Butare	02°36' S	029°44' E
Gisenyi	01°42' S	029°15' E
Kigali	01°57' S	030°04' E
Ruhengeri	01°30' S	029°38' E

SAINT KITTS AND NEVIS . . . . . page 147

City	Latitude	Longitude
Basseterre	17°18' N	062°43' W
Brown Hill	17°08' N	062°33' W
Cayon	17°22' N	062°43' W
Challengers	17°18' N	062°47' W
Charlestown	17°08' N	062°37' W
Cotton Ground	17°11' N	062°36' W
Half Way Tree	17°20' N	062°49' W
Mansion	17°22' N	062°46' W
Monkey Hill Village	17°19' N	062°43' W
Newcastle	17°13' N	062°34' W
New River	17°09' N	062°32' W
Newton Ground	17°23' N	062°51' W
Old Road Town	17°19' N	062°48' W
Sadlers	17°24' N	062°49' W
Saint Paul's	17°24' N	062°49' W
Sandy Point Town	17°22' N	062°50' W
Verchild's	17°20' N	062°48' W
Zetlands	17°08' N	062°34' W

SAINT LUCIA . . . . page 148

City	Latitude	Longitude
Anse La Raye	13°57' N	061°03' W
Canaries	13°55' N	061°04' W
Castries	14°01' N	061°00' W
Dauphin	14°03' N	060°55' W
Dennery	13°55' N	060°54' W
Grande Anse	14°01' N	061°45' W
Gros Islet	14°05' N	060°58' W
Laborie	13°45' N	061°00' W
Micoud	13°50' N	060°54' W
Praslin	13°53' N	060°54' W
Sans Soucis	13°59' N	061°01' W
Soufrière	13°52' N	061°04' W

SAINT VINCENT AND THE GRENADINES . . . . page 149

City	Latitude	Longitude
Ashton	12°36' N	061°27' W
Barrouallie	13°14' N	061°17' W
Calliaqua	13°08' N	061°12' W
Chateaubelaír	13°17' N	061°15' W
Georgetown	13°16' N	061°08' W
Kingstown	13°09' N	061°14' W

SAMOA . . . . page 150

City	Latitude	Longitude
Apia	13°50' S	171°44' W
Fa'aala	13°45' S	172°16' W
Faleasi'u	13°48' S	171°54' W
Le'auva'u	13°45' S	171°51' W
Lotofaga	13°59' S	171°50' W
Matavai (Asau)	13°28' S	172°35' W
Safotu	13°27' S	172°24' W
Sagone	13°39' S	172°35' W
Samatau	13°54' S	172°02' W
Sili	13°43' S	172°21' W
Si'umu	14°01' S	171°47' W
Solosolo	13°51' S	171°36' W

SAN MARINO . . . . page 151

City	Latitude	Longitude
San Marino	43°56' N	012°25' E

SÃO TOMÉ AND PRÍNCIPE . . page 152

City	Latitude	Longitude
Infante Don Henrique	01°34' N	007°25' E
Neves	00°22' N	006°33' E
Porto Alegre	00°02' N	006°32' E
Santana	00°16' N	006°45' E
Santo Amaro	00°22' N	006°42' E
Santo António	01°39' N	007°25' E
São Tomé	00°20' N	006°44' E
Trindade	00°15' N	006°40' E

SAUDI ARABIA . . . page 153

City	Latitude	Longitude
Abhā	18°13' N	042°30' E
Abqaiq (Buqayq)	25°56' N	049°40' E
ʿAfif	23°55' N	042°56' E
Al-Bāhah	20°01' N	041°28' E
Al-Badīʿ	22°02' N	046°34' E
Al-Bātin Hafar	28°27' N	045°58' E
Al-Bi'ār	22°39' N	039°40' E
Al-Dammām	26°26' N	050°07' E
Al-Hā'ir	24°23' N	046°50' E
Al-Hufūf	25°22' N	049°34' E
Al-Ju'aydah	19°40' N	041°34' E
Al-Jubayl	27°01' N	049°40' E
Al-Khubar	26°17' N	050°12' E
Al-Mish'āb	28°12' N	048°36' E
Al-Mubarraz	25°25' N	049°35' E
Al-Qaṭīf	26°33' N	050°00' E
Al-Qunfudhah	19°08' N	041°05' E
Al-Sulayyil	20°27' N	045°34' E
Al-Ta'if	21°16' N	040°25' E
Al-Ulā	26°38' N	037°55' E
Ar'ar	30°59' N	041°02' E
As-Ṣafrā'	24°02' N	038°56' E
Az-Zilfī	26°18' N	044°48' E
Badanah	30°59' N	040°58' E
Birkah	23°48' N	038°50' E
Buraydah	26°20' N	043°59' E
Buraykah	22°21' N	039°20' E
Hā'il	27°33' N	041°42' E
Halabān	23°29' N	044°23' E
Harajah	17°56' N	043°21' E
Jidda (Jiddah)	21°29' N	039°12' E
Jizān (Qizān)	16°54' N	042°32' E
Khamīs Mushayṭ	18°18' N	042°44' E
Khawsh	18°59' N	041°53' E
Laylā	22°17' N	046°45' E
Madā'in Sālih	26°48' N	037°57' E
Mecca (Makkah)	21°27' N	039°49' E
Medina (al-Madinah; Yathrib)	24°28' N	039°36' E
Miskah	24°49' N	042°56' E
Muṣābih	18°42' N	042°01' E
Na'jān	24°05' N	047°10' E
Najrān	17°26' N	044°15' E
Qanā	27°47' N	041°25' E
Rābigh	22°48' N	039°02' E
Rafhā'	29°38' N	043°30' E
Ras Tanura	26°42' N	050°06' E
Riyadh (ar-Riyad)	24°38' N	046°43' E
Sahwah	19°19' N	042°06' E
Sakākah	29°59' N	040°12' E
Shidād	21°19' N	040°03' E
Tabūk	28°23' N	036°35' E
Taymā'	27°38' N	038°29' E
Turayf	31°41' N	038°39' E
ʿUsfan	21°55' N	039°22' E
Yanbuʿ	24°05' N	038°03' E
Zahrān	17°40' N	043°30' E
Zalim	22°43' N	042°10' E

SENEGAL . . . . page 154

Bakel . . . . 14°54' N, 012°27' W
Bignona . . . . 12°49' N, 016°14' W
Dagana . . . . 16°31' N, 015°30' W
Dakar . . . . 14°40' N, 017°26' W
Diourbel . . . . 14°40' N, 016°15' W
Fatick . . . . 14°20' N, 016°25' W
Joal . . . . 14°10' N, 016°51' W
Kaffrine . . . . 14°06' N, 015°33' W
Kaolack . . . . 14°09' N, 016°04' W
Kédougou . . . . 12°33' N, 012°11' W
Kolda . . . . 12°53' N, 014°57' W
Koungheul . . . . 13°59' N, 014°48' W
Linguère . . . . 15°24' N, 015°07' W
Louga . . . . 15°37' N, 016°13' W
Mbacké . . . . 14°48' N, 015°55' W
Mbour . . . . 14°24' N, 016°58' W
Mékhé . . . . 15°07' N, 016°38' W
Podor . . . . 16°40' N, 014°57' W
Richard-Toll . . . . 16°28' N, 015°41' W
Saint Louis . . . . 16°02' N, 016°30' W
Sédhiou . . . . 12°44' N, 015°33' W
Tambacounda . . . . 13°47' N, 013°40' W
Thiès . . . . 14°48' N, 016°56' W
Tivaouane . . . . 14°57' N, 016°49' W
Vélingara . . . . 13°09' N, 014°07' W
Ziguinchor . . . . 12°35' N, 016°16' W

SERBIA . . . . page 155

Belgrade . . . . 44°50' N, 020°30' E
Bor . . . . 44°06' N, 022°06' E
Cacak . . . . 43°54' N, 020°21' E
Gornji Milanovac . . . . 44°02' N, 020°27' E
Kikinda . . . . 45°50' N, 020°29' E
Knjaževac . . . . 43°34' N, 022°15' E
Kosovska Mitrovica (Titova Mitrovica) . . . . . . 42°53' N, 020°52' E
Kragujevac . . . . 44°01' N, 020°55' E
Kraljevo . . . . 43°44' N, 020°43' E
Kruševac . . . . 43°35' N, 021°20' E
Leskovac . . . . 42°59' N, 021°57' E
Majdanpek . . . . 44°25' N, 021°56' E
Nis . . . . 43°19' N, 021°54' E
Novi Beograd . . . . 44°49' N, 020°27' E
Novi Pazar . . . . 43°08' N, 020°31' E
Novi Sad . . . . 45°15' N, 019°50' E
Pancevo . . . . 44°52' N, 020°39' E
Pirot . . . . 43°09' N, 022°36' E
Priboj . . . . 43°35' N, 019°32' E
Priština . . . . 42°40' N, 021°10' E
Prizren . . . . 42°13' N, 020°45' E
Sabac . . . . 44°45' N, 019°43' E
Smederevo . . . . 44°39' N, 020°56' E
Sombor . . . . 45°46' N, 019°07' E
Sremski Karlovci . . . . 45°12' N, 019°56' E
Subotica . . . . 46°06' N, 019°40' E
Titovo Užice (Užice) . . . . . . 43°52' N, 019°51' E
Valjevo . . . . 44°16' N, 019°53' E
Vranje . . . . 42°33' N, 021°54' E
Zrenjanin . . . . 45°23' N, 020°23' E

SEYCHELLES . . . . page 156

Victoria . . . . 04°37' S, 055°27' E

SIERRA LEONE . . page 157

Bo . . . . 07°58' N, 011°45' W
Bonthe . . . . 07°32' N, 012°30' W
Freetown . . . . 08°30' N, 013°15' W
Kabala . . . . 09°35' N, 011°33' W
Kailahun . . . . 08°17' N, 010°34' W
Kambia . . . . 09°07' N, 012°55' W
Kenema . . . . 07°52' N, 011°12' W
Koidu-New Sembehun . . . . 08°38' N, 010°59' W
Lunsar . . . . 08°41' N, 012°32' W
Magburaka . . . . 08°43' N, 011°57' W
Makeni . . . . 08°53' N, 012°03' W
Mongeri . . . . 08°19' N, 011°44' W
Moyamba . . . . 08°10' N, 012°26' W
Pepel . . . . 08°35' N, 013°03' W
Port Loko . . . . 08°46' N, 012°47' W
Pujehun . . . . 07°21' N, 011°42' W
Sulima . . . . 06°58' N, 011°35' W

SINGAPORE . . . . . page 158

Singapore . . . . 01°16' N, 103°50' E

SLOVAKIA . . . . page 159

Banská Bystrica . . . . 48°44' N, 019°09' E
Bardejov . . . . 49°17' N, 021°17' E
Bratislava . . . . 48°09' N, 017°07' E
Čadca . . . . 49°26' N, 018°47' E
Fil'akovo . . . . 48°16' N, 019°50' E
Humenné . . . . 48°56' N, 021°55' E
Komárno . . . . 47°46' N, 018°08' E
Košice . . . . 48°42' N, 021°15' E
Levice . . . . 48°13' N, 018°36' E
Liptovský Mikuláš . . . . 49°05' N, 019°37' E
Lučenec . . . . 48°20' N, 019°40' E
Martin . . . . 49°04' N, 018°56' E
Michalovce . . . . 48°45' N, 021°56' E
Nitra . . . . 48°19' N, 018°05' E
Nové Zámky . . . . 47°59' N, 018°10' E
Partizánske . . . . 48°38' N, 018°23' E
Piešt'any . . . . 48°36' N, 017°50' E
Poprad . . . . 49°03' N, 020°18' E
Považská Bystrica . . . . 49°07' N, 018°27' E
Prešov . . . . 49°00' N, 021°15' E
Prievidza . . . . 48°46' N, 018°38' E
Rimavská Sobota . . . . 48°23' N, 020°02' E
Rožňava . . . . 48°40' N, 020°32' E
Skalica . . . . 48°51' N, 017°14' E
Spišská Nová Ves . . . . 48°57' N, 020°34' E

Topol'čany . . . . 48°34' N, 018°11' E
Trebišov . . . . 48°38' N, 021°43' E
Trenčín . . . . 48°54' N, 018°02' E
Trnava . . . . 48°22' N, 017°36' E
Žilina . . . . 49°13' N, 018°44' E
Zvolen . . . . 48°35' N, 019°08' E

SLOVENIA . . . . . . page 160

Celje . . . . 46°14' N, 015°16' E
Hrastnik . . . . 46°09' N, 015°06' E
Idrija . . . . 46°00' N, 014°02' E
Javornik . . . . 46°14' N, 014°18' E
Jesenice . . . . 46°27' N, 014°04' E
Kočevje . . . . 45°39' N, 014°51' E
Koper . . . . 45°33' N, 013°44' E
Kranj . . . . 46°14' N, 014°22' E
Krško . . . . 45°58' N, 015°29' E
Ljubljana . . . . 46°02' N, 014°30' E
Maribor . . . . 46°33' N, 015°39' E
Murska Sobota . . . . 46°40' N, 016°10' E
Novo Mesto . . . . 45°48' N, 015°10' E
Postojna . . . . 45°47' N, 014°14' E
Ptuj . . . . 46°25' N, 015°52' E
Trbovlje . . . . 46°10' N, 015°03' E
Velenje . . . . 46°22' N, 015°07' E
Zagorje . . . . 46°08' N, 015°00' E

SOLOMON ISLANDS . . . . page 161

Buala . . . . 08°08' S, 159°35' E
Honiara . . . . 09°26' S, 159°57' E
Kirakira . . . . 10°27' S, 161°55' E
Lata . . . . 10°44' S, 165°54' E
Maravovo . . . . 09°17' S, 159°38' E
Munda . . . . 08°19' S, 157°15' E
Sahalu . . . . 09°44' S, 160°31' E
Sasamungga . . . . 07°02' S, 156°47' E
Takwa . . . . 08°22' S, 160°48' E

SOMALIA . . . . page 162

Baardheere (Bardera) . . . . 02°20' N, 042°17' E
Baraawe (Brava) . . . . 01°06' N, 044°03' E
Baydhabo (Baidoa) . . . . 03°07' N, 043°39' E
Beledweyne (Belet Uen) . . . 04°45' N, 045°12' E
Berbera . . . . 10°25' N, 045°02' E
Boosaaso (Bender Cassim) . . . . 11°17' N, 049°11' E
Burao (Burco) . . . . 09°31' N, 045°32' E
Buulobarde (Bulo Burti) . . 03°51' N, 045°34' E
Eyl . . . . 07°59' N, 049°49' E
Hargeysa . . . . 09°35' N, 044°04' E
Hobyo (Obbia) . . . . 05°21' N, 048°32' E
Jamaame (Giamama or Jamame or Margherita) . 00°04' N, 042°45' E
Jawhar (Giohar) . . . . 02°46' N, 045°31' E
Kismaayo (Chisimayu) . . . . 00°22' S, 042°32' E
Marka (Merca) . . . . 01°43' N, 044°53' E
Mogadishu (Mogadiscio or Mogadisho) . . . . 02°04' N, 045°22' E
Seylac (Zeila) . . . . 11°21' N, 043°29' E
Xaafun . . . . 10°25' N, 051°16' E

SOUTH AFRICA . . page 163

Bellville . . . . 33°54' S, 018°38' E
Bisho . . . . 32°53' S, 027°24' E
Bloemfontein . . . . 29°08' S, 026°10' E
Calvinia . . . . 31°28' S, 019°47' E
Cape Town (Kaapstad) . . . . 33°55' S, 018°25' E
Durban (Port Natal) . . . . . . 29°51' S, 031°01' E
East London . . . . 33°02' S, 027°55' E
George . . . . 33°58' S, 022°27' E
Germiston . . . . 26°13' S, 028°11' E
Hopefield . . . . 33°04' S, 018°21' E
Johannesburg . . . . 26°12' S, 028°05' E
Kimberley . . . . 28°45' S, 024°46' E
Klerksdorp . . . . 26°52' S, 026°40' E
Krugersdorp . . . . 26°06' S, 027°46' E
Kuruman . . . . 27°28' S, 023°26' E
Ladysmith . . . . 28°33' S, 029°47' E
Margate . . . . 30°51' S, 030°22' E
Newcastle . . . . 27°45' S, 029°56' E
Oudtshoorn . . . . 33°35' S, 022°12' E
Pietermaritzburg . . . . 29°37' S, 030°23' E
Port Elizabeth . . . . 33°58' S, 025°35' E
Port Nolloth . . . . 29°15' S, 016°52' E
Pretoria . . . . 25°45' S, 028°10' E
Queenstown . . . . 31°54' S, 026°53' E
Rustenburg . . . . 25°40' S, 027°15' E
Seshego . . . . 23°51' S, 029°23' E
Soweto . . . . 26°16' S, 027°52' E
Stellenbosch . . . . 33°56' S, 018°51' E
Uitenhage . . . . 33°46' S, 025°24' E
Upington . . . . 28°27' S, 021°15' E
Vanderbijlpark . . . . 26°42' S, 027°49' E
Welkom . . . . 27°59' S, 026°42' E
Worcester . . . . 33°39' S, 019°26' E

SOUTH KOREA . . page 164

Andong . . . . 36°34' N, 128°44' E
Anyang . . . . 37°23' N, 126°55' E
Ch'ang won . . . . 35°16' N, 128°37' E
Cheju . . . . 33°31' N, 126°32' E
Ch'ŏngju . . . . 36°38' N, 127°30' E
Chŏnju . . . . 35°49' N, 127°09' E
Ch'unch'ŏn . . . . 37°52' N, 127°44' E
Inch'ŏn . . . . 37°28' N, 126°38' E
Iri . . . . 35°56' N, 126°57' E
Kumi . . . . 36°08' N, 128°20' E
Kunsan . . . . 35°59' N, 126°43' E
Kwangju . . . . 35°10' N, 126°55' E
Kyŏngju . . . . 35°50' N, 129°13' E
Masan . . . . 35°11' N, 128°34' E
Mokp'o . . . . 34°47' N, 126°23' E
P'ohang . . . . 36°02' N, 129°22' E

City	Latitude	Longitude
Pusan	35°06' N,	129°03' E
Samch'ŏnp'o	34°55' N,	128°04' E
Seoul (Soul)	37°34' N,	127°00' E
Sŏsan	36°47' N,	126°27' E
Sunch'ŏn	34°57' N,	127°29' E
Suwŏn	37°16' N,	127°01' E
T'aebaek	37°10' N,	128°59' E
Taech'ŏn	36°21' N,	126°36' E
Taegu (Daegu or Taiku)	35°52' N,	128°36' E
Taejon	36°20' N,	127°26' E
Uijŏngbu	37°44' N,	127°02' E
Ulsan	35°33' N,	129°19' E
Wŏnju	37°21' N,	127°58' E

SPAIN . . . . page 165

City	Latitude	Longitude
Albacete	38°59' N,	001°51' W
Alcalá de Henares	40°29' N,	003°22' W
Algeciras	36°08' N,	005°30' W
Alicante (Alacant)	38°21' N,	000°29' W
Avilés	43°33' N,	005°55' W
Badajoz	38°53' N,	006°58' W
Barcelona	41°23' N,	002°11' E
Bilbao	43°15' N,	002°58' W
Burgos	42°21' N,	003°42' W
Cáceres	39°29' N,	006°22' W
Cádiz (Cadiz)	36°32' N,	006°18' W
Cartagena	37°36' N,	000°59' W
Castellón de la Plana	39°59' N,	000°02' W
Ciudad Real	38°59' N,	003°56' W
Cordova (Córdoba)	37°53' N,	004°46' W
Cuenca	40°04' N,	002°08' W
Elche (Elx)	38°15' N,	000°42' W
Ferrol (El Ferrol del Caudillo)	43°29' N,	008°14' W
Gernika-Lumo (Guernica y Luno)	43°19' N,	002°41' W
Getafe	40°18' N,	003°43' W
Gijón	43°32' N,	005°40' W
Granada	37°11' N,	003°36' W
Huelva	37°16' N,	006°57' W
Jaén	37°46' N,	003°47' W
La Coruña (A Coruña)	43°22' N,	008°23' W
León	42°36' N,	005°34' W
Lérida (Lleida)	41°37' N,	000°37' E
L'Hospitalet de Llobregat	41°22' N,	002°08' E
Logroño	42°28' N,	002°27' W
Lugo	43°00' N,	007°34' W
Madrid	40°24' N,	003°41' W
Málaga	36°43' N,	004°25' W
Mérida	38°55' N,	006°20' W
Murcia	37°59' N,	001°07' W
Palencia	42°01' N,	004°32' W
Pamplona (Iruña)	42°49' N,	001°38' W
Salamanca	40°58' N,	005°39' W
San Fernando	36°28' N,	006°12' W
Santander	43°28' N,	003°48' W
Santiago de Compostela	42°53' N,	008°33' W
Saragossa (Zaragoza)	41°38' N,	000°53' W
Segovia	40°57' N,	004°07' W
Seville (Sevilla)	37°23' N,	005°59' W
Soria	41°46' N,	002°28' W
Tarragona	41°07' N,	001°15' E
Terrassa (Tarrasa)	41°34' N,	002°01' E
Teruel	40°21' N,	001°06' W
Toledo	39°52' N,	004°01' W
Valencia	39°28' N,	000°22' W
Valladolid	41°39' N,	004°43' W
Vigo	42°14' N,	008°43' W
Vitoria (Gasteiz)	42°51' N,	002°40' W

SRI LANKA . . . . . page 166

City	Latitude	Longitude
Ambalangoda	06°14' N,	080°03' E
Anuradhapura	08°21' N,	080°23' E
Badulla	06°59' N,	081°03' E
Batticaloa	07°43' N,	081°42' E
Beruwala	06°29' N,	079°59' E
Chavakachcheri	09°39' N,	080°09' E
Colombo	06°56' N,	079°51' E
Dehiwala-Mount Lavinia	06°51' N,	079°52' E
Eravur	07°46' N,	081°36' E
Galle	06°02' N,	080°13' E
Gampola	07°10' N,	080°34' E
Hambantota	06°07' N,	081°07' E
Jaffna	09°40' N,	080°00' E
Kalutara	06°35' N,	079°58' E
Kandy	07°18' N,	080°38' E
Kankesanturai	09°49' N,	080°02' E
Kegalla	07°15' N,	080°21' E
Kilinochchi	09°24' N,	080°24' E
Kotte	06°54' N,	079°54' E
Kurunegala	07°29' N,	080°22' E
Madampe	07°30' N,	079°50' E
Mannar	08°59' N,	079°54' E
Moratuwa	06°46' N,	079°53' E
Mullaittivu	09°16' N,	080°49' E
Mutur	08°27' N,	081°16' E
Negombo	07°13' N,	079°50' E
Nuwara Eliya	06°58' N,	080°46' E
Point Pedro	09°50' N,	080°14' E
Polonnaruwa	07°56' N,	081°00' E
Puttalam	08°02' N,	079°49' E
Ratnapura	06°41' N,	080°24' E
Tangalla	06°01' N,	080°48' E
Trincomalee	08°34' N,	081°14' E
Vavuniya	08°45' N,	080°30' E
Watugedara	06°15' N,	080°03' E
Weligama	05°58' N,	080°25' E
Yala	06°22' N,	081°31' E

SUDAN . . . . page 167

City	Latitude	Longitude
Ad-Damazin (Ed–Damazin)	11°46' N,	034°21' E
Ad-Dāmir	17°35' N,	033°58' E
Ad-Duwaym (Ed-Dueim)	14°00' N,	032°19' E
Al-Fūlah	11°48' N,	028°24' E
Al-Fashir (El Fasher)	13°38' N,	025°21' E
Al-Junaynah (Geneina)	13°27' N,	022°27' E

Al-Mijlad . . . 11°02' N, 027°44' E
Al-Qadārif (Gedaref) . . . 14°02' N, 035°24' E
Al-Ubbayid (El-Obeid) . . . 13°11' N, 030°13' E
An-Nuhūd (An-Nahūd) . . . 12°42' N, 028°26' E
'Aṭbarah . . . 17°42' N, 033°59' E
Bor . . . 06°12' N, 031°33' E
Dunqulah (Dongola) . . . 19°10' N, 030°29' E
Juba . . . 04°51' N, 031°37' E
Kāduqlī . . . 11°01' N, 029°43' E
Kas . . . 12°30' N, 024°17' E
Kassalā . . . 15°28' N, 036°24' E
Khartoum . . . 15°36' N, 032°32' E
Khartoum North . . . 15°38' N, 032°33' E
Kūstī . . . 13°10' N, 032°40' E
Malakāl . . . 09°31' N, 031°39' E
Marawi . . . 18°29' N, 031°49' E
Nagichot . . . 04°16' N, 033°34' E
Nāṣir . . . 08°36' N, 033°04' E
Nyala . . . 12°03' N, 024°53' E
Omdurman . . . 15°38' N, 032°30' E
Port Sudan . . . 19°37' N, 037°14' E
Rumbek . . . 06°48' N, 029°41' E
Sannār . . . 13°33' N, 033°38' E
Sawākin . . . 19°07' N, 037°20' E
Shandi . . . 16°42' N, 033°26' E
Wadi Halfa' . . . 21°48' N, 031°21' E
Wad Madanī . . . 14°24' N, 033°32' E
Wāw (Wau) . . . 07°42' N, 028°00' E

SURINAME . . . . . . page 168

Albina . . . 05°30' N, 054°03' W
Benzdorp . . . 03°41' N, 054°05' W
Bitagron . . . 05°10' N, 056°06' W
Brokopondo . . . 05°04' N, 054°58' W
Brownsweg . . . 05°01' N, 055°10' W
Goddo . . . 04°01' N, 055°28' W
Groningen . . . 05°48' N, 055°28' W
Meerzorg . . . 05°49' N, 055°09' W
Nieuw Amsterdam . . . 05°53' N, 055°05' W
Nieuw Nickerie . . . 05°57' N, 056°59' W
Onverwacht . . . 05°36' N, 055°12' W
Paramaribo . . . 05°50' N, 055°10' W
Totness . . . 05°53' N, 056°19' W
Zanderij . . . 05°27' N, 055°12' W

SWAZILAND . . . . . page 169

Hlatikulu . . . 26°58' S, 031°19' E
Kadake . . . 26°13' S, 031°02' E
Manzini (Bremersdorp) . . . 26°29' S, 031°22' E
Mbabane . . . 26°19' S, 031°08' E
Nhlangono . . . 27°07' S, 031°12' E
Piggs Peak . . . 25°58' S, 031°15' E
Siteki (Stegi) . . . 26°27' S, 031°57' E

SWEDEN . . . . page 170

Älvsbyn . . . 65°40' N, 021°00' E
Falun . . . 60°36' N, 015°38' E
Gävle . . . 60°40' N, 017°10' E
Göteborg . . . 57°43' N, 011°58' E
Halmstad . . . 56°39' N, 012°50' E
Haparanda . . . 65°50' N, 024°10' E
Hudiksvall . . . 61°44' N, 017°07' E
Jönköping . . . 57°47' N, 014°11' E
Karlskrona . . . 56°10' N, 015°35' E
Karlstad . . . 59°22' N, 013°30' E
Kiruna . . . 67°51' N, 020°13' E
Kristianstad . . . 56°02' N, 014°08' E
Linköping . . . 58°25' N, 015°37' E
Luleå . . . 65°34' N, 022°10' E
Lycksele . . . 64°36' N, 018°40' E
Malmberget . . . 67°10' N, 020°40' E
Malmö . . . 55°36' N, 013°00' E
Mariestad . . . 58°43' N, 013°51' E
Mora . . . 61°00' N, 014°33' E
Örebro . . . 59°17' N, 015°13' E
Örnsköldsvik . . . 63°18' N, 018°43' E
Östersund . . . 63°11' N, 014°39' E
Piteå . . . 65°20' N, 021°30' E
Skellefteå . . . 64°46' N, 020°57' E
Söderhamn . . . 61°18' N, 017°03' E
Stockholm . . . 59°20' N, 018°03' E
Strömsund . . . 63°51' N, 015°35' E
Sundsvall . . . 62°23' N, 017°18' E
Umea . . . 63°50' N, 020°15' E
Uppsala . . . 59°52' N, 017°38' E
Vänersborg . . . 58°22' N, 012°19' E
Västerås . . . 59°37' N, 016°33' E
Växjö . . . 56°53' N, 014°49' E
Vetalnda . . . 57°26' N, 015°04' E
Visby . . . 57°38' N, 018°18' E
Ystad . . . 55°25' N, 013°49' E

SWITZERLAND . . page 171

Aarau . . . 47°23' N, 008°03' E
Altdorf . . . 46°53' N, 008°39' E
Arbon . . . 47°31' N, 009°26' E
Appenzell . . . 47°20' N, 009°24' E
Arosa . . . 46°47' N, 009°40' E
Baden . . . 47°28' N, 008°18' E
Basel . . . 47°35' N, 007°32' E
Bellinzona . . . 46°12' N, 009°01' E
Bern . . . 46°55' N, 007°28' E
Biel (Bienne) . . . 47°10' N, 007°15' E
Chur (Coire) . . . 46°51' N, 009°30' E
Davos . . . 46°49' N, 009°50' E
Delémont . . . 47°22' N, 007°20' E
Frauenfeld . . . 47°33' N, 008°54' E
Fribourg (Freiburg) . . . 46°48' N, 007°09' E
Geneva . . . 46°12' N, 006°10' E
Glarus . . . 47°02' N, 009°04' E
Grindelwald . . . 46°37' N, 008°03' E
Gstaad . . . 46°28' N, 007°17' E
Herisau . . . 47°24' N, 009°16' E
Interlaken . . . 46°41' N, 007°51' E
La Chaux-de-Fonds . . . 47°08' N, 006°51' E
Lausanne . . . 46°32' N, 006°40' E
Liestal . . . 47°28' N, 007°44' E

Locarno (Luggarus)	46°10' N,	008°48' E
Lucerne (Luzern)	47°05' N,	008°16' E
Lugano (Lauis)	46°00' N,	008°58' E
Montreux	46°26' N,	006°55' E
Neuchatel (Neuenburg)	47°00' N,	006°58' E
Saint Gall (Sankt Gallen)	47°28' N,	009°24' E
Saint Moritz (San Murezzan, Saint-Moritz, or Sankt Moritz)	46°30' N,	009°50' E
Sarnen	46°54' N,	008°14' E
Schaffhausen	47°42' N,	008°38' E
Sion (Sitten)	46°14' N,	007°21' E
Solothurn (Soleure)	47°14' N,	007°31' E
Stans	46°58' N,	008°21' E
Thun (Thoune)	46°45' N,	007°37' E
Vevey	46°27' N,	006°51' E
Winterthur	47°30' N,	008°45' E
Zermatt	46°01' N,	007°45' E
Zug	47°10' N,	008°31' E
Zürich	47°22' N,	008°33' E

SYRIA . . . . page 172

Al-Bāb	36°22' N,	037°31' E
Al-Hasakah	36°29' N,	040°45' E
Al-Mayādin	35°01' N,	040°27' E
Al-Qāmishli (Al-Kamishly)	37°02' N,	041°14' E
Al-Raqqah (Rakka)	35°57' N,	039°01' E
Al-Safirah	36°04' N,	037°22' E
Al-Suwaydā'	32°42' N,	036°34' E
Aleppo (Ḥalab)	36°12' N,	037°10' E
A'zāz (I'zaz)	36°35' N,	037°03' E
Damascus	33°30' N,	036°18' E
Dar'ā	32°37' N,	036°06' E
Dayr azl-Zawr	35°20' N,	040°09' E
Dūmā (Douma)	33°35' N,	036°24' E
Hamāh (Hama)	35°08' N,	036°45' E
Ḥimṣ (Homs)	34°44' N,	036°43' E
Idlib	35°55' N,	036°38' E
Jablah (Jableh)	35°21' N,	035°55' E
Jarābulus	36°49' N,	038°01' E
Latakia (Al-Lādhiqīyah)	35°31' N,	035°47' E
Ma'arrat al-Nu'mān	35°38' N,	036°40' E
Ma'lūlā	33°50' N,	036°33' E
Manbij (Manbej)	36°31' N,	037°57' E
Mukharram al-Fawqāni	34°49' N,	037°05' E
Ra's al-'Ayn	36°51' N,	040°04' E
Salamīyah	35°01' N,	037°03' E
Tadmur	34°33' N,	038°17' E
Ṭarṭūs	34°53' N,	035°53' E

TAIWAN . . . . page 173

Chang-hua	24°05' N,	120°32' E
Ch'ao-chou	22°33' N,	120°32' E
Ch'e-ch'eng	22°05' N,	120°42' E
Chia-i	23°29' N,	120°27' E
Ch'ih-shang	23°07' N,	121°12' E
Chi-lung	25°08' N,	121°44' E
Chung-hsing Hsin-ts'un	23°57' N,	120°41' E
Chu-tung	24°44' N,	121°05' E
Erh-lin	23°54' N,	120°22' E
Feng-lin	23°45' N,	121°26' E
Feng-shan	22°38' N,	120°21' E
Feng-yüan	24°15' N,	120°43' E
Hsin-chu	24°48' N,	120°58' E
Hsin-ying	23°18' N,	120°19' E
Hua-lien	23°59' N,	121°36' E
I-lan	24°46' N,	121°45' E
Kang-shan	22°48' N,	120°17' E
Kao-hsiung	22°38' N,	120°17' E
Lan-yü	22°02' N,	121°33' E
Lo-tung	24°41' N,	121°46' E
Lu-kang	24°03' N,	120°25' E
Lü-tao	22°40' N,	121°28' E
Miao-li	24°34' N,	120°49' E
Nan-t'ou	23°55' N,	120°41' E
Pan-ch'iao	25°01' N,	121°27' E
P'ing-tung	22°40' N,	120°29' E
San-ch'ung	25°04' N,	121°30' E
Su-ao	24°36' N,	121°51' E
T'ai-chung	24°09' N,	120°41' E
T'ai-nan	23°00' N,	120°12' E
Taipei (T'ai-pei)	25°03' N,	121°30' E
T'ai-tung	22°45' N,	121°09' E
T'ao-yüan	25°00' N,	121°18' E
Tung-ho	22°58' N,	121°18' E
Yüan-lin	23°58' N,	120°34' E
Yung-k'ang	23°02' N,	120°15' E

TAJIKISTAN . . . . . page 174

Dushanbe	38°33' N,	068°48' E
Kalininobod	37°52' N,	068°55' E
Khorugh	37°30' N,	071°36' E
Khujand (Leninabad, or Khojand)	40°17' N,	069°37' E
Kofarniqon (Ordzhonikidzeäbad)	38°34' N,	069°01' E
Külob	37°55' N,	069°46' E
Norak	38°23' N,	069°21' E
Qayroqqum	40°16' N,	069°49' E
Qŭrghonteppa	37°50' N,	068°47' E
Uroteppa	39°55' N,	069°01' E

TANZANIA . . . . . . page 175

Arusha	03°22' S,	036°41' E
Bagamoyo	06°26' S,	038°54' E
Bukoba	01°20' S,	031°49' E
Chake Chake	05°15' S,	039°46' E
Dar es Salaam	06°48' S,	039°17' E
Dodoma	06°11' S,	035°45' E
Ifakara	08°08' S,	036°41' E

City	Latitude	Longitude
Iringa	07°46' S,	035°42' E
Kigoma	04°52' S,	029°38' E
Korogwe	05°09' S,	038°29' E
Lindi	10°00' S,	039°43' E
Mbeya	08°54' S,	033°27' E
Mkoani	05°22' S,	039°39' E
Morogoro	06°49' S,	037°40' E
Moshi	03°21' S,	037°20' E
Mpwapwa	06°21' S,	036°29' E
Mtwara	10°16' S,	040°11' E
Musoma	01°30' S,	033°48' E
Mwanza	02°31' S,	032°54' E
Newala	10°56' S,	039°18' E
Pangani	09°32' S,	035°31' E
Shinyanga	03°40' S,	033°26' E
Singida	04°49' S,	034°45' E
Songea	10°41' S,	035°39' E
Sumbawanga	07°58' S,	031°37' E
Tabora	05°01' S,	032°48' E
Tanga	05°04' S,	039°06' E
Tunduru	11°07' S,	037°21' E
Wete	05°04' S,	039°43' E
Zanzibar	06°10' S,	039°11' E

THAILAND . . . . . . page 176

City	Latitude	Longitude
Bangkok (Krung Thep)	13°45' N,	100°31' E
Chanthaburi (Chantabun)	12°36' N,	102°09' E
Chiang Mai (Chiengmai)	18°47' N,	098°59' E
Chon Buri	13°22' N,	100°59' E
Hat Yai (Haad Yai)	07°01' N,	100°28' E
Khon Kaen	16°26' N,	102°50' E
Mae Sot	16°43' N,	098°34' E
Nakhhon Phanom	17°24' N,	104°47' E
Nakhon Ratchasima (Khorat)	14°58' N,	102°07' E
Nakhon Sawan	15°41' N,	100°07' E
Nakhon Si Thammarat	08°26' N,	099°58' E
Nan	18°47' N,	100°47' E
Nong Khai	17°52' N,	102°44' E
Nonthaburi	13°50' N,	100°29' E
Pathum Thani	14°01' N,	100°32' E
Pattaya	12°54' N,	100°51' E
Phichit	16°26' N,	100°22' E
Phitsanulok	16°50' N,	100°15' E
Phra Nakhon Si Ayutthaya (Ayutthaya)	14°21' N,	100°33' E
Phuket	07°53' N,	098°24' E
Roi Et	16°03' N,	103°40' E
Sakon Nakhon	17°10' N,	104°09' E
Samut Prakan	13°36' N,	100°36' E
Samut Sakhon (Samut Sakorn)	13°32' N,	100°17' E
Sara Buri	14°32' N,	100°55' E
Trang	07°33' N,	099°36' E
Trat	12°14' N,	102°30' E
Ubon Ratchathani	15°14' N,	104°54' E
Udon Thani	17°26' N,	102°46' E
Uthai Thani	15°22' N,	100°03' E
Yala	06°33' N,	101°18' E

TOGO . . . . page 177

City	Latitude	Longitude
Aného	06°14' N,	001°36' E
Atakpamé	07°32' N,	001°08' E
Bassar	09°15' N,	000°47' E
Blitta	08°19' N,	000°59' E
Dapaong	10°52' N,	000°12' E
Kara (Lama Kara)	09°33' N,	001°12' E
Lomé	06°08' N,	001°13' E
Palimé	09°21' N,	002°37' E
Sokodé	08°59' N,	001°08' E
Tsévié	06°25' N,	001°13' E

TONGA . . . . page 178

City	Latitude	Longitude
Nuku'alofa	21°08' N,	175°12' E

TRINIDAD AND TOBAGO . . . . page 179

City	Latitude	Longitude
Arima	10°38' N,	061°17' W
Arouca	10°38' N,	061°20' W
Chaguanas	10°31' N,	061°25' W
Charlotteville	11°19' N,	060°33' W
Couva	10°25' N,	061°27' W
Point Fortin	10°11' N,	061°41' W
Port of Spain	10°39' N,	061°31' W
Princes Town	10°16' N,	061°23' W
Rio Claro	10°18' N,	061°11' W
Roxborough	11°15' N,	060°35' W
San Fernando	10°17' N,	061°28' W
Sangre Grande	10°35' N,	061°07' W
Scarborough	11°11' N,	060°44' W
Siparia	10°08' N,	061°30' W
Tunapuna	10°38' N,	061°23' W

TUNISIA . . . . page 180

City	Latitude	Longitude
Al-Ḥammāmāt (Hammamet)	36°24' N,	010°37' E
Al-Mahdīyah (Mahdia)	35°30' N,	011°04' E
Al-Metlaoui	34°20' N,	008°24' E
Al-Muknīn (Moknine)	35°38' N,	010°54' E
Al-Munastīr (Monastir or Ruspina)	35°47' N,	010°50' E
Al-Qaṣrayn (Kasserine)	35°11' N,	008°48' E
Al-Qayrawān (Kairouan or Qairouan)	35°41' N,	010°07' E
Bājah (Béja)	36°44' N,	009°11' E
Banzart (Bizerte)	37°17' N,	009°52' E
Ḥammām al-Anf (Hammam-lif)	36°44' N,	010°20' E
Jarjīs (Zarzis)	33°30' N,	011°07' E
Madanīn (Medenine)	33°21' N,	010°30' E
Makthar	35°51' N,	009°12' E
Manzil Bū Ruqaybah (Ferryville or Menzel-Bourguiba)	37°10' N,	009°48' E

Nābul (Nabeul or Neapolis) . . . 36°27' N, 010°44' E
Nafṭah (Nefta) . . . 33°52' N, 007°53' E
Qābis (Gabes or Tacape) . . 33°53' N, 010°07' E
Qafṣah (Gafsa) . . . 34°25' N, 008°48' E
Qibilī (Kebili) . . . 33°42' N, 008°58' E
Safāqis (Sfax) . . . 34°44' N, 010°46' E
Sūsah (Sousa or Sousse) . . 35°49' N, 010°38' E
Tawzar (Tozeur) . . . 33°55' N, 008°08' E
Tunis (Tunis) . . . 36°48' N, 010°11' E
Zaghwān (Zaghouan) . . . 36°24' N, 010°09' E

TURKEY . . . . page 181

Adana . . . 37°01' N, 035°18' E
Afyon . . . 38°45' N, 030°33' E
Amasya . . . 40°39' N, 035°51' E
Ankara (Angora) . . . 39°56' N, 032°52' E
Antakya (Antioch) . . . 36°14' N, 036°07' E
Antalya (Attalia or Hatay) . . . 36°53' N, 030°42' E
Artvin . . . 41°11' N, 041°49' E
Aydın . . . 37°51' N, 027°51' E
Balıkesir . . . 39°39' N, 027°53' E
Bandırma (Panderma) . . . 40°20' N, 027°58' E
Batman . . . 37°52' N, 041°07' E
Bursa (Brusa) . . . 40°11' N, 029°04' E
Çorum . . . 40°33' N, 034°58' E
Denizli . . . 37°46' N, 029°06' E
Diyarbakır (Amida) . . . 37°55' N, 040°14' E
Elâziğ . . . 38°41' N, 039°14' E
Erzincan . . . 39°44' N, 039°29' E
Erzurum . . . 39°55' N, 041°17' E
Eskisehir . . . 39°46' N, 030°32' E
Gaziantep . . . 37°05' N, 037°22' E
Iğdir . . . 39°56' N, 044°02' E
İskenderun (Alexandretta) . 36°35' N, 036°10' E
Isparta (Hamid-Abad) . . . 37°46' N, 030°33' E
Istanbul (Constantinople) . . . 41°01' N, 028°58' E
İzmir (Smyrna) . . . 38°25' N, 027°09' E
İzmit . . . 40°46' N, 029°55' E
Kahramanmaraş (Maraş) . . . 37°36' N, 036°55' E
Karabük . . . 41°12' N, 032°37' E
Karaman . . . 37°11' N, 033°14' E
Kars . . . 40°37' N, 043°05' E
Kayseri (Caesarea) . . . 38°43' N, 035°30' E
Kırıkkale . . . 39°50' N, 033°31' E
Konya (Iconium) . . . 37°52' N, 032°31' E
Kütahya . . . 39°25' N, 029°59' E
Manisa . . . 38°36' N, 027°26' E
Mardin . . . 37°18' N, 040°44' E
Mersin . . . 36°48' N, 034°38' E
Muğla . . . 37°12' N, 028°22' E
Nevşehir . . . 38°38' N, 034°43' E
Niğde . . . 37°59' N, 034°42' E
Ordu . . . 41°00' N, 037°53' E
Samsun (Amisus) . . . 41°17' N, 036°20' E
Sinop . . . 42°01' N, 035°09' E
Sivas (Sebastia) . . . 39°45' N, 037°02' E
Trabzon (Trapezus or Trebizond) . . . 41°00' N, 039°43' E
Urfa . . . 37°08' N, 038°46' E
Uşak (Ushak) . . . 38°41' N, 029°25' E
Van . . . 38°30' N, 043°23' E
Yalova . . . 40°39' N, 029°15' E
Yozgat . . . 39°50' N, 034°48' E
Zonguldak . . . 41°27' N, 031°49' E

TURKMENISTAN . page 182

Ashgabat (Ashkhabad) . . . 37°57' N, 058°23' E
Bayramaly . . . 37°37' N, 062°10' E
Büzmeyin . . . 38°05' N, 058°12' E
Chärjew . . . 39°06' N, 063°34' E
Cheleken . . . 39°26' N, 053°07' E
Chirchiq . . . 41°29' N, 069°35' E
Dashhowuz . . . 41°50' N, 059°58' E
Gowurdak . . . 37°50' N, 066°04' E
Kerki . . . 37°50' N, 065°12' E
Mary (Merv) . . . 37°36' N, 061°50' E
Nebitdag . . . 39°30' N, 054°22' E
Türkmenbashy (Krasnovodsk) . . . 40°00' N, 053°00' E
Yolöten . . . 37°18' N, 062°21' E

TUVALU . . . . page 183

Fongafale . . . 08°31' S, 179°13' E

UGANDA . . . . page 184

Entebbe . . . 00°04' N, 032°28' E
Gulu . . . 02°47' N, 032°18' E
Jinja . . . 00°26' N, 033°12' E
Kabarole . . . 00°39' N, 030°16' E
Kampala . . . 00°19' N, 032°35' E
Masaka . . . 00°20' S, 031°44' E
Mbale . . . 01°05' N, 034°10' E
Soroti . . . 01°43' N, 033°37' E
Tororo . . . 00°42' N, 034°11' E

UKRAINE . . . . page 185

Alchevsk . . . 48°30' N, 038°47' E
Berdyansk . . . 46°45' N, 036°47' E
Berdychiv . . . 49°54' N, 028°35' E
Bila Tserkva . . . 49°47' N, 030°07' E
Cherkasy . . . 49°26' N, 032°04' E
Chernihiv . . . 51°30' N, 031°18' E
Chernivtsi . . . 48°18' N, 025°56' E
Chornobyl (Chernobyl) . . . 51°16' N, 030°14' E
Dnipropetrovs'k . . . 48°27' N, 034°59' E
Donetsk . . . 48°00' N, 037°48' E
Kerch . . . 45°21' N, 036°28' E
Kharkiv . . . 50°00' N, 036°15' E
Khmelnytskyy . . . 49°25' N, 027°00' E
Kiev (Kyyiv) . . . 50°26' N, 030°31' E
Korosten . . . 50°57' N, 028°39' E

Kovel	51°13' N,	024°43' E
Krasny Luch	48°08' N,	038°56' E
Kryvyy Rih	47°55' N,	033°21' E
Luhansk	48°34' N,	039°20' E
Lutsk	50°45' N,	025°20' E
Lviv	49°50' N,	024°00' E
Makiyivka	48°02' N,	037°58' E
Marhanets	47°38' N,	034°38' E
Mariupol	47°06' N,	037°33' E
Melitopol	46°50' N,	035°22' E
Mykolayiv	46°58' N,	032°00' E
Myrhorod	49°58' N,	033°36' E
Novhorod-Siverskyy	52°00' N,	033°16' E
Odessa	46°28' N,	030°44' E
Pavlograd	48°31' N,	035°52' E
Poltava	49°35' N,	034°34' E
Pryluky	50°36' N,	032°24' E
Rivne	50°37' N,	026°15' E
Rubizhne	49°01' N,	038°23' E
Sevastopol	44°36' N,	033°32' E
Shostka	51°52' N,	033°29' E
Simferopol	44°57' N,	034°06' E
Sumy	50°54' N,	034°48' E
Syeverodonets'k	48°58' N,	038°26' E
Uzhhorod	48°37' N,	022°18' E
Vinnytsya	49°14' N,	028°29' E
Voznesensk	47°33' N,	031°20' E
Yevpatoriya	45°12' N,	033°22' E
Zaporizhzhya	47°49' N,	035°11' E
Zhytomyr	50°15' N,	028°40' E

UNITED ARAB EMIRATES .... page 186

Abu Dhabi	24°28' N,	054°22' E
'Ajmān	25°25' N,	055°27' E
Al-'Ayn	24°13' N,	055°46' E
Al-Fujayrah	25°08' N,	056°21' E
Al-Khīs	23°00' N,	054°12' E
Al-Māriyah	23°08' N,	053°44' E
'Arādah	22°59' N,	053°26' E
Ash-Shāriqah	25°22' N,	055°23' E
Diqdāqah	25°40' N,	055°58' E
Dubai	25°16' N,	055°18' E
Kalbā	25°05' N,	056°22' E
Khawr Fakkān	25°21' N,	056°22' E
Ra's Al-Khaymah	25°47' N,	055°57' E
Tarīf	24°03' N,	053°46' E
Umm Al-Qaywayn	25°35' N,	055°34' E
Wadhīl	23°03' N,	054°08' E

UNITED KINGDOM .... page 187

Aberdeen	57°09' N,	002°08' W
Belfast	54°35' N,	005°56' W
Birmingham	52°29' N,	001°51' W
Bradford	53°47' N,	001°45' W
Bristol	51°26' N,	002°35' W
Cambridge	52°12' N,	000°09' E
Cardiff	51°29' N,	003°11' W
Carlisle	54°53' N,	002°57' W
Cheltenham	51°54' N,	002°05' W
Colchester	51°54' N,	000°54' E
Coventry	52°24' N,	001°31' W
Darlington	54°32' N,	001°34' W
Dartford	51°26' N,	000°12' W
Derby	52°55' N,	001°28' W
Derry (Londonderry)	55°00' N,	007°20' W
Dundee	56°29' N,	003°02' W
Edinburgh	55°57' N,	003°10' W
Exeter	50°43' N,	003°31' W
Glasgow	55°52' N,	004°15' W
Hastings	50°52' N,	000°35' E
High Wycombe	51°38' N,	000°45' W
Hove	50°50' N,	000°11' W
Ipswich	52°03' N,	001°09' E
King's Lynn	52°45' N,	000°24' E
Kingston upon Hull	53°45' N,	000°20' W
Leeds	53°48' N,	001°32' W
Leicester	52°38' N,	001°08' W
Lincoln	53°14' N,	000°32' W
Liverpool	53°25' N,	002°57' W
London	51°30' N,	000°07' W
Maidstone	51°16' N,	000°32' E
Manchester	53°29' N,	002°15' W
Margate	51°23' N,	001°23' E
Newcastle upon Tyne	54°58' N,	001°36' W
Newtownabbey	54°40' N,	005°57' W
Norwich	52°38' N,	001°18' E
Nottingham	52°58' N,	001°10' W
Peterborough	52°35' N,	000°14' W
Plymouth	50°23' N,	004°09' W
Poole	50°43' N,	001°59' W
Portsmouth	50°49' N,	001°04' W
Rhondda	51°39' N,	003°29' W
Sheffield	53°23' N,	001°28' W
Southampton	50°55' N,	001°24' W
Stoke-on-Trent	53°01' N,	002°11' W
Swansea	51°38' N,	003°58' W
Walsall	52°35' N,	001°59' W
Warrington	53°24' N,	002°36' W
York	53°57' N,	001°06' W

UNITED STATES .... page 188-9

Aberdeen, S.D.	45°28' N,	098°29' W
Aberdeen, Wash.	46°59' N,	123°50' W
Abilene, Kan.	38°55' N,	097°13' W
Abilene, Tex.	32°28' N,	099°43' W
Ada, Okla.	34°46' N,	096°41' W
Akron, Ohio	41°05' N,	081°31' W
Alamogordo, N.M.	32°54' N,	105°57' W
Alamosa, Colo.	37°28' N,	105°52' W
Albany, Ga.	31°35' N,	084°10' W
Albany, N.Y.	42°39' N,	073°45' W

Albuquerque, N.M. . . . . 35°05' N, 106°39' W
Alexandria, La. . . . . 31°18' N, 092°27' W
Alexandria, Va. . . . . 38°48' N, 077°03' W
Alliance, Neb. . . . . 42°06' N, 102°52' W
Alpena, Mich. . . . . 45°04' N, 083°27' W
Alton, Ill. . . . . 38°53' N, 090°11' W
Alturas, Calif. . . . . 41°29' N, 120°32' W
Altus, Okla. . . . . 34°38' N, 099°20' W
Amarillo, Tex. . . . . 35°13' N, 101°50' W
Americus, Ga. . . . . 32°04' N, 084°14' W
Anaconda, Mont.. . . . . 46°08' N, 112°57' W
Anchorage, Alaska . . . . 61°13' N, 149°54' W
Andalusia, Ala. . . . . 31°18' N, 086°29' W
Ann Arbor, Mich. . . . . 42°17' N, 083°45' W
Annapolis, Md. . . . . 38°59' N, 076°30' W
Appleton, Wis.. . . . . 44°16' N, 088°25' W
Arcata, Calif. . . . . 40°52' N, 124°05' W
Arlington, Tex. . . . . 32°44' N, 097°07' W
Arlington, Va. . . . . 38°53' N, 077°07' W
Asheville, N.C.. . . . . 35°36' N, 082°33' W
Ashland, Ky. . . . . 38°28' N, 082°38' W
Ashland, Wis. . . . . 46°35' N, 090°53' W
Aspen, Colo. . . . . 39°11' N, 106°49' W
Astoria, Ore. . . . . 46°11' N, 123°50' W
Athens, Ga. . . . . 33°57' N, 083°23' W
Atlanta, Ga. . . . . 33°45' N, 084°23' W
Atlantic City, N.J. . . . . 39°21' N, 074°27' W
Augusta, Ga. . . . . 33°28' N, 081°58' W
Augusta, Me. . . . . 44°19' N, 069°47' W
Aurora, Colo.. . . . . 39°43' N, 104°49' W
Austin, Minn.. . . . . 43°40' N, 092°58' W
Austin, Tex. . . . . 30°17' N, 097°45' W
Baker, Mont. . . . . 46°22' N, 104°17' W
Baker, Ore. . . . . 44°47' N, 117°50' W
Bakersfield, Calif. . . . . 35°23' N, 119°01' W
Baltimore, Md. . . . . 39°17' N, 076°37' W
Bangor, Me. . . . . 44°48' N, 068°46' W
Bar Harbor, Me. . . . . 44°23' N, 068°13' W
Barrow, Alaska . . . . 71°18' N, 156°47' W
Bartlesville, Okla. . . . . 36°45' N, 095°59' W
Baton Rouge, La.. . . . . 30°27' N, 091°11' W
Bay City, Mich. . . . . 43°36' N, 083°54' W
Beaumont, Tex.. . . . . 30°05' N, 094°06' W
Bellingham, Wash. . . . . 48°46' N, 122°29' W
Beloit, Wis. . . . . 42°31' N, 089°01' W
Bemidji, Minn.. . . . . 47°28' N, 094°52' W
Bend, Ore. . . . . 44°04' N, 121°19' W
Berlin, N.H. . . . . 44°28' N, 071°11' W
Bethel, Alaska . . . . 60°48' N, 161°45' W
Beulah, N.D. . . . . 47°15' N, 101°46' W
Billings, Mont. . . . . 45°47' N, 108°30' W
Biloxi, Miss.. . . . . 30°24' N, 088°53' W
Birmingham, Ala. . . . . 33°31' N, 086°48' W
Bismarck, N.D. . . . . 46°48' N, 100°47' W
Bloomington, Ind. . . . . 39°10' N, 086°32' W
Blythe, Calif. . . . . 33°37' N, 114°36' W
Boca Raton, Fla. . . . . 26°21' N, 080°05' W
Bogalusa, La.. . . . . 30°47' N, 089°52' W
Boise, Idaho . . . . 43°37' N, 116°13' W
Boston, Mass. . . . . 42°22' N, 071°04' W
Boulder, Colo. . . . . 40°01' N, 105°17' W
Bowling Green, Ky. . . . . 36°59' N, 086°27' W
Bozeman, Mont. . . . . 45°41' N, 111°02' W
Bradenton, Fla. . . . . 27°30' N, 082°34' W
Brady, Tex. . . . . 31°09' N, 099°20' W
Brainerd, Minn.. . . . . 46°22' N, 094°12' W
Bremerton, Wash.. . . . . 47°34' N, 122°38' W
Brigham City, Utah . . . . 41°31' N, 112°01' W
Brookings, S.D. . . . . 44°19' N, 096°48' W
Brownsville, Tex. . . . . 25°54' N, 097°30' W
Brunswick, Ga. . . . . 31°10' N, 081°30' W
Bryan, Tex. . . . . 30°40' N, 096°22' W
Buffalo, N.Y. . . . . 42°53' N, 078°53' W
Buffalo, Tex. . . . . 31°28' N, 096°04' W
Burlington, Ia. . . . . 40°48' N, 091°06' W
Burlington, Vt.. . . . . 44°29' N, 073°12' W
Burns, Ore. . . . . 43°35' N, 119°03' W
Butte, Mont. . . . . 46°00' N, 112°32' W
Cairo, Ill. . . . . 37°00' N, 089°11' W
Caldwell, Idaho . . . . 43°40' N, 116°41' W
Canton, Ohio . . . . 40°48' N, 081°23' W
Cape Girardeau, Mo.. . . . . . . 37°19' N, 089°32' W
Carbondale, Ill. . . . . 37°44' N, 089°13' W
Carlsbad, N.M. . . . . 32°25' N, 104°14' W
Carson City, Nev. . . . . 39°10' N, 119°46' W
Casa Grande, Ariz. . . . . 32°53' N, 111°45' W
Casper, Wyo.. . . . . 42°51' N, 106°19' W
Cedar City, Utah . . . . 37°41' N, 113°04' W
Cedar Rapids, Ia.. . . . . 41°59' N, 091°40' W
Chadron, Neb.. . . . . 42°50' N, 103°00' W
Champaign, Ill. . . . . 40°07' N, 088°15' W
Charleston, S.C.. . . . . 32°46' N, 079°56' W
Charleston, W.Va. . . . . 38°21' N, 081°39' W
Charlotte, N.C. . . . . 35°13' N, 080°51' W
Chattanooga, Tenn. . . . . . . 35°03' N, 085°19' W
Chesapeake, Va. . . . . 36°50' N, 076°17' W
Cheyenne, Wyo. . . . . 41°08' N, 104°49' W
Chicago, Ill. . . . . 41°53' N, 087°38' W
Chico, Calif.. . . . . 39°44' N, 121°50' W
Chula Vista, Calif. . . . . 32°38' N, 117°05' W
Cincinnati, Ohio . . . . 39°06' N, 084°31' W
Clarksdale, Miss.. . . . . 34°12' N, 090°35' W
Clayton, N.M. . . . . 36°27' N, 103°11' W
Clearwater, Fla.. . . . . 27°58' N, 082°48' W
Cleveland, Ohio . . . . 41°30' N, 081°42' W
Clinton, Okla. . . . . 35°31' N, 098°58' W
Clovis, N.M.. . . . . 34°24' N, 103°12' W
Cody, Wyo. . . . . 44°32' N, 109°03' W
Coeur d'Alene, Idaho . . . . . 47°41' N, 116°46' W
College Station, Tex.. . . . . . . 30°37' N, 096°21' W
Colorado Springs, Colo. . . . 38°50' N, 104°49' W
Columbia, S.C.. . . . . 34°00' N, 081°03' W
Columbus, Ga.. . . . . 32°29' N, 084°59' W
Columbus, Miss. . . . . 33°30' N, 088°25' W
Columbus, Ohio . . . . 39°58' N, 083°00' W
Concord, N.H. . . . . 43°12' N, 071°32' W
Coos Bay, Ore. . . . . 43°22' N, 124°12' W
Coral Gables, Fla. . . . . 25°45' N, 080°16' W
Cordele, Ga.. . . . . 31°58' N, 083°47' W
Cordova, Alaska . . . . 60°33' N, 145°45' W
Corinth, Miss. . . . . 34°56' N, 088°31' W
Corpus Christi, Tex. . . . . . . 27°47' N, 097°24' W

Corsicana, Tex. 32°06' N, 096°28' W
Corvallis, Ore. 44°34' N, 123°16' W
Council Bluffs, Ia. 41°16' N, 095°52' W
Covington, Ky. 39°05' N, 084°31' W
Crescent City, Calif. 41°45' N, 124°12' W
Crystal City, Tex. 28°41' N, 099°50' W
Dalhart, Tex. 36°04' N, 102°31' W
Dallas, Tex. 32°47' N, 096°49' W
Dalton, Ga. 34°46' N, 084°58' W
Danville, Va. 36°36' N, 079°23' W
Davenport, Ia. 41°32' N, 090°35' W
Davis, Calif. 38°33' N, 121°44' W
Dayton, Ohio 39°45' N, 084°12' W
Daytona Beach, Fla. 29°13' N, 081°01' W
Decorah, Ia. 43°18' N, 091°48' W
Denver, Colo. 39°44' N, 104°59' W
Des Moines, Ia. 41°35' N, 093°37' W
Detroit, Mich. 42°20' N, 083°03' W
Dickinson, N.D. 46°53' N, 102°47' W
Dillingham, Alaska 59°03' N, 158°28' W
Dillon, Mont. 45°13' N, 112°38' W
Dodge City, Kan. 37°45' N, 100°00' W
Dothan, Ala. 31°13' N, 085°24' W
Dover, Del. 39°10' N, 075°32' W
Dover, N.H. 43°12' N, 070°53' W
Dubuque, Ia. 42°30' N, 090°41' W
Duluth, Minn. 46°47' N, 092°07' W
Duncan, Okla. 34°30' N, 097°57' W
Durango, Colo. 37°17' N, 107°53' W
Durham, N.C. 36°00' N, 078°54' W
Dutch Harbor, Alaska 53°53' N, 166°32' W
East St. Louis, Ill. 38°37' N, 090°09' W
Eau Claire, Wis. 44°49' N, 091°30' W
El Cajon, Calif. 32°48' N, 116°58' W
El Dorado, Ark. 33°12' N, 092°40' W
El Paso, Tex. 31°45' N, 106°29' W
Elko, Nev. 40°50' N, 115°46' W
Ely, Minn. 47°55' N, 091°51' W
Ely, Nev. 39°15' N, 114°54' W
Emporia, Kan. 38°25' N, 096°11' W
Enid, Okla. 36°24' N, 097°53' W
Erie, Pa. 42°08' N, 080°05' W
Escanaba, Mich. 45°45' N, 087°04' W
Escondido, Calif. 33°07' N, 117°05' W
Eugene, Ore. 44°05' N, 123°04' W
Eunice, La. 30°30' N, 092°25' W
Eureka, Calif. 40°47' N, 124°09' W
Eustis, Fla. 28°51' N, 081°41' W
Evanston, Wyo. 41°16' N, 110°58' W
Everett, Wash. 47°59' N, 122°12' W
Fairbanks, Alaska, 64°51' N, 147°45' W
Falls City, Neb. 40°03' N, 095°36' W
Fargo, N.D. 46°53' N, 096°48' W
Farmington, N.M. 36°44' N, 108°12' W
Fayetteville, Ark. 36°03' N, 094°09' W
Fayetteville, N.C. 35°03' N, 078°53' W
Fergus Falls, Minn. 46°17' N, 096°04' W
Flagstaff, Ariz. 35°12' N, 111°39' W
Flint, Mich. 43°01' N, 083°41' W
Florence, S.C. 34°12' N, 079°46' W
Fort Bragg, Calif. 39°26' N, 123°48' W
Fort Collins, Colo. 40°35' N, 105°05' W
Fort Dodge, Ia. 42°30' N, 094°11' W
Fort Lauderdale, Fla. 26°07' N, 080°08' W
Fort Madison, Ia. 40°38' N, 091°27' W
Fort Myers, Fla. 26°39' N, 081°53' W
Fort Pierce, Fla. 27°26' N, 080°19' W
Fort Smith, Ark. 35°23' N, 094°25' W
Fort Wayne, Ind. 41°04' N, 085°09' W
Fort Worth, Tex. 32°45' N, 097°18' W
Frankfort, Ky. 38°12' N, 084°52' W
Freeport, Ill. 42°17' N, 089°36' W
Freeport, Tex. 28°57' N, 095°21' W
Fremont, Neb. 41°26' N, 096°30' W
Fresno, Calif. 36°44' N, 119°47' W
Gadsden, Ala. 34°01' N, 086°01' W
Gainesville, Fla. 29°40' N, 082°20' W
Gainesville, Ga. 34°17' N, 083°49' W
Galena, Alaska 64°44' N, 156°56' W
Gallup, N.M. 35°31' N, 108°45' W
Galveston, Tex. 29°18' N, 094°48' W
Garden City, Kan. 37°58' N, 100°52' W
Garland, Tex. 32°54' N, 096°38' W
Gary, Ind. 41°36' N, 087°20' W
Georgetown, S.C. 33°23' N, 079°17' W
Gillette, Wyo. 44°18' N, 105°30' W
Glasgow, Ky. 37°00' N, 085°55' W
Glasgow, Mont. 48°12' N, 106°38' W
Glendive, Mont. 47°07' N, 104°43' W
Glenwood Springs, Colo. 39°33' N, 107°19' W
Goliad, Tex. 28°40' N, 097°23' W
Goodland, Kan. 39°21' N, 101°43' W
Grand Forks, N.D. 47°55' N, 097°03' W
Grand Island, Neb. 40°55' N, 098°21' W
Grand Junction, Colo. 39°04' N, 108°33' W
Grand Rapids, Mich. 42°58' N, 085°40' W
Granite Falls, Minn. 44°49' N, 095°33' W
Great Falls, Mont. 47°30' N, 111°17' W
Greeley, Colo. 40°25' N, 104°42' W
Green Bay, Wis. 44°31' N, 088°00' W
Greensboro, N.C. 36°04' N, 079°48' W
Greenville, Ala. 31°50' N, 086°38' W
Greenville, Miss. 33°24' N, 091°04' W
Greenwood, S.C. 34°12' N, 082°10' W
Griffin, Ga. 33°15' N, 084°16' W
Gulfport, Miss. 30°22' N, 089°06' W
Guymon, Okla. 36°41' N, 101°29' W
Hampton, Va. 37°02' N, 076°21' W
Hannibal, Mo. 39°42' N, 091°22' W
Harlingen, Tex. 26°12' N, 097°42' W
Harrisburg, Pa. 40°16' N, 076°53' W
Hartford, Conn. 41°46' N, 072°41' W
Hattiesburg, Miss. 31°20' N, 089°17' W
Helena, Mont. 46°36' N, 112°02' W
Henderson, Nev. 36°02' N, 114°59' W
Hialeah, Fla. 25°51' N, 080°16' W
Hilo, Hawaii 19°44' N, 155°05' W
Hobbs, N.M. 32°42' N, 103°08' W
Hollywood, Fla. 26°01' N, 080°09' W
Honokaa, Hawaii 20°05' N, 155°28' W
Honolulu, Hawaii 21°19' N, 157°52' W
Hope, Ark. 33°40' N, 093°36' W

City	Latitude	Longitude
Hot Springs, Ark.	34°31′ N,	093°03′ W
Houghton, Mich.	47°07′ N,	088°34′ W
Houston, Tex.	29°46′ N,	095°22′ W
Hugo, Okla.	34°01′ N,	095°31′ W
Huntsville, Ala.	34°44′ N,	086°35′ W
Hutchinson, Kan.	38°05′ N,	097°56′ W
Idaho Falls, Idaho	43°30′ N,	112°02′ W
Independence, Mo.	39°05′ N,	094°24′ W
Indianapolis, Ind.	39°46′ N,	086°09′ W
International Falls, Minn.	48°36′ N,	093°25′ W
Iron Mountain, Mich.	45°49′ N,	088°04′ W
Ironwood, Mich.	46°27′ N,	090°09′ W
Ithaca, N.Y.	42°26′ N,	076°30′ W
Jackson, Miss.	32°18′ N,	090°12′ W
Jackson, Tenn.	35°37′ N,	088°49′ W
Jacksonville, Fla.	30°20′ N,	081°39′ W
Jacksonville, N.C.	34°45′ N,	077°26′ W
Jamestown, N.Y.	42°06′ N,	079°14′ W
Jefferson City, Mo.	38°34′ N,	092°10′ W
Jersey City, N.J.	40°44′ N,	074°04′ W
Joliet, Ill.	41°32′ N,	088°05′ W
Jonesboro, Ark.	35°50′ N,	090°42′ W
Jonesboro, Ga.	33°31′ N,	084°22′ W
Juneau, Alaska	58°20′ N,	134°27′ W
Kaktovik, Alaska	70°08′ N,	143°38′ W
Kalamazoo, Mich.	42°17′ N,	085°35′ W
Kalispell, Mont.	48°12′ N,	114°19′ W
Kansas City, Kan.	39°07′ N,	094°38′ W
Kansas City, Mo.	39°06′ N,	094°35′ W
Kapaa, Hawaii	22°05′ N,	159°19′ W
Kearney, Neb.	40°42′ N,	099°05′ W
Kenai, Alaska	60°33′ N,	151°16′ W
Ketchikan, Alaska	55°21′ N,	131°39′ W
Key Largo, Fla.	25°06′ N,	080°27′ W
Key West, Fla.	24°33′ N,	081°49′ W
King City, Calif.	36°13′ N,	121°08′ W
Kingman, Ariz.	35°12′ N,	114°04′ W
Kingsville, Tex.	27°31′ N,	097°52′ W
Kirksville, Mo.	40°12′ N,	092°35′ W
Klamath Falls, Ore.	42°12′ N,	121°46′ W
Knoxville, Tenn.	35°58′ N,	083°55′ W
Kodiak, Alaska	57°47′ N,	152°24′ W
Kokomo, Ind.	40°30′ N,	086°08′ W
La Crosse, Wis.	43°48′ N,	091°15′ W
Lafayette, La.	30°14′ N,	092°01′ W
La Junta, Colo.	37°59′ N,	103°33′ W
Lake Charles, La.	30°14′ N,	093°13′ W
Lake Havasu City, Ariz.	34°29′ N,	114°19′ W
Lakeland, Fla.	28°03′ N,	081°57′ W
Lansing, Mich.	42°44′ N,	084°33′ W
Laramie, Wyo.	41°19′ N,	105°35′ W
Laredo, Tex.	27°30′ N,	099°30′ W
Las Cruces, N.M.	32°19′ N,	106°47′ W
Las Vegas, Nev.	36°01′ N,	115°09′ W
Las Vegas, N.M.	35°36′ N,	105°13′ W
Laurel, Miss.	31°41′ N,	089°08′ W
Lawton, Okla.	34°37′ N,	098°25′ W
Lebanon, N.H.	43°39′ N,	072°15′ W
Lewiston, Idaho	46°25′ N,	117°01′ W
Lewiston, Me.	44°06′ N,	070°13′ W
Lewiston, Mont.	47°03′ N,	109°25′ W
Lexington, Ky.	38°01′ N,	084°30′ W
Liberal, Kan.	37°02′ N,	100°55′ W
Lihue, Hawaii	21°59′ N,	159°23′ W
Lima, Ohio	40°44′ N,	084°06′ W
Lincoln, Me.	45°22′ N,	068°30′ W
Lincoln, Neb.	40°50′ N,	096°41′ W
Little Rock, Ark.	34°45′ N,	092°17′ W
Logan, Utah	41°44′ N,	111°50′ W
Long Beach, Calif.	33°47′ N,	118°11′ W
Los Alamos, N.M.	35°53′ N,	106°19′ W
Los Angeles, Calif.	34°04′ N,	118°15′ W
Louisville, Ky.	38°15′ N,	085°46′ W
Lowell, Mass.	42°38′ N,	071°19′ W
Lubbock, Tex.	33°35′ N,	101°51′ W
Lynchburg, Va.	37°25′ N,	079°09′ W
Macomb, Ill.	40°27′ N,	090°40′ W
Macon, Ga.	32°51′ N,	083°38′ W
Madison, Wis.	43°04′ N,	089°24′ W
Manchester, N.H.	43°00′ N,	071°28′ W
Mandan, N.D.	46°50′ N,	100°54′ W
Mankato, Minn.	44°10′ N,	094°00′ W
Marietta, Ohio	39°25′ N,	081°27′ W
Marinette, Wis.	45°06′ N,	087°38′ W
Marion, Ind.	40°32′ N,	085°40′ W
Marquette, Mich.	46°33′ N,	087°24′ W
Massillon, Ohio	40°48′ N,	081°32′ W
McAllen, Tex.	26°12′ N,	098°14′ W
McCall, Idaho	44°55′ N,	116°06′ W
McCook, Neb.	40°12′ N,	100°38′ W
Medford, Ore.	42°19′ N,	122°52′ W
Meeker, Colo.	40°02′ N,	107°55′ W
Melbourne, Fla.	28°05′ N,	080°37′ W
Memphis, Tenn.	35°08′ N,	090°03′ W
Meridian, Miss.	32°22′ N,	088°42′ W
Mesa, Ariz.	33°25′ N,	111°49′ W
Miami, Fla.	25°47′ N,	080°11′ W
Midland, Mich.	43°36′ N,	084°14′ W
Midland, Tex.	32°00′ N,	102°05′ W
Miles City, Mont.	46°25′ N,	105°51′ W
Milledgeville, Ga.	33°05′ N,	083°14′ W
Milwaukee, Wis.	43°02′ N,	087°55′ W
Minneapolis, Minn.	44°59′ N,	093°16′ W
Minot, N.D.	48°14′ N,	101°18′ W
Missoula, Mont.	46°52′ N,	114°01′ W
Mitchell, S.D.	43°43′ N,	098°02′ W
Moab, Utah	38°35′ N,	109°33′ W
Mobile, Ala.	30°41′ N,	088°03′ W
Moline, Ill.	41°30′ N,	090°31′ W
Monterey, Calif.	36°37′ N,	121°55′ W
Montgomery, Ala.	32°23′ N,	086°19′ W
Montpelier, Vt.	44°16′ N,	072°35′ W
Montrose, Colo.	38°29′ N,	107°53′ W
Morehead City, N.C.	34°43′ N,	076°43′ W
Morgan City, La.	29°42′ N,	091°12′ W
Morgantown, W.Va.	39°38′ N,	079°57′ W
Moscow, Idaho	46°44′ N,	117°00′ W
Mount Vernon, Ill.	38°19′ N,	088°55′ W
Murfreesboro, Ark.	34°04′ N,	093°41′ W
Murfreesboro, Tenn.	35°50′ N,	086°23′ W
Muskogee, Okla.	35°45′ N,	095°22′ W
Myrtle Beach, S.C.	33°42′ N,	078°53′ W

City	Latitude	Longitude
Naples, Fla.	26°08' N,	081°48' W
Nashville, Tenn.	36°10' N,	086°47' W
Natchez, Miss.	31°34' N,	091°24' W
Needles, Calif.	34°51' N,	114°37' W
Nevada, Mo.	37°51' N,	094°22' W
New Albany, Ind.	38°18' N,	085°49' W
Newark, N.J.	40°44' N,	074°10' W
New Bedford, Mass.	41°38' N,	070°56' W
New Bern, N.C.	35°07' N,	077°03' W
Newcastle, Wyo.	43°50' N,	104°11' W
New Haven, Conn.	41°18' N,	072°55' W
New Madrid, Mo.	36°36' N,	089°32' W
New Orleans, La.	29°58' N,	090°04' W
Newport, Ore.	44°39' N,	124°03' W
Newport, R.I.	41°29' N,	071°18' W
Newport News, Va.	36°59' N,	076°25' W
New York City, N.Y.	40°43' N,	074°00' W
Niagara Falls, N.Y.	43°06' N,	079°03' W
Nogales, Ariz.	31°20' N,	110°56' W
Nome, Alaska	64°30' N,	165°25' W
Norfolk, Va.	36°51' N,	076°17' W
Norman, Okla.	35°13' N,	097°26' W
North Augusta, S.C.	33°30' N,	081°59' W
North Platte, Neb.	41°08' N,	100°46' W
Oakland, Calif.	37°49' N,	122°16' W
Ocala, Fla.	29°11' N,	082°08' W
Oceanside, Calif.	33°12' N,	117°23' W
Odessa, Tex.	31°52' N,	102°23' W
Ogallala, Neb.	41°08' N,	101°43' W
Ogden, Utah	41°13' N,	111°58' W
Oklahoma City, Okla.	35°30' N,	097°30' W
Olympia, Wash.	47°03' N,	122°53' W
Omaha, Neb.	41°17' N,	096°01' W
O'Neill, Neb.	42°27' N,	098°39' W
Orem, Utah	40°18' N,	111°42' W
Orlando, Fla.	28°33' N,	081°23' W
Oshkosh, Wis.	44°01' N,	088°33' W
Ottawa, Ill.	41°20' N,	088°50' W
Ottumwa, Ia.	41°01' N,	092°25' W
Overton, Nev.	36°33' N,	114°27' W
Owensboro, Ky.	37°46' N,	087°07' W
Paducah, Ky.	37°05' N,	088°37' W
Pahala, Hawaii.	19°12' N,	155°29' W
Palm Springs, Calif.	33°50' N,	116°33' W
Palo Alto, Calif.	37°27' N,	122°10' W
Panama City, Fla.	30°10' N,	085°40' W
Paris, Tex.	33°40' N,	095°33' W
Parsons, Kan.	37°20' N,	095°16' W
Pasadena, Calif.	34°09' N,	118°09' W
Pasadena, Tex.	29°43' N,	095°13' W
Pascagoula, Miss.	30°21' N,	088°33' W
Paterson, N.J.	40°55' N,	074°11' W
Pecos, Tex.	31°26' N,	103°30' W
Pendleton, Ore.	45°40' N,	118°47' W
Pensacola, Fla.	30°25' N,	087°13' W
Peoria, Ill.	40°42' N,	089°36' W
Petoskey, Mich.	45°22' N,	084°57' W
Philadelphia, Pa.	39°57' N,	075°10' W
Phoenix, Ariz.	33°27' N,	112°04' W
Pierre, S.D.	44°22' N,	100°21' W
Pine Bluff, Ark.	34°13' N,	092°01' W
Pittsburgh, Pa.	40°26' N,	080°01' W
Plano, Tex.	33°01' N,	096°41' W
Plattsburgh, N.Y.	44°42' N,	073°27' W
Pocatello, Idaho	42°52' N,	112°27' W
Point Hope, Alaska	68°21' N,	166°41' W
Port Gibson, Miss.	31°58' N,	090°59' W
Port Lavaca, Tex.	28°37' N,	096°38' W
Port Royal, S.C.	32°23' N,	080°42' W
Portland, Me.	43°39' N,	070°16' W
Portland, Ore.	45°32' N,	122°37' W
Prescott, Ariz.	34°33' N,	112°28' W
Presque Isle, Me.	46°41' N,	068°01' W
Providence, R.I.	41°49' N,	071°24' W
Provo, Utah	40°14' N,	111°39' W
Pueblo, Colo.	38°15' N,	104°36' W
Pullman, Wash.	46°44' N,	117°10' W
Racine, Wis.	42°44' N,	087°48' W
Raleigh, N.C.	35°46' N,	078°38' W
Rapid City, S.D.	44°05' N,	103°14' W
Red Bluff, Calif.	40°11' N,	122°15' W
Redding, Calif.	40°35' N,	122°24' W
Redfield, S.D.	44°53' N,	098°31' W
Reno, Nev.	39°31' N,	119°48' W
Rice Lake, Wis.	45°30' N,	091°44' W
Richfield, Utah	38°46' N,	112°05' W
Richmond, Ind.	39°50' N,	084°54' W
Richmond, Va.	37°33' N,	077°27' W
Riverside, Calif.	33°59' N,	117°22' W
Riverton, Wyo.	43°02' N,	108°23' W
Roanoke, Va.	37°16' N,	079°56' W
Rochester, Minn.	44°01' N,	092°28' W
Rochester, N.Y.	43°10' N,	077°37' W
Rock Hill, S.C.	34°56' N,	081°01' W
Rock Island, Ill.	41°30' N,	090°34' W
Rock Springs, Wyo.	41°35' N,	109°12' W
Rockford, Ill.	42°16' N,	089°06' W
Rolla, Mo.	37°57' N,	091°46' W
Rome, Ga.	34°15' N,	085°09' W
Roseburg, Ore.	43°13' N,	123°20' W
Roswell, N.M.	33°24' N,	104°32' W
Sacramento, Calif.	38°35' N,	121°29' W
Saginaw, Mich.	43°26' N,	083°56' W
Salem, Ore.	44°56' N,	123°02' W
Salina, Kan.	38°50' N,	097°37' W
Salinas, Calif.	36°40' N,	121°39' W
Salmon, Idaho	45°11' N,	113°54' W
Salt Lake City, Utah	40°45' N,	111°53' W
San Angelo, Tex.	31°28' N,	100°26' W
San Antonio, Tex.	29°25' N,	098°30' W
San Bernardino, Calif.	34°07' N,	117°19' W
San Diego, Calif.	32°43' N,	117°09' W
San Francisco, Calif.	37°47' N,	122°25' W
San Jose, Calif.	37°20' N,	121°53' W
San Luis Obispo, Calif.	35°17' N,	120°40' W
Sanderson, Tex.	30°09' N,	102°24' W
Santa Ana, Calif.	33°46' N,	117°52' W
Santa Barbara, Calif.	34°25' N,	119°42' W
Santa Fe, N.M.	35°41' N,	105°57' W
Santa Maria, Calif.	34°57' N,	120°26' W
Sarasota, Fla.	27°20' N,	082°32' W
Sault Ste. Marie, Mich.	46°30' N,	084°21' W

City	Latitude	Longitude
Savannah, Ga.	32°05' N,	081°06' W
Scott City, Kan.	38°29' N,	100°54' W
Scottsbluff, Neb.	41°52' N,	103°40' W
Scottsdale, Ariz.	33°29' N,	111°56' W
Searcy, Ark.	35°15' N,	091°44' W
Seattle, Wash.	47°36' N,	122°20' W
Sebring, Fla.	27°30' N,	081°27' W
Seguin, Tex.	29°34' N,	097°58' W
Selawik, Alaska	66°36' N,	160°00' W
Seldovia, Alaska	59°26' N,	151°43' W
Selma, Ala.	32°25' N,	087°01' W
Sharpsburg, Md.	39°28' N,	077°45' W
Sheboygan, Wis.	43°45' N,	087°42' W
Sheridan, Wyo.	44°48' N,	106°58' W
Show Low, Ariz.	34°15' N,	110°02' W
Shreveport, La.	32°31' N,	093°45' W
Sierra Vista, Ariz.	31°33' N,	110°18' W
Silver City, N.M.	32°46' N,	108°17' W
Sioux City, Ia.	42°30' N,	096°24' W
Sioux Falls, S.D.	43°33' N,	096°44' W
Skagway, Alaska	59°28' N,	135°19' W
Snyder, Tex.	32°44' N,	100°55' W
Socorro, N.M.	34°04' N,	106°54' W
Somerset, Ky.	37°05' N,	084°36' W
South Bend, Ind.	41°41' N,	086°15' W
Sparks, Nev.	39°32' N,	119°45' W
Spencer, Ia.	43°09' N,	095°10' W
Spokane, Wash.	47°40' N,	117°24' W
Springfield, Ill.	39°48' N,	089°38' W
Springfield, Mo.	37°13' N,	093°17' W
St. Augustine, Fla.	29°54' N,	081°19' W
St. Cloud, Minn.	45°34' N,	094°10' W
St. George, Utah	37°06' N,	113°35' W
St. Joseph, Mo.	39°46' N,	094°50' W
St. Louis, Mo.	38°37' N,	090°11' W
St. Maries, Idaho	47°19' N,	116°35' W
St. Paul, Minn.	44°57' N,	093°06' W
St. Petersburg, Fla.	27°46' N,	082°39' W
State College, Pa.	40°48' N,	077°52' W
Ste. Genevieve, Mo.	37°59' N,	090°03' W
Steamboat Springs, Colo.	40°29' N,	106°50' W
Stillwater, Minn.	45°03' N,	092°49' W
Sumter, S.C.	33°55' N,	080°21' W
Sun Valley, Idaho	43°42' N,	114°21' W
Superior, Wis.	46°44' N,	092°06' W
Syracuse, N.Y.	43°03' N,	076°09' W
Tacoma, Wash.	47°14' N,	122°26' W
Tallahassee, Fla.	30°27' N,	084°17' W
Tampa, Fla.	27°57' N,	082°27' W
Tempe, Ariz.	33°25' N,	111°56' W
Temple, Tex.	31°06' N,	097°21' W
Terre Haute, Ind.	39°28' N,	087°25' W
Texarkana, Ark.	33°26' N,	094°03' W
Thief River Falls, Minn.	48°07' N,	096°10' W
Tifton, Ga.	31°27' N,	083°31' W
Titusville, Fla.	28°37' N,	080°49' W
Toledo, Ohio	41°39' N,	083°33' W
Tonopah, Nev.	38°04' N,	117°14' W
Topeka, Kan.	39°03' N,	095°40' W
Traverse City, Mich.	44°46' N,	085°38' W
Trenton, N.J.	40°14' N,	074°46' W
Trinidad, Colo.	37°10' N,	104°31' W
Troy, Ala.	31°48' N,	085°58' W
Troy, N.Y.	42°44' N,	073°41' W
Tucson, Ariz.	32°13' N,	110°58' W
Tulsa, Okla.	36°10' N,	095°55' W
Tupelo, Miss.	34°16' N,	088°43' W
Tuscaloosa, Ala.	33°12' N,	087°34' W
Twin Falls, Idaho	42°34' N,	114°28' W
Tyler, Tex.	32°21' N,	095°18' W
Ukiah, Calif.	39°09' N,	123°12' W
Utica, N.Y.	43°06' N,	075°14' W
Uvalde, Tex.	29°13' N,	099°47' W
Valdez, Alaska	61°07' N,	146°16' W
Valdosta, Ga.	30°50' N,	083°17' W
Valentine, Neb.	42°52' N,	100°33' W
Vero Beach, Fla.	27°38' N,	080°24' W
Vicksburg, Miss.	32°21' N,	090°53' W
Victoria, Tex.	28°48' N,	097°00' W
Vincennes, Ind.	38°41' N,	087°32' W
Virginia Beach, Va.	36°51' N,	075°59' W
Waco, Tex.	31°33' N,	097°09' W
Wahpeton, N.D.	46°15' N,	096°36' W
Wailuku, Hawaii	20°53' N,	156°30' W
Walla Walla, Wash.	46°04' N,	118°20' W
Warren, Pa.	41°51' N,	079°08' W
Washington, D.C.	38°54' N,	077°02' W
Waterloo, Ia.	42°30' N,	092°21' W
Watertown, N.Y.	43°59' N,	075°55' W
Waycross, Ga.	31°13' N,	082°21' W
Wayne, Neb.	42°14' N,	097°01' W
Weiser, Idaho	44°45' N,	116°58' W
West Palm Beach, Fla.	26°43' N,	080°03' W
Wheeling, W.Va.	40°04' N,	080°43' W
Wichita, Kan.	37°42' N,	097°20' W
Wichita Falls, Tex.	33°54' N,	098°30' W
Williamsport, Pa.	41°15' N,	077°00' W
Wilmington, N.C.	34°14' N,	077°55' W
Winfield, Kan.	37°15' N,	096°59' W
Winnemucca, Nev.	40°58' N,	117°44' W
Winslow, Ariz.	35°02' N,	110°42' W
Winston-Salem, N.C.	36°06' N,	080°14' W
Worcester, Mass.	42°16' N,	071°48' W
Worthington, Minn.	43°37' N,	095°36' W
Wrangell, Alaska	56°28' N,	132°23' W
Yakima, Wash.	46°36' N,	120°31' W
Yankton, S.D.	42°53' N,	097°23' W
Yazoo City, Miss.	32°51' N,	090°25' W
Youngstown, Ohio	41°06' N,	080°39' W
Yuba City, Calif.	39°08' N,	121°37' W
Yuma, Ariz.	32°43' N,	114°37' W
Zanesville, Ohio	39°56' N,	082°01' W

URUGUAY . . . . . .page 190

City	Latitude	Longitude
Aiguá	34°12' S,	054°45' W
Artigas	30°24' S,	056°28' W
Belén	30°47' S,	057°47' W
Bella Unión	30°15' S,	057°35' W
Carmelo	34°00' S,	058°17' W
Castillos	34°12' S,	053°50' W

Casupá	34°07' S,	055°39' W
Chuy	33°41' S,	053°27' W
Colonia	34°28' S,	057°51' W
Constitución	31°05' S,	057°50' W
Dolores	33°33' S,	058°13' W
Durazno	33°22' S,	056°31' W
Florida	34°06' S,	056°13' W
Lascano	33°40' S,	054°12'W
Las Piedras	34°44' S,	056°13' W
Maldonado	34°54' S,	054°57' W
Melo	32°22' S,	054°11' W
Mercedes	33°16' S,	058°01' W
Minas	34°23' S,	055°14' W
Montevideo	34°53' S,	056°11' W
Nuevo Berlín	32°59' S,	058°03' W
Pando	34°43' S,	055°57' W
Paysandú	32°19' S,	058°05' W
Rio Branco	32°34' S,	053°25' W
Rivera	30°54' S,	055°31' W
Rocha	34°29' S,	054°20' W
Salto	31°23' S,	057°58' W
San Carlos	34°48' S,	054°55' W
San Gregorio	32°37' S,	055°40' W
San José	34°20' S,	056°42' W
Santa Clara	32°55' S,	054°58' W
Suárez (Tarariras)	34°17' S,	057°37' W
Tacuarembó (San Fructuoso)	31°44' S,	055°59' W
Tranqueras	31°12' S,	055°45' W
Treinta y Tres	33°14' S,	054°23' W
Trinidad	33°32' S,	056°54' W
Vergara	32°56' S,	053°57' W
Young	32°41' S,	057°38' W

UZBEKISTAN .... page 191

Andijon	40°45' N,	072°22' E
Angren	41°01' N,	070°12' E
Bekobod	40°13' N,	069°14' E
Beruniy (Biruni)	41°42' N,	060°44' E
Bukhara (Bokhoro)	39°48' N,	064°25' E
Chirchiq	41°29' N,	069°35' E
Denow	38°16' N,	067°54' E
Fergana (Farghona)	40°23' N,	071°46' E
Guliston	40°29' N,	068°46' E
Jizzakh	40°06' N,	067°50' E
Kattaqürghon	39°55' N,	066°15' E
Khiva (Khiwa)	41°24' N,	060°22' E
Khonqa	41°28' N,	060°47' E
Kogon	39°43' N,	064°33' E
Marghilon	40°27' N,	071°42' E
Namangan	41°00' N,	071°40' E
Nawoiy	40°09' N,	065°22' E
Nukus	42°29' N,	059°38' E
Olmaliq	40°50' N,	069°35' E
Qarshi	38°53' N,	065°48' E
Qŭqon	40°30' N,	070°57' E
Samarkand	39°40' N,	066°58' E
Tashkent (Toshkent)	41°20' N,	069°18' E
Termiz	37°14' N,	067°16' E
Urganch	41°33' N,	060°38' E
Zarafshon	41°31' N,	064°15' E

VANUATU .... page 192

Ipayato	15°38' S,	166°52' E
Isangel	19°33' S,	169°16' E
Lakatoro	16°07' S,	167°25' E
Lalinda	16°21' S,	168°03' E
Laol	16°41' S,	168°16' E
Loltong	15°33' S,	168°09' E
Luganville	15°32' S,	167°10' E
Lumbukuti	16°55' S,	168°32' E
Natapao	17°37' S,	168°13' E
Norsup	16°04' S,	167°23' E
Port Olry	15°03' S,	167°04' E
Unpongkor	18°49' S,	169°01' E
Veutumboso	13°54' S,	167°27' E
Vila (Port-Vila)	17°44' S,	168°18' E

VENEZUELA ..... page 193

Barcelona	10°08' N,	064°42' W
Barinas	08°38' N,	070°12' W
Barquisimeto	10°04' N,	069°19' W
Cabimas	10°23' N,	071°28' W
Caicara (Caicara de Orinoco)	07°37' N,	066°10' W
Caicara	09°49' N,	063°36' W
Caracas	10°30' N,	066°55' W
Ciudad Bolívar	08°08' N,	063°33' W
Ciudad Guayana (San Felix)	08°23' N,	062°40' W
Coro	11°25' N,	069°41' W
Cumaná	10°28' N,	064°10' W
Guasdualito	07°15' N,	070°44' W
La Asunción	11°02' N,	063°53' W
Maracaibo	10°40' N,	071°37' W
Maracay	10°15' N,	067°36' W
Maturín	09°45' N,	063°11' W
Mérida	08°36' N,	071°08' W
Pariaguán	08°51' N,	064°43' W
Petare	10°29' N,	066°49' W
Puerto Ayacucho	05°40' N,	067°35' W
Punto Fijo	11°42' N,	070°13' W
San Carlos de Río Negro	01°55' N,	067°04' W
San Cristóbal	07°46' N,	072°14' W
San Fernando de Apure	07°54' N,	067°28' W
San Fernando de Atabapo	04°03' N,	067°42' W
Santa Elena	04°37' N,	061°08' W
Tucupita	09°04' N,	062°03' W
Upata	08°01' N,	062°24' W
Valencia	10°11' N,	068°00' W
Valera	09°19' N,	070°37' W

VIETNAM .... page 194

Bac Can	22°08' N,	105°50' E
Bac Giang	21°16' N,	106°12' E

Bac Lieu . . . 09°17' N, 105°43' E
Bien Hoa . . . 10°57' N, 106°49' E
Buon Me Thuot (Lac Giao) . . . 12°40' N, 108°03' E
Ca Mau . . . 09°11' N, 105°08' E
Cam Pha . . . 21°01' N, 107°19' E
Cam Ranh . . . 11°54' N, 109°13' E
Can Tho . . . 10°02' N, 105°47' E
Chau Doc . . . 10°42' N, 105°07' E
Da Lat . . . 11°56' N, 108°25' E
Da Nang (Tourane) . . . 16°04' N, 108°13' E
Dong Ha . . . 16°49' N, 107°08' E
Dong Hoi . . . 17°29' N, 106°36' E
Go Cong . . . 10°22' N, 106°40' E
Ha Giang . . . 22°50' N, 104°59' E
Hai Duong . . . 20°56' N, 106°19' E
Haiphong (Hai Phong) . . . 20°52' N, 106°41' E
Hanoi (Ha Noi) . . . 21°02' N, 105°51' E
Ha Tinh . . . 18°20' N, 105°54' E
Hoa Binh . . . 20°50' N, 105°20' E
Ho Chi Minh City (Saigon) . . . 10°45' N, 106°40' E
Hoi An . . . 15°52' N, 108°19' E
Hong Gai (Hon Gai) . . . 20°57' N, 107°05' E
Hue . . . 16°28' N, 107°36' E
Kon Tum (Cong Tum or Kontun) . . . 14°21' N, 108°00' E
Lai Chau . . . 22°04' N, 103°10' E
Lao Caí . . . 22°30' N, 103°58' E
Long Xuyen . . . 10°23' N, 105°25' E
Minh Hoa . . . 17°47' N, 106°01' E
My Tho . . . 10°21' N, 106°21' E
Nam Dinh . . . 20°25' N, 106°10' E
Nha Trang . . . 12°15' N, 109°11' E
Phan Rang . . . 11°34' N, 108°59' E
Phan Thiet . . . 10°56' N, 108°06' E
Pleiku (Play Cu) . . . 13°59' N, 108°00' E
Quan Long . . . 09°11' N, 105°08' E
Quang Ngai . . . 15°07' N, 108°48' E
Qui Nhon . . . 13°46' N, 109°14' E
Rach Gia . . . 10°01' N, 105°05' E
Sa Dec . . . 10°18' N, 105°46' E
Soc Trang . . . 09°36' N, 105°58' E
Son La . . . 21°19' N, 103°54' E
Tam Ky . . . 15°34' N, 108°29' E
Tan An . . . 10°32' N, 106°25' E
Thai Binh . . . 20°27' N, 106°20' E
Thai Nguyen . . . 21°36' N, 105°50' E
Thanh Hoa . . . 19°48' N, 105°46' E
Tuy Hoa . . . 13°05' N, 109°18' E
Viet Tri . . . 21°18' N, 105°26' E
Vinh . . . 18°40' N, 105°40' E
Vung Tau . . . 10°21' N, 107°04' E
Yen Bai . . . 21°42' N, 104°52' E

YEMEN . . . page 195

Aden ('Adan) . . . 12°46' N, 045°02' E
Aḥwar . . . 13°31' N, 046°42' E
Al-Bayḍā' . . . 13°58' N, 045°35' E
Al-Ghayḍah . . . 16°13' N, 052°11' E
Al-Ḥudaydah . . . 14°48' N, 042°57' E
Al-Luḥayyah . . . 15°43' N, 042°42' E
Al-Mukallā . . . 14°32' N, 049°08' E
Balḥāf . . . 13°58' N, 048°11' E
Dhamār . . . 14°33' N, 044°24' E
Ibb . . . 13°58' N, 044°11' E
Laḥij . . . 13°04' N, 044°53' E
Madīnat al-Sha'b . . . 12°50' N, 044°56' E
Ma'rib . . . 15°25' N, 045°21' E
Min'ar . . . 16°43' N, 051°18' E
Mocha (al-Mukha) . . . 13°19' N, 043°15' E
Niṣāb . . . 14°31' N, 046°30' E
Raydah . . . 15°50' N, 044°03' E
Sa'dah . . . 16°57' N, 043°46' E
Ṣalīf . . . 15°18' N, 042°41' E
Ṣan'ā' . . . 15°21' N, 044°12' E
Sayḥūt . . . 15°12' N, 051°14' E
Saywūn (Say'un) . . . 15°56' N, 048°47' E
Shabwah . . . 15°22' N, 047°01' E
Shahārah . . . 16°11' N, 043°42' E
Ta'izz . . . 13°34' N, 044°02' E
Tarīm . . . 16°03' N, 049°00' E
Zabīd . . . 14°12' N, 043°19' E
Zinjibār . . . 13°08' N, 045°23' E

ZAMBIA . . . page 196

Chililabombwe (Bancroft) . . . 12°22' S, 027°50' E
Chingola . . . 12°32' S, 027°52' E
Chipata (Fort Jameson) . . . 13°39' S, 032°40' E
Isoka . . . 10°08' S, 032°38' E
Kabwe (Broken Hill) . . . 14°27' S, 028°27' E
Kalabo . . . 14°58' S, 022°41' E
Kalulushi . . . 12°50' S, 028°05' E
Kasama . . . 10°13' S, 031°12' E
Kawambwa . . . 09°47' S, 029°05' E
Kitwe . . . 12°49' S, 028°13' E
Livingstone (Maramba) . . . 17°51' S, 025°52' E
Luanshya . . . 13°08' S, 028°25' E
Lusaka . . . 15°25' S, 028°17' E
Mansa (Fort Rosebery) . . . 11°12' S, 028°53' E
Mazabuka . . . 15°51' S, 027°46' E
Mongu . . . 15°17' S, 023°08' E
Monze . . . 16°16' S, 027°29' E
Mpika . . . 11°50' S, 031°27' E
Mumbwa . . . 14°59' S, 027°04' E
Mwamfuli (Samfya) . . . 11°21' S, 029°33' E
Nchelenge . . . 09°21' S, 029°44' E
Ndola . . . 12°58' S, 028°38' E
Senanga . . . 16°07' S, 023°16' E
Serenje . . . 13°14' S, 030°14' E
Zambezi . . . 13°33' S, 023°07' E

ZIMBABWE . . . page 197

Beitbridge . . . 22°13' S, 030°00' E
Bulawayo . . . 20°09' S, 028°35' E

City	Latitude	Longitude
Chimanimani (Mandidzudzure, or Melsetter)	19°48' S,	032°52' E
Chinhoyi (Sinoia)	17°22' S,	030°12' E
Chipinge	20°12' S,	032°37' E
Chiredzi	21°03' S,	031°40' E
Chitungwiza	18°47' S,	032°37' E
Empress Mine Township	18°27' S,	029°27' E
Gweru (Gwelo)	19°27' S,	029°49' E
Harare (Salisbury)	17°50' S,	031°03' E
Hwange (Wankie)	18°22' S,	026°29' E
Inyanga	18°13' S,	032°45' E
Kadoma (Gatooma)	18°21' S,	029°55' E
Kariba	16°31' S,	028°48' E
Karoi	16°49' S,	029°41' E
Kwekwe (Que Que)	18°55' S,	029°49' E
Marondera (Marandellas)	18°11' S,	031°33' E
Mashava	20°03' S,	030°29' E
Masvingo (Fort Victoria, or Nyanda)	20°05' S,	030°50' E
Mhangura	16°54' S,	030°09' E
Mount Darwin	16°47' S,	031°35' E
Mvuma	19°17' S,	030°32' E
Mutare (Umtali)	18°58' S,	032°40' E
Norton	17°53' S,	030°42' E
Redcliff	19°02' S,	029°47' E
Shamva	17°19' S,	031°34' E
Shurugwi (Selukwe)	19°40' S,	030°00' E
Triangle	21°02' S,	031°27' E
Tuli	21°55' S,	029°12' E
Victoria Falls	17°56' S,	025°50' E

World's Largest Lakes

Name and location	Area (square miles)
WORLD	
Caspian Sea, *Turkmenistan–Kazakstan–Russia–Azerbaijan-Iran*	149,200
Superior, *Canada–United States*	31,700
Victoria, *Kenya–Tanzania–Uganda*	26,828
Huron, *Canada–United States*	23,000
Michigan, *United States*	22,300
Aral Sea, *Kazakstan–Uzbekistan*	13,000
Tanganyika, *Burundi–Tanzania–Dem. Rep. Congo–Zambia*	12,700
Baikal, *Russia*	12,200
AFRICA	
Victoria, *Kenya-Tanzania–Uganda*	26,828
Tanganyika, *Burundi–Tanzania-Dem. Rep. Congo–Zambia*	12,700
Nyasa (Malawi), *Malawi–Mozambique–Tanzania*	11,430
Chad, *Cameroon–Chad–Niger–Nigeria*	6,875
Bangweulu, *Zambia*	3,800
AMERICA, NORTH	
Superior, *Canada–United States*	31,700
Huron, *Canada–United States*	23,000
Michigan, *United States*	22,300
Great Bear, *Northwest Territories, Canada*	12,028
Great Slave, *Northwest Territories, Canada*	11,031
AMERICA, SOUTH	
Maracaibo, *Venezuela*	5,150
Titicaca, *Peru–Bolivia*	3,200
Poopó, *Bolivia*	1,000
Buenos Aires (General Carrera), *Chile–Argentina*	865
Chiquita, *Argentina*	714
ASIA	
Caspian Sea, *Turkmenistan–Kazakstan–Russia–Azerbaijan-Iran*	149,200
Aral Sea, *Kazakstan–Uzbekistan*	13,000
Baikal, *Russia*	12,200
Balkhash, *Kazakstan*	6,650
Tonle Sap, *Cambodia*	2,525
EUROPE	
Ladoga, *Russia*	6,826
Onega, *Russia*	3,753
Vänern, *Sweden*	2,156
Iso Saimaa, *Finland*	1,690
Peipsi, *Estonia–Russia*	1,373
OCEANIA	
Eyre, *South Australia*	3,600
Torrens, *South Australia*	2,230
Gairdner, *South Australia*	1,845
Frome, *South Australia*	900

World's Longest Rivers

Name	Outflow	Length (miles)
WORLD		
Nile	Mediterranean Sea	4,132
Amazon–Ucayali–Apurimac	South Alantic Ocean	4,000
Chang (Yangtze)	East China Sea	3,915
Mississippi–Missouri–Red Rock	Gulf of Mexico	3,710
Yenisey–Baikal–Selenga	Kara Sea	3,442
Huang (Yellow)	Bo Hai (Gulf of Chihli)	3,395
Ob–Irtysh	Gulf of Ob	3,362
Paraná	Río de la Plata	3,032
AFRICA		
Nile	Mediterranean Sea	4,132
Congo	South Alantic Ocean	2,900
Niger	Bight of Biafra	2,600
Zambezi	Mozambique Channel	2,200
Kasai	Congo River	1,338
AMERICA, NORTH		
Mississippi–Missouri–Red Rock	Gulf of Mexico	3,710
Mackenzie–Slave–Peace	Beaufort Sea	2,635
Missouri–Red Rock	Mississippi River	2,540
St. Lawrence–Great Lakes	Gulf of St. Lawrence	2,500
Mississippi	Gulf of Mexico	2,340
AMERICA, SOUTH		
Amazon–Ucayali–Apurimac	South Alantic Ocean	4,000
Paraná	Río de la Plata	3,032
Madeira–Mamoré–Guaporé	Amazon River	2.082
Jurua	Amazon River	2,040
Purus	Amazon River	1,995
ASIA		
Chang (Yangtze)	East China Sea	3,915
Yenisey–Baikal–Selenga	Kara Sea	3,442
Huang (Yellow)	Bo Hai (Gulf of Chihli)	3,395
Ob–Irtysh	Gulf of Ob	3,362
Amur–Argun	Sea of Okhotsk	2,761
EUROPE		
Volga	Caspian Sea	2,193
Danube	Black Sea	1,770
Ural	Caspian Sea	1,509
Dnieper	Black Sea	1,367
Don	Sea of Azov	1,162
OCEANIA		
Darling	Murray River	1,702
Murray	Great Australian Bight	1,609
Murrumbidgee	Murray River	981
Lachlan	Murrumbidgee River	992

World's Tallest Mountains

Name and location	Height (feet)
AFRICA	
Kilimanjaro (Kibo Peak), *Tanzania*	19,340
Mt. Kenya (Batian Peak), *Kenya*	17,058
Margherita, Ruwenzori Range, *Dem. Rep. Congo–Uganda*	16,795
Ras Dashen, Simyen Mts., *Ethiopia*	15,157
AMERICA, NORTH	
McKinley, Alaska Range, *Alaska, U.S.*	20,320
Logan, St. Elias Mts., *Yukon, Canada*	19,524
Citlaltépetl (Orizaba), Cordillera Neo-Volcánica, *Mexico*	18,406
St. Elias, St Elias Mts., *Alaska, U.S.–Canada*	18,009
AMERICA, SOUTH	
Aconcagua, Andes, *Argentina–Chile*	22,831
Ojos del Salado, Andes, *Argentina–Chile*	22,615
Bonete, Andes, *Argentina*	22,546
Tupungato, Andes, *Argentina–Chile*	22,310
Pissis, Andes, *Argentina*	22,241
ANTARCTICA	
Vinson Massif, Sentinel Range, Ellsworth Mts.	16,066
Tyree, Sentinel Range, Ellsworth Mts.	15,919
Shinn, Sentinel Range, Ellsworth Mts.	15,751
Kirkpatrick, Queen Alexandra Range	14,856
ASIA	
Everest (Chomolungma), Himalayas, *Nepal–Tibet, China*	29,028
K2 (Godwin Austen), Karakoram Range, *Pakistan–Xinjiang, China*	28,251
Kānchenjunga I, Himalayas, *Nepal–India*	28,169
Lhotse I, Himalayas, *Nepal–Tibet, China*	27,940
EUROPE	
Mont Blanc, Alps, *France–Italy*	15,771
Dufourspitze (Monte Rosa), Alps, *Switzerland–Italy*	15,203
Dom (Mischabel), Alps, *Switzerland*	14,911
Weisshorn, Alps, *Switzerland*	14,780
OCEANIA	
Jaya (Sukarno, Carstensz), Sudirman Range, *Indonesia*	16,500
Pilimsit (Idenburg), Sudirman Range, *Indonesia*	15,750
Trikora (Wilhelmina), Jayawijaya Mts., *Indonesia*	15,580
Mandala (Juliana), Jayawijaya Mts., *Indonesia*	15,420
CAUCASUS	
Elbrus, Caucasus, *Russia*	18,510
Dyhk-Tau, Caucasus, *Russia*	17,073
Koshtan-Tau, Caucasus, *Russia*	16,900
Shkhara, Caucasus, *Russia–Georgia*	16,627

Acronyms for International Organizations

ACP	African, Caribbean, and Pacific Convention
ADB	Asian Development Bank
APEC	Asia-Pacific Economic Cooperation Council
CARICOM	Caribbean Community and Common Market
EEC	European Economic Community
EU	The European Union
FAO	Food and Agriculture Organization
GCC	Gulf Cooperation Council
I-ADB	Inter-American Development Bank
IDB	Islamic Development Bank
ILO	International Labour Organization
IMF	International Monetary Fund
ITU	International Telecommunications Union
OAS	Organization of American States
OAU	Organization of African Unity
OPEC	Organization of Petroleum Exporting Countries
SPC	South Pacific Commission
UNICEF	United Nations Children's Fund
UNESCO	United Nations Educational, Scientific, and Cultural Organization
WHO	World Health Organization
WTO	World Trade Organization (formerly General Agreement on Tariffs and Trade, GATT)

Country	National Capital	Population of National Capital	United Nations (date of admission)	UNICEF	FAO	ILO
Afghanistan	Kābul	700,000	1946	•	•	•
Albania	Tiranë	354,304	1955	•	•	•
Algeria	Algiers	1,790,700	1962	•	•	•
Andorra	Andorra la Vella	20,787	1993			
Angola	Luanda	2,783,000	1976	•	•	•
Antigua and Barbuda	Saint John's	23,600	1981	•	•	•
Argentina	Buenos Aires	2,768,772	1945	•	•	•
Armenia	Yerevan	1,246,100	1992	•	•	•
Australia	Canberra	339,727	1945	•	•	•
Austria	Vienna	1,550,123	1955	•	•	•
Azerbaijan	Baku	1,817,900	1992	•	•	•
Bahamas, The	Nassau	210,832	1973	•	•	•
Bahrain	Al-Manamah	143,035	1971	•	•	•
Bangladesh	Dhākā (Dacca)	5,644,235	1974	•	•	•
Barbados	Bridgetown	6,070	1966	•	•	•
Belarus	Minsk	1,682,900	1945	•		•
Belgium	Brussels	136,730	1945	•	•	•
Belize	Belmopan	12,300	1981	•	•	•
Benin	Cotonou (official)	650,660	1960	•	•	•
	Porto-Novo (de facto)	232,756				
Bhutan	Thimphu	45,000	1971	•	•	
Bolivia	La Paz (administrative)	789,585	1945	•	•	•
	Sucre (judicial)	193,873				
Bosnia and Herzegovina	Sarajevo	380,000	1992	•	•	•
Botswana	Gaborone	186,007	1966	•	•	•
Brazil	Brasília	2,094,100	1945	•	•	•
Brunei	Bandar Seri Begawan	27,285	1984			
Bulgaria	Sofia	1,096,389	1955	•	•	•
Burkina Faso	Ouagadougou	709,736	1960	•	•	•
Burundi	Bujumbura	346,000	1962	•	•	•
Cambodia	Phnom Penh	1,109,000	1955	•	•	•
Cameroon	Yaoundé	903,649	1960	•	•	•
Canada	Ottawa	774,072	1945	•	•	•
Cape Verde	Praia	94,757	1975	•	•	•
Central African Republic	Bangui	553,000	1960	•	•	•
Chad	N'Djamena	530,965	1960	•	•	•
Chile	Santiago	5,623,000	1945	•	•	•
China	Beijing (Peking)	7,699,297	1945	•	•	•
Colombia	Bogotá	6,850,205	1945	•	•	•
Comoros	Moroni	34,168	1975	•	•	•
Congo, Democratic Republic of the	Kinshasha	4,655,313	1960	•	•	•
Congo, Republic of the	Brazzaville	856,410	1960	•	•	•
Costa Rica	San José	309,762	1945	•	•	•
Cote d'Ivoire	Abidjan	2,877,948	1960	•	•	•
Croatia	Zagreb	691,724	1992	•	•	•
Cuba	Havana	2,175,900	1945	•	•	•
Cyprus	Lefkosia	47,832	1960	•	•	•
Czech Republic	Prague	1,161,938	1993	•	•	•
Denmark	Copenhagen	501,285	1945	•	•	•
Djibouti	Djibouti	465,300	1977	•	•	•

IMF	ITU	UNESCO	WHO	WTO	Common-wealth of Nations	EU	GCC	OAS	AU	PC	ACP	ADB	APEC	CARICOM	I-ADB	IDB	OPEC	Country
•	•	•	•									•				•		Afghanistan
•	•	•	•	•												•		Albania
•	•	•	•						•							•	•	Algeria
	•	•	•															Andorra
•	•	•	•	•					•		•							Angola
•	•	•	•	•	•			•			•			•				Antigua and Barbuda
•	•	•	•	•				•							•			Argentina
•	•	•	•	•								•						Armenia
•	•	•	•	•	•					•		•	•					Australia
•	•	•	•	•		•						•			•			Austria
•	•	•	•									•				•		Azerbaijan
•	•	•	•		•			•			•			•	•			Bahamas, The
•	•	•	•	•			•									•		Bahrain
•	•	•	•	•	•							•				•		Bangladesh
•	•	•	•	•	•			•			•			•	•			Barbados
•	•	•	•															Belarus
•	•	•	•	•		•						•			•			Belgium
•	•	•	•	•	•			•			•			•	•			Belize
•	•	•	•	•					•		•					•		Benin
•	•	•	•									•						Bhutan
•	•	•	•	•				•							•			Bolivia
•	•	•	•															Bosnia and Herzegovina
•	•	•	•	•	•				•		•							Botswana
•	•	•	•	•				•							•			Brazil
•	•	•	•	•	•								•			•		Brunei
•	•	•	•	•														Bulgaria
•	•	•	•	•					•		•					•		Burkina Faso
•	•	•	•	•					•		•							Burundi
•	•	•	•	•								•						Cambodia
•	•	•	•	•	•				•		•					•		Cameroon
•	•	•	•	•	•			•				•	•		•			Canada
•	•	•	•						•		•							Cape Verde
•	•	•	•	•					•		•							Central African Republic
•	•	•	•	•					•		•					•		Chad
•	•	•	•	•				•			•				•			Chile
•	•	•	•	•								•	•					China
•	•	•	•	•				•							•			Colombia
•	•	•	•						•		•					•		Comoros
•	•	•	•	•					•		•							Congo, Democratic Republic. of the
•	•	•	•	•					•		•							Congo, Republic. of the
•	•	•	•	•				•							•			Costa Rica
•	•	•	•	•					•		•					•		Cote d'Ivoire
•	•	•	•	•											•			Croatia
	•	•	•	•								•						Cuba
•	•	•	•	•	•	•												Cyprus
•	•	•	•	•		•												Czech Republic
•	•	•	•	•		•						•			•			Denmark
•	•	•	•	•					•		•					•		Djibouti

Country	National Capital	Population of National Capital	United Nations (date of admission)	UNICEF	FAO	ILO
Dominica	Roseau	20,200	1978	•	•	•
Dominican Republic	Santo Domingo	1,817,754	1945	•	•	•
East Timor	Dili	51,700	2002		•	•
Ecuador	Quito	1,399,378	1945	•	•	•
Egypt	Cairo	6,789,479	1945	•	•	•
El Salvador	San Salvador	479,600	1945	•	•	•
Equatorial Guinea	Malabo	92,900	1968	•	•	•
Eritrea	Asmara	500,600	1993	•	•	•
Estonia	Tallinn	400,378	1991	•	•	•
Ethiopia	Addis Ababa	2,112,737	1945	•	•	•
Fiji	Suva	77,366	1970	•	•	•
Finland	Helsinki	559,716	1955	•	•	•
France	Paris	2,123,261	1945	•	•	•
Gabon	Libreville	362,386	1960	•	•	•
Gambia, The	Banjul	34,828	1965	•	•	
Georgia	Tbilisi	1,081,700	1992	•	•	•
Germany	Berlin	3,388,434	1973	•	•	•
Ghana	Accra	1,551,200	1957	•	•	•
Greece	Athens	745,514	1945	•	•	•
Grenada	Saint George's	3,908	1974	•	•	•
Guatemala	Guatemala City	942,348	1945	•	•	•
Guinea	Conakry	1,851,800	1958	•	•	•
Guinea-Bissau	Bissau	305,700	1974	•	•	•
Guyana	Georgetown	137,330	1966	•	•	•
Haiti	Port-au-Prince	917,112	1945	•	•	•
Honduras	Tegucigalpa	769,061	1945	•	•	•
Hungary	Budapest	1,775,203	1955	•	•	•
Iceland	Reykjavik	112,490	1946	•	•	•
India	New Delhi	294,783	1945	•	•	•
Indonesia	Jakarta	8,347,083	1950	•	•	•
Iran	Tehrān	6,758,845	1945	•	•	•
Iraq	Baghdad	5,423,964	1945	•	•	•
Ireland	Dublin	495,781	1955	•	•	•
Israel	Jerusalem (Yerushalayim, Al-Quds)	680,400	1949	•	•	•
Italy	Rome (Roma)	2,546,804	1955	•	•	•
Jamaica	Kingston	96,052	1962	•	•	•
Japan	Tokyo	8,134,688	1956	•	•	•
Jordan	Amman	1,147,447	1955	•	•	•
Kazakhstan	Astana	313,000	1992	•	•	•
Kenya	Nairobi	2,143,354	1963	•	•	•
Kiribati	Bairiki	36,717	1999	•	•	•
Kuwait	Kuwait (Al-Kuwayt)	28,859	1963	•	•	•
Kyrgyzstan	Bishkek (Frunze)	750,327	1992	•	•	•
Laos	Vientiane (Viangchan)	194,200	1955	•	•	•
Latvia	Rīga	747,157	1991	•	•	•
Lebanon	Beirut (Bayrūt)	1,171,000	1945	•	•	•
Lesotho	Maseru	160,100	1966	•	•	•
Liberia	Monrovia	543,000	1945	•	•	•
Libya	Tripoli (Ṭarābulus)	591,060	1955		•	•
Liechtenstein	Vaduz	4,949	1990			

IMF	ITU	UNESCO	WHO	WTO	Commonwealth of Nations	EU	GCC	OAS	AU	PC	ACP	ADB	APEC	CARICOM	I-ADB	IDB	OPEC	Country
●	●	●	●	●	●			●			●			●				Dominica
●	●	●	●	●				●			●				●			Dominican Republic
●		●	●								●	●						East Timor
●	●	●	●	●				●							●			Ecuador
●	●	●	●	●					●							●		Egypt
●	●	●	●	●				●							●			El Salvador
●	●	●	●						●		●							Equatorial Guinea
●	●	●	●						●		●							Eritrea
●	●	●	●	●		●												Estonia
●	●	●	●						●	●	●							Ethiopia
●	●	●	●	●							●	●						Fiji
●	●	●	●	●		●				●		●			●			Finland
●	●	●	●	●		●						●			●			France
●	●	●	●	●					●		●					●		Gabon
●	●	●	●	●	●				●		●					●		Gambia, The
●	●	●	●															Georgia
●	●	●	●	●		●						●			●			Germany
●	●	●	●	●	●				●		●							Ghana
●	●	●	●	●		●												Greece
●	●	●	●	●	●			●			●			●				Grenada
●	●	●	●	●				●							●			Guatemala
●	●	●	●	●					●		●					●		Guinea
●	●	●	●	●					●		●					●		Guinea-Bissau
●	●	●	●	●	●			●			●			●	●			Guyana
●	●	●	●	●				●			●			●	●			Haiti
●	●	●	●	●				●							●			Honduras
●	●	●	●	●		●												Hungary
●	●	●	●	●														Iceland
●	●	●	●	●	●							●						India
●	●	●	●	●								●	●			●	●	Indonesia
●	●	●	●													●	●	Iran
●	●	●	●													●	●	Iraq
●	●	●	●	●		●												Ireland
																		Israel
●	●	●	●	●											●			
●	●	●	●	●		●						●			●			Italy
●	●	●	●	●	●			●			●			●	●			Jamaica
●	●	●	●	●								●	●		●			Japan
●	●	●	●	●												●		Jordan
●	●	●	●									●				●		Kazakhstan
●	●	●	●	●	●				●	●	●							Kenya
●	●	●	●		●						●	●						Kiribati
●	●	●	●	●			●									●	●	Kuwait
●	●	●	●	●								●				●		Kyrgyzstan
●	●	●	●									●						Laos
●	●	●	●	●		●												Latvia
●	●	●	●													●		Lebanon
●	●	●	●	●	●				●		●							Lesotho
●	●	●	●						●		●							Liberia
●	●	●	●						●							●	●	Libya
	●			●														Liechtenstein

Country	National Capital	Population of National Capital	United Nations (date of admission)	UNICEF	FAO	ILO
Lithuania	Vilnius	553,038	1991	•	•	•
Luxembourg	Luxembourg	76,688	1945	•	•	•
Macedonia	Skopje (Skopije)	467,257	1993	•	•	•
Madagascar	Antananarivo	1,403,449	1960	•	•	•
Malawi	Lilongwe	597,619	1964	•	•	•
Malaysia	Kuala Lumpur	1,297,526	1957	•	•	•
Maldives	Male	74,069	1965	•	•	
Mali	Bamako	1,016,167	1960	•	•	•
Malta	Valletta	7,199	1964	•	•	•
Marshall Islands	Majuro	20,800	1991	•	•	
Mauritania	Nouakchott	558,195	1961	•	•	•
Mauritius	Port Louis	144,303	1968		•	•
Mexico	Mexico City	8,605,239	1945	•	•	•
Micronesia, Federated States of	Palikir	6,227	1991	•	•	
Moldova	Chişinău	662,400	1992	•	•	•
Monaco	Monaco	32,020	1993	•	•	
Mongolia	Ulaanbaatar (Ulan Bator)	760,077	1961	•	•	•
Montenegro	Podgorica					
Morocco	Rabat	623,457	1956	•	•	•
Mozambique	Maputo (Lourenço Marques)	989,386	1975	•	•	•
Myanmar	Yangôn (Rangoon)	4,454,500	1948	•	•	•
Namibia	Windhoek	220,000	1990	•	•	•
Nauru	Yaren	672	1999	•	•	
Nepal	Kāthmāndu	671,846	1955	•	•	•
Netherlands, The	Amsterdam (capital)	735,080	1945	•	•	•
	The Hague (seat of gov.)	463,841		•	•	•
New Zealand	Wellington	178,000	1945	•	•	•
Nicaragua	Managua	864,201	1945	•	•	•
Niger	Niamey	674,950	1960	•	•	•
Nigeria	Abuja	420,000	1960	•	•	•
North Korea	P'yŏngyang	2,741,260	1991	•	•	
Norway	Oslo	517,401	1945	•	•	•
Oman	Muscat	56,410	1971	•	•	•
Pakistan	Islāmābād	524,500	1947	•	•	•
Palau	Koror	13,303	1994	•	•	
Panama	Panama City	469,307	1945	•	•	•
Papua New Guinea	Port Moresby	254,158	1975	•	•	•
Paraguay	Asunción	513,399	1945	•	•	•
Peru	Lima	316,322	1945	•	•	•
Philippines	Manila	1,581,082	1945	•	•	•
Poland	Warsaw (Warszawa)	1,671,670	1945	•	•	•
Portugal	Lisbon	564,657	1955	•	•	•
Qatar	Doha	338,760	1971	•	•	•
Romania	Bucharest	1,921,751	1955	•	•	•
Russia	Moscow	10,101,500	1991	•	•	•
Rwanda	Kigali	608,141	1962	•	•	•
St. Kitts and Nevis	Basseterre	13,220	1983	•	•	•
St. Lucia	Castries	12,439	1979	•	•	•
St. Vincent and The Grenadines	Kingstown	16,209	1980	•	•	•

IMF	ITU	UNESCO	WHO	WTO	Common-wealth of Nations	EU	GCC	OAS	AU	PC	ACP	ADB	APEC	CARICOM	I-ADB	IDB	OPEC	Country
•	•	•	•	•		•												Lithuania
•	•	•	•	•		•						•						Luxembourg
•	•	•	•	•														Macedonia
•	•	•	•	•					•		•							Madagascar
•	•	•	•	•	•				•		•							Malawi
•	•	•	•	•	•							•	•			•		Malaysia
•	•	•	•	•	•							•				•		Maldives
•	•	•	•	•					•		•					•		Mali
•	•	•	•	•	•	•				•								Malta
•	•	•	•								•	•						Marshall Islands
•	•	•	•	•	•				•		•					•		Mauritania
•	•	•	•	•	•				•		•							Mauritius
																		Mexico,
•	•	•	•	•				•		•			•		•			Federated States of
•	•	•	•								•	•						Micronesia
•	•	•	•	•														Moldova
•	•	•	•															Monaco
•	•	•	•	•								•						Mongolia
					•													Montenegro
•	•	•	•	•												•		Morocco
																		Mozambique
•	•	•	•	•	•				•		•					•		
				•								•						Myanmar
•	•	•	•	•					•		•							Namibia
	•	•	•		•					•	•	•						Nauru
•	•	•	•	•								•						Nepal
•	•	•	•	•		•						•			•			Netherlands, The
•	•	•	•	•														
•	•	•	•	•	•					•		•	•					New Zealand
•	•	•	•	•				•							•			Nicaragua
•	•	•	•	•					•		•					•		Niger
•	•	•	•	•	•				•		•						•	Nigeria
	•	•	•															North Korea
•	•	•	•	•								•			•			Norway
•	•	•	•	•			•									•		Oman
•	•	•	•	•	•							•				•		Pakistan
•		•	•							•					•			Palau
•	•	•	•	•				•							•			Panama
•	•	•	•	•	•					•	•	•	•					Papua New Guinea
•	•	•	•	•				•							•			Paraguay
•	•	•	•	•				•					•		•			Peru
•	•	•	•	•								•	•					Phillippines
•	•	•	•	•		•												Poland
•	•	•	•	•		•									•			Portugal
•	•	•	•	•			•									•	•	Qatar
•	•	•	•	•														Romania
•	•	•	•										•					Russia
•	•	•	•	•					•		•							Rwanda
•		•	•	•	•			•			•							St. Kitts and Nevis
•	•	•	•	•	•			•			•			•				St. Lucia
														•				St. Vincent and the
•	•	•	•	•	•			•			•							Grenadines

Country	National Capital	Population of National Capital	United Nations (date of admission)	UNICEF	FAO	ILO
Samoa	Apia	38,836	1976	•	•	•
San Marino	San Marino	4,483	1992	•	•	•
São Tomé and Príncipe	São Tomé	51,886	1975	•	•	•
Saudi Arabia	Riyadh (Ar-Riyadh)	2,776,096	1945	•	•	•
Senegal	Dakar	919,683	1960	•	•	•
Serbia	Belgrade (executive,					
	legislative)	1,120,092	1945	•	•	•
	Podgorica (judicial)	139,100				
Seychelles	Victoria	24,701	1976	•	•	•
Sierra Leone	Freetown	1,070,200	1961	•	•	•
Singapore	Singapore	4,171,300	1965	•		•
Slovakia	Bratislava	428,672	1993	•	•	•
Slovenia	Ljubljana	258,873	1992	•	•	•
Solomon Islands	Honiara	50,100	1978	•	•	•
Somalia	Mogadishu	1,212,000	1960	•	•	•
South Africa	Bloemfontein (judicial)	333,769	1945	•	•	•
	Cape Town (legislative)	2,415,408				
	Pretoria (executive)	1,104,479				
South Korea	Seoul (Sŏul)	10,280,523	1991	•	•	•
Spain	Madrid	2,938,723	1955	•	•	•
Sri Lanka	Colombo	642,163	1955	•	•	•
Sudan, The	Khartoum	947,483	1956	•	•	•
Suriname	Paramaribo	218,500	1975	•	•	•
Swaziland	Mbabane	57,992	1968	•	•	•
Sweden	Stockholm	758,148	1946	•	•	•
Switzerland	Bern (Berne)	122,707	2002	•	•	•
Syria	Damascus (Dimashq)	1,614,500	1956	•	•	•
Taiwan	Taipei (T'ai-pei)	2,641,856	-			
Tajikistan	Dushanbe	575,900	1992	•	•	•
Tanzania	Dar es Salaam (acting)	2,336,055	1961	•	•	•
Thailand	Bangkok	6,320,174	1946	•	•	•
Togo	Lomé	676,400	1960	•	•	•
Tonga	Nuku'alofa	22,400	1999	•	•	
Trinidad and Tobago	Port-of-Spain	49,031	1962	•	•	•
Tunisia	Tunis	695,500	1956	•	•	•
Turkey	Ankara	3,203,362	1945	•	•	•
Turkmenistan	Ashkhabad (Ashgabat)	773,400	1992	•	•	•
Tuvalu	Funafuti	4,492	2000	•	•	
Uganda	Kampala	1,208,544	1962	•	•	•
Ukraine	Kiev (Kyyiv)	2,611,327	1945	•	•	•
United Arab Emirates	Abu Dhabi (Abū Ẓaby)	552,000	1971	•	•	•
United Kingdom	London (Greater London)	7,172,091	1945	•	•	•
United States	Washington, D.C.	563,384	1945	•	•	•
Uruguay	Montevideo	1,378,707	1945	•	•	•
Uzbekistan	Tashkent	2,142,700	1992	•	•	•
Vanuatu	Vila	29,356	1981	•	•	•
Venezuela	Caracas	1,836,000	1945	•	•	•
Vietnam	Hanoi	1,420,400	1977	•	•	•
Yemen	Ṣan'ā'	1,590,624	1947	•	•	•
Zambia	Lusaka	1,084,703	1964	•	•	•
Zimbabwe	Harare	1,444,534	1980	•	•	•

IMF	ITU	UNESCO	WHO	WTO	Commonwealth of Nations	EU	GCC	OAS	AU	PC	ACP	ADB	APEC	CARICOM	I-ADB	IDB	OPEC	Country
•	•	•	•		•				•	•	•	•		•				Samoa
•	•	•	•															San Marino
•	•	•	•						•		•					•	•	São Tomé and Príncipe
•	•	•	•				•									•	•	Saudi Arabia
•	•	•	•	•					•		•					•		Senegal
																		Serbia
•	•	•	•															
•	•	•	•		•				•		•							Seychelles
•	•	•	•	•	•				•		•					•		Sierra Leone
•	•		•	•	•							•	•					Singapore
•	•	•	•	•		•												Slovakia
•	•	•	•	•		•									•			Slovenia
•	•	•	•	•	•					•	•	•						Solomon Islands
•	•	•	•						•		•					•		Somalia
•	•	•	•	•	•				•		•							South Africa
•	•	•	•	•								•	•		•			South Korea
•	•	•	•	•		•						•			•			Spain
•	•	•	•	•	•							•						Sri Lanka
•	•	•	•						•		•					•		Sudan, The
•	•	•	•	•				•			•				•	•		Suriname
•	•	•	•	•	•				•		•			•				Swaziland
•	•	•	•	•		•						•			•			Sweden
•	•	•	•	•								•			•			Switzerland
•	•	•	•													•		Syria
				•								•	•					Taiwan
•	•	•	•									•				•		Tajikistan
•	•	•	•	•	•				•		•							Tanzania
•	•	•	•	•								•	•					Thailand
•	•	•	•	•					•		•					•		Togo
•	•	•	•		•					•	•	•						Tonga
•	•	•	•	•	•			•			•		•		•			Trinidad and Tobago
•	•	•	•	•					•							•		Tunisia
•	•	•	•	•								•				•		Turkey
•	•	•	•									•				•		Turkmenistan
	•	•	•		•					•	•	•						Tuvalu
•	•	•	•	•	•				•		•					•		Uganda
•	•	•	•															Ukraine
•	•	•	•	•			•									•	•	United Arab Emirates
•	•	•	•	•	•	•						•			•			United Kingdom
•	•	•	•	•				•		•		•	•		•			United States
•	•	•	•	•				•							•			Uruguay
•	•	•	•									•				•		Uzbekistan
•	•	•	•		•					•	•	•						Vanuatu
•	•	•	•	•				•							•		•	Venezuela
•	•	•	•									•	•					Vietnam
•	•	•	•													•		Yemen
•	•	•	•	•	•				•		•							Zambia
•	•	•	•	•					•		•							Zimbabwe